our trip **with**

For Dummies

Covering the most pop___ ___stinations in North America and Europe,
For Dummies travel g___ ___ the ultimate user-friendly trip planners.
Available where___ ___ ___s are sold or go to www.dummies.com

KT-162-424

And book it with
our online partner,
Frommers.com

- ✔ **Book airfare, hotels and packages**
- ✔ **Find the hottest deals**
- ✔ **Get breaking travel news**
- ✔ **Enter to win vacations**
- ✔ **Share trip photos and stories**
- ✔ **And much more**

*Frommers.com, rated the
#1 Travel Web Site by PC Magazine*

WILEY

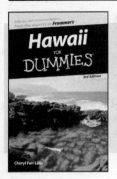
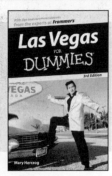
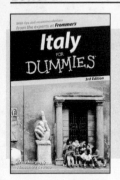

Scotland
FOR
DUMMIES®
3RD EDITION

by Barry Shelby

WILEY

Wiley Publishing, Inc.

Scotland For Dummies, 3rd Edition

Published by
Wiley Publishing, Inc.
111 River St.
Hoboken, NJ 07030-5774
www.wiley.com

Copyright © 2005 by Wiley Publishing, Inc., Indianapolis, Indiana

Published simultaneously in Canada

For general information on our other products and services, please contact our Customer Care Department within the U.S. at 800-762-2974, outside the U.S. at 317-572-3993, or fax 317-572-4002.

For technical support, please visit www.wiley.com/techsupport.

Wiley also publishes its books in a variety of electronic formats. Some content that appears in print may not be available in electronic books.

Library of Congress Control Number: Library of Congress Control Number is available from the publisher.

ISBN-13: 978-07645-7862-5

ISBN-10: 0-7645-7862-6

Manufactured in the United States of America

10 9 8 7 6 5 4 3 2 1

1B/TQ/QT/QV/IN

WILEY

About the Author

Barry Shelby was born in 1960 in Berkeley, California, where he later attended the University of California. He received a master's degree in journalism from Northwestern University in Illinois in 1984, after which he was an editor at *World Press Review* magazine in Manhattan. He moved to Scotland in 1997, where he has worked as a caretaker for a small and privately owned castle on the Clyde Coast, as a "temp" with the privatized national railway company, and as a food and drink writer and editor for newspapers and magazines, including the *Guardian, Glasgow Herald,* and *The List.* He is married to a Scot and lives in Glasgow.

Publisher's Acknowledgments

We're proud of this book; please send us your comments through our Dummies online registration form located at www.dummies.com/register/.

Some of the people who helped bring this book to market include the following:

Editorial

Editors: Traci Cumbay, Project Editor, Kendra Falkenstein, Development Editor

Copy Editor: Elizabeth Rea

Cartographer: Roberta Stockwell

Editorial Manager: Jennifer Ehrlich

Editorial Assistant: Nadine Bell

Senior Photo Editor: Richard Fox

Cover Photos:

Front Cover: Scenic of Castle Stalker, Loch Linnhe © Garry Black/Masterfile

Back Cover: Man in kilt, jumping © Eric Schmidt/Masterfile

Cartoons: Rich Tennant (www.the5thwave.com)

Composition Services

Project Coordinator: Michael Kruzil

Layout and Graphics: Lauren Goddard, Barry Offringa, Lynsey Osborn, Heather Ryan, Julie Trippetti

Proofreaders: Leeann Harney, Jessica Kramer, Joe Niesen, Carl Pierce, TECHBOOKS Production Services

Indexer: TECHBOOKS Production Services

Publishing and Editorial for Consumer Dummies

Diane Graves Steele, Vice President and Publisher, Consumer Dummies

Joyce Pepple, Acquisitions Director, Consumer Dummies

Kristin A. Cocks, Product Development Director, Consumer Dummies

Michael Spring, Vice President and Publisher, Travel

Kelly Regan, Editorial Director, Travel

Publishing for Technology Dummies

Andy Cummings, Vice President and Publisher, Dummies Technology/General User

Composition Services

Gerry Fahey, Vice President of Production Services

Debbie Stailey, Director of Composition Services

Contents at a Glance

Maps at a Glance

Table of Contents

Introduction

*T*his guide is a departure from conventional travel guidebooks. Rather than just throwing out dizzying reams of information for you to sift through until you're too tired to tell Edinburgh from Inverness, *Scotland For Dummies,* 3rd Edition, separates the proverbial wheat from the chaff for you.

This book walks you through the whole process of putting together your trip to Scotland, from the ins and outs of a manageable itinerary to advice on choosing the right places to stay or how much time to allot to attractions and activities. My recommendations may not be perfect for everyone, of course. The goal here is to help you see what may interest you (whether it's castles, museums, pubs, or open countryside) and what probably will not. Your time is valuable, so this book strives to get right to the point. *Scotland For Dummies,* 3rd Edition, is designed to give you a clear picture of what you need to know and what your options are, so that you can make informed decisions easily and efficiently about traveling in Scotland.

About This Book

Some parts of Scotland are bound to interest you more than others, so don't feel as if you have to read this book cover to cover. If you want to focus on the metropolitan life, for example, then simply concentrate on Part III's chapters devoted to Edinburgh and Glasgow. If the lore of the Loch Ness monster intrigues you, then you can find valuable information in Part VI. And if you're interested in picturesque settings that are less touristy than the famous loch, then *Scotland For Dummies,* 3rd Edition, can point you in the right direction.

Although the information is laid out in the logical order of a step-by-step manual, you don't need to read the book in order from front to back. You're also not expected to remember everything you read — you can just look up and revisit specific information as you need it. Each section and chapter is as self-contained as possible, a feature that allows you to concentrate on what's important to you (and skip the rest).

Of course this guide has up-to-date information on the best hotels and restaurants in Scotland's major cities and regions. But it also has information on shopping and nightlife, attractions, walking tours, helpful historical asides, and details on those things that make Scotland unique, too — whether that's golf courses or the tallest mountains and most pristine seas in the entire United Kingdom.

Dummies Post-it® Flags

As you're reading this book, you'll come across information that you may want to reference as you plan or enjoy your trip — whether it be a new hotel, a must-see attraction, or a must-try walking tour. Use the handy Post-it® Flags included in this book to mark particular pages and make your trip planning easier!

Please be advised that travel information is subject to change at any time — and this is especially true of prices. It never hurts to check the Internet or write or call ahead for confirmation of the "current" situation when making your travel plans. The author, editors, and publisher can't be held responsible for the experiences of readers while traveling. Your safety is important to us, however, so we encourage you to stay alert and be aware of your surroundings. Keep a close eye on cameras, purses, and wallets, all favorite targets of thieves and pickpockets.

Conventions Used in This Book

The goal of *Scotland For Dummies,* 3rd Edition, is to be a quick read in any order that you desire, so the listings for hotels, restaurants, and sights are consistently standardized throughout the chapters. Each listing offers you an idea of what the place is like and then gives you details about specific addresses, prices, and hours of operation.

Other conventions include:

- ✔ The abbreviations for commonly accepted credit cards used throughout this book are:
  - AE: American Express
  - DC: Diners Club
  - DISC: Discover
  - MC: MasterCard
  - V: Visa
- ✔ Hotels, restaurants, and attractions are listed alphabetically in each chapter.
- ✔ Wherever possible, page references for maps are given to help you locate hotels, restaurants, attractions, and the like. If a hotel, restaurant, or attraction is in an out-of-the-way area, however, it may not appear on a map. In chapters on the major cities, information about bus routes, and, in Glasgow, subway stops, is given as well.

✔ All prices are in British pounds sterling (£), with the dollar equivalent given in parentheses. The conversion rate (always changing in the real world, of course) used to make these calculations is £1 equals $1.85.

Price is normally a factor when choosing hotels and restaurants. The relative costs of accommodations and meals are indicated with dollar signs. Specific prices are given, too, but the dollar signs are a quick way for you to see if a place is in your price category before reading any more information. My scale for accommodations and restaurants ranges from one dollar sign ($) to four ($$$$). Most hotel prices are per night for double rooms (rather than per person per night). The cost of a meal generally means dinner with at least two courses and a drink per person. The following table helps you decipher what the dollar signs mean.

Cost	Hotel	Restaurant
$	Less than £65 ($120)	Less than £10 ($19)
$$	£65–£125 ($120–$231)	£10–£25 ($19–$46)
$$$	£125–£250 ($231–$463)	£25–£35 ($46–$65)
$$$$	More than £250 ($463)	More than £35 ($65)

The hotels in Chapters 11 and 12 are divided into two categories — favorites and those that don't quite make the preferred list but still get seals of approval. Don't hesitate to consider the "runner-up" hotels — the amenities and the services they offer make them all reasonable choices as you decide where to rest your head at night.

Foolish Assumptions

This book makes some assumptions about you and what your needs may be as a traveler. Here's what I've assumed about you:

✔ You're an experienced traveler who hasn't had much time to explore Scotland but wants expert advice when you finally do get a chance to enjoy any part of the country.

✔ You're an inexperienced traveler looking for guidance when determining whether to take a trip to Scotland and how to plan for it.

✔ You're not looking for a book that provides all the information available about Scotland or that lists every hotel, restaurant, or attraction available to you. Instead, you want a book that focuses on the places that will give you the best or most unique experience in Scotland.

If you fit any of these criteria, then *Scotland For Dummies,* 3rd Edition, is the book for you.

How This Book Is Organized

Scotland For Dummies, 3rd Edition, consists of five parts. The chapters within each part cover specific components in detail.

Part I: Introducing Scotland

This part introduces you to the very best of Scotland and touches on issues you need to consider before actually getting down to the nitty-gritty of trip planning. It includes a brief history of Scotland as well as recommended reading, when and where to go, and detailed itineraries to consider.

Part II: Planning Your Trip to Scotland

This part gets down to the nuts and bolts of travel planning, including information on managing your money, how best to get to Scotland, getting around the country, and reserving hotel rooms. It also addresses special considerations for families, seniors, travelers with disabilities, and students as well as gay and lesbian travelers.

Part III: Edinburgh and Glasgow

You may only have time to see the two major cities in Scotland, and so I've devoted an entire chapter to each, with details on hotels, restaurants, top attractions, shopping, walking tours, and nightlife. Plus, you can find information on how to get around, how much time you need to see things, suggested itineraries, and recommended side trips.

Part IV: The Major Regions

This part offers chapters on Scotland's major regions: from Southern Scotland to the Highlands, from Ayrshire and Argyll to the Hebridean Islands. Each chapter has suggestions on accommodations, places to dine out, and attractions, not to mention some useful information on shopping and nightlife. For a more thorough overview of Scotland, including a brief description of these regions, flip to Chapter 3.

Part V: The Part of Tens

Every *For Dummies* book has a Part of Tens. These more breezy chapters have quick and handy lists that highlight the best golf courses, castles, natural attractions, and more in Scotland.

In back of this book I've included an *appendix* — your Quick Concierge — containing lots of handy information you may need when traveling in Scotland, like phone numbers and addresses of emergency personnel or area hospitals and pharmacies, lists of local newspapers and magazines, protocol for sending mail or finding taxis, and more. Check out this appendix when you're faced with the little questions that may come up as you travel. The Quick Concierge is easy to find because it's printed on yellow paper.

Icons Used in This Book

You can't miss the icons (little pictures) sprinkled throughout the margins of this book. Think of them as signposts that highlight special tips, draw your attention to things you don't want to miss, and give you a heads-up on a variety of topics.

 Keep an eye out for the Bargain Alert icon as you seek out money-saving tips and/or great deals.

 Best of the Best icons highlight the best each destination has to offer in all categories — hotels, restaurants, attractions, activities, shopping, and nightlife.

 Watch for the Heads Up icon to identify annoying or potentially dangerous situations such as tourist traps, unsafe neighborhoods, budgetary rip-offs, and other things to beware.

 This icon points to useful advice on things to do and ways to schedule your time.

 Look to the Kid Friendly icon for attractions, hotels, restaurants, and activities that are particularly hospitable to children or people traveling with kids.

 This icon points out secret little finds or useful resources that are worth the extra bit of effort to get to or find.

Where to Go from Here

This travel guide isn't designed to be read from beginning to end (although you're certainly welcome to do so). Instead, it provides detailed and well-organized information on loads of topics — from getting your passport to finding the best restaurants. So, choose your own adventure and look for the topics or destinations you want to explore by using the Table of Contents or the Index.

As you start to prepare for your visit to Scotland, remember this: The planning is half the fun. Don't make choosing your destinations and solidifying the details feel like a chore. Make the homebound part of the process a voyage of discovery, and you'll end up with a vacation that's much more rewarding and enriching. See you in Scotland!

Part I

Introducing Scotland

"It's the room next door. They suggest you deflate your souvenir bagpipes before trying to pack them in your luggage."

In this part . . .

Scotland — with its rich and evocative past — has much to offer the traveler. But visitors don't come here just for the history: The country's vibrant cities, natural beauty, indigenous culture, and friendly people are all additional draws.

This part suggests Scotland's best, from hotels and restaurants to castles and art galleries. You'll find useful itineraries to help you decide what to see if your time is limited. This part also contains a condensed history, a glossary of the Scots language, a list of suggested books and films to help get you in the mood, and lots more. When's the best season to visit? Are discounts available for seniors or children? What, for heaven's sake, is haggis? Look no further; the answers are here.

Chapter 1

Discovering the Best of Scotland

- -

- -

1 begin this book with the highlights: the best of what Scotland has to offer visitors, from top "travel experiences" to hotels, restaurants, castles, museums, golf courses, pubs, and more. These attractions are highlighted by a "Best of the Best" icon when they appear elsewhere in this book.

The Best Travel Experiences

✔ **Ardnamurchan Peninsula:** One of the more easily reached but seemingly remote areas of the Highlands, the peninsula is the most westerly point in the entire British mainland. See Chapter 18.

✔ **Butt of Lewis:** On the Isle of Lewis, these beautiful high cliffs over the ocean have views that are worth the drive to the tip of the island. You can see seabirds, seals, and spectacular windblown waves crashing against the rocks. See Chapter 19.

✔ **Edinburgh Old Town:** This area is probably the most visited location in Scotland and not without good reason. Running along the spine of a hill and extending from the castle to the Palace of Holyroodhouse, Old Town is a delight to wander through. Make sure you take time to explore the alleyways. See Chapter 11.

✔ **Glasgow City Centre:** This area shows off the thriving heart of a modern European city, with some of the finest examples of Victorian architecture in all the world. It's set out on a grid, so you don't need to worry about getting lost. See Chapter 12.

✔ **Glen Coe:** With a visitor center near Glencoe village, Glen Coe is such a beautiful valley that it's hard to reconcile the natural beauty with the bloody historical event that took place there. See Chapter 18.

✔ **Jacobite Cruises:** Jacobite offers arguably the most efficient and best organized cruises on Loch Ness. See Chapter 18.

✔ **Jacobite Steam Train:** This train is accessible from the Fort William and Mallaig railway stations, and it takes you on one of the most picturesque rail journeys you'll find anywhere. See Chapter 18.

✔ **Loch Lomond:** Located in Argyll, the loch is the largest inland body of water in all of Great Britain. It's only about a 30- to 45-minute drive or train ride from the Glasgow city limits. When you reach the loch, you can hike, canoe, or just relax. See Chapter 15.

✔ **Loch Ness:** This loch is mysterious and legendary — if somewhat overrated. In addition to looking for the elusive monster, you should seek out other local attractions, such as Urquhart Castle. See Chapter 18.

✔ **Sands of Morar:** Near Mallaig, the Sands of Morar offer beautiful bleached beaches set against postcard-pretty seas. You can see the Hebridean islands Rhum and Eigg from here. See Chapter 18.

✔ **Sandwood Bay:** This area near Blairmore has a beach that, by most accounts, is the most beautiful and unsullied in all of Great Britain's mainland. See Chapter 18.

The Best Accommodations in Edinburgh and Glasgow

Edinburgh

✔ **Best Boutique Hotel: The Bonham.** In an upscale, western New Town neighborhood, The Bonham offers some of the most alluring accommodations in a city filled with fine hotels. See Chapter 11.

✔ **Best Traditional Hotel: Balmoral.** With a Michelin-star restaurant, doormen in kilts, and a romantic pile to rival any others, Balmoral is legendary, and its location is smack in the heart of the capital. See Chapter 11.

✔ **Best Rooms near the Castle: The Witchery by the Castle.** As its list of celebrity guests testifies, the Witchery offers opulence and individuality in a manner not seen anywhere else in the Old Town. See Chapter 11.

✔ **Best Hotel in Leith: Malmaison.** At the port of Leith, Malmaison is about a 15-minute ride north of Edinburgh's center. Named after Joséphine's mansion outside Paris, the hotel celebrates the Auld

Alliance of France and Scotland and occupies a Victorian building built in 1900. See Chapter 11.

✔ **Best Hotel Health Spa: Sheraton Grand.** Near the city's conference center, the Sheraton Grand has wonderful facilities in an adjoining building. Especially noteworthy is the roof-top indoor/outdoor pool. See Chapter 11.

Glasgow

✔ **Best Boutique Hotel: One Devonshire Gardens.** In a West End neighborhood filled with similar sandstone-fronted town houses, One Devonshire Gardens still stands out. It's a re-creation of a high-bourgeois, very proper Scottish home from the early 1900s, boasting antique furnishings and discreetly concealed modern comforts. See Chapter 12.

✔ **Best Hip Hotel: Brunswick Hotel.** With only 18 rooms, the Brunswick Hotel exudes cool in the city's Merchant City. The design is modern and minimalist but is executed with character and class. See Chapter 12.

✔ **Best in the Commercial Centre: Malmaison.** Linked to the hotel with the same name in Edinburgh (see listing in previous section), this Malmaison is in a building that dates from the 1800s. It welcomes visitors with Scottish hospitality and houses them with quite a bit of style. See Chapter 12.

✔ **Best Moderately Priced Hotel: The ArtHouse.** Unique to Glasgow, The ArtHouse was converted from a 1911 Edwardian-era school administration building. The building has been dramatically renovated and offers first-class comfort and affordable prices, all part of a striking design. See Chapter 12.

The Best Small and Country House Hotels

✔ **Ardanaiseig,** Kilchrenan: This stone Scottish baronial pile built in the 1830s offers a bit of luxury in an out-of-the-way corner. See Chapter 15.

✔ **Ballachulish House,** Ballachulish: This 17th-century laird's house includes a history said to be the inspiration for key passages in Robert Louis Stevenson's masterpiece, *Kidnapped.* See Chapter 18.

✔ **Burts Hotel,** Melrose: This whitewashed hotel dates to 1722 and is well-known for its award-winning food. See Chapter 14.

✔ **Darroch Learg,** Ballater: This hotel is one of the more highly regarded hotels in the Royal Deeside region near the Queen's estate at Balmoral. See Chapter 17.

✔ **Glenapp Castle,** Ballantrae: Glenapp is a beautifully decorated pile close to Stranraer, with Victorian baronial splendor and antiques, oil paintings, and elegant touches. See Chapter 15.

- ✔ **Glengarry Castle Hotel,** Invergarry: The 26-room Victorian mansion, with its own castle ruins (the real Glengarry Castle), is on extensive wooded grounds with nice views of Loch Oich. See Chapter 18.

- ✔ **Hotel Eilean Iarmain,** Isleornsay: This hotel on the Isle of Skye offers quintessential island hospitality combined with tranquility and beautiful surroundings. See Chapter 19.

- ✔ **Prestonfield,** Edinburgh: This hotel rises in Jacobean splendor amid gardens, pastures, and woodlands below Arthur's Seat. See Chapter 11.

- ✔ **Roman Camp,** Callander: A cozy old hotel located near Roman ruins, it was once the home of the Dukes of Perth. See Chapter 16.

- ✔ **Town House,** Glasgow: One of the most charming of the city's B&Bs, Town House is also a less expensive alternative to One Devonshire Gardens, which is just around the corner. See Chapter 12.

The Best Dining in Edinburgh and Glasgow

Edinburgh

- ✔ **Best French Restaurant: Restaurant Martin Wishart.** With one of the city's precious Michelin stars and its most talented chef/owner, Restaurant Martin Wishart is where the leading out-of-town chefs dine when they visit Edinburgh. See Chapter 11.

- ✔ **Best Cafe: Spoon.** In the heart of Old Town, Spoon forks out some the best salads and sandwiches in Edinburgh — and the freshly made soups are even better. See Chapter 11.

- ✔ **Best Italian Restaurant: Santini.** Although many of the more established Italian restaurants in town don't like hearing it, Santini continually gets rave reviews and sets the highest standards. See Chapter 11.

- ✔ **Best Modern Scottish Restaurant: Atrium.** Owned by Andrew and Lisa Radford, Atrium offers dishes prepared with flair and imagination but not excessive amounts of fuss or over-fancy presentation. See Chapter 11.

- ✔ **Best Restaurant Views: Oloroso** and **Forth Floor.** This category is a dead heat between Oloroso and Forth Floor at Harvey Nichols. Both offer wonderful preparation of fresh Scottish produce to go with those scenic vistas. See Chapter 11.

- ✔ **Best on a Budget: Rogue.** Rogue looks far too stylish to fall into this category, but nowhere else in the capital can you get food this good at these prices. See Chapter 11.

Glasgow

- ✔ **Best Fish Restaurant: Gamba.** Arguably the best restaurant in the entire city, Gamba specializes in superb seafood, showing off some of Scotland's best natural produce. See Chapter 12.

- ✔ **Best Indian Restaurant: Mother India.** Glasgow loves its Indian cuisine, and Mother India offers a concise menu of south Asian dishes, with a touch of Glasgow-style curry as well. See Chapter 12.

- ✔ **Best Contemporary Restaurant: étain.** Seeing as it's owned by the Conran group, you would expect étain to be sharp-looking, and it is. But it has also surprised many with its smart French-influenced cooking. See Chapter 12.

- ✔ **Best Cafe: Café Gandolfi.** Perhaps more of a bistro than cafe, Café Gandolfi offers straightforward and delicious dishes, whether you choose a bowl of Cullen skink (smoked haddock chowder) or a sirloin steak sandwich. See Chapter 12.

- ✔ **Best Pub Food: Stravaigin.** With an award-winning restaurant in the basement, the ground-floor pub Stravaigin offers similarly top-notch quality food — at a fraction of the restaurant price. See Chapter 12.

- ✔ **Best on a Budget: Wee Curry Shop.** A brief stroll from the shopping precincts of Sauchiehall Street, the Wee Curry Shop is a tiny gem of a restaurant, serving freshly prepared Indian cuisine at bargain prices. See Chapter 12.

The Best Rural Restaurants

- ✔ **Andrew Fairlie at Gleneagles,** Auchterarder: It may be the finest dining experience in the country, and Fairlie is arguably the most talented chef in Scotland at present. See Chapter 16.

- ✔ **Applecross Inn,** Applecross: The inn may not be the easiest place in Scotland to reach, but many visitors agree that the twists and turns of the road to Applecross are well worth the journey for a meal here. See Chapter 18.

- ✔ **Braidwoods,** Dalry: One of the standout restaurants in Ayrshire and holder of a Michelin star and other accolades, Braidwoods is expensive but worth the price. See Chapter 15.

- ✔ **Creagan House,** Straheyre: Run by Cherry and Gordon Gunn, the restaurant is part of a charming inn in a 17th-century farm house. See Chapter 16.

- ✔ **Peat Inn,** Cupar: Built in 1760, the Peat Inn is currently a post office, inn, and restaurant offering David Wilson's exceptional cuisine. See Chapter 16.

- ✔ **Plumed Horse,** Castle Douglas: This restaurant is a small place with a big reputation (and a Michelin star!) in Southern Scotland. See Chapter 14.

✔ **Port-Na-Craig Inn,** Pitlochry: The restaurant here captured the attention of the Michelin inspectors a few years back, when they bestowed upon the owners an award for good food at reasonable prices. See Chapter 17.

✔ **Three Chimneys Restaurant,** Colbost: Probably the most popular restaurant on Skye, the Three Chimneys serves superb Scottish cuisine paired with produce from Skye, its island home. See Chapter 19.

The Best Castles

✔ **Blair Castle,** Blair: Blair's chock-full o' stuff: art, armor, flags, stag horns, and more goodies not typically found on the standard furniture-and-portrait castle tour. See Chapter 17.

✔ **Caerlaverock Castle,** Dumfries: Long a target of English armies, Caerlaverock remains one of Scotland's more classic Medieval castles. See Chapter 14.

✔ **Castle Tioram,** Blain: This classic medieval fortress now in ruins sits along the picturesque shores of Loch Moidart. You can enjoy some good hiking trails near the castle, too. See Chapter 18.

✔ **Cawdor Castle,** Cawdor: Cawdor is one of my favorites, largely because the room-by-room self-guided tour cards are well written and humorous. See Chapter 18.

✔ **Doune Castle,** Stirling: Fans of the film *Monty Python and the Holy Grail* may recognize Doune. Thanks to its limited restoration, visitors get a good idea of what living here in the 14th century may have been like. See Chapter 16.

✔ **Duart Castle,** Craignure: Duart was abandoned in 1751, but thanks to the efforts of Fitzroy Maclean, it was restored from ruins in 1911. Making your way up the narrow, twisting stairs is worth it because you can walk outside on the parapet at the top of the castle. See Chapter 19.

✔ **Edinburgh Castle,** Edinburgh: This castle in Old Town is surely the most famous in the country and one of a few places in Scotland filled with so much lore. See Chapter 11.

✔ **Eilean Donan,** Dornie: This is probably the most photographed stone pile in Scotland (after Edinburgh Castle, that is). On an islet in Loch Duich, Eilean Donan is a quintessential castle. See Chapter 18.

✔ **Kilchurn Castle,** Loch Awe: A stunning ruin that dates to the 16th century, the castle is as much fun to get to as it is to explore. See Chapter 15.

✔ **Stirling Castle,** Stirling: This castle was the residence of Mary Queen of Scots, her son James VI of Scotland (and later James I of England), and other Stuart monarchs. Recently restored, the Great

Hall stands out for miles thanks to the creamy, almost yellow exterior that apparently replicates its original color. See Chapter 16.

✔ **Threave Castle,** Castle Douglas: Threave is a massive 14th-century tower house on an island in the middle of the River Dee (a boatman ferries visitors across). See Chapter 14.

The Best Cathedrals, Churches, and Abbeys

✔ **Dunfermline Abbey and Palace,** Dunfermline: This abbey is on the site of a Celtic church and an 11th-century house of worship dedicated to the Holy Trinity; traces of this history are visible beneath gratings in the floor of the old nave. See Chapter 16.

✔ **Glasgow Cathedral,** Glasgow: This cathedral is also known as the cathedral of St. Kentigern or St. Mungo's, and it dates to the 13th century. The edifice is mainland Scotland's only complete medieval cathedral. See Chapter 12.

✔ **High Kirk of St. Giles,** Edinburgh: Just a brief walk downhill from Edinburgh Castle, this church — and its steeple, in particular — is one of the most important architectural landmarks along the Royal Mile. See Chapter 11.

✔ **Iona Abbey and Nunnery,** Iona: This spiritual landmark is a significant shrine to the earliest days of Christianity in Scotland. See Chapter 19.

✔ **Jedburgh Abbey,** Jedburgh: This abbey is one of four Borders abbeys commissioned by Scots King David I in the 12th century. See Chapter 14.

✔ **Melrose Abbey,** Melrose: The heart of Scots King Robert the Bruce is rumored to be buried somewhere on the grounds of this abbey, which sits amidst somewhat spectacular ruins. See Chapter 14.

✔ **St. Vincent Street Church,** Glasgow: This church offers limited access to visitors, but it's the most visible landmark attributed to the city's great architect, Alexander "Greek" Thomson. See Chapter 12.

The Best Art Galleries

✔ **The Burrell Collection,** Glasgow: This gallery houses the treasures left to Glasgow by Sir William Burrell, a wealthy ship owner and industrialist who had a lifelong passion for art. He started collecting at age 14 and only ceased when he died at the age of 96 in 1958. See Chapter 12.

✔ **Centre for Contemporary Art (CCA),** Glasgow: CCA is one of three premier venues in Glasgow for the exhibition of contemporary art — usually of a conceptual nature — by both local artists and those of international reputation. See Chapter 12.

✔ **Gallery of Modern Art (GOMA),** Glasgow: This gallery is housed in the former Royal Exchange. The permanent collection has works by Stanley Spencer and John Bellany as well as art from the "new Glasgow boys." See Chapter 12.

✔ **Hunterian Art Gallery,** Glasgow: The Hunterian holds the artistic estate of James McNeill Whistler, with some 60 of his paintings as well as some by the Scottish Colourists. It also boasts a collection of Charles Rennie Mackintosh–designed furnishings. See Chapter 12.

✔ **National Gallery of Scotland,** Edinburgh: The National Gallery offers a collection that has been chosen with great care and expanded by bequests, gifts, loans, and purchases. See Chapter 11.

✔ **Scottish National Gallery of Modern Art,** Edinburgh: This gallery houses Scotland's national collection of 20th-century art in a converted 1828 school set on 12 acres of grounds. See Chapter 11.

✔ **Scottish National Portrait Gallery,** Edinburgh: Designed by Rowand Anderson, the gallery gives you a chance to stand before the faces of many famous people from Scottish history. See Chapter 11.

The Best Museums and Historic Attractions

✔ **Bannockburn,** Stirling: Bannockburn is believed to be the famous battlefield site where King Robert the Bruce's soldiers vanquished the English troops of Edward II. The heritage centre offers an excellent audiovisual presentation of the site's unique history. See Chapter 16.

✔ **Burns Cottage and Museum,** Alloway: This attraction may be basic, but it remains a must-see for even casual fans of Scots poet Robert Burns. See Chapter 15.

✔ **Calanais Standing Stones,** Lewis: This ancient cross-shaped formation of large stones is best known as the "Scottish Stonehenge." See Chapter 19.

✔ **Calton Hill,** Edinburgh: This landmark rises about 350 feet above the city and is crowned with monuments. It's mainly responsible for Edinburgh's being called the "Athens of the North." See Chapter 11.

✔ **Culloden Moor Battlefield,** Culloden Moor: This battlefield is where the hopes of Bonnie Prince Charlie's Jacobite uprising of 1745 (begun at Glenfinnan) ended in complete defeat in 1746. See Chapter 18.

✔ **Gladstone's Land,** Edinburgh: This 17th-century merchant's house, looking suitably weathered and aged, is decorated in period-style furnishings, features colorful paintings of flowers and fruit, and has a sensitively restored timber ceiling. See Chapter 11.

✔ **Glasgow School of Art,** Glasgow: This building was designed by Scotland's great architect Charles Rennie Mackintosh, whose global reputation rests in large part on this magnificent building on Garnethill above Sauchiehall Street. See Chapter 12.

✔ **Glenfinnan Monument,** Glenfinnan: This monument marks the hopeful start of the 1745 Jacobite rebellion, led by Bonnie Prince Charlie, who was trying to reclaim the English and Scottish crowns for his Stuart family lineage. See Chapter 18.

✔ **Highland Folk Museum,** Kingussie: This interesting museum in a reconstructed crofter's (small farmer's) home describes the last 400 years of Highland life. See Chapter 18.

✔ **Kilmartin House Museum,** Kilmartin: This museum traces Scotland's earliest civilizations, history, and culture. See Chapter 15.

✔ **Museum of Scotland,** Edinburgh: A most impressive modern sandstone building not far from the Royal Mile, the museum is home to exhibits that follow the story of Scotland, including archaeology, technology, science, the decorative arts, royalty, and geology. See Chapter 11.

✔ **The Palace of Holyroodhouse,** Edinburgh: The palace was built in the 16th century adjacent to an Augustinian abbey that David I established in the 12th century. Today, the royal family stays here whenever they visit Edinburgh. When they're not in residence, which is most of the time, the palace is open to visitors. See Chapter 11.

✔ **Skara Brae,** Orkney: This is the best-preserved prehistoric beachside village in northern Europe. For an idea of what you'll see here, think Pompeii-meets-the-Neolithic. See Chapter 20.

The Best Historic Houses and Gardens

✔ **Abbotsford,** Roxburghshire: Abbotsford is the mansion that Scotland's best known novelist Sir Walter Scott built and lived in from 1817 until his death. You can visit extensive gardens and grounds on the property, plus the private chapel added after Scott's death. See Chapter 14.

✔ **Culzean Castle,** South Ayrshire: This castle overlooking the Firth of Clyde is a fine example of Robert Adam's "castellated" style (built with turrets and ramparts). It replaced an earlier castle keep as the family seat of the powerful Kennedy clan. See Chapter 15.

✔ **Hill House,** Helensburgh: The design of the house was inspired by Scottish Baronial style, but it's still pure Charles Rennie Mackintosh, from the asymmetrical juxtaposition of windows and clean lines that blend sharp geometry and gentle curves to the sumptuous but uncluttered interior. See Chapter 13.

✔ **Holmwood House**, Glasgow: This 1858 villa designed by Alexander "Greek" Thomson is probably the best example of his innovative style as applied to stately Victorian homes. See Chapter 12.

✔ **Inverewe Garden,** Poolewe: On the south-facing shores of Loch Ewe, Inverewe is the most impressive garden in the Highlands. See Chapter 18.

✔ **Little Sparta,** Dunsyre: This garden was devised by one of Scotland's most intriguing artists of the 20th and 21st centuries, Ian Hamilton Finlay. See Chapter 14.

✔ **Logan Botanic Garden,** Port Logan: This garden has palms, tree ferns, and other exotic plants that you wouldn't expect to see in Scotland, such as towering flowering columns of echium pininanas native to the Canary Islands. See Chapter 14.

✔ **Mount Stuart,** Isle of Bute: This mansion belongs to the Marquess of Bute's family, but it's open to the public for much of the year. See Chapter 15.

✔ **Royal Botanic Garden,** Edinburgh: Royal Botanic, with its acres of land to explore, is one of the grandest gardens in all of Great Britain, which is certainly saying something. See Chapter 11.

✔ **Traquair House,** Innerleithen: This house dates to the 10th century and is perhaps Scotland's most romantic house, rich in its association with Mary Queen of Scots and the Jacobite uprisings. See Chapter 14.

The Best Small Towns

✔ **Culross:** Thanks largely to the National Trust for Scotland, Culross shows what a Scottish village from the 16th to 18th centuries was like, with its cobbled streets lined by stout cottages featuring crow-stepped gables. See Chapter 16.

✔ **Dirleton:** Midway between North Berwick and Gullane, Dirleton has been cited as the prettiest village in Scotland. It's picture postcard perfect, not like a real town at all, but rather one that appears to have been created for a movie set. See Chapter 13.

✔ **Plockton:** Located not far from Eilean Donan castle, Plockton is the prettiest village in the Highlands. It sits on the shores of Loch Carron. See Chapter 18.

✔ **Portpatrick:** A small holiday resort on the Rhinns of Galloway, Portpatrick is most certainly one of the most picturesque towns in southwest Scotland. See Chapter 14.

✔ **Ullapool:** This town is the busiest fishing port in the northwest of Scotland, and it's also a popular resort — the last outpost before the sparsely populated north. See Chapter 18.

The Best Distilleries

  ✔ **Edradour Distillery,** Pitlochry: Visitors get a good primer on the whisky-making process at this mini-distillery. See Chapter 17.

  ✔ **Laphroaig Distillery,** Islay: Laphroaig is the home of a whisky that has a distinctive peaty flavor with a whiff of sea air (some say they can even taste a little seaweed). See Chapter 15.

  ✔ **Talisker Distillery,** Carbost: This distillery on the Isle of Skye may just offer the best whisky distillery tour in all Scotland. See Chapter 19.

The Best Golf Courses

  ✔ **Muirfield Golf Course,** Gullane: Muirfield is ranked among the world's great golf courses. It's the home course of the Honorable Company of Edinburgh Golfers — the world's oldest club. See Chapter 13.

  ✔ **St. Andrews:** Surely Scotland's most famous golf mecca, St. Andrews offers five 18-hole courses as well as one 9-hole course for beginners and children, all owned by a trust and open to the public. See Chapter 16.

  ✔ **Troon:** The city and its environs offer several sandy links courses, most prominently the Royal Troon Golf Club. But try the municipal courses for a bargain round as well. See Chapter 15.

  ✔ **Turnberry Hotel Golf Courses, Turnberry:** Like the Royal Troon Golf Club, Turnberry has been the scene of Open tournaments and other professional golfing events over the years. Guests of the Westin Turnberry hotel get priority here. See Chapter 15.

The Best Pubs and Bars

  ✔ **Café Royal Circle Bar,** Edinburgh: This New Town pub stands out as a longtime favorite, boasting lots of atmosphere and Victorian trappings. It attracts a sea of drinkers, locals as well as visitors. See Chapter 11.

  ✔ **Claichaig Inn,** Glencoe: This hotel has a rustic pub with a wood-burning stove, although it's really the staff's sunny dispositions that warm the woody lounge and bar. Claichaig Inn is especially popular with hikers. See Chapter 18.

  ✔ **Drover's Inn,** Inverarnan: This hotel has an atmospheric pub with an open fire burning, barmen in kilts, and plenty of travelers by foot and car nursing their drinks at the north end of Loch Lomond. See Chapter 15.

✔ **The Horse Shoe,** Glasgow: With its long, horseshoe-shaped bar and central location, this pub is a throwback to the days of so-called Palace Pubs in Scotland. See Chapter 12.

✔ **Mishnish,** Tobermory: This pub on the island of Mull is a rather big quayside bar for such a diminutive town. See Chapter 19.

✔ **The Pot Still,** Glasgow: This pub gets the nod because of its selection of single malts that numbers easily into the hundreds. See Chapter 12.

✔ **Prince of Wales,** Aberdeen: With the longest bar in town and a convivial atmosphere, this pub is possibly the best place to grab a pint in Aberdeen. See Chapter 17.

✔ **The Shore,** Edinburgh: This pub in Leith fits seamlessly into its seaside port surroundings without resorting to a lot of the usual decorations of cork and netting. It has excellent food, too. See Chapter 11.

✔ **Whistlebinkies,** Stirling: The name may make Whistlebinkies sound like a place for kids, but adults will appreciate the comfortable booths and selection of good beers and whiskys. The building dates to 1595 and originally housed Stirling Castle's blacksmith. See Chapter 16.

Chapter 2

Digging Deeper into Scotland

*I*n this chapter, I give you a concise bit of history to elevate your knowledge of a country whose national origins are among the oldest in Europe. I also show you how to tackle the language. Yes, it's English but not the same English you're used to. I also cover the basics of Scottish food, which is often as misunderstood as the native's accents. Interested in golf or the Scottish folk music scene? You can find that info here, plus a suggested list of must-see films set in Scotland and books about the country and its people.

History 101: The Main Events

The key to comprehending — and in fact enjoying — Scotland is understanding at least a bit of the country's long and sometimes complex history. For most of its existence, Scotland has had full (if disputed) autonomy from England, its larger, more populous, and sometimes-pushy neighbor to the south. Although the Scottish and English crowns were joined (1603) and the countries were unified into Great Britain (1707), they remain — distinct nations.

Scotland is small: The country fills about 78,761 sq. km (30,410 sq. miles), which is about the size of South Dakota. Scotland encompasses more than 750 islands, although only about a fourth are inhabited. No resident in Scotland lives more than about 65km (40 miles) from the sea (whether that's the Atlantic Ocean, the Irish Sea, or the North Sea).

Is that a chip I spy?

Scots are often thought to be English by foreigners. Any visitors should avoid that faux pas. Scotland's union with England in 1707 effectively relegated Scotland to little more than an administrative region within Great Britain. Even though Edinburgh — called the Athens of the North — has long been an intellectual center and Glasgow was the "Second City" of the British Empire, many written histories of "Britain" tend to ignore developments in Scotland. Even worse, in some cases, Scotland is treated with condescension, which in part explains why Scots sometimes act as if they have terrible chips on their shoulders.

Early history

Standing stones, *brochs* (circular stone towers), and burial chambers are signs of Scotland's earliest residents, but little is known about these first tribes. When the Romans invaded in AD 82, the land was occupied by a people they called the **Picts** (Painted Ones). Despite some spectacular bloodletting, the Romans never conquered the indigenous people in Scotland, and the building of Hadrian's Wall (well south of the current border) effectively marked the northern limits of Rome's influence. Sometime before AD 500, however, the Irish, called "Scots," successfully colonized the land.

The Dark & Middle Ages

The Scots and the Picts were united around 843, while pressures of invasion from the south and Scandinavia helped mold Scotland into a relatively cohesive unit. Under Malcolm II (1005–1034), tribes who occupied the southwest and southeast parts of the Scottish mainland were merged with the Scots and the Picts.

However small, Scotland's terrain is full of lochs (or lakes; see "Braving the Burr: Scottish English" for more local terminology) and mountains that effectively divide the territory, and the country was often preoccupied with the territorial battles of clan allegiances.

Some of Scotland's most legendary heroes lived during the 13th century, particularly **William Wallace** (1270–1305), who drove the English out of Perth and Stirling. Later, **Robert the Bruce** (1274–1329) beat English forces at Bannockburn. Crowned at Scone in 1306, he decisively defeated Edward II of England in 1314.

In 1320, after decades of war against English invaders and occupiers, barons loyal to Scottish King Robert the Bruce put their names on a letter to the Pope, the **Declaration of Arbroath.** The letter not only clearly affirmed the country's independence but also addressed notions of freedom and liberty — abstract ideals that most nations didn't contemplate for hundreds of years.

The Reformation

The passions of the Reformation arrived on an already turbulent Scottish scene in the 16th century. The main protagonist was undoubtedly **John Knox,** a devoted disciple of the Geneva Protestant John Calvin. Knox had a peculiar mixture of piety, conservatism, strict morality, and intellectual independence that many see as a pronounced feature of the Scottish character today.

Knox helped shape the democratic form of the Scottish Church: Primary among his tenets were provisions for a self-governing congregation, including schools. Thus, Knox effectively encouraged literacy.

Knox was vehemently opposed to the reign of Scotland's most famous monarch: **Mary Queen of Scots** (1542–1587). When she eventually took up her rule, she was a Roman Catholic Scot of French upbringing trying to govern a land (about which she knew little) in the throes of the Reformation.

Following some disastrous political and romantic alliances, Mary fled Scotland to be imprisoned in England — her life eventually ended by the executioner's ax on orders of her cousin, Elizabeth I. Ironically, Mary's son — **James VI of Scotland** — succeeded the childless Elizabeth and became king of England (James I) in 1603.

Union & the Jacobites

In the 17th century, Scotland's sovereignty ebbed away as the Scottish kings spent most of their time in London. In 1689, the final Stuart king, the staunchly Catholic James VII (and II of England) fled London to France, and his daughter, the Protestant Mary, and her Dutch husband William succeeded to the throne, thus effectively ending the rule of Scots over Scotland, England, and its territories. In 1707, Scotland had little choice but to merge formally with England and create Great Britain. Although this union abolished the Scottish Parliament, those loyal to the Stuarts (known as the Jacobites) vainly attempted in 1715 to restore the Stuart line of royalty. Despite defeat, the Jacobites didn't give up.

In 1745, Charles Edward (the Young Pretender), better known as **Bonnie Prince Charlie,** picked up the gauntlet. He was the central figure in the 1745 revolt. Although initially successful, starting from the Highlands and easily reaching Derby, only 125 miles from London, they made an ill-conceived tactical retreat to Scotland and were eventually crushed at the **Battle of Culloden,** near Inverness.

The Scottish Enlightenment and economic growth

During the 18th century, rapid progress in the emerging industrial age produced prominent Scots who made broad and sweeping contributions to all fields of endeavor. Many of the inventions that altered the history of the developing world — such as the steam engine — were either invented or installed by Scottish genius and industry.

Scotland timeline

- ✔ 6000 BC: The earliest known residents of Scotland establish settlements on the Argyll Peninsula.

- ✔ 3000 BC: Celtic tribes invade, making the use of Gaelic widespread.

- ✔ AD 90: Romans abandon the hope of conquering Scotland, retreating to England and the relative safety of Hadrian's Wall.

- ✔ 1272: Edward I of England embarks on an aggressive campaign to conquer both Wales and Scotland but is deflected by William Wallace, among others.

- ✔ 1314-1328: The Scots, under Robert the Bruce, defeat English armies. England formally recognizes Scotland's sovereignty.

- ✔ 1587: Mary, Queen of Scots is executed on orders of her cousin, Queen Elizabeth.

- ✔ 1603: Mary's son, James VI of Scotland, accedes to the throne of England as James I — thus unifying the crown.

- ✔ 1707: The union of England and Scotland takes place, the Scottish Parliament is dissolved, and Great Britain is born.

- ✔ 1750–1850: Britain experiences rapid industrialization. The Clearances strip many crofters of their farms, creating epic bitterness and forcing new patterns of Scottish migrations.

- ✔ Late 19th century: Astonishing success in the sciences propels Scotland into the role of arbiter of industrial know-how around the globe.

- ✔ Mid–20th century: The decline of traditional industries, especially shipbuilding, painfully redefines the nature of Scottish industry.

- ✔ 1970: The discovery of oil deposits in the North Sea brings new vitality to Scotland.

- ✔ 1997: Scotland passes a referendum on "devolution" within Great Britain.

- ✔ 1999: Elections for the Scottish Parliament are held, and soon after Queen Elizabeth opens the first Scottish Parliament in almost 300 years.

- ✔ 2004: The controversially expensive and much delayed Parliament building opens in Edinburgh.

Scotland's union with England and Wales began to reap dividends, and the Scottish economy underwent a radical transformation. As trade with British overseas colonies increased, the port of Glasgow, in particular, flourished. Its merchants grew rich on the tobacco trade with Virginia and the Carolinas.

The infamous **Highland Clearances** (1750–1850) expelled small farmers, or *crofters,* from their ancestral lands to make way for sheep grazing.

Similarly, people in the Scottish Lowlands were forcibly moved. Increased industrialization and migration into urban centers changed the national demographics forever, while a massive wave of emigration created a global **Scottish Diaspora.**

Edinburgh's **New Town** was begun in the mid-1700s and today is a World Heritage Site recognized by the United Nations. Later, Victorian builders turned Glasgow into a showcase of 19th-century architecture.

The 20th and 21st centuries

By the 1960s and 1970s, Scotland found that its industrial plants couldn't compete with the emerging industrial powerhouses of Asia and else-where. A glimmer of light appeared on the Scottish economic horizon in the 1970s: The discovery of **North Sea oil** lifted the British economy considerably.

In 1997, under a newly elected Labour government in London, the Scottish electorate voted on **devolution** — a fancy word for limited sovereignty. The referendum passed, allowing Scotland to have its own legislature for the first time since the 1707 union with England. The **Scottish Parliament,** centered at Edinburgh, has limited taxing powers and can enact laws regarding health, education, transportation, and public housing — but it has no authority over matters of finance, defense, immigration, and foreign policy.

Taste of Scotland: From Haddock to Haggis

Traditional Scottish cooking is good and hearty. Staples of its cuisine include **fish** (often haddock), **potatoes** (called tatties), **turnips** (called neeps), **oatcakes, porridge,** and local game such as **grouse** or **venison.**

For too many years, restaurants in Scotland were known for boiled meats and watery, overcooked vegetables. But in the past 20 years or so, inde-pendent restaurants have opened in spades showing significant improve-ment in Scottish cookery, where the best ingredients that the country produces have been married with other styles and influences.

One of Scotland's best-known food exports is **Aberdeen Angus beef,** but equally fine is free-range **Scottish lamb,** known for its tender, tasty meat. **Fish,** in this land of seas, rivers, and lochs, is a mainstay, from wild brown trout to the herring that's transformed into the elegant kipper (see the sidebar "Culinary lingo"). Scottish smoked salmon is, of course, a delicacy known around the globe. Scottish shellfish is world-class, whether lob-sters and langoustines or oysters and crabs. Ranging from woodcock and grouse to rabbit and venison, **game** also has a key spot in the Scottish nat-ural larder. And **haggis** remains Scotland's national dish — though it's per-haps more symbolic than gustatory.

Culinary lingo

Here are a few foods that you're likely to come across in Scotland:

- **black pudding:** savoury sausage of pigs' blood and oats
- **bridie:** meat and potato pie
- **cullen skink:** smoked haddock chowder
- **haggis:** sheep organs (heart, liver, lungs, and so on), oatmeal, and spices stuffed into intestines or bag and boiled
- **kippers:** smoked herrings
- **neeps:** turnips
- **tattie:** potato
- **toastie:** toasted sandwich

Heather-infused honey is top notch, and jams make use of Scotland's abundant harvest of soft fruits. Scottish **raspberries,** for example, are said to be among the finest in the world. You definitely need to try some of Scotland's excellent **cheeses** as well. One of the best is Criffel, from the south of the country: a creamy and rich semi-soft cheese made from the milk of Shorthorn cows that graze only in organic pastures.

At your hotel or B&B, one traditional meal you're sure to have and enjoy is a Scottish breakfast or **full fry-up,** as the locals may call it. Expect most or all of the following: **eggs, bacon** and **sausage, black pudding, grilled tomatoes** and **mushrooms, fried bread** and/or **potato scones, coffee** or **tea, cereal** or **muesli.** A feast this size can often keep you going right through the afternoon.

These days, the word "eclectic" describes Scotland's **restaurant scene,** particularly in Edinburgh and Glasgow. Indian restaurants abound, as do French, Italian, and Thai options. Scots today can eat better than ever before, although much of population still seems to subsist on take-away fish and chips or, as the locals prefer to call them, **fish suppers.**

Braving the Burr: Scottish English

Yes, English is spoken in Scotland, but between the local expressions, heavy accents, and thick burr (trilling of the letter "r"), at times it sounds like a foreign language. Don't worry, sometimes even Scots from one region don't know what someone from another area is saying!

The standard joke about England and Scotland is "two countries divided by a common language." Differences of Scottish English include: r's being rolled, "ch" takes a hard throaty sound, and the "g" is often dropped in words ending in "ing."

Gaelic and Scots

In Scotland's earliest history, the prevailing tongue was a Celtic language, **Gaelic.** Northumbrian English was introduced from the south, and the language known as Lowland Scottish, or **Scots,** then developed; Scots borrowed from Gaelic, Scandinavian dialects, Dutch, and French.

After the royal court moved to England in 1603, the population of Scotland mostly spoke vernacular English, the language of their beloved Bible, and the Scots language was looked upon as a rather awkward, coarse tongue. In the 18th century, English also became the language of university instruction. By the end of the 20th century, TV and radio had begun to even out some of the more pronounced burrs and lilts of the Scottish accent. However, the dialect and speech patterns of the people in Scotland remain rich and evocative.

Meanwhile, Gaelic, while not widely spoken, is certainly not dead. Scottish public affairs TV airs some programs in the language, and particularly in places like the Isle of Skye, about 60 percent of the population still speaks Gaelic.

 Glaswegians (residents of Glasgow) are very friendly to tourists, so don't feel intimidated by their heavy accents and colorful local expressions. Be patient and ask those you don't understand to repeat themselves or to slow down. And if someone says to you, "Hi, how ye dae'in?" Reply with, "I canna complain." You just may be mistaken for a local — for a minute, anyway.

To save you from having to maintain one of those polite but puzzled smiles on your face while talking to locals, review this handy glossary of some common words from both Gaelic and Scots as well as some standard British English substitutions for North American English.

auld	old	**glen**	valley
aye	yes	**hen**	woman
bonnie	pretty	**howff**	meeting place or pub
boot	car trunk	**ken**	know or known
burn	creek	**lad**	boy
cairn	stone landmark	**lassie**	girl
ceilidh	social dance	**lift**	elevator
cheers	thanks	**loch**	lake
dinnae	don't or didn't	**pavement**	sidewalk

petrol	gasoline	take-away	to-go
messages	groceries or the shopping	till	cash register
		tins	canned goods
quid	pound sterling	torch	flashlight
stramash	disturbance	wee	little
stushie	fuss		

Pub Life in Scotland

Much socializing in Scotland centers on the local pub. The pub's more than a watering hole, however; it can be a gathering place for the entire community, where the locals go to share news and gossip. At certain pubs, pickup sessions of traditional and folk music are common.

Even if you're not a big drinker, going out for a pint of lager, a dram of whisky, or even just a bite to eat at a Scottish *howff* can be a memorable part of your trip, since you're almost guaranteed to meet real Scots.

 Don't tip the bar staff: You'll immediately be sussed as an outsider, and it won't get you a free round of drinks. On the issue of rounds, it's quite common for individuals in groups to buy a round during any session of drinking. Don't pass on your turn — it's bad manners.

Join 'em for a pint of beer

From region to region, you'll find a number of local breweries and a growing lot of microbreweries. The most widely available Scottish beers are Tennents and McEwens, and each has different types of beers, from light-colored lagers to dark ales. Among those produced on a smaller scale, Deuchars IPA and Orkney's Dark Island are standouts. The most popular stout is Guinness, from neighboring Ireland, and the potent Stella Artois, from the continent, is the best-selling premium lager.

A bit of whisky terminology

Scotland's home to a host of whisky experts, and in case you meet some, here are a few helpful terms to keep in mind.

- **dram:** A shot of spirits (usually whisky), roughly 50 milliliters or 1.7 ounces
- **neat:** Whisky served without ice or water
- **nip:** A whisky chaser to a pint of beer
- **usige beatha** (ooshka Bay): Water of life; Gaelic for the word whisky

Traditionally, the strength of Scottish ale (as distinct from lager) is labeled by shillings (for example, Belhaven 80/-), The higher the number, the stronger the beer. Today, with cask-conditioned ales, the bar can tell you the alcohol content, ABV: four is standard, six is strong.

 Remember, practically all beer in Scotland has a higher alcohol content than any sold in North America. And that even goes for familiar American brands like Budweiser. So, take it easy.

Whisky galore!

If you're in Scotland (or almost anywhere in Europe), you don't need to identify it as **Scotch** whisky. If you want a North American whiskey, however, you need to name the brand. Most connoisseurs prefer varieties of single malt Scotch, whose taste depends largely on where it's distilled: sweet Lowland, peaty Island, or smooth and balanced Highland. Single malts are seen as sipping whiskies and should never be served with ice or diluted with any thing other than a few drops of tap water. If you want a cocktail made with whisky, expect it to be a well-known blend, like Famous Grouse or Bell's and not a single malt, such as Glemorangie or Laphroaig.

 If you're ordering whisky, ask for a "wee dram" (a small shot), and the bartender will think you've been drinking in Scotland forever. Again, the established way to drink the spirit is neat — that is, nothing added — but some say a few drops of tap water bring out the aroma and flavor.

Other cocktail concoctions

 If you order a mixed drink (such as a gin and tonic), don't be surprised if the barkeep hands you a glass with a little ice and the alcohol, and, to the side, a small bottle of mixer. That's just how it's done. Also, the expression "fresh orange" usually means bottled orange juice.

Tuning Your Ear to Scottish Music

Scottish music is considerably more than "Scotland the Brave" played on bagpipes, although you may well hear that during your stay as well.

The Gaelic-influenced songs and sounds of the Hebridean Islands and the Highlands have been around for centuries. The fiddle, accordion, flute, and Celtic drum are all part of the musical tradition. The best chance to hear the real deal is at a jam session in a pub or at a more formal (but still fun) social dance called a *ceilidh* (pronounced *kay*-lee). Bagpipes and the rousing, indeed ear-shattering, sounds they can create are entrenched in the national identity and culture of Scotland.

Every summer, Glasgow hosts an international piping competition that draws thousands of pipers (many of whom also perform as part of

Edinburgh's Military Tattoo, a show featuring music, marching, and military exercises). A lone piper may pop up anywhere, however.

Visiting Golf's Hallowed Ground

Golf may have originated in mainland Europe, but Scotland gets the credit for developing the sport and codifying its rules. Golf has been played here for more than 500 years. In places such as eastern Fife or north Ayrshire, you're as likely to see someone golfing around a park as you are to see kids playing basketball in Chicago or the suburbs of L.A.

If you need a caddy, don't be surprised if he isn't young — the average age of a golf caddy here is about 50. Don't expect courses to provide carts, and *do not* play a championship course if you're a beginner or intermediate. You can play on many public and private courses (Chapter 21 lists the best), but at private clubs, members receive priority for tee times. Many courses have dress codes, so play it safe and wear a shirt with a collar as well as proper golf shoes if you're heading to the links.

Exploring Scotland's Great Outdoors

Scotland has long had world-class fishing, and its hill-walking and hiking are first rate, too. Unlike most other countries in Europe, Scotland doesn't require a national license to fish. Instead, you buy permits locally at bait and tackle shops or request permission from landowners. Local tourism offices can provide you with more information.

The hiking in Scotland can take you through wooded glens, beach dunes, or wind-swept mountains. If you're hiking in the Highlands, you must take all the precautions you would if you were climbing in Alpine conditions, however. The weather can change dramatically.

As for eco-tourism, the marshes of Scotland teem with migratory birds, the seas offer whale watching, and the Highlands have eagles' nests.

Background Check: Recommended Movies and Books

If you're looking to find out more about Scotland than just what's in this book, you have a variety of films and books at your disposal. The following sections list some suggestions.

Films

The ten films listed below are among the most popular made about Scotland and its people.

✔ *Braveheart* (1995): Mel Gibson stars as the 13th-century patriot William Wallace in this sweeping Academy Award-winning epic. The movie — hardly historically accurate but moving nonetheless — probably did more to stir overseas interest in Scotland than any promotional campaign ever cooked up by the tourist board.

✔ *Gregory's Girl* (1981): This simple story of an awkward high school student (John Gordon-Sinclair) in a modern (and hideous) 20th-century Edinburgh is quirky but loveable.

✔ *I Know Where I'm Going!* (1945): This is a charming, funny WWII-era black and white film from the great British team of Powell and Pressburger. It takes a young English fiancée on a suspenseful adventure to the Western Islands.

✔ *Local Hero* (1983): In this sweetly eclectic comedy, villagers on a gorgeous stretch of Scottish coast (actually Morar near Malliag) expect to cash in big time because of Texan oil industry interest.

✔ *My Name is Joe* (1998): Although not entirely lacking humor and romance, this film paints an ultimately grim if accurate picture of Glaswegians struggling with their addictions and inner demons.

✔ *Orphans* (1997): Actor Peter Mullan (star of *My Name is Joe*) wrote and directed this outlandish and very, very dark comedy with lots of foul language about the day the Flynn family in Glasgow tried to bury their recently deceased mother.

✔ *Rob Roy* (1994): Liam Neeson stars as the strong-willed, heroic Rob Roy MacGregor, who gets his revenge on an evil and double-crossing 18th-century English laird in a story of honor and bravery.

✔ *The 39 Steps* (1935): Director Alfred Hitchcock and scriptwriter Charles Bennett almost completely reset the tale of spies and intrigue by Scottish novelist John Buchan. Instead of sticking to the Borders, the film transports the hero to the Highlands.

✔ *Trainspotting* (1996): Based one of the most popular books by a Scottish author (Irvine Welsh), *Trainspotting*, which stars Ewan McGregor, is the gritty and often hilarious account of a group of unrepentant drug-addled characters in Edinburgh in the 1980s.

✔ *Whiskey Galore* (1949): Re-titled *Tight Little Island* in America, this classic movie is based on a true story. The residents of a small Scottish isle get an intoxicating windfall when a ship carrying 50,000 cases of whisky crashes off their coast during WWII.

Books

There are too many books about Scotland to mention, so I've chosen to highlight my favorites in four main categories: travel, biography, fiction, and history.

Travel

For centuries, English writers have been fascinated (and confounded) by the perceived idiosyncrasies of their neighbors to the north. Without contest, the most influential (and perhaps the most curmudgeonly) of these observers was Samuel Johnson, whose usually negative impressions were recorded by Scottish-born James Boswell in *James Boswell's Journal of a Tour to the Hebrides with Samuel Johnson* (1773, reprinted by Littlefield, Adams in 1978). In the same vein is Donald E. Hayden's *Wordsworth's Travels in Scotland* (University of Oklahoma Press, 1988).

Biography

- ✔ *Bonnie Prince Charlie* by Fitzroy Maclean (Canongate, 1989) tells the tale of one of the most romantic royal characters in Scottish history.

- ✔ *The Life of Robert Burns* by Catherine Carswell (Canongate Classics, 1998) is the groundbreaking look at the life of Scotland's national poet. First published in the 1930s, Carswell's assessment was so frank — particularly regarding the poet's romantic and sexual liaisons — that many took offense. But that honesty is precisely what makes her version of the poet's story indispensable.

- ✔ *Robert Louis Stevenson: A Biography* by Frank McLynn (Random House, 1994) maintains that the frail adventurer and author of *Treasure Island* and other classics was Scotland's greatest writer. The book documents the tragic life of the Edinburgh-born author.

- ✔ *The Sound of Sleat: A Painter's Life* by Jon Schueler (Picador, 1999) is a remarkable autobiography by American–born abstract impressionist Schueler, who found his muse in the land and especially the sky of Scotland. He even made a second home near the Western Highland port of Mallaig.

Fiction

- ✔ *The Heart of Midlothian* by Sir Walter Scott (Penguin Classics) was declared a masterpiece in 1818 and remains Scott's seminal piece of fiction, influencing the later works of authors such as Balzac, Hawthorne, and Dickens.

- ✔ *Kidnapped* by Robert Louis Stevenson (Penguin Classics) follows the adventures of young David Balfour after he's spirited out of Edinburgh and ends up on the wrong side of the law in the Western Highlands. The story is as entertaining today as it was upon publication in 1886.

- ✔ *Lanark: A Life in Four Books* by Alasdair Gray (Pub Group West, 2003) is perhaps the most important contemporary novel to be published in Scotland in the last 100 years. Gray is an eccentric of the first order, but this work of fiction (first published in 1981 and illustrated by the author, too), despite some fantastical detours, gets to the core of urban Scotland.

✔ *The Prime of Miss Jean Brodie* by Muriel Spark (Perennial Classics, 1999) and *Trainspotting* by Irvine Welsh (W. W. Norton & Company, 1996) are both better known for their cinematic adaptations, but in their own very different ways, both novels manage to capture elements of Edinburgh life.

History

✔ *Scotland: A New History* by Michael Lynch (Pimlico, 1992) is a good take on Scottish history from ancient times up to the 1990s.

✔ *The Scottish Enlightenment: The Scot's Invention of the Modern World* by American historian Arthur Herman (Crown, 2001) offers a clear and extremely readable explanation of the impact that Scottish thinkers had on the world.

✔ *The Scottish Nation: 1700–2000* by academic Tom Devine (Penguin, 2001) is a good, recently published historical overview of Scotland. With this book, Devine is one of the few to examine how people were driven from the Scottish Lowlands, as well as more famous and lamentable clearances from the Highlands.

✔ *Stone Voices: The Search for Scotland* by Neal Ascherson (Hill & Wang, 2003) is a quest for the national character of Scotland. Still, in a series of anecdotes and reflections, Ascherson helps readers understand the worthy sentiments behind Scottish independence and begins to redress the imbalance of Scottish histories so often written by the English. (British histories written by the English generally don't adequately address history outside of England.)

Chapter 3

Deciding Where and When to Go

In This Chapter

▶ Understanding Scotland's terrain and major regions

▶ Evaluating when to go, season by season

▶ Anticipating Scotland's changeable weather

▶ Planning for festivals and events

The next time you meet people who've recently been to Scotland, ask them what the place is like, and they may well give you a wistful, far-away look. That's because a trip to Scotland has the potential for magic. With the vitality and culture of Edinburgh and Glasgow, the countryside's sometimes breathtakingly barren scenery, and some of the friendliest people in the world, Scotland is bound to leave evocative memories. From urban chic to ancient castles, from misty glens to legendary golf courses, Scotland is a dream (as well as dreamy) destination.

This chapter starts with a geographic breakdown of the country, giving you a better idea of what the various regions have to offer and how long you may want to stay in each spot, given your particular interests and budget. The success of a Scottish vacation may depend on when you go. Good planning ensures that certain factors — such short winter days, too many tourists, being stuck in one place for too long, or not giving yourself enough time to see the big attractions — don't distract from a great trip.

In this chapter, I offer advice and insight on when to travel — from details about the weather to a calendar of events — so that you can more easily determine the best way to spend your Scotland vacation.

Going Everywhere You Want to Be

The first thing to understand about Scotland is this: It may be a small country, but it's one divided by mountains, rivers, and lochs, especially in the north. Most roads don't travel in straight lines. So, although the mileage may seem short, your trip can — and probably will — take longer than expected.

To further trip you up, the boundary of the Highlands runs diagonally across the country, from the southwest to the northeast. If you draw a straight line, west to east (say from the Isle of Mull to the River Tay), you may at first have rocky islands and distinctive Highland mountain terrain but end up with the moorland and rolling hills of the upper Lowlands.

Finally, any division of Scotland is bound to be a bit arbitrary: There's often no clean line to divide one region from another, but I've done my very best to present the regions accurately and logically.

For more information on the country's cities and regions, check out Part III, which discusses Scotland's two major cities: Edinburgh and Glasgow. Part IV has the lowdown on major regions in Scotland, which are introduced from south to north, starting with the Borders and south-west regions and finishing with the islands in the northernmost part of Scotland.

Edinburgh and Glasgow

Let's face it: Many and possibly most visitors to Scotland never get any farther than the country's two principal cities. And that's okay. They're excellent destinations in their own right and from them, travelers can take side trips to experience Scotland's other charms (see Chapter 13).

Although only a 55-minute train ride apart, **Edinburgh** (Chapter 11) and **Glasgow** (Chapter 12) are exceptionally different but equally fasci-nating and culturally rich. Think of them as the McCartney and Lennon of Scotland, making their own unique contributions and creating a dynamic duo.

Edinburgh (pronounced *eddin*-burra, with a short "e" as in "Edward") is the capital of Scotland. It has a historic Old Town as well as a so-called New Town that is actually slightly older than the United States! As the second most popular tourist destination in the UK (London's the first), Edinburgh and its charms are internationally recognized, as is the city's annual summer Festival. In addition, it boasts a striking cityscape — a castle on a hill being just one of several noteworthy landmarks — as well as the royal Palace of Holyroodhouse.

Glasgow (pronounced *glaz*-go, with a short "a" as in "at") is older than Edinburgh but appears more modern these days. Traditionally viewed as a working-class industrial metropolis, Glasgow thrived as the "Second City" of the empire in the 18th and 19th centuries, and today it offers the best concentration of Victorian architecture in the UK. After an eco-nomic decline in the 20th century and a reputation (deserving or not) of crime, grime, and gangsters, Glasgow emerged in the 1980s and 1990s as the cultural hot spot of Scotland, boasting leading artists and best-selling Indie rock bands.

Southern Scotland

The southernmost regions of Scotland are the **Borders,** aptly named because it borders Northumberland in northern England, and **Dumfries and Galloway,** which stretches southwest along the Solway Firth (which clearly divides England and Scotland) to the Mull of Galloway. Chapter 14 is devoted to these regions, which certainly have their own charm and attractions, whether Abbotsford, the house that Sir Walter Scott built; or the Logan Botanic Gardens, with its almost tropical plants. The town of Dumfries (dum-*frees*) was the final home to the national poet Robert Burns, and the ruins of several ancient abbeys commissioned by King David I in the 12th century can be found in and around the village of Melrose. If you have the time, both regions are worth a day or two of exploring.

Ayrshire and Argyll

Ayrshire (air-*shur*) is the long and primarily coastal region southwest of Glasgow best known for housing "Burns Country," where most of the landmarks and attractions associated with the great poet are located. But Ayrshire is also home to some of the best links-style golf courses in Scotland and perhaps the world. **Argyll** encompasses the West Coast of Scotland, its remote peninsulas, and the southernmost islands, such as Jura, Bute, and Arran. (See Chapter 15 for more information on both Ayrshire and Argyll.)

If you have time, the beautiful **Kintyre Peninsula** and the isle of **Arran** (sometimes described as Scotland in miniature) are certainly worth including, as are the port of **Oban** (oh-*bin*), the gateway to the Hebrides, and **Inveraray** on the shores of Loch Fyne. But even if you don't have time to explore the region fully, you would be remiss to skip places such as **Culzean Castle** or **Loch Lomond,** which are close enough to make good daytrips from Glasgow.

Fife and the Trossachs

North of Edinburgh, across the Firth of Forth, is the ancient Kingdom of **Fife;** moving west across the country takes in the historic city of **Stirling** and the **Trossach** mountains — rather like the Highlands only smaller, less dramatic, and more wooded (discussed in more detail in Chapter 16).

Fife is a reasonably compact area and is perhaps best known for the town of **St. Andrews,** because golfers make the pilgrimage here from all over the world. But St. Andrews isn't only a hallowed ground for golf; it's also a pretty great little East Coast college town. Another golf mecca lies inland: the famous Gleneagles resort with its first-class hotel and perhaps the best restaurant in Scotland, Andrew Fairlie at Gleneagles.

History buffs enjoy a visit to the town of Stirling, with its castle, Old Town wall, and picturesque monument to William Wallace (of *Braveheart* fame). And if you'll forgive more name-dropping, the **Trossachs** are the old

Glossary of place names

Picture this: You're passing through a quaint Highland town with an even quainter name. Wonder what it means? Use this glossary to mix and match parts of names to get closer to their meanings.

- ✔ **alt:** stream
- ✔ **ben:** mountain
- ✔ **brae:** hill
- ✔ **craig:** rock
- ✔ **drum:** ridge
- ✔ **dun:** hill fort
- ✔ **eilean:** island

- ✔ **firth:** sea inlet
- ✔ **glen:** valley
- ✔ **inver:** river mouth
- ✔ **loch:** lake
- ✔ **mor:** great
- ✔ **ness:** headland

stomping grounds of the legendary Rob Roy and provided the setting for Walter Scott's romantic poetry. Like some landmarks in Ayrshire, highlights of Fife, Stirling, and the Trossachs can be covered in daytrips from Edinburgh and Glasgow.

Tayside and Northeast Scotland

North of Fife and east of the Highlands are the **River Tay** and the city of **Dundee.** Farther north sit the **Grampian Mountains, Royal Deeside** (home of the monarchy's retreat at Balmoral castle), and the now oil-rich city of **Aberdeen.** This region, called Tayside, offers castles, whisky distilleries, and handsome countryside. For details on this area, flip to Chapter 17.

The Highlands

The **Highlands,** discussed at length in Chapter 18, is a huge and justifiable tourist draw. For better or worse, however, the area's main attraction is still a mythical creature swimming in the waters of **Loch Ness.** Don't get me wrong, the loch is a big, dark, and brooding body of water, but it's not the best thing about the Highlands. You're not likely to see any monster and may feel that the place has elements of a tourist trap, so see it if you must, but then move on. The unofficial capital of the Highlands, **Inverness,** although not particularly exciting, provides a good jumping off spot for exploring the Black Isle or other parts of the Highlands nearby.

The craggy Western Highlands are the proverbial soul of Scotland. Although steeped in proud lore and sad tragedy, from the Jacobite uprising and the once-mighty clans to the massacre of **Glencoe** and the

Not quite ready for prime time

This book can't possibly cover every part of Scotland. The northernmost areas of the mainland, towns such as Tongue, Wick, and Scrabster, aren't addressed. My apologies for that, especially to any surfers among the readership: The north coast is becoming a mecca for those seeking new breakers. Most of the nearly 800 Scottish islands are uninhabited, and only 60 are larger than about 3 square miles, so I don't have the space to deal with places such as Jura or Tiree in any detail. Sorry. I've also kept the chapter on Shetland and Orkney concise and don't go into great detail about Aberdeenshire and Moray. I intend no offense but generally feel that these are destinations for long-term visitors or for travelers with specific interests. If you want to visit an uninhabited island or spend time in a location not adequately dealt with in *Scotland For Dummies,* please visit a Scottish tourist office to get any supplemental information you may need.

Highland Clearances, the scenery here is what leaves indelible marks on visitors' memories. The mountains are ancient and rise from the sea with utter majesty; the beach sands on the "Road to the Isles" west of Fort William near Mallaig are brilliantly white and unspoiled. Villages such as **Plockton** look like picture postcards, set near the sea in the shadow of nearby peaks. North of the port of **Ullapool,** the country is beautifully desolate and sparsely populated, and **Cape Wrath** feels like the end of the earth.

The Hebridean Islands

If you have time to conquer part of the Highlands, you may also be able to squeeze in one or two of the country's many, many islands. The **Hebrides** (pronounced *heb*-ri-deez) includes a few large inhabited islands and several smaller ones (see Chapter 19). The **Isle of Skye** is the biggest, most accessible, and *arguably* the most beautiful.

Worth a ferry trip and overnight stays if you have the time are other islands such as **Mull** and its little sister **Iona,** an ancient landmark of Celtic Christianity in Scotland. Day-trippers may just go to **Eigg** from the tiny port village of **Arisaig.** Feeling a little more adventurous? Head to the wind-swept Outer Hebrides, such as **Lewis** and **Harris**.

Shetland and Orkney islands

The far northern island chains of **Shetland** and **Orkney** are remote and rural (so they're only discussed briefly in Chapter 20). Unless you have the time and inclination, they may not be worth the trouble to visit. On the other hand, their very remoteness makes them a welcome reprieve from the tourist trail.

Scheduling Your Time

The temptation to any visitor, and especially the curious and ambitious ones, is trying to see everything, but most of us end up missing as much as we see in the frantic effort to "do it all." Plus, we're just exhausted at the end of it all.

This book covers most of the country and gives you itineraries that take you from one side of the country to the other and back again. But if your time is limited, you should consider simply staying in Edinburgh and Glasgow, which have plenty to offer, and using them as bases for any excursions. Chapter 13 and the first chapters of Part IV are full of attractions within striking distance of the country's two biggest cities.

Of course, the Highlands are spectacular. But if you don't fancy the idea of sleeping in a different bed every night, find a location that offers a variety of sights to see and things to do in the vicinity of other places you want to visit. For example, from the pretty seaside village of Arisaig, you can easily get to Skye, see Glenfinnan and Fort William to the east, or go south to Movern and Ardnamurchan.

Ultimately, you can't really go wrong wherever you choose to go. If you don't see it all in one go, then you'll just have to plan a return trip — or use this book to vicariously experience the bits you missed.

Mild weather thanks to the Gulf Stream

No matter what time of year you choose to visit Scotland, chances are slim that you'll make it back home without Scottish raindrops falling on your head. Always have a waterproof coat handy.

Certain places in Scotland get more rain than others. For example, the Isle of Mull in the west is notoriously prone to precipitation, while the Moray coast in the northeast is probably the most consistently sunny spot.

Still, as far as temperature goes, Scotland is reasonably mild year-round (see Table 3-1). Not much risk of frostbite here, except on mountaintops and during occasional cold snaps.

Table 3-1		Average Monthly Temperature in Scotland									
	Jan	Feb	Mar	Apr	May	June	July	Aug	Sep	Oct	Nov	Dec
°F	33–42	34–43	35–48	39–52	42–58	49–63	52–67	51–67	47–61	42–55	35–48	34–43
°C	1–6	2–7	3–8	4–12	6–14	9–18	12–20	11–20	8–17	6–13	3–8	2–7

Here comes the sun

The amount of daylight varies greatly in Scotland's northern latitudes. The price paid for long, languid days during the summer is short, dark ones during winter. So, if you depend upon natural light to see the sights that you're most interested in, visiting from May through September allows you to take advantage of the longer days.

Before you leave home, get up-to-date weather forecasts on the Internet. The BBC Web site www.bbc.co.uk/weather is a good source for Scottish weather forecasts.

Revealing the Secrets of the Seasons

You've no doubt heard all about Scottish weather: The Scots like to joke about getting "four seasons in one day." But weather isn't the only consideration to make when planning your trip to Scotland. The high season brings crowds, and the low season carries the possibility that some attractions and hotels are closed. No matter when you travel to Scotland, however, each season boasts certain advantages and drawbacks, which I share in this section.

Summer

The most popular and arguably the best time to tour Scotland is summer, when the country's geared to receive tourists and the weather's usually (though not always) warmer than other times of the year. For the unsure traveler, traveling in the summer is your best bet; you have lots of company and plenty of leads to follow.

The upside

In the summer, all attractions, hotels, and restaurants — no matter how remote — are open for visitors and business. All tourist information centers are open, too — some seven days a week and well into the evening hours.

Summer's the busiest tourist season, but crowds aren't always bad things. Streets teeming with people may actually enhance your trip. Scotland's a friendly place, so throwing a ton of visitors into the mix can create a spirited atmosphere. Plus, the Edinburgh Festival in August is quite possibly the biggest annual cultural event in all of Europe.

The days are long during this time of year. In fact, if you're in the far north, the sun never really appears to set. Even down in Edinburgh, sunlight lasts well into the evening, and closer to the west coast, you can discern a glimmer of fading light as late as 11 p.m. Of course, the sun rises about 4:30 in the morning here, too.

The weather? Well, if you've got your heart set on fine and dry weather; if you're allergic (either physically or emotionally) to drizzle, fog, or rain; if it's your tan you want to work on, then don't go to Scotland. The place is almost never balmy. Instead, summer conditions can be comfortably warm and breezy during the day and drop to that perfect light-sweater temperature at night. You may get caught in some rain, especially on the islands, in June, July, or August.

The downside

During the summer, tourists can overwhelm many popular attractions and towns. The influx of visitors, especially in Edinburgh from late July to early September, may mean that hotels don't have any available rooms. Plus, normally quiet villages like Pitlochry or Plockton start to resemble Fifth Avenue, with crowds pouring off tour buses. So, if you're craving a break from the masses, summer is not the time to come to Scotland unless you plan to travel to the country's very extremities.

Seasonal rates are the other major downside to visiting in the summer: Accommodations can be significantly more expensive in summer than in other seasons.

For many travelers, the worst thing about summer in the Western Highlands and islands are the *midges* — blood-sucking no-see-um bugs that can drive you to serious distraction and leave a plethora of tiny but extremely itchy bites on your body. Make sure you have netting and some strong bug spray if you're coming to these parts in the summer.

 Summers on the western islands can be quite rainy because they take the brunt of the prevailing trade winds. The best times to visit this region are usually in May or September, when dry periods are more prevalent, although it may be a tad cooler.

Fall

Fall, which Scots know only as autumn, is probably the most underrated time to visit Scotland. The weather can be spectacular, with a good chance of sunny, dry stretches. Even when it's stormy, the fronts often move through quickly. The prospect of mild days without too much rain (except out in the islands) and daylight extending to 8 or 9 p.m. (until the clocks go back) is great for marathon sightseeing.

The upside

Beginning in mid-September, the high season has run its course and prices begin to fall. Everything is less crowded. The pubs and restaurants "belong" to the locals again as they reclaim their turf from the tourist hordes. So, in the autumn, you're more likely to find bars filled with locals rather than tourists.

Days are still long, and if you're traveling in the West, the midges usually get knocked back by the first cool nights. What a relief.

The downside

A few of the more seasonal and far flung attractions, as well as some tourist offices, begin to shut down or at least restrict their hours in the fall.

Autumn may mean fewer tourists, but plenty of people still travel this time of year. Autumn nights in Scotland can start to be surprisingly cool, and some of the guesthouses don't have central heating, so you may end up buried in blankets or layering more clothes over your pajamas. In the Highlands, you may even experience a light frost or snow flurry.

Winter

Winter conditions are less than ideal, but Scottish winters are quite a bit less severe than they're often made out to be. Anyone visiting from Iowa or Illinois will find them quite mild. From November through March, the main cities function as normal, and golf along the southwest coast remains a lure. Days are very short, however, plus tourist attractions and some inns in the countryside may well be closed for the season.

The upside

Prices are at their lowest all across the country in the winter, and you're likely to find the cheapest airfares of the year. Because it's the least popular time to travel, more special rates and package deals are offered. The exceptions to winter travel deals are Christmas and New Year's, when rates pop up to equal those of the high season.

If you dislike crowds, winter's the best time for you to visit Scotland. It's also a good time to visit museums, galleries, and year-round attractions. And the landscape is almost as beautiful as during the full swing of summer.

For snowboarding and skiing, a few resorts offer adequate facilities in the Highlands. If golf is your bag, then head for the links courses in Ayrshire. They're sandy and drain well, allowing play through the winter.

The downside

The winter weather can be *driech* (Scottish slang for gloomy and wet). It's often cold, rainy, and windy from January through March. The temperature rarely dips to extreme lows, but the elements can be pretty miserable. Snowfall isn't as heavy as it used to be, but blizzards can still hit. The sun usually doesn't rise until 9:30 a.m., and then it's gone by 4 p.m.

Some attractions are shuttered for a few months every winter. Many rural hotels, B&Bs, and restaurants close for the season, as well, and lots of places have shorter hours during the winter months. This reduced activity is all because tourism slows to a crawl. You still can find plenty of things to do, but the tour you get is abbreviated and offers fewer highlights than the one you get in the other seasons.

Spring

Spring can be slow to start in Scotland, and even in May, the weather can still feel rather wintry at times. But the days quickly lengthen, and some people consider this to be the ideal time to travel in Scotland.

The upside

Warmer temperatures and longer days combine to make for wonderful springtime conditions for touring the countryside. The ground's carpeted in spring greenery, and the plants are beginning their displays (the rhododendrons, in particular, are breathtaking). Any rain showers are isolated and last only part of the day.

By the time spring rolls around, tourist industry folks have had their breaks and are ready to resume playing host. Country inns and travel information offices reopen, but because the high season hasn't hit yet, crowds are manageable.

The downside

Scotland can get pretty rainy from March through June, and a snow flurry or two isn't unusual. Nights remain cool even if days are warming slowly up, so packing for the weather can be a chore.

Easter traditionally marks the beginning of the high season, so prices start to go up at that point. But these days, foreign visitors start flooding in (especially to Edinburgh) before that magic date, so it looks as if the tourist season is stretching its normal boundaries.

Perusing a Calendar of Events

Scotland has its share of festivals and special events throughout the year, with the centerpiece being the Edinburgh Festival, which is really several festivals in one, in August. Highland games are held in most regions from summer to early autumn. Log onto www.visitscotland.com for information on many of the events highlighted below.

January

The best attended annual festival in Glasgow and the largest of its kind in the world, **Celtic Connections** kicks off the year every January. The main venue for performances is the Royal Concert Hall, which produces the event. Guests include traditional acts of folk music and dance as well as contemporary artists. For details, call Glasgow Royal Concert Hall, Sauchiehall Street (☎ **0141-353-8000;** www.grch.com). Mid-January.

On **Burns Night,** the poet Robert Burns's birthday, special suppers (usually involving haggis) are held across the country — but particularly in Ayrshire. It's an evening of storytelling, whisky, and traditional Scottish fare. January 25.

March

In Lanark, south of Glasgow, the **Whuppity Scourie Festival** aims to beat the winter blahs. The town sponsors dancing, singing, music, and storytelling activities. March 1.

For one week, the Isle of Mull becomes the theatrical capital of Scotland thanks to the **Mull Drama Festival in Tobermory.** Production companies head over to do a short run of their shows. Last week in March.

April

For two weeks, Scotland hosts the world's largest science festival at various venues throughout Edinburgh. At the **Edinburgh International Science Festival,** adults and kids alike find the festival's 250 shows, workshops, exhibitions, and lectures lots of fun and quite interesting. For details, call ☎ **0131-530-2001** or visit www.sciencefestival.co.uk. Second and third week in April.

The **Melrose Seven,** held in Melrose, is an international rugby event that features seven high-octane players on each side. Call ☎ **01343-542-666** for the scoop. Mid-April.

Under a big top tent in Glasgow's George Square, art galleries from across the UK set up stalls and show off the work of artists they represent during **RAW: Real Art Weekend.** This is the second biggest art show of its type in the UK. Mid-April.

May

When the **Pitlochry Festival Theatre's** season kicks off in May, the Highlands' gateway town hosts a series of events. For details, call ☎ **01796-484-600** or visit www.pitlochry.org.uk. Mid-May.

Football fans flock to Glasgow in May for the **Scottish FA Cup Final.** This game is the deciding match for Scotland's premier football (that's soccer) cup tournament. The center of the festivities, merriment, and fanaticism is Hamden Park. Mid-May.

The **Perth Festival of the Arts,** the city's annual festival of music, art, and drama, features local and international artists. Call ☎ **01738-47-2706** or visit www.perthfestival.co.uk for more information. Last ten days in May.

Edinburgh hosts the **Children's International Theatre Festival,** Britain's largest performing-arts festival for young people. Renowned companies from around the world sponsor shows, workshops, and storytelling. Visitors under the age of 15 are easily engaged, and the festival has enough to keep parents interested as well. For details, call ☎ **0131-225-8050** or surf to www.imaginate.org.uk. Last week in May.

The best in modern and old-school jazz culminates in a series of concerts and late-night events during the **Dundee Jazz Festival.** The three main venues are the Dundee Rep Theatre, the Westport Bar, and the Dundee Contemporary Arts Centre. For information, call ☎ **01382-223-530.** Last week in May.

June

During the **Common Riding,** hundreds of riders parade around Selkirk, Hawick, Annan, and other Borders towns in a magnificent display of horsemanship. The event commemorates a 16th-century battle that left only one survivor to sound the alarm for the city. Throughout June.

St. Magnus Fest, on the Orkney Islands, is an excellent music festival that showcases new singing and composing talent and mixes up modern and classical sounds to the delight of fans. Music is the main focus of the festival, but local arts-and-crafts folks come out as well. Log onto www. stmagnusfestival.com for information. Third week in June.

One highlight of Scotland's country calendar is the **Royal Highland Show** in Ingliston, near Edinburgh. This agriculture and food fair is a great opportunity to get up close and personal with pedigree livestock, flowers, show jumping, crafts, and more. For information, call ☎ **0131-335-6200** or visit www.rhass.org.uk. Late June.

July

During the **Royal Bank Glasgow Jazz Festival,** top Scottish and some international jazz performers converge on the city for a long weekend of concerts. Call ☎ **0141-552-3552** or visit www.jazzfest.co.uk for information. First weekend in July.

T in the Park, in Balado, Fife, is considered Scotland's "Woodstock." This annual outdoor music show is the biggest and best pop festival in the country. Big acts from the United States and the UK play on five stages; fans enjoy good food and craft stalls and plenty of camping space. For more information, visit www.tinthepark.com. Second weekend in July.

The longest-running jazz festival in the UK is the **Edinburgh International Jazz & Blues Festival.** During the festival, the whole city opens its doors to host the best jazz and blues performances. Venues aren't limited; concert halls, theaters, clubs, pubs, and even the streets feature all styles of jazz played by artists who hail from the four corners of the globe. For more information, call ☎ **0131-667-7776** or 0131-225-2202 or point your browser to www.jazzmusic.co.uk. Last week of July and into August.

August

The cultural highlight of Edinburgh's year comes every August during the **Edinburgh International Festival** and **Festival Fringe.** Since it began in 1947, the International Festival has attracted artists and performance companies of the highest caliber, whether in classical music, opera, ballet, or theater. Running almost simultaneously is the Fringe, an opportunity for anybody — professional or nonprofessional, an individual, a group of friends, or a whole company — to put on a show wherever they can find an empty stage or street corner. HQ for the International Festival is The

Hub, Castle Hill (☎ **0131-473-2000;** www.eif.co.uk). The Fringe is based at 180 High St. (☎ **0131-226-0000;** www.edfringe.com). Throughout August.

As if the International Festival and the Fringe weren't enough, Edinburgh also hosts (at about the same time) a variety of other festivals. In Charlotte Square, the **Edinburgh International Book Festival** has become a huge annual event, drawing authors such as J.K. Rowling and Toni Morrison. You can also find the **Edinburgh International Film Festival,** the **Jazz Festival** (see events listing for June), and the **Edinburgh International Television Festival.** One of the season's more popular spectacles is the **Military Tattoo,** featuring music, marching, and military exercises on the floodlit esplanade of Edinburgh Castle. For information on these and other Edinburgh festivals, visit www.edinburghfestivals.co.uk.

The largest bagpipe band gathering, the **World Pipe Championships,** takes place every year in Glasgow. Nearly 200 bands from around the world gather at Glasgow Green to compete for the highest honors in piping. The competition gives the playing sports-like fervor, and the weeklong event includes some Highland game action, as well. Call ☎ **0141-221-5414** for details. Mid-August.

September

Braemar Royal Highland Games & Gathering is one of the largest Highland games and is almost always attended by members of the Windsor family, given their Royal Highland spread is nearby. Spectators take in piping, dancing, and strength competitions. Call ☎ **01339-755-377** for details or log onto www.braemargathering.org. First weekend in September.

For a couple weekends every September, the **Doors Open Days** event arranges for the doors at buildings normally closed to the public to be opened. Thus, visitors have rare opportunities to see the interiors of historic and architecturally significant edifices all over Scotland. For more information, visit www.scottishcivictrust.org.uk/doors.htm. Throughout September.

October

A large festival of Gaelic music, culture, and song, the **Royal National Mod** moves from one city to the next every year. In 2005, for example, it's to be held in Stornoway on the Isle of Lewis. The performing arts competition and all the good food and crafts that surround the Mod make it worth checking to see whether the festival may be in or near a city on your itinerary. For information, call ☎ **01463-709-705** or visit www.the-mod.co.uk. Mid-October.

November

St. Andrews Night celebrates the patron saint of Scotland; festivities including exhibits, concerts, and fireworks displays are held in St. Andrews and other locations around the country. The Scots would like to see St. Andrews Night be as big a celebration as St. Patrick's Day — doing for Scotland what the other has done for Ireland in terms of good PR. Alas, St. Patrick's Day is in March, at the beginning of spring, and St. Andrew's Day is at the end of gloomy November. November 30.

December

In Scotland's capital, the end of the year, known as **Hogmanay,** turns into a weeklong festival with dozens of indoor and outdoor events (many free), culminating with a New Year's Eve Street Party, rock concert, and fireworks display. Glasgow also has Hogmanay celebrations that usually include outdoor concerts in the city center. For the scoop on Edinburgh's Hogmanay, call ☎ **0131-473-2001** or log onto www.edinburghshogmanay.org; for Glasgow information, visit www.glasgows-hogmanay.co.uk. Last week in December.

Chapter 4

Following an Itinerary: Five Great Options

*M*any people like to have a bit of structure when they travel. Most of us are willing to leave a few things to chance, but we still basically want to know the whats, wheres, and whens of our travel breaks. With that in mind, this chapter suggests a clutch of practical itineraries. The first two are appropriate if you have only one or two weeks to explore Scotland. With the next itinerary, I tackle a seven-day route designed particularly for those traveling with family. Finally, if you want to focus on the outdoors, I've put together two different one-week itineraries that focus on the wonderful Highlands and Scottish islands.

In each itinerary, I direct you to the proper chapters to find in-depth information on the sights and attractions listed. Alternatively, you can look up specific attractions in the Index at the back of the book, which directs you to the appropriate city and region chapters in Parts III and IV.

You may be planning to rent a car for your stay in Scotland. If you want to see Edinburgh and Glasgow, however, you're better off without one. You may find that some side trips are more difficult to make without an automobile, but regions such as Fife and Ayrshire and cities such as Stirling can be easily visited by train or by bus. Even the shores of Loch Lomond can be reached by train, so don't feel obliged to use a gas guzzler unless you want the utter freedom to explore and take all sorts of back roads.

Seeing Scotland's Highlights in One Week

If you have seven days to explore, you're not going to see everything that Scotland has to offer. Worry not: With a bit of enterprise, you can see quite a lot despite the time restrictions of your vacation.

With only a week to spend, I strongly suggest that you principally visit Edinburgh and Glasgow, using them as bases for excursions into the countryside. The one-week itinerary in this section offers the option of one overnight stay on the fringes of the Highlands or south of the principal cities. You may prefer to try and cover more of the country by staying in different places every night. If that's the case, then you may want to combine part of this section with parts of the next section on a two-week trip in Scotland.

Day 1

Start in the capital, **Edinburgh.** In your inaugural 24 hours, familiarize yourself with the city by taking one of the hop-on hop-off, open-top **tour buses.** Then stick to the city's **Old Town** and stroll the **Royal Mile,** taking in the attractions, such as **Edinburgh Castle, Gladstone's Land, St. Giles Cathedral,** and the **Palace of Holyroodhouse.** Later **pop into a pub** for a drink and dine at one of the city's fine restaurants. You can find complete information on Old Town and its major attractions, pubs, and restaurants in Chapter 11.

Day 2

Your priority today is Edinburgh's museums and galleries. If you're a history buff, the **Museum of Scotland** should top your list. For art, hit as many **National Galleries** as possible, whether the main collection on **the Mound,** more recent works at the **Modern Art Gallery,** or luminaries depicted in the **National Portrait Gallery.** For details on all these (and more), see Chapter 11.

Day 3

Take your first daytrip outside the city today. I offer three choices here not because I can't make up my mind but because I want you to know your options. Pick between the **Kingdom of Fife,** which is just across the Forth River from Edinburgh (see Chapter 16); the ancient city and castle of **Stirling** (see Chapter 16); or East Lothian and the Borders (see Chapters 13 and 14). Each choice provides a break from the city and exposes you to the readily available countryside.

Day 4

It's a travel day, but you're only going some 45 miles west to Scotland's biggest city, **Glasgow.** Leave as early as possible to avoid rush hour crowds on the trains or traffic on the motorway. As in Edinburgh, I advise one of the hop-on hop-off **tour bus** rides that leave frequently from George Square in the heart of the city. Return to the commercial center after your tour and explore some of the city's **free museums,** visit the medieval **Glasgow Cathedral,** or follow my walking tour (in Chapter 12) to admire the famous **Victorian architecture.** Flip to Chapter 12 for more information on Glasgow, including hints on the city's top pubs and restaurants.

Day 5

One of today's priorities is the **Burrell Collection,** which requires a trip to the Pollok Country Park on the city's South Side. Return to explore the leafy environs of Glasgow's most desirable district, the **West End,** which is home to the city's 500-plus year-old university and more art (especially in the **Kelvingrove Art Museum and Gallery,** which reopens in 2006). Shop, drink, and dine on **Byres Road.** You can find more information on all Glasgow has to offer in Chapter 12, where you can also take note of my suggested one-, two-, and three-day or more itineraries for Glasgow.

Day 6

Time is running short, so why not make another daytrip, with the option of an overnight stay? Take the high road from Glasgow to the Highlands, stopping along the bonnie banks of **Loch Lomond** before heading west over the pass known as **Rest and be Thankful** and arriving at Loch Fyne, where some of the best shellfish in the world is raised. Inveraray Castle sits near the banks of Loch Fyne, and the town of Inveraray itself has its own charm as well. The old jail, which has been converted into a museum of Scottish crime and punishment, is particularly interesting. You can make it back to Glasgow, but you may prefer to stay in the country this evening. See Chapter 15 for details on this region.

Day 7

Unbelievably, your time is almost up. You may want to go south of Glasgow to **Burns Country** in Ayrshire, an excursion that can include visits to the poet's birthplace as well as stops at golfing hotspots such as **Turnberry** and a tour of historic properties such as **Culzean Castle,** with its magnificent seaside prospect, gardens, and parkland. (See Chapter 15 for more information on these and other attractions in the area.) If you passed on Stirling earlier in your visit, you can get there just as easily from Glasgow. Chapter 16 has all the details.

Touring the Best of Scotland in Two Weeks

In two weeks, you can see all the major regions of Scotland and a fair number of the major attractions, too.

Days 1, 2, and 3

Obviously, I don't want to exclude Edinburgh and Glasgow from this itinerary, so you can spend your first two days in Edinburgh, following the itinerary outlined in the previous section. But give the capital an extra 24 hours, so that on the third day you can pick-up some additional quality time in this fabulous city or take a quick daytrip to either Stirling or Fife. See Chapters 11, 13, and 15 for more information. (After a detour south, this itinerary takes you to Glasgow, too, on Days 6 and 7.)

Day 4

Now's your chance to see some of **Southern Scotland.** Head for **Melrose** and its historic abbey and see **Abbotsford,** the home of Sir Walter Scott. Then, journey west to Dumfries and Galloway. Dumfries is a pleasant southern town, sometimes referred to as the "Queen of the South," with poet Robert Burns's final home, which is now a museum. If you have the inclination, head to the lovely harbor town of **Portpatrick** on the Rhinns of Galloway, a picturesque coastal settlement boasting a natural harbor with excellent seaside views. See Chapter 14.

Day 5

Travel north toward Glasgow, seeing the sights of Culzean and Burns Country, which is outlined in Day 7 of "Seeing Scotland's Highlights in One Week."

Days 6 and 7

These are your days to spend in Glasgow; consider following my suggestions for what to see and do in "Seeing Scotland's Highlights in One Week." For details on Glasgow and its offerings, jump to Chapter 12.

Day 8

Head north of the city toward the **Highlands,** via **Loch Lomond.** Depending on your ambitions, this journey can include a detour to Loch Fyne and Loch Awe, but I suggest it's probably best to head for **Oban** (see Chapter 15).

Day 9

Spend today touring the isles of **Mull** and the ancient Christian settlement of **Iona.** To get to these places, catch an early ferry from Oban or join a guided tour. If you want to spend the night on Mull, you may consider the **Western Isles Hotel** in **Tobermory.** See Chapter 19 for more information on the islands.

Day 10

From the port of Tobermory you can take a ferry (in season) to the remote peninsula of **Ardnamurchan.** Along the way, you can stop to take in **Castle Tioram, Arisaig, Sands of Morar,** and **Mallaig.** From Mallaig, another ferry departs to the **Isle of Skye.** The ferry will also take you to the mainland where you can travel north and link up with the "Road to the Isles." See Chapters 18 and 19 for details on these areas and attractions.

Day 11

As you near the end of your tour, visit the **Cuillin Hills** of Skye and stop at **Portree** before heading back to the mainland via the bridge at the **Kyle of Lochalsh.** If you're making good time, stop at **Eilean Donan** castle and the picturesque town of **Plockton** before you start the long but lovely drive to **Inverness** and the northern shores of **Loch Ness.** For details on the area, flip to Chapter 18.

Day 12

Here's your chance to see Nessie, the Loch Ness Monster. Don't spend too much time at Loch Ness, however, because you need to get across the mountains to Royal Deeside. Here, it's worth your time to have a gander at a few castles, such as **Braemar** and **Blair Atholl,** and perhaps make a stop at a whisky distillery. See Chapter 17 for more on the area.

Day 13

As you head back toward the center of Scotland, take in **Perth** as well as the golfing mecca and ancient settlement of **St. Andrews** (see Chapter 17).

Day 14

On the last day of your tour, visit Stirling if you haven't already done so, or alternatively, tour Fife on your way back to Edinburgh, where this itinerary began a fortnight ago.

Discovering Scotland with Kids

Touring history-heavy castles or art-laden museums with children in tow doesn't have to be a big headache or a battle of patience and wills. Plenty of attractions appeal to all ages. If you're traveling with little ones, following the loose itinerary in this section can be the path of least resistance. When you're following this tour through Edinburgh and Glasgow, you don't need a car; public transportation and an occasional taxi should suffice. However, upon leaving those two cities, a car becomes necessary to complete this tour.

As you follow the cross-references in this section and jump to other chapters in this book, look for the Kid Friendly icon, which points out the best attractions, restaurants, and so on to visit with children.

Begin in **Edinburgh**, and make sure to visit **Edinburgh Castle**. The self-guided audio tour may confuse little kids, but the castle is interesting and fun to explore even without any commentary. Nearby, the **Camera Obscura** usually fascinates children. You can make a trip to the **Edinburgh Zoo** to see the penguin parade, and while in town, visit the toy-filled **Museum of Childhood**. See Chapter 11 for more information on Edinburgh's attractions.

Next it's on to **Glasgow**, where you can break up your other sightseeing with kiddie favorites such as the **Museum of Transport**; interactive exhibits at the **Science Centre;** and the fun, hands-on **People's Palace**. For a breath of fresh air (and to burn off any excess energy), take a romp around **Glasgow Green.**

A couple of side trips from Glasgow can take two entire days. You can head south along the coast, where the kids can comb beaches, see the cottage where poet Robert Burns was born, and romp about the adventure playground at **Culzean Castle.** In the other direction is Stirling, with a bit of history and education at **Bannockburn,** good exploring in **Stirling Castle,** and some entertainment (and frights) in the tour of Stirling's **Old Town Jail.**

From Glasgow, you may want to head north through spectacular **Glen Coe** and perhaps spend a day exploring the area around Fort William, hiking or mountain biking around **Ben Nevis,** the highest peak in Great Britain. Next comes the **Loch Ness** region, which is generally a load of fun for children. Check out one of the Loch Ness exhibitions and one of the sonar-scoping monster-hunting cruises.

On the road back to Edinburgh, you can stop at **J.M. Barrie's Birthplace** (he wrote *Peter Pan*) in Kirriemuir; see **Discovery Point,** the home of the adventure ship RRS *Discovery,* in Dundee; and visit **Deep Sea World,** just north of Edinburgh in North Queensferry.

Touring Scotland's Great Highlands

Scotland has no shortage of things to see, and most regions have their own unique attractions. But the best among all regions has to be the wild terrain of the Highlands. Why not try to get all the way to the top of Scotland (and the UK, too, for that matter) and see some of the wide-open spaces? For this seven-day itinerary (I didn't break it down into exact days, so you can adjust the plans as you like), you can take the train from anywhere up to Inverness and rent a car there. For more details on the attractions and for lists of accommodations and restaurants in this area, see Chapter 18.

From **Inverness**, head north across the Black Isle, through **Tain,** and across the Dornoch Firth. Make a brief stop to see the cathedral in **Dornoch,** and then head up through Lairg to the northern shore.

Beware of the midge

I love the western extremities of Scotland, but for many, the region's home to the nastiest beast in the nation. The *midge* (pronounced midgy) is a tiny flying insect that leaves a terrifically itchy bite. If you can't resist the call of the west, arm yourself with some powerful bug spray.

At Tongue, you may want to stop to see the Highland cattle that roam the beaches here, and then go west to **Durness,** a settlement that John Lennon visited as a child, which is why a small monument stands in his memory. One natural curiosity is **Smoo Cave,** although what's really spectacular is the craggy shoreline, which leads to remote **Cape Wrath.** For some excellent crafts, visit **Balnakeil** — an artists' colony that's a throwback to the 1960s if there ever was one.

From Durness, you head south along more beautiful, unspoiled shoreline towards **Scourie.** But before you get there, you really must detour out to Blairmore, park the car, and hike into the most unspoiled beach in Great Britain, at **Sandwood Bay.** You can also hike to Cape Wrath from Sandwood, if you're ambitious.

To appreciate just how wild, beautiful, and un-populated the Western Highlands region of Scotland truly is, detour at Kylesku to the peninsula with the stone monument known as the **Old Man of Stoer** or simply carry on to the active fishing port of **Ullapool.** It's hardly a big town, but it seems like the height of civilization after you've spent time further north.

Inverewe Garden is the next highlight, although your drive south provides ample opportunities to stop and sightsee, like at **Gruinard Bay,** where you may just see some sea otters splashing in the surf.

The road south twists and turns past Gairloch, Loch Torridon, and the road to **Applecross** (where the inn serves famously delicious meals) before arriving in perhaps the most picturesque village in the Highlands: **Plockton.** Kick back, relax, and toast your Highland excursion on your final night of this tour.

Finally, drive to Loch Duich and see **Eilean Donan,** the most photographed castle in the Highlands. Then hit the road through Invermoriston to **Loch Ness,** where you can take a brief cruise and see if Nessie raises her knurled head, before you return to Inverness.

Touring the Western Highlands and Islands

If you don't want to cover the hundreds of miles necessary to get to places such as Durness, Sandwood Bay, and Inverewe Garden, then the itinerary in this section is the one for you. It's less strenuous but still brings you into the Highlands and includes a taste of the islands, too. For more details on the places mentioned in this section, see Chapters 15, 18, and 19.

From Glasgow, where you should rent a car for this tour after you've seen the city, head northwest along the bonnie banks of **Loch Lomond,** stop for refreshment at the **Drovers Inn,** carry on to Crianlarich, and enter the Highlands via the gorgeously desolate **Rannoch Moor** and verdant **Glen Coe.**

The region south of Fort William is a great place to spend the night. You can choose from inexpensive B&Bs as well as posher lodges, such as **Ballachulish House.** In **Fort William,** satisfy your shopping urges, and then get on the "Road to the Isles," which takes you to the **Glenfinnan Monument** at the tip of Loch Shiel.

Get off the beaten track and explore a bit of Moidart and **Ardnamurchan,** which has the most westerly peninsula in the British mainland. Take time to see **Castle Tioram** before backtracking to Lochailort and resuming the trek north to **Arisaig.**

From Arisaig, with its pleasant little harbor, you can take a cruise to one of the small islands, **Eigg.** The trip often includes some whale sightings. Just past Arisaig, golfers may want to try the tricky (if short) **Traigh** course, before everyone enjoys the lovely **Sands of Morar.**

Next on this tour is **Mallaig** and the ferry to Armadale on the isle of **Skye,** which is the largest island of the Hebrides. Just north of the ferry terminal is the **Clan Donald** visitor center. You have time to visit the center and drive up to **Portree,** Skye's main port, before heading back to the mainland via the bridge at the **Kyle of Lochalsh.**

From Skye, head back to the mainland, where area highlights include the attractions of lovely **Plockton** on Loch Carron and **Eilean Donan** castle. Take the scenic drive to **Invergarry,** where you may want to spend the night at the **Glengarry Castle Hotel.**

On your final day, head back to Fort William, where you may have time to explore the **Ben Nevis** region, before retracing your steps through Glen Coe and Rannoch Moor. But this time around, stop at the touristy shops in **Tyndrum** for some souvenirs before hitting the shores of Loch Lomond and the busy highway back to Glasgow.

Planning Your Trip: Mileage Chart

Use Table 4-1 to help you plan your travel itinerary in Scotland, but remember: Roads can be narrow and winding, so allot more time than would be ordinarily necessary to get from point A to point B.

Table 4-1 Distances (In Miles) Between Some of Scotland's Towns and Cities

	Aberdeen	Ayr	Edinburgh	Fort William	Glasgow	Inverness	Perth	Stirling	Ullapool
Ayr	179								
Edinburgh	129	79							
Fort William	157	141	131						
Glasgow	146	33	45	116					
Inverness	105	207	154	64	175				
Perth	84	95	45	106	62	117			
Stirling	119	64	36	96	27	143	35		
Ullapool	158	258	208	109	222	56	165	193	

It's important to be realistic about the amount of time you'll spend in the car or bus burning up precious daylight hours. If you try to hit Ullapool and Inverness in one full (and tiring) day, then you spend most of your day driving the distance between the two cities and see only a few big sights. Try to get up and out early — that means breakfast at 8:30 a.m. instead of 11 a.m. And don't try to cram too much into each day. If you're constantly rushing from one place to the next, then you won't enjoy anything you see.

Part II
Planning Your Trip to Scotland

By Rich Tennant

"They said they offered a very inexpensive package tour."

In this part . . .

The chapters in Part II are designed to get down to the nitty-gritty of planning your trip: making a sensible budget; finding out which airlines go where (and finding the smartest value in airfares); deciding the best ways to get around Scotland once you're there; figuring out how to drive on Scotland's roads; finding the right accommodations for your needs; and managing passports.

In this part you'll find advice on what to do if you get sick in Scotland and whether you should invest in travel insurance. If you're a traveler with special needs and interests, issues important to you are covered here, as well. In short, the following pages are filled with all the info you need to plan your trip to Scotland.

Chapter 5

Managing Your Money

. . . .

In This Chapter

▶ Budgeting for your trip

▶ Reviewing money-saving tips

▶ Understanding the local currency and how best to get it

▶ Carrying money conveniently and safely

. . . .

*A*n important consideration for any vacation is your budget. How much will the trip cost and where will the money go? You don't want to waste good money, but you probably don't want to be tied down to a bare-bones budget that restricts you from seeing the best that Scotland has to offer.

The smart way to travel is to plan your spending in advance: In large part, this means understanding ahead of time what things will cost. But keep in mind that sometimes you get what you pay for.

In this chapter, I cover what you can expect to pay for transportation, accommodation, dining, and sightseeing while in Scotland. Plus, I include some money-saving tips. As a hands-on bonus, I provide a budget work-sheet (Table 5-2) that you can use to plot out your expenses.

Keep in mind that exchange rates are constantly changing. Scotland, like the rest of the United Kingdom, doesn't use the euro. In general, the British pound is worth somewhere between 50 to 100 percent more than the US dollar. Throughout this book, I've calculated the exchange rate at one US dollar being equal to one British pound and eighty-five pence ($1=£1.85). As the pound is worth more than the dollar, goods and services may seem more expensive than what you're used to.

 Goods in Scotland often carry the same price in pounds as they would in dollars back home. For example, a camera that costs $350 in New York might be priced £350 in Edinburgh. But, of course, that means it's quite a bit more expensive in Scotland: almost $300 more costly (using my conversion rate).

Obviously, you want to enjoy your stay and don't want to be constantly converting pounds to dollars before making every purchase. But if your desire is to keep costs down, be wary and make sure you're getting a bargain or at least spending your money wisely.

Planning Your Budget

As far as destinations go, Scotland is neither the cheapest nor the most expensive place to visit. Can you do Scotland on $10 a day? No, quite honestly. On $50 a day? Possibly, if you don't mind camping or hostel bunk beds and convenience-store dinners. Being realistic, however, you can bet on a figure more like $125 to $175 per person per day — more if you factor in full-time car rental and gasoline (petrol) costs. And that figure doesn't include the cost of actually getting to Scotland.

But as I said before, sometimes you do get what you pay for. In this case, Scotland more than compensates for the proverbial price of admission.

Transportation

Car rental (or *car hire* per local vernacular) isn't especially exorbitant, but visitors will likely find the cost of gasoline to be staggeringly high. Remember, here it's called *petrol* and is priced in liters not gallons. It costs about 3.5 times more than the average in the United States. On the plus side, however, your rental car will get exceptional miles per gallon, and the driving distances across Scotland are miniscule compared to cross-country travel in the United States, Canada, or Australia. Usually the car hire rates include unlimited mileage. Check with your auto insurance company to see if you need to buy extra coverage for when you're in Scotland. (I discuss insurance coverage for travelers in Chapter 10.)

Although it may limit your mobility, using public transportation can cut your costs significantly. If you're only planning to visit Edinburgh, Glasgow, and some side destinations, you don't really need to rent a car.

Lodging

Hotel rooms in Scotland aren't cheap. If, however, you do your homework and scour accommodation Web sites, you *will* find rates considerably lower than the standard "tariff" that's quoted by each hotel. If you want luxury or a spectacular view, however, you will have to pay a premium. If you just need a leak-proof roof over your head, a place to wash, and a clean bed, then you can easily save money on your accommodations.

Generally speaking, a double room runs about $120 to $180; those on the low end are around $80 to $100, and on the high end $300 or more. Self-catering cottages rented by the week and country B&Bs are almost always less expensive.

Dining

American visitors with their calculators at the ready will quickly find out that food is about 50 percent more expensive in Scotland than in the U.S. But you can cut your dining expenses by not choosing the ritziest restaurant in town every night of the week. Keep an eye out for lunch specials and pre-theater menus — they offer considerable savings. On the Web, investigate www.5pm.co.uk, which offers reductions on early evening dining options.

A good per-person allowance for lunch is $15 to $20, and for dinner between $20 and $40. Many hotels and lodges include breakfast in the room rate, so at least you don't have to figure that meal into your daily food budget.

Sightseeing

The price of admission to many tourist attractions in Scotland is slightly more modest than what you may expect to find in other Western European countries. In Edinburgh, the permanent exhibitions of the Scottish national galleries are priced just right: absolutely free. And similarly, in Glasgow, the city museums don't cost a pence to enter. All the natural beauty of the countryside, from the Ayrshire coastline to the Grampian Mountains, doesn't cost you a thing and is indeed priceless

Even if you see two or three attractions each day, a fair amount to budget for sights is $15 per person per day.

Shopping

Jump back up to the introduction to this chapter and recall what I've already said about goods and their UK prices. A pair of Calvin Kleins may have the same sticker price as its counterpart in the U.S. but will actually cost nearly twice as much given the exchange rate. Still, you can find "home-grown" commodities in Scotland that are less expensive when purchased here: woolen goods or cashmere, local crafts and arts, and more. So, be selective in your purchases and your wallet will thank you.

Nightlife

Here, as with sightseeing, you may find that things are cheaper than you anticipated, particularly the theater, dance, and even opera. In pubs and bars, prices of alcohol are at the higher end but not ridiculously so. Expect to pay between £1.80 and £2.50 ($3.30–$4.60) for a pint of lager or ale. A dram of whisky is sometimes as little as £1.50 ($2.70), but cocktails are often around £5 ($9.25). In general, I'm talking the equivalent of big city (Toronto, San Francisco, or Melbourne) prices for nightlife in Scotland.

Better too much than not enough

Make sure you have access to emergency money in case you need it. If you golf, add up greens fees and the price of renting clubs (assuming you're not lugging your own around the country). Horseback riding and fishing also make for added costs. Perhaps the best reason for having a supply of money available is shopping. Do you plan to buy clothes, jewelry, crystal, and antiques, or just pick up a few postcards, a snow globe, and a couple of cheap souvenirs? A modest piece of crystal can set you back $80; a nice Edinburgh sweatshirt, about $50. So gauge your impulse-buying tendencies and factor that into your budget, as well.

In Table 5-1, I take the daily estimates laid out in this section and add them up for a projection of how much it typically costs to accommodate and entertain one person for one week in Scotland.

Table 5-1	Per Person Expenses for a Typical Week in Scotland
Expense	**Cost**
Airfare (round-trip New York City to London to Glasgow/Edinburgh)	$500–$700
Rental car	$400
Two to three tanks of gas	$100–$150
Seven nights in hotels ($60 per person average)	$420
Seven lunches ($15 each average)	$105
Seven dinners ($28 each average)	$196
Sightseeing admissions ($20 per day average)	$140
Souvenirs and miscellaneous ($10 per day average)	$70
TOTAL	$1,931–$2,181

Cutting Costs without Cutting the Fun

If worries about travel costs mean you're hesitant to go to Scotland, you have two options: simply stay home and miss all that the country has to offer or get over it. Sure, Scotland isn't the cheapest European country to visit, but it *can* be affordable. Make sensible decisions and look for those bargains that don't cheapen the experience, and you should be fine.

Some tourists demand to be pampered in five-star hotels, but those places are exceptionally expensive in Scotland. If you're flexible when it comes to the pampering, you should seek out the smaller lodges and guesthouses that are priced to fit most travel budgets. A nice perk of most Scottish accommodations is the breakfast that's included in the price of the room. Sometimes it's even hearty enough to keep you full until dinner.

Also, many attractions are free. Even if you stick to seeing things that cost nothing (although you shouldn't skip the other sights just because of the cost), you'll still experience a vast amount of the country.

You can find plenty of ways, some little and some big, to cut down on costs. Here are some smart ways to save on your trip to Scotland:

✔ **Go in mid-season or off-season.** Traveling between mid-October and mid-April can save you plenty on airfare and accommodations. The days leading up to and just after Christmas, New Year's Eve, and Easter are the exceptions, and prices jump up during those periods. (See Chapter 3 for more info on Scotland's seasons.)

✔ **Travel on off-days of the week.** Most everybody wants to travel on the weekends, but those willing to travel on a Tuesday, Wednesday, or Thursday can usually find cheaper flights. When inquiring about airfares, ask if you get a cheaper rate if you fly on a different day. Also remember that staying over a Saturday night can occasionally cut airfares by half.

✔ **Remember that group rates can save money.** And you don't necessarily have to be one of a busload to get them. Sometimes a party as small as three people qualifies for group rates.

✔ **Get the Explorer Pass.** An Explorer Pass offers multiple entries to all the sightseeing attractions run by Historic Scotland, from Iona Abbey to St. Andrews Cathedral to Edinburgh Castle. The pass is sold at many of the 74 historic sites run by the organization. For more information, call ☎ **0131-668-8800** or visit www.historic-scotland.gov.uk.

✔ **Try a package deal.** Many people believe that planning a trip entirely on their own is less expensive, but they're not necessarily correct. Travel packages can save not only money but also time. A single phone call to a travel agent or package tour operator can take care of your flight, accommodations, transportation within the country, and sightseeing arrangements. Even if you're not up for a complete package — if you'd prefer to pay for your plane tickets with frequent-flier miles, say, or if you don't like some of the things the package tour operators offer — you can book room-car deals (which include a free rental car) or other combo packages directly through many hotels. Chapter 6 contains more details on package deals.

✔ **Always ask about discounts.** Membership in AAA, frequent-flier plans, trade unions, AARP, university alumni associations, or other groups often qualifies you for discounted rates on plane tickets, hotel rooms, and (mainly with U.S.-based companies) car rentals. Some car-rental companies give discounts to employees of companies that have corporate accounts. With valid identification, students, teachers, youths, and seniors may be entitled to discounts. Many attractions have discounted family prices. Ask about everything — you may be pleasantly surprised.

✔ **Book your rental car at weekly rates, when possible.** Weekly rentals are most often offered at a discounted rate.

✔ **Know where to buy petrol.** The United Kingdom has some of the highest gasoline prices in Europe, and parts of rural Scotland have the highest prices in the UK. One way to ease the burden of these exhorbitant rates is to fill your tank in larger towns (the farther south, the better) as you drive through the Highlands. For the most part, the smaller the town, the higher the price of gas. Also, you may find lower gas prices at petrol stations at large supermarkets.

✔ **Don't rent a gas guzzler.** Renting a smaller car is cheaper, and you save on gas to boot. Unless you're traveling with kids and need lots of space, don't go beyond the economy size. For more on car rentals, see Chapter 7.

✔ **Walk.** All cities in the country are easy to explore on foot, even Glasgow and Edinburgh. So, avoid the bus and cab fares and hoof it to save a few extra pounds (and even burn off a few from your waistline). As a bonus, you'll get to know your destination more intimately as you explore at a slower pace.

✔ **Skimp on souvenirs.** As a general rule, souvenirs specially created for the tourist market are poorly made and over-priced. If you're concerned about money, you can definitely do without the T-shirts, key chains, and other trinkets.

✔ **Use American Express to exchange money.** Amex offers the best exchange rate and exchanges American Express traveler's checks for free (although you may have to pay a fee for the traveler's checks when you first get them at home). Amex charges a flat fee (under $5) to exchange dollars to pounds or pounds to dollars, but that beats the competition, which invariably charges a percentage of the cash exchanged. Make the exchange office your last stop before you head to the airport at the end of your trip, as well; there's no in joy going home with a pocketful of useless, weighty "souvenir" coins.

✔ **Use libraries for Internet access.** Because of Western tourists' growing use of the Internet, online access is popping up all over Scotland. Most town libraries have access, and they usually don't charge or require you to be a member. This policy may change in the coming years, but for now, libraries are a good, cheap option for surfing the Web.

✔ **Pick up free, coupon-packed visitor pamphlets and magazines.** Detailed maps, feature articles, dining and shopping directories, and discount and freebie coupons make these pocket-size giveaways a smart pickup. You'll find these types of materials in tourist board offices and, perhaps, in the lobby of your hotel.

✔ **Skip the fantabulous hotel room views.** Rooms with great views are the most expensive in any hotel. Unless you're planning to hang out in your room all day, why hand over the extra dough?

✔ **Get out of town.** In many places, hotels located just outside popular tourist areas may be a great bargain and require only a little more driving — and they may even offer free parking. Sure, you may not get all the fancy amenities, and you'll probably have to carry your own bags, but the rooms may be just as comfortable and a whole lot cheaper.

✔ **Ask whether your children can stay in your room for free.** Although many accommodations in Scotland charge by the head, some may allow your little ones to stay for free. Even if you have to pay $10 or $15 for a rollaway bed, in the long run you'll save hundreds by not having to pay for two rooms.

✔ **Never make phone calls from a hotel.** The inflated fees that hotels charge for phone calls are scandalous. Walk to the nearest Coin-Phone or Card-Phone to make calls within and out of the country.

✔ **Consider rooms that aren't *en-suite*.** Rooms without a bathroom are cheaper, although they're increasingly hard to find. Sharing a bathroom may be a small sacrifice when it comes to saving money, and it doesn't really detract from your trip. Group hostel rooms are even cheaper if you're willing to rough it a bit more.

✔ **Check out accommodations with kitchens.** By renting self-catering apartments or cottages for a week or more, you can save money overall on accommodations (especially if you're traveling with a group) and on food, because you can prepare your own meals in the kitchen. By avoiding big-ticket restaurant meals, you'll save a heck of a lot of money.

✔ **Have the same meal for less money.** If you enjoy a late lunch (or an early evening meal) at a nice restaurant and settle for a snack later, your wallet will thank you. Lunch and pre-theater menus often offer the same food as dinner menus, but the prices are much less expensive.

✔ **Before you leave home, check prices on items you think you may want to buy.** This way, you'll know whether you're really getting a bargain by buying items abroad. Spending a little time surfing the Web is an easy way to find the information you need.

✔ **Dress respectably, but not too well.** You want merchants to know you're a potential paying customer and not riffraff, but you don't want to give them the idea that you're loaded — especially in markets, where prices can go up on the spot if you look like you're willing to pay anything.

✔ **Look before you tip.** Some restaurants include a service fee or gratuity on the bill, especially if you're with a group. Study your bill: You could be paying a double tip by mistake. And don't tip bartenders for drinks — they don't expect it.

Table 5-2	Your Scotland Budget Worksheet
Expense	*Amount*
Airfare (multiplied by number of people traveling)	
Car rental (if you expect to rent one)	
Gas (expect to need a tankfull, at about $50 per, for every four to five days of driving)	
Lodging (multiplied by the number of nights you'll be in the country)	
Breakfast (your room rate likely includes it)	
Lunch (multiplied by the number of days in the country)	
Dinner (multiplied by the number of days in the country)	
Attractions (admission charges to museums, gardens, tours, theaters, nightclubs, and so on)	
Souvenirs (T-shirts, postcards, and that antique you just gotta have)	
Tips (think 15 percent of your meal total plus $1 a bag every time a bellhop moves your luggage)	
Incidentals (whisky, snacks, and so on)	
Getting from your hometown to the airport, plus long-term parking (if applicable)	
Grand Total	

Handling Money

After you settle on a budget for your trip, you can start figuring out the nuts and bolts of carrying money abroad. How much money do you want to bring along? Do you want to carry cold hard cash, credit cards, traveler's checks, or all three? How can you get more money after you're in

Scotland? What's the best way to exchange dollars for pounds? And how can you ensure that your money will be safe and secure while you're vacationing?

You're the best judge of how much cash you feel comfortable carrying or what alternative form of currency is your favorite. That's not going to change much just because you're on vacation. True, you'll probably be moving around more and incurring more expenses than you generally do (unless you happen to eat out every meal when you're at home), and you may let your mind slip into vacation mode and not be as vigilant about your safety as when you're in work mode. But, those factors aside, the only type of payment that won't be quite as available to you away from home is your personal checkbook. This section offers just about everything you need to know about money matters in Scotland.

The local currency: What it's worth to you

The currency in Scotland, *British pence* and *pounds sterling,* is quite similar to American cents and dollars. The denominations are almost the same: A few exceptions include the coins for 2 pence and 1 and 2 pound denominations as well as a 20 pence coin (there's no equivalent to the U.S. quarter). Pence are often just referred to as "p," like in "Do you have 20p for the pay phone?" A pound is also known colloquially as a "quid." Some people may refer to a "bob" — this is equivalent to 5p, which used to be known as a "shilling" before the decimal system was imposed in 1971.

Although the Bank of England controls monetary matters across Great Britain and Northern Ireland, a few banks in Scotland, such as the Royal Bank of Scotland, have permission to print Scottish bills in 1-, 5-, 10-, and 20-pound denominations. There's no value difference between these pound notes and those printed in England, and both are accepted throughout Scotland.

 Be careful if you travel to England with Scottish bank notes. Although they're perfectly legal tender in England, Scottish bank notes aren't always accepted by shops and restaurants. Err on the side of caution and go to a bank and exchange any Scottish bills for Bank of England notes before heading south of the border.

As I've said throughout this chapter, goods and services are often more expensive in Scotland than they would be in the U.S. or in other English-speaking countries. Many items sold in Scotland are priced with the same numerical amount as they would be in the U.S. — for instance, if a soda costs a dollar in the U.S., it's often priced at a pound (about $1.85) in Scotland. But because you get less than 60 pence for every dollar you exchange, things cost between 50 percent and 100 percent more in Scotland. This increase isn't true of all items, but it gives you a general idea of how far your new cash and weighty coins will go.

The exchange rate fluctuates daily (by small amounts). The best source for up-to-date currency exchange information is www.xe.com/ucc. The average rates are shown in Table 5-3.

Table 5-3	Typical Currency Exchange Rates
One Dollar	*Equals*
$1 U.S.	54p
$1 Canadian	45p
$1 Australian	42p
$1 New Zealand	38p
One British Pound	*Equals*
£1	$1.85 U.S.
£1	$2.23 Canadian
£1	$2.40 Australian
£1	$2.64 New Zealand

You can exchange money anywhere you see the **Bureau de Change** sign. You usually see it at travel agencies, banks, post offices, and tourist information offices. Generally, you'll get the best rates at banks; the local tourist office can tell you the location of the bank branch nearest you.

Using ATMs and carrying cash

The easiest and best way to get cash away from home is from an ATM (automated teller machine). The **Cirrus** (☎ **800-424-7787;** www.master card.com) and **PLUS** (☎ **800-843-7587;** www.visa.com) networks span the globe; look at the back of your bank card to see which network you're on, then call or check online for ATM locations at your destination. Be sure you know your personal identification number (PIN) and your daily withdrawal limit before you leave home. Also keep in mind that many banks impose a fee every time your card is used at a different bank's ATM, and that fee can be higher for international transactions (up to $5 or more) than for domestic ones (where the fee's rarely more than $1.50). On top of this charge, the bank from which you withdraw cash may charge its own fee, although that's rare in Scotland. For international withdrawal fees, contact your bank.

Despite the withdrawal charges, however, the expansion and integration of ATMs (or "cash points," as the locals prefer to call them) have made obtaining cash a cinch in Scotland's cities. Slip in your card, type in your PIN, and withdraw money in pounds sterling from your bank at home. The exchange rates are usually as good as you'll get anywhere else.

What's up with the euro?

Europe's common currency, the *euro,* isn't used in the UK as of this writing. A major debate has raged among politicians and common folk alike about whether to phase out the pound and phase in the euro. Since 1997, the Labour government has waffled polit- ically and only confused the issue by introducing some spurious economic hurdles. Many people doubt that it ever will be used in place of the British pound. If countries on the Continent begin to reject the euro, then the UK will likely never agree to make the switch — even if it's in the country's best interests to do so. An independent Scotland would probably accept the euro more quickly than the UK, but nobody expects full Scottish automomy any time soon.

You may see euro equivalents calculated on some money transactions, but that's only designed to get consumers familiar with the new money. A few euro-friendly busi- nesses in Scotland happily accept the euro — otherwise it's about as useful as a dollar.

Not all cash points — or cash machines — are connected to the global banking networks. This is especially true in rural areas and in small banks in Scotland. So, don't depend solely on ATMs for cash when you're travel- ing. Also, the security risks are the same here as at home. If someone steals your card and knows your personal identification number (PIN), the crook will try to drain your bank account. Recently, machines have been rigged to "swallow" cards, which are later extracted and used illegally. All this is rare in Scotland, but, nevertheless, you should exercise caution and avoid using ATMs late at night or in poorly lit urban areas.

 Be sure to check your daily withdrawal limit with your bank before you set off on your trip. Remember, if your limit is $250, you'll be able to withdraw only about £135.

 If you lose your ATM card, contact your bank at home and report the loss immediately. You don't want your bank account depleted in the event that the card (and, in a worst-case scenario, personal identifica- tion number) falls into the wrong hands.

Charging ahead with credit cards

Credit cards are invaluable when traveling. They're a safe way to carry money, they provide a convenient record of all your expenses, and they generally offer relatively good exchange rates. You can also withdraw cash advances from your credit cards at banks or ATMs, provided you know your PIN. If you've forgotten yours or didn't even know you had one, call the number on the back of your credit card and ask the bank to send it to you. Do this in advance of your trip because the number usually takes five to seven business days to arrive, although some banks will provide the number over the phone if you tell them your mother's maiden name or some other personal information that verifies your identity.

Keep in mind that when you use your credit card abroad, most banks assess a 2 percent fee above the 1 percent fee charged by Visa or MasterCard or American Express for currency conversion on credit charges. But credit cards still may be the smartest way to go when you factor in things like exorbitant ATM fees and high traveler's check exchange rates (and service fees).

Visa and MasterCard are both widely used in Scotland. American Express is accepted by most major businesses, but Diner's Club is less frequently accepted.

Some credit card companies recommend that you notify them of any impending trip abroad so that they don't become suspicious when the card is used numerous times in a foreign destination and consequently block your charges. Even if you don't call your credit card company in advance, you can always call the card's toll-free emergency number if a charge is refused — a good reason to carry the phone number with you. But perhaps the most important lesson here is to carry more than one card with you on your trip; a card may not work for any number of reasons, so having a backup is the smart way to go. Also, make certain you have the credit card companies' toll free or collect call numbers to phone them from Scotland. You may want to keep multiple copies of these numbers, in case your card (with the number on the back) is lost or stolen.

If you're an **American Express** card member, bring a single blank personal check and keep it in a separate place from your card. If the card is lost or stolen, you can use that check to draw a cash advance against your account. Just bring it, unsigned, into any Amex office, and it'll be cashed on the spot.

Toting traveler's checks

These days, traveler's checks are less necessary because most cities have 24-hour ATMs that allow you to withdraw small amounts of cash as needed. However, keep in mind that you're likely to be charged an ATM withdrawal fee if the bank isn't your own, so if you're withdrawing money every day, you may be better off with traveler's checks — provided that you don't mind showing identification every time you want to cash one.

You can get traveler's checks at almost any bank. **American Express** (with city center offices in both Edinburgh and Glasgow) offers denominations of $20, $50, $100, $500, and (for cardholders only) $1,000. You'll pay a service charge ranging from 1 to 4 percent. You can also get American Express traveler's checks over the phone by calling ☎ 800-221-7282; Amex gold and platinum cardholders who use this number are exempt from the 1 percent fee.

Visa offers traveler's checks at Citibank locations nationwide, as well as at several other banks. The service charge ranges between 1.5 percent and 2 percent; checks come in denominations of $20, $50, $100, $500, and $1,000. Call ☎ **800-732-1322** for information. AAA members can obtain Visa checks without a fee at most AAA offices or by calling ☎ **866-339-3378. MasterCard** also offers traveler's checks; call ☎ **800-223-9920** for a location near you.

 If you choose to carry traveler's checks, be sure to keep a record of their serial numbers separate from your checks in the event that they're stolen or lost. You'll get a refund faster if you know the numbers.

Taking Taxes into Account

All goods and services in Scotland have a tax or tariff similar to the local sales taxes in the U.S. In Scotland, it's called the Value Added Tax (VAT) and is a rather whopping 17.5 percent. The good news is that, as a tourist, you're entitled to get a refund on any VAT paid at stores that are part of the Retail Export Scheme (signs are posted in the window). The tax-back scheme in Scotland is great for tourists who spend a good deal of money on books, jewelry, musical instruments, clothes — you name it. But many tourists come to Scotland, spend a good deal of money, and never find out how to get their VAT back or don't bother because they don't fully understand how it works. To ensure that you don't make the same mistake, here's your quick guide to the VAT.

When you make your purchase, show your passport and ask for the VAT form. Fill out the form, and when you leave the UK, submit the form to Customs for approval. After Customs has stamped it, mail the form back to the shop with the envelope provided — but you must do this before you leave the country. Your refund will then be mailed to you.

 Not all VATs are refundable. For the most part, taxes added to services aren't refundable. Hotels, restaurants, and car rentals, for example, charge VAT that you can't get back.

Protecting Yourself and Your Money

Rest easy: You're going to a pretty darn safe place. The occurrence of violent crime and theft is pretty low in Scotland. You're actually safer there than in most major American cities. Handguns are banned in the UK, and Scotland has so few pistols on the streets that police don't even carry them as a rule. As a tourist, the most important thing you can do is guard yourself against theft. Pickpockets look for people who seem to have the most money on them and know the least about where they are. Standing on a street corner at night with your nose in this book will immediately make you a target.

Scotland is quite safe, but crime is a fact of modern life. And it's always more prevalent in larger cities. In remote areas, people don't even bother locking their house doors for the most part.

Here are a few simple precautions that can help safeguard you against crime:

- ✔ **Leave the gold cufflinks at home.** You don't need to bring valuable jewelry or irreplaceable heirlooms with you when you travel. If possible, arrange to store excess cash, traveler's checks, passports, plane tickets, and other valuables in a hotel safe or security box. If you carry traveler's checks, keep the list of numbers and denominations and the emergency refund phone number separate from the checks.

- ✔ **Don't carry more cash than you'll need for a particular day or evening.** Leave excess money in the hotel safe. While you're out, keep half of your money in your wallet or purse and "hide" the rest — perhaps in the small, or fifth, pocket of your jeans or pants or in a slim wallet that you can wear under your clothes (check out travel or outdoors shops for these types of wallets). This way, if you're mugged or your pocket is picked, you aren't forking over all your cash.

- ✔ **Be aware of your surroundings.** It's not likely to happen, but if you're feeling lost in a "dodgy" area, don't act frightened or confused or even look in your guidebook to orient yourself — all these reactions make you a potential target. Proceed calmly and assuredly till you come to a shop or public building where you can safely ask for assistance.

If your wallet is lost or stolen, don't panic. Contact all your credit card companies the minute you discover the loss. Most credit card companies have an emergency toll-free number to call if your card is lost or stolen; they may be able to wire you a cash advance immediately or deliver an emergency credit card in a day or two.

Contact the police by going to a station, stopping a passing cop, or dialing ☎ **999** on any telephone. In order to cancel charges or cover your loss, your credit card company or insurer may require a police report; plus, contacting the police ensures that any lost items can easily be returned to you if they're found.

Except for the cash, everything in your wallet is replaceable, and you probably can get emergency cash by contacting your bank. Most larger banks will accept collect calls. You may be able to get cash from your checking account wired as a Moneygram and sent to a travel agent or perhaps to your hotel in Scotland. Fees will apply, but at least you won't starve. If you need emergency cash over the weekend when all banks and American Express offices are closed, you can have money wired to you via **Western Union** (☎ **800-325-6000;** www.westernunion.com).

Most Scottish merchants are careful about checking the signatures on receipts against credit cards, but a smart thief will quickly master the fine art of forging your signature. Make sure your cards really are lost before reporting them gone, but after you're certain they're gone, make the calls. You're expected to phone immediately upon realizing your credit cards are gone.

The phone numbers to report lost or stolen credit cards while you're in Scotland are:

  ✔ **Visa** (☎ **0800-891-725**)

  ✔ **MasterCard** (☎ **0800-964-767**)

  ✔ **American Express** (☎ **0800-587-6023**)

  ✔ **Diner's Club** (☎ **702-797-5532**; members can call collect)

For other credit cards, call the toll-free number directory at ☎ **800-555-1212.**

Identity theft or fraud are potential complications of losing your wallet, especially if you've lost your driver's license along with your cash and credit cards. Notify the major credit reporting bureaus immediately; placing a fraud alert on your records may protect you against liability for criminal activity. The three major U.S. credit reporting agencies are **Equifax** (☎ **800-766-0008**; www.equifax.com), **Experian** (☎ **888-397-3742;** www.experian.com), and **TransUnion** (☎ **800-680-7289;** www.transunion.com). Finally, if you've lost all forms of photo ID, call your airline and explain the situation; the airline may allow you to board the plane if you have a photocopy of your passport or birth certificate and a copy of the police report you've filed.

Chapter 6

Getting to Scotland

- -

In This Chapter
▶ Flying to Scotland with the best airfares
▶ Taking the train from England to Scotland
▶ Weighing the pros and cons of escorted or package tours

- -

*V*isiting castles, relaxing in local pubs, and exploring the Highlands are the easy parts of traveling to Scotland. The difficult part is making all the plans to get yourself there and around after you arrive. Several resources, however, make planning your travel to Scotland almost painless. This chapter discusses how to find those resources in addition to helpful hints on things from bargain airfares to the lowdown on love-'em-or-hate-'em package tours.

Flying to Scotland

Unless you fancy a long boat ride, you're most likely to fly into the United Kingdom, arriving in Scotland directly or via England or some other European hub, such as Dublin, Reykjavik, or Amsterdam.

Identifying your airline options

Some U.S. carriers fly directly from New York, Newark, Boston, or Chicago to Glasgow (and more recently Edinburgh), but often the service is seasonal (May–Sept) and seems to change every year. Airlines don't yet appear convinced that the market is solid enough to make a long-term commitment to direct flights to Scotland.

Still, almost every airline in the world seems to fly into one of London's airports, so getting north from there to Scotland will entail only a short flight (45 minutes to one hour, unless you're headed to the Highlands) or a four- to five-hour train ride.

 Air Canada is one carrier that consistently offers direct flights to Scotland, allowing you to bypass London. You can fly directly from Toronto year-round on Air Canada.

If you're traveling from down under, no airlines currently fly directly from Australia or New Zealand to Scotland. All flights on international airlines from these two countries go through London.

Some of the airlines listed below offer direct UK flights. Be sure to call more than one airline to compare prices.

- ✔ **Air Canada** (☎ **888-247-2262;** www.aircanada.ca)

- ✔ **American Airlines** (☎ **800-433-7300;** www.aa.com)

- ✔ **British Airways** (☎ **800-247-9297;** www.britishairways.com)

- ✔ **Continental Airlines** (☎ **800-231-0856;** www.continental.com)

- ✔ **Delta Airlines** (☎ **800-241-4141;** www.delta.com)

- ✔ **Northwest Airlines** (☎ **800-447-4747;** www.nwa.com)

- ✔ **United Airlines** (☎ **800-538-2929;** www.united.com)

- ✔ **Virgin Atlantic** (☎ **800-862-8621;** www.virgin-atlantic.com)

If you travel via London, you can opt for a short flight to Scotland. **BMI** (☎ **0870-6070-555;** www.flybmi.com) offers internal UK and international flights. **Flybe** (☎ **0871-700-0535** or ☎ **44-01392-268520** from outside the UK; www.flybe.com) is a new, discount airline that crisscrosses the UK.

Regardless of whether you're coming to Scotland directly or from a transfer point, you'll most likely fly into Glasgow or Edinburgh. Both airports are easy to get in and out of and offer easy transportation into the cities. Because of the frequency of flights into these airports, you're more likely to find a cheap fare to them compared to flights to smaller Scottish cities, such as Inverness, Aberdeen, or Dundee. Both Edinburgh and Glasgow offer perfectly fine airports, and neither option outweighs the other in terms of proximity to a city.

Glasgow International Airport (☎ **0870-040-0008**) is at Abbotsinch, near Paisley, only about 16km (10 miles) west of the city via M8. On Monday through Friday, British Airways runs almost hourly shuttle service (a short flight) between London's Heathrow Airport and Glasgow. **Edinburgh International Airport** (☎ **0870-040-0007**) is about 10km (6 miles) west of the city's center and has become a growing hub of flights both within the British Isles as well as to and from Continental Europe. South of Glasgow is **Prestwick International Airport** (☎ **0871-223-0700;** www.gpia.co.uk), which is favored by some of the low-budget airlines such as **RyanAir**. Prestwick's on the railway line to Ayr, about a 45-minute ride from Glasgow's Central Station. (For pointers on planning your itinerary, which helps you decide where you should fly in and out of, see Chapter 4; for details on getting to Edinburgh or Glasgow, see Chapters 11 and 12.)

Getting the best deal on your airfare

Competition among the major airlines is unlike that of any other industry. Every airline offers virtually the same product, yet prices can vary by hundreds of dollars.

If you can book your ticket far in advance, stay over Saturday night, and are willing to travel midweek (Tues–Thurs), you can qualify for the least expensive price — usually a fraction of the full fare. Obviously, planning ahead pays.

The airlines also periodically hold sales, in which they lower the prices on their most popular routes. As you plan your vacation, keep your eyes open for these sales, which tend to take place in seasons of low travel volume — in Scotland, the off-season generally runs from the beginning of October to early April. You almost never see a sale around the peak summer vacation months of July and August or around Christmas and New Years.

Consolidators, also known as bucket shops, are great sources for well-priced international tickets. Start by looking in Sunday newspaper travel sections; U.S. travelers should focus on the *New York Times, Los Angeles Times,* and *Miami Herald.*

Bucket shop tickets are usually nonrefundable or rigged with stiff cancellation penalties, often as high as 50 to 75 percent of the ticket price, and some put you on charter airlines with questionable safety records.

The now well-established Cheapflights Web site, www.cheapflights. co.uk, often offers tickets on low-cost flights that have been obtained from consolidators. Another predominantly Internet-based company in Staffordshire, Flight Find (☎ **01782-844-831;** www.flightfind.co.uk) acts as a consolidator in the United Kingdom.

Several reliable consolidators operate worldwide and are available on the Web. **STA Travel** (☎ **800-781-4040;** www.statravel.com), the world's leader in student-aimed travel, offers good fares for travelers of all ages. **ELTExpress** (☎ **800-TRAV-800;** www.flights.com) started in Europe and has excellent fares worldwide, but particularly to that continent. Flights.com also has "local" Web sites in 12 countries. **LowestFare. com** (☎ **800-FLY-CHEAP;** www.1800flycheap.com) is owned by package-holiday megalith MyTravel and so has especially good access to fares for sunny destinations. **Air Tickets Direct** (☎ **800-778-3447;** www.airticketsdirect.com) is based in Montreal and leverages the currently weak Canadian dollar for low fares.

Booking your flight online

The "big three" online travel agencies, **Expedia** (www.expedia.com), **Travelocity** (www.travelocity.com), and **Orbitz** (www.orbitz.com) sell most of the air travel tickets purchased via the Internet. (Canadian travelers should try www.expedia.ca and www.travelocity.ca; UK residents can go for www.expedia.co.uk and www.opodo.co.uk.) Each online agency has different arrangements with the airlines and may offer different fares on the same flights, so shopping around is wise. If you register for the service, Expedia and Travelocity will send you an **e-mail notification** when a cheap fare becomes available to your favorite destination. Of the smaller travel agency Web sites, **SideStep** (www.sidestep.com) receives good reviews from users. It's a browser add-on that purports to "search 140 sites at once" but in reality beats competitors' fares no more than other sites do.

If you're willing to give up some control over your flight details, use an *opaque fare service* such as **Priceline** (www.priceline.com) or **Hotwire** (www.hotwire.com). Both offer rock-bottom prices in exchange for travel on a "mystery airline" at a mysterious time of day, often with a mysterious change of planes en route. The airlines are all major, well-known carriers — and the possibility of being sent from Philadelphia to Scotland via Dallas is remote. But your chances of getting a 6 a.m. or 11 p.m. flight are pretty high. Hotwire tells you flight prices before you buy; Priceline usually has better deals than Hotwire, but you have to play their "name your price" game. *Note:* In 2004 Priceline added non-opaque service to its roster. You now have the option to pick exact flights, times, and airlines from a list of offers (at prices similar to other non-opaque Web sites) — or opt to bid on opaque fares as before.

Great last-minute deals are also available directly from the airlines themselves through a free e-mail service called *e-savers*. Each week, the airline sends you a list of discounted flights. You can sign up for all the major airlines at one time by logging on to **Smarter Living** (www.smarterliving.com), or you can go to each individual airline's Web site. Airline sites also offer schedules, flight booking, and information on late-breaking bargains.

Taking the Train

Taking a train to Scotland from London or from other cities with airports, such as Manchester, isn't as fast as flying, but you may save money (and lessen damage to the environment) — plus you get to admire the countryside and you'll arrive at your destination right in the heart of town. The five hours (increasingly less) on the train to Edinburgh or Glasgow from London represents precious time (when you could be sightseeing in Scotland), so you may want to enquire about red-eye trips that let you sleep on the train (because you're traveling during the night).

The trains that link London to Edinburgh (via Newcastle) on the so-called East Coast Main Line are reasonably fast, efficient, and generally relaxing with restaurant and bar service as well as air-conditioning. Trains depart from London's Kings Cross Station (call National Railway Enquiries ☎ **08457-48-49-50** for rail info) every hour or so and arrive in Edinburgh at **Waverley Station** in the heart of the city. The trip generally takes 4½ hours. Standard class off-peak fares bought in advance range from around £25 to £36 ($46–$66); first class off-peak fares purchased in advance cost about £60 ($111); and the fully flexible "buy anytime, travel anytime" standard open return fare is upwards of £180 ($333). The Caledonian Sleeper service for overnight travel can cost about £90 ($166) if purchased in advance. You can easily make taxi and bus connections at Waverley Station, which also serves Glasgow with a **First ScotRail** (www.firstgroup.com/scotrail) shuttle service every 15 minutes during the day and every 30 minutes in the evenings until about 11:30 p.m. The round-trip shuttle fare during off-peak times (travel between 9:15 a.m. and 4:30 p.m. and after 6:15 p.m.) is £7.90 ($14.50).

Trains from London arrive in Glasgow at **Central Station** in the heart of the city (call National Rail Enquiries ☎ **08457-48-49-50** for rail and fare info). The trains that directly link London and Glasgow (via Preston and Carlisle) on the so-called West Coast Main Line don't have the reputation for timeliness and efficiency of those going to Edinburgh. The semi-privatized company responsible for railway maintenance, Network Rail, is spending literally billions to upgrade the line and create a faster service. But work has been slow, and while it's ongoing, travel is subject to frequent delays. The trains (operated by Virgin ☎ **08457-222-333;** www.virgintrains.co.uk) on the West Coast Main Line depart from London's Euston Station every hour or so and the trip generally takes 5½ hours. If you plan a trip on the West Coast Main Line, however, call and find out if any major "track works" are scheduled during your trip. If so, you can expect delays and the possibility of a bus replacing a portion of your train trip.

You may prefer trains — run by operators GNER — from London's Kings Cross up the East Coast Main Line via Newcastle, Edinburgh, and across (via Motherwell) to Glasgow. The time it takes is about the same as the West Coast Line. Standard class off-peak fares bought in advance range from around £25 to £36 ($46–$66); first class off-peak fares purchased in advance cost about £60 ($111); and the fully flexible "buy anytime, travel anytime" standard open return fare is upwards of £180 ($333). The Caledonian Sleeper service for overnight travel can cost about £90 ($166) if purchased in advance.

Glasgow's Central Station is also the terminus for trains arriving from the southwest of Scotland and a hub for numerous trains to city suburbs in most directions. A ten-minute walk away (or via shuttle bus 398) is **Queen Street Station.** From here, a **First ScotRail** (www.firstgroup.com/scotrail) shuttle service to and from Edinburgh runs every 15 minutes during the day and every 30 minutes in the evenings until about 11:30 p.m. The round-trip fare during off-peak times (travel between 9:15 a.m. and 4:30 p.m. and after 6:30 p.m.) is £7.90 ($14.50). The trip takes just under an hour.

Trains to points north of Edinburgh and Glasgow depart from both cities about three to five times daily, although frequency on many lines is reduced during the low season (from the end of September to about Easter).

Joining an Escorted Tour

You may be one of the many people who love escorted tours. The tour company takes care of all the details and tells you what to expect on each leg of your journey. You know your costs upfront and, in the case of the tame ones, you don't get many surprises. A great thing about escorted tours is that they can take you to the maximum number of sights in the minimum amount of time with the least amount of hassle.

 If you decide to go with an escorted tour, purchasing travel insurance is strongly recommended, especially if the tour operator asks to you pay your trip costs upfront. But don't buy insurance from the tour operator! If the tour operator doesn't fulfill its obligation to provide you with the vacation you paid for, there's no reason to think that it will fulfill its insurance obligations either. Get travel insurance through an independent agency. (You can find out more about the ins and outs of travel insurance in Chapter 10.)

When choosing an escorted tour, along with finding out whether you have to put down a deposit and when final payment is due, ask a few simple questions before you buy:

- ✔ **What is the cancellation policy?** Can the operator cancel the trip if it doesn't get enough people? How late can you cancel if you're unable to go? Do you get a refund if you cancel? If the operator cancels?

- ✔ **How jam-packed is the schedule?** Does the tour schedule try to fit 25 hours worth of activity into a 24-hour day, or does it give you ample time to relax by the pool or shop? If getting up at 7 a.m. every day and not returning to your hotel until 6 or 7 p.m. sounds like a grind, certain escorted tours may not be for you.

- ✔ **How large is the group?** The smaller the group, the less time you spend waiting for people to get on and off the bus. A tour operator may give you an evasive answer to this question because it may not know the exact size of the group until everybody has made reservations, but it should be able to give you a rough estimate. Also, get an idea of the general age range of the group; whether the tour's geared to seniors, students, families, or some other demographic may affect your decision to sign up.

✔ **Is there a minimum group size?** Some tours have a minimum group size and may cancel the tour if it doesn't book enough people. If a quota exists, find out what it is and how close the operator is to reaching it. Again, tour operators may be evasive in their answers, but the information may help you select a tour that's sure to happen.

✔ **What exactly is included?** Don't assume anything. You may have to pay to get yourself to and from the airport. A box lunch may be included in an excursion, but drinks may be extra. How much flexibility do you have? Can you opt out of certain activities, or does the bus leave once a day with no exceptions? Are all your meals planned in advance? Can you choose your entree at dinner?

Depending on your recreational passions, one of the following escorted tour companies may suit you:

✔ **CIE Tours International** (☎ 800-CIE-TOUR; www.cietours.com) does tours of the United Kingdom and offers a five-day, four-night escorted tour of Scotland, among other tours. The Web site features a helpful tour index with package prices, descriptions, and itineraries. Expect to pay around $700 (not counting airfare) per person.

✔ **Globus** (☎ 866-755-8581; www.globusandcosmos.com) is a first-class, worldwide tour company. Globus has comprehensive 9- and 15-day tours of Scotland. You can book a whole package (including airfare, meals, hotels, and so on) or find your own cheap plane ticket (good for those travelers racking up frequent-flier miles) and book only the bus-tour part with Globus. Prices (including airfare) range from about $1,775 to $3,250 per person.

✔ **Scottish Tours** (☎ 0131-557-8008; www.scottishtours.co.uk) offers six mini-tours in air-conditioned buses departing from Edinburgh. The most elaborate is a three-day, two-night excursion that goes from the Scottish capital to Inverness on day one and then visits the northeastern tip of the country. Per person rates start at around £31 ($57) for one-day trips and go up to £225 ($416) for two nights (including breakfast and accommodation).

✔ **Cosmos** (☎ 800-276-1241; www.cosmosvacations.com) is the budget arm of Globus and offers scaled down versions of the Globus trips (although you don't see a great price difference), with a tour guide and motorcoach on hand at all times. Prices (including airfare) run from $1,400 to $1,900 per person.

Choosing a Package Tour

For many destinations, package tours can be a smart way to go. A package tour that includes airfare, hotel, and transportation to and from the airport often costs less than the hotel alone on a tour you book yourself. That's because packages are sold in bulk to tour operators, who resell them to the public.

Some packagers offer a better class of hotels than others; others provide the same hotels for lower prices. Some book flights on scheduled airlines; others sell charter flights. In some packages, your choice of accommodations and travel days may be limited. Some let you choose between escorted vacations and independent vacations, and others allow you to add on just a few excursions or escorted day trips (also at discounted prices) without booking an entirely escorted tour.

To find package tours, check out the travel section of your local Sunday newspaper or the ads in the back of national travel magazines such as *Travel & Leisure, National Geographic Traveler,* and *Condé Nast Traveler.* **Liberty Travel** (call ☎ **888-271-1584** to find the store nearest you; www.libertytravel.com) is one of the biggest packagers in the Northeast and usually boasts a full-page ad in Sunday papers.

Another good source of package deals is the airlines themselves. Most major airlines offer air/land packages, including **American Airlines Vacations** (☎ 800-321-2121; www.aavacations.com), **Delta Vacations** (☎ 800-221-6666; www.deltavacations.com), **Continental Airlines Vacations** (☎ 800-301-3800; www.covacations.com), and **United Vacations** (☎ 888-854-3899; www.unitedvacations.com). Several big **online travel agencies** — Expedia, Travelocity, Orbitz, Site59, and Lastminute.com — also do a brisk business in travel packages.

 If you're unsure about the pedigree of a smaller packager, check with the Better Business Bureau in the city where the company is based or go online at www.bbb.org. If a packager won't tell you where it's based, don't purchase anything from it.

Depending on your interests, one of the following packaged tour companies may suit you:

- ✔ **CIE Tours International** (☎ **800-CIE-TOUR;** www.cietours.com). See details in the section "Joining an Escorted Tour" earlier in this chapter.

- ✔ **Brian Moore International Tours** (☎ **800-982-2299;** www.bmit.com) offers "Air Inclusive" vacations to Edinburgh from around $500 during the low season.

- ✔ **Freedom Scotland Holidays** (☎ **0132-487-8617;** www.freedom scotland.com) is slightly different than other packaged tour operators in that it asks what interests you and then sets up an itinerary and accommodations based on your interests and what you wish to pay. Fees vary.

- ✔ **Thistle Golf (Scotland) Limited** (☎ **0141-248-4554;** www.thistle golf.co.uk) offers various golfing tours, such as one that covers both Ayrshire in the southwest and St. Andrews northeast of Edinburgh. Prices depend on the touring region and the length of your stay, so contact the company for details.

Chapter 7

Getting Around Scotland

*Y*ou have a multitude of choices when it comes to getting around Scotland: **train, car, bus, ferry, bicycle,** or **on foot.** Most visitors to Scotland rent a car for the duration of their visits because cars provide the sense of mobility that travelers appreciate. Indeed, in the Highlands especially, cars are almost essential because the cities are few and far between and public transportation doesn't cover much ground. If you're traveling to the islands, a ferry ride is almost unavoidable.

If your budget, length of stay, and specific destinations make driving out of the question, however, a variety of public transportation options can get you where you need to go.

If your trip is primarily to Edinburgh and/or Glasgow, you don't really need a car at all. But outside the cities, the country is a virtual archipelago, populated by settlements separated by deep valleys, ragged mountains, and especially long lochs; you may have to travel 100 miles to cover 50 miles as the crow flies, so journeys that don't seem very far can take longer than anticipated. The downside of cars is that you may, unfortunately, spend so much time in your car that you miss a lot of the beauty of the country as you zip around at speeds of 40 to 70 miles per hour.

Getting Around by Car

Seeing Scotland by car definitely has its advantages, most notably the lack of timetables to keep in mind and the control over where you want to go and when you want to go there. But still you need to be aware of some driving-related issues that you may encounter while exploring Scotland by car. Expect to pull over to the side of the road on a regular basis to take in the scenery and snap a few pictures; you should factor those delays into the car trip planning, too.

To drive a car in Scotland for a limited period (up to twelve months), be certain that you have a valid driver's license issued by local authorities where you live permanently; you don't need any special license.

Getting along with fewer road signs

One of the biggest complaints that tourists have about driving around Scotland is the relative paucity of road signs. Most major attractions are well marked, but the motorways around cities can be confusing, and country roads seem to lack the necessary signage. Having a good map close at hand (as well as a navigator who can read it) to help track your progress is always helpful. When in doubt, however, simply stop and ask for directions.

Keeping up with street name switches

You're in a city, you're driving along such-and-such street, and then magically that street has a new name. This curiosity comes up often as you navigate city boulevards. It's actually common for street names in Scotland to change. For example, the famous Royal Mile in Edinburgh between the castle and Holyrood actually takes five different names along the way, from Castlehill to Canongate. Now that's royally confusing. Again, keep a map handy and refer to it often.

Driving on the left, roundabouts, and other differences

If you're used to driving on the right-hand side of the road, driving on the left-hand side is a shock initially. Perhaps what feels the strangest is that the wheel is on the right-hand side of the car and the gearshift is on the left (the relative positions of the clutch, brake pedal, and accelerator are the same, however). *Note:* Like the rest of Europe, most cars in Scotland are manual transmission. If you need an automatic, make sure you request one when you make your rental reservation.

You merge to the right to get on highways, and you pass cars on the right while slower traffic stays in the left lanes. Don't pass cars (or "overtake" in local parlance) by using a left-hand, outside lane. Overtake slower traffic only by using the inside, right-hand lanes meant for faster traffic, and after you've safely passed someone, return to a left lane.

Roundabouts (traffic circles) are slightly tricky: Traffic that approaches from the right in the roundabout has the right of way — in other words, you're driving around the circle in a clockwise direction. You use your left turn signal to indicate which exit you intend to take from a roundabout. If you find yourself driving in an inside (right-hand) lane in a roundabout and can't get safely to your desired exit (on the left), don't barge across. Simply go around the circle again and prepare to exit the next time you pass your exit.

Staying safe on "single-track" roads

When you're driving through the rural countryside or in small villages, it's quite common to find only one-lane, or single-track, roads carrying two-way traffic. Don't panic. These roads will always have passing places, often marked with a black and white striped pole or sign. If you see a car approaching in the opposite direction, pull into the passing place if it's on your left and allow the car to pass. You can confirm your intentions by putting on your left turn signal (and you may find that some drivers will flash their headlights in recognition).

If, however, the passing place is to the right on the single-track road, *do not* pull into it. Stop where you are and just stay put (put on your left turn signal if you like) and allow the oncoming vehicle to use the pull-over space to slide by.

In general, the driver who gets to a passing place first is meant to use it, but don't get involved in games of "chicken" to see who pulls off first. Play it safe and be the one to give way.

It's a simple courtesy to acknowledge the other driver (who's passing you or whom you're passing) with a small wave, sometimes as simple as a raised finger (not the middle one) from the steering wheel.

Planning your gasoline expenditures

Gas, called *petrol* in Scotland, is very costly. Remember that the prices posted here are per *liter,* not per gallon. So, in essence, you're paying about four times what you would in the U.S. In order to get the best gas mileage, get the smallest car you can. (A small car also helps you more easily navigate narrow roads.)

Laying down the law on parking

In Scotland, you often see parked cars facing in both directions on one side of the road, which makes it tough to tell if you're going the wrong way on a one-way street.

In towns, you may find some parking garages and outdoor car lots. Street parking is also fine, but don't assume that the absence of American-style meters means that parking on the street is free. Check the signs. You may have to buy a ticket from a nearby machine that indicates how long you can stay. Purchase a ticket and use the sticky backing paper to affix it to your window. This system is used in some parking lots, too. Some residential neighborhoods in the cities are very restrictive and allow only local residents to park in available places.

Safety tips to know before you get behind the wheel

Here are some important traffic rules and laws to help you get around safely and legally.

- ✔ At intersections marked with an inverted triangle or at round-abouts, yield to traffic coming from your right.

- ✔ You should not make left-hand turns (the equivalent of right-hand turns in America) when the traffic light is red.

✔ The general speed limit on the open road is 60 mph (96km/h) unless otherwise posted. Standard 60 mph signs bear only a black circle with a slash mark through it. When the speed limit is other than 60 mph, you see a sign with a red circle and the limit written inside in black. You often see these signs when entering small towns where you should reduce your speed to 30 mph. On motorways, the speed limit is generally 70 mph.

✔ A flashing yellow light means yield to pedestrian traffic but proceed with caution when clear.

✔ A sign with a red circle and a red "X" through the middle means no stopping or parking during posted hours. A zig-zag white line along the curb also means no parking or stopping unless it's due to traffic signals or congestion.

✔ Drivers and front-seat passengers must wear seat belts. If your car has back-seat belts, passengers seated there must wear them also.

Renting a car

Car rental rates can vary even more than airline fares. The price depends on the size of the car, the length of time you keep it, where and when you pick it up and drop it off, where you take it, and a host of other factors. Asking a few key questions may save you hundreds of dollars.

✔ Weekend rates may be lower than weekday rates. If you're keeping the car five or more days, a weekly rate may be cheaper than the daily rate. Ask if the rate is the same for pickup on Friday morning as it is on Thursday night.

✔ Some companies may assess a drop-off charge if you don't return the car to the same rental location.

✔ Ask if the rate is cheaper if you pick up the car at a location in town rather than at the airport.

✔ Find out whether age is an issue. Some car rental companies add on a fee for drivers under 25, but some don't rent to them at all.

✔ If you see an advertised price, be sure to ask for that specific rate; otherwise you may be charged the standard (higher) rate. Don't forget to mention membership in AAA, AARP, trade unions, and other associations such as university alumni groups. These memberships may entitle you to discounts.

✔ Check your frequent-flier accounts for special deals.

✔ As with other aspects of planning your trip, using the Internet can make comparison shopping for a car rental much easier. You can check rates at most of the major rental agencies' Web sites. Plus, all the major travel sites — **Travelocity** (www.travelocity.com), **Expedia** (www.expedia.com), **Orbitz** (www.orbitz.com), and **Smarter Living** (www.smarterliving.com), for example — have search engines that can dig up discounted car-rental rates. Just enter the car size you want and the pickup and return dates and locations, and the server returns a price. You can even make the reservation through any of these sites.

In addition to the standard rental prices, other optional charges apply to most car rentals (and some not-so-optional charges, such as taxes). Many credit card companies cover the *Collision Damage Waiver* (CDW), which requires you to pay for damage to the car if you're involved in a collision. Check with your credit card company before you go so you can avoid paying this hefty fee (as much as $20 a day).

The car rental companies also offer additional *liability insurance* (if you harm others in an accident), *personal accident insurance* (if you harm yourself or your passengers), and *personal effects insurance* (if your luggage is stolen from your car). Your insurance policy on your car at home probably covers most of these unlikely occurrences. However, if your own insurance doesn't cover you for rentals, or if you don't have auto insurance, definitely consider purchasing the additional coverage (ask your car rental agent for more information). Unless you're toting around the Hope diamond, you can probably skip the personal effects insurance, but driving around without liability or personal accident coverage is never a good idea. Even if you're a good driver, other people may not be, and liability claims can be complicated.

Some companies also offer *refueling packages,* in which you pay for your initial full tank of gas up front and can then return the car with an empty gas tank. The refueling package prices can be competitive with local gas prices, but you don't get credit for any gas remaining in the tank when you return the car. If you decline this option, you pay only for the gas you use, but you have to return the car with a full tank — otherwise the rental company will charge you (at higher than usual gas prices) for any shortfall.

Because the driver's side is the right-hand front seat in Scotland, your left hand, not your right, controls the stick shift. Rental companies have few cars with automatic transmissions, so inquire specifically if you don't know how to drive a manual. Mini-vans, or *people movers,* are more likely to offer the option of automatic transmissions.

As for the class of car available, you can expect three levels: **economy** (small), **compact** (medium), and **intermediate** (large). Companies often offer upgrades. You may think you want a larger vehicle, but keep in mind that roads are narrow. Try to get the smallest car you can, taking into consideration your driving comfort, the comfort of your fellow travelers, and the amount of luggage you're carrying. **Air-conditioning** and **unlimited mileage** are standard.

The following are a couple of issues you need to address when arranging for your rental car.

✔ **Where and when to pick up the car:** If you fly into Edinburgh or Glasgow and plan to stay in the city for two or more days, wait to get the car until you're just about to head out to the countryside. In the city, you don't need a car. Some companies have pick-up locations in or near the city. If you're planning to leave town immediately or early the next morning, however, getting the car upon arrival is a good idea. You can set out according to plan, and you save the time and hassle of having to go back to the airport or locate the rental agency the next day.

✔ **How to pay for the car:** Some companies require a deposit, generally on a credit card, when you make your reservation. If you book by phone, the clerk may ask for the card number then; otherwise you use your credit card at the rental desk.

 If you're not sure how long you need a car (if, maybe, you're thinking about coming back to Glasgow early to see more city sights), book your rental for the shorter amount of time and extend it from the road with a simple phone call rather than bringing the car back early. If you've booked a car for a week but bring it back after only four days, for example, the company will post the refund to your credit card.

Rental-car companies in Scotland

All the major rental agencies are represented at the country's two primary airports. In addition, in Glasgow, you can find

✔ **Avis Rent-a-Car:** 70 Lancefield St. (☎ 0141-221-2827)

✔ **Budget Rent-a-Car:** 101 Waterloo St. (☎ 0141-221-9241)

✔ **Europcar:** 38 Anderson Quay (☎ 0141-248-8788)

✔ **Arnold Clark:** multiple locations (☎ 0845-607-4500)

In Edinburgh city, try

✔ **Avis:** West Park Place (☎ 0131-337-6363)

✔ **Hertz:** Picardy Place (☎ 0131-556-8311)

✔ **Thrifty:** Haymarket Terrace (☎ 0131-337-1319)

Taking the Train

First ScotRail runs the trains in Scotland. It's not a publicly owned company, but rather a state-subsidized private firm that recently won the contract to operate the trains. To confuse matters, the railway lines are owned by a different, pseudo-private company called Network Rail (formerly Railtrack). Privatization of the railways has proved to be a poor decision for most of Great Britain, a country that once led the way in the development of the railroad.

Does your boot go in your luggage or your luggage in your boot?

To spare you the confusion of car-related words and phrases in Scotland, here's a list of the most commonly used (and most commonly confused) terms you may come across:

- **roundabouts:** traffic circles (or "rotaries" if you're a New Englander); make sure you go left and yield to the right
- **boot:** trunk
- **bonnet:** hood
- **pavement:** sidewalk
- **motorways:** freeways
- **petrol:** gasoline

The advantage of train travel in Scotland is that it's reasonably fast, efficient, and comfortable. On the downside, trains are more expensive than in most European countries, and they travel to fewer destinations than would be ideal. Nevertheless, when they run on time, train travel is a relaxing way to get from one part of the country to another.

Generally speaking, you should have no problem buying **tickets** a half-hour before departure, but during the high season, it never hurts to call the day before to confirm availability. For 24-hour rail and fare information, call National Rail Enquiries ☎ **0845-748-4950** or log onto www.firstscotrail.com. For special package deals and short break reservations, call ScotRail at ☎ **0870-161-0161** (Monday to Friday from 9 a.m. to 5 p.m. — recorded messages play outside normal office hours) or from overseas at ☎ **44-1844-353-077.**

Seeing Scotland by Bus

Buses are a pretty good way to see Scotland. They make more stops than the trains, but they cost less. However, the usual downsides apply to bus travel: Unlike when you have a rental car, you're not free to stop wherever and whenever you want, you're stuck with the same people for hours at a time, and not all buses have toilets. Regardless, the seating is comfortable, and the bus is a good way to meet people.

Scottish Citylink is the country's primary bus company. It offers service to towns and cities across Scotland, including Glasgow, Edinburgh, Dundee, Aberdeen, Stirling, Perth, Inverness, Aviemore, Thurso, Ullapool, Oban, Campbeltown, Lochgilphead, Fort William, Portree,

Glencoe, Dunfermline, and Dumfries. Information, prices, times, and routes can be obtained by calling ☎ **0141-332-9644** or ☎ **0870-550-5050** or by visiting www.citylink.co.uk.

Sightseeing bus tours based in Edinburgh can give a taste of the often-stunning countryside on one-, two-, and three-day excursions. If this is your kind of travel, consider the following tour companies:

- ✔ **Scottish Tours** (☎ **0131-557-8008;** www.scottishtours.co.uk) has six mini-tours in air-conditioned buses. The most elaborate is a three-day, two-night excursion that goes from the Scottish capital to Inverness on day one and then visits the northeastern tip of the country. Prices start at around £31 ($57) for one-day trips and go to £225 ($416) for two nights (including breakfast and accommodation).

- ✔ **Timberbush Tours** (☎ **0131-226-6066;** www.timberbush-tours. co.uk) use mini-buses to take small groups to the Highlands. Prices for a two-day tour range from £52 ($96) in low season to £62 ($115) at the height of summer. Prices only cover transportation and guide.

- ✔ **Heart of Scotland Tours** (☎ **0131-558-8855;** www.heartof scotlandtours.co.uk) offers one-day mini-bus tours of the Highlands that depart from Edinburgh's Waterloo Place near Calton Hill at 8 a.m. and 9 a.m., returning to Edinburgh between 6 p.m. and 8 p.m. Prices range from £23 to £30 ($42.50–$55.50).

- ✔ **MacBackpackers** (☎ **0131-558-9900;** www.macbackpackers.com) offers "hop-on, hop-off" bus service for more intrepid adventurers. This bus does a circuit of Scotland, stopping at Pitlochry, Inverness, Kyle of Lochalsh, Fort William, Oban, and Glasgow. The basic price is £65 ($120).

Finally, by Ferry

The preferable way to get from one island to the next in the Hebrides (see Chapter 19) is by ferry. Few rides are more sublime. One company, **Caledonian MacBrayne,** runs the major routes between islands. You can take your car on most of the ferries, but a few are vehicle-free and want to stay that way. Remember to call the day before you hope to go out, because heavy seas can cancel ferry travel.

- ✔ **Caledonian MacBrayne** (☎ **01475-650-100;** www.calmac.co.uk), or CalMac, as it's more colloquially known, serves 22 islands and 4 peninsulas over the western coast of Scotland.

- ✔ **P&O Scottish Ferries** (☎ **01224-572-615;** www.poscottish ferries.com), part of the European ferry company, has quite a few routes in Scotland (including to Shetland and Orkney) as well as routes from Scotland to Ireland and to Belgium.

Chapter 8

Booking Your Accommodations

In This Chapter

▶ Knowing what to expect accomodation-wise
▶ Estimating how much you'll pay to stay
▶ Determining your lodging needs
▶ Finding the best rates and reserving the best rooms

*I*n this chapter, I provide an overview of the types of accommodations available in Scotland, helping you choose what feels right in terms of style, comfort, and budget. Individual accommodation listings appear in each city and regional chapter later in this book (Parts III and IV).

Getting to Know Your Options

The **Scottish Tourist Board,** or as it prefers to be called in the computer age **visitscotland.com,** has instituted a **grading system** that ranks all types of accommodations on the basis of their available amenities as well as more subjective criteria such as hospitality, ambience, food, and the condition of the property. This ranking system can be useful, but it can also be misleading. The ranking may be lower than the place actually deserves simply because a room lacks a telephone or an accommodation doesn't include a television. Decide if certain amenities such as a mini-bar or trouser press in your room are important to you and then find out what's being offered by hotels or B&Bs.

Accommodations involved in the grading system display a blue plaque or sticker (usually on or by the door) showing the number of stars earned. If you don't see the plaque and the lodging isn't in the grading system, it's not necessarily a bad place to stay, but if you have a bad experience, the tourist board has no authority to reprimand the establishment.

The tourist board's grading system doesn't rate the size or location of the place, the price, or the range of facilities (restaurant, pool, and so on). It also only rates those establishments that pay to join the tourist board and its scheme (which can put off some more frugal or independent-minded operators).

Knowing What You'll Pay

You can expect to pay a good deal for accommodations in Scotland, although I've tried to include some options for the budget-minded, too. Generally speaking, the cost of a **double room** — one room for you and a guest to stay in together — is listed for each accommodation. The figures usually indicate a range of prices from the off-season (the lower price) to the high season (the higher cost). Note that price differences aren't only seasonal but may also reflect room size, views (important in Edinburgh or along the sea, for example), extra-large beds, and so on. Most places offer a **full breakfast** — or at least a light Continental breakfast — as part of the rate.

Each hotel listing is prefaced with a number of dollar signs ranging from one ($) to four ($$$$), corresponding to price. Use Table 8-1 as a pricing scale for quick reference; it shows you what you can expect in terms of room size and standard amenities in each of these price categories:

Table 8-1	Key to Hotel Dollar Signs	
Dollar Sign(s)	*Price Range*	*What to Expect*
$	Less than £54 ($100)	These accommodations are relatively simple and inexpensive. Rooms will likely be small, and televisions are not necessarily provided. Parking is likely not provided, and you're on your own to find a spot on the street.
$$	£55–£108 ($101–$200)	A bit classier, these mid-range accommodations offer more room, more extras, and a more convenient location than the preceding category. Parking is not necessarily provided.
$$$	£109–£162 ($201–$300)	Higher-class still, these accommodations begin to look plush. Think chocolates on your pillow, a restaurant, underground parking garages, and maybe even views of the water.
$$$$	£163 ($301) and up	These top-rated accommodations come with luxury amenities such as valet parking, on-premise spas, and in-room hot tubs and CD players — but you pay through the nose for 'em.

Determining Your Accommodations Needs

You probably won't be staying in a castle or a cottage during your trip to Scotland — although you certainly can. Check the Internet or local tourism boards for just the right 30-room mansion or ivy-covered cottage in the heather for you. However, it's much more likely that you'll be staying in the more common choices for accommodations in Scotland: **hotels, B&Bs,** and **guesthouses.**

Wherever you stay, you can expect generally friendly service, clean rooms, and a decent breakfast. Smaller hotels with dining rooms, however, can be quite restrictive about when food is available.

The quality of food offered can vary dramatically from inn to inn. You may be frustrated to find that although you're staying in a hotel at the edge of a plentiful loch, the fish on the menu is frozen and deep-fried. If cuisine is important to you, do a bit of homework before you decide where you're going to stay, especially if dinners are included in the room price.

Other accommodation options include **self-catering properties,** which have kitchen facilities, and youth **hostels.**

You can find out much about the country's different types of accommodations and available package deals at the tourist board's Web site, www. visitscotland.com. The site lists a range of lodging choices, including hotels, guesthouses, bed-and-breakfasts, caravan and camping parks, and self-catering cottages.

Hello? Is this Scotland?

If you want to book your room over the phone, or if the place you want to stay at doesn't have Internet booking abilities, you need to know **how to call Scotland.** To call Scotland from anywhere in the world, dial the international access code (for example, 011 from the U.S.), then the country code (44 for the UK), then the city or local code (for example, Glasgow is 141), and then the number. (Note: When you're calling from within Great Britain, you need to add a zero before the city code.)

For example, if you're in the States and you want to call a favorite watering hole in Glasgow, the Babbity Bowster, just to make sure they'll have enough wine ready when you get there, you dial:

Int'l	Country	City	Number
011 +	44 +	141 +	552-5055

Remember, Scotland is five hours ahead of eastern time in the U.S. (eight hours ahead of the West Coast). If it's 1 p.m. in Philadelphia, it's 6 p.m. in Peterhead. So, if you're trying to call a business in Scotland, call before noon EST to be safe (before 9 a.m. in San Francisco).

Hotels

Most hotels will have tea- and instant coffee-making equipment (electric kettles and cups) in their rooms. Bellhops aren't so common, however, except in the posh places. And smaller hotels sometimes lock the doors at certain (late) hours, so you may have to ring the bell or knock to be let in after hours. Let a hotel staff person know if you plan to be out late.

Hotels are used to catering to tourists, and many will be helpful. You can expect the furnishings to be comfortable, and many of the larger and chain hotels have gyms, room service, and an in-house restaurant and pub. Because you're a resident, hotels are required to keep the bar open until you retire for the night (but don't abuse the privilege).

Chains have hotels in Scotland's cities and larger towns. In some cases, taverns or restaurants have overnight rooms, too. If you choose to take a room in a pub, just be certain you're not going to be troubled if the Saturday night karaoke goes on until midnight.

 Weekends can be the cheapest time to stay at the highest-ranking hotels in Scotland's cities because they normally cater to business visitors. Hotels are eager to keep the house as full as possible, so they may offer deals to tourists on weekends. It's definitely worth asking about.

Bed-and-breakfasts (B&Bs)

Many Scottish B&Bs take their hospitality seriously. You usually get to know the owners (likely the same folks who cook and serve your breakfast) — and you may come away feeling that you've made a new friend or two. A *guesthouse* is, for the most part, the same thing as a B&B, although possibly a little larger.

Some B&Bs offer just a spare and comfortable bedroom (usually with a bathroom attached) in their home. Some B&B rooms, however, aren't *en suite,* meaning each room doesn't have a private bathroom. So, if you're completely averse to sharing facilities with the folks down the hall, make sure you ask for a room with its own bathroom (which may cost a bit more).

Bed-and-breakfasts aren't large — many have only four to eight rooms. The better-known B&Bs tend to fill up quickly during the high season, so make your reservations as early as possible. A lot of B&Bs don't accept credit cards, so be prepared to pay in cash.

 One advantage of choosing B&Bs over hotels is the price: They can be much less expensive, but you don't get the amenities of a hotel.

Self-catering cottages

Properties offered as *self-catering* run the gamut from modern apartments to rooms within castles to country cottages. Taking a self-catering accommodation is essentially similar to renting a condo. They're a place

to settle into and do things like you might at home. At self-catering properties, you can cook your own meals and make your own beds (or not).

Be certain you know what is provided in a self-catering facility — for
example, the provision of towels and bed linens can incur extra costs.

With self-catering properties, the price isn't calculated per person and is
generally set for the week (although some also rent by the weekend, for
two to three days). When you take into account the amount of money you
would pay for hotels and B&Bs, staying in a self-catering lodging can cut
costs considerably. Food costs also decrease when you're buying your
own and cooking it yourself. So, if you're budget-minded, self-catering
properties are an option worth checking out.

A good place to begin researching self-catering properties is the **Association of Scotland's Self-Caterers** (www.assc.co.uk), whose members
include owners and operators of a wide range of self-catering properties,
from cottages to chalets to lodges to castles.

Hostels

Hostels have a reputation of being the accommodation of choice for students and frugal travelers. If the image you have of hostels is a place full
of young, perky travelers who can go for long stretches without showers
or food, you're partly correct (though only partly). Hostels are for independent travelers who cherish flexibility and want to stick to an accommodations budget. And although these accommodations are called
"youth hostels," they take anyone of any age, although most of the
people you encounter are in their late teens or early 20s. They're also
usually really great places to meet fellow travelers.

Hostels sometimes don't allow guests to remain in the building during the
day. You may have to get out and about from 11 a.m. to 4 p.m., whether
you like it or not.

Hostels across Scotland vary in quality and services. Some offer commu-
nal kitchens for you to bring in and cook your own food. Some even have
private rooms with en-suite bathrooms. Families can also stay in hostels,
renting a room with four bunks. The majority of hostels, though, are
places where people sleep dorm-style — anywhere from four to dozens
of people to a room, usually in bunk beds.

Hostels provide a blanket and pillow and sometimes sheets, but to be
safe, you should bring your own sleeping bag or sleep sack (or expect to
rent sheets from the hostel).

As for the bathrooms: Think of high school gym restrooms or your college
dorm — tiles, a row of sinks, toilet cubicles, and shower stalls, sometimes
spotlessly immaculate, sometimes appallingly grimy. You may not love it,
but it gets the job done.

You can usually get a warm hostel bed for £10 ($18.50) a night and will rarely pay more than £20 ($37).

One general resource to check out is www.hostels.com. And if you know you'll be taking the backpacking route through Scotland, you may want to contact the Scottish Youth Hostel Association (☎ **0870-155-3255** for reservations or ☎ **01786-891-400** for general enquiries; www.syha.org.uk).

Security isn't a major problem in Scotland's hostels, but it's something to consider. Any time you're sleeping in a room full of strangers, take precautions to ensure the safety of yourself and your personal belongings. If your hostel doesn't provide lockers, lock your luggage, if it seems appropriate, or make your bags as difficult to get into as possible. Stack them, for example, with the most valuable items at the bottom. Also, bring your wallet, passport, purse, and any other valuables into bed with you for safekeeping.

Finding the Best Room at the Best Rate

The *rack rate* is the maximum rate a hotel charges for a room. It's the rate you get if you walk in off the street and ask for a room for the night. You sometimes see these rates printed on the fire/emergency exit diagrams posted on the back of your hotel room door.

Hotels are happy to charge you the rack rate, but you can almost always do better. In all but the smallest accommodations, the rate you pay for a room depends on many factors.

Reserving a room through the hotel's toll-free number may result in a lower rate than calling the hotel directly. On the other hand, the central reservations number may not know about discount rates available at specific locations. Your best bet is to call both the local number and toll-free number and see which one gives you a better deal.

Room rates (even rack rates) change with the season, as occupancy rates rise and fall. But even within a given season, room prices are subject to change without notice, so the rates quoted in this book may be different from the actual rate you receive when you make your reservation. Be sure to mention membership in AAA, AARP, frequent-flier programs, and any other corporate rewards programs you can think of when you call to book. You never know when the affiliation may be worth a few dollars off your room rate.

Remember, in Scotland, accommodation rates fall from about the beginning of October until Christmas and New Years (when they jump up to high season prices for a couple of weeks), and then they stay more affordable until mid-March or Easter time. Some of the nicer country house hotels close entirely in January. See Chapter 3 for a discussion of

Scotland's high and low travel seasons. If you think you want a package tour that includes accommodation, flip to Chapter 6.

Surfing the Web for hotel deals

Independent Internet hotel booking agencies representing hotels and guesthouses in Scotland have multiplied in mind-boggling numbers of late, and it's the best way to get a reduced price for a room. Such competitiveness can be a boon to consumers who have the patience and time to shop and compare the online sites for good deals — but shop they must, for prices can vary considerably from site to site. And keep in mind that hotels at the top of a site's listing may be there for no other reason than that they paid money to get the placement.

Of the "big three" sites, **Expedia** offers a long list of special deals and "virtual tours" or photos of available rooms that allow you to see what you're paying for. **Travelocity** posts unvarnished customer reviews and ranks its properties according to the AAA rating system. Also reliable are **Hotels.com** and **Quikbook.com**. An excellent free program, **TravelAxe** (www.travelaxe.net), helps you search multiple hotel sites at once, even ones you may never have heard of, and conveniently lists the total price of the room, including the taxes and service charges. Another booking site, **Travelweb** (www.travelweb.com), is partly owned by the hotels it represents (including the Hilton, Hyatt, and Starwood chains). It's a good idea to get a confirmation number and make a printout of any online booking transaction you make.

In the opaque Web site category, **Priceline** and **Hotwire** are even better for hotels than for airfares; with both, you're allowed to pick the neighborhood and quality level of the hotel you want before offering up your money. (However, as with all opaque Web sites, the name of the hotel is not revealed until you pay.) Priceline's hotel product even covers Europe and Asia, though it's much better at getting five-star lodging for three-star prices than at finding anything at the bottom of the scale. On the downside, many hotels stick Priceline guests in their least desirable rooms. Be sure to go to the BiddingforTravel Web site (www.bidding fortravel.com) before bidding on a hotel room on Priceline; it features a fairly up-to-date list of hotels that Priceline uses in major cities. For both Priceline and Hotwire, you pay upfront and the fee is nonrefundable. *Note:* Some hotels don't provide loyalty program credits or points or other frequent-stay amenities when you book a room through opaque online services.

For online hotel reservations services in Scotland, try www.visit scotland.com or www.hotelreviewscotland.com. If you're looking for something more unusual, you may want to consider a farm stay; you can find information at www.scotfarmhols.co.uk.

Reserving the best room

After you make your reservation, asking one or two more pointed questions can go a long way toward making sure you get the best room for your money. (If you've booked your stay over the Internet, it's time to pick up the telephone and call the hotel or guesthouse directly.)

- ✔ Always ask for a corner room. They're usually larger, quieter, and have more windows and light than standard rooms, and they don't always cost more.

- ✔ Ask if the hotel is renovating; if it is, request a room away from the renovation work. Or, in the case of Edinburgh or Glasgow, there may be nearby construction works. Workers don't go on jackhammering into the evening hours, but the racket may start quite early in the morning. So ask.

- ✔ In the case of a view, sometimes it will cost you more. But you never know.

- ✔ Inquire, too, about the location of the restaurants and bars in the hotel — they're potential sources of annoying noise. And if you aren't happy with your room when you arrive, talk to someone at the front desk. If the hotel has another available room, they should be happy to accommodate you, within reason.

Chapter 9

Catering to Special Travel Needs or Interests

*S*cotland's population is generally a friendly one that welcomes visitors of all stripes. No matter where you are, however, some aspects of travel can be challenging for people with special needs. This chapter provides basic advice to help make your trip successful for everyone involved.

Traveling with the Brood: Advice for Families

Scotland may not top the list of countries that ease the burden of traveling with children, but it *is* getting better. Some posh country house hotels actually discourage families with children and/or prohibit toddlers from the dining room at night. Throughout this book, I've flagged (with the kid-friendly icon) those spots that are particularly appealing prospects for families.

You can find good family-oriented vacation advice on the Internet at:

✔ **Family Travel Files** (www.thefamilytravelfiles.com): A site that offers an online magazine and a directory of off-the-beaten-path tours and tour operators for families

✔ **Family Travel Forum** (www.familytravelforum.com): A comprehensive site that offers customized trip planning

✔ **Family Travel Network** (www.familytravelnetwork.com): An award-winning site that offers travel features, deals, and tips

  ✔ **Traveling Internationally with Your Kids** (www.travelwithyour kids.com): A comprehensive site that offers customized trip planning

Familyhostel (☎ **800-733-9753;** www.learn.unh.edu/familyhostel) takes the whole family, including kids ages 8 to 15, on moderately priced domestic and international learning vacations. A team of academics leads lectures, field trips, and sightseeing excursions.

To help ensure a peaceful trip with children in tow, take care of a few preliminaries before lift-off:

  ✔ Check what your children have packed. You want to make sure that they have the clothes necessary for any changes in the weather and make sure they haven't overpacked.

  ✔ Bring a few toys for younger children, but nothing that can't be replaced if it's lost along the way.

  ✔ Music and even books on tape or CD are great diversions. Small games work well for those times when the scenery isn't sufficiently engaging. Having a deck of cards handy is a good idea for restaurant visits.

Getting to Scotland and exploring with kids

Remember, each child regardless of age is expected to have a passport. Some airlines offer child-companion fares and have a children's menu upon request.

Car-rental companies in Scotland will provide necessary car seats, and all vehicles have rear seatbelts. The law requires that children be buckled in no matter whether they're in the front or back seats.

Keep in mind that most attractions and some public transportation options offer reduced prices for children. And most attractions, even places that don't seem particularly family-oriented, offer family group prices (usually for two adults and two or three children).

For the female traveler

Scotland very well could be, in general, a safer place than most for people traveling alone — especially women — but be careful not to be lulled into a false sense of security. To find out more about safety for women travelers, pick up a copy of *Safety and Security for Women Who Travel,* by Sheila Swan Laufer and Peter Laufer (Travelers' Tales Guides), which caters to the concerns of the female traveler.

Finding a family-friendly hotel

Contact your hotel, guesthouse, or B&B before you go to find out about potential cost-cutting accommodations for families with children. Many times, an extra cot for a child is just a small additional cost — a welcome exception to the per-person pricing standard in Scotland. Also, some places have a babysitter list in case you opt for a grown-ups' night out.

Making Age Work for You: Advice for Seniors

Most of the paid attractions in Scotland offer discounts to seniors ("pensioners" or "OAPs" — which stands for *old age pensioners* — in local lingo). Most public transportation is less costly for these people, too, although local service may require a special ID that's too much of a bother to obtain if you're only in town for a day or two.

Many hotels offer discounts for seniors. People over the age of 60 usually qualify for reduced admission to theaters, museums, and other attractions as well as discounted fares on public transportation.

Members of **AARP** (formerly known as the American Association of Retired Persons), 601 E St. NW, Washington, DC 20049 (☎ **888-687-2277** or 202-434-2277; www.aarp.org), are eligible for discounts on hotels, airfares, and car rentals.

Elderhostel (☎ **877-426-8056**; www.elderhostel.org) arranges study programs in more than 80 countries around the world for those aged 55 and over (and a companion of any age). Most courses last for two to four weeks abroad, and many include airfare, modest accommodations, meals, and tuition.

Recommended publications offering travel resources and discounts for seniors include: the quarterly magazine *Travel 50 & Beyond* (www.travel50andbeyond.com); *Travel Unlimited: Uncommon Adventures for the Mature Traveler* (Avalon); *101 Tips for Mature Travelers,* available from Grand Circle Travel (☎ **800-221-2610** or 617-350-7500; www.gct.com); *The 50+ Traveler's Guidebook* (St. Martin's Press); and *Unbelievably Good Deals and Great Adventures That You Absolutely Can't Get Unless You're Over 50,* by Joann Rattner Heilman (McGraw-Hill).

Many senior-targeted tours of Scotland are of the tour-bus variety, with free trips thrown in for those who organize groups of 20 or more. If you're seeking more independent travel, you should probably consult a regular travel agent to make your travel plans (see Chapter 6).

Accessing Scotland: Advice for Travelers with Disabilities

Most disabilities shouldn't stop anyone from traveling. Scotland's cities are reasonably well equipped to accommodate the disabled. However, not everything in Scotland will be easy. Many train stations are decidedly inaccessible and historical attractions, such as castles, by their very nature, with cobbles and stone stairs, are difficult for even some able-bodied visitors to navigate. Some rural B&Bs aren't suitable, either.

Call ahead to attractions and B&Bs to check their facilities, but you can feel fairly confident that most restaurants and newer hotels will be entirely accessible.

The "Information for Visitors with Disabilities" guide, published by the National Trust of Scotland, is available at most tourist offices. It lists attractions in Scotland and details the accessibility of each portion of the attraction (for example, the castle may be accessible but the gardens and toilets may not be). The publication even details access points and views that are available from a wheelchair.

Travel agencies and organizations

Many travel agencies offer customized tours and itineraries for travelers with disabilities.

- ✔ **Access-Able Travel Source** (☎ 303-232-2979; www.access-able.com) offers extensive access information and advice for traveling around the world with disabilities.

- ✔ **Accessible Journeys** (☎ 800-846-4537 or 610-521-0339; www.disabilitytravel.com) offers travel planning and information for mature travelers, slow walkers, wheelchair travelers, and their families and friends.

- ✔ **Flying Wheels Travel** (☎ 507-451-5005; www.flyingwheelstravel.com) offers escorted tours and cruises that emphasize sports and private tours in minivans with lifts.

Organizations that offer assistance to disabled travelers include:

- ✔ **American Foundation for the Blind (AFB)** (☎ 800-232-5463; www.afb.org): A referral resource for the blind or visually impaired that includes information on traveling with Seeing Eye dogs.

- ✔ **MossRehab ResourceNet** (www.mossresourcenet.org): Provides a library of accessible-travel resources online.

- ✔ **Society for Accessible Travel & Hospitality (SATH)** (☎ 212-447-7284; www.sath.org): Offers a wealth of travel resources for people with all types of disabilities and recommendations on destinations, access guides, travel agents, tour operators, vehicle rentals, and companion services. Annual membership costs are $45 for adults and $30 for seniors and students.

For more information specifically targeted to travelers with disabilities, the community Web site **iCan** (www.icanonline.net) has destination guides and several regular columns on accessible travel. Also, check out **Twin Peaks Press** (☎ 360-694-2462), offering travel-related books for people with special needs, and *Open World Magazine,* published by SATH (subscription is $13 per year, $21 outside the U.S.).

Transportation

Avis Rent a Car has a program called "Avis Access" (☎ 888-879-4273; www.avis.com) that offers special car features such as swivel seats, spinner knobs, and hand controls.

Following the Rainbow: Advice for Gay and Lesbian Travelers

Although not considered the most open-minded country in Europe, Scotland is safe for gay and lesbian travelers. Glasgow and Edinburgh are progressive cities home to substantial (though perhaps subdued, depending on what you're used to) gay populations. Smaller towns and villages are less tolerant, and open displays of affection may be frowned upon. For more information and support, contact the **Gay and Lesbian Switchboard** (☎ 0141-847-0447) in Glasgow, which also operates the LGBT Centre (☎ 0141-221-7203), which offers health advice, workshops, and cultural events in the community. On the Web, visit www.eusa.ed.ac.uk/societies/blogs, which is run by Edinburgh University's Bisexual, Lesbian, Gay or Transgendered Society.

The International Gay and Lesbian Travel Association (IGLTA) (☎ 800-448-8550 or 954-776-2626; www.iglta.org) offers an online directory of gay- and lesbian-friendly travel businesses; on the organization's Web site, click "Members" for a detailed list.

Many agencies offer tours and travel itineraries specifically for gay and lesbian travelers.

- ✔ **Above and Beyond Tours** (☎ 800-397-2681; www.abovebeyondtours.com) is the exclusive gay and lesbian tour operator for United Airlines.

- ✔ **Now, Voyager** (☎ 800-255-6951; www.nowvoyager.com) is a well-known San Francisco–based gay-owned and -operated travel service.

The following travel guides are available at most travel bookstores and gay and lesbian bookstores, or you can order them from **Giovanni's Room Bookstore** (☎ 215-923-2960; www.giovannisroom.com):

- ✔ The *Damron* guides (www.damron.com) include annual books for gay men and lesbians.

- ✔ *Frommer's Gay & Lesbian Europe* (www.frommers.com) is an excellent travel resource.

- ✔ *Gay Travel A to Z: The World of Gay & Lesbian Travel Options at Your Fingertips* by Marianne Ferrari (Ferrari International; Box 35575, Phoenix, AZ 85069) is a very good gay and lesbian guidebook series.

- ✔ *Out and About* (☎ 800-929-2268 or 415-644-8044; www.outandabout.com) offers guidebooks and a newsletter ($20/yr; 10 issues) packed with solid information on the global gay and lesbian scene.

- ✔ *Spartacus International Gay Guide* (Bruno Gmünder Verlag; www.spartacusworld.com/gayguide) and *Odysseus* are both good, annual English-language guidebooks focused on gay men.

Uncovering your Scottish roots

If you have a surname beginning with Mac (which simply means "son of") or one of the common lowland Scottish monikers from Burns to Armstrong, you're probably a descendant of Scotland and may have ties to a clan — a group of kinsmen with common ancestry.

Clans and clan societies maintain their own museums throughout Scotland, and local tourist offices can give you details about where to locate them. Bookstores here also sell clan histories and maps.

Genealogical records are kept at the **General Register Office for Scotland,** New Register House, 3 W. Register St., Edinburgh (☎ 0131-334-0380), where you can search for a fee. The system is strictly self-service, and the office gets very crowded in summer.

The official government source for genealogical data has also been added to the Web. Log onto www.scotlandspeople.gov.uk. A basic search through the computerized archive costs £6 (about $11). The Web site's census data goes back more than 100 years.

Chapter 10

Taking Care of the Remaining Details

. . . .

In This Chapter

▶ Getting your passport

▶ Investigating insurance needs

▶ Staying healthy

▶ Getting in touch by cellphone or e-mail

▶ Keeping up with airport security measures

. . . .

*B*efore boarding the plane to Scotland, you need to take care of some important business. The information I provide in this chapter should help you get all your ducks in a row.

Getting a Passport

A valid passport is the only legal form of identification accepted around the world. You can't cross an international border without one. Getting a passport is easy, but the process takes some time, so you need to plan ahead. For an up-to-date country-by-country listing of passport requirements around the world, go to travel.state.gov/travel/foreign entryreqs.html, which is maintained by the U.S. State Department.

Applying for a U.S. passport

If you're applying for a first-time passport, follow these steps:

1. Complete a passport application in person at a U.S. passport office; a federal, state, or probate court; or a major post office. To find your regional passport office, either check the **U.S. State Department** Web site, travel.state.gov/passport/index.html, or call the **National Passport Information Center** (☎ 877-487-2778) for automated information.

2. Present a certified birth certificate as proof of citizenship. (Bringing along your driver's license, state or military ID, or social security card is also a good idea.)

3. Submit two identical passport-sized photos, measuring 2-x-2-inches in size. A variety of business, including pharmacies and major post offices, take these photos.

4. Pay a fee. For people 16 and over, a passport is valid for ten years and costs $85. For those 15 and under, a passport is valid for five years and costs $70.

 Allow plenty of time before your trip to apply for a passport; processing normally takes three weeks but can take longer during busy periods (especially spring).

If you have a passport in your current name that was issued within the past 15 years (and you were over age 16 when it was issued), you can renew the passport by mail for $55. Whether you're applying in person or by mail, you can download passport applications from the U.S. State Department Web site at `travel.state.gov/passport/index.html`. For general information, call the **National Passport Agency** (☎ **202-647-0518**).

Applying for other passports

The following list contains passport information for citizens of Australia, Canada, New Zealand, and the United Kingdom.

✔ Australians can visit a local post office or passport office, call the **Australia Passport Information Service** (☎ **131-232** toll-free from Australia), or log onto `www.passports.gov.au` for details on how and where to apply.

✔ Canadians can pick up applications at passport offices throughout Canada, post offices, or from the central **Passport Office, Department of Foreign Affairs and International Trade,** Ottawa, ON K1A 0G3 (☎ **800-567-6868;** `www.ppt.gc.ca`). Applications must be accompanied by two identical passport-sized photographs and proof of Canadian citizenship. Processing takes five to ten days if you apply in person or three weeks by mail.

✔ New Zealanders can pick up a passport application at any New Zealand Passports Office or download it from the main office's Web site, `www.passports.govt.nz`. For information, contact **Passports Office** at ☎ **0800-225-050** or visit the Web site.

✔ United Kingdom residents can pick up applications for a standard 10-year passport (5-year passport for children under 16) at passport offices, major post offices, or travel agencies. For information, contact the **United Kingdom Passport Service** (☎ **0870-521-0410;** `www.ukpa.gov.uk`).

Playing It Safe with Travel and Medical Insurance

Three kinds of travel insurance are available to you: trip-cancellation insurance, medical insurance, and lost luggage insurance. The cost of travel insurance varies widely depending on the cost and length of your trip, your age and health, and the type of trip you're taking, but expect to pay between 5 percent and 8 percent of the cost of the vacation itself.

For more information on travel insurance, contact one of the following insurers: **Access America** (☎ 866-807-3982; www.accessamerica.com); and **Travelex Insurance Services** (☎ 888-457-4602; www.travelex-insurance.com).

Trip-cancellation insurance

Trip-cancellation insurance helps you get your money back if you have to back out of a trip, if you have to go home early, or if your travel supplier goes bankrupt. Permissible reasons for cancellation can range from sickness to natural disasters to the state department declaring your destination unsafe for travel.

A good resource for information on trip-cancellation and travel-related scams is **Travel Guard Alerts,** a list of companies considered high-risk by Travel Guard International (www.travelguard.com). Protect yourself further by paying for the insurance with a credit card — by law, a consumer can get his money back on goods and services not received if he paid with a credit card and reports the loss within 60 days after the charge is listed on his credit card statement.

Many tour operators include insurance in the cost of the trip or can arrange insurance policies through a partnering provider, a convenient and often cost-effective way for the traveler to obtain insurance. Make sure the tour company is a reputable one, however: Some experts suggest you avoid buying insurance from the tour or cruise company you're traveling with, saying it's better to buy from a "third party" insurer than to put all your money in one place.

Medical insurance

Most existing health policies cover you if you get sick away from home — but verify your coverage before you go, particularly if you're insured by an HMO.

For travel overseas, most health plans (including Medicare and Medicaid) don't provide coverage; those that do often require you to pay for services upfront and only reimburse you after you've returned home and filed the necessary paperwork. In Scotland, health care is nationalized and free to residents. The hospital's emergency rooms will treat anyone at no cost, regardless of whether you're a local or a tourist. For stays in the hospital and follow-up care, however, they will seek payment. As a safety net, you may want to buy travel medical insurance. If you require additional medical insurance, try **MEDEX Assistance** (☎ 410-453-6300; www.medex assist.com) or **Travel Assistance International** (☎ 800-821-2828; www. travelassistance.com).

Lost luggage insurance

Lost luggage insurance isn't necessary for most travelers. On domestic flights in the U.S., checked baggage is covered up to $2,500 per ticketed passenger. On international flights (including U.S. portions of international trips), baggage coverage is limited to approximately $9.07 per pound, up to approximately $635 per checked bag. If you plan to check items more valuable than the standard liability, see if your valuables are covered by your homeowner's insurance policy, or get baggage insurance as part of your comprehensive travel-insurance package. Don't buy insurance at the airport — it's usually overpriced.

Be sure to take any valuables or irreplaceable items with you in your carry-on luggage, because many valuables (including books, money, and electronics) aren't covered by airline policies.

If your luggage is lost, immediately file a lost-luggage claim at the airport, detailing the luggage contents. For most airlines, you must report delayed, damaged, or lost baggage within four hours of arrival. Airlines are required to deliver found luggage directly to your house or destination free of charge.

Staying Healthy When You Travel

If you have a serious and/or chronic illness, talk to your doctor before leaving on a trip. For conditions such as epilepsy, diabetes, or heart problems, wear a **MedicAlert identification tag** (☎ 888-633-4298; www.medic alert.org), which immediately alerts doctors to your condition and gives them access to your records through MedicAlert's 24-hour hotline. Contact the **International Association for Medical Assistance to Travelers** (IAMAT) (☎ 716-754-4883 or, in Canada, 416-652-0137; www. iamat.org) for tips on travel and health concerns in Scotland and lists of local doctors. Also, the United States **Centers for Disease Control and Prevention** (☎ 800-311-3435; www.cdc.gov) provides up-to-date information on health hazards by region or country and offers tips on food safety.

In Scotland, health care is nationalized and free. Hospital emergency rooms will treat anyone, regardless of whether they're local residents or tourists.

Avoiding "economy-class syndrome"

Deep vein thrombosis (or as it's know in the world of flying, "economy-class syndrome") is a blood clot that develops in a deep vein. It's a potentially deadly condition that can be caused by sitting in cramped conditions — such as an airplane cabin — for long periods of time. Symptoms of deep vein thrombosis include leg pain or swelling or even shortness of breath.

During a flight (especially a long one), get up, walk around, and stretch your legs every 60 to 90 minutes. Other things you can do to prevent deep vein thrombosis include frequent flexing of the legs while sitting, drinking lots of water, and avoiding alcohol and sleeping pills. If you have a history of deep vein thrombosis, heart disease, or other condition that puts you at high risk for deep vein thrombosis, some experts recommend wearing compression stockings or taking anticoagulants when you fly; always ask your physician about the best course of action for you.

Staying Connected by Cellphone or E-mail

Staying in touch while traveling is easier than ever, thanks to cellphones and the Internet. Of course, if what you're interested in is an escape, you may want to skip the section below. Otherwise, read on.

Using a cellphone outside the U.S.

First of all, they're called "mobiles" (*moe*-bye-alls) in Scotland. The three letters that define much of the world's wireless capabilities are GSM (Global System for Mobiles), a big, seamless network that makes for easy cross-border cellphone use throughout Europe and dozens of other countries worldwide. In the U.S., T-Mobile, AT&T Wireless, and Cingular use this quasi-universal system; in Canada, Microcell and some Rogers customers are GSM, and all Europeans and most Australians use GSM.

If your cellphone is on a GSM system and you have a world-capable multiband phone such as many Sony Ericsson, Motorola, or Samsung models, you can make and receive calls across much of the globe, from Andorra to Uganda. Just call your wireless operator and ask for "international roaming" to be activated on your account. Unfortunately, per-minute charges on the network can be high.

If you have an unlocked phone — one that allows you to install removable computer memory phone chips (called SIM cards) — you can switch over to a cheap, prepaid SIM card (found at a local retailer) in Scotland. (Show your phone to the salesperson when you go to buy a SIM card; not all phones work on all networks.) With the new card, you get a local phone number and much, much lower calling rates. If your phone is locked, you may be able to have it unlocked. Just call your cellular operator and say you'll be going abroad and want to use the phone with a local provider.

If you don't have a cellphone, or if your phone is locked, then renting a phone is another possibility. Although you can rent a phone from any number of overseas sites, including kiosks at airports and at car-rental agencies, I suggest renting the phone before you leave home. That way you can give loved ones and business associates your new number, make sure the phone works, and take the phone wherever you go; getting the phone before you leave is especially helpful if you're planning to visit Scotland and then go overseas through several other countries, where local phone-rental agencies often bill in local currency and may not let you take the phone to another country.

Phone rental isn't cheap. You'll usually pay $40 to $50 per week, plus airtime fees of at least $1 per minute. If you're traveling to the UK or Europe, though, local rental companies often offer free incoming calls within their home country, which can save you big bucks. Shop around.

Two good wireless rental companies in the States are **InTouch Global** (☎ **800-872-7626**; www.intouchglobal.com) and **RoadPost** (☎ **888-290-1606** or 905-272-5665; www.roadpost.com). Give the company your itinerary, and someone will tell you what wireless products you need. For no charge, InTouch also advises you on whether your existing phone will work overseas; simply call ☎ **703-222-7161** between 9 a.m. and 4 p.m. EST, or go to intouchglobal.com/travel.htm.

In the UK, you can rent (or "hire") phones from

> ✔ **Cellhire UK** (☎ **0800-610-610** within the UK, ☎ **44-1904-610-610** outside the UK, or ☎ 1-866-246-6546 within the U.S.; www.cellhire.co.uk)

> ✔ **Adam Phones** (☎ **0800-123-000** within the UK; ☎ **44-20-8742-0101** outside the UK, or ☎ **1-866-GSM-HIRE** within the U.S.; www.adamphones.com)

Accessing the Internet

Travelers have any number of ways to check their e-mail and access the Internet on the road. Of course, using your own laptop — or even a PDA (personal digital assistant) or electronic organizer with a modem — gives you the most flexibility. But even if you don't have a computer, you can still access your e-mail and even your office computer from cybercafes.

It's hard nowadays to find a city that *doesn't* have a few cybercafes. Although no definitive directory for cybercafes exists — these are independent businesses, after all — two places to start looking are at www.cybercaptive.com and www.cybercafe.com. In Scotland, cybercafes pop up near universities more than anywhere else.

Aside from formal cybercafes, most youth hostels nowadays have at least one computer you can use to access the Internet. And most public libraries across the world offer Internet access free or for a small charge. Avoid hotel business centers unless you're willing to pay exorbitant rates.

To retrieve your e-mail, ask your Internet Service Provider (ISP) if it has a Web-based interface tied to your existing e-mail account. If your ISP doesn't have such an interface, you can use the free service from **mail2web** (www.mail2web.com) to view and reply to your home e-mail. For more flexibility, you may want to open a free, Web-based e-mail account with **Yahoo! Mail** (mail.yahoo.com). Your home ISP may be able to forward your e-mail to the Web-based account automatically.

If you need to access files on your office computer while you're away, look into a service called **GoToMyPC** (www.gotomypc.com). The service provides a Web-based interface for you to access and manipulate a distant PC from anywhere — even a cybercafe — provided your "target" PC is on and has an always-on connection to the Internet (such as with digital cable).

If you're bringing your own computer with you as you travel, the buzzword in computer access to familiarize yourself with is *wi-fi* (wireless fidelity). More and more hotels, cafes, and retailers are signing on as wireless "hotspots," allowing you to get a high-speed connection without cable wires, networking hardware, or a phone line.

You can get wi-fi connection in one of several ways. Many laptops sold in the last year have built-in wi-fi capability (an 802.11b wireless Ethernet connection). Mac owners have their own networking technology called Apple AirPort. For those with older computers, an 802.11b/wi-fi card can be purchased for around $50 and plugs into your laptop. You sign up for wireless access service much as you do cellphone service, through a plan offered by one of several commercial companies that have made wireless service available in airports, hotel lobbies, and coffee shops, primarily in the U.S. (followed by the UK and Japan). **T-Mobile Hotspot** (www.t-mobile.com/hotspot) serves up wireless connections at more than 1,000 Starbucks coffee shops nationwide. **Boingo** (www.boingo.com) and **Wayport** (www.wayport.com) have set up networks in airports and high-class hotel lobbies. **iPass** (www.ipass.com) providers also give you access to a few hundred wireless hotel lobby setups.

Certain places also provide free wireless networks in cities around the world. To locate these free hotspots, go to www.wififreespot.com.

If wi-fi isn't available at your destination, most business-class hotels throughout the world offer dataports for laptop modems, and many hotels in Europe now offer free high-speed Internet access using an Ethernet network cable. You can bring your own cables, but most hotels rent them for around $10. Call your hotel in advance to find out about your options.

In addition, major Internet Service Providers (ISPs) have local access numbers around the world, allowing you to go online simply by placing a local call. Check your ISP's Web site or call its toll-free number and ask how you can use your current account away from home and how much it costs. If you're traveling outside the reach of your ISP, the **iPass** network has dial-up numbers in most countries. You have to sign up with an iPass provider, who then tells you how to set up your computer for your destination(s). For a list of iPass providers, go to www.ipass.com and click on "Individual Purchase." One solid provider is **i2roam** (☎ **866-811-6209** or 920-235-0475; www.i2roam.com).

Wherever you go, bring a connection kit of the right power and phone adapters, a spare phone cord, and a spare Ethernet network cable — or find out whether your hotel supplies them to guests.

Scotland Unplugged: Getting Your Electric Stuff to Work

The plugs in Scotland are different than in the U.S. and Canada. You can buy a cheap adapter, but it won't address the problem of different voltages. In the U.S. and Canada, the current is 110 volts. In Scotland, it's 240 volts. So, if you plug in your hair dryer, even with an adapter, the machine could light up like a Roman candle or blow a fuse. You can buy a voltage transformer (check out www.walkabouttravelgear.com), but they can be expensive and not worth the cost if you're planning a short stay.

Some travel appliances, such as shavers and irons, have a nice feature called dual voltage that adapts to the change, but unless your appliance gives a voltage range (such as 110v–220v), don't chance it. Bring a battery-operated alarm clock (for when you can't get a wake-up call) and shaver (if you're averse to disposables) as well as a battery-powered personal stereo (if you can't bear to be without your tunes). And don't forget extra batteries.

If you plan to travel with a video camera, bring enough battery packs *and* enough blank videotape. Blank cassette tapes in Scotland may look identical to yours, but they won't work in your camera.

Keeping Up with Airline Security Measures

With the federalization of airport security, procedures at U.S. airports are more stable and consistent than ever. Generally, arriving at the airport two hours before an international flight should be sufficient.

Don't leave home without a current, government-issued photo ID such as a driver's license and your passport. Keep your ID at the ready to show at check-in, the security checkpoint, and sometimes even the gate.

In 2003, gate check-in was phased out at all U.S. airports. And e-tickets have made paper tickets nearly obsolete. With an e-ticket, you can beat the ticket-counter lines by using airport electronic kiosks or even online check-in from your home computer.

If you're using a kiosk at the airport, bring the credit card you used to book the ticket or your frequent-flier card. (You may not be able to print out your boarding pass without the credit card used for purchase, and you want to make sure your frequent-flier miles are credited properly.) Print out your boarding pass from the kiosk and simply proceed to the security checkpoint with your pass and photo ID. If you're checking bags or looking to snag an exit-row seat, you can do so using most airline kiosks.

Curbside check-in is also a good way to avoid lines, although a few airlines still ban curbside check-in, so call and check.

Security checkpoint lines are getting shorter than they were in 2002, but some doozies remain. Speed up security by not wearing metal objects such as big belt buckles. If you've got metallic body parts, a note from your doctor can prevent a long chat with the security screeners. Keep in mind that only ticketed passengers are allowed past security, except for folks escorting disabled passengers or children.

Federal rules dictate what you can carry on a plane and what you can't. The general rule is that sharp things are out, nail clippers are okay, and food and beverages must be passed through the X-ray machine — but screeners can't make you drink from your coffee cup. Bring food in your carry-on rather than checking it, because explosive-detection machines used on checked luggage have been known to mistake food (especially chocolate, for some reason) for bombs. Travelers in the U.S. are allowed one carry-on bag, plus a "personal item" such as a purse, briefcase, or laptop bag. Carry-on hoarders can stuff all sorts of things into a laptop bag; as long as it has a laptop in it, it's still considered a personal item. The TSA has issued a list of restricted items; check its Web site (www. tsa.gov/public/index.jsp) for details.

Airport screeners may decide that your checked luggage needs to be searched by hand. You can now purchase luggage locks that allow screeners to open and re-lock a checked bag if hand-searching is necessary. Look for Travel Sentry certified locks at luggage or travel shops and Brookstone stores (you can buy them online at www.brookstone.com). These locks, approved by the TSA, can be opened by luggage inspectors with a special code or key. For more information on the locks, visit www.travelsentry. org. If you use something other than TSA-approved locks, your lock may be cut off your suitcase if a TSA agent needs to hand-search your luggage.

Part III
Edinburgh and Glasgow

The 5th Wave   By Rich Tennant

"We were in Edinburgh this summer. I loved the
New Town section but Edward preferred the
medieval feel of Old Town."

In this part . . .

You find out about the charms and attractions of Scotland's two major cities, Edinburgh and Glasgow, and about some of the sights that are within easy striking distance of each or both of the cities. Though noticeably different from one another, each city is worth a visit, and you'll find plenty of suggestions here of what to do and see. Edinburgh, Scotland's capital, is most famous for its castle and picturesque setting, while Glasgow, once one of the greatest shipbuilding centers of the world, is a more modern and bustling big city (though not too big).

The chapters in Part III offer everything from advice on getting there to getting around — and discovering the best places to stay and dine. You also get the lowdown on the cities' finest sights and attractions, insider tips on quintessential Scottish pubs and cafes, and walking tours for each city.

Chapter 11

Edinburgh

* *

In This Chapter

▶ Getting around Edinburgh

▶ Discovering the best places to stay and eat

▶ Exploring the city's sights and attractions

▶ Shopping for quintessential Scottish souvenirs

▶ Finding the best spots for pints, music, and pub grub

* *

*E*dinburgh is often referred to as one of Europe's fairest cities and as the "Athens of the North." And what most experienced travelers to the United Kingdom say is true: If you can visit only two cities in all of Great Britain, hit London first and Edinburgh second. The Scottish capital began as a small, fortified settlement on a craggy hill. Indeed, because of its defensive attributes, Edinburgh (remember "burgh" is always pronounced *burra* in Scotland) became an important place for the country's rulers. Somewhat ironically, it has become the crossroads of Scotland — the spot at which most visitors to this country north of England are likely to stop.

The city is filled with historic, intellectual, and literary associations. People such as Mary Queen of Scots and her nemesis, Protestant reformer John Knox; pioneer economist Adam Smith and philosopher David Hume; authors Sir Walter Scott, Robert Louis Stevenson, and Sir Arthur Conan Doyle; as well as inventor Alexander Graham Bell are all part of Edinburgh's past. Today, the city is most famous for its world-class cultural festival, the **Edinburgh International Festival,** which is actually several festivals in one: films, books, comedy, drama, classical music, dance, and more.

But this ancient seat of Scottish royalty also attracts visitors year-round. Indeed, when the festival-goers have returned home, the city's pace is more relaxed, the prices are lower, and the inhabitants — though not celebrated for their bonhomie — are under less pressure and offer a more hospitable welcome.

Built on extinct volcanoes atop an inlet (the Firth of Forth) of the North Sea and enveloped by lakes, forests, and rolling hills (several of which offer panoramic views), Edinburgh is a city that lends itself to walking. Its **Old Town** and **New Town** sport moody, cobbled alleys; elegant streetscapes; handsome squares; and placid parks. Additionally, Edinburgh is home to the several excellent **National Galleries** of Scotland and is well situated for interesting daytrips. Notable nearby attractions include Linlithgow, where Mary Queen of Scots was born; the Borders, with rolling hillsides to the south; the Kingdom of Fife on the opposite shore of the Firth of Forth; and St. Andrews. (Turn to Chapter 13 for more information on these attractions and your daytrip options.) Any trip to Scotland should allow Edinburgh at least two days — and, if you have the time, you won't regret staying longer than that.

Getting to Edinburgh

Although a few flights to Edinburgh from North America are direct, a stopover in London's Heathrow airport is common. If you're coming from London, your best options are flying or taking the train. If you're coming from elsewhere in Scotland, the major bus and train routes serve Edinburgh. Having a car in Edinburgh isn't strictly necessary (nor indeed preferable), but the city is easily accessed from freeways if you choose to drive.

By air

Edinburgh is only about an hour's flying time from London, which is 633km (393 miles) south. **Edinburgh International Airport (☎ 0131-333-1000)** is about 10km (6 miles) west of the city's center, and has become a growing hub for flights both within the British Isles as well as to and from Continental Europe.

Remember, however, that Glasgow International Airport is only about 90km (55 miles) away and shouldn't be discounted if you're coming to Edinburgh, because it traditionally greets more long-haul flights, especially from North America. For information on arriving in Glasgow by air, see Chapter 12.

Orienting yourself

Edinburgh's airport is small (about the length of two football fields) and contained in one terminal, so there's little possibility of getting lost. Immigration control and customs agents are vigilant, but the scene is quite a bit more relaxed than at a giant air terminal such as London's Heathrow. Usually you find just one line (queue) for visitors from outside the European Union. Arrivals with EU passports are able to breeze right through. Before heading into town, you may want to stop at the airport's **information and accommodation desk (☎ 0131-333-2167)**, which is generally open Monday through Saturday from 6:15 a.m. to 7:45 p.m. and Sunday from 9 a.m. to 4:30 p.m.

Getting into town

From Edinburgh airport, the Airlink bus (look for the sign) makes the trip to the city center about every 10 minutes during peak times, terminating at Waverley Bridge near the central railway station. The fare is £3.30 ($6.10) one-way or £5 ($9.25) round-trip; an "Airsaver" ticket for £4.20 ($7.75) provides not only the one-way trip into town but also unlimited bus travel within the city for the day as well. The trip from the airport into town takes about 25 minutes (sometimes longer during rush hours). Overnight service is provided by Night Buses N22. Visit www.flybybus.com for details of Airlink bus service.

A taxi into the city costs about £12 ($22) or more, depending on traffic, and the ride takes about the same time as the bus. Look for the taxi line-up area when exiting the airport.

By train

The trains that link London to Edinburgh (via Newcastle) on the so-called East Coast Main Line are reasonably fast, efficient, and generally relaxing, with restaurant and bar service as well as air-conditioning. Trains depart from London's Kings Cross Station (contact National Railway Enquiries at ☎ 0845-748-4950 for rail info) every hour or so and arrive in Edinburgh at **Waverley Station** in the heart of the city. The trip generally takes 4½ hours. Standard class "off-peak" fares bought in advance range from around £25 to £36 ($46–$66); "off-peak" first class fares purchased in advance cost about £60 ($111). (Off-peak travel times are listed at the end of this paragraph.) The fully flexible "buy anytime, travel anytime" standard open return fare is upwards of £180 ($333). The Caledonian Sleeper service for overnight travel can cost about £90 ($166) if purchased in advance. Taxi and bus connections are easily made at Waverley Station, which also serves Glasgow, with shuttle service every 15 minutes during the day and every 30 minutes in the evenings until about 11:30 p.m. The round-trip shuttle fare during off-peak times (travel between 9:15 a.m. and 4:30 p.m. and after 6:15 p.m., to avoid the rush hour) is £7.90 ($14.50).

By bus

The journey from London to Edinburgh by bus can take up to 10 hours. Nevertheless, it gets you there for only about £40 ($74) round-trip. Scottish CityLink coaches depart from London's Victoria Coach Station and deliver you to Edinburgh's **Bus Station** near St. Andrew Square (☎ 0870-550-5050 for information).

By car

Edinburgh is 74km (46 miles) east of Glasgow and 169km (105 miles) north of Newcastle-upon-Tyne in England. Unfortunately, no express motorway links London directly to Edinburgh. The M1 from London takes you most of the way north, but you have to come into Edinburgh via secondary roads — either the coastal A1 or inland A68. Alternatively, you can travel the well-used motorways in the west of the UK. From London, take the M1 to the M6 (near Coventry), which links to the M74 at Carlisle. Then travel to the M8 southeast of Glasgow, which takes you Edinburgh's ring road or beltway. Allow 8 hours or more for the drive north from London.

Orienting Yourself in Edinburgh

Central Edinburgh is divided into an **Old Town** and larger **New Town.**
Many visitors find lodgings in the New Town (or elsewhere) and tend to
visit Old Town for sightseeing, dining, and drinking — although there are
accommodations in Old Town on the **High Street** and in the **Grassmarket,**
which is both a district and a street, a common occurrence in Britain.

Once called "Auld Reekie" because of its smoky atmosphere, today's Old
Town is chock-a-block with tourist attractions, shops, and out-of-town
visitors for most months of the year. The **Royal Mile** is the main thoroughfare of the Old Town, running from Edinburgh Castle in the west
to the Palace of Holyroodhouse in the east. Both British **royalty** and
Scotland's **Parliament** (revived in 1999) are based in the Old Town, as are
city government and the country's legal elite. Another more infamous
street at the southern base of the castle is the **Grassmarket,** where con-
victed criminals were once hanged on the gallows. Today it's home to
restaurants, pubs, and hotels.

New Town is actually fairly old. North of the Old Town, across what is
today Princes Street Gardens, New Town was first settled in the 18th
century. By the end of that century, classic squares, streets, and town
houses were complete, and the original New Town was soon expanded
with more Georgian designs. New Town represents the golden age of
Edinburgh, a designation aided by the presence of world-famous **Princes
Street.** The city's main shopping precinct, Princes Street boasts broad
sidewalks and a park running its entire length — all with panoramic
views of Old Town and Edinburgh Castle.

North of and running parallel to Princes Street is New Town's second
great boulevard, **George Street.** It begins at St. Andrew Square and runs
west to Charlotte Square. Directly north of George Street is another
impressive thoroughfare, **Queen Street,** which opens onto Queen Street
Gardens on its north side and features views of the Firth of Forth. You
may also hear a lot about **Rose Street,** between Princes Street and
George Street, and its many pubs, shops, and restaurants.

Edinburgh's **South Side** and **West End** are primarily residential. The
South Side is home to both the city's well-regarded Edinburgh University
(which makes parts of the area quite lively) and the sprawling park
known as the Meadows. The West End includes the last of the New Town
developments begun at the beginning of the 19th century. It has theaters,
several small B&Bs, and swank boutique hotels as well as the city's most
exclusive central neighborhoods.

Leith is Edinburgh's historic port where the Water of Leith meets the
Firth of Forth. It briefly served as the Scottish capital in the middle of
the 16th century, and its strategic location was so strong that Oliver
Cromwell's invading forces built a citadel there. Leith remained an independent burgh until the 20th century. Fans of Irvine Welsh (author of

Trainspotting) probably know that the area has a rough and tumble reputation. But today, most of its shipping and the sailors have gone, and lots
of luxury apartments are being built instead. Still, Leith remains an
evocative area and offers a good selection of seafood restaurants and
nautical-themed pubs. It's also now the home of the royal yacht
Britannia.

Despite the hills, Edinburgh is a very walkable city. Many little alleys
(wynds) and passageways (closes) are accessible only by foot. So bring
a pair of comfortable shoes and start walking — you'll get a great feel for
what the city has to offer.

Introducing the neighborhoods

Edinburgh has a host of districts, some of which appear to include only
a few streets and many that can be folded into the broader areas of the
Old and New Towns.

Old Town

Old Town is where Edinburgh began. Its spine is the **Royal Mile,** a
medieval thoroughfare stretching for about 1.6km (1 mile) from Edinburgh
Castle downhill to the Palace of Holyroodhouse. The neighborhood's composed of streets bearing four names: Castlehill, Lawnmarket, High Street,
and Canongate. English author Daniel Defoe wrote of the Royal Mile, "This
is perhaps the largest, longest, and finest street for buildings and number
of inhabitants in the world." Old Town also includes the areas of
Grassmarket and Cowgate.

New Town

Lying predominantly north of Old Town, the first New Town bloomed
between 1766 and 1840 as one of the largest Georgian developments in
the world. It grew to encompass the northern half of the heart of the city.
New Town is the largest conservation area in Britain and has at least
25,000 residents. New Town is made up of a network of squares, streets,
terraces, and circuses, reaching from Haymarket in the west to almost
Leith Walk in the east. The neighborhood also extends from Canonmills in
the north to Princes Street, its most famous artery, on the south.

Stockbridge

Today part of the New Town area, Stockbridge is a one-time village that
still feels rather like a small town because of its tightly knit community.
Northwest of the castle and straddling the Water of Leigh, it's a good
place for visitors to the city to relax, especially in the friendly cafes,
pubs, restaurants, and shops.

Haymarket and Dalry

West of the city center by about 1.5km (1 mile), these two districts may
be off the beaten path for most visitors. Haymarket centers on the
Haymarket railway station (an alternative to Waverley for travelers to

and from Glasgow and the west or places much further north). Just a bit farther out of town is Murrayfield, the Scottish national rugby stadium. Dalry is slowly opening some interesting though largely neighborhood-oriented restaurants.

Tollcross and West End

Edinburgh's theater district and Conference Center are in the area west of the Castle. The West End neighborhoods near Shandwick Place are rather exclusive. Although the district of Tollcross appears a bit rough, it's rapidly changing and becoming more visitor-friendly.

South Side: Marchmont and Bruntsfield

About 1.5km (1 mile) south of High Street, Marchmont was constructed between 1869 and 1914 to offer new housing to people who could no longer afford to live in New Town. Its northern border is the Meadows. Sometimes visitors go south to this neighborhood seeking an affordable B&B in one of the little homes that receive guests.

Bruntsfield is west of the Meadows and is named for Bruntsfield Links (a short-hole public golf course). Now a largely residential district, the area was the ground on which James IV apparently gathered the Scottish army that he marched to defeat at Flodden in 1513. You can find many low-cost B&Bs in this vicinity.

Calton

Encompassing Calton Hill with its Regent and Royal terraces (streets), this district borders the so-called Pink Triangle, Edinburgh's version of a gay-friendly district. Edinburgh has a lively gay population, which focuses socially on an area from the top of Leith Walk to Broughton Street. The area is not, however, a dedicated gay district like San Francisco's Castro or Christopher Street in Manhattan's Greenwich Village. It's just part and parcel of lively Calton with its bars, nightclubs, and restaurants.

Leith Walk and the Port of Leith

Leith Walk isn't technically a neighborhood but is instead the main artery that connects Edinburgh's city center to Leith. Off it are Easter Road (home of Hibernian football club) and the districts of Pilrig and South Leith. A foray down Leith Walk presents you with an honest cross section of Edinburgh.

The **Port of Leith** lies only a few kilometers north of Princes Street and is the city's major harbor, opening onto the Firth of Forth. In terms of maritime might, the port isn't what it used to be; its glory days were back when stevedores unloaded cargoes by hand. The area is currently experiencing urban renewal, however, and visitors come here for the restaurants and pubs, many of which specialize in seafood.

Finding information after you arrive

The **Edinburgh Information Centre** (☎ **0131-473-3800** or 0845-225-5121; www.edinburgh.org), located atop the Princes Mall near Waverley Station, can provide you with sightseeing information and arrange lodgings. The center sells bus tours, theater tickets, and Edinburgh souvenirs. It also has racks and racks of free brochures. It's open year-round, and typically the hours are Monday through Saturday from 9 a.m. to 7 p.m. and Sunday from 10 a.m. to 7 p.m., although it's open later during the Edinburgh International Festival and closes earlier in the winter months.

Getting Around Edinburgh

Because of its narrow lanes, wynds, and closes, you can only honestly explore the Old Town in any depth on foot. Edinburgh is fairly convenient for the visitor who likes to walk (see the section "Taking a walking tour," later in this chapter), because most of the major attractions are located along the Royal Mile, Princes Street, or one of the major streets of New Town. The city doesn't have a subway system, although there has been discussion about reintroducing a tramway.

By bus

Because Edinburgh has no underground or subway and only limited commuter train service, the city's rather numerous buses provide the chief method of public transportation. Buses are plentiful, and most travel down Princes Street at some point on their routes.

Bus fares depend on the distance traveled, with the one-way (single) minimum fare set at 80 pence ($1.50). That fare covers the central Edinburgh districts. Children ages 4 and under ride free. Children between 5 and 15 years old are charged a flat rate of 60p ($1.10), but kids ages 13 to 15 are expected to carry a **teen card** (available at bus travelshops) as proof of age. If you're planning to take multiple trips in one day, purchase a **Day Saver** ticket that allows one day of unlimited travel on city buses at a cost of £2.50 ($4) for adults and £2 ($3.70) for children. Bus drivers, by the way, don't make change, so be sure to carry the correct amount in coins or expect to pay more. One-week **Ridacard** passes, which allow unlimited travel on buses, can be purchased at travelshops for £12 ($22) for adults, £10 ($18.50) for students, and £8 ($15) for juniors (ages 5 to 15).

The tourist buses that terminate at Waverley Bridge also offer hop-on hop-off service at any of their stops on the established circuit of primarily Old and New Towns. Tickets — £8.50 ($15.70) for adults and £2.50 ($4.60) for children — are valid for 24 hours (although the buses make their final runs in the early evening).

You can get advance tickets and further information on bus transportation in the city center at the **Waverley Bridge Travelshop,** Waverley

Edinburgh Orientation

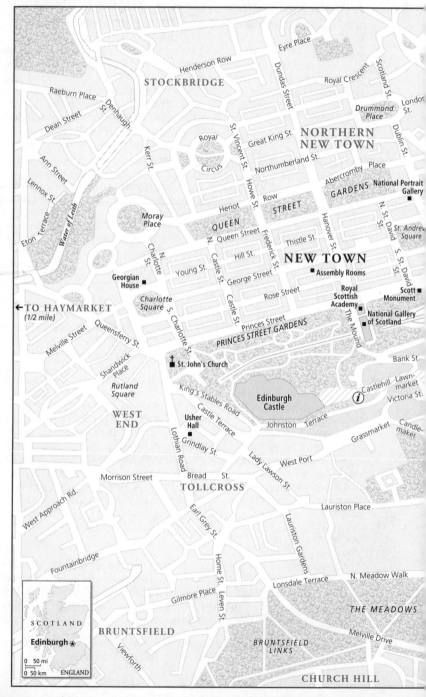

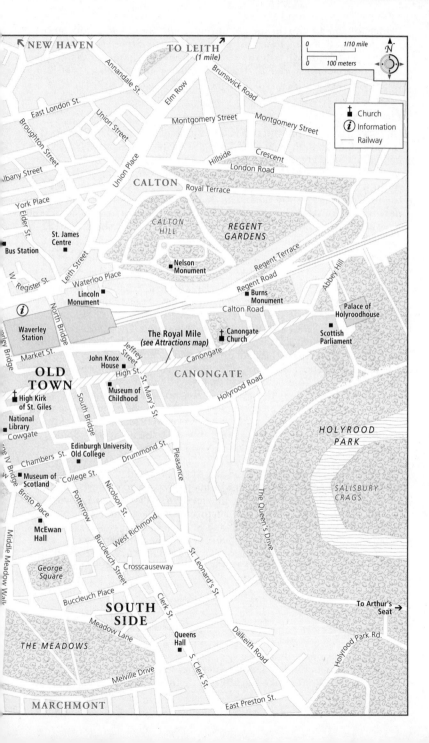

↖ NEW HAVEN

TO LEITH ↗
(1 mile)

0   1/10 mile

0   100 meters

N

✝ Church
ⓘ Information
— Railway

Annandale St.

Elm Row

Brunswick Road

East London St.

Union Street

Montgomery Street

Montgomery Street

Broughton Street

Union Place

Hillside

Crescent

London Road

Albany Street

CALTON

Royal Terrace

York Place

Elder St.

CALTON
HILL

REGENT
GARDENS

■ Bus Station

St. James
Centre

Leith Street

Nelson
Monument

Regent Terrace

W. Register St.

Waterloo Place

Regent Road

Abbey Hill

Lincoln
Monument

Burns
Monument

Palace of
Holyroodhouse

ⓘ

North Bridge

Calton Road

Waverley
Station

The Royal Mile
(see Attractions map)

✝ Canongate
Church

Scottish
Parliament

Market St.

Jeffrey St.

Canongate

OLD
TOWN

John Knox
House

High St.

St. Mary's St.

CANONGATE

Holyrood Road

✝ High Kirk
of St. Giles

South Bridge

Museum of
Childhood

HOLYROOD
PARK

National
Library

Cowgate

Edinburgh University
Old College

Drummond St.

Pleasance

Chambers St.

IV Bridge

■ Museum of
Scotland

College St.

Potterrow

Nicolson St.

SALISBURY
CRAGS

Bristo Place

McEwan
Hall

West Richmond

The Queen's Drive

George
Square

Buccleuch Street

Crosscauseway

Middle Meadow Walk

Buccleuch Place

SOUTH
SIDE

Clerk St.

St. Leonard's St.

To Arthur's
Seat →

Meadow Lane

Queens
Hall

Dalkeith Road

Holyrood Park Rd.

THE MEADOWS

Melville Drive

S. Clerk St.

MARCHMONT

East Preston St.

Bridge, open Monday through Saturday from 8:30 a.m. to 6 p.m. and
Sunday from 9:30 a.m. to 5 p.m., or at 27 Hanover Street Travelshop,
open Monday through Saturday from 8:30 a.m. to 6 p.m. For details on
fares and timetables, call ☎ **0131-555-6363** or log onto www.lothian
buses.co.uk.

By taxi

One way to get around the city is to either hail a taxi or pick one up at a
taxi stand. Meters begin at £2 ($3.20) and a typical trek across town may
cost about £6 ($11). Taxi ranks (stands) are at High Street near North
Bridge, Waverley and Haymarket stations, Hanover Street, North St.
Andrew Street, and Lauriston Place. Fares are displayed on the front of
the taxi, and charges are posted, including extra fees for night drivers or
destinations outside the city limits. You can also call a taxi ahead of time.
Try **City Cabs** at ☎ **0131-228-1211** or **Central Radio Taxis** at ☎ **0131-
229-2468.**

By car

Unless you absolutely can't avoid it, don't drive in Edinburgh — it's a
tricky and frustrating business, even for natives. Speed bumps, one-way
streets, dedicated bus lanes, and the promise of tolls (which has been
under debate in 2004) are all good reasons to forego the automobile.
Parking is expensive and also can be difficult to find. Metered parking is
available, but you need the right change and have to watch out for traffic
wardens who issue tickets. Some zones are marked PERMIT HOLDERS ONLY —
and they mean it! Your vehicle will be towed if you don't have a permit. A
double yellow line along the curb indicates no parking at any time. A
single yellow line along the curb may allow you to park; check for posted
restrictions or you may incur a ticket there as well. Major parking lots (car
parks) are at Castle Terrace (near Edinburgh Castle), Waverley Station,
and St James Centre (close to the east end of Princes Street).

You may want a rental car for touring the countryside or heading
onward. Many agencies grant discounts to those who reserve cars in
advance (see Chapter 7 for more information). Most rental agencies will
accept your foreign driver's license, provided you've held it for more
than a year and are over age 21. Most of the major car-rental companies
maintain offices at the Edinburgh airport in case you want to rent a car
on the spot. In the city, try **Avis** on West Park Place (☎ **0131-337-6363**),
Hertz on Picardy Place (☎ **0131-556-8311**), or **Thrifty** on Haymarket
Terrace (☎ **0131-337 1319**).

By bicycle

Bicycles are a more common mode of transportation in Edinburgh than
in Glasgow. Nevertheless, biking is probably a good idea only for visitors
in good shape, given that the city's set on a series of ridges and the
streets are often cobbled. If you're determined to bike your way through
Edinburgh, try **Rent-a-Bike Edinburgh,** 29 Blackfriars St., near the High

Famous Edinburghers

Famous Edinburgh residents include *Harry Potter* author J.K. Rowling, who has become one of the best-selling writers in history. She lives in the shadow of Edinburgh Castle and wrote her first book in one of the city's coffee shops. David Hume lived at James Court in Old Town in the 18th century. James Boswell, Robert Louis Stevenson, Sir Walter Scott, and Flora MacDonald also made their homes here. One of the city's most famous former residents, Sean Connery, grew up in the Fenton Bridge tenements, and Queen Elizabeth knighted him in 2000 at the Palace of Holyroodhouse. The actor, most widely known for his many James Bond films, had previously dismissed the idea of knighthood as long as Scotland was denied independent rule. (See Chapter 2 for more on the political history of Scotland.)

Street (☎ 0131-556-5560; www.cyclescotland.co.uk; Bus: 35). Depending on the type of bike you rent, charges average around £15 ($28) per day or £70 ($130) for the week, But partial-day hires are also possible. A credit card imprint will be taken as security. The same company that operates Rent-a-Bike Edinburgh also runs **Scottish Cycle Safaris,** which organizes tours in the city and across Scotland. They can equip you for excursions, and because they have branches in places such as Oban, Inverness, and Skye, you can drop off your bike and equipment there at the end of your trip if it's more convenient.

On foot

Walking Edinburgh is definitely the best way to see the city center and most of the town. (But I also recommend using buses or taxis if the distances seem too great.)

Staying in Style

Edinburgh offers a variety of accommodations for visitors, from super posh and ridiculously pricey five-star hotels to down-and-dirty bunkhouses and youth hostels. It's a city that anticipates bundles of tourists and travelers, whether backpackers, families, or business types in the Scottish capital on commercial or governmental matters.

During the three- to four-week period of the Edinburgh Festival every summer, the hotels fill up quickly. If you're planning a visit during that time, be sure to reserve your accommodation as far in advance as possible. Otherwise you'll end up in a town or village as much as 40km (55 miles) from the city center. And don't be surprised if the room rates in Edinburgh are higher during August, particularly at guesthouses and smaller hotels.

Edinburgh Accommodations

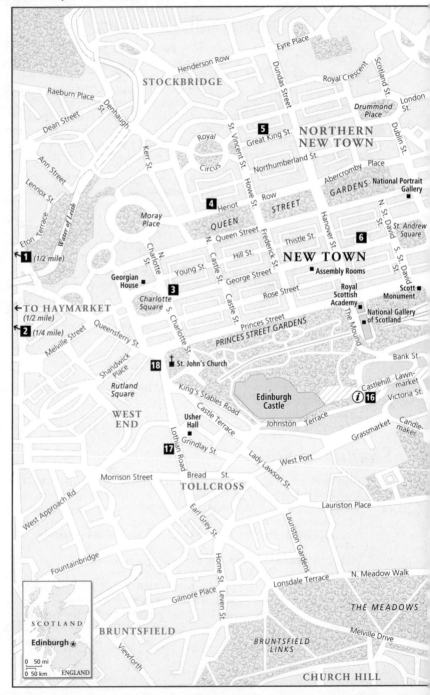

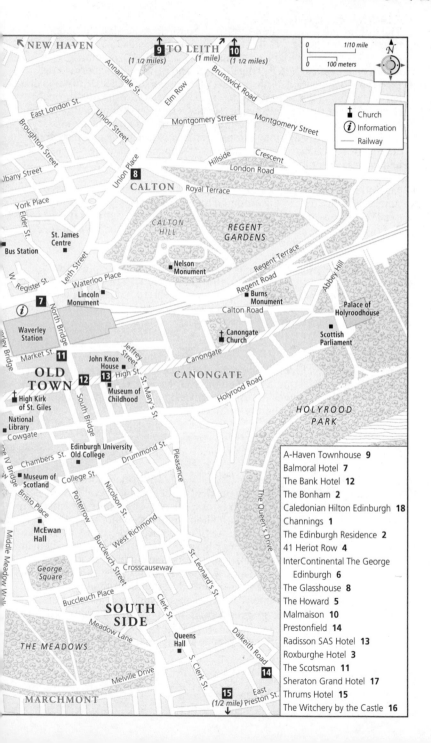

NEW HAVEN
TO LEITH
(1 1/2 miles) (1 mile) (1 1/2 miles)

0   1/10 mile
0   100 meters

N

† Church
ⓘ Information
— Railway

Annandale St.
Elm Row
Brunswick Road
East London St.
Union Street
Montgomery Street
Montgomery Street
Broughton Street
Hillside
Crescent
London Road
Albany Street
Union Place
CALTON
Royal Terrace
York Place
8
Elder St.
St. James
Centre
CALTON
HILL
REGENT
GARDENS
Bus Station
Leith Street
Nelson
Monument
Regent Terrace
W. Register St.
Waterloo Place
Regent Road
Abbey Hill
ⓘ
7
Lincoln
Monument
North Bridge
Burns
Monument
Calton Road
Palace of
Holyroodhouse
Waverley
Station
† Canongate
Church
Scottish
Parliament
Market St.
11
Jeffrey Street
Canongate
**OLD
TOWN**
John Knox
House
St. Mary's St.
CANONGATE
12
13
High St.
Holyrood Road
† High Kirk
of St. Giles
South Bridge
Museum of
Childhood
**HOLYROOD
PARK**
National
Library
Cowgate
Edinburgh University
Old College
Drummond St.
Chambers St.
College St.
Pleasance
■ Museum of
Scotland
Nicolson St.
Bristo Place
Potterrow
West Richmond
St. Leonard's St.
McEwan
Hall
Buccleuch Street
George
Square
Crosscauseway
The Queen's Drive
Buccleuch Place
**SOUTH
SIDE**
Clerk St.
Dalkeith Road
THE MEADOWS
Meadow Lane
Queens
Hall
14
Melville Drive
S. Clerk St.
15
East
MARCHMONT
(1/2 mile) Preston St.

The **Edinburgh Information Centre,** atop the Princes Mall shopping center at 3 Princes St. (☎ **0131-473-3800** or ☎ **0845-225-5121;** Fax: 0131-473-3881; www.edinburgh.org; Bus: 3, 8, 22, 25, or 31), maintains a lengthy list of small hotels, guesthouses, and private homes providing B&B-type lodging for as little as £20 ($37) per person. A £3 ($5.50) booking fee is charged and a 10 percent deposit is expected if you book through the center. For the best availability, make your reservation about 4 weeks in advance, especially during summer. The center is open year-round; typically the hours are Monday through Saturday from 9 a.m. to 7 p.m. and Sunday from 10 a.m. to 7 p.m., although it's open later during the Festival and closes earlier in the winter months.

The Internet can be a treasure trove of discounted rates if you have the time and inclination to dig around a bit. In some cases, bargains are only available when you use Web-based booking services. Some of these special prices and promotions are noted below. See Chapter 8 for more details on booking your hotel.

If you have an early flight out and need a hotel that's convenient to the airport, consider the 244-unit **Edinburgh Marriott,** 111 Glasgow Rd. (☎ **0131-334-9191**), off A8 on Edinburgh's western outskirts. It offers doubles from about £150 ($277), including breakfast. Facilities include an indoor pool, gym, sauna, and restaurant.

The top hotels

Here's a list of my favorite places to stay in Edinburgh. **Rack rates** are the maximum rates that a hotel charges for a room. Hardly anybody pays this price, however, except in high season or on holidays. Parking is available at all of the hotels, for a fee.

Balmoral Hotel
$$$$ New Town

This legendary place opened in 1902 as the North British Hotel, and it was one of the grandest hotels in the north of Great Britain. It reopened in 1991 after a £35-million ($64-million) restoration, and even more recently, the rooms received a £7-million ($13-million) refurbishment. Almost directly above the Waverley Rail Station, the hotel features one of the city's landmarks: a soaring clock tower famously set five minutes fast for the benefit of those on the way to the trains. Kilted doormen supply a Scottish atmosphere from the start. Afternoon tea is served in the high-ceilinged Palm Court. In addition to the standard rates, Internet offers include "simply Balmoral" seasonal discounts. All rooms are elegant and distinctive.

See map p. 128. 1 Princes St. ☎ *800-223-6800 in the U.S., or 0131-556-2414. Fax: 0131-557-3747. www.thebalmoralhotel.com. Bus: 3, 8, 22, 25, 30. Rack rates: £225–£290 ($416–$536) double; £245–£310 ($453–$573) superior double; from £465 ($860) suite. AE, DC, MC, V.*

The Bonham
$$$$ New Town

One of Edinburgh's most stylish hotels, the Bonham is actually three connected town houses that functioned as a nursing home in the 19th century and then more recently as dorms for the university. In 1998, a team of entrepreneurs poured millions of pounds into the buildings' refurbishment, pumped up the design, and outfitted each high-ceilinged guest room in a hip blend of old and new. Perhaps the jewel in the crown of The Town House Company group of hotels in Edinburgh, each of the Bonham's rooms has an individual theme, plush upholsteries, and a TV with a keyboard hooked up to the Internet — apparently the first setup of its kind in Europe. In addition to the standard rates, mid- and off-season special rates for dinner, bed, and breakfast are available for two people staying for at least two nights.

See map p. 128. 35 Drumsheugh Gardens. ☎ *0131-226-6050. Fax: 0131-226-6080.* www.thebonham.com. *Bus: 19, 37. Rack rates: £195–£240 ($360–$444) standard double; £340 ($629) suite. Rates include continental breakfast. AE, DC, MC, V.*

Caledonian Hilton Edinburgh
$$$$ New Town

This hotel remains one of the city's landmarks and offers commanding views toward the nearby Edinburgh Castle and over Princes Street Gardens. The public rooms are reminiscent of Edwardian splendor, and the guest rooms (many of which are exceptionally spacious) are conservatively styled with reproduction furniture. (Be aware that the fifth-floor rooms are the smallest.) Bathrooms are equipped with combination tub/showers. Although the accommodations are equal to those of other first-class, multi-star hotels in Edinburgh, the competition has moved ahead with its leisure facilities. Formal meals are served in Pompadour Restaurant, and a traditional tea is featured in the high-ceilinged lounge. On its Web site, the Caledonian offers discounts not available elsewhere.

See map p. 128. Princes St. ☎ *0131-222-8888. Fax: 0131-222-8889.* www.caledonian. hilton.com. *Bus: 33. Rack rates: £200–£380 ($370–$703) double; from £340 ($630) suite. Children age 15 and under stay free in parent's room. AE, DC, MC, V.*

Channings
$$$ Between West End and Old Town

Five Edwardian terrace houses combine to create this hotel, located just outside New Town and near Stockbridge in a tranquil residential area. Channings maintains the atmosphere of a Scottish country house, with oak paneling, ornate fireplaces, molded ceilings, and antiques. The guest rooms are outfitted in a modern style; the front units get the views, but the rear ones offer more seclusion. The most desirable rooms are the "Executives," most of which have bay windows and wingback chairs. Even if you're not a guest, consider a meal here; Channings Restaurant offers fine fare (see the listing in the section "The top restaurants and cafes" later in this chapter), while Ochre Vita, also in the hotel, is more casual and Mediterranean in orientation.

See map p. 128. 15 South Learmonth Gardens. ☎ 0131-623-9302. Fax: 0131-332-9631. www.channings.co.uk. Bus: 37. Rack rates: £120–£185 ($222–$342) double. Rates include breakfast. AE, DC, MC, V.

The Edinburgh Residence
$$$$ New Town

Part of the Townhouse group, this is one of the finest luxury hotels in Scotland. The Edinburgh Residence offers a series of elegant suites installed in a trio of architecturally beautiful and sensitively restored Georgian buildings. As you enter, grand staircases and classic wood paneling greet you. But the units have all the modern conveniences that befit five-star accommodation. This hotel is on the same level as its siblings — the Bonham, the Howard, and Channings — although it lacks their accomplished restaurants. Still, the rooms are the ultimate in comfort, with a trio of suites having their own private entrances. All units are spacious. If you're traveling off-season, inquire about "short break" promotions that recently offered two nights at the Edinburgh Residence for £75 ($138) per person.

See map p. 128. 7 Rothesay Terrace. ☎ 0131-226-3380. Fax: 0131-226-3381. www.theedinburghresidence.com. Bus: 36. Rack rates: £150–£265 ($277–$490) suite; £260–£395 ($481–$730) apt. AE, MC, V.

The Howard
$$$$ New Town

Dubbed one of the most exclusive five-star hotels in the city, this lovely hotel is made up of a set of linked Georgian terraced houses in the Northern New Town, just down the hill from the Queen Street Gardens. Some of the aura of a private home remains. Accommodations are midsize to spacious; each unit is individually and rather elegantly decorated, with some of the best bathrooms in town — featuring power and double showers and, in some, a Jacuzzi. The décor is traditional and modern, using both antiques and reproductions. Service is a hallmark of The Howard, with a dedicated butler who can tend to your individual needs, even unpacking your luggage, should you so desire. This place is definitely an oasis of Georgian charm and class. If you're on a budget, weekend breaks can bring rates to as low as £99 ($183) per person.

See map p. 128. 34 Great King St. ☎ 0131-557-3500. Fax: 0131-557-6515. www.thehoward.com. Bus: 23, 27. Rack rates: £180–£275 ($333–$508) double; £243–£475 ($450–$878) suite. Rates include breakfast. AE, DC, MC, V.

InterContinental The George Edinburgh
$$$$ New Town

Designed by famed architect Robert Adam and only yards from St. Andrew's Square, the building that houses the George opened in 1755 and was turned into a hotel in 1972. The public rooms have retained the style, elegance, and old-fashioned comfort of a country house. The guest rooms come in various sizes and have undergone frequent refurbishments. The best units, which open onto views, are those on the fourth floor and above in the new wing. Le Chambertin is the formal choice for dining at the George, which, at the time of this writing, has been offering "Scottish Night" deals at £35 ($65) per person on Sunday, Tuesday, and Friday.

See map p. 128. 19–21 George St. ☎ *800-327-0200 in the U.S., or 0131-225-1251. Fax: 0131-226-5644.* www.edinburgh.intercontinental.com. *Bus: 24, 28, 45. Rack rates: £190–£275 ($351–$508) double; from £460 ($851) suite. AE, DC, MC, V.*

Malmaison
$$–$$$ Leith

This is Leith's stylish boutique hotel, located amid the old harbor district, only a few steps from the Water of Leith. Malmaison was converted from an 1883 seamen's mission/dorm and is capped by a stately stone clock-tower. Overall, it's a hip, unpretentious place with a minimalist décor. Rooms are average in size but well equipped. The facilities are sparse, but you'll find a brasserie, cafe, and wine bar good enough to be favored by locals.

See map p. 128. 1 Tower Place. ☎ ***0131-555-6868***. *Fax: 0131-468-5002.* www.malmaison.com. *Bus: 16, 35. Rack rates: £99–£129 ($183–$238) double. AE, DC, MC, V.*

Prestonfield
$$$$ South Side

Prestonfield, rising in Jacobean splendor amid 5.3 hectares (13 acres) of gardens, pastures, and woodlands below Arthur's Seat, underwent a £3-million ($5.5-million) refurbishment in 2003 and is now in the hands of James Thomson, who owns the Witchery (see listing later in this section). The pile was built in the 17th century, serving first as the home of the city's Lord Provost (mayor), and has entertained a varied group of luminaries over the years from David Hume and Benjamin Franklin to pop stars and actors such as Sean Connery and Minnie Driver. Guests appreciate the traditional atmosphere and 1680s architecture as well as the peacocks and Highland cattle that strut and stroll across the grounds. The spacious bedrooms (now five-star rated by the tourist board) hide all mod conveniences (such as Bose sound systems, DVD players, and plasma, flat-screened TVs) behind velvet lined walls. The restaurant, Rhubarb, is as theatrical as they come, with a period stage set, plush furnishings, and décor to match the mansion. Reduced mid-week rates are sometimes available.

See map p. 128. Priestfield Rd. ☎ ***0131-225-7800***. *Fax: 0131-668-3976.* www.prestonfield.com. *Bus: 2, 14, 30. Rack rates: £195 ($360) double; from £250 ($462) suite. Rates include breakfast. AE, MC, V.*

The Scotsman
$$$–$$$$ Old Town

Located on North Bridge, only minutes from the Royal Mile or Princes Street, the Scotsman is probably the brightest and most stylish hotel to open recently in Edinburgh. Its name honors the newspaper that was published in the building for nearly a century before relocating to modern facilities near Holyroodhouse. Traditional styling and cutting-edge design are harmoniously wed in the 1904 baronial limestone pile, a city landmark since it was first constructed. The 68 units, from the Study Room to the Baron Suite, vary in size (from 300 sq. ft. to a whopping 1,110 sq. ft.) and views (choose between views of the castle or toward Calton Hill and the Firth of Forth). Rooms include state-of-the-art bathrooms and such extras as two-way service closets, which means your laundry can be picked up virtually unnoticed. The two-floor Penthouse suite is in a category of its own, with a private elevator and balcony with barbecue. The in-house dining options include the smart North Bridge Brasserie & Bar as well as the more exclusive fine-dining option in the basement, Vermilion. In addition to standard rates, weekend break promotions are available.

See map p. 128. 20 North Bridge. ☎ **0131-556-5565.** *Fax: 0131-652-3652.* www. scotsmanhotels.com. *Bus: 3, 8, 14, 29. Rack rates: £200–£295 ($370–$545) double; from £395 ($730) suite; £1,200 ($2,220) penthouse. AE, DC, MC, V.*

Sheraton Grand Hotel
$$$$ West End

This building near the West End theatres is a six-story postmodern structure housing both a glamorous hotel and an office complex. The hotel is elegant, with soaring public rooms and carpeting in rich tones. Boasting a good location — as well as state-of-the-art spa and leisure facilities (including a rooftop indoor/outdoor pool) — the hotel pretty much has it all. The spacious, well-furnished units have double-glazed windows; glamorous suites are available, as are rooms for nonsmokers and travelers with disabilities. The castle-view rooms on the top floors are the best (and the most expensive). The main restaurant, The Terrace, with views of the Festival Square, presents well-prepared meals and a lavish Sunday buffet, while an annex houses the Italian Santini restaurant below the spa.

See map p. 128. 1 Festival Sq. ☎ **800-325-3535** *in the U.S. and Canada, or 0131-229-9131. Fax: 0131-228-4510.* www.sheraton.com. *Bus: 10, 22, 30. Rack rates: June–Sept £190–£260 ($351–$481) double, from £300 ($555) suite; off-season £115 ($212) double, £215 ($397) suite. AE, DC, MC, V.*

Thrums Hotel
$–$$ South Side

In the Newington district southwest of the Meadows, Thrums is a pair of connected Georgian buildings. The hotel contains high-ceilinged guest rooms with period Georgian furnishings. Six rooms come with a shower-only bathroom, but the rest are equipped with combination tub and shower. Children are particularly welcome here, and some accommodations are set aside as family rooms. One notable example of the child-friendly approach is an outdoor area in which kids can play. *See map p. 128. 14–15 Minto St.* ☎ **0131-667-5545.** *Fax: 0131-667-8707.* www. thrumshotel.com. *Bus: 3, 8, 29. Rack rates: £55–£110 ($101–$203) double. Rates include breakfast. MC, V.*

The Witchery by the Castle
$$$$ **Old Town**

This is a sumptuous and theatrically decorated address of Gothic antiques and elaborate tapestries near the top of the Royal Mile. Most of the hype about the suites at the Witchery — "the perfect lust-den," "Scotland's most romantic hotel," "a jewel-box setting," and "one of the 50 best places in the world for honeymooners" — is true. *Cosmopolitan* magazine and others have hailed this place as one of the world's "most wonderful" places to stay. Each lavishly decorated suite (named the Library, Vestry, Armoury, and the like) features splendid furnishings fit for a lord and his lady and such extras as books, chocolates, a Bose sound system, and a complimentary bottle of champagne. Expect a huge bath built for two in each suite. The building dates to the 17th century and is filled with open fires, opulent beds, luxurious sitting areas, and wall-to-wall luxury. Previous guests have included Michael Douglas, Catherine Zeta-Jones, Pierce Brosnan, and Andrew Lloyd Webber. *See map p. 128. Castlehill, The Royal Mile.* ☎ **0131-225-5613.** *Fax: 0131-220-4392.* www.thewitchery.com. *Bus: 28. Rack rates: from £250 ($462). Rates include continental breakfast and champagne or the option of a full breakfast. AE, DC, MC, V.*

Runner-up hotels and B&Bs

A-Haven Townhouse
$ **Leith**   Guest rooms here vary in size and are outfitted with traditional furnishings and shower-only bathrooms. Some rooms are large enough to accommodate families if cots are used. *See map p. 128. 180 Ferry Rd.* ☎ **0131-554-6559.** www.a-haven.co.uk.

The Bank Hotel
$$ **Old Town**   This hotel offers better value than many of its competitors in this congested area on the Royal Mile. From the 1920s to the 1990s, it was a branch of the Royal Bank of Scotland, and the past is still evident in its Greek influenced design. Inside you'll discover high ceilings, well-chosen furnishings, and king-size beds. *See map p. 128. 1 S. Bridge St.* ☎ **0131-622-6800.** www.festival-inns.co.uk.

41 Heriot Row
$$ **New Town**   This handsome stone town house was built in 1806 on one of Edinburgh's most prestigious residential streets — the very one where Robert Louis Stevenson enjoyed his childhood. The two comfortable rooms

here have attractive and upscale furnishings, with attractive prints, flagstone floors, Persian rugs, brass beds, unusual books, and antique furnishings. *See map p. 128. 41 Heriot Row.* ☎ *0131-225-3113.* www.edinburgh accommodation.org.uk.

The Glasshouse

$$$ New Town (Calton)   A recently developed property, this hotel is not only one of the most modern but among the top so-called boutique hotels of Edinburgh. It combines the old and the new, and many of the well-furnished bedrooms offer panoramic views of the city. *See map p. 128. 2 Greenside Place.* ☎ *0131-525-8200.* www.theetoncollection.com/hotels/glasshouse.

Radisson SAS Hotel

$$$ Old Town   Until recently known as the "Crowne Plaza," this baronial-style building lies midway along the Royal Mile. The hotel is thoroughly modernized and offers first-class facilities, although it lacks the old world charm of some of Edinburgh's grand dame hotels. Most of the bedrooms are spacious and well-decorated; bathrooms have heated floors for those chilly Scottish mornings. Check the Radisson Web site for "hot deals." *See map p. 128. 80 High St.* ☎ *0131-473-6590.* www.radisson.com.

Roxburghe Hotel

$$–$$$ New Town   On a tree-filled square a short walk from Princes Street, the traditional atmosphere here is reflected in the drawing room with its ornate ceiling and woodwork, antique furnishings, and tall arched windows. In 1999, the hotel was expanded into two neighboring buildings. The largest rooms are in the original building and maintain features such as imposing fireplaces. The new rooms have more recent furnishings and more up-to-date plumbing. *See map p. 128. 38 Charlotte St. (at George Street).* ☎ *0131-240-5500.* www.macdonaldhotels.co.uk.

Dining Out

Cuisine in Scotland is perhaps the most misunderstood aspect of the country. Too many people think that food here begins and ends with haggis, but there's a lot more to the country's larder than the famous stuffed sheep's stomach. Thank goodness!

The city of Edinburgh boasts some of the best restaurants in Scotland, and the choices the capital has to offer are more diverse today than ever before. You can find an array of contemporary Scottish and modern British restaurants and French, fish, and brasserie-style eateries along with cuisines from around the world, particularly India and Asia. Plus, several restaurants cater to vegetarians exclusively.

Scotland's reputation for excellent fresh produce is growing. So look out for the following delights in season: shellfish such as oysters, mussels, or scallops; locally landed finned fish (such as bream or sea bass); and spring lamb or Aberdeen Angus beef. Fresh vegetables include asparagus, peas, and, of course, potatoes — some claim that the spuds grown in Ayrshire's sandy soils are unparalleled for fluffy texture and rich taste.

If you're dining out, the majority of restaurants close in the afternoon, so if you're looking for lunch, don't leave it for too late in the day. The hours I provide in the listings that follow reflect when food may be ordered, but bars on the premises may keep longer hours. Many restaurants also close for business on either Sunday or Monday — and sometimes both. But during the annual Edinburgh Festival from late July to the end of August, many restaurants also offer extended hours. Given the crowds during this time, you should always reserve a table in advance.

For more ideas on dining options, buy *The List* magazine's annual **Eating & Drinking Guide,** a publication that reviews hundreds of restaurants, bars, and cafes in Edinburgh (and Glasgow).

Scotland is getting better at welcoming families, but it's still a far cry from the family-friendliness of, say, Italy or France. That said, give the local restaurants a try and resist the temptation to resort to well-known international chains or fast-food outlets.

Prices

Given the strength of the UK's currency since 2002, prices may seem expensive, especially in comparison to the simultaneously weak American dollar. Still, you can find a range of choices for most budgets. The prices I list here already include the 17.5 percent VAT, so you don't see any hidden surprises when the bill comes. If you're looking for bargains, inquire about pre-theatre special menus, which can be as much as half the price of the regular dinner menu.

Log onto www.5pm.co.uk for a list of restaurants offering early dining deals.

Lunch menus in Edinburgh offer the same food as the full dinner menus but at a much better price. So, if you're trying to save money on your food bills, have a big late lunch or early meal in the evening.

Tipping

A 10 percent gratuity is the minimum for service, although you shouldn't hesitate to leave nothing if you were badly treated. On the other hand, if you were truly impressed, consider leaving 15 to 20 percent. In a few restaurants, service is included in the bill automatically, but the charge can be deleted if the service was genuinely dreadful.

Smoking

Most restaurants have sections reserved for nonsmokers, and an ever-growing number simply don't allow smoking in their dining rooms at all — at least during peak dining times. In 2004, the country's parliament was

Edinburgh Dining

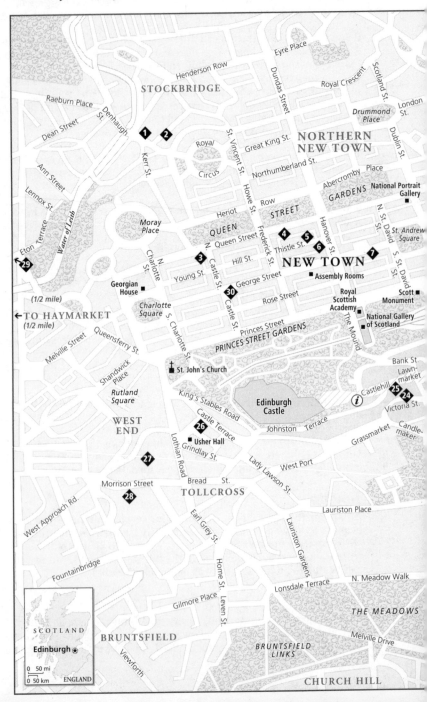

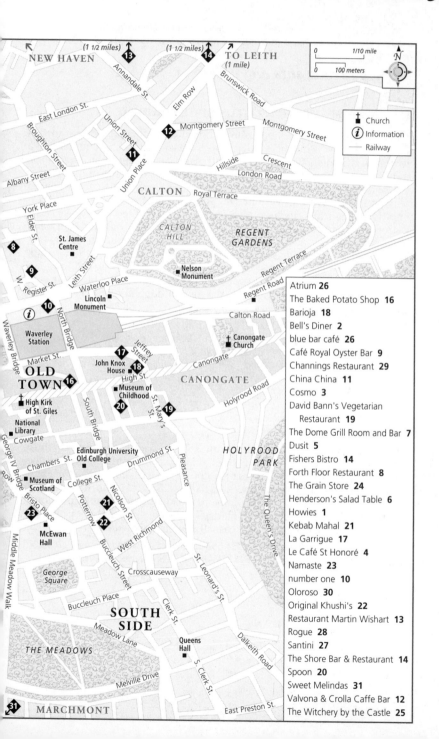

NEW HAVEN (1 1/2 miles) 13 (1 1/2 miles) 14 TO LEITH (1 mile)

0 1/10 mile
0 100 meters
N

✝ Church
ⓘ Information
— Railway

Annandale St.
Brunswick Road
East London St.
Elm Row
Union Street
Montgomery Street 12
Montgomery Street
Broughton Street
Union Place 11
Hillside
Crescent
London Road
Albany Street
CALTON
Royal Terrace
York Place
Elder St.
St. James Centre
CALTON HILL
REGENT GARDENS
8
W. Register St.
9
Leith Street
Waterloo Place
Nelson Monument
Lincoln Monument 10
ⓘ
Calton Road
Regent Terrace
Regent Road
Waverley Bridge
Waverley Station
North Bridge
Market St.
Jeffrey Street
John Knox House 17 18
Canongate
† Canongate Church
OLD TOWN 16
High St.
Museum of Childhood
CANONGATE
Holyrood Road
✝ High Kirk of St. Giles
South Bridge
20
St. Mary's St.
19
National Library
Cowgate
Edinburgh University Old College
Drummond St.
Pleasance
HOLYROOD PARK
George IV Bridge
Chambers St.
College St.
The Queen's Drive
■ Museum of Scotland
Bristo Place
23
Nicolson St.
Potterrow
21
McEwan Hall
22
Buccleuch Street
West Richmond
Crosscauseway
St. Leonard's St.
George Square
Middle Meadow Walk
Buccleuch Place
SOUTH SIDE
Clerk St.
Meadow Lane
Queens Hall
Dalkeith Road
THE MEADOWS
Melville Drive
S. Clerk St.
31
MARCHMONT
East Preston St.

Atrium **26**
The Baked Potato Shop **16**
Barioja **18**
Bell's Diner **2**
blue bar café **26**
Café Royal Oyster Bar **9**
Channings Restaurant **29**
China China **11**
Cosmo **3**
David Bann's Vegetarian Restaurant **19**
The Dome Grill Room and Bar **7**
Dusit **5**
Fishers Bistro **14**
Forth Floor Restaurant **8**
The Grain Store **24**
Henderson's Salad Table **6**
Howies **1**
Kebab Mahal **21**
La Garrigue **17**
Le Café St Honoré **4**
Namaste **23**
number one **10**
Oloroso **30**
Original Khushi's **22**
Restaurant Martin Wishart **13**
Rogue **28**
Santini **27**
The Shore Bar & Restaurant **14**
Spoon **20**
Sweet Melindas **31**
Valvona & Crolla Caffe Bar **12**
The Witchery by the Castle **25**

considering a complete ban on all smoking in pubs and restaurants, following the precedent set in Ireland, California, and New York City.

The top restaurants and cafes

Atrium
$$$ West End   MODERN SCOTTISH/INTERNATIONAL

Since 1993, Atrium has been one of the most acclaimed restaurants in Edinburgh. In an atmosphere that's both classy and welcoming (kind of a fusion of a stylish Beverly Hills bistro and an Argentinean hacienda), upholstered metal chairs and tables that seem to be made of old railway sleepers envelope no more than 60 diners at a time. Dishes are prepared with taste and flair but without excessive amounts of fuss or fancy presentation. Favorites include dishes such as roasted sea bass with Dauphinois potatoes, baby spinach, charcoal-grilled eggplant, and baby fennel; or seared scallops served with chilis and garlic on lemon linguini. The desserts are equally superb. The wine list is excellent but not cheap, with most bottles costing in excess of £20 ($37). No smoking is allowed in the dining room. Diners on a stricter budget should try the **blue bar café** located on the same premises (see the description later in this chapter).

See map p. 138. 10 Cambridge St. (adjacent the Traverse Theatre, about a 5-min. walk from Princes Street). ☎ *0131-228-8882.* www.atriumrestaurant.co.uk. *Reservations recommended, especially on weekends. Bus: 2, 28. Fixed-price 2-course lunch: £14 ($26); main courses dinner: £17–£22 ($31–$40). AE, MC, V. Open: Mon–Fri noon–2 p.m. and 6–10 p.m.; Sat 6–10 p.m. Closed Sun and for 1 week at Christmas.*

Barioja
$–$$ Old Town   SPANISH

Just off the Royal Mile (near the World's End Close) with views north to Calton Hill and the Royal High School, this tapas bar is the partner to the fine-food Spanish restaurant Iggs next door. With a casual atmosphere and staffed by natives of Spanish-speaking nations, Barioja is fun, friendly, and often lively. The kitchen's tapas come in reasonably substantial portions, whether you order tender fried squid, garlicky king prawns, spicy chorizo sausages, or plenty of other choices, all of which are excellent.

See map p. 138. 19 Jeffrey St. ☎ *0131-557-3622. Bus: 35. Fixed-price lunch: £8.50 ($16), main courses: £4–£10 ($7.50–$18.50). AE, MC, V. Open: Mon–Sat 11 a.m.–11 p.m. Closed Sun.*

Bell's Diner
$ Stockbridge   AMERICAN

If you're desperate for a chargrilled patty of real ground beef, please resist any urge to visit the ubiquitous international fast-food chains. You can patronize them at home. Instead, seek out wee Bell's Diner in Stockbridge. Open for over 30 years, the diner's burgers are cooked to order with a variety of toppings (from cheese to garlic butter) and are served with fries, salad, and a full array of condiments. The only drawback of Bell's, aside from its limited space, is its limited hours of operation: Only open in the evenings, except on Saturdays when Bell's is open for both lunch and dinner.

See map p. 138. 17 St. Stephen St. ☎ *0131-225-8116. Reservations recommended. Bus: 24, 29, 42. Main courses: £6.50–£9 ($12–$16). Open: Sun–Fri 6–10:30 p.m., Sat noon–10:30 p.m.*

Picnic fare

The Edinburgh weather doesn't always lend itself to outdoor dining on an expanse of lawn, but there are certainly days when the sun shines warmly enough to enjoy a picnic at Princes Street Gardens, the Meadows, Holyrood Park, along the Water of Leith, or in the Botanic Gardens.

If you're in the central area of town, the best place to pick up some deli goods is undoubtedly **Valvonna & Crolla**, 19 Elm Row (at the top of Leith Walk; ☎ 0131-556-6066). This Italian shop has an excellent reputation across the UK and offers a wonderful range of cheeses, cured meats, and fresh fruit and vegetables, plus baked goods from rolls to sourdough loaves, all the condiments you may need, and wine. Another option in New Town is the food hall at the top of **Harvey Nichols** department store, 30–34 St. Andrews Sq. (☎ 0131-524-8388). Freshly prepared salads, lots of dried goods, and fresh fruit and vegetables are all stocked here.

Near the Water of Leith in Stockbridge, the **Circus Café and Food Hall** at 15 Northwest Circus Place (☎ 0131-220-0333), has a range of goods, while **IJ Mellis Cheesemongers**, on nearby Bakers Place (☎ 0131-225-6566), sells award-winning British and Irish cheeses. The Mellis staff really know their stuff, and you can find the shop in Old Town on Victoria Street and south of the city center on Morningside Road, as well.

If you're on the south side of the city near the Meadows, **Peckham's** on Bruntsfield Place (☎ 0131-229-7054) is a solid choice for filling a picnic basket. But if you like Mexican food — Monterrey Jack cheese, real tortillas, and the like — visit **Lupe Pintos** in Tollcross, at 24 Leven St. (near the King's Theatre; ☎ 0131-228-6241). The shop also stocks some American goods, such as beef jerky, dill pickles, and peanut butter.

Heading toward the Botanic Gardens on the other side of town in Canonmills, **Au Gourmand,** on Brandon Terrace (☎ 0131-624-4666), as you might guess from the name, specializes in French goodies, whether charcuterie and cheeses or sweet pastries and freshly baked bread. Across the nearby roundabout is a nice Spanish deli called **Dionika** (☎ 0131-652-3993). In the port of Leith, **Relish** at 6 Commercial St. (☎ 0131-476-1920) — not to be confused with a modern hamburger joint on the Royal Mile — is a modern delicatessen offering a broad selection from its reasonably small shop.

blue bar café
$–$$ West End   INTERNATIONAL/BRITISH

Located in the building containing the Traverse Theatre, this attractive bistro is the less expensive sibling of Atrium (see the listing above). Here you'll find a minimalist décor with touches of azure hues, solid oak tables, and a cheerful staff. The sophisticated menu is divided between dishes that can serve either as starters or a light main meal and a list of more substantial meals. The menu can change periodically but often includes seared scallops; succulent breast of duck; and a perfect charcoal-grilled tuna which comes with either basil-flavored noodles or bubble and squeak (that's cabbage, potatoes, and maybe some meat all fried together — yum).

See map p. 138. 10 Cambridge St. ☎ *0131-221-1222.* www.bluebarcafe.com. *Reservations recommended. Bus: 2, 28. Fixed-price 2-course lunch: £9.95 ($18); main courses: £10–£15 ($18.50–$28). AE, MC, V. Open: Mon–Sat noon–3 p.m. and 6–10:30 p.m.*

Café Royal Oyster Bar
$$–$$$ New Town   FISH/SEAFOOD

The Café Royal has been here for some 140 years, and thankfully, its many splendorous Victorian touches remain intact. The main menu offers more than just oysters (although don't leave without sampling some); salmon, venison, langoustines, lobster, beef, and rabbit are often featured menu selections. The restaurant closes after lunch and reopens for dinner, but the ground-level Circle Bar is open throughout the day. The menu there is more limited but also less pricey. A highlight of this stylish room is the tile pictures of notable inventors. Upstairs, a second drinking hole, the Bistro Bar, has an ornate ceiling but a less classy atmosphere.

See map p. 138. 17a West Register St. ☎ *0131-556-4124. Bus: 8, 13. Fixed-price 2-course lunch: £15 ($27); main courses dinner: £15–£20 ($27–$37). AE, MC, V. Main restaurant open: Mon–Sun noon–2 p.m. and 7–10 p.m.; Circle and Bistro bars open: Mon–Wed 11 a.m.–11 p.m., Thurs 11 a.m.–midnight, Fri–Sat 11 a.m.–1 a.m.*

Channings Restaurant
$$$ New Town   SCOTTISH/FRENCH

Channings is the main restaurant in the charming Edwardian hotel of the same name, located in the Comely Bank district of the city's western New Town. Amid traditional but subtle décor, elegant service comes courtesy of a well-trained staff. The chefs aren't bad either. Cuisine emphasizes the natural flavors of the superior-quality Scottish ingredients and more recently has been pushed in a French direction. For dinner, you may opt for roast pheasant with dried fig purée or sea bream with creamed butter endive. For dessert (or "pudding" as they say in the UK), you may want to consider chocolate fondant served with a sweet and sour guacamole. The restaurant is proud of its extensive wine list, which incorporates the old standards and newer, more exciting choices. No smoking is allowed in the dining room. A less formal conservatory dining room found in the rear beyond the wine bar, Ochre Vita, serves Mediterranean-style lunches and dinners.

See map p. 138. Channings Hotel, 15 South Learmonth Gardens. ☎ **0131-315-2225.**
www.channings.co.uk. *Reservations recommended, especially on weekends.*
Bus: 37. Fixed-price 2-course lunch: £16 ($30); main courses dinner: £14–£18 ($26–$33).
AE, MC, V. Open: Tues–Sat 12:30–2 p.m. and 6:30–10 p.m. Closed Sun and Mon.

Cosmo
$$$ New Town ITALIAN

Even after three decades in business, Cosmo remains one of the most pop-
ular Italian restaurants in Edinburgh, combining class (silver service),
Mediterranean courtesy, professional efficiency, and consistent quality.
The soups and pastas are always freshly made by hand; especially good is
a plate of ravioli. The kitchen is known for its *saltimbocca* (veal with ham)
and Italian-inspired preparations of fish (such as West Coast shellfish) or
Aberdeen Angus. Don't let the subtle exterior fool you, this is definitely
one of the best Italian restaurants in the city.

See map p. 138. 58a N. Castle St. ☎ **0131-226-6743.** www.cosmo-restaurant.
co.uk. *Reservations recommended. Bus: 13, 41. Fixed-price lunch: £14.50 ($27); main
courses dinner: £15–£22 ($28–$40). AE, MC, V. Open: Mon–Fri 12:30–2:15 p.m.,
Mon–Sat 7–10:45 p.m. Closed Sun.*

David Bann's Vegetarian Restaurant
$$ Old Town VEGETARIAN

Chef David Bann has been at the forefront of meat-free cooking in Edinburgh
for more than a decade. He comes from the school of thought that vegetarian meals can be healthy *and* tasty. The menu at his eponymous restaurant
(located just a short stroll south of Royal Mile) is eclectic: Dishes have
international influences, from Mexico to Thailand. The dining room is as
stylish as the cooking, and to top it off, the prices are very reasonable.

See map p. 138. 56–58 St. Mary's St. ☎ **0131-556-5888.** www.davidbann.com.
*Reservations recommended. Bus: 35. Main courses lunch: £7.50 ($16); main courses
dinner: £7.50–£10 ($16–$18.50). AE, MC, V. Open: Sun–Thurs 11 a.m.–10 p.m., Fri–Sat
11 a.m.–midnight.*

The Dome Grill Room and Bar
$$–$$$ New Town INTERNATIONAL

Thanks to its restored Victorian-era Royal Bank of Scotland premises, with
Corinthian columns, intricate mosaic tile flooring, marble-topped bar,
potted palms, and towering flower arrangements (all under an elaborate
domed ceiling), it's only honest to say that most people come here for the
look of the place, which oozes class and elegance. Alas, the last time I visited, the ambience was ruined by a loud, modern pop/R'n'B soundtrack
that belonged at the All Bar One branch across the street. What were they
thinking? Occasionally, you may get lucky and visit on a night when live
jazz is on the roster. Regardless of the mood, the selection of food includes
dishes such as smoked salmon starters, mussels in chili, and chicken
Bourguignon.

See map p. 138. 14 George St. ☎ *0131-624-8624.* www.thedomeedinburgh.com. *Reservations recommended. Bus: 24, 25, 28. Main courses lunch: £9–£16 ($16.50–$30); main courses dinner: £10–£22 ($18.50–$40). AE, DC, MC, V. Open: restaurant Sun–Thurs noon–10:15 p.m. and Fri–Sat noon–10:45 p.m.; bar Mon–Thurs 10 a.m.– 11 p.m., Fri–Sat 10 a.m.–1 a.m., Sun noon–11 p.m.*

Dusit
$$$ New Town   THAI

Although little more than a slender lane with narrow sidewalks, Thistle Street has become a hotbed for dining out in recent years, and this unassuming restaurant has quickly developed a reputation for being one of the best in the city for Thai cuisine. The menu is not typical and has a tendency toward the prosaic, with names such as "Three Colour Jewel" or "Loving Couple." Despite the name, "Pretty Duck" is pretty delicious: chargrilled with nuts, mango, and shallots. Some of the main courses incorporate Scottish produce, such as venison, and the seafood options are plentiful.

See map p. 138. 49a Thistle St. ☎ *0131-220-6846. Reservations recommended. Bus: 24, 42. Main courses lunch and dinner: £10–£16 ($18.50–$30). AE, MC, V. Open: Mon–Sat noon–3 p.m. and 6–11 p.m., Sun noon–11 p.m.*

Fishers Bistro
$$–$$$ Leith   FISH/SEAFOOD

Seeing as how you've come down to the shore (Leith), you may as well enjoy some fish. Fishers Bistro is a favorite for its seafood and view of the harbor at Leith. Naturally, a nautical theme prevails with fish nets, pictures of the sea, and various marine memorabilia. The Miller family founded the restaurant in the early 1990s, and their chefs offer such enticing dishes as fresh Loch Fyne oysters, acclaimed as among Britain's finest; mussels in white wine sauce; and breaded and crispy fish cakes. Of course the fresh fish choices depend on what's been landed: It may be salmon, trout, sole, or cod. If you can't make it to Leith, you can also find a branch of the restaurant in New Town on Thistle Street (☎ **0131-225-5109**).

See map p. 138. 1 The Shore. ☎ *0131-554-5666. Reservations recommended. Bus: 16, 36. Main courses: £12–£18 ($22–$33). AE, MC, V. Open: Mon–Sat noon–10:30 p.m., Sun 12:30–10:30 p.m.*

Forth Floor Restaurant
$$$ New Town   MODERN SCOTTISH

No, that's not a misspelling of the name; this restaurant at the top of the Harvey Nichols department store has excellent views of the Firth of Forth from the fourth floor of the building. It combines excellent contemporary Scottish cooking with those commanding vistas. Many Edinburgh residents were slow to warm to the posh Harvey Nicks after its summer 2002 launch, but any similar bias would be misapplied to this up-market bar, brasserie, and restaurant. Although you do feel like you're dining in a department store annex (despite the slick, minimalist décor), the food can be phenomenal, whether a succulent and robust braised oxtail or a light salad with endive and seasonal truffles. The kitchen uses notably fresh produce. The brasserie menu, while less extensive than the restaurant's selections, is an excellent value.

See map p. 138. Harvey Nichols, 30–34 St. Andrew Sq. ☎ *0131-524-8350.* www.harvey nichols.com. *Reservations recommended. Bus: 8. Main courses lunch: £10–£16 ($18.50–$29); main courses dinner: £12–£20 ($22–$37). AE, DC, MC, V. Open: Sun noon–3 p.m. and 7–9 p.m., Mon noon–3 p.m. and 7–10:30 p.m., Tues–Fri noon–3 p.m. and 6–10 p.m., and Sat noon–3 p.m. and 7–10:30 p.m.*

The Grain Store
$$–$$$ Old Town   SCOTTISH/MODERN BRITISH

With its dining room up some unassuming stairs and wooden tables set amid raw stone walls, the Grain Store capably captures Old Town essence and atmosphere. The cooking of owner Carlo Coxon is ambitious and innovative; for example, the menu may include dishes such as a saddle of Scottish venison with a beetroot fondant or a medley of sea bass and scallops served with fennel, olives, and tomato. While the á la carte menu isn't cheap, the fixed-price options are certainly moderately priced. A favorite of many, the Grain Store is considered to be among the best restaurants in the capital.

See map p. 138. 30 Victoria St. ☎ *0131-225-7635.* www.grainstore-restaurant. co.uk. *Reservations recommended. Bus: 35, 41. Fixed-price 2-course lunch: £10 ($18.50); fixed-price 2-course dinner: £17.50 ($32); dinner main courses: £14–£20 ($26–$37). AE, MC, V. Open: Mon–Thurs noon–2 p.m. and 6–10 p.m., Fri–Sun noon–3 p.m. and 6–11 p.m.*

Henderson's Salad Table
$ New Town   VEGETARIAN

Right in the heart of the New Town, Henderson's Salad Table (and Henderson's Bistro around the corner) is a long-time stalwart of healthy, inexpensive vegetarian cuisine in Edinburgh. During the day, the Salad Table half of the operation offers counter service only. In the evening, however, the menu is expanded a bit and table service is offered. Dishes such as vegetable stroganoff or Greek moussaka complement what you might expect from the name: a wide array of salads. Wines include organic options.

See map p. 138. 94 Hanover St. ☎ *0131-225-2131. Bus: 23, 27. Fixed-price 2-course lunch: £8 ($14); main courses dinner: £6–£8 ($11–$14). MC, V. Open: Mon–Fri 7 a.m.–10:30 p.m., Sat 8 a.m.–10:30 p.m. Closed Sun.*

Howies
$–$$ New Town   SCOTTISH/CONTINENTAL

David Howie Scott opened his eponymous restaurant with modest ambitions (for example, guests brought their own wine) and then created a minor empire in Edinburgh, with a couple branches elsewhere in Scotland, as well. In the capital city, you can find two New Town outlets: in Stockbridge, near the Water of Leith;, and on Calton Hill, on Waterloo Place just off Princes Street. Elsewhere, you'll find Howies locations on Victoria Street in Old Town and in the South Side on Bruntsfield Place. The mini-chain's motto is "fine food without the faff" — and I'd add "sold at reasonable prices," as well. Typical dishes include pan-seared supreme of chicken, honey-cured Scottish salmon, and gnocchi with fresh basil pesto. You can still bring your own bottle, but the wine list at Howies is as reasonably priced as its menu.

See map p. 138. 4–6 Glanville Place, Stockbridge. ☎ *0131-225-5553.* www.howies. uk.com. *Reservations recommended. Bus: 24, 29, 42. Fixed-price 2-course lunch: £8.75 ($16); fixed-price 2-course dinner: £16 ($30). AE, MC, V. Open: Mon–Sun noon–2:30 p.m. and 6–10 p.m.*

Kebab Mahal
$ South Side   INDIAN

The kebab is usually a late-night meal scarfed down by students standing in the streets after they've danced their heads off in a club. And although the late weekend hours of this simple diner mean it indeed attracts that crowd, too, Kebab Mahal is much more. Drawing a cross-section of the city, whether dusty construction workers on break or tweed-clad professors grading papers, this basic Indian restaurant — where you may have to share your table with others — has become a landmark. Although the counter is full of hot food, most of the main courses are prepared separately in a kitchen at the rear. True to the faith of its Islamic owners, Kebab Mahal doesn't have a license to serve alcohol, doesn't allow diners to bring their own, either, and closes for an hour on Friday afternoon for prayers.

See map p. 138. 7 Nicolson Sq. ☎ *0131-667-5214. Bus: 3, 8, 29. Main courses lunch and dinner: £4–£6 ($7.50–$11). No credit cards accepted. Open: Sun–Thurs noon–midnight, Fri–Sat noon–2 a.m.*

La Garrigue
$$–$$$ Old Town   FRENCH

The chef and proprietor of La Garrigue, Jean Michel Gauffre, hails from the southern French region of Languedoc, and he attempts to recreate the fresh and rustic cooking of his home here in Edinburgh. The feeling of the dining room is casual but smart, with some stylish handmade furniture and almost naïve paintings on the wall. The menu may feature a hearty roast or cassoulet (stew) with beans and meat as well as a more delicate pan-fried fillet of bream. The wines are from southern France, too. Often, chef Gauffre ventures into the dining room to see how things are going and have a friendly chat or two; he knows the small touches can go a long way.

See map p. 138. 31 Jeffrey St. ☎ *0131-557-3032.* www.lagarrigue.co.uk. *Reservations recommended. Bus: 35. Fixed-price 2-course lunch: £10 ($18.50); fixed-price 2-course dinner: Sun–Thurs £15.05 ($28.50), Fri–Sat £18 ($33); main courses à la carte dinner: £10–£18 ($18.50–$33). AE, MC, V. Open: daily noon–2:30 p.m. and 6:30–10:30 p.m.*

Le Café St Honoré
$$ **New Town** **FRENCH BISTRO**

This brasserie with a classic black-and-white checkered floor is a deliberately rapid-paced place at lunchtime and then becomes a much more relaxed and sedate affair at dinner (ideal for romantic couples). The menu is completely revised daily based on what's fresh and what the chefs feel inspired to cook. An upbeat and usually enthusiastic staff serves cuisine that may include baked oysters with smoked salmon, venison with juniper berries and wild mushrooms, local pheasant in wine and garlic sauce, or baked cod with asparagus. Pre-theatre prices from 5:30 to 6:45 p.m. are a bargain, as are those on the wine list at any time.

See map p. 138. 34 NW Thistle Street Lane. ☎ *0131-226-2211.* www.cafesthonore. com. *Reservations recommended. Bus: 24, 42. Main courses lunch: £8–£12 ($15–$22); main courses dinner: £16–£20 ($30–$37). AE, MC, V. Open: Mon–Sat noon–2:15 p.m. and 6–10 p.m. Closed Sun.*

Namaste
$$ **Old Town** **INDIAN**

In 2004, this unassuming, casual, and cozy restaurant, which features cuisine from the region of India known as the North Frontier, moved from a South Side location somewhat off the beaten track to a more central site near the Museum of Scotland. But that's about all that has changed. The feeling is still relaxed and the cooking excellent. Unlike so many Indian restaurants, Namaste doesn't have a menu with 200-plus dishes. Instead, it concentrates of a select number, whether the succulent tandoori fish starter or a spicy lamb jalfrezi. The vegetarian options are numerous, with the black lentil stew (dhal makhani) particularly recommended.

See map p. 138. 15 Bristo Place. ☎ *0131-225-2000. Reservations recommended. Bus: 2, 41, 42. Main courses dinner: £6.25–£10 ($11.50–$18.50). AE, MC, V. Open: Mon–Fri noon–2:30 p.m. and 5:30–11 p.m., Sat–Sun 5:30–11 p.m.*

number one
$$$$ **New Town** **SCOTTISH/CONTINENTAL**

This is the premier restaurant in the city's premier central hotel: an intimate, mostly crimson-colored enclave whose walls are studded with Scottish memorabilia. Recently, it earned a vaunted star from the widely respected Michelin Guide for its superior cuisine and service. Sample the likes of pan-seared Isle of Skye monkfish with saffron mussel broth or perhaps roulade of Dover sole with langoustine, oyster, and scallop garnish. Dessert brings a variety of sorbets, cheeses, and more exotic choices like mulled wine parfait with a cinnamon sauce. Wines are excellent although pricey. number one is definitely the place to go for a special treat while you're in Edinburgh.

Family-friendly fare

The Baked Potato Shop (56 Cockburn St. ☎ 0131-225-7572): Children generally delight in being taken to this favorite lunch spot, just off the High Street in Old Town, where they can order fluffy baked potatoes with a choice of half a dozen hot fillings along with all sorts of other dishes, including chili and a variety of salads. It's cheap, too.

China China (near the top of Leith Walk at 10 Antigua St. ☎ 0131-556-9791): Edinburgh has recently seen a boom in Chinese buffet restaurants. This bright and bustling place was the first and remains perhaps the best. For families, it represents excellent value for the money because kids from 5 to 12 years old eat for half price and those younger than 5 eat for free (as long as parents are paying).

Valvona & Crolla Caffe Bar (19 Elm Row; ☎ 0131-556-6066): Also at the top of Leith Walk, this place is best known as one of the UK's finest Italian delis. But if you can get past the tempting salamis, cheeses, and other delicacies, V&C offers a cafe that welcomes children in that way that Italians seem to do best.

See map p. 138. Balmoral Hotel, 1 Princes St. ☎ *0131-557-6727.* www.thebalmoral hotel.com/restaurant1.html. *Reservations recommended. Bus: 3, 8, 25, 29. Main courses from £20 ($37); fixed-price 2-course lunch: £16.50 ($30.50); fixed-price 3-course dinner: £42.50 ($79); fixed-price 6-course dinner: £55 ($102). AE, DC, MC, V. Open: Mon–Thurs noon–2 p.m. and 7–10 p.m., Fri noon–2 p.m. and 7–10:30 p.m., Sat 7–10:30 p.m., Sun 7–10 p.m.*

Oloroso
$$$ New Town   SCOTTISH/INTERNATIONAL

Oloroso's chef and owner, Tony Singh, is a Scottish-born Indian with an imaginative approach to cooking Scottish produce. Here in his roof-top restaurant with an ample veranda and excellent panoramic views both north over the city to the Forth River and back toward Old Town and Edinburgh Castle, the feeling is contemporary and swanky. Oloroso (intentionally) boasts little decoration, because the views provide enough interest. The menu includes dishes such as steamed asparagus with light cream sauce and flakes of parmesan cheese, pan-seared pigeon with confit leg, and chump of roast lamb with couscous and roasted peppers. You can also choose from a "grill menu" with a variety of cuts of Scottish beef. Watch out for extras, however, as they can increase the cost of the "set-price" courses considerably. No smoking is allowed in the dining room. The bar, which mixes some mean cocktails, is usually open until 1 a.m.

See map p. 138. 33 Castle St. ☎ *0131-226-7614.* www.oloroso.co.uk. *Reservations recommended. Bus: 13, 19, 41. Main courses lunch and dinner: £17 ($34). MC, V. Open: Mon–Sun noon–2:30 p.m. and 7–10:30 p.m.*

Original Khushi's
$$ South Side INDIAN

The oldest Indian restaurant in Edinburgh and probably one of the oldest in Scotland, Kushi's opened a few years after the end of World War II. Until a few years ago, it was housed in a real throwback to the 1960s and 1970s — a cramped dining room that time had forgotten. But today Khushi's is a spacious and modern Indian cafe/restaurant with lots of windows looking onto the sidewalk. The menu is concise and features Khushi's specialty, slow-marinated meats. Although the restaurant has no license to sell alcohol, you can bring your own. Alternatively, you may want to try one of Khushi's freshly made creamy yogurt drinks.

See map p. 138. 26–30 Potterrow. ☎ *0131-667-0888.* www.khushis.com. *Bus: 2, 42. Main courses lunch and dinner: £4–£6 ($7.50–$11). MC, V. Open: Mon–Sat noon–11 p.m., Sun 5–11 p.m.*

Restaurant Martin Wishart
$$$$ Leith MODERN FRENCH

Despite a vaunted Michelin star and plenty of other local awards to his name, chef and owner Martin Wishart remains the antithesis of the high-profile prima-donna chef. He takes his accolades in stride and strives to continually improve the quality of his high-priced establishment in this increasingly fashionable part of the Leith docklands. The décor is minimalist, featuring white walls and modern art. The menu, which changes frequently, is kept short and sweet, taking advantage of the best of the season. For example, an aromatic gratin of sea bass with a soft, herby crust or roast saddle of rabbit with puy lentils and puree of celeriac are popular offerings. And, as I've asked before: Where can you get a good pot roast pig's cheek if not here? If you're on an unlimited budget, I recommend that you — as the Scots say — push the boat out and go for the tasting menu; get the sommelier to open a different wine to match each course. The meal may cost a month's wages, but it's heavenly and worth it. Be warned: No smoking is allowed in the dining room.

See map p. 138. 54 The Shore. ☎ *0131-553-3557.* www.martin-wishart.co.uk. *Reservations required. Bus: 22, 36. Fixed-price lunch: £18.50 ($34); main courses dinner: £20–£25 ($37–$46); tasting menu (5 or 6 courses): £48 or £55 ($89 or $102). AE, MC, V. Open: Tues–Fri noon–2 p.m. and 6:45–10 p.m., Sat 6:45–10 p.m. Closed Sun and Mon.*

Rogue
$$ West End SCOTTISH/CONTINENTAL

Given the dramatic setting of this modern restaurant (almost cinematic in its minimalist white-on-white décor), you may expect to pay a whole lot more. But Rogue's owner/host, the irrepressible and gravel-voiced David Ramsden, decided in 2004 to keep prices down, and thankfully the quality doesn't appear to have suffered. Rogue has a NYC-style destination-restaurant feel to it given that it's stuck amid offices in the West End and isn't particularly well sign-posted. The menu is positively eclectic, with dishes such as pan-roasted guinea fowl, bourbon-barbecue burgers, chili mussels, and lamb shank with rosemary and barley broth. The wine list offers equally good value.

See map p. 138. Scottish Widows Building, 67 Morrison St. ☎ *0131-228-2700. www.rogues-uk.com. Reservations recommended. Bus: 2. Main courses: £6–£11 ($11–$20). AE, MC, V. Open: Mon–Sat noon–3 p.m. and 6–11 p.m. Closed Sun.*

Santini
$$$ West End   ITALIAN

A relative newcomer, this modern restaurant in a building adjacent to the Sheraton (and below the hotel's spa) offers what many consider to be the capital's best Italian cuisine. As one of a small international restaurant chain owned by Italian-born Gino Santini (the other branches are in Milan and London, no less), Santini offers more authenticity than other area Italian restaurants. Dishes such as fish antipasti offer fresh foodstuffs — in this case, seared whitefish and chargrilled prawns. No smoking is allowed in the dining room. If you're only in the mood for pasta dishes or pizza, then opt for **Santini Bis** — the more casual option located under the same roof.

See map p. 138. 8 Conference St. ☎ *0131-221-7788. Bus: 2. Fixed-price 2-course lunch: £21 ($38); main courses dinner: £15–£22 ($28–40). AE, MC, V. Open: Mon–Fri noon–2:30 p.m. and 6:30–10:30 p.m., Sat 6:30–10:30 p.m. Closed Sun.*

The Shore Bar & Restaurant
$$ Leith   FISH/SEAFOOD

Whether you choose to eat in the unassuming pub or in the only slightly more formal dining room to one side, you should appreciate the simplicity and ease of this operation, which is dedicated to fresh fish and seafood. The menu changes daily, offering un-fussy dishes from mussels with white wine, garlic, and onions to salmon fillet with herby oil and balsamic vinegar reduction. And when food isn't being served, the bar is still one of the best in Leith. It often has live music in the evenings, good ale on tap, and an unforced and sincere seaport ambience at all times. No smoking is allowed in the dining room.

See map p. 138. 3/4 The Shore. ☎ *0131-553-5080. Bus: 16, 36. Fixed-price lunch: £15 ($28); main courses dinner: £12–£18 ($22–$33). AE, MC, V. Open: Mon–Fri noon–2:30 p.m. and 6:30–10 p.m., Sat–Sun 12:30–3 p.m. and 6:30–10 p.m.*

Spoon
$ Old Town   CAFE

This particular spoon is far from greasy. Just off the High Street, this cafe offers a contemporary setting by combining a relaxed ambience, first-rate espresso-based coffees, and the assured hand of a classically trained chef.

The soups are superb, whether you try the meat-free options — such as lentil and red onion or roasted pepper and eggplant — or go for Italian ham and pea soup. Sandwiches are prepared fresh using quality ingredients (one of my favorites is the free-range chicken breast with tarragon on a toasted Italian roll). Alternatively, you can simply drop in for piece of moist, homemade carrot or rich chocolate cake. Yum.

See map p. 138. 15 Blackfriars St. ☎ *0131-556-6922. Soups from £2.80 ($5); sandwiches and salads from £4.50 ($8). MC, V. Open: Mon–Sat 8 a.m.–6 p.m. Closed Sun.*

Sweet Melindas
$$ Marchmont (South Side)   SCOTTISH/SEAFOOD

The capital's Marchmont neighborhood, although just south of the Meadows, is far enough from the well-trod traveler's trail to seem miles away from touristy Edinburgh. This locally owned and operated restaurant is a neighborhood favorite and merits a visit from those outsiders who admire simple and amiable surroundings. The cooking tends to emphasize fish (which the chefs purchase from the shop next door) in dishes such as crispy squid salad or roast cod with a sesame and ginger sauce. But the menu isn't limited to the fruits of the sea. Sweet Melindas often serves up seasonal game, whether wood pigeon or venison, and a reasonable selection of vegetarian options as well.

See map p. 138. 11 Roseneath St. ☎ *0131-229-7953. Reservations recommended. Bus: 24. Main courses lunch: £8–£10 ($15–$18.50); main courses dinner: £10–£15 ($18.50–$28). AE, MC, V. Open: Mon 7–10 p.m., Tues–Sat noon–2 p.m. and 7–10 p.m. Closed Sun.*

The Witchery by the Castle
$$$–$$$$ Old Town   SCOTTISH

This award-winning landmark restaurant bills itself as the oldest and most haunted restaurant in town. The building's link to witchcraft dates back to 1470. Between then and the 1720s, more than 1,000 people were apparently burned alive nearby, and one of the victims is alleged to haunt the Witchery. Today, the restaurant serves classy Scottish food in classy surroundings, with dishes that feature ingredients such as Angus beef, Scottish lobster, or Loch Fyne oysters. Such well-prepared old-time British favorites as an omelet Arnold Bennett (made with cream and smoked fish) contrast with specials such as pan-roasted monkfish with a thyme and lemon risotto. Atmospheric and good for special occasions, the Witchery is also ideal for a sumptuous late meal. In addition to the dining room nearest the street, there's also the "Secret Garden" dining area further down the narrow close.

See map p. 138. Boswell Court, Castlehill, Royal Mile. ☎ *0131-225-5613.* www.the witchery.com. *Reservations required. Bus: 28. Fixed-price 2-course lunch or pre-/ post-theatre dinner: £10 ($18.50); main courses dinner: £18–£25 ($33–$46). AE, DC, MC, V. Open: daily noon–4 p.m. and 5:30–11:30 p.m.*

Tea for two?

If you're looking for a bit of a break while sightseeing in Old Town, try **Plaisir du Chocolat,** 251–253 Canongate (☎ 0131-556-9524). The cafe is a modern representative of the Auld Alliance between Scotland and France — when England was the nemesis of both countries. You can find more than 100 types of tea here, but if you need a boost of energy, go for one of the cafe's specialties: hot chocolate. It's as effective as coffee, believe us. Plaisir du Chocolat is open Monday through Saturday from 10 a.m. to 6 p.m. and Sunday from 10 a.m. to 4:45 p.m.

Another choice for a relaxing pick-me-up is **Clarinda's Tearoom,** 69 Canongate (☎ 0131-557-1888), especially if you're in the mood for the more classically British experience of afternoon tea: lace tablecloths, china, and Wedgwood plates on the walls. Clarinda's has plenty of teas from which to choose, plus a long list of tempting homemade cakes and sweets. If you want a more formal teatime experience, try the Palm Court at the **Balmoral Hotel,** Princes Street (☎ 0131-556-2414).

Exploring Edinburgh

Edinburgh's reputation is enormous, and the city lives up to all the hype. The second most popular destination after London for visitors to Great Britain, the Scottish capital is one of the most picturesque cities in Europe. Built on a set of hills, it's unarguably dramatic.

The **Old Town** lies at the city's heart, featuring the dramatic Edinburgh Castle at one end of the **Royal Mile,** which follows the spine of a hill down to the Palace of Holyroodhouse. For many visitors, this *is* Edinburgh, with its mews, closes, and alleyways.

But across the valley to the north, a valley now filled by the verdant Princes Street Gardens, is the city's **New Town,** which dates to the 1770s. Here you can find tidy streets and broad avenues, with shops, squares, and attractions such as the **National Portrait Gallery.** New Town reaches out to the village-like setting of Stockbridge, from which one can walk along the city's narrow meandering river, the Water of Leith, to Dean Village (another district that feels almost rural in nature), home of the **National Gallery of Modern Art** and its sister art venue, the **Dean Gallery.**

South of Old Town is the sprawling **Meadows,** with its acres of grass, the precincts of Edinburgh University, and suburbs such as Marchmont. To the north is the port of **Leith** and the Firth of Forth, which empties into the North Sea.

The only problem with Edinburgh's many attractions is deciding what you have time to see. You would need at least a few days to visit every place listed in this section, so you need to make some decisions depending on how long you're planning to be in the city. If you have children in tow, fewer galleries and more family attractions would probably be best; if you like art, more museums and fewer wanders may be in store.

Edinburgh's world famous annual cultural celebration — the **Edinburgh Festival** — brings in tourists and lovers of all forms of art from around the world. But if you prefer a bit more space and smaller crowds, avoid the month of August in Edinburgh.

 During the Edinburgh Festival, many museums that are normally closed on Sunday are open, and hours are generally extended. Some museums that open only in summer are also open on public holidays.

The top attractions

Calton Hill
New Town

Rising 106m (350 ft.) above sea level, this bluff full of monuments is mainly responsible for Edinburgh's being called the "Athens of the North." People visit the promontory not only to see the monuments up close but also to enjoy the panoramic views of the Firth of Forth and the city. The Parthenon-like structure at the summit, the **National Monument,** was meant to honor the Scottish soldiers killed during the Napoleonic wars. However, money for the project ran out in 1829, and the William H. Playfair–designed structure (sometimes referred to as "Edinburgh Disgrace") was never finished. The **Nelson Monument,** containing relics of the hero of Trafalgar, dates from 1815 and rises more than 30m (100 ft.) above the hill. A time ball at the top of the monument falls at 1 p.m. Monday through Saturday, and historically, it helped sailors in Leith set their timepieces. The monument is open from April through September, Monday from 1 to 6 p.m. and Tuesday through Saturday from 10 a.m. to 6 p.m.; from October through March, it's open Monday through Saturday from 10 a.m. to 3 p.m. Admission is £2.50 ($4.50).

Down the hill toward Princes Street, in the Old Calton Burial Grounds, is a curiosity of special interest to visitors from the United States. The **Emancipation Monument,** erected in 1893, was dedicated to the soldiers of Scottish descent who lost their lives in America's Civil War. It features a statue of Abraham Lincoln with a freed slave at his feet. Some famous Scots are buried here, too, with elaborate tombs honoring their memories (notably the Robert Adam–designed tomb for philosopher David Hume).

See map p. 154. www.undiscoveredscotland.co.uk/edinburgh/calton hill. *Walk up Calton Hill from the north end of Princes Street or from Leith Street. It's a steep 5-minute walk from the staircase at Waterloo Place. You can also drive up and park.*

Edinburgh Attractions

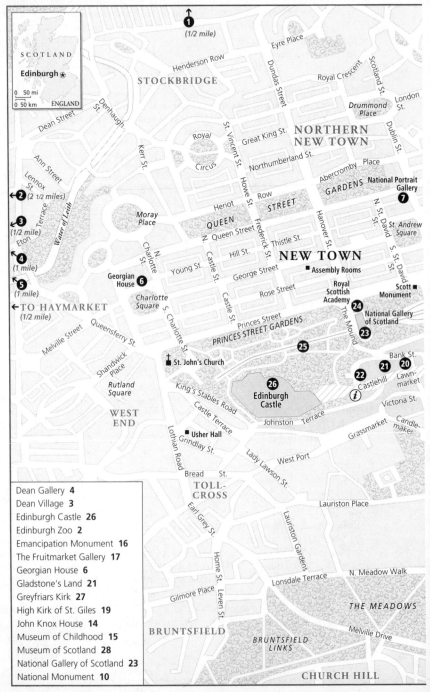

SCOTLAND

Edinburgh

0   50 mi
0   50 km   ENGLAND

① (1/2 mile)

STOCKBRIDGE

Henderson Row

Eyre Place

Royal Crescent

Scotland St.

Dundas Street

London St.

Drummond Place

NORTHERN NEW TOWN

Dean Street

Denhaugh St.

Ann Street

Lennox St.

②(2 1/2 miles)

③(1/2 mile)

④(1 mile)

⑤(1 mile)

Water of Leith

Eton Terrace

Kerr St.

Royal Circus

St. Vincent St.

Great King St.

Howe St.

Northumberland St.

Abercromby Place

GARDENS

National Portrait Gallery ⑦

Moray Place

Heriot Row

QUEEN STREET

N. Queen Street

Frederick St.

Thistle St.

Dublin St.

N. St. David St.

St. Andrew Square

Georgian House ⑥

Charlotte Square

N. Charlotte St.

Young St.

Castle St.

Hill St.

George Street

Hanover St.

NEW TOWN

■ Assembly Rooms

S. St. David St.

←TO HAYMARKET (1/2 mile)

Melville Street

Queensferry St.

S. Charlotte St.

Castle St.

Rose Street

Royal Scottish Academy ㉔

Scott ■ Monument

National Gallery of Scotland

Princes Street

PRINCES STREET GARDENS

The Mound

㉓

Shandwick Place

Rutland Square

King's Stables Road

✝ St. John's Church

㉕

㉒ ㉑ ㉒⓪

Castlehill

Bank St.

Lawn-market

WEST END

Castle Terrace

㉖ Edinburgh Castle

Johnston Terrace

ⓘ

Victoria St.

Grassmarket

Candle-maker

■ Usher Hall

Lothian Road

Grindlay St.

Lady Lawson St.

West Port

Bread   St.

TOLL-CROSS

Earl Grey St.

Lauriston Place

Lauriston Gardens

N. Meadow Walk

Home St.

Gilmore Place

Leven St.

Lonsdale Terrace

THE MEADOWS

BRUNTSFIELD

BRUNTSFIELD LINKS

Melville Drive

CHURCH HILL

Dean Gallery **4**
Dean Village **3**
Edinburgh Castle **26**
Edinburgh Zoo **2**
Emancipation Monument **16**
The Fruitmarket Gallery **17**
Georgian House **6**
Gladstone's Land **21**
Greyfriars Kirk **27**
High Kirk of St. Giles **19**
John Knox House **14**
Museum of Childhood **15**
Museum of Scotland **28**
National Gallery of Scotland **23**
National Monument **10**

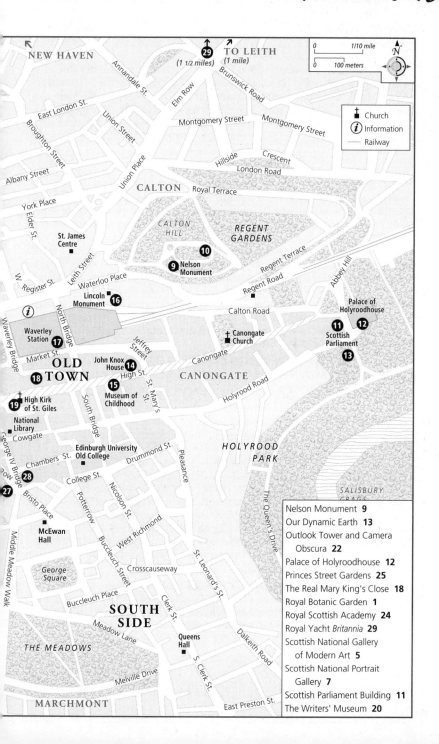

NEW HAVEN

↑ 29 ↗ TO LEITH
(1 1/2 miles) (1 mile)

0   1/10 mile
0   100 meters
N

Annandale St.

Elm Row

East London St.
Broughton Street
Union Street
Union Place

Montgomery Street   Montgomery Street

Brunswick Road

✝ Church
ⓘ Information
— Railway

Albany Street

York Place

Hillside   Crescent
London Road

CALTON   Royal Terrace

Elder St.

St. James
Centre

CALTON
HILL

REGENT
GARDENS

W. Register St.
York Place

Leith Street
Waterloo Place

🔟

9 Nelson
Monument

Regent Terrace

Regent Road

Abbey Hill

Palace of
Holyroodhouse

Lincoln
Monument 16

ⓘ

North Bridge

Waverley
Station 17

Calton Road

✝ Canongate
Church

Calton Road

11 12
Scottish
Parliament

13

Market St.

Waverley Bridge

OLD
18 TOWN

John Knox
House 14

Jeffrey Street

High St.

Canongate

CANONGATE

George IV Bridge

✝ High Kirk
19 of St. Giles

15
Museum of
Childhood

St. Mary's St.

Holyrood Road

National
Library
Cowgate

South Bridge

Edinburgh University
Old College

Drummond St.

Pleasance

HOLYROOD
PARK

SALISBURY
CRAGS

Chambers St.

28

27

College St.

Bristo Place

Potterrow

Nicolson St.

West Richmond

Buccleuch Street

Crosscauseway

St. Leonard's St.

The Queen's Drive

McEwan
Hall

George
Square

Buccleuch Place

Clerk St.

SOUTH
SIDE

Middle Meadow Walk

THE MEADOWS

Meadow Lane

Queens
Hall

Dalkeith Road

Melville Drive

S. Clerk St.

MARCHMONT

East Preston St.

Edinburgh Castle
Old Town

Few places in Scotland are filled with as much lore as Edinburgh Castle. The castle's very early history is somewhat vague, but in the 11th century, Malcolm III (Canmore) and his queen (later venerated as St. Margaret) founded a castle on this spot. The only fragment left of their original pile — in fact, the oldest structure in Edinburgh — is St. Margaret's Chapel. Built in the Norman style, the oblong structure dates principally from the 12th century.

After centuries of destruction, demolition, and upheaval, the buildings that stand as Edinburgh Castle today are basically those that came out of the castle's role as a military garrison in the past 300 years or so. And much of the displays are devoted to military history. The castle vaults served as prisons for foreign soldiers in the 18th century, and these great storerooms housed hundreds of Napoleonic soldiers in the early 19th century. In fact, some of the prisoners made wall carvings still seen today. Among the batteries of armaments that protected the castle is a Medieval siege cannon, known as Mons Meg, which weighs more than 5 tons. Other interesting sights include the place where Mary Queen of Scots gave birth to James VI of Scotland (later James I of England); the Great Hall, where Scottish Parliaments convened; and the Scottish Crown Jewels, used at coronations, along with the scepter and sword of the state of Scotland and infamous Stone of Scone.

See map p. 154. Castlehill. ☎ *0131-225-9846. Bus: 28 or 35. Admission: £9.50 ($17.50) adults, £7 ($13) seniors and students, £2 ($3.70) children age 15 and under. Open: Apr–Sept daily 9:30 a.m.–6 p.m.; Oct–Mar daily 9:30 a.m.–5 p.m.*

Edinburgh Zoo
Corstorphine, west of Murrayfield

Scotland's largest animal collection is located 4½km (3 miles) west of Edinburgh's city center on 32 hectares (80 acres) of hillside parkland offering unrivaled views from the Pentlands to the Firth of Forth. Operated by the Royal Zoological Society of Scotland, the zoo emphasizes its role in the conservation of wildlife and contains more than 1,500 animals, including endangered species such as snow leopards, white rhinos, pygmy hippos. The zoo boasts the largest penguin colony in Europe, with four species, and the world's largest penguin enclosure. From April to September, a penguin parade is held daily at 2:15 p.m.

See map p. 154. 134 Corstorphine Rd. ☎ *0131-334-9171.* www.edinburghzoo.org. uk. *Bus: 12, 26, or 31. Admission: £8.50 ($15.75) adults, £5.50 ($10) children ages 3 to 14, £26 ($48) families (2 adults and 2 children), £33 ($61) family (2 adults and 4 children). Open: Apr–Sept daily 9 a.m.–6 p.m.; Oct and Mar daily 9 a.m.–5 p.m.; Nov–Feb daily 9 a.m.–4:30 p.m.*

Gladstone's Land
Old Town

Now run by the National Trust for Scotland, which rescued the property from demolition in the 1930s, this 17th-century merchant's house is decorated in period-style furnishings. It's not very large, though, and is perhaps worth a visit if only to get an impression of how confining living conditions were some 400 years ago, even for the reasonably well-off. Note as well how small the doorways are — just don't bump your head. The merchant Gladstone (then spelled Gledstane) expanded the original 16th-century structure he purchased in 1617 both upwards and toward the street. In the front room added to the second floor, you can see the original facade with its classical friezes of columns and arches. Notice the sensitively restored timber ceiling, looking suitably weathered and aged, with colorful paintings of flowers and fruit.

See map p. 154. 477B Lawnmarket. ☎ *0131-226-5856. Bus: 28 or 35. Admission: £5 ($9.25) adults; £3.75 ($7) seniors, students, and children; £13.50 ($25) family. Open: Apr–Oct Mon–Sat 10 a.m.–5 p.m., Sun 2–5 p.m.*

Museum of Childhood
Old Town

Allegedly the world's first museum devoted solely to the history of childhood, this popular and free museum is just past the intersection of High and Blackfriars streets. The contents of its four floors range from antique toys to games to exhibits on health, education, and costumes, plus video presentations and an activity area. Not surprisingly, this is often the noisiest museum in town.

See map p. 154. 42 High St. ☎ *0131-529-4142. Bus: 35. Admission: free. Open: Mon–Sat 10 a.m.–5 p.m.; during the Edinburgh Festival, also open Sun noon–5 p.m.*

For fans of Mr. Hyde

Not far from Gladstone's Land is **Brodie's Close,** a stone-floored alley off the Lawnmarket. It was named after the well-respected cabinet-making father of the notorious William Brodie, who was a respectable councilor and deacon of trades by day — but a notorious thief and ne'er-do-well by night. Brodie's apparent split personality (actually he was simply calculating and devious) was likely the inspiration for Robert Louis Stevenson's *The Strange Case of Dr. Jekyll and Mr. Hyde.* Brodie was finally caught and hanged for his crimes in 1788. In a final irony, the mechanism used in the hangman's scaffold was perfected by none other than Brodie himself — and he tried to defy its action by secretly wearing a steel collar under his shirt. Alas, it didn't work. Across the street from Brodie's Close is one of the more famous pubs along the Royal Mile: **Deacon Brodie's Tavern,** 435 Lawnmarket (☎ **0131-225-6531**).

Museum of Scotland
Old Town

Opened in 1998, this impressive modern sandstone building not far from the Royal Mile offers exhibits that follow the story of Scotland, including archaeology, technology, science, the decorative arts, royalty, and geology. Hundreds of millions of years of Scottish history are distilled on each of the museum's floors. There's a total of some 12,000 items, ranging from 2.9-billion-year-old rocks found on the island of South Uist to a cute Hillman Imp, one of the last of 500 automobiles manufactured in Scotland. One gallery is devoted to Scotland's centuries as an independent nation before it merged with England and Wales to form Great Britain in the first decade of the 18th century. Another gallery, devoted to industry and empire from 1707 to 1914, includes exhibits on shipbuilding, whisky distilling, railways, and such textiles as the tartan and paisley. The roof garden has excellent views, the **Tower Restaurant** offers superb lunches, and adjacent to the Museum of Scotland is the **Royal Museum,** with its well-preserved and airy Victorian-era Main Hall and some 36 more galleries.

See map p. 154. Chambers St. ☎ *0131-225-7534.* www.nms.ac.uk. *Bus: 41 or 42. Admission: free. Open: Mon and Wed–Sat 10 a.m.–5 p.m., Tues 10 a.m.–8 p.m., Sun noon–5 p.m.*

National Gallery of Scotland
New Town

While the art collection held by Scotland may seem small according to the standards of larger countries, it has been chosen with great care and gradually expanded by bequests, gifts, loans, and purchases. The National Gallery has only enough space to display part of the entire collection. One recent major acquisition is Botticelli's *The Virgin Adoring the Sleeping Christ Child.* Also, the Duke of Sutherland has lent the museum two Raphaels as well as Titian's two Diana canvases and *Venus Rising from the Sea.* The galleries also feature works by El Greco and Velázquez and Dutch art by Rembrandt and Van Dyck. Impressionism is represented by Cézanne, Degas, van Gogh, Renoir, Gauguin, and Seurat. In the basement wing (opened in 1978), Scottish art is highlighted. Henry Raeburn is at his best in the whimsical *The Rev. Robert Walker Skating on Duddingston Loch,* and the late 19th century Glasgow School is represented by artists such as Sir James Guthrie.

Next door is the **Royal Scottish Academy** (☎ **0141-624-6200**), a gallery now connected to the National Gallery by the Weston Link, which opened in the summer of 2004. The RSA was renovated in 2003 and 2004 and now hosts blockbuster exhibitions for works by Monet and Titian among others.

See map p. 154. 2 The Mound. ☎ *0131-624-6200.* www.nationalgalleries.org. *Bus: 3, 25, 28, or 41. Admission to both National Gallery and Royal Scottish Academy: free to permanent collections, admission prices vary for special exhibitions. Open: Fri–Wed 10 a.m.–5 p.m., Thurs 10 a.m.–7 p.m; (extended hours daily during the Edinburgh Festival). Closed Dec 25–26.*

Outlook Tower and Camera Obscura
Old Town

The 150-year-old camera obscura, the periscope-like lens at the top of the Outlook Tower throws an image of nearby streets and buildings onto a circular table, and the image can be almost magically magnified with just a bit of cardboard. Tower guides reveal this trick, help to identify landmarks, and discuss highlights of Edinburgh's history. In addition, the observation deck offers free telescope use, and several exhibits in the "World of Illusions" have an optical theme that will keep some children occupied. What's most disappointing about the attraction, however, is the utter dearth of information on the man responsible for the camera obscura, Sir Patrick Geddes, a polymath (all-around smart guy) who worked tirelessly to improve the fortunes of the Old Town in the 19th and 20th centuries and kept it from being torn down.

See map p. 154. Castlehill. ☎ *0131-226-3709. Bus: 28 or 35. Admission: £5.95 ($11) adults, £4.75 ($9) seniors and students, £3.80 ($7) children. Open: Apr–June and Sept–Oct daily 9:30 a.m.–6 p.m.; July–Aug daily 9:30 a.m.–7:30 p.m.; Nov–Mar daily 10 a.m.–5 p.m.*

The Palace of Holyroodhouse
Old Town

In the 16th century, James IV built his palace adjacent to an Augustinian abbey that David I had established in the 12th century. The nave of the abbey church, now in ruins, still stands, but only the north tower of James's palace remains. The palace you see today was mostly built by Charles II. One wing was the scene of Holyroodhouse's most dramatic incident. Mary Queen of Scots's Italian secretary, David Rizzio, was stabbed repeatedly by her jealous husband, Lord Darnley, and his accomplices. A plaque marks the spot where he died on March 9, 1566. And one of the more curious exhibits is a piece of needlework done by Mary depicting a cat-and-mouse scene (her cousin, Elizabeth I, is the cat).

The palace suffered long periods of neglect, but it basked in brief glory during a ball thrown by Bonnie Prince Charlie in the mid-18th century, during the peak of his feverish (and doomed) rebellion to restore the Stuart line to monarchy. And later Holyroodhouse's fortunes were revived — as were other royal holdings in Scotland — by Queen Victoria. Today the royal family stays here whenever they visit Edinburgh. When they're not in residence, which is most of the time, the palace is open to visitors.

Palace highlights include the oldest surviving section, King James Tower, where Mary Queen of Scots lived on the second floor with Lord Darnley's rooms below. Some of the rich tapestries, paneling, massive fireplaces, and antiques from the 1700s are still in place. The Picture Gallery boasts many portraits of Scottish monarchs. More recently, the **Queen's Gallery** (with separate admission) opened to display works from the royal collection, including Mughal art and Dutch paintings.

Behind Holyroodhouse is **Holyrood Park,** Edinburgh's largest park. With rocky crags, a loch, sweeping meadows, and the ruins of a chapel, it's a wee bit of the Scottish countryside in the city and a great place for a picnic. If you climb 250m (823 ft) up Holyrood Park, you come to **Arthur's Seat,** from which the panorama is breathtaking. The name doesn't refer to King Arthur, as many people assume, but perhaps is a reference to Prince Arthur of Strathclyde or a corruption of *Ard Thor,* Gaelic for "height of Thor."

See map p. 154. Canongate, at the eastern end of the Royal Mile. ☎ *0131-556-5100. www.royal.gov.uk. Bus: 35, open-top tours. Admission (includes audio tour): £8 ($15) adults, £6.50 ($12) seniors and students, £4 ($7) children age 17 and under, £20 ($37) families (up to 2 adults and 3 children). Open: Apr–Oct daily 9:30 a.m.–6 p.m.; Nov–Mar 9:30 a.m.–3:45 p.m. Closed 2 weeks in mid-May and late June and at Christmas.*

Princes Street Gardens
New Town

A drained loch to the north of Old Town is now filled by the Princes Street Gardens, the most-used outdoor public space in the city. With Edinburgh Castle above, this is one of the most picturesque parks in Europe.

If you want a little exercise, climb the 287 steps to the 200-foot Scott Monument in the East Gardens for a great view of the castle. Resembling a church spire on a continental European cathedral, the Gothic-inspired monument is one of Edinburgh's most recognizable landmarks. In the center of the tall spire is a large seated statue of Sir Walter Scott and his dog, Maida, with Scott's heroes carved as small figures in the monument.

See map p. 154. Princes Street. Bus: 3, 10, 12, 17, 25, or 44. Admission: garden: free; Scott monument: £2.50 ($4.50).

Royal Botanic Garden
New Town

This is one of the grandest gardens in all of Great Britain, which is certainly saying something. Sprawling across 28 hectares (70 acres), the Royal Botanic Garden dates from the late 17th century, when it was originally used for medical studies. In spring, the various rhododendrons (from ground cover to gigantic shrubs) are reason alone to visit. The planting in various areas, from the rock garden to the deep "herbaceous borders," assures year-round interest. When it comes to research, only London's Kew Gardens does more. The grounds in Edinburgh include numerous glass houses, the Palm House (Britain's tallest) being foremost among them. Inverleith House is a venue for art exhibitions and has the Terrace Café, too.

See map p. 154. Inverleith Row. ☎ *0131-552-7171. www.rbge.org.uk. Bus: 8, 17, 23, or 27. Admission: by voluntary donation. Open: Jan–Feb daily 10 a.m.–4 p.m.; Mar and Oct–Dec daily 10 a.m.–6 p.m.; Apr–Sept daily 10 a.m.–7 p.m.*

Hume in Nor' Loch

When Princes Street Gardens were still a bog, the great philosopher David Hume fell into the bog, couldn't remove himself, and called for help from a passing woman. She recognized him, pronounced him an atheist, and refused to offer her umbrella to pull him out of the mire until he recited the Lord's Prayer. Presumably, he obliged.

Royal Yacht Britannia
Leith

The royal yacht *Britannia* launched on April 16, 1953, and traveled more than one million miles before it was decommissioned in December 1997. Several cities competed to permanently harbor the ship as a tourist attraction. The port of Leith won, and today the ship is moored next to the Ocean Terminal shopping mall some 3km (2 miles) from Edinburgh's center. After you're on board, you're guided around by a 90-minute audio tour. You can see where Prince Charles and Princess Diana strolled the deck on their honeymoon, visit the drawing room and the Royal apartments, and explore the engine room, galleys, and captain's cabin. All tickets should be booked as far in advance as possible.

See map p. 154. Ocean Terminal, Ocean Drive, Leith. ☎ *0131-555-5566.* www.royal yachtbritannia.co.uk. *Bus: 22, 34, 35, or the Britannia Tour Bus. Admission: £8 ($15) adults, £6 ($11) seniors, £4 ($7.40) children ages 5 to 17, free for children age 4 and under, £20 ($37) family ticket. Open: Apr–Sept first tour beginning at 9.30 a.m. and the last tour at 4:30 p.m.; Oct–Mar daily 10 a.m.–3:30 p.m. Closed Dec 25 and Jan 1.*

Scottish National Gallery of Modern Art
New Town/West End

Scotland's national collection of 20th-century art occupies a gallery converted from an 1828 school set on 4.8 hectares (12 acres) of grounds, about a 20-minute walk from the Haymarket. The collection is international in scope and quality despite its modest size, with works ranging from Matisse, Braque, Miró, and Picasso to Balthus, Lichtenstein, and Hockney. Recently, dramatic grassy terraces and a pond turned the grounds in front of the museum into a piece of art itself called Landform. A cafe on premises sells light refreshments and salads.

The easiest way to see the Scottish National Galleries is by catching the courtesy bus that stops at each museum.

See map p. 154. 75 Belford Rd. ☎ *0131-556-8921.* www.nationalgalleries.org. *Bus: 13. Admission: free, except for some temporary exhibits. Open: Fri–Wed 10 a.m.– 5 p.m., Thurs 10 a.m.–7 p.m. Closed Dec 25–26.*

Scottish National Portrait Gallery
New Town

Housed in a red-stone Victorian neo-Gothic pile designed by Rowand Anderson, the country's portrait gallery gives you a chance to see many of the famous people of Scottish history. The portraits, many by Ramsay and Raeburn, include everybody from Mary Queen of Scots and Flora Macdonald to early golfers and enlightenment thinkers. But the gallery's not all historical characters; modern portraits include contemporary figures such as Sean Connery and Billy Connolly.

See map p. 154. 1 Queen St. ☎ *0131-624-6200.* www.nationalgalleries.org. *Bus: 18, 20, or 41. Admission: free, except for some temporary exhibits. Open: Fri–Wed 10 a.m.–5 p.m., Thurs 10 a.m.–7 p.m. Closed Dec 25–26.*

Scottish Parliament Building
Old Town

After much controversy over its cost — the better part of £500 million ($925 million) — and the time it took to construct, the new Scottish Parliament finally opened in autumn of 2004. Designed by the late Barcelona-based architect Enric Miralles, it's a remarkable bit of modern design and perhaps worth the expense and delays. The abstract motif repeated on the facade was apparently inspired by Raeburn's painting *The Rev. Robert Walker Skating on Duddingston Loch,* which hangs in the National Gallery of Art (see listing above). Visitors can take a free, self-guided tour or pay to be led by a guide.

See map p. 154. Holyrood Rd. ☎ *0131-348-5000.* www.scottish.parliament.uk. *Bus: 35. Admission: guided tour £3.50 ($6.50) adult; £1.75 ($3.25) seniors, students, and children over 5. Open: business days (when Parliament is in session) Tues–Thurs 9 a.m.–7 p.m.; all non-business days (when Parliament is in recess and all Mon and Fri) Apr–Oct 10 a.m.–6 p.m., Nov–Mar 10 a.m.–4 p.m.; year-round Sat–Sun 10 a.m.–4 p.m. Last admission 45 minutes before closing. Closed Dec 25–26 and Jan 1–2.*

More cool things to see and do

Dean Gallery
New Town/West End

Opened in 1999 across the way from the Scottish National Gallery of Modern Art, the Dean Gallery provides a home for surrealist art and includes a replica of the studio of Leith-born pop art pioneer Eduardo Paolozzi. Paolozzi gave an extensive body of his private collection to the National Galleries of Scotland, including prints, drawings, plaster maquettes, and molds. The artist's mammoth composition of the robotic Vulcan dominates the entrance hall. Elsewhere works by Salvador Dalí, Max Ernst, and Joan Miró are displayed, while the Dean also hosts traveling or changing exhibitions of modern art.

See map p. 154. 73 Belford Rd. ☎ *0131-624-6200.* www.nationalgalleries.org. *Bus 13. Admission: free to permanent collection; prices vary for special exhibitions. Open: Fri–Wed 10 a.m.–5 p.m., Thurs 10 a.m.–7 p.m. Closed Dec 25–26.*

The Fruitmarket Gallery
New Town

Near Waverley Station, the Fruitmarket is the city's leading contemporary art gallery. The location is an old cavernous market dramatically updated and modernized by architect Richard Murphy in the early 1990s. The gallery draws exhibits from both local and internationally renowned modern and conceptual artists, including Louise Bourgeois, Cindy Sherman, Yoko Ono, Chad McCail, and Nathan Coley. The Fruitmarket's bookshop and cafe are equally appealing. Across the street is the Edinburgh **City Art Centre** (☎ **0131-529-3993**).

See map p. 154. 45 Market St. ☎ *0131-225-2383.* www.fruitmarket.co.uk. *Admission: free. Open: Mon–Sat 11 a.m.–6 p.m., Sun noon–5 p.m., hours extended during the Edinburgh Festival.*

Georgian House
New Town

Charlotte Square, designed by the great Robert Adam, was the final piece in the city's first New Town development. The National Trust for Scotland has two bits of property on Charlotte Square: No. 28, on the southern side of the square (the square's HQ with a small gallery), and, on the northern side, Georgian House, a town house that has been refurbished and opened to the public. The furniture is mainly Hepplewhite, Chippendale, and Sheraton, all from the 18th century. A sturdy old four-poster bed with an original 18th-century canopy occupies a ground-floor bedroom. The nearby dining room has a table set with fine Wedgwood china as well as a chamber pot that was apparently passed around after the womenfolk had retired.

See map p. 154. 7 Charlotte Sq. ☎ *0131-226-3318.* www.nts.org.uk. *Bus: 19, 36, or 41. Admission: £5 ($9.25) adults; £3.75 ($7) children, students, and seniors. Open: Apr–Oct daily 10 a.m.–5 p.m.; Nov–Dec and Mar daily 11 a.m.–3 p.m.. Closed Jan–Feb.*

Greyfriars Kirk
Old Town

Although the churches of Scotland aren't generally on the same scale as the cathedrals of the Continent, they generate their own slightly austere allure. Dedicated in 1620, this kirk was the first "reformed" church in Edinburgh and became the center of a good bit of history. It was built amid a cemetery proposed by Queen Mary in 1562 because no more burial space was available at St. Giles Cathedral on the Royal Mile. By the middle of the 17th century, the church had become a barracks for Cromwell's forces and, then, in the 18th century, the original tower exploded when gunpowder stored there caught fire. The kirkyard has a bit of the Flodden Wall (a wall built after the battle of Flodden, ostensibly to protect the city from invasion) and is full of 17th-century monuments. Its most celebrated grave, however, contains a 19th-century policeman whose faithful dog, Bobby, reputedly stood watch in the cemetery for years. The tenacious terrier's statue is at the top of Candlemaker Row, just outside the pub named in his honor.

See map p. 154. Greyfriars Pl. ☎ *0131-226-5429.* www.greyfriarskirk.com. *Bus: 2, 41, or 42. Admission: free. Open: Apr–Oct Mon–Fri 10:30 a.m.–4:30 p.m., Sat 10:30 a.m.–2:30 p.m.; Nov–Mar Thurs 1:30–3:30 p.m.*

High Kirk of St. Giles
Old Town

A brief walk downhill from Edinburgh Castle, this church — and its steeple in particular — is one of the most important architectural landmarks along the Royal Mile. It's where Scotland's own Martin Luther, John Knox, preached his sermons on the Reformation. Often called St. Giles Cathedral, the building combines a dark and brooding stone exterior (the result of a Victorian-era restoration) with surprisingly graceful buttresses. Only the tower reflects the Medieval era of the church. One of the church's outstanding features is Thistle Chapel, which houses beautiful stalls and notable heraldic stained-glass windows.

See map p. 154. High St. ☎ *0131-225-9442. Bus: 35. Admission: free, but £1 ($1.85) donation suggested. Open: Easter–Sept Mon–Fri 9 a.m.–7 p.m., Sat 9 a.m.–5 p.m., Sun 1–5 p.m.; Oct–Easter Mon–Sat 9 a.m.–5 p.m., Sun 1–5 p.m.*

John Knox House
Old Town

Born in East Lothian, John Knox is acknowledged as the father of the Presbyterian Church of Scotland, the Protestant tenets of which he established in 1560. Although some regard him as a prototypical Puritan, he actually proposed progressive changes in the ruling of the church and in education, and he was quite renowned for his sharp wit and sarcasm. But Knox lived at a time of great religious and political upheaval; he spent two years as a galley slave for agitating against papal authority and later lived in exile in Geneva (ruled by John Calvin). Upon his return, he became minister of St. Giles and worked with the English crown to ensure Protestant victory in Scotland.

Knox was also a writer/historian, perhaps best known for the inflammatory treatise, *The First Blast of the Trumpet Against the Monstrous Regiment of Women,* written in exile and inspired by his loathing of the reign of the three Roman Catholic queens in Scotland, France, and England. Even if you're not interested in the firebrand reformer (who probably never lived here anyway), you may want to visit this late 15th-century house. With its timbered gallery, it's characteristic of the "lands" (properties) that used to flank the Royal Mile, and the Oak Room is noteworthy for its frescoed ceiling as well as its Knox memorabilia. The house was shut for renovations in 2003 and is expected to reopen in 2005.

See map p. 154. 43-45 High St. ☎ *0131-556-9579. Bus: 35. Admission: £2.25 ($4.15) adults, £1.75 ($3.25) children ages 7 to 15, free for children 6 and under. Open: year-round Mon–Sat 10 a.m.–4:30 p.m.; July–Aug also open Sun noon–4:30 p.m.*

The Meadows
South Side

South of Old Town, this expansive public park separates the city center from the suburbs and leafy neighborhoods that popped up in the 18th and 19th centuries. The park dates to the 1700s, when a loch on the location was drained. Tree-lined paths crisscross the soccer, rugby, and cricket playing fields, but you can find plenty of additional space for having a picnic or flying a kite. At the far western end of the Meadows is Bruntsfield Links, a short-hole course that has a hallowed place in golf history and can still be played during the summer.

See map p. 154. Melville Dr. Bus: 24 or 41.

Our Dynamic Earth
Old Town

Under a futuristic tent-like canopy near the new Scottish Parliament, Our Dynamic Earth celebrates the evolution and diversity of the planet with emphasis on the seismological and biological processes that led from the Big Bang to the world we know today. The discovery center has been called "physical evolution as interpreted by Disney" because of its audio and video clips; buttons you can push to simulate earthquakes and meteor showers; and views of outer space. Kids delight in the slimy green primordial soup where life began and the series of specialized aquariums, some with replicas of early life forms, others with actual living sharks, dolphins, and coral. The skies of a simulated tropical rainforest darken at 15-minute intervals, offering torrents of rainfall and creepy-crawlies underfoot. Located on the premises are a restaurant, a cafe, a children's play area, and a gift shop.

See map p. 154. Holyrood Rd. ☎ 0131-550-7800. www.dynamicearth.co.uk. Bus 35. Admission: £8.95 ($16.50) adults, £5.45 ($10) children ages 5 to 15, free for children under 5. Open: Apr–Oct daily 10 a.m.–5 p.m.; Nov–Mar Wed–Sun 10 a.m.–5 p.m. Last admissions are at 3:50 p.m.

The Real Mary King's Close
Old Town

Beneath the City Chambers on the Royal Mile lies a warren of hidden streets where people lived and worked for centuries. When the Royal Exchange (now the City Chambers) was constructed in 1753, the top floors of the existing buildings were torn down but the lower sections were left standing and used as the foundations, leaving a number of dark, mysterious passages largely intact. These underground "closes," originally very narrow walkways with houses on either side, date back centuries. In 2003, tour groups — led by guides dressed up as characters from the past — began visiting these dwellings for the first time in perhaps 250 years. During the tours, visitors return to the turbulent and plague-ridden days of the 17th century. Dim lighting and an audio track are intended to add to the experience.

See map p. 154. 2 Warriston Close, High St. ☎ *0870-243-0160. Bus: 35. Admission: £7 ($13) adults, £6 ($11) students, £5 ($9.25) children (none under age 5 allowed). Reservations recommended. Open: Apr–Oct daily 10 a.m.–9 p.m.; Nov–Mar Sun–Fri 10 a.m.–4 p.m. and Sat 10 a.m.–9 p.m. Closed Dec 25.*

The Writers' Museum
Old Town

This remnant of a 17th-century house is a trove of portraits, relics, and manuscripts relating to Scotland's greatest men of letters: Robert Burns (1759–1796), Sir Walter Scott (1771–1832), and Robert Louis Stevenson (1850–1894). The Writers' Museum is often a surprisingly uncrowded space. The basement is perhaps the best part, with a good deal of items from the life of Stevenson (including his fishing rod and riding boots) as well as a gallery of black-and-white photographs taken when he lived in the South Pacific. The main floor is devoted to Scott, with his dining room table from 39 Castle St., his pipe, chess set, and original manuscripts. Another set of rooms gives details of Burns's life (note his page-one death notice in a copy of London's *Herald* from July 27, 1796) along with a glimpse of his writing desk, rare manuscripts, portraits, and other items. The house, with narrow passages and low clearances, was originally built in 1622 for Edinburgh merchant Sir William Gray.

See map p. 154. In Lady Stair's House, off Lawnmarket. ☎ *0131-529-4901. Admission: free. Bus: 28 or 35. Open: year-round Mon–Sat 10 a.m.–5 p.m.; Aug also open Sun noon–5 p.m.*

Guided tours

For an entertaining, one-hour overview and introduction to the principal attractions of Edinburgh, consider the **Edinburgh Bus Tours** that leave every 20 minutes or so from Waverley Bridge from April to late October. You can see most of the major sights along the Royal Mile, the Grassmarket, Princes Street, George Street, and more from the double-decker open-top motor coaches. Three tours — Edinburgh Tour (green buses), City Sightseeing (red buses), and Mac Tours (vintage buses) — all cover roughly the same ground in Old Town and New Town. The Majestic Tour buses, however, make short work of the city center as they go down to Leith as well. Tickets are valid for 24 hours, and you can hop on and hop off the bus at designated stops as you choose. The first tour is at 9:30 a.m., and the last is usually around 5:40 p.m. (slightly later from July through September). For more information on Edinburgh Bus Tours call ☎ 0131-220-0770 (www.edinburghtour.com). Tickets are £8.50 ($15.75) adults, £7.50 ($14) seniors and students, £2.50 ($4.50) children ages 5 to 15 (under 5 ride free), and £19.50 ($36) for a family of 2 adults and up to 3 children.

The **Literary Pub Tour** traces the footsteps of such literary greats as Robert Burns, Robert Louis Stevenson, and Sir Walter Scott. Tours go into the city's taverns, highlighting the tales of Dr. Jekyll and Mr. Hyde or the erotic love poetry of Burns. They leave at 7:30 p.m. from the Beehive

Inn on the Grassmarket nightly from May through September; Thursday through Sunday in April and October; and just on Fridays from November through March. For more information, call ☎ **0131-226-6665** (www.edinburghliterarypubtour.co.uk). Reservations are recommended for groups during the high season. You can purchase tickets at the Beehive; prices are £6–£8 ($11–$15), but you can get a reduced price if you book on the Internet.

Edinburgh's history is filled with tales of ghosts, gore, and witchcraft, and **The Witchery Tours** are enlivened by "jumper-ooters" — characters who leap out of seemingly nowhere to startle you when you least expect it. Two tours — the 90-minute Ghost & Gore and the 75-minute Murder & Mystery — overlap in parts. Under the cloak of darkness, you visit scenes of horrific torture, murder, and supernatural occurrence in the Old Town. The ghost tour (runs May through August) departs nightly at 7 p.m. and 7:30 p.m., with the murder tour (runs year-round) leaving at 9 p.m. and 9:30 p.m. All tours depart from the outside of the Witchery Restaurant on Castlehill. For tickets — £7 ($13) — visit the tour office at 84 West Bow (☎ **0131-225-6745;** www.witcherytours.com). Reservations are required.

The father of Dr. Jekyll and Mr. Hyde

Robert Louis Stevenson (1850–1894) was a restless character. Born in Edinburgh, he found the place too cold and dreary for his frail constitution and spent much of his life traveling. He has been alternately hailed as Scotland's greatest writer and dismissed as nothing more than the creator of tall tales for children.

The son of a Scottish civil engineer famed for buildings, bridges, and lighthouses, Stevenson was a sickly child and, as an adult, something of disappointment to his accomplished father. When at age 22 he announced he was an agnostic, his father declared, "My son has rendered my whole life a failure." One of the author's favorite bars still stands today: Rutherford's on Drummond Street near South Bridge. Determined to roam ("I shall be a nomad"), he traveled to France, and in 1876, he met American Fanny Osborne, who divorced her husband to wed Stevenson. She proved a dubious judge of his work: She didn't like *The Sea-Cook* (1881), which became the ever-popular *Treasure Island*. That work was followed by *Kidnapped* (1886). Perhaps his most evocative book, it reflects the troubled political times after the 1745 rebellion of Bonnie Prince Charlie and takes the protagonist on an adventure across the Western Highlands. But his most famous work — thanks to later Hollywood adaptations — is no doubt *The Strange Case of Dr. Jekyll and Mr. Hyde* (1886).

Eventually Stevenson and Fanny settled in Samoa, hoping to find a climate that would suit his tuberculosis-damaged lungs. While there, Stevenson worked on *The Ebb-Tide* (1894), the unfinished classic *Weir of Hermiston* (published posthumously in 1896), and translated one of his tales into Samoan. On December 3, 1894, at only 43 years old, he collapsed and died soon after.

Edinburgh's big summer events

The cultural highlight of Edinburgh's year comes every August during the **Edinburgh International Festival** and **Festival Fringe**. Since 1947, the International Festival has attracted artists and companies of the highest standards, whether in classical music, opera, ballet, or theater. Running almost simultaneously is the Fringe, an opportunity for anybody — professionals or nonprofessionals, individuals, groups of friends, or a whole company — to put on a show wherever they can find an empty stage or street corner. For many people today, the Fringe is *the* festival thanks to its late-night revues, contemporary drama, university theater presentations, and even full-length opera. Over the years, the Fringe has become increasingly established (and sponsored) though no less experimental and unexpected.

As if the International Festival and the Fringe weren't enough, Edinburgh also hosts at about the same time a variety of other festivals. In Charlotte Square, the **Book Festival** has become a huge annual event, drawing authors such as J.K. Rowling and Toni Morrison. You may also stumble upon the international **Film Festival**, a **Jazz Festival**, and a **Television Festival**. One of the season's more popular spectacles is the **Military Tattoo** on the floodlit esplanade of Edinburgh Castle. The show features precision marching of not only Scottish regiments but also soldiers and performers (including bands, drill teams, and gymnasts) from dozens of countries.

Ticket prices for festivals, the Fringe, and other shows or events vary from £1 ($1.85) to £50 ($92.50). The headquarters for the International Festival is The Hub, Castle Hill (☎ 0131-473-2000). The Fringe is based at 180 High St. (☎ 0131-226-0000). General information on festivals and most events can be found on the Web at www.edinburghfestivals.co.uk.

Mercat Tours is a well-established company that conducts popular walking tours of the city that cover a range of interests from "Secrets of the Royal Mile" to a haunted underground experience and the ghost trail. The Secrets of the Royal Mile tour, for example, leaves daily at 10:30 a.m. from the Mercat Cross, outside of St. Giles Cathedral on the Royal Mile. The tour office is located at Mercat House, Niddry Street (☎ 0131-557-6464; www.mercat-tours.co.uk). Tickets cost £6 ($11), and reservations are recommended.

Suggested 1-, 2-, and 3-day itineraries

You may just want to wander around Edinburgh, which is easy enough — it's a small place and many of the tourist attractions are within the central part of the city. However, if your time in the capital is limited to a few days, here are some suggested itineraries that highlight some of the very best things to do and see.

If you have 1 day

If you're unfortunate enough to only have one day in Edinburgh, I suggest that you stick to the city's famous Royal Mile and Old Town. The area's every bit a day's worth of activity, with plenty of history and attractions from Edinburgh Castle to the Palace of Holyroodhouse, not to mention shops, restaurants, and pubs. Wander down some of the alleys off the Royal Mile, too.

If you have 2 days

Follow my one-day itinerary for your first day, and on your second day, take the hop-on, hop-off bus tour that emphasizes the New Town. Your ticket is good for 24 hours (although the buses stop running in the late afternoon/early evening). Get off on Calton Hill for the views, which Robert Louis Stevenson said were the best in the city. Amble down Princes Street for a bit of shopping and afterwards take a break in Princes Street Gardens. Then go admire some of the fine art nearby at the National Gallery (on the Mound).

If you have 3 days

Days 1 and 2 should be filled with the activities I suggest in the previous two sections. On Day 3, take in **Leith,** Edinburgh's once rough-and-tumble port. Now increasingly gentrified, it's still evocative. A seaside village that is now part of Edinburgh, Leith has a rich history of its own. Today it also offers some good restaurants and lively pubs. On your way back into the city center, also worth a visit is the Botanic Gardens. It's one of the best in Britain — and that's saying a lot. If you have any time to spare, visit Stockbridge or the Meadows, which have an off-the-main-tourist-tracks feel to them.

If you (are lucky and) have 4 days or more

Start with my recommendations from the previous sections, and then on Day 4 climb Arthur's Seat for views of the city and the sea. Take the family to the Edinburgh Zoo, or appreciate the country's modern art collection at the Dean Gallery, or get out of town with an excursion up to St. Andrews or to nearby historic Linlithgow.

Taking a walking tour

Given that Edinburgh is a relatively compact city, walking is one of the best ways to see it. This fact is especially true in the Old Town, where passages and alleys — or "closes" (pronounced *clozes*) and "vennels," as the locals prefer — run off both sides of the main street like ribs from a spine. You really owe it to yourself to wander down a few of them to appreciate the medieval core of the Scottish capital. Beyond the Old Town to the north is the classic Georgian-era New Town, another part of the city that now has World Heritage Site status. If you want to leave the tourist trail, however, the following walk south of the Royal Mile gives you a notion of what "real" Edinburgh is like — as well as takes you past some architectural highlights. The route's only about 2 miles long and shouldn't take you more than an hour or so to complete (if you don't go into buildings or get distracted, that is).

Hogmanay

Hogmanay is what the Scots call New Year's Eve, and Edinburgh now hosts one of the biggest New Year's Eve parties on the planet. In Scotland, the festivities traditionally don't really even begin until the clock strikes midnight and then they continue until daybreak or later. In 1993, the Edinburgh City Council began a three-day Hogmanay festival featuring rock bands, street theater, and a lively procession. By 1997, the event had become so big that participation is now reserved for ticket holders. For information, visit www.edinburghshogmanay.com.

Start the walk at:

1. West Bow

Initially this street zigzagged right up the steep slope from the Grassmarket to Castlehill. With the 19th-century addition of Victoria Street, however, West Bow links more easily with the Royal Mile via George IV Bridge. The combination of Victoria Street and West Bow create a charming and winding road of unpretentious shops, bars, and restaurants. At the base of the street is the West Bow Well, which was built in 1674. To the west is the Grassmarket.

Go southeast from Cowgate Head up Candlemaker Row to:

2. Greyfriars Kirk

This isn't the church you see ascending Candlemaker Row but instead lies to the right at the top. Greyfriars Kirk was completed in 1620 (for some history, flip back to the church's listing in the section "More cool things to see and do," earlier in this chapter).

Cross George IV Bridge to Chambers Street and the:

3. Museum of Scotland

Directly in front of you as you leave Greyfriars is the impressive and modern Museum of Scotland. It was designed by architects Benson and Forsyth and constructed mostly with sandstone from the northeast of Scotland. Opened in 1998, the museum's purpose is to host exhibitions that chart the history of Scotland: the land, wildlife, and people. (A bonus if you have free time, next door is the Royal Museum.) Chambers Street is named after a 19th-century lord provost (the equivalent of a mayor) whose statue stands in front of the museum's Victorian Great Hall. Further down off Chambers Street on what is today Guthrie Street you can find Sir Walter Scott's birthplace.

Continue east on Chambers Street to South Bridge, turning right (south). At this corner is the:

4. Old College

The 1781 exteriors of the University of Edinburgh Old College have been called the greatest public work of Robert Adam. The university was first established in 1583 by James VI (and later James I of England), and this Old College actually replaced an earlier Old College. Construction of the quadrangle of buildings was suspended during the Napoleonic wars, and William Playfair designed the Quad's interiors in 1819. In the southwest corner is the entrance to the Talbot Rice gallery (www.trg.ed.ac.uk), which displays contemporary art. On nearby Drummond Street is one of Robert Louis Stevenson's favorite saloons — the Rutherford Bar — and a plaque commemorating his admiration for it is posted at the corner. Across Drummond Street is more literary history — but of more recent vintage. A cafe here on the second floor is reputedly where J.K. Rowling began writing the Harry Potter series. More recently, it became a Chinese restaurant.

At Drummond Street, South Bridge becomes Nicolson Street. Continue south on it to:

5. Nicolson Square

The impressive building you passed on the left (across from the modern Festival Theatre) before arriving at this square was the Surgeons' Hall, designed by William Playfair in the 1830s. Nicolson Square dates to 1756, and the buildings along its north fringe apparently were the first to be built here. In the square's park you can see the Brassfounders' Column created by James Gowans in 1886.

Leave the square at the west on Marshall Street, turn left (south) onto Potterrow, and turn right (west) at the parking lot entrance and Crichton Street to:

6. George Square

Almost entirely redeveloped by the University of Edinburgh in the 20th century, George Square originally had uniform if less than startling mid-18th century town houses. The square predates the city's New Town developments, and some of the early buildings are still standing on the western side of the square. The park provides a quiet daytime retreat. Walter Scott played in this park as a child. (A little trivia: The square was named after the brother of the designer James Brown and not a king.)

Exit the square at the southwest corner, turning right (west) into:

7. The Meadows

This sweeping park separates from central Edinburth the southern suburbs, such as Marchmont, that were largely developed in the 19th century. The area once had a loch, but today it's a green expanse crisscrossed by tree-lined paths. At the Western end is Bruntsfield Links, which some speculate entertained golfers in the 17th century and still has a short course with many holes available for play today.

Turn right a short distance later (at the black cycle network marker) and follow the bike/pedestrian path, Meadow Lane, north to:

8. Teviot Place

The triangle of land formed by Teviot Place, Forrest Road, and Bristo Place is a hotbed of university life today, with its cafes and bars. To the right (east) is the Medical School. To the left (west) on Lauriston Place is the Royal Infirmary of Edinburgh. George Watson's Hospital on the grounds dates to the 1740s, but Scots baronial (a type of architecture) buildings superceded it in the 19th century, adopting the open-plan dictates of Florence Nightingale.

Walk west on Lauriston Place to:

9. George Heriot's School

Heriot was nicknamed "the Jinglin' Geordie," and as jeweler to James VI, he exemplified the courtiers and royal hangers-on who left Scotland and made their fortunes in London after the unification of the crowns. Heriot, at least, decided to pay Edinburgh back by leaving more than £20,000 to build a facility for disadvantaged boys. Of the 200-odd windows in the Renaissance pile, only two are exactly alike. Today, the building's a private school for both boys and girls.

Continue on Lauriston Place to the edge of the campus and turn right on Heriot Place. Continue down the vennel to the:

10. Grassmarket

Located just at the top of the steep steps of the vennel is another piece of the Flodden Wall, the southwest bastion, indicating how the Grassmarket was enclosed in the city by the 16th century. Now home to loads of bars and restaurants, the Grassmarket — in the shadow of the castle — hosted a weekly market for more than 400 years. Until the 1780s, the Grassmarket also was the site of public gallows and a place where zealous Protestants — known as the Covenators — were hung, as was Maggie Dickson, who came back to life according to legend. She at least has a pub named after her today. At the nearby White Hart Inn, both Burns and Wordsworth are said to have lodged.

Shopping in Edinburgh

Edinburgh doesn't have quite as many shopping options as you can find in Glasgow, but it does have a combination of traditional department stores, such as the classic Jenners, and newfangled boutiques. With the recent addition of every fashionista's favorite, Harvey Nichols, Edinburgh is definitely beginning to challenge the more style-conscious city to the west.

Best shopping areas

New Town's **Princes Street** is the main shopping artery in the Scottish capital; it's home to leading department stores including the homegrown Jenners and the British staple Marks & Spencer. But for the posher shops, such as Cruise or Laura Ashley, **George Street** tops the lot. In between, is **Rose Street,** a narrow pedestrian lane that's best known for its pubs but is actually full of more shops.

For tourists on the hunt for more traditional souvenirs, the **Royal Mile** on the hill of Old Town presents the Mother Lode, whether it's tartan or trinkets you seek.

Shopping hours in Edinburgh are generally only from 9 or 10 a.m. to 6 p.m. Monday through Wednesday and on Friday and Saturday. Thursday is the so-called late shopping day with many shops opening at 9 or 10 a.m. and remaining open to 7 or 8 p.m. Shops open Sundays from 11 a.m. or noon and close at around 5 p.m., although smaller operations may remain closed on Sunday.

Shopping complexes

In addition to the primary shopping districts in New Town and Old Town, a few shopping malls with a concentration of shops are scattered around. The newest is in Leith: **Ocean Terminal** (☎ 0131-555-8888; www.ocean terminal.com). Although it was designed by the firm run by Habitat (a landmark home decorating shop) founder Sir Terrance Conran, Ocean Terminal is ultimately just another modern mall. Debenhams, French Connection, Gap, and other stores have set out their stalls in this retail cathedral, which gets a lot of footfall from tourists because the royal yacht *Britannia* is moored here as well.

Above Waverley train station and beneath the city's main tourist information center, **Princes Mall** (☎ 0131-557-3759; www.princesmall-edinburgh.co.uk) appears to have something for everyone — except a leading department store. About 80 shops sell fashions, accessories, gifts, books, jewelry, and beauty products, and a food court offers the typical fast-food outlets.

St James Centre (☎ 0131-557-0050; www.stjamesshopping.com) is slightly more upscale than Princes Mall. At the top of Leith Walk near Calton Hill, this shopping center is anchored by John Lewis's department store, giving the place a nice touch of respectability.

What to look for and where to find it

If your shopping intentions are less of the browsing variety, here are some of Edinburgh's specialized shopping options.

Books

✔ **Blackwell's** is the new name for the once venerable James Thin bookstore, Edinburgh's most respected seller. Despite the new corporate owners, the shop has at least maintained a knowledgeable staff and a wide-ranging stock of fiction and non-fiction. 53 South Bridge (☎ **0131-622-8222;** www.blackwells.co.uk)

✔ **McNaughtan's Bookshop** is one of the city's best antiquarian and secondhand book purveyors. Consider it a must-stop for book lovers. 3a–4a Haddington Place at the top of Leith Walk near Gayfield Sq. (☎ **0131-556-5897;** www.mcnaughtansbookshop.com)

✔ **Waterstone's** is a giant Barnes and Noble–like operation with plenty of stock and a lot of soft seats. It's the most prominent book retailer in the city center and has a good Scottish section on the ground floor. Other branches in New Town are at the western end of Princes Street and on George Street. 128 Princes St. (☎ **0131-226-2666**)

Crystal

✔ **Edinburgh Crystal** is some 16km (10 miles) south of Edinburgh. It's devoted to handmade crystal glassware. The visitor center contains the factory shop where the world's largest collection of Edinburgh Crystal and inexpensive factory seconds are sold. Waterford may be a more prestigious name, but Edinburgh Crystal is a serious competitor. Eastfield, Penicuik, just off A701 to Peebles (☎ **01968-672-244;** www.edinburgh-crystal.co.uk)

Clothing

✔ **Arkangel** is in the city's affluent West End, which offers a host of boutique shops. This one specializes in women's designers and sells brands that no other store in Scotland does. UK designer duds sold here include Marilyn Moore. 4 William St., West End (☎ **0131-226-4466**)

✔ **Corniche** is one of the more sophisticated boutiques in Edinburgh; if it's the latest in Scottish fashion, expect to find it here. Offerings have included "Anglomania kilts" created by that controversial lady of clothing design, Vivienne Westwood, as well as fashions by Gautier, Katherine Hamnett, and Yamamoto. 2 Jeffrey St. near the Royal Mile (☎ **0131-556-3707**)

✔ **Cruise** is commonly associated with Glasgow, but this home-grown fashion outlet began in Edinburgh's Old Town — not generally considered fertile ground for the avant-garde. You can still find a shop off the Royal Mile, but this New Town outlet is the focus for couture. 94 George St. (☎ **0131-226-3524**)

✔ **The Earth Collection** tags all its clothing "eco-friendly," meaning the clothes are made from cotton, silk, ramie, and hemp. The natural fibers are also colored using only natural dyes. This shop mostly stocks women's clothing but sells some items for men and children. 2/3 North Bank St. (☎ **0131-226-1925**)

✔ **Walker Slater** is a handsome shop full of well-made and contemporary (if understated) men's clothes, usually made of cotton and dyed in rich, earthy hues. It also carries Mackintosh overcoats and accessories for the smart gentleman about town. 20 Victoria St. (☎ **0131-220-2636**)

Crafts and jewelry

✔ **Alistir Wood Tait** is a jewelry store with a reputation for Scottish gems and precious metals such as agates, Scottish gold, garnets, and sapphires. Ask to see the artful depictions of Luckenbooths — two entwined hearts capped by a royal crest, usually fashioned as pendants. 116A Rose St. (☎ **0131-225-4105**; www.alistirtaitgem. co.uk)

✔ **Hamilton & Inches** has sold gold and silver jewelry, porcelain and silver, and gift items including quaichs since 1866. Folkloric *quaichs* (drinking vessels now mostly used to give as gifts) originated in the West Highlands as whisky measures crafted from wood or horn. They were later gentrified into something like silver chafing dishes, each with a pair of lugs (ears) fashioned into Celtic or thistle patterns. 87 George St. (☎ **0131-225-4898**; www.hamiltonandinches.com)

✔ **Ness Clothing** is filled with whimsical accessories scoured from around the country — from the Orkney Islands to the Borders. Ness offers hand-loomed cardigans and tasteful scarves, amid much more. 367 High St. (☎ **0131-226-5227**)

Department stores

✔ **Harvey Nichols** opened in 2002 with much celebration but was a tad slow to catch on. Perhaps traditional shoppers were not quite prepared for floors of expensive labels and designers such as Jimmy Choo or Alexander McQueen. But they're learning. 30–34 St. Andrew's Sq. (☎ **0131-524-8388**; www.harveynichols.com)

✔ **Jenners** opened in 1838, and the shop's neo-Gothic facade is almost as much an Edinburgh landmark as the Scott Monument just across Princes Street. The store's array of local and international merchandise is well-known, and it has a food hall with a wide array of gift-oriented Scottish products, including heather honey, Dundee marmalade, and a vast selection of shortbreads. 48 Princes St. (☎ **0131-225-2442**)

✔ **John Lewis** is the largest department store in Scotland, and this branch is many people's first choice when it comes to shopping for clothes, appliances, furniture, toys, and more. St James Centre near Picardy Place at the top of Leith Walk (☎ **0131-556-9121**)

Edibles

See the sidebar "Picnic fare" earlier in this chapter for select food markets with Scottish specialties.

Hats, knits, and woolens

✔ **Bill Baber** is a workshop/store that turns out artfully modernized adaptations of traditional Scottish patterns for both men and women. Expect to find traditional knits spiced up with strands of Caribbean-inspired turquoise or aqua or rugged-looking blazers or sweaters suitable for treks or bike rides through the moors. 66 Grassmarket (☎ 0131-225-3249; www.billbaber.com)

✔ **Edinburgh Woollen Mill Shop** is one of several in the capital and of about 280 outlet shops throughout the United Kingdom that sell practical Scottish woolens, knitwear, skirts, gifts, and travel rugs. Note: Whatever the name of the shop, most of the merchandise is made in England. 139 Princes St. (☎ 0131-226-3840; www.ewm.co.uk)

✔ **Fabhatrix** has hundreds of handmade felt hats and caps, many practical as well as attractive and some downright frivolous but extremely fun. Remember: Keep your head warm and your whole body stays warm. 13 Cowgatehead, near Grassmarket (☎ 0131-225-9222)

✔ **Ragamuffin** sells what's termed "wearable art," created by some 150 designers from all over the UK. The apparel here is one-of-a-kind unique. Well, not exactly — Ragamuffin also has a shop way up north on the Isle of Skye. 276 Canongate, Royal Mile (☎ 0131-557-6007; www.ragamuffinonline.co.uk)

Gifts

✔ **Geraldine's of Edinburgh** is also known as the "Doll Hospital." Each of the heirloom-quality dolls here requires days of labor to create and has a hand-painted porcelain head and sometimes an elaborate coiffure. Also available are fully jointed, all-mohair teddy bears. 35a Dundas St. (☎ 0131-556-4295)

✔ **Tartan Gift Shops** has a chart indicating the place of origin (in Scotland) of family names, accompanied by a bewildering array of hunt and dress tartans for men and women, all sold by the yard. The shop also carries a line of lambswool and cashmere sweaters. 54 High St. (☎ 0131-558-3187)

Music

✔ **Avalanche** usually has a bunch of harmless goth kids hanging out in front of it. You can find this branch of the excellent CD shop where the steep steps of the Fleshmarket Close meet Cockburn Street. It's best for new releases of indie bands. Another Avalanche shop is on West Nicolson Street. 60 Cockburn St., near the Royal Mile (☎ 0131-225-3939)

✔ **Fopp** offers books and rock, pop, jazz, and dance CDs. Fopp's Rose Street branch even has a bar selling beer, so you can swill while you sample at a listening station. Another branch is located on Cockburn Street. 7–15 Rose St. (☎ **0131-220-0310**)

✔ **Virgin Megastore** is where you find one of the biggest selections of records, CDs, videos, and tapes in Scotland. The shop has traditional and Scottish music as well as the mainstream offerings. 125 Princes St. (☎ **0131-220-2230**)

Tartans and kilts

✔ **Anta** sells some of the most stylish tartans. Woolen blankets with hand-purled fringe are woven here on old-style looms. 32 High St. (☎ **0131-557-8300**)

✔ **Geoffrey (Tailor) Kiltmakers** has a list of customers that includes Sean Connery, Charlton Heston, Dr. Ruth Westheimer, members of Scotland's rugby teams, and Mel Gibson. It stocks 200 of Scotland's best-known tartan patterns and is revolutionizing the kilt by establishing a subsidiary called 21st Century Kilts, which makes them in fabrics ranging from denim to leather. 57–59 High St. (☎ **0131-557-0256**)

✔ **Hector Russell**, a well-known kiltmakers shop on the Royal Mile, creates bespoke — that's made-to-order— clothes made from tartans. Another branch is located on Princes Street. 137–141 High St. (☎ **0131-225-3315**)

✔ **James Pringle Weavers** produces a large variety of wool items, including cashmere sweaters, tartan and tweed ties, travel rugs, tweed hats, and tam o' shanters. In addition, it boasts a clan ancestry center with a database containing more than 50,000 family names. 70–74 Bangor Rd., Leith (☎ **0131-553-5161**)

Living It Up After Dark

Every summer, Edinburgh becomes the cultural capital of Europe and the envy of every other tourist board in the UK when it hosts the **International Festival, Festival Fringe, Book Festival, Film Festival,** and **Jazz Festival.** All totaled, these festivals bring in thousands of visitors to see hundreds of world-class acts — whether in drama, dance, music, comedy, or more. In August, the Scottish capital becomes a proverbial "city that never sleeps."

Although the yearly festivals (www.edinburghfestivals.co.uk) are no doubt the peak of Edinburgh's social calendar, the city offers a pretty good selection of entertainment choices throughout the year. Visitors can busy themselves with the cinema, clubs, theater, opera, ballet, and other diversions such as a night at the pub.

178 Part III: Edinburgh and Glasgow

For a complete rundown of what's happening in Edinburgh, pick up a copy of *The List,* a biweekly magazine available at all major newsstands and bookshops. It previews, reviews, and gives the full details of arts events here — and in Glasgow.

The performing arts

The West End is the cradle of theatre and music, home to the legendary and innovative **Traverse Theatre** as well as the **Royal Lyceum Theatre** and the classic **Usher Hall** for concerts.

✔ **Edinburgh Festival Theatre** reopened in 1994 after serious renovations in time for the Edinburgh Festival (hence the name). Located on the south side of the city about a ten-minute walk from the Royal Mile and right near the University of Edinburgh Old Campus, the 1,900-seat theater hosts the national opera and ballet, touring companies, and orchestras. Tickets are £5–£45 ($9.25–$83). 13–29 Nicolson St. (☎ **0131-529-6000** box office; 0131-662-1112 administration; www.eft.co.uk; Bus: 5, 7, 8, or 29)

✔ **Edinburgh Playhouse** is best known for hosting popular plays or musicals and other mainstream acts when they come to town, whether it's *Miss Saigon* or *Lord of the Dance.* Formerly a cinema, the playhouse is the largest theater in Great Britain, with more than 3,000 seats. Tickets are £8–£35 ($15–$65). 18–22 Greenside Place (☎ **0870-606-3424**; www.edinburgh-playhouse.co.uk; Bus: 5 or 22)

✔ **Kings Theatre** is a 1,300-seat late-Victorian era venue with a domed ceiling and rather Glasgow-style stained glass doors and red-stone frontage. Located on the edge of Tollcross southwest of the castle, it offers a wide repertoire, especially traveling West End productions, productions of the Scottish National Theatre, other classical entertainment, ballet, and opera. During December and January, it's the premier theatre for popular pantomime productions in Edinburgh. Tickets range from £5–£20 ($9.25–$37). 2 Leven St. (☎ **0131-529-6000**; www.eft.co.uk; Bus: 11, 15, or 17)

✔ **Royal Lyceum Theatre** has a most enviable reputation with presentations that range from the most famous works of Shakespeare to new Scottish playwrights. It's home to the leading theatre production company in the city, often hiring the best Scottish actors such as Brian Cox, Billy (Lord of the Rings) Boyd, and Siobhan Redmond — when they're not preoccupied with Hollywood, that is. Grindlay Street (☎ **0131-248-4848** box office; 0131-238-4800 general inquiries; www.lyceum.org; Bus: 1, 10, 15, or 34)

✔ **Traverse Theatre** is just around the corner from the Royal Lyceum and is something of a local legend. Beginning in the 1960s as an experimental theater company that doubled as a bohemian social club, it still produces the contemporary drama at its height in Scotland. This custom-made subterranean complex actually contains two theaters, seating 100 and 250, respectively, on the benches. Upstairs, the Traverse Bar is where you find the hippest dramatists, actors, and their courtiers. Tickets are £4–£14 ($7–$26). 10 Cambridge St. (☎ **0131-228-1404;** www.traverse.co.uk; Bus: 11 or 15)

✔ **Usher Hall** is unbeatable when it comes to concerts. Built thanks to the bequest of distiller Andrew Usher in the 1890s, this beaux-arts building is Edinburgh's equivalent of Carnegie Hall. During the International Festival, the horseshoe-shaped auditorium hosts such ensembles as the Cleveland or London Philharmonic orchestras. But Usher Hall isn't only a venue for classical music; top touring jazz, world music, and pop acts play here throughout the year. Lothian Road (☎ **0131-228-1155;** www.usherhall.co.uk; Bus: 1, 10, 15, or 34)

Club and music scene

Clubbing is a popular pastime in Edinburgh. Clubs here offer not only some first-class DJs who play a wide range of dance music but also an opportunity to keep drinking after the bars and pubs have closed. Arguably, Glasgow has more lively contemporary music scene, but Edinburgh has the edge when it comes to jazz.

Late-night eats

Okay, it's Friday or Saturday night. You've been out to a play, the pub, or a dance club and now you're utterly starving. But it's sometime between 11 p.m. and 2 a.m. (you're not exactly sure because your watch seems to be keeping Australian time at the moment). Food will help you get back on track. If you're in the West End, Lothian Road is your best bet. Try **Lazio,** 95 Lothian Rd. (☎ **0131-229-7788**), for a bit of pizza or pasta. It's open until midnight during the week and until 2 a.m. on Friday and Saturday nights (technically, that's Saturday and Sunday mornings). In Old Town, another Italian eatery caters to night owls: **Gordon's Trattoria** on the High Street (☎ **0131-225-7992**) is open until 3 a.m. on the weekends (until midnight Sunday through Thursday). For something a bit more modern and trendy, **Favorit** is a NYC-style diner. The branch on Leven Street (☎ **0131-221-1800**) is open until 1 a.m. daily, while the other location near the university, on Teviot Place (☎ **0131-220-6880**), stays open until 3 a.m. daily.

Comedy

Given the importance of the Edinburgh Festival Fringe, where the vaunted Perrier Award for comedy can launch a career, the stand-up comedian is . . . err, taken very seriously in the Scottish capital.

 ✔ **Jongleurs Comedy Club** is a corporate-owned entity from down south with more than a dozen venues across the UK. Jongleurs came to Scotland a few years back, dragging along its own cadre of house funnymen (and funnywomen) as well as some touring comedians from overseas. After the shows and continuing until 3 a.m., the club features 1970s-style disco dancing — just in case you haven't already had enough laughs. Tickets are £4–£15 ($7.50–$28). Omni Centre, Greenside Place (☎ **0870-787-0707;** www.jongleurs.com; Bus: 7 or 22)

 ✔ **The Stand,** just down the hill from St. Andrew's Square, is the premier local comedy venue. Big acts are reserved for weekend nights, while local talent tries their jokes and tales during the week. On Sundays, no admission is charged for brunch performances. Tickets range from £1–£8 ($1.85–$15). 5 York Place (☎ **0131-558-7272;** www.thestand.co.uk; Bus: 8 or 17)

Folk music

Although touring folk acts — performers such as Gillian Welsh are huge in Scotland — get booked into the larger music halls, the day-to-day folk scene in Edinburgh takes place in unassuming public houses.

 ✔ **Assembly Rooms** is a popular host for ceilidhs — or Scottish country dances. They're known as the "National Theatre of the Fringe," seeing as some of the biggest acts perform here. There are six separate performance spaces, the largest of which is the 600 seat Music Room. 54 George Street, New Town (☎ **0131-220-4349;** www.assemblyroomsedinburgh.co.uk. Bus: 24, 41, 42).

 ✔ **The Royal Oak** is where Old Town meets the South Side, just a few minutes' walk from the Royal Mile off South Bridge. The pub is the home of live Scottish folk music. On Sundays from 8:30 p.m. on, various guests play at the "Wee Folk Club." Tickets are £3 ($5.50). The Royal Oak is open daily until 2 a.m. 1 Infirmary St. (☎ **0131-557-2967;** Bus: 3, 5, 8, or 2)

 ✔ **Sandy Bell's** offers live folk or traditional music virtually every night from about 9 p.m. and all day Saturday and Sunday. This small pub near the Museum of Scotland is a landmark for Scottish and Gaelic culture. Sandy Bell's is open Monday through Saturday from 11:30 a.m.to 1 a.m. and Sunday from 12:30 p.m. to 11 p.m. 25 Forrest Rd. (☎ **0131-225-2751;** Bus: 2 or 42)

Rock, pop, and jazz

Although it's not listed here, the very big acts — whether Bob Dylan, REM, or Robbie Williams, for example — that come to Edinburgh are likely to play outdoors at the national rugby facility, **Murrayfield Stadium.**

✔ **Corn Exchange,** in the West End, is a bit of a haul out of the city center. But this venue was meant to compete with the likes of Glasgow's infamous Barrowland ballroom, where touring groups absolutely love to appear. The comparison isn't really fair, but the Corn Exchange isn't a bad medium-to-small size hall (capacity 3,000) to see rock acts just on the verge of a major breakthrough or indie bands and DJ acts with more cult-like followings, such as the Hives, Massive Attack, or the Streets. 11 New Market Rd. (☎ **0131-477-3500;** www.ece.uk.com; Bus: 4 or 28)

✔ **The Liquid Room** has space for less than 1,000. This is Edinburgh's best venue for seeing the sweat off the brows of groups. Mostly booked by local bands like Mull Historical Society and visiting indie acts such as the Datsuns, it's also a busy dance club when not hosting such groups. 9c Victoria St. (☎ **0131-225-2564;** www.liquidroom.com; Bus: 35)

Dance clubs

Clubbing isn't quite as popular now as it was in the 1980s and 1990s, but it still draws more people than the folk, jazz, and classic music scenes combined. In this section, I've listed just a sampling of the clubs in and around Edinburgh.

✔ **Bongo Club** offers a varied music policy throughout the week — funk, dub, and experimental. This venue has more reasonably priced drinks than many. The cover charge can be up to £8 ($15). The club's open daily from 10 p.m. to 3 a.m. Moray House, 37 Holyrood Rd. (☎ **0131-558-7604;** www.outoftheblue.org; Bus: 35)

✔ **Po Na Na** is a branch of a successful chain of clubs in Britain. The theme is a Moroccan casbah with décor to match thanks to wall mosaics, brass lanterns, and artifacts shipped in from Marrakech. The dance mix varies from hip hop and funk to disco and sounds of the 80s. The cover can be up to £5 ($9). Po Na Na's open daily until 3 a.m. 43B Frederick St. (☎ **0131-226-2224;** www.ponana.co.uk; Bus: 80)

✔ **Venue** was, at the time of this writing, perhaps the most important mainstream club on the scene and a place to catch live music, too. Techno and house appear to rule the roost, although with three floors, you may well find something different on each level. The cover charge varies from £3–£12 ($5.50–$22). Venue's open Thursday through Sunday from 10:30 p.m. to 3 a.m. 15–21 Calton Rd. (☎ **0131-557-3073;** www.edinvenue.com; Bus: 2 or 35)

Bars and pubs

The most active areas for pubs and clubs are the **Cowgate** and **Grassmarket** in the Old Town and **Broughton Street** in New Town, although the university precincts on the South Side are lively, as are the pubs near **The Shore** in the Port of Leith. Most bars and pubs are open Sunday through Thursday from 11 a.m. or noon until 11 p.m. or midnight, often closing later on Fridays and Saturdays.

✔ **The Abbotsford's** bartenders have been pouring pints since around 1900. (Not the same bartenders, of course!) The gaslight era is still alive here thanks to the preservation of the dark paneling and ornate plaster ceiling. The ales on tap change about once a week, and you can find a good selection of single malt whiskies, too. Drinks are served Monday through Saturday from 11 a.m. to 11 p.m. Platters of food are dispensed from the bar Monday through Saturday from noon to 3 p.m. and 5:30 to 10 p.m. 3 Rose St. (☎ **0131-225-5276;** Bus: 3, 28, or 45)

✔ **Black Bo's** is a stone's throw from the Royal Mile. Many visitors may find its dark walls and mix-and-match furniture downright plain, but I think it has a rather unforced hipness. And due to its proximity to the hostels of Blackfriars Street, Black Bo's often hosts chatty groups of young foreigners enjoying a pint or two. DJs play from Wednesday to Saturday; downstairs is a pool room with juke box, and next door is a mostly vegetarian restaurant — although no food is served in the bar itself. Drinks are served daily from 5 p.m. to 1 a.m. 57 Blackfriars St. (☎ **0131-557-6136;** Bus: 35)

✔ **Bow Bar,** located just below Edinburgh Castle, is a classic Edinburgh pub that appears little changed by time or tampered with by foolish trends. Surprise: It's only a few more than a dozen years old. Nevermind that, though. The pub looks the part of a classic and features some eight cask-conditioned ales, which change regularly. The Scottish brewed options may include the dark and smooth Lia Fail (Gaelic for "Stone of Destiny," the rock on which Scottish kings were crowned until the 13th century) from the Perthshire-based Inveralmond Brewery. Bow Bar's open Monday through Saturday from noon to 11:30 p.m. and Sunday from 12:30 to 11 p.m. 80 West Bow (☎ **0131-226-7667;** Bus: 2 or 35)

✔ **Café Royal Circle Bar** is a well-preserved Victorian-era pub. Spacious booths combined with plenty of room around the island bar create a comfortable and stylish place to drink. The bar's hours are Monday through Wednesday from 11 a.m. to 11 p.m., Thursday from 11 a.m. to midnight, Friday and Saturday from 11 a.m. to 1 a.m., and Sunday from 12:30 to 11 p.m. Above-average food from the same kitchen as the neighboring oyster bar/restaurant is served daily until about 1 p.m. 17 W. Register St. (☎ **0131-556-1884;** Bus: 8 or 13)

✔ **Opal Lounge,** in New Town, is an excellent example of the so-called modern style bar. After opening in 2001, it became the haunt of Prince William when the handsome heir to the British throne attended St. Andrew's University. Opal Lounge draws a predominantly young, well-dressed, and affluent crowd, combining a long list of cocktails with a cavernous underground space. Drinks are served daily from noon to 3 a.m.; food of an Asian-fusion nature is served from daily from noon to 10 p.m. 51a George St. (☎ **0131-226-2275**; Bus: 13, 19, or 41)

✔ **The Outhouse** is one of the more contemporary outfits on busy Broughton Street. The bar was renovated in 2003 with rich brown hues. During good weather spells, a beer garden out back offers an excellent open-air retreat and some outdoor heaters help take the chill off the night. Drinks are served daily from 11 a.m. to 1 a.m. 14 Broughton St. (☎ **0131-557-6688**; Bus: 8 or 17)

✔ **The Shore,** down in Leith, fits seamlessly into the seaside port ambience without resorting to a lot of the usual decorations of cork and netting. The place is small, but on nice days they put a few seats out front to soak in the afternoon sun. On three nights of the week, you can find live folk and jazz music. Drinks are served Monday to Saturday from 11 a.m. to midnight and Sunday from 12:30 p.m. to midnight. Food is served both in the bar and in the adjoining dining room Monday through Friday from noon to 2:30 p.m. and 6:30 to 10 p.m. and Saturday and Sunday from 12:30 to 3 p.m. and 6:30 to 10 p.m. 3–4 The Shore (☎ **0131-553-5080**; Bus: 16 or 36)

Going to the cinema

✔ **The Cameo,** is perhaps the Edinburgh movie house with the most character. It screens just about everything (*Trainspotting* received its premier here), but it normally carries repertory, art house, foreign, and independent films. Every Sunday, a double bill matinee is offered. There's a bar on the premises, and you can take your drink along to the movie. Tickets are £3.50–£5.20 ($6.50–$9.50). 38 Home St. (☎ **0131-228-4141;** www.picturehouses.co.uk; Bus: 10 or 45)

✔ **The Filmhouse,** the capital's most important cinema, is the focus of the Edinburgh Film Festival — one of the oldest annual film festivals in the world. The movies shown here are foreign and art house, classic and experimental, documentary and shorts. Plus, the Filmhouse hosts discussions and lectures with directors during the Festival and at other points throughout the year. The cafe/bar does drinks, serves light meals, and remains open late. Consider this a must-stop for any visiting film buffs. Tickets range from £1.20–£5.50 ($2–$10). 88 Lothian Rd. (☎ **0131-228-2688;** www.filmhousecinema.com; Bus: 10, 22, or 30)

Fast Facts: Edinburgh

American Express

The office is at 69 George St., at Frederick Street (☎ 0131-718-2501; Bus: 13, 19, or 41). It's open Monday, Tuesday, Thursday, and Friday from 9 a.m. to 5:30 p.m. On Wednesdays, the hours are 9:30 a.m. to 5:30 p.m. and on Saturdays 9 a.m. to 5 p.m.

Babysitters

The most reliable services are provided by Guardians Baby Sitting Service, 13 Eton Terrace (☎ 0131-337-4150).

Business Hours

In Edinburgh, banks are usually open Monday through Friday from 9 or 9:30 a.m. to 4 or 5 p.m., with some branches sometimes shutting early one day a week and opening late on another. Shops are generally open Monday through Saturday from 9 or 10 a.m. to 6 p.m.; on Thursdays, retail stores are open late, usually until about 8 p.m. Many shops are now open on Sundays, as well. In general, business hours are Monday through Friday from 9 a.m. to 5 p.m., although some offices will close early on Fridays. Food supermarkets generally keep later hours.

Currency Exchange

Many banks in the Old and New Towns exchange currency. Post offices run *bureaux de change* as does the Edinburgh Information Office (☎ 0131-473-3800). Major hotels also exchange currency but charge a premium for the service. ATM machines in the city center are linked to major banking systems such as Cirrus and Plus, so you'll almost definitely be able to draw money directly from your bank account at home.

Dentists

If you have a dental emergency, go to the Edinburgh Dental Institute, 39 Lauriston Place (☎ 0131-536-4900; Bus: 35), open Monday through Friday from 9 a.m. to 3 p.m. Alternatively, call the National Health Service Helpline (☎ 0800-224-488).

Doctors

You can seek help from the Edinburgh Royal Infirmary, 1 Lauriston Place (☎ 0131-536-1000; Bus: 35). The emergency department is open 24 hours.

Emergencies

Call ☎ **999** in an emergency to summon the police, an ambulance, or firefighters. This is a free call.

Hot Lines

Edinburgh and Lothian Woman's Aid is available by calling ☎ 0131-229-1419. Lothian Gay and Lesbian Switchboard (☎ 0131-556-4049) offers advice from 7:30 p.m. to 10 p.m. daily; the Lesbian Line is ☎ 0131-557-0751. You can reach the Rape Crisis Centre at ☎ 0141-331-1990.

Internet Access

EasyEverything, at 58 Rose St., between Frederick and Hanover streets (www.easyeverything.com; Bus: 42), is open daily from 7:30 a.m. to 10:30 p.m. It has 448 terminals. You can get online here for as little as 50p (93¢, although some shops require £1 coins.

Laundry/Dry Cleaning

For your dry cleaning needs, the most central service is probably at Johnson's Cleaners, 23 Frederick St. (☎ 0131-225-8095; Bus: 13, 19, or 42), which is open Monday through Friday from 8 a.m. to 5:30 p.m. and Saturday from 8:30 a.m. to 4 p.m.

Luggage Storage/Lockers

Given the tenor of the times, left luggage can prove problematic if an alert is in place. Generally speaking, you can store luggage in lockers at Waverley Station or with your hotel.

Newspapers

Published since 1817, *The Scotsman* is a quality daily newspaper with a national and international perspective, while its sister publication, the *Evening News,* concentrates more on local affairs. For comprehensive arts and entertainment listings and reviews of local shows, buy *The List* magazine, which is published every other Thursday and weekly during the Festival. *Metro,* a free daily (Monday through Friday) available on buses and in train stations, also gives listings of daily events.

Pharmacies

There are no 24-hour drugstores (called *chemists*) in Edinburgh. The one with probably the longest hours is the branch of Boots at 48 Shandwick Place, west of Princes Street (☎ 0131-225-6757; Bus: 12 or 25). It's open Monday through Friday from 8 a.m. to 8 p.m., Saturday from 8 a.m. to 6 p.m., and Sunday from 10:30 a.m. to 4:30 p.m.

Post Office

The Edinburgh Branch Post Office, St James Centre, is open Monday through Saturday from 9 a.m. to 5:30 p.m. For general postal information and customer service, call ☎ 0845-722-3344.

Restrooms

These are found at rail stations, terminals, restaurants, hotels, pubs, and department stores. A system of public toilets, often marked wc, is in place at strategic corners and squares throughout the city. They're safe and clean but likely to be closed late in the evening.

Safety

Edinburgh is generally thought to be safer than Glasgow — in fact, it's one of Europe's safest capitals for a visitor to stroll. But that doesn't mean crimes, especially muggings, don't occur. They do, largely because of Edinburgh's problems with drug abuse.

Weather

For weather forecasts of the day and 24 hours in advance, and for severe road-condition warnings, call the Met Office at ☎ 0870-900-0100. An advisor offers forecasts for the entire region and beyond. For online weather forecasts, check www.weather.com.

Chapter 12

Glasgow

*G*lasgow is only about 74km (46 miles) west of Scotland's capital, Edinburgh, but there's a noticeable contrast between the two cities. Glasgow (pronounced *glaaz*-go by natives) doesn't offer a fairy-tale setting but compensates with a lively culture, big-city feel, and gregarious locals.

Glasgow's origins are ancient, making Edinburgh seem comparatively young. Archeologists have uncovered evidence of Roman settlements in the city. In the sixth century, St. Kentigern (or St. Mungo) is believed to have begun a monastery at the site of **Glasgow Cathedral,** on a hillside along a burn (creek) that feeds into the **River Clyde.** The site's a logical one for settlement because it allows convenient access to ford the mighty Clyde before it widens on its way to the sea some 32km (20 miles) away.

Aside from the Cathedral itself, practically none of this medieval ecclesiastical center (which included a university) remains, and much of Glasgow's historical records (kept at the Cathedral) were lost during the Reformation. The city became Scotland's economic powerhouse in the 18th century and quickly grew into the country's largest city (it's still among the biggest in the UK). The boom began in earnest with the tobacco trade to the New World, in which Glasgow outpaced rivals such as London and Bristol. The city then became famous worldwide for shipbuilding and docks that produced the *Queen Mary, Queen Elizabeth,* and other fabled ocean liners. It was, for a while, the Second City of the Empire. But post-industrial decline gave Glasgow a poor reputation as a city of slums, particularly in contrast to the enduring charms of Edinburgh. Internationally, the city still struggles to convince those who may have seen Glasgow in the 1970s that it's a safe, vibrant, and cosmopolitan city today.

In the 1980s, Glasgow reversed its fortune by becoming Scotland's contemporary **cultural capital,** drawing talent from across the UK, whether in art or rock 'n' roll. Decades of grime were sandblasted away from its monumental Victorian buildings and one of Europe's best collections of art — the **Burrell** — found a permanent home. In 1990, the city was deemed the European Capital of Culture (a prestigious honor awarded by the European Council of Ministers), thus certifying the changes that occurred.

Glasgow's not a city without flaws, however. Serious pockets of poverty remain in its peripheral housing projects (called *estates* or *schemes*). A major motorway cuts a scar through the center of town, and although the splendor of what critics hailed as "the greatest surviving example of a Victorian city" is evident, Glasgow still prefers to knock buildings down and erect new structures.

Glasgow is a good gateway for exploring **Burns Country** in Ayrshire to the southwest. From Glasgow, you can also tour **Loch Lomond** and see some of the **Highlands,** and you're less than an hour away from **Stirling** and the **Trossach mountains.** Also on Glasgow's doorstep is the scenic estuary of the **Firth of Clyde,** with islands only a short ferry ride away.

Getting to Glasgow

Glasgow is centrally located in terms of transportation options. Most flights into Glasgow Airport from North America connect in London, but some major airlines offer direct service from the U.S. and Canada. If you're traveling from London, you can easily take the train to Glasgow's downtown station or fly to Glasgow Airport. If you're coming from elsewhere in Scotland, highway, train, and bus routes service the city in all directions. The bus station is a couple of blocks from George Square, and the two main train stations are both in the heart of the city. Figuring out the best way to come into Glasgow is easy — it all depends on the time you have and the flexibility you desire.

By air

Glasgow International Airport (☎ **0870-040-0008** or 0141-887-1111) is located at Abbotsinch, near Paisley, only about 16km (10 miles) west of the city via M8. Monday through Friday, British Airways runs almost hourly shuttle service between London's Heathrow Airport and Glasgow. The first flight departs London at 7:15 a.m. and the last flight leaves at 9:15 p.m.; service is reduced on weekends, depending on volume. For flight schedules and fares, call British Airways in London at ☎ **0870-551-1155** or log onto www.britishairways.com, which offers a slight discount on ticket prices. The British Airways Travel Shop in Glasgow is at 66 Gordon St. (☎ **0845-606-0747**).

The schedule of direct flights from North America to Glasgow is subject to change. In recent years, **American Airlines** (☎ **800-433-7300** or 0845-778-9789; www.aa.com or www.americanairlines.co.uk) has offered a daily nonstop flight to Glasgow from Chicago between mid-May and October, **Continental** has offered similar direct service out of Newark International, and **Air Canada** has flown nonstop between Glasgow and Toronto.

BMI (formerly British Midland; ☎ **0870-607-0555**; www.flybmi.com) offers internal UK and international flights. **Aer Lingus** (☎ **800-223-6537** or ☎ 0845-084-4444 at Dublin Airport; www.aerlingus.ie) flies daily from Dublin to Glasgow.

South of Glasgow is **Prestwick International Airport** (☎ **0871-223-0700**), which is favored by some of the low-budget airlines, such as **RyanAir.** Prestwick's on the railway line to Ayr, about a 45-minute ride from Glasgow's Central Station. Remember, as well, that **Edinburgh International Airport** is only about 90km (55 miles) away and shouldn't be discounted seeing as it greets many European and internal UK flights.

Orienting yourself

Like Edinburgh's, Glasgow's airport is fairly small and therefore presents little possibility of getting lost. Immigration control and customs agents are vigilant, but the scene is quite a bit more relaxed than at a giant air terminal such as London's Heathrow. Usually there is just one line (called a *queue*) for visitors from outside the European Union. Arrivals with EU passports can breeze right through.

Getting into town from the airport

Regular Glasgow CityLink bus service runs between the airport and the city center, terminating at the Buchanan Street Bus Station. The ride takes only about 20 minutes (but much longer during rush hours) and costs £4 ($7.40). A taxi to the city center costs about £15 ($28).

By train

Trains from London arrive in Glasgow at **Central Station** in the heart of the city (call National Rail Enquiries; ☎ **08457-48-49-50** for rail and fare info). The trains that directly link London and Glasgow (via Preston and Carlisle) on the so-called West Coast Main Line don't have the same reputation for timeliness and efficiency as those going to Edinburgh. However, the semi-privatized company responsible for railway mainte-nance, Network Rail, is spending literally billions to upgrade the line and create a faster service.

But work has been slow, and while it's ongoing, travel is subject to frequent delays. The trains (operated by Virgin; ☎ **08457-222-333**; www.virgin.com/trains) on the West Coast Main Line depart from London's Euston Station every hour or so and the trip to Glasgow gen-erally takes 5½ hours these days. If you plan a trip on the West Coast

Main Line, however, call and find out if any major "track works" are scheduled during your journey. If so, you can expect delays and the possibility of riding on a bus for a portion of the trip.

You may prefer trains run by operators GNER (www.gner.co.uk) from London's Kings Cross station up the East Coast Main Line via Newcastle, Edinburgh, and across (via Motherwell) to Glasgow. The trip takes about the same amount of time as one on the West Coast Main Line. Standard class off-peak fares bought in advance range from around £25 to £36 ($46–$66); off-peak first class fares purchased in advance cost about £60 ($111); and the fully flexible, "buy anytime, travel anytime" standard open return fare is upwards of £180 ($333). The Caledonian Sleeper service for overnight travel can cost about £90 ($166) if purchased in advance.

Glasgow's Central Station is also the terminus for trains from the southwest of Scotland and a hub for numerous trains to city suburbs in most directions. A ten-minute walk away (or via shuttle bus 398) is **Queen Street Station.** From here, a **ScotRail** shuttle service to and from Edinburgh runs every 15 minutes during the day and every 30 minutes in the evenings until about 11:30 p.m. The round-trip fare during off-peak times (travel between 9:15 a.m. and 4:30 p.m. and after 6:30 p.m.) is £7.90 ($14.50), and the trip takes just under an hour.

Trains to the north (Stirling, Aberdeen, and such Highland destinations as Oban, Inverness, and Fort William) as well as to Glasgow's suburbs also run frequently through Queen Street Station. By the way, Glasgow has the biggest commuter rail network in Britain after London.

By bus

The journey from London to Glasgow by bus can take at least 8 hours. **National Express** (☎ **0870-580-8080;** www.nationalexpress.com) runs buses daily (typically at 9 a.m., noon, and 10:30 p.m. for direct service) from London's Victoria Coach Station to Glasgow's **Buchanan Street Bus Station** (☎ **0870-608-2608**), about two blocks north of the Queen Street Station on North Hanover Street. The round-trip fare is £37 ($68), although it's cheaper if you book more than seven days in advance. Scottish **CityLink** (☎ **0870-550-5050;** www.citylink.co.uk) also has frequent bus service to and from Edinburgh, with a one-way ticket costing £3 to £5 ($5.50–$9.25).

By car

Glasgow is 74km (46 miles) west of Edinburgh, 356km (221 miles) north of Manchester, and some 625km (388 miles) north of London. From England and the south, you reach Glasgow by the M1 or M5 to the M6 in the Midlands, which becomes the M74 at Carlisle. The M74 runs north to southeastern conurbation of greater Glasgow, where drivers can link with the M8, which runs right through the city's center before heading west. The M8 also links Glasgow and Edinburgh.

Other routes into the city are M77 (A77) from Ayr and A8 from the west (this becomes M8 around the port of Glasgow). A82 comes in from the northwest (the Western Highlands) on the north bank of the Clyde, and A80 also goes into the city. (This route is the southwestern section of M80 and M9 from Stirling.)

Orienting Yourself in Glasgow

The monumental heart of Glasgow lies north of the **River Clyde.** The area's divided between the larger and mostly Victorian **Commercial Centre** and the more compact district now designated the **Merchant City** (in honor of the tobacco and cotton "lords" who lived and ran businesses there from the 1700s). The Commercial Centre is a vibrant modern city that offers loads of shopping opportunities on the pedestrian-friendly stretches of Argyle, Buchanan, and Sauchiehall streets. You can find art galleries, theatres, multiplex cinemas, music halls, and literally hundreds of bars and restaurants. Meanwhile the adjacent Merchant City is to Glasgow as SoHo is to Manhattan — full of warehouses recently converted to condos, stylish bars, and trendy restaurants. If the river creates a southern boundary for "downtown" Glasgow, then the M8 motorway creates both its western and northern limits. The eastern boundary is set by the **High Street,** which is historically the heart of the city.

Medieval Glasgow was demolished by the well-meaning though history-destroying urban renewal schemes of late Georgian and Victorian Glasgow. Practically nothing remains to give any idea of how the city looked before the 18th-century boom, which is a particular shame because, by some accounts, it was once one of Europe's most attractive medieval burghs. Still standing on the hill at the top of the High Street, however, is **Glasgow Cathedral,** an excellent example of pre-Reformation Gothic architecture that dates in part to the 12th century. Across the square is Provand's Lordship, the city's oldest house, built in the 1470s. Down the High Street you find the Tolbooth Steeple (1626) at Glasgow Cross, and nearer the River Clyde is **Glasgow Green,** one of Britain's first large-scale public parks. Glasgow has more green spaces per resident than any other European city.

The city's salubrious and leafy **West End,** home to the University of Glasgow, is just a short journey from the city center, on the other side of the M8. The terraces of Woodlands Hill, rising to Park Circus, afford excellent views. Across Kelvingrove Park is a red sandstone palace, the city's **Art Gallery and Museum** (closed for renovation until 2006). Nearby, the tower of Glasgow University dominates Gilmorehill. **Byres Road,** the social and entertainment destination in the West End, is a street full of restaurants, cafes, bars, and shops.

The city's **South Side** sprawls from the River Clyde and is largely residential. Aside from the city's shiny **Science Centre** on the south bank, the area may offer little of immediate interest to the casual visitor. But a

little more than 5km (3 miles) southwest of Glasgow's center in wooded
Pollok Country Park is the vaunted **Burrell Collection.** This museum of
antiquity and art has become one of Scotland's top tourist attractions.
The commercial heart of the South Side is **Shawlands,** which offers an
increasing number of good restaurants, and nearby **Queens Park** is a
hilly classic of Victorian planning.

Glasgow's **East End** is only slowly redeveloping after its industrial heyday.
Once the site of coal mining and steel production, it's the least affluent
district in Glasgow and, according to surveys, is one of the poorest and
least healthy areas in all of Europe. But statistics don't tell the entire
story. Visitors to the East End's **Gallowgate** on the weekend should see
the flea market stalls of the **Barras.** And East End neighborhoods such
as **Dennistoun** are gradually drawing young, creative types who can no
longer afford apartments in the West End or on the South Side — a renaissance is simmering.

Introducing the neighborhoods

Glasgow's composed of a variety of neighborhoods, from the compact
area of imposing buildings in Merchant City to the University of Glasgow-
dominated Hillhead.

City Centre

Cathedral (Townhead)

St. Mungo apparently arrived here in AD 543 and built his little church in
what's now the northeastern part of the city's center. **Glasgow Cathedral**
was at one time surrounded by a variety of buildings: prebendal manses
and the so-called Bishops Castle, which stood between the cathedral's
west facade and the Provand's Lordship, which still exists in largely its
original form. East of the Cathedral is one of Britain's largest Victorian
cemeteries, Glasgow's Central Necropolis.

Merchant City

The city's first New Town development lies southeast of the city's modern
core. Merchant City extends from Trongate and Argyle Street in the south
to George Street in the north. Because the medieval closes off the High
Street were regarded as festering sores, the affluent moved to develop
areas to the west. Now, Merchant City is one of few inner city areas of
Glasgow in which people reside.

Gallowgate

Once one of the streets that prosperous city businessmen strolled,
Gallowgate is the beginning of the city's East End today. The Saracen's
Head Inn stood here and took in such distinguished guests as Dr. Samuel
Johnson and James Boswell in 1774 after the duo's famous tour of the
Hebrides. Today, Gallowgate is best known for the Barras market and
Barrowland, a one-time ballroom that now is a popular live music venue.

Saltmarket

The first settlements in Glasgow were on the hill by the Cathedral, but existing almost as early were dwellings in this area at the opposite end of the High Street, along the banks of the Clyde. Saltmarket served as the trading post where the river could be forded. The Bridgegate leads to Victoria Bridge, the first crossing erected over the Clyde. Constructed in the 1850s, this bridge is the oldest Clyde crossing in Glasgow.

Commercial Centre

The biggest of the central districts of Glasgow, Commercial Centre includes areas of 19th-century development, such as **Blythswood** and **Charing Cross** (although the latter was severed from the city by the M8 freeway). This area offers Victorian architecture at its finest. Luckily, even though the city had a mind to tear it all to the ground in the middle to late 1960s, city leaders realized that it had something of international interest and preserved the area instead.

Broomielaw

It has been said that, "the Clyde made Glasgow." From docks here in Broomielaw, Glasgow imported tobacco, cotton, and rum and shipped its manufactured goods around the world. After becoming a rather lost and neglected part of the city, Broomielaw today is targeted for renewal, with luxury flats planned along the riverbank.

Garnethill

Up the steep slopes north of Sauchiehall Street, this neighborhood is best known for the Charles Rennie Mackintosh-designed Glasgow School of Art. Developed in the late 1800s, Garnethill offers good views of the city and is also home to the first proper synagogue built in Scotland.

West End

Woodlands

Centering on Park Circus at the crown of Woodlands Hill, this neighborhood is the first one just west of the M8 freeway. Woodlands is a mix of residential tenements and retail stretches, particularly on Woodland and Great Western roads. South to the river lies the district of **Finnieston,** whose most visible landmark is the old shipbuilding crane that stands like some giant dinosaur. Along the Clyde is the Scottish Exhibition Centre. West of Woodlands is **Kelvingrove,** with its Art Gallery and Museum and the impressive park.

Hillhead

With the Gilmorehill campus of the University of Glasgow, Hillhead is rather dominated by academia. Its main boulevard is Byres Road, which is the High Street of the West End. In addition to the university, two other major institutions reside in Hillhead: BBC Scotland on Queen Margaret Drive and NHS Western Infirmary next to the University.

Partick

The railway station at Partick is one of the few in the city to translate the stop's name into Gaelic: Partaig. Indeed, the neighborhood has a bit of Highland pride, although there's no particular evidence that Highland people have settled here in great masses. Partick is one of the less pretentious districts of the central West End. To the north are leafy and affluent **Hyndland** and **Dowanhill.**

South Side

Gorbals

In the early part of the twentieth century, this neighborhood, just across the Clyde from the city's center, developed a rather notorious reputation for mean streets and unsanitary tenements. So, the city demolished Gorbals in the early 1960s and erected sets of modern high apartment towers, which in turn developed a reputation for unsavory and unpleasant conditions. Today, the towers are coming down and the New Gorbals has been developed on a more human scale, although the fabric of the place still seems torn and frayed. One good thing is that it's home to the Citizens' Theatre, one of the most innovative and democratic in the UK.

Govan

Govan was settled as early as the 10th century, making it another ecclesiastical focal point along with St. Kentigern's north of the river. Until 1912, it was an independent burgh and was one of the key shipbuilding districts on the south banks of the Clyde. The first shipyard in the neighborhood, Mackie & Thomson, opened in 1840. But with the demise of shipbuilding, the fortunes of Govan fell, too. Today, the Science Centre and other developments planned in area (such as a new Transport Museum) are hoped to revive Govan's fortunes.

Pollokshaws

Along with **Pollokshields** and **Crosshill,** these neighborhoods form the heart of the city's more modern South Side suburbs. Pollok Park and the Burrell Collection are the primary tourist attractions, and Queens Park is perhaps better and more verdant than Kelvingrove Park, even if it lacks the monuments and statues of that park in the West End.

Finding information after you arrive

The **Greater Glasgow and Clyde Valley Tourist Board,** 11 George Sq. (☎ **0141-204-4400;** Underground: Buchanan Street), is possibly the country's most helpful office. In addition to piles of brochures, you can find a small bookshop, *bureau de change,* and a hotel reservation service that charges a booking fee of £2 ($3.70) for local accommodations. During peak season, the office is open Monday through Saturday from 9 a.m. to 7 p.m. and Sunday from 10 a.m. to 6 p.m. Hours are more limited during winter months. Gathering information about travel can be a bit more frustrating. Traveline (☎ **0870-608-26078**) offers bus timetable information and advice on routes but can't quote ticket prices.

Getting Around Glasgow

One of the best ways to explore Glasgow is by foot. The center of town is laid out on a grid, which makes map reading relatively easy. However, some of the city's significant attractions, such as the Burrell Collection, are in surrounding districts and for those you'll need to rely on public transportation or a car.

By subway

The underground, affectionately called the "Clockwork Orange" (due to the vivid hues of the trains, which travel in a virtual circle), offers a 15-stop system linking the City Centre, West End, and a bit of the South Side. Generally, the wait for trains is no more than five to eight minutes, but trains run at longer intervals on Sunday and at night. The one-way fare is £1 ($1.85), or you can buy a 20-trip ticket for £12.50 ($23). The underground runs Monday through Saturday from 6:30 a.m. to about 11:30 p.m. and Sunday from 11 a.m. to about 6 p.m.

The **Transcentre** (local ticket sales only) at St. Enoch Square, two blocks from the Central Station (Underground: St. Enoch), is generally open Monday through Saturday from 8:30 a.m. to 5:30 p.m., but it closes early on Wednesday. On Sunday, the hours are 10 a.m. to 5 p.m.

Glasgow and the surrounding region have the largest train network in Great Britain after London, and these suburban trains are useful for visitors. Like the subway, the system is operated by **Strathclyde Passenger Transport (SPT),** and service runs to both Central (upper and lower levels) and Queen Street (lower level only) stations. During the day, trains run as frequently as every ten minutes or so to destinations in the West End and on the South Side. Service is less frequent after the evening rush hour and terminates around midnight. The trains aren't cheap by European standards; a typical round-trip (return) fare is £1.70 ($3.15).

For families on an excursion, the **Daytripper** ticket is an excellent value. For £15 ($28), two adults and up to four children (5–15 years old) can travel anywhere in the system (including broad swaths of Ayrshire) by suburban train, the underground, most buses, and even a few ferries. For one adult and two children the fare is £8.50 ($16).

For information on SPT tickets only, call ☎ **0141-333-3708** Monday through Saturday from 9 a.m. to 5 p.m., or log onto www.spt.co.uk.

By bus

Glasgow has an extensive (and somewhat confusing) bus service run by the privately owned **First** company. Recently, First rather cleverly began marketing the network as the "Over Ground." Routes tend to run between east and west or north and south, with all buses coming though the center of Glasgow. Service is frequent during the day. After 11 p.m. service is curtailed on most routes, but some (for example the 9, 12, 40, and 62) run all-night fares. Typically, one-way (single) fares cost no more than

Glasgow Orientation

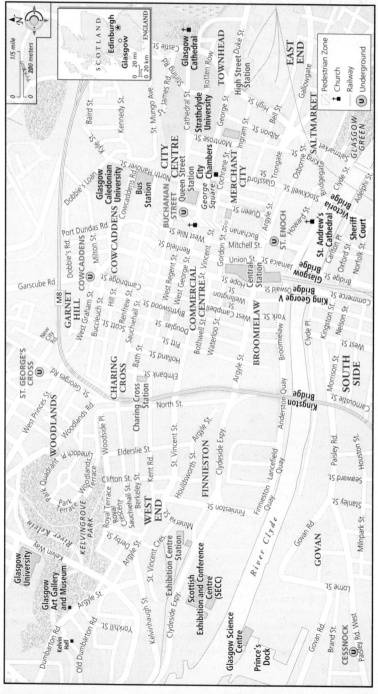

£1.15 ($2), and for £2.20 ($4), you can use the buses all day long with few restrictions. A weeklong ticket costs £11 ($20). The city bus station is the **Buchanan Street Bus Station,** located at Killarmont Street. The "Traveline" number (☎ **0870-608-2608**) gives timetable information (but not fares). You can also log onto www.firstgroup.com for more detailed information about bus service.

By taxi

Metered taxis are the same excellent ones as found in Edinburgh or London — the so-called Fast Black, which you can hail or pick up at taxi ranks in the central city. Alternatively, you can call **TOA Taxis** at ☎ **0141-429-7070.** No matter the company, fares are displayed on a meter next to the driver. When a taxi is available on the street, a sign on the roof is lit. Most taxi trips within the city cost £4 to £6 ($7.50–$11). A surcharge is imposed for late night/early morning runs. Generally speaking, you should give the driver a ten percent tip. **Private hire** cars run by various companies are also available, but they can't be hailed.

By car

You're better off using public transportation (especially at rush hour) than driving, but Glasgow goes a long way toward accomodating car use by offering several multi-story parking lots. Metered parking is available but expensive, and you need plenty of coins to feed the meter, which issues a ticket that you must then affix to your windshield. Some zones in residential areas are marked PERMIT HOLDERS ONLY — your vehicle may be towed if you lack a permit. A double yellow line along the curb indicates no parking at any time. A single yellow line along the curb indicates restrictions, too, so be sure and read the signs on what the limitations are for a particular area before choosing a spot.

If you want to rent a car, it's best to arrange the rental in advance. But if you want to rent a car locally, most companies will accept your foreign driver's license. All the major rental agencies are represented at the airport. In addition, **Avis Rent-a-Car** is at 70 Lancefield St. (☎ **0141-221-2827**), **Budget Rent-a-Car** is at 101 Waterloo St. (☎ **0141-221-9241**), **Europcar** is at 38 Anderson Quay (☎ **0141-248-8788**), and **Arnold Clark** offices can be found at multiple locations (☎ **0845-607-4500**).

By bicycle

Although bikes aren't as widely used in Glasgow as in Edinburgh, most parts of the city are fine for biking. For what the Scots call "cycle hire," go to a well-recommended shop about a kilometer (½ mile) west of the town center, just off Byres Road: **West End Cycles,** 16–18 Chancellor St. (☎ **0141-357-1344**; Underground: Hillhead or Kelvinhall or Bus: 9 or 18). The shop's close to the National Cycle Trail that leads to Loch Lomond, and it rents bikes well suited to the hilly terrain of Glasgow and surrounding areas. Payment of £15 ($28) per day or £85 ($157) per week and a cash deposit of £100 ($185) or the imprint of a valid credit card are necessary for security.

On foot

Walking Glasgow is the best way to see the city center and most of the town (but using trains, buses, or taxis if the distances seem too great is perfectly okay, too). Some streets have even been made into pedestrian malls. But as in any bustling metropolis that's now rather over-dependent on the use of cars, pedestrians should always exercise caution at intersections and other crossing points. Glasgow drivers (including those behind the wheels of city buses) can be a tad aggressive at times.

Cars drive on the left, so when you cross a street, make certain to look both ways.

Staying in Style

The tourist trade in Glasgow is less seasonal than in Edinburgh, with fewer visitors in general coming to Scotland's largest city. However, Glasgow has become a popular spot for business conferences, and the increase in budget-airline flights from the European continent seems to have increased the overall number of visitors. So if, for example, an international association of dentists is in town, finding accommodations may be difficult. Until recently, many tourism industry observers said Glasgow suffered from a shortage of hotel rooms, but new places such as the Radisson SAS have altered the equation.

Whenever you decide to visit, I recommend that you reserve a room in advance. Some rates are predictably high (especially so if the pound remains strong), but many business-oriented hotels offer bargains on weekends, and the number of budget options is increasing. Plus, the Internet can be a real treasure trove of reduced room rates. The Glasgow and Clyde Valley Tourism Office (www.visitscotland.com) offers an **Information & Booking Hot Line** (☎ **0845-225-5121** from within the UK and ☎ **4-1506-832-121** from outside the UK). Lines are open (local time) Monday through Friday from 8 a.m. to 8 p.m., Saturday from 9 a.m. to 5:50 p.m. and Sunday from 10 a.m. to 4 p.m. The fee for this booking service is £3 ($5.50).

The top hotels and B&Bs

The ArtHouse
$$$ Commerical Centre

This handsome Edwardian building, only a few blocks from both Central Street and Queen Street train stations, was originally built to house school board offices. But more recently, it became one of the most striking hotels in the city's center, with clientele that ranges from travelers with style sense to the occasional top-ranking pop musician. Dramatic colors and textures blend in perfectly with the older structure while commissioned art and period pieces evoke some of the original splendor. In 2004, new owners took over the operation, but whatever the changes, expect the

Glasgow Accommodations

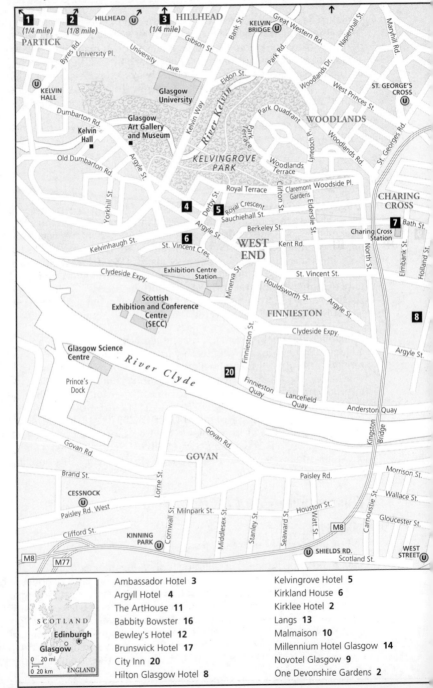

Ambassador Hotel **3**
Argyll Hotel **4**
The ArtHouse **11**
Babbity Bowster **16**
Bewley's Hotel **12**
Brunswick Hotel **17**
City Inn **20**
Hilton Glasgow Hotel **8**

Kelvingrove Hotel **5**
Kirkland House **6**
Kirklee Hotel **2**
Langs **13**
Malmaison **10**
Millennium Hotel Glasgow **14**
Novotel Glasgow **9**
One Devonshire Gardens **2**

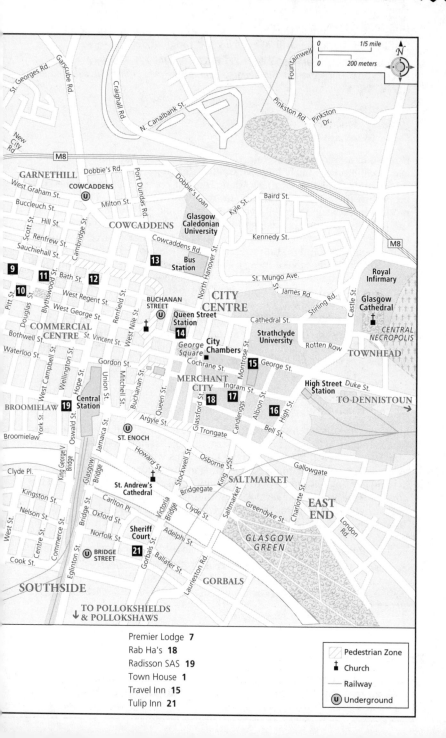

Premier Lodge **7**
Rab Ha's **18**
Radisson SAS **19**
Town House **1**
Travel Inn **15**
Tulip Inn **21**

Pedestrian Zone
✚ Church
— Railway
Ⓤ Underground

sleek furniture and state-of-the-art bathrooms to remain. The hotel's busy restaurant, Arthouse Grill, serves a good range of dishes.

See map p. 198. 129 Bath St. ☎ **0141-221-6789.** *Fax: 0141-221-6777.* www.arthouse hotel.com. *Underground: Buchanan Street. Rack rates: from £110 ($203) double. AE, DC, MC, V.*

Babbity Bowster
$–$$ Merchant City

Housed in a reconstructed late 18th century house, the Babbity Bowster is a small inn with fairly large character, due in part to the classic design by brothers James and Robert Adam; the rest comes courtesy of the acerbic wit of owner Fraser Laurie (he with the eye patch). The units are modest but reasonably well-appointed (a couple only have showers). But the Babbity Bowster is designed to appeal to travelers who don't spend too much time in their rooms, anyway. The location is convenient to the many local pubs and restaurants in the nightlife hotbed of the Merchant City, and you only have a five- to ten-minute walk to the heart of central Glasgow. The Babbity's ground-level pub is convivial and notably civilized, with a sheltered beer garden, excellent bar meals, and live acoustic Scottish folk sessions on Saturdays. The second-floor restaurant, **Schottische,** offers French-influenced cooking in the evenings only.

See map p. 198. 16–18 Blackfriars St. (off High Street). ☎ **0141-552-5055.** *Fax: 0141-552-7774. Underground: Buchanan Street. Rack rates: £45–£80 ($83–$148) double. Rates include full breakfast. AE, MC, V.*

Brunswick Hotel
$$ Merchant City

In the heart of the Merchant City, the Brunswick Hotel is one of the hippest places to stay in Glasgow. The modern, minimalist design — from the popular cafe/bar **Brutti Ma Buoni** to the bedrooms with their sleek look — has aged well since the Brunswick's opening in the 1990s. The units are soothing and inviting with neutral tones, comfortable mattresses, and small but adequate bathrooms (several with both tub and shower). For all its trendiness, however, the Brunswick is far from pretentiously run. The owners are fun-loving cosmopolitans. Indeed, the cafe's name literally means "ugly but good," which may accurately describe the misshapen pizzas that the kitchen churns out but actually says more about the place's sense of humor.

See map p. 198. 106–108 Brunswick St. ☎ **0141-552-0001.** *Fax: 0141-552-1551.* www.brunswickhotel.co.uk. *Underground: Buchanan Street. Rack rates: £55–£100 ($100–$185) double; £400 ($740) penthouse suite. Rates include buffet breakfast. AE, DC, MC, V.*

Hilton Glasgow Hotel
$$$$ Commerical Centre

Glasgow's only true five-star hotel is centrally located but oddly situated, looking over the stretch of M8 freeway that slashes through the city.

Perhaps the caliber of guests ensures that they all take taxis or have private cars, because actually trying to get to and from the place on foot can be a bit of a nightmare. Still, the Hilton's a dignified and modern hotel, one that has a good deal of class and shine. The numerous units — plush and conservative — in the 20-story building offer fine city views. Residents on the executive floors enjoy complimentary breakfasts and evening canapes and cocktails in the Executive lounge. Dining options include a casual New York deli-style buffet, **Minsky's,** and a recently added Italian restaurant, **La Primavera,** as well as the posh **Camerons,** with its first-rate and expensive modern Scottish cuisine.

See map p. 198. 1 William St. ☎ *800-445-8667 in the U.S. and Canada, or* ☎ *0141-204-5555. Fax: 0141-204-5004.* www.glasgow.hilton.com. *Suburban train: Central Station. Rack rates: £100–£180 ($185–$333) double; from £140 ($260) suite. Weekend discounts often available. AE, DC, MC, V.*

Kelvingrove Hotel
$$ **West End**

Three generations of Somerville family women have made their marks on this guesthouse since buying it in October 2002. They're welcoming hoteliers with 30 years experience running small lodges in Edinburgh, Inverness, and the isle of Arran. Usually either Muriel, Valerie, or Mandy is on duty during the day, orienting new arrivals, answering questions, booking cabs, or chatting with visitors. The Kelvingrove's rooms are comfortable, have mainly modern furnishings, and are set within the converted flats on the ground and garden levels. Room 24 is a particularly bright and reasonably spacious family room with kitchenette. The Kelvingrove was elevated in 2004 to one of the 'best in its category' hotels in Glasgow.

See map p. 198. 944 Sauchiehall St. ☎ *0141-339-5011. Fax: 0141-339-6566.* www.kelvingrove-hotel.co.uk. *Underground: Kelvin Hall. Bus: 18, 62, or city sightseeing bus. Rack rates: £60 ($111) double. Rates include Scottish breakfast. MC, V.*

Langs
$$$ **Commercial Centre**

This contemporary hotel close to Glasgow Royal Concert Hall, the city's bus station, Buchanan Galleries shopping mall, and the towering UGC multiplex cinema calls itself an urban oasis. The main public space is **Oshi,** a Zen-influenced bar and restaurant with a 40-foot pool of water that runs between a waterfall and cauldron of fire. Very impressive, if just a little over the top. Bedrooms in various shapes, sizes, and configurations are available, and each room offers a certain flair. The smallest units are the studios, but guests can opt for a duplex, theme room, or a large suite. The beautiful bathrooms have power showers with body jets. Visitors also can be pampered at the hotel's own spa. In addition to Oshi's Asian fusion cuisine, **Las Brisas** offers excellent Scottish produce such as Aberdeen Angus or fresh fish in Mediterranean-style dishes.

See map p. 198. 2 Port Dundas Place. ☎ *0141-333-1500. Fax: 0141-333-5700.* www.langshotels.com. *Underground: Buchanan Street. Rack rates: £110–£160 ($203–$296) double. AE, DC, MC, V.*

Malmaison
$$$ **Charing Cross** **Commerical Centre**

Today, hip and sophisticated Malmaisons are spread across the UK, but the hotel chain began in Scotland. This one, a converted church with a fine Greek-styled exterior, offers only a few of the original details on the inside; the hotel's décor is sleek and modern. Units vary in size from quite cozy to average, but all are chic and well-appointed with special extras such as CD players, specially commissioned art, and top-of-the-line toiletries. You can find a popular brasserie and champagne bar in the vaulted spaces below reception.

See map p. 198. 278 W. George St. ☎ *0141-572-1000. Fax: 0141-572-1002.* www. malmaison.com. *Suburban train: Charing Cross. Rack rates: from £99 ($183) double weekend; from £129 ($239) double weeknights; from £165 ($305) suite. AE, DC, MC, V.*

Millennium Hotel Glasgow
$$$$ **George Square** **Commerical Centre**

Following a $5-million upgrade, this landmark hotel (once called the Copthorne and erected at the beginning of the 19th century) has been modernized with all the amenities and services you'd expect of any highly rated hotel. Just off the boundary of the Merchant City and adjacent to Queen Street Station, the hotel has a conservatory space for dining and drinks. It faces the city's central plaza, George Square, and offers views of the opulent Glasgow city chambers. The best units are at the front of the building; those in the rear offer no views worth writing home about. The ground-floor restaurant, **Brasserie on George Square,** offers an elegant, neo-colonial — but not stuffy — dining experience, while the hotel's more recently recast **Georgics Bar** has an excellent selection of wines, many served by the glass.

See map p. 198. George Square. ☎ *0141-332-6711. Fax: 0141-332-4264.* www. millenniumhotels.com. *Underground: Buchanan Street. Rack rates: from £165 ($305) double, from £220 ($407) suite. AE, DC, MC, V.*

One Devonshire Gardens
$$$$ **West End**

This hotel is the most glamorous the city has to offer — the place where the famous traditionally stay, whether gorgeous George Clooney or, er, interesting Michael Jackson. The town houses along this lane parallel to always busy Great Western Road were built in 1880 and are possibly more elegant today than in their heyday. Of the units, number 29, the so-called "luxury town house," is the most impressive. The suite includes a sitting room (with its own toilet) as well as a separate dressing chamber and master bedroom with four-poster bed and a full bathroom with spa, separate shower with computerized controls, and twin basins.

See map p. 198. 1 Devonshire Gardens. ☎ *0141-339-2001. Fax: 0141-337-1663.* www. onedevonshiregardens.com. *Underground: Hillhead. Rack rates: £145 ($268) double, £225–£485 ($416–$897) suites. AE, DC, MC, V.*

No frills in the City Centre

For basic, inexpensive accommodation from the better-known chains, Glasgow has a few options. Near Sauchiehall Street in the Charing Cross district is the **Novotel Glasgow** (181 Pitt St.; ☎ **0141-222-2775**; www.novotel.com) with 139 rooms at £65 ($122). Just across the Clyde in the gentrified New Gorbals, the **Tulip Inn** (80 Ballater St.; ☎ **0141-429-4233**) offers double rooms from £45 ($83) and has lots of free car parking. Above the Charing Cross railway stop is the 278-unit **Premier Lodge** (10 Elmbank Gardens; ☎ **0870-700-1394**; www.premierlodge.com) with rooms at £46 ($85).

Radisson SAS
$$$ **Commerical Centre**

Still shiny and new since its November 2002 opening, the Radisson has set architectural standards for hotels in Glasgow. Its dramatic and curving facade is just a stone's throw from Central Station, but it's in a slightly risky location on the fringe of a portion of the City Centre that's still being redeveloped. Contemporary units with blonde wood details and Scandinavian cool have all the modern conveniences. The 15,000-square-foot club and fitness facility includes a 15-meter pool and state of the art gym. **Collage** and **TaPaell'ya** offer two distinct dining options.

See map p. 198. 301 Argyle St. ☎ 0141-204-3333. Fax: 0141-204-3344. www.radisson sas.com. *Underground: St. Enoch. Rack rates: from £120 ($222) double. AE, DC, MC, V.*

Town House
$$–$$$ **West End**

This remains one of the most charming of the city's B&Bs — and a less expensive alternative to One Devonshire Gardens, which is just around the corner. The terraced stone Victorian house, which faces the rugby fields of Hillhead sports grounds, came under new ownership in January 2003. Eventually each of the 10 units will be restored with all the proper period details, such as ceiling rosettes or the wedding cake cornicing of the atmospheric main lounge with its Persian carpet, coal-burning fire, and art work (original paintings and prints) from the owner's own private collection. A shared computer in a common area provides guests with free Internet access. The only possible gripe about the individual units may be the less-attractive box rooms in several that contain shower, sink, and toilet. But otherwise, the hospitality, comfort, and ambience are excellent.

See map p. 198. 4 Hughenden Terrace (near Great Western and Hyndland roads). ☎ 0141-357-0862. Fax: 0141-339-9605. www.thetownhouseglasgow.com. *Underground: Hillhead. Rack rates: £72 ($133) double. Rate includes full breakfast. MC, V.*

Runner-up hotels and B&Bs

Ambassador Hotel

$$ West End   This small hotel in a circa-1900 Edwardian town house is one of the better B&Bs in Glasgow. After a refurbishment in 2002, the hotel looks quite stylish. It's well situated for exploring the West End, with many good restaurants or brasseries nearby on Byres Road. *See map p. 198. 7 Kelvin Dr.* ☎ *0141-946-1018. Fax: 0141-945-5377.* www.glasgowhotelsand apartments.co.uk.

Argyll Hotel

$$ West End   The Argyll lives up to its Scottish name: full of tartan and kilts. You almost expect this traditional feel to be part of a Highland lodge rather than urban inn. The hotel has a clutch of spacious family rooms, and one double has a firm four-poster bed and corner-filling bath tub. Note: All rooms are nonsmoking, but smoking is allowed in the hotel's bar. *See map p. 198. 969–973 Sauchiehall St.* ☎ *0141-337-3313. Fax: 0141-337-3283.* www.argyllhotelglasgow.co.uk.

Bewley's Hotel

$-$$ Commercial Centre   Bewley's Hotel rises impressively from the street, with oddly angled windows that appear to look down on the ground below. Run by an Ireland-based group, Bewley's basic room rate applies to larger units that can accommodate families. At 38 Bath St., Bewley's also lets one- and two-bedroom apartment suites suitable for families from £99 ($183) to £129 ($239). *See map p. 198. 110 Bath St.* ☎ *0141-353-0800. Fax: 0141-353-0900.* www.bewleyshotels.com.

City Inn

$$ West End   This smart hotel with its waterside terrace isn't exactly in the heart of the action — but neither is it very far away. Part of small chain with other hotels in London, Birmingham, Bristol, and Manchester, the City Inn is modern and contemporary with good facilities. *See map p. 198. Finnieston Quay.* ☎ *0141-240-1002. Fax: 0141-248-2754.* www.cityinn.com.

Kirkland House

$$ West End   The Kirkland is an impeccably maintained Victorian house (circa 1832). A mix of antiques and reproductions are used in the large units, where guests are served breakfast. Note: Credit cards are not accepted. *See map p. 198. 42 St. Vincent Crescent.* ☎ *0141-248-3458. Fax: 0141-221-5174.* www.kirkland.net43.co.uk.

Kirklee Hotel

$$ West End   A red-sandstone Edwardian terraced house with elegant bay windows near the West End's diverse night life, the Kirklee is often recommended locally. It's graced with a rose garden that has won several awards. Most of the high-ceilinged guest rooms are average size, but some are large enough to accommodate families. *See map p. 198. 11 Kensington Gate.* ☎ *0141-334-5555. Fax: 0141-339-3828.* www.kirkleehotel.co.uk.

Rab Ha's

$$ **Merchant City**   This small boutique hotel has overnight rooms above a popular and urbane pub on the ground level as well as a modern restaurant in the basement. The recently redesigned units have dark slate flooring in the bathrooms, specially commissioned glass, photographic prints, and flat screen televisions. *See map p. 198. 83 Hutcheson St.* ☎ *0141-572-0400. Fax: 0141-572-0402.* www.rabhas.com.

Travel Inn

$ **Merchant City**   A branch of an inexpensively priced chain of hotels, this hotel is functional if not particularly full of character. A fair amount of new construction is going on in the area, so the neighborhood can be noisy during the day. Rooms that overlook the old kirkyard and cemetery are preferable to those facing busy George Street and the Strathclyde University parking lot across the road. *See map p. 198. 187 George St.* ☎ *0870-238-3320. Fax: 0141-553-2719.* www.travelinn.co.uk.

Dining in Glasgow

Glasgow has seen tremendous growth in the number of restaurants since the mid-1990s, and the choices are now excellent. Although the city may not boast the Michelin stars that a couple of Edinburgh restaurants have earned, Glasgow has some seriously stylish dining rooms, budget-minded bistros, and a mix of ethnic eateries.

Today, some of the best fresh Scottish produce is served up here, whether it's shellfish and seafood from the nearby West Coast sea lochs, Ayrshire meat such as pork and lamb, or Aberdeen Angus steaks. You can also find an ever-increasing number of ethnic restaurants. The immigrant groups who have most influenced cuisine in the city are Italians and families from the Asian subcontinent, mainly the Punjab region. There's a surfeit of Italian and Indian restaurants, as well as a good choice of Chinese and Greek restaurants.

A lot of restaurants close on Sunday or Monday (sometimes both), and many lock up after lunch, reopening again for dinner at around 6 p.m. The hours listed here are for when food is served; bars on the premises may stay open longer.

For ideas on dining options, buy *The List* magazine's annual **Eating & Drinking Guide,** a comprehensive review of hundreds of eateries in Glasgow (and Edinburgh).

Scotland is getting better at welcoming families, but it's still a far cry from the Continental approach of, say, Italy or France. That said, give the local restaurants a try and resist the temptation to resort to well-known international chains or fast-food outlets.

Glasgow Dining

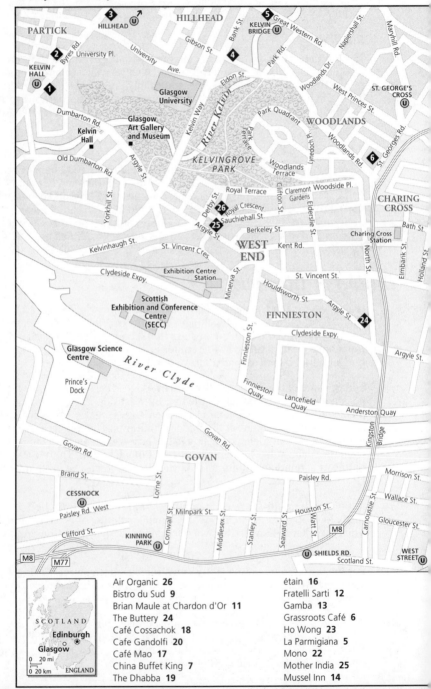

Air Organic **26**	étain **16**
Bistro du Sud **9**	Fratelli Sarti **12**
Brian Maule at Chardon d'Or **11**	Gamba **13**
The Buttery **24**	Grassroots Café **6**
Café Cossachok **18**	Ho Wong **23**
Cafe Gandolfi **20**	La Parmigiana **5**
Café Mao **17**	Mono **22**
China Buffet King **7**	Mother India **25**
The Dhabba **19**	Mussel Inn **14**

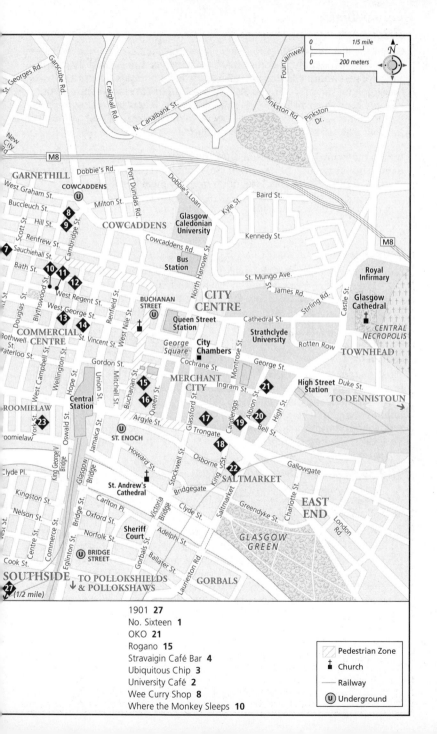

1901 **27**
No. Sixteen **1**
OKO **21**
Rogano **15**
Stravaigin Café Bar **4**
Ubiquitous Chip **3**
University Café **2**
Wee Curry Shop **8**
Where the Monkey Sleeps **10**

Pedestrian Zone
✝ Church
— Railway
Ⓤ Underground

Prices

Given the strength of the UK's currency since 2002, prices may well seem expensive, especially in comparison to the weak American dollar. Still, a range of restaurant choices is available for most budgets. The prices listed here include the 17.5 percent VAT (Value Added Tax), so you shouldn't see any hidden surprises when the bill comes. If you're looking for bargains, inquire about pre-theatre special menus, which can be as much as half the price of the regular dinner menu.

Lunch menus in Glasgow often offer the same food as the full dinner menus but at a much better price. So, if you're trying to save money on your food bills, have a big late lunch or early meal in the evening.

Log onto www.5pm.co.uk for a list of restaurants offering early dining deals.

Tipping

A gratuity of 10 percent is the minimum for service, although leave nothing if you were badly treated. On the other hand, if you were truly impressed with the service you received, consider leaving 15 to 20 percent. In a few restaurants, service is included in the bill automatically, but this charge can be deleted if the service was dreadful.

Smoking

Most restaurants have sections reserved for nonsmokers, and a growing number simply don't allow smoking in their dining rooms at all — at least during peak dining times. In 2004, the country's parliament voted unanimously on a complete ban on all smoking in pubs and restaurants, following the pattern set by nearby Ireland as well as California and New York City. The ban is set to be in force starting Spring 2006.

The top restaurants and cafes

Air Organic
$$–$$$ **West End**   SCOTTISH

After a change of ownership in 2004, the unique space-age décor of Air Organic has been removed in favor of a less adventurous but still modern design. The kitchen has shaken things up, too. Gone are most of the references to organic produce on the menu and the "fusion" cooking, but the quality of ingredients still appears strong, favoring local suppliers, and the preparation is still top notch. Dishes include braised rump of black-face lamb, crispy pork belly, seared hand-dived (rather than dredged) scallops, and a twice-baked smoked cheddar soufflé.

See map p. 206. 36 Kelvingrove St. ☎ 0141-564-5200. Reservations recommended. Underground: Kelvinhall. Fixed-price lunch: £12.50 ($23); fixed-price dinner: £24 ($44); bento boxes: £12–£16.50 ($19–$26). AE, DC, MC, V. Open: Sun–Thurs noon–10 p.m., Fri–Sat noon–10:30 p.m.

Brian Maule at Chardon d'Or
$$$–$$$$ Commerical Centre   FRENCH/SCOTTISH

Chef Brian Maule was born in Ayrshire near Glasgow, but he trained with some of the best chefs in France and became part of the team working with the highly respected Roux brothers in London. After rising in rank to head chef at their vaunted Michelin-star winning Gavroche restaurant, he decided to go north and return to Scotland with his young family, opening his own restaurant in Glasgow in 2001. His place is considered among the finest in the city, with excellent ingredients and an ambience that's classy but not at all stuffy. Fresh fish and lamb dishes come highly recommended. Smoking is not permitted in the dining room.

See map p. 206. 176 West Regent St. ☎ *0141-248-3801.* www.lechardondor.com. *Reservations recommended. Underground: Buchanan Street. Fixed-price lunch: £14.50 ($27); main courses dinner: £15–£20 ($28–$37). AE, MC, V. Open: Mon–Fri noon–2:30 p.m. and 6–10 p.m., Sat 6–10 p.m. Closed Sun (and bank holidays).*

The Buttery
$$$–$$$$ Commerical Centre   SCOTTISH/FRENCH

One of the best-known and most long-established restaurants in Glasgow, The Buttery exudes old world charm — from its rich, sumptuous bar and lounge to the wood-paneled dining room with white linen. This restaurant and its Victorian tenement home have been standing here since 1870 or so. The Buttery seems out of the way only because it's on "the wrong side" of the M8 freeway that bisects the city. Although the place was briefly closed a few years back, restaurateur Ian Fleming and executive chef Willie Deans revived it in 2002, and it's now doing better than ever, especially after snagging the best restaurant in Scotland award from the prestigious AA (the UK's Automobile Association) in 2004. Although the setting is traditional, the cooking is progressive: rabbit served with roasted coriander seed sauce or halibut with a pea puree. Smoking is not permitted in the dining room.

See map p. 206. 652 Argyle St. ☎ *0141-221-8188. Reservations recommended. Suburban train: Anderston. Fixed-price lunch: £16 ($30); fixed-price dinner: £34 ($63). AE, DC, MC, V. Open: Tues–Fri noon–2 p.m. and 7–10 p.m., Sat 6–10 p.m.*

Café Cossachok
$$ Merchant City   RUSSIAN

A combination of small restaurant and gallery space where live music frequently is played, the Atlas family's Café Cossachok is an entertaining place to eat. The restaurant's located just south of the Trongate on art-gallery filled King Street. The chefs concentrate on hearty Slavic fare: primarily Russian, Georgian, and Ukrainian specialties. Come here to feast on famous dishes such as borscht beet root soup with sour cream or some savory blinis, the Russian equivalent of pancakes. Cossachok's chicken Vladimir, a breaded breast of chicken with a mushroom sauce resting under a cheese topping, is an excellent main course, as is the chicken chakhokhbili (a Georgian dish made with a tomato, paprika, basil, mint, and tarragon sauce).

Armenian moussaka successfully blends eggplant, tomatoes, mushrooms, and coriander. For the full Russian experience, throw down a refreshing shot from one (or several) of the freezer's variety of vodka bottles. *See map p. 206. 10 King St.* ☎ *0141-553-0733.* www.cossachok.com. *Reservations recommended. Underground: St. Enoch. Main courses: £7–£14 ($13–$26). MC, V. Open: Tues–Sat 11:30 a.m.–10:30 p.m., Sun 4–10 p.m. Closed Mon.*

Cafe Gandolfi

$–$$ **Merchant City** **SCOTTISH/CONTINENTAL**

Many local foodies who live on a budget will tell you that this popular place in Merchant City is their favorite dining-out spot: It offers solid cooking and a friendly ambience at the right price. Owner Seumas MacInnes comes from a Highland/Hebredian family, and so the black pudding comes down from Stornoway while the haggis hails from Dingwall. Particularly recommended is the black pudding (a savoury sausage made of pigs' blood and oats), Gandolfi's creamy Cullen skink (smoked haddock chowder), or one of the light pasta dishes. If you're really hungry, go for the steak sandwich. The ground floor room has original, organic, and comfortable wooden furniture created by the Tim Stead workshop in Scotland. A recent addition to the premises is **Bar Gandolfi,** up the steel staircase in the attic space. With a ceiling sky-light, however, it's anything but dark and dank.

See map p. 206. 64 Albion St. ☎ *0141-552-6813.* www.cafegandolfi.com. *Underground: Buchanan Street. Main courses: £7.50–£12 ($14–$22). MC, V. Open: Mon–Sat 9 a.m.–11:30 p.m., Sun noon–11:30 p.m.*

Picnic fare

According to some translations, Glasgow or glascau means "dear green place." And this "dear green place" has no shortage of spots for a picnic, whether in sprawling Glasgow Green or along the Clyde near the city center, Kelvingrove Park or the Botanic Gardens in the West End, not to mention Pollok Country Park or Queens Park on the South Side.

If you're in the city center, gravitate towards **Pekhams** in the Merchant City near George Square, 61 Glassford St. (☎ **0141-553-0666**), which has a full delicatessen with fresh bread and a wine shop.

In the West End, the options include the wonderful **Heart Buchanan Fine Food and Wine,** near the Botanic Gardens at 380 Byres Rd. (☎ **0141-334-7626**); **Delizique,** 66 Hyndland St. (☎ **0141-339-2000**); another branch of **Pekhams,** 124 Byres Rd. (☎ **0141-357-1454**); and, new in 2004, **Kember & Jones Fine Food Emporium,** 134 Byres Rd. (☎ **0141-337-3851**).

Next door to Kember & Jones is **Patisserie Françoise,** good for French-style pastries and breads. For some of the best cheese in the UK, visit the **IJ Mellis Cheesemonger** branch in Glasgow at 492 Great Western Rd. (☎ **0141-339-8998**). Towards the City Centre area is the Glasgow branch of **Lupe Pintos** at 313 Great Western Rd. (☎ **0141-334-5444**), the perfect stop for Mexican and American foodstuffs.

Café Mao
$$ **Merchant City** **ASIAN**

This restaurant's a lively place for a meal, situated just north of the Trongate in the Merchant City district. With the big Andy Warhol-style portraits of Chairman Mao prominently displayed in the window-filled corner location, you can't really miss the place. Part of a small chain of Asian eateries curiously based in Ireland, Café Mao offers the casual setting of a spacious, modern, and stylish bistro The place can be quiet during lunchtime, but it's almost always hopping at night, with a buzz you would expect more at a popular bar. Dishes include starters such as spring rolls stuffed with pumpkin and main courses such as Indonesian nasi goreng (fried rice) and Vietnamese beef and noodles, all prepared in the open kitchen where you can see flames licking at the chefs' bibs.

See map p. 206. 84 Brunswick St. ☎ *0141-564-5161.* www.cafemao.com. *Reservations recommended. Underground: St. Enoch. Fixed-price lunch: £8 ($15); main courses: £6–£9 ($11–$17). AE, MC, V. Open: daily noon–11 p.m.*

The Dhabba
$$–$$$ **Merchant City** **INDIAN**

Glaswegians love their Indian food, as visitors can tell from the sheer number of Indian restaurants in the city. However, the Dhabba, which opened in late 2002, isn't your typical Glasgow curry house; it's a bit more refined, slightly more expensive, and considerably more stylish than the norm. In an attempt to be more authentic, the Dhabba specializes in North Indian dishes, so it largely foregoes the bright food coloring that so many other restaurants use. In addition to spicy dishes featuring lamb, chicken, and prawns, the menu also features an excellent selection of vegetarian dishes, which are noticeably less costly than the meat options. Marinated fish cooked in tandoori spices is recommended, as are the many baked breads, whether naan, rotis, or parathas.

See map p. 206. 44 Candleriggs. ☎ *0141-553-1249.* www.thedhabba.com. *Reservations recommended. Underground: St Enoch. Main courses: £8–£15 ($15–$28). AE, MC, V. Open: Mon–Fri noon–2 p.m. and 5–11 p.m., Sat 1 p.m.–midnight, Sun 1–11 p.m.*

étain
$$–$$$ **Commercial Centre** **SCOTTISH/FRENCH**

Sir Terrance Conran, the UK designer who founded Habitat (a furniture store; www.habitat.net) and then became a restaurateur, surprised many when he opened his first "destination" restaurant outside of London here in Glasgow a few years back. Adjacent to a branch of Conran's Zinc Bar & Grill, around the backside of the posh Princes Square shopping center, you enter étain (French for "pewter") either through the mall or via a dedicated glass elevator down an alley (with the glorified name of Springfield Court) from Queen Street. Chef Geoff Smeddle has an assured touch with contemporary French cooking using excellent Scottish produce, whether he's working with lobster, lamb, scallops, crab, or venison. Memorable touches include handmade truffles served after dinner, and service is generally excellent. Despite corporate ownership, étain feels very much like a locally-owned and -operated restaurant, with attention both to detail and to the needs of customers.

See map p. 206. The Glass House, Springfield Court. ☎ *0141-225-5630. Reservations recommended. Underground: Buchanan Street. Fixed-price lunch: £16 ($30); main courses dinner: £14–£20 ($26–$37). AE, MC, V. Open: Mon–Fri noon–2:30 p.m. and 7–11 p.m., Sat 7–11 p.m., Sun noon–3 p.m.*

Fratelli Sarti
$–$$ Commerical Centre   ITALIAN

You can find a few Fratelli Sarti restaurants in town, but my favorite remains the original on Wellington Street. Owned by the Sarti brothers, it feels like a family-run cafe/bistro crossed with a delicatessen. Indeed, you can still buy dried goods and wines here, although they stopped carrying deli meats and cheeses a couple of years ago. The restaurant's pizzas are excellent, with thin, crispy crusts and modest amounts of sauce, cheese, and toppings, which prevent them from becoming a sloppy mess. Pasta dishes, such as "al forno" with penne, sausage, and spinach, are filling. Come here even if you just want a real Italian espresso and pastry. If you want a slightly more formal setting, try the Sarti restaurant around the corner on Bath Street (which is connected to this one via a stairwell) or the Fratelli Sarti on 21 Renfield St. (☎ 0141-572-7000).

See map p. 206. 133 Wellington St. ☎ *0141-204-0440.* www.fratellisarti.com. *Underground: Buchanan Street. Reservations recommended. Main courses: £6–£10 ($11–$18.50). AE, MC, V. Open: Mon–Thurs 8 a.m.–10:30 p.m., Fri–Sat 8 a.m.–11 p.m., Sun noon–10:30 p.m.*

Gamba
$$$$ Commercial Centre   FISH/SEAFOOD

Gamba is arguably the best restaurant in Glasgow and is today the place where famous visitors to the city are likely to eat. For many, Gamba wins hands down on the strength of its fresh fish and seafood dishes prepared by chef and co-owner Derek Marshall. The food is complemented by the professional and cordial staff. The basement venture is modern and stylish without feeling excessively fancy. Diners often begin with a cocktail or glass of champagne in the small bar where they can look at the menu and order before moving through to the dining room. Starters include Marshall's signature fish soup or a sashimi dish with succulent slices of salmon and scallops. Main courses may include whole lemon sole in browned butter or delicate pan-seared sea bream. And desserts aren't an afterthought, whether smooth panna cotta or ice cream infused with Scotch whisky. Nothing here is particularly cheap, but it feels like value nonetheless. If you're on a tight budget, try the lunch or pre-theatre fixed price menu. Smoking is not permitted in the dining room.

See map p. 206. 225a West George St. ☎ 0141-572-0899. www.gamba.co.uk.
Reservations required. Underground: Buchanan Street. Fixed-price lunch: £15 ($28);
main courses dinner: £16–£22 ($30–$40). AE, MC, V. Open: Mon–Sat noon–2:30 p.m.
and 5–10:30 p.m. Closed Sun.

Grassroots Café
$ West End   VEGETARIAN

Tied to the whole-foods shop located just around the corner, Grassroots
is the city's leading vegetarian restaurant. The feel is casual and relaxed,
with sofas at the front of the dining space and booths separated by gauzy
curtains along one wall. A good selection of non-alcoholic fruit drinks and
organic bottled beers from Britain complement a menu that has international influences. Cakes of risotto-style rice with goat cheese and pine nuts,
tempura-battered vegetables, and a Middle Eastern tagine with couscous
are delicious examples of what you'll find here.

See map p. 206. 93–97 St. Georges Rd. (parallel to the M8 freeway). ☎ 0141-333-0534.
Underground: St. George's Cross. Main courses: £5–£8 ($9–$15). MC, V. Open:
Mon–Fri 10 a.m.–10 p.m., Sat–Sun 10 a.m.–3:45 p.m. and 5–10 p.m.

Ho Wong
$$$ Broomielaw/Commercial Centre   CHINESE

Probably the city's finest Chinese restaurant, this outpost of Jimmy Ho's
and David Wong's Hong Kong establishment is on a rather inauspicious
block between the river and Argyle Street, just southwest of Glasgow's
Central Station. The ambience is refined and even a bit romantic. The
menu traditionally contains at least eight duck dishes, a few types of fresh
lobster, plenty of fish options, and some sizzling platters as well. If you
have trouble deciding, the banquet option makes life a bit easier.

Family-friendly fare

Just off Sauchiehall Street, **Bistro du Sud**, 97 Cambridge St (☎ 0141-332-2666), is a
small, locally owned cafe/bistro that loves to have children in its midst. Instead of being
lulled by the familiar multi-national chain operations, try something tasty at this modern
Italian/French eatery. Open daily from 8:30 a.m. to 10 p.m. (from noon on Sundays).

Just like in Edinburgh, the all you can eat buffet-only Chinese restaurant has taken
Glasgow by storm. **China Buffet King**, 349 Sauchiehall St. (☎ 0141-333-1788), is centrally
located, with a good variety of Chinese food and some European dishes, at discount
prices for children. Open daily from noon to 11 p.m.

A "Knickerbocker Glory" is an extremely elaborate ice-cream sundae (with fruit, jelly, and
more) and few places do it better than the **University Café**, 87 Byres Rd (☎ 0141-339-
5217). This Art Deco landmark has all its original features, from booths to counter. Open
Wednesday through Monday from 9 a.m. to 10 p.m. or so.

See map p. 206. 82 York St. ☎ 0141-221-3550. www.ho-wong.com. *Reservations recommended. Suburban train: Central Station. Fixed-price lunch: £9.50 ($17.50); main courses: £15–£20 ($28–$37); fixed-price banquet (5-courses): £27 ($43). AE, MC, V. Open: Mon–Fri noon–2 p.m. and 6 p.m.–midnight, Sun 6 p.m.–midnight.*

La Parmigiana
$$$ West End   ITALIAN

Providing a cosmopolitan and Continental atmosphere, this place seems to be everyone's favorite up-market Italian restaurant in Glasgow. A well-established, quarter century–old business of the Giovanazzi family, Parmigiana is often recommended for its fish and seafood dishes. The menu offers an array of pasta concoctions, some especially delectable, such as the lobster-stuffed ravioli served in creamy basil sauce. Try the chargrilled scallops cooked quickly in olive oil and served with fresh lemon juice. Veal is often served with Parma ham, mozzarella, and a tomato sauce. The house wine is excellent, but the list affords the opportunity to sample some fine wines at corresponding costs. Service by waiters in smart black vests is usually impeccable.

See map p. 206. 447 Great Western Rd. ☎ 0141-334-0686. www.laparmigiana. co.uk. *Reservations required. Underground: Kelvinbridge. Fixed-price lunch: £10.50 ($16); pre-theatre dinner: £13.50 ($25); main courses dinner: £15–£20 ($28–$37). AE, DC, MC, V. Open: Mon–Sat noon–2:30 p.m. and 6–11 p.m. Closed Sun.*

Mono
$ Merchant City   VEGAN

Technically outside the Merchant City in the nearby Saltmarket district closer to the River Clyde, Mono is the best choice for meat-free meals in this part of town. Not just a bar and a cafe/restaurant, Mono also houses a store selling free-trade goods and a CD shop with the latest in indie rock and non-mainstream music. The restaurant's completely vegan (that means no dairy products, either), which makes Mono unique in Scotland, let alone Glasgow. If this all sounds a tad too "politically correct," relax: It's a welcoming and casual place with a mixed and varied clientele. Sweet pepper and zucchini potato cakes and veggie burgers with fries are typical dishes, and the Thai curry and stir-fried vegetables reveals a bit of an Asian influence. Mono brews its own organic ales, and you have a selection of organic wines to choose from, too. Live music of an acoustic nature is sometimes featured on the weekends.

See map p. 206. 12 Kings Ct. ☎ 0141-553-2400. www.gomono.com. *Underground: St. Enoch. Main courses: £5–£7 ($9–$13). AE, MC, V. Open: daily noon–10 p.m.*

Mother India
$$ West End   INDIAN

After a decade in business, this restaurant seems to have established itself as the most respected Indian restaurant in Glasgow. Others have been open longer and certainly have their own loyal followings, but Mother India is the one that people in the know most often recommend. Unlike the norm for Indian restaurants, the menu here isn't overloaded with hundreds of different dishes. Oven-baked fish, which comes wrapped in foil, is seasoned with aromatic spices, while chicken and zucchini squash are served with a sauce that includes pan-roasted cumin and cardamom. Whether seated on the ground floor or in the dining room above, diners are likely to find the staff courteous and attentive.

Down the road toward the heart of the West End, a second branch of Mother India with less expensive, small thali-style dishes has more recently opened: **Mother India's Café.**

See map p. 206. 28 Westminster Terrace (Sauchiehall Street at Kelvingrove Street). ☎ *0141-221-1663. Reservations required. Underground: Kelvinhall. Main courses: £7.50–£12 ($14–$22). Open: Mon–Tues 5:30–10:30 p.m., Wed–Thurs noon–2 p.m. and 5:30–10:30 p.m., Fri noon–2:30 p.m. and 5:30–11 p.m., Sat 1–11 p.m., Sun 4:30–10 p.m.*

Mussel Inn
$$–$$$ Commerical Centre FISH/SEAFOOD

Sister restaurant to the original on Rose Street in Edinburgh, the Mussel Inn has the distinction of being owned by shellfish farmers in the West of Scotland. The kilo pot of mussels you eat here on any given evening may have been harvested only earlier the same day. The feel at the Glasgow branch is casual, with an open kitchen, light wood tables, and high ceilings, recreating the feel you may find if it were located right at the seashore. In addition to the house specialty of steamed mussels served with a choice of broths (from spicy to white wine with garlic), the queen scallop salad is tasty and refreshing, creamy chowders are hearty and filling, and the menu always features a fresh catch of the day.

See map p. 206. 157 Hope St. ☎ *0141-572-1405.* www.mussel-inn.com. *Reservations recommended for weekend nights. Underground: St. Enoch. Main courses: £8–£14 ($15–$26). AE, MC, V. Open: Mon–Fri noon–2:30 p.m. and 5:30–10 p.m., Sat noon–10 p.m., Sun 5–10 p.m.*

1901
$$ South Side FRENCH/CONTINENTAL

Not too far from the Burrell Collection, 1901 is perhaps your best choice after a visit to Pollok Park. The owner once ran a French restaurant in the city, and the décor of the dining room, which is back behind the traditional pub, nods to this background with its use of blue, white, and red. The menu offers a range of French-influenced and Continental food, almost all served in large portions. Dishes include lamb shanks with garlic and thyme, pasta with chicken, or the classic steak frites.

See map p. 206. 1534 Pollokshaws Rd. ☎ *0141-632-0161. Reservations recommended. Fixed-price lunch: £7.50 ($14); main courses: £10–£15 ($18.50–$28). MC, V. Open: Mon–Fri noon–2:30 p.m. and 5–9:30 p.m., Sat–Sun noon–9:30 p.m.*

No. Sixteen
$$–$$$ **West End SCOTTISH**

No. Sixteen has a slightly homey feel — small and slightly cramped with dining on the ground floor and a tiny mezzanine above. A story's been told of a couple visiting Glasgow who came here on their first night in town for dinner and returned every subsequent night because they were so pleased with the food. Near the base of Byres Road, this Scottish bistro offers inventive cooking from local ingredients. White fish can be served with an olive tapenade or rabbit may come atop a barley risotto. The vaunted Michelin inspectors have repeated given No. Sixteen a "bib gourmand" award, which denotes good food at reasonable prices. Smoking is not permitted.

See map p. 206. 16 Byres Rd. ☎ 0141-339-2544. Reservations recommended. Underground: Kelvinhall. Fixed-price lunch: £10.50 ($18.50); main courses: £12–£20 ($22–$37). AE, MC, V. Open: Mon–Sat noon–2:30 p.m. and 5:30–10 p.m., Sun 12:30–4 p.m. and 5:30–9:30 p.m.

OKO
$$ **Merchant City JAPANESE**

The centerpiece of this restaurant is the large rectangular sushi bar with a conveyor belt that moves the clear-plastic covered and color-coded plates of various raw fish and sticky rice around and around, almost literally under the noses of diners. Given the availability of fresh fish in Scotland, you would expect the sushi to be good here — and it is, whether salmon, bream, or scallops. In addition to sushi, OKO also offers cooked Japanese food such as breaded and fried chicken katsu, barbecued beef teriyaki, miso soup, and even some spicy Korean dishes featuring marinated cabbage. The prices of the dishes vary, and what seems like an inexpensive option at the start of the visit can become pricey. But it's just too tempting not to try another maki or tempura as the plates pass by. Smoking is not permitted in the dining room.

See map p. 206. 68 Ingram St. ☎ 0141-572-1500. www.okorestaurants.com. *Reservations recommended. Underground: Buchanan Street. Typical sushi meal: £15 ($28). AE, MC, V. Open: Tues–Thurs noon–3 p.m. and 6–11 p.m., Fri–Sat noon–midnight, Sun 5:30–11:30 p.m. Closed Mon.*

Rogano
$$$–$$$$ **Commerical Centre FISH/SEAFOOD**

Rogano is the best-known City Centre restaurant in Glasgow. Its well-preserved Art Deco interior patterned after the Queen Mary ocean liner dates back to the opening of the oyster bar here in 1935. Since then, the space has expanded and Rogano has hosted virtually every visiting celebrity to the city. Visitors enjoy their dinners amid etched mirrors, ceiling fans, semicircular banquettes, and potted palms. Service is attentive and informed. The menu always emphasizes seafood, with dishes such as halibut in champagne-and-oyster sauce or lobster Thermidor. Although these are traditional (if possibly old-fashioned) recipes, they have their fans; some people wouldn't dream of having scallops done any other way than in a creamy cheese sauce. If you just want to experience the glamour, stay in the bar and enjoy a cocktail with a plate of oysters. Smoking is not permitted in the dining room.

A less expensive menu is offered downstairs in **Cafe Rogano,** where the prices of main courses hover around the £10 ($15) mark.

See map p. 206. 11 Exchange Place. ☎ *0141-248-4055.* www.rogano.co.uk. *Reservations recommended. Underground: Buchanan Street. Fixed-price lunch: £16.50 ($30.50); main courses dinner: £17–£34 ($31–$63). AE, DC, MC, V. Open: restaurant daily noon–2:30 p.m. and 6:30–10:30 p.m.; cafe Sun–Thurs noon–11 p.m., Fri–Sat noon–midnight.*

Stravaigin Café Bar
$$ West End SCOTTISH/GLOBAL

The motto of Stravaigin (which roughly translates from the Scottish vernacular to "wanderin" in English) is "think global, eat local." Although the basement restaurant here near the University of Glasgow is no slouch and is in fact an award-winning enterprise, I tend to prefer the less expensive but still memorably made food served at the ground level pub/cafe, with its recently expanded balcony area. Every afternoon and evening, people squeeze in for a drink and a meal. Scottish produce gets international twists: cheese and herb fritters with sweet chili sauce or roast lamb served with coriander couscous. But you also find staples such as a hearty fish and chips. The atmosphere is always cordial, and prices are lower still during the busy pre-theatre seating. In the downstairs restaurant, expect concoctions such as Vietnamese-inspired marinated quail served on a candy smoked eggplant concasse or mullet served on a bed of Thai noodles with bits of mussels and mushrooms.

Tea for two?

For tea and a snack, why not join the rest of the tourists in Glasgow and try to secure a table at the landmark **Willow Tea Rooms,** 217 Sauchiehall St. (☎ **0141-332-0521;** Underground: Cowcaddens)? When the famed Mrs. Cranston opened the Willow Tea Rooms in 1904, it was something of a sensation due to its unique Charles Rennie Mackintosh design. The building's white facade still stands out from the crowd more than 100 years later. The dining room (one floor above street level) is open Monday to Saturday from 9 a.m. to 5 p.m. and Sunday from noon to 5 p.m. A second branch on Buchanan Street is similarly appointed if less authentic.

For a more contemporary experience, in the West End overlooking the River Kelvin, **Tchai Ovna,** 42 Otago St. (☎ **0141-357-4524),** has a selection of some 80 teas served in fairly eccentric and bohemian surroundings. In the evenings, you may find live music, poetry, or comedy. Tchai Ovna is open daily from 11 a.m. to 11 p.m.

If you like Stravaigin, you may consider visiting its sister bistro near Byres Road, called, appropriately enough, **Stravaigin 2,** Ruthven Lane (☎ **0141-334-7156**).

See map p. 206. 28 Gibson St. ☎ *0141-334-2665. Reservations required in restaurant. Underground: Kelvinbridge. Bar/cafe main courses: £6–£10 ($11–$18.50); restaurant fixed-price dinner: £23 ($42.50). AE, MC, V. Open: bar/cafe daily 11 a.m.–10:30 p.m.; restaurant Tues–Sun 5–11:30 p.m., Fri–Sat noon–2:30 p.m. Closed Mon.*

Ubiquitous Chip
$$–$$$$ **West End   SCOTTISH**

Quite possibly no other restaurant has been more responsible for the culinary renaissance in Scotland than the Ubiquitous Chip. Opening the Chip in 1971, chef/owner Ronnie Clydesdale was one of the first to concentrate on bringing the best Scottish ingredients into his kitchen — and then to the attention of diners. The restaurant proudly states the source of its produce on its menus, a practice now commonplace in better restaurants. Inside the walls of a former stable, the restaurant has a roomy interior courtyard with a fountain and masses of climbing vines. Many Glaswegians favor the place for anniversaries and special occasions, although the reputation of the venerable Chip has been a bit up and down in the past few years. Still, many wouldn't dream of going anywhere else. The menu can feature free-range chicken, Aberdeen Angus beef, shellfish with crispy seaweed snaps, or wild rabbit. Upstairs is a neighborhood pub and small brasserie, **Upstairs at the Chip,** where similar quality fare is available at a fraction of the price.

See map p. 206. 12 Ashton Lane, off Byres Road. ☎ *0141-334-5007.* www.ubiquitous chip.co.uk. *Reservations recommended. Underground: Hillhead. Restaurant fixed-price lunch: £22 ($40); fixed-price dinner: £33 ($61); brasserie main courses: £10–£15 ($18.50–28). AE, DC, MC, V. Open: restaurant Mon–Sat noon–2:30 p.m. and 5:30–11 p.m., Sun 12:30–3 p.m. and 6:30–11 p.m.; brasserie Mon–Sat noon–11 p.m., Sun 12:30–11 p.m.*

Wee Curry Shop
$ **Commerical Centre   INDIAN**

This tiny place is hardly big enough to swing a cat in, but the aptly named Wee Curry Shop offers the best low-cost Indian dishes in the city. Just about five tables are crammed between the front door and the open kitchen where the chefs prepare everything to order. The menu is concise, with a clutch of opening courses, such as fried pakora, and a half dozen or so main courses, such as spicy chili garlic chicken. Despite the cheap prices, portions are large. Although it may feel off the beaten track, the Wee Curry Shop is actually only a short walk from the shopping precincts of Sauchiehall Street. Smoking is not permitted.

See map p. 206. 7 Buccleuch St. (near Cambridge Street.). ☎ *0141-353-0777. Reservations recommended. Underground: Cowcaddens. Fixed-price lunch: £4.75 ($9); main courses: £5–£7 ($9.25–$13). Open: Mon–Sat noon–2 p.m. and 5:30–10:30 p.m. Closed Sun.*

Where the Monkey Sleeps
$ **Commerical Centre** CAFE

Near Blythswood Square, this downstairs singular cafe-cum-gallery is one of the best places for cappuccinos, soups, and sandwiches in the Commercial Centre area of Glasgow. You know you've found it when you see all the waiting messenger bikes, the riders of which seem to live here when they're not on the streets delivering special letters and business packages. As the name indicates, Where the Monkey Sleeps is no ordinary cafe; it's owned and operated by artistic types (including two graduates from the nearby Art School) who learned their barista skills at Starbucks but wanted to be free of corporate constraints.

See map p. 206. 182 West Regent St. ☎ *0141-226-3406.* www.wherethemonkey sleeps.com. *Underground: Buchanan Street. Lunch: usually less than £10 ($18.50); main courses dinner: £7–£12 ($13–$22). Open: Mon–Fri 8 a.m.–5 p.m., Sat 10 a.m.–6 p.m. Closed Sun.*

Exploring Glasgow

Glasgow is a compact city roughly the size of San Francisco. The part that many visitors may describe as "downtown," Glasgow's city center is laid out on a grid, so the commercial heart of the city is user-friendly. Most visits begin here, amid the rich **Victorian architecture,** whether 19th-century banks (many of which have been converted to other uses such as restaurants and bars), office buildings, warehouses, or churches. Three main boulevards — Argyle, Buchanan, and Sauchiehall streets — form a Z-shape and have been made into predominantly car-free pedestrian zones that offer a wealth of shopping opportunities. Culturally, the choices in the heart of Glasgow include the **Gallery of Modern Art** (GOMA), the **Lighthouse** (devoted to design and architecture), and the **Centre for Contemporary Art** (CCA). These are all within a fairly short walking distance of one another.

Adjacent to the Commercial Centre is the **Merchant City,** where loft conversions over the past 20 years have created a hip, happening quarter with many lively bars and restaurants. This district skirts the historic heart of Glasgow, but little if anything remains of the medieval city — most of it has been knocked down over the years in various urban renewal schemes. But at either end of the historic High Street, you can see two of the city's more ancient landmarks: **Glasgow Cathedral,** which dates to the 13th century, and the Renaissance **Tolbooth** steeple.

Of course, a river runs through Glasgow, but the city has yet to capitalize fully on the real potential of the **Clyde.** The shipbuilding that made the river famous is long gone, yet there isn't even an active, attractive marina for leisure boats today. Concrete redevelopment of the waterfront done toward the end of the 20th century hasn't aged particularly well, although the riverbank, which has a national bicycle path, has a certain run-down urban charm.

Glasgow Attractions

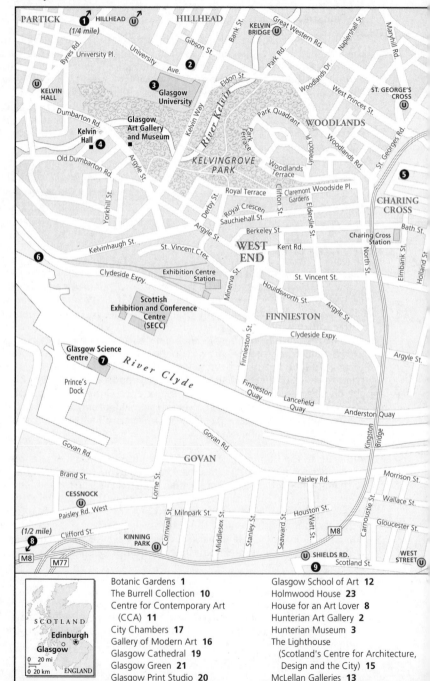

Botanic Gardens **1**	Glasgow School of Art **12**
The Burrell Collection **10**	Holmwood House **23**
Centre for Contemporary Art	House for an Art Lover **8**
(CCA) **11**	Hunterian Art Gallery **2**
City Chambers **17**	Hunterian Museum **3**
Gallery of Modern Art **16**	The Lighthouse
Glasgow Cathedral **19**	(Scotland's Centre for Architecture,
Glasgow Green **21**	Design and the City) **15**
Glasgow Print Studio **20**	McLellan Galleries **13**

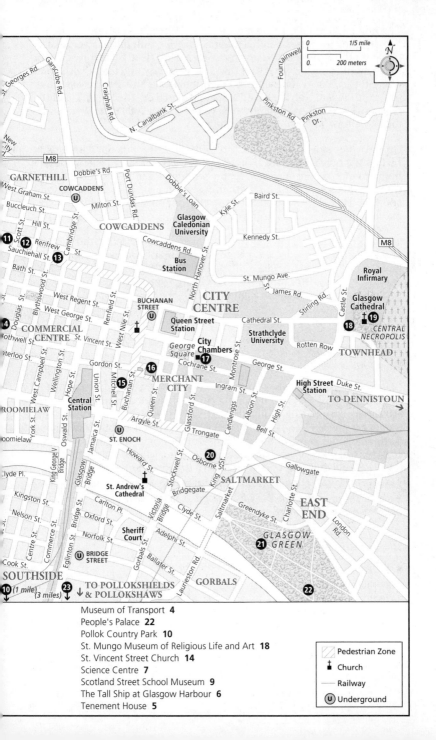

Museum of Transport **4**
People's Palace **22**
Pollok Country Park **10**
St. Mungo Museum of Religious Life and Art **18**
St. Vincent Street Church **14**
Science Centre **7**
Scotland Street School Museum **9**
The Tall Ship at Glasgow Harbour **6**
Tenement House **5**

Pedestrian Zone
✝ Church
— Railway
Ⓤ Underground

The affluent and urbane **West End** has the city's top university and the Scottish headquarters (until a planned move south of the river takes place) of the British Broadcasting Corporation (BBC). The presence of these institutions ensures that this area is trendy and lively, with some of the city's best restaurants and nightlife. Leafy and attractive thanks to the sprawling **Kelvingrove Park,** another river (the Kelvin), and the **Glasgow Art Gallery and Museum** (closed until 2006), the West End is many visitors' favorite place to explore.

On the other side of the Clyde, the South Side spreads out with mostly residential neighborhoods. Some say this is the "real" Glasgow, and it's home to at least one major, arguably world-class attraction, the **Burrell Collection,** as well as several other destinations that merit excursions south of the River Clyde. Like all the city-run museums, visiting the permanent collection costs nothing.

 You'd need at least a few days to visit every place listed in this section and you'd be more than exhausted by the end of your romp, so you'll have to make some decisions. If you have children in tow, fewer galleries and more family attractions would be best; if you like art, more museums and fewer wanders may be right up your alley.

The top attractions

Botanic Gardens
West End

Glasgow's Botanic Gardens aren't as extensive or exemplary as the Royal Botanic Gardens in Edinburgh. Nevertheless, they cover some 16 hectares (40 acres). An extensive collection of tropical plants lives in Kibble Palace, the Victorian cast iron glasshouse that was restored in 2004. The plant collection includes some rather acclaimed orchids and begonias. The Botanic Gardens is a good place to unwind and wander, whether through the working vegetable plot or along the banks of the River Kelvin.

See map p. 220. Great Western Road. ☎ *0141-334-2422. Admission: free. Underground: Hillhead. Open: gardens daily dawn–dusk; greenhouses daily 10 a.m.–4:45 p.m. (only until 4:15 p.m. in the winter).*

The Burrell Collection
South Side

This museum houses the treasures left to Glasgow by Sir William Burrell, a wealthy ship owner and industrialist who had a lifelong passion for art. He started collecting at age 14 and stopped only when he died at the age of 96 in 1958. His tastes were eclectic: Chinese ceramics, French paintings from the 1800s, tapestries, stained-glass windows from churches, even stone doorways from the Middle Ages. You can see a vast aggregation of furniture, textiles, ceramics, stained glass, silver, art objects, and pictures in the dining room, hall, and drawing room reconstructed from Sir William's home, Hutton Castle at Berwick-upon-Tweed. Ancient artifacts, Asian art, and European decorative arts and paintings are all featured. There's a cafe on site, and you can roam through the surrounding park, 5km (3 miles) south of the River Clyde.

Nearby **Pollok House** (☎ 0141-616-6521) dates to the 18th century. Now run by the National Trust for Scotland, it features interiors as they were in the Victorian/Edwardian era. Open daily with an admission charge of £6 ($11) adults.

See map p. 220. Pollok Country Park, 2060 Pollokshaws Rd. ☎ 0141-287-2550. www. glasgowmuseums.com. *Suburban train: Pollokshaws West. Bus: 45 or 57. Admission: free. Open: Mon–Thurs and Sat 10 a.m.–5 p.m., Fri and Sun 11 a.m.–5 p.m. Closed Jan 1 and Dec 25.*

Centre for Contemporary Art (CCA)
Commerical Centre

The CCA is one of three premier venues in Glasgow for the exhibition of contemporary art, usually of a conceptual nature, by both local artists and those of international reputation. Because it's owned by the city, the CCA charges no entrance fees. The main, atrium-like space is actually given over to the CCA's cafe, **Tempus,** but you can visit the other exhibition rooms, plus a small theater that screens art-house and foreign films coordinated by the Glasgow Film Theatre. Housed in a recently restored building designed by Alexander "Greek" Thomson, the CCA annually hosts art by the nominees for the Beck Futures Awards, which has become one of the leading judges of young talent in Britain.

See map p. 220. 350 Sauchiehall St. ☎ 0141-352-4900. www.cca-glasgow.org. *Underground: Cowcaddens. Suburban train: Charing Cross. Bus: 16, 18, 44, or 57. Admission: free. Open: Tues–Wed and Fri–Sun 11 a.m.–6 p.m., Thurs 11 a.m.–8 p.m. Closed Mon and for two weeks during Christmas and New Years holidays.*

Gallery of Modern Art
Merchant City

GOMA, as it's better known, is housed in the former Royal Exchange at Royal Exchange Square, where Ingram Street meets Queen Street. The building was built as a mansion for an 18th-century tobacco magnate. It was later expanded by one of the city's busy 19th-century architects, David Hamilton, who added a dramatic portico to the front. Now the pile and its square are at the heart of the city, near George Square and Buchanan Street. The galleries on different floors are slightly pretentiously named after earth, fire, air, and water. The permanent collection has works by Stanley Spencer and John Bellany as well as art from the "new Glasgow boys" who emerged in the 1980s — Peter Howson, Ken Currie, and Steven Campbell. Before becoming a museum in the mid 1990s, the building was used as a public library and recently the basement was converted to serve that function again.

See map p. 220. Royal Exchange Square, Queen Street. ☎ **0141-229-1996.**
www.glasgowmuseums.com. *Underground: Buchanan Street. Bus: 12, 18, 40, 62,
or 66. Admission: free. Open: Mon–Wed and Sat 10 a.m.–5 p.m., Thurs 10 a.m.–8 p.m.,
Fri and Sun 11 a.m.–5 p.m.*

Glasgow Cathedral
Townhead

Also known as the cathedral of St. Kentigern or St. Mungo's, this structure
dates to the 13th century. The edifice is mainland Scotland's only complete
medieval cathedral, making it the most important ecclesiastical building of
that era in the entire country. Unlike other cathedrals on the mainland,
this one survived the Reformation practically intact, but 16th-century zeal
purged it of all monuments of idolatry. Later, misguided "restoration" led to
the demolition of its western towers, thus altering the cathedral's appear-
ance. Gothic design reigns in the lower Church, which has an array of pointed
arches and piers. Its vaulted crypt is said to be one of the finest in Europe
and holds St. Mungo's tomb, where a light always burns. Other highlights
of the interior include the Blackadder aisle and the 15th-century nave with
a stone screen (unique in Scotland) showing the seven deadly sins.

For one of the best views of the cathedral — and the city, for that matter —
cross the ravine into the **Central Necropolis.** Built on a proud hill and dominated by a statue of John Knox, this graveyard (patterned in part on the
famous Pere Lachaise cemetery in Paris) was opened in the 1830s. Coinci-
dentally emblematic of the mixing of ethnic groups in Glasgow, the first
person to be buried here was Jewish because Jews were first to receive
permission to use part of the hill for burial grounds.

See map p. 220. Glasgow Cathedral, Cathedral Square, Castle Street. ☎ **0141-552-6891.**
www.historic-scotland.gov.uk. *Underground: Buchanan Street. Suburban
train: High Street. Bus: 12, 28, 56, or 89. Admission: free. Open: Apr–Sept Mon–Sat
9:30 a.m.–6 p.m., Sun 1–5 p.m.; Oct–Mar Mon–Sat 9:30 a.m.–4 p.m., Sun 1–4 p.m. Sun
church services at 11 a.m. and 6:30 p.m.*

Glasgow School of Art
Commerical Center

Architect Charles Rennie Mackintosh's global reputation rests in large part
on this magnificent building on Garnethill above Sauchiehall Street, a highlight of the Mackintosh trail that legions of his fans from across the world
follow through the city. Completed in two stages (1899 and 1909), the
building offers a mix of ideas promoted by the Arts and Crafts and Art
Nouveau movements. The building is even more amazing because
Mackintosh was not yet 30 when he designed the place. It's still a working
and much respected school of art. Guided tours are the only way to see the
entire building, and a highlight of the tour is the library. If you just drop in,
however, the first floor offers a gift shop, and the airy landing one flight
up serves as the school's exhibition space: the Mackintosh Gallery.

See map p. 220. 167 Renfrew St. ☎ **0141-353-4526**. www.gsa.ac.uk. *Underground: Cowcaddens. Suburban train: Charing Cross. Bus: 16, 18, 44, or 57. Admission: tours £5 ($9). Open: Mackintosh Gallery Mon–Thurs 10 a.m.–7 p.m., Fri 10 a.m.–5 p.m., Sat 10 a.m.–2 p.m; tours Mon–Fri 11 a.m. and 2 p.m., Sat 10:30 a.m. and 11:30 a.m. Advance reservations recommended for tours.*

Holmwood House
South Side

This villa, designed by Alexander "Greek" Thomson and built in 1858, is probably the best example of his innovative style as applied to stately Victorian homes. Holmwood House is magnificently original, and its restoration (which is ongoing) has revealed that the architect was concerned with almost every element of the house's design, right down to the wallpaper and painted friezes. Visitors have access to most parts of the building and surrounding gardens. Most impressive is the overall exterior design as well as the home's parlor with its circular bay window, the cupola over the staircase, and the detailed cornicing around the ceiling in the dining room.

See map p. 220. 61–63 Netherlee Rd., Cathcart, about 6km (4 miles) south of the city's center. ☎ **0141-637-2129**. www.nts.org.uk. *Suburban train: Cathcart. Bus: 44 or 66. Admission: £4 ($7.50) adult, £2 ($3.75) children. Open: Apr–Oct daily noon–5 p.m. Closed Nov–Mar.*

Unappreciated genius: Alexander "Greek" Thomson

Even though architect and designer Charles Rennie Mackintosh (1868–1928) is well known and his world-wide popularity has spurred a cottage industry of "mock-intosh" fakes from jewelry to stationery, a precursor of his was perhaps even more important and innovative. Alexander "Greek" Thomson (1817–1875) brought a vision to Victorian Glasgow that was unrivaled by his contemporaries. Although the influence of classical Greek structures — the so-called Greek Revival — was nothing new, Thomson didn't so much replicate Grecian design as hone it to essentials and then mix in Egyptian, Assyrian, and other Eastern-influenced motifs. As with Mackintosh later, Thomson increasingly found himself out of step with fashion, which architecturally was moving toward Gothic Revival.

An unforgivable number of structures created by the reasonably prolific and successful Thomson have been lost to the wrecker's ball, but some key works remain: terraced houses such as **Moray Place** (where he lived) in the city's South Side and **Eton Terrace** in the West End, churches such as the derelict **Caledonian Road Church** and the still-used **St. Vincent Street Church**, detached homes such as the **Double Villa** or **Holmwood House**, and commercial structures such as the **Grecian Buildings** (which today houses the CCA) and **Egyptian Halls.** Just as a Mackintosh trail has been created so that fans can revisit his works, Thomson deserves no less and in time may receive his full due.

Hunterian Art Gallery
West End

In 1783, the University of Glasgow inherited the artistic estate of James McNeill Whistler; some 60 of his paintings, many of which are hanging in this gallery, were bestowed by his sister-in-law. The Hunterian also boasts a collection of Charles Rennie Mackintosh furnishings, and one wing of the building has a recreation of the architect's home on three levels, decorated in the original style. The main gallery exhibits 17th- and 18th-century paintings (Rembrandt to Rubens) and 19th- and 20th-century Scottish works. Temporary exhibits, selected from Scotland's largest collection of prints, are presented in the print gallery.

See map p. 220. University of Glasgow, 22 Hillhead St. ☎ *0141-330-5431.* www. hunterian.gla.ac.uk. *Underground: Hillhead. Bus: 44. Admission: free. Open: Mon–Sat 9:30 a.m.–5 p.m. (Mackintosh House closed 12:30–1:30 p.m.). Closed Jan 1, Jul 21, Sept 29, Dec 25.*

The Lighthouse (Scotland's Centre for Architecture, Design and the City)
Commercial Centre

The Lighthouse opened in 1999, a year in which the city hosted an international celebration of its architecture. The Lighthouse is housed in Charles Rennie Mackintosh's first public commission, home of the *Glasgow Herald* newspaper from 1895. Unoccupied for 15 years, the building is now the site of a seven-story, state-of-the-art exhibition center with a unique blue neon-tracked escalator that leads to four galleries, education suites, and a cafe. The **Mackintosh Centre** on the third level is the Lighthouse's only permanent exhibition and provides an overview of Mackintosh's art, design, and architecture. A glass timeline wall documents his achievements. The **Wee People's City** on the second floor provides an interactive play area for children between ages three and eight. Visitors can also ride an elevator to a viewing platform that offers a unique panorama of the city.

See map p. 220. 11 Mitchell Lane. ☎ *0141-221-6362.* www.thelighthouse.co.uk. *Underground: St. Enoch. Admission to Lighthouse and Mackintosh Interpretation Centre: £3 ($5.50). Open: Mon and Wed–Sat 10:30 a.m.–5 p.m., Tues 11 a.m.–5 p.m., Sun noon–5 p.m.*

McLellan Galleries
Commercial Centre

Not normally a top attraction, the McLellan was given more prominence in 2003 when it became temporary home to some of the city's best art work — usually found in the **Kelvingrove Art Gallery and Museum,** which closed for massive renovation work until at least 2006. Seeing as the Kelvingrove Art Gallery is the repository of a municipal collection that many consider among the best of its type in the world, the McLellan has become a necessary stop. The exhibit called **Art Treasures of Kelvingrove** includes works by the Scottish Colourists such as J.D. Fergusson and F.C. Cadell; works of the Glasgow Boys (Sir James Guthrie, for example); and more recent art by Anne Redpath and Joan Eardley. The collection also includes French impressionists and 17th-century Dutch and Flemish paintings. *See map p. 220. 270 Sauchiehall St. ☎ 0141-565-4100.* www.glasgowmuseums.com. *Bus: 16, 18, or 44. Underground: Cowcaddens. Admission: free. Open: Mon–Thurs and Sat 10 a.m.–5 p.m., Fri and Sun 11 a.m.–5 p.m.*

People's Palace
East End

This museum reveals the social history of Glasgow through exhibits on how "ordinary people" have lived in the city, especially since the industrial age. It also attempts to explain the Glasgow vernacular — speech patterns and expressions that even Scots from outside the city can have trouble deciphering. Further noteworthy are the murals painted by "new Glasgow boy" Ken Currie. The spacious Winter Gardens to the rear of the building, in a restored Victorian glass house with cafe facility, offers a nice retreat. *See map p. 220. Glasgow Green. ☎ 0141-554-0223.* www.glasgowmuseums.com. *Bus: 16 or 18. Admission: free. Open: Mon–Thurs and Sat 10 a.m.–5 p.m., Fri and Sun 11 a.m.–5 p.m.*

Ahead of his time: Charles Rennie Mackintosh

Although he's legendary today, architect, designer, and decorater Charles Rennie Mackintosh (1868–1928) was largely forgotten in Scotland at the time of his death. His approach, poised between Arts and Crafts and the Art Nouveau eras, had its fans, however, and history has compensated for any slights he received during his lifetime.

Mackintosh used forms of nature, especially plants, in his interior design motifs, which offered a simplicity and harmony that was not the Victorian fashion. Nonetheless, in 1896, Mackintosh's design for the **Glasgow School of Art** won a prestigious competition. Other Mackintosh landmark buildings in the city include the exterior of the old Glasgow Herald building, now the **Lighthouse,** the **Willow Tea Rooms** on Sauchiehall Street, and the **Scotland Street School.** His own West End home from 1906 to 1914 (with wife and collaborator Margaret Macdonald) was itself a work of art, eschewing the fussy clutter of the age for clean, elegant lines. Its interiors have been recreated by the University of Glasgow's Hunterian Gallery. Twenty-five miles west of Glasgow in Helensburgh is perhaps his greatest singular achievement: **Hill House,** designed for publisher Walter Blackie in 1902.

Later failures to win commissions locally led Mackintosh to move out of Glasgow, to the southern coast of England and later to Port Vendres in France. In both places, however, his artistic talents were not wasted. He painted watercolors of flowers and landscapes that are as distinctive as his architectural and interior design work.

St. Mungo Museum of Religious Life and Art
Townhead

Opened in 1993, this eclectic museum near Glasgow Cathedral embraces a collection that spans the centuries and highlights various religious groups. It has been hailed as unique in that Buddha, Ganesha, and Shiva, amongst other spiritual leaders, saints, and historic figures, are all treated equally. The centerpiece of the various exhibits has to be the infamous painting by Spanish surrealist Salvador Dalí: *Christ of St. John of the Cross.* Purchased at great expense by the city, it's point of view looks down upon a crucified man set against a stark black background. A more recent acquisition is Kenny Hunter's statue of Jesus. The grounds include a Zen garden of stone and gravel.

See map p. 220. 2 Castle St. ☎ *0141-552-2557.* www.glasgowmuseums.com. *Bus: 11, 36, 38, 42, or 89. Admission: free. Open: Mon–Thurs and Sat 10 a.m.–5 p.m., Fri and Sun 11 a.m.–5 p.m.*

St. Vincent Street Church
Commerical Center

Access is limited here, but the church is the most visible landmark attributed to the city's *other* great architect, Alexander "Greek" Thomson. Built originally for Presbyterians in 1859, the stone church offers two classic Greek porticos facing north and south beside a clock tower decorated in exotic yet sympathetic Egyptian, Assyrian, and even Indian-looking motifs and designs. The interior is surprisingly colorful.

See map p. 220. 265 St. Vincent St. Suburban train: Charing Cross. Sunday services at 11 a.m. and 6:30 p.m. Interiors open only during services.

Science Centre
South Side

The Science Centre has been called Britain's most successful "millennium project," but with so many stinkers constructed to commemorate the year 2000, that compliment can be read as faint praise. Indeed, a millennium jinx has hit even here. The tall, slender tower atop which an observatory room was designed to give breathtaking views closed shortly after the Science Centre opened in 2001, and in 2004, it remained off-limits. Still, on the banks of the River Clyde and opposite the Scottish Exhibition and Conference Centre, this futuristic-looking, silver-skinned edifice (the first titanium-clad building in Britain) is the focal point of Glasgow's drive to redevelop the once run-down former docklands. The overall theme of the centre's exhibitions is to document 21st-century challenges as well as Glasgow's contribution to science and technology in the past, present, and future. Families should enjoy the hands-on and interactive activities, whether they're taking three-dimensional head scans or starring in their own digital videos.

The Science Centre is also home to Scotland's first IMAX Theatre, which uses film with a frame size some 10 times larger than the standard 35mm film. The projected picture is the size of a five-story building. The theater charges separate admission: £5.95 ($11) for adults, £4.45 ($8) for students and children, and £17.95 ($33) for a family ticket for two adults and two children. The theatre's open Sunday through Wednesday from 11 a.m. to 6 p.m. and Thursday through Saturday from 11 a.m. to 8 p.m.

See map p. 220. 50 Pacific Quay. ☎ *0141-420-5010.* www.gsc.org.uk. *Underground: Cessnock. Suburban train: Exhibition Centre, then walk across the footbridge over the Clyde. Bus: 89 or 90. Admission: £6.95 ($13) adults, £4.95 ($9) students and seniors, £18.95 ($35) family pass. Open: daily 10 a.m.–6 p.m.*

More cool things to do and see

City Chambers
Merchant City

Located on George Square, Glasgow's city hall is even more impressive on the inside than on the outside. Even if you don't take the free tour, at least pop your head in to see the cruciform front hall (the only part open to visitors who don't take the tour). Ceiling tile work and magnificent marble columns appear throughout the building. In fact, the palatial interior has been used in many films as a stand-in for both the Vatican and the Kremlin, as well as for an interior shot in *Dr. Zhivago*. The office of the city's Lord Provost (essentially the mayor) is here as well. Outside, Yanks will note a little Statue of Liberty atop the facade, just below the flag.

See map p. 220. George Square. ☎ *0141-287-2000. Underground: Buchanan Street. Admission: free. Open: tours offered Mon–Fri at 10:30 a.m. and 2:30 p.m.*

Glasgow Green
East End

Glasgow Green's the city's oldest park, probably dating from medieval times. Running along the River Clyde southeast of the Commercial Centre, this huge stretch of green had paths laid and shrubs planted in the middle of the 18th century but didn't formally became a public park until some 100 years later. Its landmarks include the **People's Palace** (see listing earlier in this chapter) social history museum and adjoining Winter Garden, Nelson's Monument, and the Doulton Fountain. At one end of the green, the influence of the Doges' Palace in Venice can be seen in the colorful facade of the old Templeton Carpet Factory. Near here is a large children's play area. The southern side of Glasgow Green offers dulcet walks along the river.

See map p. 220. Greendyke Street (east of Saltmarket). ☎ *0141-287-5098.* www.glasgow.gov.uk. *Underground: St. Enoch. Bus: 16, 18, 40, 61, 62, or 64. Admission: free. Open: daily dawn–dusk.*

Glasgow Print Studio
Merchant City

Some of the strongest contemporary art being made in Glasgow today comes from the Print Studio's stable of artists, from the eccentric color-filled collages of Ashley Cook to Ian McNicol's meticulous etchings of streetscapes. The gallery space holds exhibits of local artists as well as international print makers. King Street is also home to the **Streetlevel** gallery (☎ 0141-552-2151), which focuses on contemporary photography, and **Intermedia** (☎ 0141-552-2540), a contemporary art gallery.

See map p. 220. 22 and 25 King St. ☎ 0141-552-0704. www.gpsart.co.uk. *Underground: St. Enoch. Bus: 18, 40, 61, or 62. Admission: free. Open: Tues–Sat 10 a.m.–5:30 p.m.*

House for an Art Lover
South Side

This "house," which opened in 1996, is based on an unrealized and incomplete 1901 competition entry from Charles Rennie Mackintosh. The building, with its elegant interiors, is therefore really a modern architect's interpretation of what Mackintosh had in mind. The tour begins in the main hall and leads through the dining room, with its gesso panels, and on to the music room, which shows Mackintosh designs at their most inspirational. A popular cafe and gift shop are located on the premises, all surrounded by a parkland setting adjacent to Victorian walled gardens.

See map p. 220. Bellahouston Park, 10 Dumbreck Rd. ☎ 0141-353-4770. www.house foranartlover.co.uk. *Underground: Ibrox. Bus: 9 or 54. Admission: £3.50 ($5.60) adults; £2.50 ($4) children, students, and seniors. Open: Apr–Sept Mon–Wed 10 a.m.– 4 p.m., Thurs–Sun 10 a.m.–1 p.m.; Oct–Mar Sat–Sun 10 a.m.–1 p.m. Cafe and shop open daily 10 a.m.–5 p.m.*

Hunterian Museum
West End

Opened in 1807 in the main Glasgow University buildings 3km (2 miles) west of the heart of the city, this is Glasgow's oldest museum. It's named after William Hunter, its early benefactor, who donated his private collections to get the museum going. The collection is wide-ranging, from dinosaur fossils to coins to relics of the Roman occupation and plunder by the Vikings. The story of Captain Cook's voyages is pieced together in ethnographic material from the South Seas. The museum has a few shops and an 18th-century–style coffeehouse.

See map p. 220. University of Glasgow, Main/Gilbert-Scott Building. ☎ 0141-330-4221, ext. 4221. www.hunterian.gla.ac.uk. *Underground: Hillhead. Admission: free. Open: Mon–Sat 9:30 a.m.–5 p.m., additional hours for special exhibits vary. Closed Jan 1, July 21, Sept 29, Dec 25.*

The legend behind Glasgow's coat of arms

Glasgow's coat of arms is displayed throughout the city, including a modified version on many lampposts. What's with those fish and bells? At the top of the armorial insignia is St. Kentigern (better known as St. Mungo, the patron saint of Glasgow), and on the other three sides are salmon with gold rings in their mouths surrounding a tree with a bird and bell in it. This coat of arms may look a tad odd, but it has a legend behind it.

The fish and rings are from lore of St. Mungo's recovery of a ring that was a gift to the Queen of Cadzow from her husband. The queen secretly gave the ring to a knight (presumably her lover), and the jealous king stole the ring from the sleeping knight and threw it into the River Clyde. The next day, the king demanded the ring from his wife, and when she could not produce it, he threatened to kill her. St. Mungo instructed one of his monks to go fishing and return with the first fish caught — the salmon pulled from the River Clyde contained the ring.

The tree represents the one that, according to legend, St. Mungo was able to light on fire by praying over it. The bird represents a wild robin tamed by St. Mungo's master, St. Serf; St. Mungo brought the robin back to life after it was accidentally killed. The bell represents one that the pope gave to St. Mungo; the treasure rang often before it disappeared.

Museum of Transport
West End

This museum contains a collection of all forms of transportation and related technology. Displays include a simulated 1938 Glasgow street with period shop-fronts, era-appropriate vehicles, and a reconstruction of one of the original Glasgow Underground stations. The superb and varied ship models in the Clyde Room reflect the significance of Glasgow and the River Clyde as one of the world's foremost areas of shipbuilding and engineering.

See map p. 220. 1 Bunhouse Rd., Kelvin Hall. ☎ *0141-287-2720.* www.glasgow museums.com. *Underground: Kelvin Hall. Admission: free. Open: Mon–Thurs and Sat 10 a.m.–5 p.m., Sun and Fri 11 a.m.–5 p.m. Closed Jan 1 and Dec 25.*

Pollok Country Park
South Side

In the South Side part of the city, this large, hilly expanse of open space is the home to both the Burrell Collection and Pollok House but merits a visit for its own attributes. Rhododendrons, Japanese maples, and azaleas are part of the formal plantings created at the end of the 19th century by Sir John Stirling Maxwell, whose family long-resided in Pollok House. However, the park is best for its glens and pastures, which lend themselves to grazing Highland cattle.

See map p. 220. 2060 Pollokshaws Rd. ☎ *0141-632-9299.* www.glasgow.gov.uk. *Suburban train: Pollokshaws West. Bus: 45 or 57. Admission: free. Open: daily dawn–dusk.*

Scotland Street School Museum
South Side

Another of Charles Rennie Mackintosh's designs, this building was commissioned by the local school board near the beginning of the 20th century. Surrounded by light-industrial parks and facing the M8 motorway, the school seems to be in an odd location. But that's only because all the surrounding tenements have been torn down. The museum that today occupies this admittedly lesser work from the great architect is devoted to the history of education in Scotland, with reconstructed examples of classrooms from the Victorian, World War II, and 1960s eras. It also has displays on Mackintosh's design for the building.

See map p. 220. 225 Scotland St. ☎ *0141-287-0500.* www.glasgowmuseums.com. *Underground: Shields Road. Bus: 89 or 90. Admission: free. Open: Mon–Thurs and Sat 10 a.m.–5 p.m., Sun and Fri 11 a.m.–5 p.m.*

The Tall Ship at Glasgow Harbour
West End

Here you have a chance to board one of the last remaining Clydebuilt sailing ships, the s.v. *Glenlee.* Built in 1896, she circumnavigated Cape Horn 15 times. Restored in 1999, the vessel is one of only five Clydebuilt sailing ships that remain afloat. You can explore the ship and take in an exhibition detailing *Glenlee's* cargo-trading history while you're onboard.

If maritime topics float your boat, also consider visiting the **Clydebuilt Scottish Maritime Museum** (☎ **0141-886-1013;** www.scottishmaritime museum.org/renfrew.htm) in the Braehead Shopping Centre. Tickets are £3.50 ($6.50) for adults and £1.75 ($3) for children and seniors.

See map p. 220. 100 Stobcross Rd. ☎ *0141-222-2513.* www.glenlee.co.uk. *Suburban train: Exhibition Centre. Bus: tour buses. Admission: £4.50 ($8) adults, £3.25 ($6) seniors. One child is free with each adult or senior; additional children: £2.50 ($4.65). Open: Mar–Oct daily 10 a.m.–5 p.m., Nov–Feb daily 10 a.m.–4 p.m.*

Tenement House
Commercial Centre

Many Glasgwegians lived in tenements (or apartment buildings) from the middle of 19th century on. And many still live in such buildings today (although the conditions are dramatically improved). Run by the National Trust for Scotland, this "museum" is a typical flat, preserved with all the fixtures and fittings from the early part of the 20th century: coal fires, box bed in the kitchen, and gas lamps. Indeed, the resident, Miss Agnes Toward, apparently never threw out anything from 1911 to 1965, so the

museum has displays of all sorts of memorabilia, from tickets stubs and letters to ration coupons and photographs from trips down the Clyde.
See map p. 220. 145 Buccleuch St. ☎ *0141-333-0183.* www.nts.org.uk. *Underground: Cowcaddens. Bus: 20, 41, or 66. Admission: £4 ($7.50) adults, £2 ($3.75) children. Open: Mar–Oct daily 1–5 p.m. Closed Nov–Feb.*

Guided tours

The **City Sightseeing Glasgow** tours circle the town in brightly colored and open-topped buses. They operate from April through October, departing from George Square about every 15 to 20 minutes between 9:30 a.m. and 4:30 p.m. You can hop on and off at some 22 designated stops such as Glasgow Green, the University, or the Royal Concert Hall. Passes are valid for 24 hours after purchase. The live commentary can be quite entertaining and informative, and fortunately the company offers multi-lingual versions, too. For more information, contact the office at 153 Queen St. at George Square (☎ **0141-204-0444;** www.citysightseeing.co.uk). Tickets are £3 to £8 ($5.50–$13), and £19.50 ($36) for a family.

Operated by a privately owned company that has had a virtual monopoly on municipal bus routes in Glasgow, **First City Tour** buses are rather cute mustard and green 1950s-style vintage models. The First City tour, which runs from April through October, follows roughly the same route as other tour buses, with 17 stops. The first bus leaves George Square at 9:30 a.m., and service is continuous throughout the day until 4:30 p.m. More information can be obtained by calling ☎ **0141-636-3190** or going online, www.firstcitytour.co.uk. Tickets are £3 to £8 ($5.50–$13) or £19.50 ($36) for a family.

If you prefer to keep your feet on the ground and your focus on the more ghoulish aspects of Glasgow, the **Mercat Glasgow** walking tours are happy to oblige. In season (Easter through October), they depart every evening from the Tourist Information Centre at George Square at about 7:30 p.m. Guides recreate macabre Glasgow — a parade of goons including hangmen, ghosts, murderers, and body snatchers. The tours take about 1½ hours. The company also does Historic Glasgow tours on request. For information, contact Mercat at 25 Forth Rd., Bearsden (☎ **0141-586-5378;** www.mercat-glasgow.co.uk). Tickets are £7 ($13).

And if the sea floats your boat, check out **Waverley Excursions** (☎ **0141-221-8152** or 0845-130-4647; www.waverleyexcursions.co.uk). The *Waverley,* considered the world's last "seagoing" paddle steamship, was built on the Clyde in 1947. During the summer and depending on weather conditions, it continues to ply the river. One-day trips beginning at Waverley Terminal (at Anderston Quay in Broomielaw) in Glasgow take passengers "doon the watter" to historic and scenic places along the Firth of Clyde, sometimes going as far as the Isle of Arran. As you sail along, you can take in what were once vast shipyards, turning out more than half the earth's tonnage of oceangoing liners. Boat tours cost £8.95 to £29.95 ($16.50–$55).

A festival all its own

There's no doubt that if history could be rewritten, Glasgow would love to be the host of the annual International Festival instead of Edinburgh. But, the city to the west is not bereft of annual happenings. **Celtic Connections** is the best attended annual festival in Glasgow and the largest of its kind (a folk festival plus more than that description implies) in the world. It kicks off the year every January. The main venue for performances is the Royal Concert Hall, which produces the event. Guests include folk musicians, dancers, and contemporary artists. For more information, contact ☎ **0141-353-8000** or visit www.grch.com.

Suggested 1-, 2-, and 3-day itineraries

If you feel a bit overwhelmed by all the options of things to do and see in Glasgow, you're not alone. I've laid out a few itineraries in this section to help you focus on your interests and use your time most efficiently, while giving you a good sampling of what Glasgow has to offer. Remember, these are just my ideas — feel free to tailor these itineraries to suit your own schedule and taste.

If you have 1 day

From George Square (the city's main plaza in front of Glasgow City Chambers and the Queen Street station), catch one of the open-topped Glasgow **tour buses.** Depending on your guide, the trip can be as entertaining as it is informative. The buses circumnavigate the city from historic **Glasgow Cathedral** and the sprawling riverside park, **Glasgow Green,** in the east to **Glasgow University** and trendy **Byres Road** in the West. These open tour buses are the best way for visitors to get oriented and understand the city's layout and topography. Tickets are valid for 24 hours, and you can get off and on as much as you desire. Visit at least one of the city-run museums (they're free) and a bona-fide Glasgow pub, such as the **Horse Shoe.**

If you have 2 days

Spend your first day as I suggest in the one-day itinerary. Then, for your second day, go south and visit the **Burrell Collection.** This remarkable assortment of art and cultural artifacts from ancient to modern is the pride of the city; it's housed in an attractive, specially designed contemporary building amid verdant Pollok Country Park. Take in a bit of real **Charles Rennie Mackintosh,** by way of an organized tour of the **Art School** on Garnethill or an unguided visit to the interiors of his family house reconstructed at Glasgow University's **Hunterian Art Gallery.**

If you have 3 days

After London, Glasgow is the second best city for shopping in the entire UK. But don't be content with the familiar department stores (House of

When facing the bridge at the infantry memorial, go right (north) and follow one of the two paths that run along the river and exit the park at:

6. Gibson Street

Leaving the park, turn left (west) and cross the short road bridge that brings you into the Hillhead district, which includes the main campus of the University of Glasgow on Gilmorehill, the Western Infirmary, as well as the Scottish headquarters of the BBC.

Continue west on Gibson Street to Bank Street, go right (north) one block to Great George Street, then left (west) one block to Oakfield Avenue and:

7. Eton Terrace

Here, on the corner across from Hillhead High School, the unmistakable work of architect Alexander Thomson is evident in an impressive (if today poorly kept) terrace of eight houses completed in 1864 (following his similarly designed Moray Place). Two temple-like facades serve as bookends, both pushing slightly forward and rising one floor higher than the rest, and have double porches apparently fashioned after the Choragic Monument of Thrassylus in Athens. Funnily enough, for all his admiration of Eastern design, Thomson never traveled outside the UK.

Return to the corner of Great George Street and follow Oakfield Avenue, crossing Gibson Street to University Avenue; then turn right up the hill to the:

8. University of Glasgow

Aficionados rightfully bemoan the loss of the original campus east of the High Street, which may have offered the best examples of 17th-century architecture in Scotland. The university moved to its current location in the 1860s, and the city could have done worse — a lot worse. The setting high above Kelvingrove Park is befitting of a center of learning. Englishman Sir George Gilbert Scott controversially won the design commission and his Gothic Revival is punctuated by the 100-foot tower that rises from the double quadrangle — a virtual beacon on the horizon of the West End. Fragments of the original university can be seen, too, in the facade of Pearce Lodge as well as the salvaged Lion and Unicorn Stair at the chapel. The cloistered vaults and open columns under the halls between the two quads are evocative. From here you can enter the Hunterian Museum, whose exhibits include ancient coins, geology, and archeology.

Cross University Avenue north to Hillhead Street and the:

9. Hunterian Art Gallery

Built in the 1980s next to the university library, this gallery houses the school's permanent collection, which includes 18th- and 19th-century Scottish art as well as many works by James McNeill

Whistler. Scots-Italian contemporary artist Eduardo Paolozzi designed the chunky cast aluminum internal doors to the main exhibition space.

Incorporated into the building (past the gift shop) is:

10. Mackintosh House

Charles Rennie Mackintosh's and wife Margaret Macdonald's West End home (originally nearby and demolished by the university in the 1960s) is replicated here with furniture and interiors designed by the pair. Visitors enter from the side (the front door is actually several feet above the level of the plaza outside) and see the dining room, sitting room with study, and the couple's bedroom. At the top is a replication of a bedroom Mackintosh designed for a house in England, his final commission.

Return to University Avenue, exit Mackintosh House turning right to:

11. University Gardens

This fine row of houses was designed primarily by J.J. Burnet in the 1880s, but it's worth stopping especially to admire No. 12, done by J. Gaff Gillespie in 1900; that house exemplifies Glasgow style and the influences of Mackintosh and Art Nouveau.

Continue down University Gardens past Queen Margaret Union and other university buildings, going left down the stairs just past the Gregory Building. At the bottom of the stairs, follow the sidewalk and turn right onto:

12. Ashton Lane

This cobbled mews is the heart of West End nightlife, although it bustles right through the day, too, with a mix of students, University instructors, and staff, as well as local residents. The host of bars, cafes, and restaurants here includes the venerable Ubiquitous Chip, which can be credited for starting (in 1971) the ongoing renaissance of excellent cooking of fresh Scottish produce.

Go left past Ubiquitous Chip down the narrow lane to Byres Road. Just to the right, you can catch the underground (Hillhead station) back to the city center (Buchanan Street station). Or turn right on:

13. Byres Road

Ashton Lane's primary entrance is midway along the proverbial Main Street of this part of Glasgow: Byres Road, which is full of bars, cafes, restaurants, and shops. Rarely less than buzzing, the road exemplifies the West End for many people. If you aren't in a hurry, the streets running west from Byres Road, such as Athole or Huntly Gardens, merit a brief wander to see the proud town houses.

Proceed north up Byres Road to:

14. Great Western Road

It took an act of Parliament in London in 1836 to create this street, then a new turnpike road into the city. Today, its four lanes remain one of the main thoroughfares into and out of Glasgow. A stroll west for five or six blocks from this intersection (Byres and Great Western roads) reveals the opulent terraces (including one by Thomson) along Great Western's southern flank. Going in the opposite direction takes you to more retail and commercial shops.

Cross Great Western Road to the:

15. Botanic Gardens

Neither as extensive nor as grand as the Royal Botanic Gardens in Edinburgh, this hilly park is pleasant nonetheless. One main attraction, Kibble Palace, a giant domed cast iron and glass Victorian conservatory with exotic plants, was being restored in 2004. Other greenhouses house orchid collections, while the outdoor planting includes a working vegetable plot, roses and rhododendrons, and beds with lots of flowering perennials.

Shopping in Glasgow

After London, which of course is the capital of Great Britain and a city at least ten times the size of Glasgow, Glasgow has the most retail space in all of the UK. It's a shopping mecca for everyone in the west of the country and draws visitors from northern England, too.

Among the few retail goods that are high quality *and* competitively priced here are fine wool knits, particularly cashmere scarves and sweaters — or as the Scots prefer, "jumpers." Expect anything produced within the country (with the exception of whisky, which is taxed as heavily as all alcoholic products) to be less expensive than at home — that goes for smoked salmon, shortbread, and Caithness glass (those beguiling clear paper weights with swirling, colorful designs). Second-hand shops, often run by charities such as Oxfam, are potential gold mines for bargain hunters. Finally, given the number of artists in the country, getting an original piece of art to bring home may represent the most value for your shopping money in Glasgow.

For visitors from abroad, prices in the UK aren't a major selling point. In recent years, the British currency (the pound sterling) has been trading strongly against other major currencies, such as the US dollar and the euro (which most of Britain's partners in the European Union now use). The good news is that prices for most products in Scotland have been stable since the mid-1990s, and in some cases (for example, clothes) prices have come down in real terms. Nevertheless, many items carry the same numerical price in pounds as they would in American dollars. For example, a digital camera that costs $300 in New York may well be priced £300 in Glasgow, making it 50 to 100 percent more expensive.

Best shopping areas

The main area for retail therapy is defined by the pedestrian malls of **Argyle Street, Buchanan Street,** and **Sauchiehall Street,** which join together and form a Z shape right in the heart of the city. But for more unique shops and fashions, it pays to venture to the **Merchant City** and the **West End.** And perhaps the city's most unique shopping experience is at the flea market-like stalls at the weekend **Barras** market, in the East End of Glasgow.

In general, shops in the city are open Monday to Wednesday, Friday, and Saturday from 9 a.m. or 10 a.m. until 6 p.m. And be warned, they tend to close sharply, regardless of the number of potential shoppers still out on the sidewalks. Only on Thursday do the shops stay open "late," until 8 p.m. Most established stores are now open in the afternoon on Sunday, too.

Shopping complexes

Of course, any shopping city worth its salt these days must offer indoor malls. In Glasgow, **Princes Square** (Buchanan Street; ☎ 0141-204-1685; www.princessquare.co.uk) is the city's most stylish and up-market shopping center. Housed in a modernized and renovated Victorian building, the mall has many specialty stores, men's and women's fashion outlets, and restaurants, cafes, and bars.

Nearby, between Argyle Street and the River Clyde is the **St. Enoch Shopping Centre** (☎ 0141-204-3900), whose merchandise is less expensive and a lot less posh than what you find at Princes Square. St. Enoch's resembles a fairly conventional mall, with a couple major department stores and a food court at one end.

If you're after a fancy watch or gold ring, go to the **Argyll Arcade,** the main entrance to which is at 30 Buchanan St. Even if the year of its construction (1827) weren't posted above the entrance, you'd still know that this collection of shops beneath a curved glass ceiling is historic. The L-shaped arcade contains one of the largest concentrations of retail **jewelers,** both antique and modern, in all of Europe. Purchasing a wedding band here is considered lucky.

The latest contribution to mall shopping in the city center is the **Buchanan Galleries** (☎ 0141-333-9898; www.buchanangalleries.co.uk), found at the top of Buchanan Street. Completed in 1999, this mammoth development is hardly groundbreaking, but it does include the rightfully respected **John Lewis** department store.

On the western outskirts of town, the **Braehead Shopping Centre** (☎ 0141-885-1441; www.braehead.co.uk) opened most recently and somewhat controversially because it appears to be taking people away from the city center. Braehead's major draw is a sprawling Ikea store.

What to look for and where to find it

If your shopping intentions are less of the browsing variety, here are some of Glasgow's specialized shopping options.

Antiques

✔ **Victorian Village** offers a warren of shops and a pleasantly claustrophobic clutter of goods. Much of the merchandise isn't particularly noteworthy, but you can find some worthwhile pieces if you know what you're after and are willing to go hunting. 93 W. Regent St. (☎ 0141-332-0808)

Art

✔ **Compass Gallery** was opened by Cyril Gerber (see next bullet) to offer affordable pieces of contemporary art by local artists. You can find something special for as little as £20 ($37) here, depending on the show. The pre-Christmas sale is particularly good. 178 W. Regent St. (☎ 0141-221-6370)

✔ **Cyril Gerber Fine Art** is one of Glasgow's best small galleries and shops. It veers away from the avant-garde, specializing in British painting of the 19th and 20th centuries. It has good Scottish landscapes and cityscapes, especially works by Colourists and the Glasgow Boys. Gerber has been the city's most respected art authority for several decades, with lots of contacts in art circles throughout Britain. 148 W. Regent St. (☎ 0141-221-3095; www.cyrilgerberfineart.com)

✔ **Glasgow Print Studio** includes a shop that sells limited edition etchings, wood blocks, aquatints, and screen prints by members of the prestigious collective as well as other notable artists. Prices are good, and there's a framing facility on the premises. 25 King St. (☎ 0141-552-0704; www.gpsart.co.uk)

Books

✔ **Borders** offers a multi-story shop at the back of Royal Exchange Square. You find a gratifying emphasis on the culture of Scotland and plenty of places to sit and read. Borders also has the best selection of international periodicals in Scotland. 98 Buchanan St. (☎ 0141-222-7700; www.borders.com)

✔ **Caledonia Books** is one of the few remaining secondhand and antiquarian shops in the city of Glasgow. Charming and well run, the stock here tends to favor quality over quantity. 483 Great Western Rd., West End (☎ 0141-334-9663; caledoniabooks.co.uk)

✔ **Waterstones** is a giant Barnes and Noble–like operation with plenty of stock, a cafe, and a lot of soft seats. The ground floor features a good Scottish section. 174 Sauchiehall St. (☎ 0141-248-4814; www.waterstones.co.uk)

Clothes

- **Cruise** has the best selection of designer togs in town — better bring your credit cards! Labels include Prada, Armani, D&G, Vivienne Westwood, and more. At the second branch nearby (223 Ingram St.), the Oki-Ni shop within the shop offers limited edition Adidas and Levi. 180 Ingram St., Merchant City (☎ **0141-572-3232**)

- **Dr. Jives** began as a vintage clothing shop for men in the late 1980s but has evolved into the hippest boutique in town for cutting-edge designer looks, especially for the skater crowds at the dance clubs. 111 Candleriggs, Merchant City (☎ **0141-552-4551**)

- **Gap** at Buchanan Galleries offers its familiar and comfortable range of mostly cotton blouses, shirts, and trousers. Another central outlet is on Argyle Street. 220 Buchanan St. (☎ **0141-333-9699**)

- **Jigsaw** was recently relocated under the glorious dome of the Baroque-style former Savings Bank of Glasgow. This is the fashionable UK chain of women's wear, juniors, and accessories. Using its own design team in Kew, West London, Jigsaw opened its first shop in Hampsted some 30 years ago. 177 Ingram St., at Glassford Street (☎ **0141-552-7639**)

- **Starry Starry Night** shows just how tiny those Victorians and Edwardians were — although they wore some pretty stunning gowns. This shop (with a branch in the Barras market) normally has a few items worth dusting off. It also stocks secondhand kilts and matching attire. 19 Dowanside Lane, West End (☎ **0141-337-1837**)

Department stores

- **Debenhams** is a sturdy department store with mid-range prices. St. Enoch Shopping Centre, 97 Argyle St. (☎ **0141-221-0088**)

- **House of Fraser** is Glasgow's version of Harrods. A Victorian-era glass arcade rises up four stories, and on the various levels you find everything from clothing to Oriental rugs, from crystal to handmade local artifacts of all kinds. 21–45 Buchanan St., at Argyle Street (☎ **0141-221-3880;** www.houseoffraser.co.uk)

- **John Lewis** is a close equivalent to Macy's, with quality brand names, assured service, and a no-questions-asked return policy on damaged or faulty goods. Buchanan Galleries, 220 Buchanan St. (☎ **0141-353-6677**)

- **Marks & Spencer** has had its share of problems with shareholders and in board rooms, as anyone who reads international finance pages will know. But the chain carries on with clothing and very good food halls. The two branches in Glasgow are on Argyle and Sauchiehall streets. 2–12 Argyle St. (☎ **0141-552-4546**); 172 Sauchiehall St. (☎ **0141-332-6097**)

Edibles

See the sidebar "Picnic fare," earlier in this chapter, for a list of select food markets with Scottish specialties.

Gifts and design

✔ **Catherine Shaw** is named after the long-deceased matriarch of the family that runs the place today. It's a somewhat cramped gift shop that has cups, mugs, postcards, jewelry, and souvenirs — a good place for easy-to-pack gifts. 24 Gordon St. (☎ **0141-204-4762**). Look for another branch at 31 Argyll Arcade (☎ **0141-221-9038**); entrances to the arcade are on both Argyll and Buchanan streets.

✔ **Felix & Oscar** is a wacky and fun shop for off-beat cards and toys, kitsch accessories, fuzzy bags, perfumes and toiletries, and a selection of T-shirts that you're not likely to find anywhere else in Glasgow. (In addition to the flagship, two others are located on Cresswell Lane and Otago Street.) 459 Great Western Rd., West End (☎ **0131-339-8585**)

✔ **Mackintosh Shop** is a small gift shop in the Glasgow School of Art that prides itself on a stock of books, cards, stationery, mugs, glassware, and sterling-and-enamel jewelry created from or inspired by the original designs of Charles Rennie Mackintosh. Glasgow School of Art, 167 Renfrew St. (☎ **0141-353-4500**)

✔ **National Trust for Scotland Shop** offers "Glasgow-style" contemporary arts and crafts, pottery, furniture, and jewelry designed exclusively by local artists. Hutcheson Hall, 158 Ingram St. (☎ **0141-552-8391**)

Music

✔ **Avalanche** is the indie music CD store to beat all others. It's small and cramped (near Queen Street Station) but is the best for the latest releases by everybody from White Stripes to local stars Belle & Sebastian and up-and-comers like Glasgow's own Dogs Die in Hot Cars. 34 Dundas St. (☎ **0141-332-2099**)

✔ **Fopp** is Glasgow's most accomplished record outlet. It offers one of the best selections of CDs, ranging from classics to hottest hits and including music books and vinyl, too. Fopp also stocks a good number of re-releases priced at only £5 ($9.25). 358 Byres Rd., West End (☎ **0141-357-0774**). In addition to the West End flagship, a larger, multi-story branch is in the city center on Union Street (☎ **0141-222-2128**).

✔ **HMV** is, along with Virgin, Great Britain's largest purveyor of mainstream music CDs, DVDs, and videos. 154 Sauchiehall St. (☎ **0141-332-6631;** www.hmv.com)

Kilts and tartan

✔ **Geoffrey (Tailor) Kiltmakers and Weavers** is both a retailer and a manufacturer of tartans, which means they have all the clans and have also created their own range of 21st-century–style kilts — for better or worse. 309 Sauchiehall St. (☎ **0141-331-2388**; www.geoffreykilts.co.uk)

✔ **Hector Russell** was founded in 1881 and remains Scotland's long-established kiltmaker. Crystal and gift items are sold on street level, but the real heart and soul of the place is below, where impeccably crafted and reasonably priced tweed jackets, tartan-patterned accessories, waistcoats, and sweaters of top-quality wool for men and women are displayed. 110 Buchanan St. (☎ **0141-221-0217**)

✔ **James Pringle Weavers** has been in business since 1780. This shop is known for its traditional clothing that includes well-crafted, bulky wool sweaters and a tasteful selection of ties, kilts, and tartans. Some of the merchandise is unique to this shop. Ever slept in a tartan nightshirt? 130 Buchanan St. (☎ **0141-221-3434**)

Living It Up After Dark

Today, some say that Glasgow — and not Edinburgh — is the center of contemporary culture in Scotland. It's an arguable, not to say locally controversial, point of view, however.

The truth is this: Both cities contribute mightily — and equally — to the cultural vibrancy of the nation. Their strength as a *pair* of lively cities, separated by only about 50 miles, is considerably more important than which has the most to offer individually. With this idea in mind, the country would do well to improve the public transportation links between the two cities, especially in the wee small hours. Nightlife in both Edinburgh and Glasgow would benefit if officials made it easier to move between the two city centers after dark.

But there's no doubt that Glasgow has seen the most progress since the middle of the 20th century, when the shipping boom went bust and gave way to an image of profound decline that was reversed in the late 1970s and throughout the 1980s. Despite the periods of decline, however, Glasgow's local arts scene was always alive.

Although the Scottish capital to the east is home to the country's national art galleries and museums, Glasgow is where the national opera and ballet companies as well as **the Scottish National Orchestra** are based. It's also the city where young talent is nurtured at the **Royal Scottish Academy of Music and Drama**. Additionally, Glasgow's home to several theaters, including two that rank highly across the UK for staging groundbreaking drama: the **Citizens** and the **Tron**. Even more experimental performance can be seen at the **Arches** and **Tramway**.

The performing arts

Although hardly competition for a drama giant like London, Glasgow's theater scene is the equal of Edinburgh's. Young Scottish playwrights often make their debuts here, and you're likely to see anything from Steinbeck's *The Grapes of Wrath* to Beckett's *Waiting for Godot* to Shakespeare's *Romeo and Juliet* done in Edwardian dress.

✔ **The Arches** is located within the vaulted brick arches beneath the railway lines in and out of Central Station. The Arches offers a range of inexpensive drama and performances — that includes edgy new plays as well as Shakespeare — by its own unit as well as visiting companies. But the Arches also has space for a fairly full schedule of live music of all description, regular dance clubs, and visual art exhibits. Although it receives grants from government arts bodies, the Arches is an independent entity. Every April, the venue even hosts its own Theatre Festival. The cafe/bar at the Arches is, like at the Traverse in Edinburgh, a scene unto itself. Tickets are £4 to £10 ($7.50–$18). 253 Argyle St. (☎ **0141-565-1023;** www.thearches.co.uk; Underground: St. Enoch)

✔ **Citizens Theatre** is perhaps the prime symbol of Glasgow's verve and democratic approach to theater. Located in the Gorbals, just across the River Clyde from the Commercial Centre area of Glasgow, the "Citz" is home to a repertory company and has three performance spaces: a main auditorium and two smaller theaters. In 2004, new artistic director Jeremy Raison made his debut. Prices are always reasonable. Tickets are £5 to £15 ($9–$28). 119 Gorbals St. (☎ **0141-429-0022;** www.citz.co.uk; Bus: 5, 12, 20, or 66)

✔ **Glasgow Royal Concert Hall** is the home of the **Royal Scottish National Orchestra,** which plays its yearly Winter–Spring series and Pops seasons in the main auditorium. Very little is subtle about this modern music hall, which is the most prestigious performance space in the city for everything from touring ballet companies to pop/rock acts such as Elvis Costello or Jackson Browne. The hall also produces the city's annual Celtic Connections festival every January. Tickets are £10 to £35 ($18.50–$65). 2 Sauchiehall St. (☎ **0141-353-8000;** www.grch.com; Underground: Buchanan Street)

✔ **The King's Theatre** celebrated its 100th birthday in 2004. This magnificent, red-sandstone hall is the place where famous touring Broadway and West End spectacles, such as *Miss Saigon,* are likely to appear — as well as locally produced popular and light entertainment, whether comedies, musicals, or family-oriented plays. During December and January, the King's is best noted for its over-the-top pantomime presentations, often starring well-known Scottish actors. Tickets are £6 to £26 ($11–$48). 297 Bath St. (☎ **0141-240-111;** www.theambassadors.com/kings; Suburban train: Charing Cross; Bus: 16 or 18)

✔ **Pavilion Theatre** is, compared to the King's Theatre, an equally historic if less architecturally distinguished venue. It specializes in family entertainment, variety shows, light drama, tribute acts, and bands, as well as comedy and occasional modern versions of vaudeville (which, as they assure you around here, is still alive). The Pavilion's a prime location for pantomime around Christmas time. Tickets are £10 to £25 ($16–$40). 121 Renfield St. (☎ **0141-332-1846;** www.paviliontheatre.co.uk; Underground: Buchanan Street; Bus: 21, 23, or 38)

✔ **Theatre Royal** is the home of the ambitious, well respected, but also financially beleaguered **Scottish Opera,** as well as the **Scottish Ballet.** The theater also hosts visiting companies from around the world. Called somewhat exaggeratedly by the *Daily Telegraph* "the most beautiful opera theatre in the kingdom," the auditorium does offer splendid Victorian plasterwork and some glittering chandeliers. However, it's not the décor but the daunting repertoire — Wagner's *Ring* cycle or *La Boheme,* for example — that traditionally has attracted opera-goers. But budget cutbacks announced in 2004 have put this all at risk, according to some critics. Tickets range from £3.50 (standby) to £55 ($6.50–$102). 254 Hope St. (☎ **0141-332-9000;** www.theatreroyalglasgow.com; Underground: Cowcaddens; Bus: 20, 40, or 41)

✔ **Tramway** is a post-industrial, huge hangar of an arts venue and one of the only places in Glasgow able to stage sprawling performance art and modern theatre, such as Peter Brook's *The Mahabharata,* which came here in the late 1980s. In 2004, however, the city, which owns Tramway, was controversially considering the option of renting it to the national ballet company as rehearsal space. In addition to drama, the former repair shop for the city's trams houses art exhibits. Tickets range from £4 to £12 ($7.50–$22). 25 Albert Dr., Pollokshields, South Side (☎ **0141-330-3050;** www.tramway.org; Bus: 38 or 45; Suburban train: Pollokshields East)

✔ **Tron Theatre** is housed in a part of the former Tron Church, which dates back to the 15th century. The venue offers one of Scotland's leading stages for new and sometimes experimental dramatic performances. The stage is often the place where contemporary local companies, such as Cryptic or Vanishing Point, debut works. In addition to theater, the hall is used for music and dance. The Tron also has a modern bar/cafe as well as a beautifully restored Victorian bar/restaurant serving lunch and dinner, including vegetarian dishes, as well as a fine selection of beer and wine. Tickets are £3 to £20 ($5.50–$37). 63 Trongate (☎ **0141-552-4267;** www.tron.co.uk; Underground: St. Enoch)

For a complete rundown of what's happening in the city, pick up a copy of *The List,* a biweekly magazine available at all major newsstands and book shops. *The List* reviews, previews, and gives the details of arts and events in Glasgow and Edinburgh. Alternatively, the Glasgow *Herald* publishes a weekend events supplement called "Going Out" every Thursday morning.

Comedy

✔ **Jongleurs Comedy Club** is a corporate-owned entity from down south, with more than a dozen venues across the UK. The cover charge is £12 ($22). UGC Building, Renfield and Renfrew streets (☎ **0870-787-0707;** Underground: Buchanan Street)

✔ **The Stand** opened a second venue in Glasgow after starting and thriving in Edinburgh. The city's only purpose-built comedy club, its presence has helped to establish an annual International Comedy Festival every spring in the city. Usually, Tuesday night, called "Red Raw," is reserved for amateurs. The cover charge is £2 to £8 ($4–$15). 333 Woodlands Rd. (☎ **0870-600-6055;** www. thestand.co.uk; Underground: Kelvinbridge)

Folk

✔ **Oran Mor** opened in the summer of 2004 as an ambitious center for the performing arts that includes bars and restaurants as well as different spaces for live music. Byres and Great Western roads (☎ **0870-013-2652;** Underground: Hillhead)

✔ **St. Andrews in the Square** is a sympathetically restored and con- verted 18th-century church that is now dedicated to folk and tradi- tional Scottish music. The program includes concerts and ceilidhs (Scottish country dances) in the main hall upstairs. In the basement, **Café Source** serves wholesome Scottish nosh and hosts regular ses- sions of jazz and Scottish music, which may be rather reverentially enjoyed by the patrons. Tickets are £4 to £8 ($7.50–$15). 1 St. Andrews Sq. (☎ **0141-548-6020;** www.standrewsinthesquare.com; Underground: St. Enoch)

✔ **Scotia Bar** is one beam in a triangle of pubs that frequently offer live music that includes but is not solely folk. The others pubs of this sort are nearby: **Clutha Vaults** and **Victoria.** No cover charge is required. 112 Stockwell St. (☎ **0141-552-8681**)

Rock, pop, and jazz

✔ **Barrowland** has no seats and may stink of beer, but this former ballroom is the top place in the city to see visiting bands. The hall rocks, and groups generally rank it among the best venues in the UK in which to perform. With room for about 2,000, Barrowland isn't exactly intimate, but if you can withstand the mosh pit, you'll feel the sweat of the performers. 244 Gallowgate (☎ **0141-552-4601;** Underground: St. Enoch; Bus: 61, 62, or 24)

✔ **Carling Academy** is a 2,500-capacity ex-Bingo hall that opened as a live music venue in 2003. It's part of a chain, which includes the leg- endary Brixton Academy in London, and thus has a booking strength with touring bands. Pity its corporate sponsor has to be so promi- nent in the name. 121 Eglinton Rd. (☎ **0141-418-3000;** Underground: Bridge St.)

✔ **Grand Ole Opry,** a sprawling sandstone building 2.5km (1½ miles) south of the city center, is the largest club in Europe devoted to country and western music. (And they love their country and western music in Glasgow!) The Opry has a bar and dancing (Texas line-style) on two levels and a chuck-wagon eatery that serves affordable steaks and other such fare. Performers are usually from the UK, but a handful of artists from the States turn up, too. The cover charge is £3 to £10 ($5.50–$30). 2–4 Govan Rd., Paisley Toll Road (☎ **0141-429-5396;** Bus: 9 or 54)

✔ **King Tut's Wah-Wah Hut** is a crowded rock bar that has been in business for more than a decade. It's a good place to check out the Glasgow music and arts crowd as well as local bands and the occasional international act. Successful Scottish acts such as Teenage Fan Club got their starts here. The cover is usually about £5 ($9). 272 St. Vincent St. (☎ **0141-221-5279;** Bus: 9 or 62)

✔ **Nice 'n' Sleazy** books live acts to perform in the dark, basement space. The cover is quite reasonable, but it can get more expensive if you catch a more established act, such as ex-head Lemonhead, Evan Dando. Holding some 200 patrons, it provides a rare opportunity to catch such musicians in an intimate setting. The cover charge is £5–£20 ($9.25–$37). 421 Sauchiehall St. (☎ **0141-333-9637;** Bus: 18 or 44; Suburban train: Charing Cross)

✔ **The Scottish Exhibition & Conference Centre,** which incorporates the slightly more intimate Clyde Auditorium (also called the "Armadillo" because of its exterior design), may indeed be charmless, but it provides Scotland with the only indoor space large enough to host major touring acts, from Ozzie Osbourne to Justin Timberlake. Finnieston Quay (☎ **0141-275-6211;** www.secc.co.uk)

Dance clubs

✔ **Bamboo** is a stylish basement club with three distinct rooms, one of which is a rather posh cocktail lounge. One room, the Disco Badger club of house and R&B music, gets good notices. Bamboo's open daily from 10 p.m. to 3 a.m. The cover charge is £5 to £8 ($9–$15). 51 West Regent St. (☎ **0141-332-1067;** Underground: Buchanan Street)

✔ **Fury Murry's** draws a crowd of mostly youths looking for nothing more complicated than a good, sometimes rowdy, time listening to upbeat disco. It's a short walk from the St. Enoch Shopping Centre and is open Thursday through Sunday from 10:30 p.m. to 3:30 a.m. The cover charge is £2 to £6 ($3.20–$9.60). 96 Maxwell St. (☎ **0141-221-6511;** Underground: St. Enoch)

Some top bars and pubs

Finally, you have the city's many pubs and bars to consider. Most are friendly places where the locals are likely to strike up a conversation

Late night eats

Famished at four minutes past midnight? The options in Glasgow are fairly well focused on Sauchiehall Street. Try **Canton Express**, 407 Sauchiehall St. (☎ **0141-332-0145**), which looks as if it belongs on some side street in Hong Kong. You don't get anything fancy, but it *is* fast Chinese food, and the place is open daily until 4 a.m. Midway between the city center and the West End, **Insomnia Underground** (Lynedoch Street and Woodlands Road; ☎ **0141-564-1800**) does a whopping full fry-up breakfast at all hours of the day and night through the weekend. Several Indian restaurants are open until 1 a.m., but **Spice Gardens**, on the southern bank of the River Clyde (Clyde Place near Bridge Street; ☎ **0141-429-4422**), trumps the lot by staying open until 4 a.m. every day.

with you. A fine night out trawling the city's many drinking holes is not only entertaining, but it can prove to be educational as well.

Pubs and bars are concentrated in the City Centre, Merchant City, and the West End. Hours vary, but most stay open until 11 p.m. or midnight on weeknights, and many have license to remain open until 1 a.m. on the weekends.

✔ **Babbity Bowster** is a civilized place for a pint, with no pounding soundtrack of mindless pop to distract you from conversation. The wine selection is good, and the food is worth sampling, as well. Some outdoor seating (although it's rarely in full sun) is also available. Every Saturday from about 4 p.m. on, folk musicians arrive for spontaneous jamming. Drinks are served daily from noon to midnight, food until about 10 p.m. 16 Blackfriars St. (☎ **0141-552-5055**; Underground: Buchanan Street)

✔ **Bar 10** is perhaps the grand-daddy of the Glasgow-style bar, but since opening it has mellowed into a comfortable place for drinking. The groovy design is still apparent but more important is the good mix of folk and the convenient City Centre location just opposite the Lighthouse architecture center on tiny Mitchell Lane. Comforting food is served from noon to about 5 p.m. Drinks are served Monday through Saturday from noon to midnight and Sunday from 12:30 p.m. to midnight. The place gets even livelier when DJs spin on the weekends. 10 Mitchell Ln. (☎ **0141-572-1448**; Underground: St. Enoch)

✔ **Blackfriars** has a decent selection of rotating beers, including some from the Continent, even though real ales are less plentiful in Glasgow than in Edinburgh. Jazz is featured in Blackfriars' basement space on Saturdays and Sundays. Drinks are served Monday through Saturday from noon to midnight and Sunday from 12:30 p.m. to midnight. 36 Bell St. (☎ **0141-552-5924**; Underground: St. Enoch)

✔ **Bon Accord** is an amiable pub that's the best in the city for hand-pulled cask-conditioned real ale. The pub boasts an array of hand-pumps — a dozen are devoted to real English and Scottish ales — and the rest of the draft and bottled beers and stouts hail from the Czech Republic, Belgium, Germany, Ireland, and Holland. The pub is likely to satisfy your taste in malt whisky as well and offers affordable pub food. Bon Accord's open Monday through Saturday from noon to midnight and Sunday from noon to 11 p.m. 153 North St. (☎ 0141-248-4427; Bus: 6, 8, or 16; Suburban train: Charing Cross)

✔ **Brel** is possibly the best of the West End's trendy Ashton Lane's many pubs and bars. Brel has a Belgian theme, with beers and cuisine favoring that French-speaking country, but it's not overplayed. The music policy is eclectic, with DJs and live acts adding atmosphere to the former stables. The bar is open daily from 10 a.m. to midnight. Food is served Monday through Friday from noon to 3 p.m. and from 5 p.m. to 10:30 p.m., and on Saturday and Sunday from noon to 10:30 p.m. 39–43 Ashton Lane (☎ 0141-342-4966; Underground: Hillhead)

✔ **Heraghty's Free House** on the city's South Side is the real McCoy among Glasgow's trendy Irish-themed pubs. It serves up perfect pints of Guinness and Irish craic (banter) in almost equal portions. No food, though. Heraghty's is open Monday through Thursday from 11 a.m. to 11 p.m., Friday and Saturday from 11 a.m. to midnight, and Sunday from 12:30 p.m. to 11 p.m. 708 Pollokshaws Rd. (☎ 0141-423-0380; Bus: 38, 45, or 56)

✔ **The Horse Shoe** is the pub you should hit if you can only visit one in Glasgow (and I'm hoping that's not the case). It's one of the last remaining "Palace Pubs" that opened around the turn of the century. The circular, island bar is one of the longest in Europe. Drinks are inexpensive and so is the food from the upstairs buffet. Karaoke draws crowds to the second floor lounge every night of the week, but conversation and football on the televisions provide the entertainment in the main bar. Drinks are served Monday through Saturday from noon to midnight and Sunday from 12:30 p.m. to midnight. The buffet is open daily until 7:30 p.m. except on Sunday when it closes down at 5 p.m. 17 Drury St. (☎ 0141-229-5711; Underground: St. Enoch)

✔ **Lismore Lounge** in Partick is tastefully decorated in a modern manner that still recognizes traditional Highland culture. The whisky selection is good, and at £1.50 ($3) for a dram, the malt of the month is always a bargain. The lounge features live Scottish and Gaelic music Tuesday and Thursday nights. The bar is open Sunday through Thursday from 11 a.m. to 11 p.m. and Friday and Saturday from 11 a.m. to midnight. No food is served. 206 Dumbarton Rd. (☎ 0141-576-0103; Underground: Kelvinhall)

✔ **Liquid Ship** is a fairly recent addition to the West End scene. Owned by the same people who run Stravaigin (see the listing in the section "The top restaurants and cafes," earlier in this chapter), Liquid

Ship's unpretentious and smart but not precisely stylish, with the main bar up a few steps and a lounge in the basement. Drinks are served Monday through Thursday from noon to 11 p.m., Friday and Saturday from noon to midnight, and Sunday from 12:30 p.m. to 11 p.m. Food, platters, and tasty sandwiches on toasted Italian bread are served daily from noon until about 8 p.m. 171 Great Western Rd. (☎ 0141-331-1901; Underground: St. George's Cross)

✔ **The Pot Still** is the best place for sampling malt whiskies. You can taste from a selection of hundreds and hundreds of them, at a variety of styles (peaty or sweet), strengths, and maturities (that is, years spent in casks). The Pot Still's open Monday through Thursday from noon to 11 p.m., Friday and Saturday from noon to midnight, and Sunday from 12:30 p.m. to 11 p.m. 154 Hope St. (☎ 0141-333-0980; Underground: Buchanan Street)

✔ **Vroni's Wine Bar** is for those who favor the grape over the grain, Bordeaux to brown ale, Sancerre over cider. The feeling of this small bar is Continental, with banquette seating and candlelit tables. It's open Monday through Saturday from 10 a.m. to midnight and Sunday from 12:30 p.m. to midnight, and food is served Monday through Thursday from noon to 7 p.m. and until 3 p.m. on Friday. 47 W. Nile St. (☎ 0141-221-4677; Underground: Buchanan Street)

Going to the movies

✔ **Glasgow Film Theatre** has two screens for a well-programmed daily output of independent, foreign, repertory, and art-house films. The building was originally the Cosmo, an Art Deco cinema built in the late 1930s. Café Cosmo is good for a pre- or post-theatre beverage. Tickets are £3 to £5 ($5.50–$9). 12 Rose St. (☎ 0141-332-8128; www.gft.org.uk; Underground: Buchanan Street). The GFT also schedules the films screened at the **Centre for Contemporary Art** (CCA), located at 350 Sauchiehall St.

Gay & lesbian Glasgow

Glasgow and its environs are said to have the largest concentration of gays and lesbians in the UK outside of London. But there's no identifiable district in the city where the gay and lesbian community is particularly concentrated, although part of the Merchant City has been dubbed the "gay triangle." The **Polo Lounge,** 84 Wilson St., offers a gay but hetero-friendly club often described as a cross between an urbane gentleman's club and a Highland country lodge. It's open daily from 5 p.m. to 1 a.m. (until 3 a.m. on Friday and Saturday). A £5 ($9) cover is charged after 10 p.m. or so. Nearby, **Revolver Bar** on John Street is gay-owned and -operated. The bar has always tried to be a bit more grown-up and to dismiss some of the more cheesy and stereotypical elements of the gay scene. But that doesn't mean that it's not fun or popular. Conversation generally rules, but the jukebox is free. Drinks are served daily from noon to midnight.

✔ **The Grosvenor** in the West End was recently refurbished and restored. It has a bar and two downstairs screening rooms with comfy big leather chairs and sofas that you can rent. The cinema screens a mix of mainstream and independent movies. Tickets are £2.50 to £6.50 ($4.50–$12). Ashton Lane (☎ **0141-339-8444; Underground: Hillhead)**

✔ **UGC Renfrew Street** is the best multiplex in Glasgow. Tickets are £3.25 to £5.35 ($6–$10). 7 Renfrew St. (☎ **0871-200-2000;** www. ugccinemas.co.uk)

Fast Facts: Glasgow

American Express

The office is at 115 Hope St. (☎ 0141-222-1401; Underground: St. Enoch). It's open Monday through Friday from 8:30 a.m. to 5:30 p.m. (except Wednesday from 9.30 a.m.) and Saturday from 9 a.m. to noon.

Business Hours

Most offices are open Monday through Friday from 9 a.m. to 5 or 5:30 p.m. Some companies close their doors at 4:30 p.m. on Fridays. Most banks are usually open Monday through Friday from 9 or 9:30 a.m. to 4 or 5 p.m., with some branches sometimes closing early on one day a week and opening late on another. Opening times can vary slightly from bank to bank. Shops are generally open Monday through Sunday from 10 a.m. to 6 p.m. On Thursdays, many remain open until 8 p.m.

Currency Exchange

The tourist office at 11 George Sq. (☎ 0141-204-4400) and the American Express office (see listing above) exchange major foreign currencies. Thomas Cook operates a currency exchange at Central Station (generally open until 6 p.m.). Many banks in the city center operate *bureaux de change*, too, and nearly all banks cash traveler's checks if you have the proper ID. Most ATMs (cash points) in the city center can also draw money directly from your bank account at home.

Dentists

In an emergency, go to the Accident and Emergency Department of Glasgow Dental Hospital, 378 Sauchiehall St. (☎ 0141-211-9600). Its hours are Monday through Friday from 9:15 a.m. to 3:15 p.m. and Sunday and public holidays from 10:30 a.m. to noon. It's closed on Saturdays. For additional assistance or for emergencies when the Hospital is closed, call the National Health Service line (☎ 0800-224-488).

Emergencies

Call ☎ **999** in an emergency to summon the police, an ambulance, or firefighters. This is a free call.

Hospitals

The main hospital for emergency treatment (24 hours) in the city is the Royal Infirmary, 82–86 Castle St. (☎ 0141-211-4000). For additional assistance, call the National Health Service line (☎ 0800-224-488).

Hot lines

The Centre for Women's Health is at Sandyford Place, Sauchiehall Street (☎ 0141-211-6700). Gays and lesbians can call the Strathclyde Gay and Lesbian Switchboard at ☎ 0141-847-0447. The Rape Crisis Centre can be reached at ☎ 0141-331-1990.

Internet Access

You can send or receive e-mail and surf the Net at EasyEverything, 57–61 St. Vincent St. (www.easyeverything.com; Underground: Buchanan Street). This outlet offers more than 350 computers and good rates. It's open Monday through Friday from 7 a.m. to 10 p.m. and Saturday and Sunday from 8 a.m. to 9 p.m.

Laundry/Dry Cleaning

The most central service is Garnethill Cleaners, 39 Dalhousie St. (☎ 0141-332-2387; Underground: Cowcaddens), which is open Monday through Saturday from about 7:30 a.m. to 6:30 p.m. and Sunday from 8 a.m. to 5 p.m.

Library

The Mitchell Library is on North Street at Kent Road (☎ 0141-287-2999; Suburban train: Charing Cross; Bus: 9 or 16). The 19th-century building is home to one of the largest libraries in Europe. Newspapers and books, as well as miles of microfilm, are available. The library's open Monday through Thursday from 9 a.m. to 8 p.m. and Friday and Saturday from 9 a.m. to 5 p.m.

Newspapers and Magazines

Published since 1783, the *Herald* is the major newspaper with national, international, and financial news, sports, and cultural listings. The *Evening Times* offers local news, and the *Daily Record* is for tabloid enthusiasts only. For complete events listings, *The List* magazine is published every other week. On the buses and trains, pick up a free *Metro,* which also has event listings. For international newspapers, go to Borders at 98 Buchanan St. (☎ 0141-222-7700; Underground: Buchanan Street).

Pharmacies

Your best bet is Boots at 200 Sauchiehall St. (☎ 0141-332-1925), which is open Monday through Saturday from 8 a.m. to 6 p.m. (until 7 p.m. on Thursday), and Sunday from 11 a.m. to 5 p.m.

Police

In a real emergency, call ☎ **999.** This is a free call. For other inquiries, contact Strathclyde police headquarters on Pitt Street at ☎ 0141-532-2000.

Post Office

The main branch is at 47 St. Vincent's St. (☎ 0141-204-3689; Underground: Buchanan Street). It's open Monday through Friday from 8:30 a.m. to 5:45 p.m. and Saturday from 9 a.m. to 5:30 p.m. For general postal information, call (☎ 0845-722-3344).

Restrooms

Public toilets can be found at rail stations, bus stations, air terminals, restaurants, hotels, pubs, and department stores. Glasgow also has a system of public toilets, often marked "wc." Don't hesitate to use them, but they're likely to be closed late in the evening.

Safety

While Glasgow may be the most dangerous city in Scotland, it's relatively safe when compared to cities of its size in the United States. Muggings do occur, and often they're related to Glasgow's drug problem. The famed razor gangs of Calton, Bridgeton, and the Gorbals are no longer around to earn the city a reputation for violence, but you still should stay alert.

Weather

For weather forecasts of the day and 24 hours in advance, and for severe road-condition warnings, call the Met Office at ☎ 0870-900-0100. An advisor offers forecasts for the entire region and beyond. You can also check www.weather.com.

Chapter 13

Going Beyond Edinburgh and Glasgow: Daytrips

Although Edinburgh has a full complement of attractions and plenty of activities to entertain visitors, you can find some other worthwhile destinations nearby, outside the city. The closest regions are West and East Lothian, located on either side of the city. The highlights in these areas include the impressive ruins of **Linlithgow Palace,** a favorite of the Stuart dynasty; 18th-century **Hopetoun House;** and the seaside town of **North Berwick,** with its views of Bass Rock.

From Glasgow, day-trippers can easily reach **Helensburgh** on the Firth of Clyde and visit one of architect Charles Rennie Mackintosh's remarkable achievements, **Hill House.** By going upriver (that's south) into the Clyde Valley, day-trippers can also visit **New Lanark.**

In addition to the places I mention here, you can see a good deal of the attractions in Chapters 14, 15, and 16 on daytrips from Scotland's two major cities. So, if you're staying in one of the cities, your options are practically endless!

East Lothian

As the largest town in the area, the royal burgh of North Berwick (the "w" is silent) — where the Firth of Forth meets the North Sea — is a good place to kick off a daytrip. The town dates to the 14th century; in the more modern Victorian and Edwardian times, it was rebuilt to serve as an up-market holiday resort, drawing visitors to its beaches, harbor, and golf courses.

Daytrips from Edinburgh

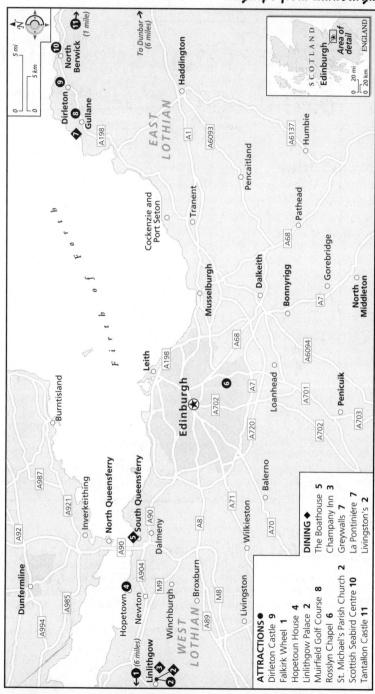

To Dunbar
(6 miles) →

(1 mile) →

SCOTLAND
Edinburgh
Area of
detail
ENGLAND

20 mi
0
0   20 km

5 mi
0
0   5 km

11 North Berwick

10

9 Dirleton
8 Gullane
7 A198

EAST
LOTHIAN

Haddington

A1
A6093
A6137
○ Humbie

Pencaitland ○

F i r t h   o f   F o r t h

Cockenzie and
Port Seton

Tranent ○

A68
Pathead ○

○ Gorebridge
A7

Dalkeith ○

Bonnyrigg ○

North
Middleton

Musselburgh ○

A198
Leith ○

A68

A6094

6 A7

Loanhead ○

A701
○ Penicuik

Burntisland ○

Edinburgh ✪

A702

A720
A702
A703

Balerno ○

A71
A70
○ Wilkieston

South Queensferry **5**
North Queensferry ○

Inverkeithing ○

A921
A987

A90

Dalmeny ○

A8
○ Livingston

Dunfermline ○

A92
A985
A994

Hopetoun ○
Newton ○ **4**
A904
M9
Winchburgh ○
○ Broxburn
M8
A89

WEST
LOTHIAN

1 (6 miles) →
Linlithgow
3
2 2

ATTRACTIONS ●
Dirleton Castle **9**
Falkirk Wheel **1**
Hopetoun House **4**
Linlithgow Palace **2**
Muirfield Golf Course **8**
Rosslyn Chapel **6**
St. Michael's Parish Church **2**
Scottish Seabird Centre **10**
Tantallon Castle **11**

DINING ◆
The Boathouse **5**
Champany Inn **3**
Greywalls **7**
La Pontinière **7**
Livingston's **2**

Daytrips from Glasgow

0	5 mi
0	5 km

Drymen

Stirling

A82

2 Helensburgh

3

Dunoon Gourock

River Clyde

Greenock **1**

Port
Glasgow

A78

Dumbarton

Kirkintilloch

*Owemyss
Bay*

INVERCLYDE

A8

M8

Clydebank

*Isle of
Bute*

Johnstone Paisley **Glasgow**

Largs

A726

Barrhead

AYRSHIRE

East Kilbride

Hamilton

M8

A77

New Lanark →
(9 miles)

Stewarton

Ardrossan Saltcoats

A736

4 4 →
(9 miles)

A735

Irvine

Ferry to Arran

Kilmarnock

A71

*Firth of
Clyde*

A78

Galston

Troon

A77

Ferry to Belfast

A719

Mauchline

ATTRACTIONS ●
Glenarn Garden **2**
Hill House **3**
Newark Castle **1**
New Lanark **4**

Prestwick

A758

Ayr

A76

SCOTLAND

*Area of
detail* Edinburgh ✴

Glasgow

0   20 mi

0 20 km   ENGLAND

DINING ◆
Prego **4**

A719

Alloway

Cumnock

Getting there

About 36km (21 miles) east of Edinburgh, North Berwick is on a direct rail
line from Edinburgh; the trip takes about 30 minutes. Or you can hit the
road on the bus service from Edinburgh, which takes 1¼ hours and leaves
from Edinburgh Bus Station. If you're driving, take the coastal road east
from Leith, or use the A1 (marked THE SOUTH and DUNBAR), to the A198 (via
Gullane) to North Berwick.

Orienting yourself

At North Berwick's tourist office on Quality Street (☎ **01620-892-197**), you can get information on boat trips to offshore islands, including **Bass Rock,** a breeding ground inhabited by about 10,000 gannets (the second largest colony in Scotland) as well as puffins and other birds. You can see the rock from the harbor, but the viewing is even better at **Berwick Law,** a volcanic lookout point that rises up behind the town.

Seeing the sights

Dirleton Castle
Dirleton

A rose-tinted 13th-century castle with equally ancient surrounding gardens, Dirleton Castle looks like a fairy-tale fortification, with towers and arched entries. Reputed to have been completely sacked by Cromwell in 1650, another story holds that the building was only partially destroyed by his army but was further torn down by a local family who apparently desired a romantic ruin on their land after building nearby Archiefield House. You can see what remains of Dirleton's Great Hall and kitchen as well as the lord's chamber. Look for the hole in the 16th-century main gate through which boiling tar or water would have been poured to deter hostile visitors. The castle's country garden and a bowling green are still in use. Allow about 1 hour.

See map p. 255. On the A198, 2 miles west of North Berwick. ☎ ***01620-850-330.*** www. historic-scotland.gov.uk. *Admission: £3 ($5.50) adults, £2.30 ($4.25) seniors, £1 ($1.85) children. Open: Apr–Sept daily 9:30 a.m.–6 p.m.; Oct–Mar daily 9:30 a.m.–4:30 p.m.*

Rosslyn Chapel
Roslin, Midlothian

Built in 1446, this chapel has seen a revival in international interest recently thanks to its depiction in the best-selling novel, *The DaVinci Code,*

Dirleton: Prettiest village in Scotland?

Dirleton, midway between North Berwick and Gullane, is one of the prettiest villages in Scotland. It's as picture-perfect as a postcard. In fact, its quaintness and beauty make it seem almost surreal. Undoubtedly high levels of home maintenance make each cottage here look as if it's waiting to be photographed. Because the main road bypasses the village, there's very little traffic. Even the railway station is closed — the last train ran through Dirleton in the mid-1950s! The biggest event for Dirleton occurred in the 1940s, when President Roosevelt and Sir Winston Churchill met here to plan D-Day landings.

Dunbar: Birthplace of John Muir

The man who "discovered" the Yosemite Valley in California, founded the Sierra Club, and was single-handedly responsible for establishing the national park system in the United States was born in the humble harbor town of Dunbar about 15km (9 miles) southeast of North Berwick. Only fairly recently have Scots begun to capitalize on Muir's international stature and celebrate the life of the explorer, naturalist, and ground-breaking conservationist. In Dunbar, you can visit his birthplace (126 High St.; ☎ 01368-865-899; www.jmbt.org.uk) which now houses a museum about Muir, his travels, and his work. It is a modest, locally run museum, but if you're a fan of John Muir and appreciate the environmental movement, then a visit here is merited.

---

and indeed there are references to the Knights Templar and Free Masons in this medieval structure. But the Gothic church also contains bibical and pagan images. The attraction is in Midlothian (rather than neighboring East Lothian) and can be easily reached by A701, which runs south from Edinburgh. Allow about 1 hour here.

See map p. 255. Just off the A701. ☎ *0131-440-2159.* www.rosslyn-chapel.com. *Admission: £5 ($7.50) adults, free for children under 18. Open: Apr–Sept Mon–Sat 10 a.m.–5 p.m. and Sun noon–4:45 p.m.; Oct–Mar Mon–Sat 10 a.m.–4:30 p.m. and Sun noon–4:30 p.m.*

Scottish Seabird Centre
North Berwick

From this popular attraction in North Berwick you can watch all the bird action (gannets and puffins) out on Bass Rock (see the section "Orienting yourself" earlier in this chapter) as well as colonies of seals thanks to live video links — or in modern parlance: "Big Brother" cameras. The Seabird Centre also has a cafe/bistro and activities geared toward families. Allow about 2 hours here.

See map p. 255. North Berwick. ☎ *01620-890-202.* www.seabird.org. *Admission: £5.95 ($11) adults, £3.95 ($7.30) seniors, £16.50 ($30.50) family of four. Open: Apr–Oct daily 10 a.m.–6 p.m.; Nov–Jan Mon–Fri 10 a.m.–4 p.m. and Sat–Sun 10 a.m.–5:30 p.m.; Feb–Mar Mon–Fri 10 a.m.–5 p.m. and Sat–Sun 10 a.m.–5:30 p.m.*

Tantallon Castle
Tantallon

From its construction in the 14th century, this castle was the ancient stronghold of the powerful and somewhat trouble-making Douglas family (Earls of Angus). Like most strongholds in the region, it endured a fair number of seiges, and Cromwell's troops sacked it in the 16th century.

Overlooking the Firth of Forth, the ruins remain formidable, however, with a square, five-story central tower. Allow 1 hour.

See map p. 255. On the A198, some 2 miles east of North Berwick. ☎ *01620-892-727.* www.historic-scotland.gov.uk. *Admission: £3 ($5.50) adults, £2.30 ($4.25) seniors, £1 ($1.85) children. Open: April–Sept daily 9:30 a.m.–6:30 p.m.; Oct–Dec Sat–Wed 9:30 a.m.–4:30 p.m.; Jan–Mar Mon–Wed and Sat 9:30 a.m.–4:30 p.m., Thurs 9:30 a.m.–noon, Fri and Sun noon–4:30 p.m.*

Dining locally

Creel Restaurant
$$–$$$ Dunbar   MEDITERRANEAN/MODERN SCOTTISH

A two-story stone building near the harbor in Dunbar is home to the Creel Restaurant, a casual bistro that recently introduced "lighter lunch-time dishes" such as pasta with spiced sausage, Cajun chicken Caesar salad, and grilled sea bream. Main courses in the evening include prime Scottish sirloin steak, rosemary chicken with chorizo and tomatoes, and local Dunbar trout fillets served with almonds and Stilton cheese.

25 Lamer St., Dunbar. ☎ *01368-863-279.* www.creelrestaurant.co.uk. *Main courses dinner: £8.50–£12 ($15.75–$22). MC, V. Open: Wed–Sun noon–2:30 p.m. and 6–9:30 p.m. Closed Mon–Tues.*

Gullane and Muirfield Golf Course

Lying 3 miles west of North Berwick and about 19 miles east of Edinburgh in East Lothian, Gullane (pronounced *gill*-in by many, *gull*-an by others) is another Scottish resort with a fine beach and a famous golf course. On the edge of the village, **Gullane Hill** provides a nature reserve and bird sanctuary where over 100 species of birds have been spotted. You cross a small wood footbridge from the car park to enter the reserve. Gullane doesn't get any direct rail service, but the nearest station is only about 4km (2½ miles) south in Drem. Buses depart to Gullane from the Edinburgh bus terminal near St. Andrew's Square (☎ **0800-23-23-23** for information) and take 20 to 25 minutes.

Muirfield Golf Course (☎ **01620-842-123**) is ranked among the world's great golf courses, and as such, it occasionally hosts the Open Championship in Great Britain. Muirfield is the home course of the Honorable Company of Edinburgh Golfers — the world's oldest club — which began at Leith Links in Edinburgh. Developed on a boggy piece of low-lying land in 1891, Muirfield was originally a 16-hole course designed by the legendary Old Tom Morris, whose face recently popped up on a £5 note in Scotland that commemorated 250 years of the club at St. Andrews. Guests are welcome to visit Muirfield on Tuesdays and Thursdays. Greens fees are £110 ($203) for a single round and £140 ($260) for the day. Peak times book quickly, but the course usually has availability from mid-October to the end of March.

Greywalls
$$$ Gullane SCOTTISH/FRENCH

This elegant Edwardian country house was designed in 1901 by the most renowned architect of the day, Sir Edwin Lutyens, and the grounds were laid out by one of England's most respected gardeners, Gertrude Jekyll. The light, Scottish/French-style dishes (Scottish haute cuisine is often French in style) served in the elegant dining room, which overlooks the 10th tee of Muirfield (see the sidebar "Gullane and Muirfield Golf Course"), are almost as appealing to the eye as to the palate; specialties include fresh seafood such as seared fillet of line-caught seabass with saffron risotto cake. If you decide to make a night of it, Greywalls also has guest rooms.

See map p. 255. Duncur Road, Gullane. ☎ ***01620-842-144.*** *Fax: 01620-842-241.* www. greywalls.co.uk. *Fixed-price dinner: £40 ($75). Reservations required. AE, DC, MC, V. Open: daily 7:30–9 p.m. Closed Oct 15–Apr 15.*

La Potinière
$$$ Gullane FRENCH/VARIED

This rather legendary restaurant that at one time earned a Michelin star was closed by its former owners, and the Michelin star was not renewed. It was opened again a short time later, however, by new owners, chefs Keith Marley and Mary Runciman, in 2003. The three-course lunches and four-course dinners offer dishes that are often French-inspired, but don't be shocked if the selection includes a Thai-influenced soup, too. The menu is seasonal and the produce is usually purchased locally; everything is tasty and freshly made on the premises.

See map p. 255. Main Street, Gullane. ☎ ***01620-843-214.*** www.la-potiniere. co.uk. *Fixed-price lunch: £15.50 ($28.50), fixed-price dinner: £35 ($65). MC, V. Open: Wed–Sun noon–2 p.m. and 7–9 p.m. Closed Mon–Tues.*

West Lothian

Linlithgow, where Mary Queen of Scots was born, is the principal town in West Lothian and its ancient palace is the main tourist attraction.

Getting there

Linlithgow is only 25.6km (16 miles) west of Edinburgh. Trains depart frequently from Edinburgh Waverley Station for the 20-minute ride. If you're driving from Edinburgh, follow the M8 toward Glasgow, take exit 2 onto the M9, and follow the signs to Linlithgow.

Orienting yourself

The tourist information center is on the road that leads up to the palace. It's open daily from Easter through October.

Seeing the sights

Falkirk Wheel
Falkirk

Just a bit west of Linlithgow in the largely industrial burgh of Falkirk is a modern engineering feat that has revived a 19th-century industrial achievement. The Falkirk Wheel is a towering structure with a rotating arm that has replaced the 11 locks once necessary to link the Union Canal and the Forth & Clyde Canal, connecting the North Sea to the Atlantic in the west. The wheel is the world's first and only rotating boat lift. The attraction includes a visitor center and the "Falkirk Wheel Experience," a 45-minute canal boat excursion. Allow about 2 hours here.

See map p. 255. Lime Road, Tamfourhill. ☎ *08700-500-208.* www.thefalkirk wheel.co.uk. *Admission: free for visitor center; for boat ride: £8 ($15) adults, £6 ($11) seniors and students, £4 ($7.50) children, £21 ($39) family. Reservations recommended. Open: Apr–Oct daily 9 a.m.–6 p.m.; Nov–Mar daily 9:30 a.m.–5 p.m.*

Hopetoun House
Near South Queensferry

On the margins of South Queensferry, amid beautifully landscaped grounds, Hopetoun House is one of Scotland's best examples of 18th-century palatial Georgian architecture; it features design work by Sir William Bruce and three members of the architecturally inclined Adam family. You can wander through splendid reception rooms filled with period furniture, Renaissance paintings, statuary, and other artwork. The views of the Firth of Forth are panoramic from the roof-top observation deck. After touring the house, visitors can explore more than 100 acres of parkland, including a walled garden, a trail along the shorefront, and a deer park. Allow 2 hours.

See map p. 255. Off the A904, 2 miles from the Forth Road Bridge near South Queensferry, South Queensferry. ☎ *0131-331-2451.* www.hopetounhouse.com. *Admission: £6.50 ($12) adults, £5.50 ($10) seniors, £3.50 ($6.50) children, £18 ($33) family of four. Open: Apr–Sept daily 10 a.m.–5:30 p.m. (last admission at 4:30 p.m.). Closed Oct–Mar.*

Linlithgow Palace
Linlithgow

Birthplace of Mary, Queen of Scots, this palace was once a favorite residence of royalty and is now one of Scotland's most poignant ruins, set on the shores of Linlithgow Loch. Enough of the royal apartments are still sufficiently intact to let visitors get an idea of how grand the palace used to be. Linlithgow is a landmark bit of architecture in the country — the first building to be called a palace — and a romantic touchstone of Scottish history and lore. The English king Edward I occupied the tower in the 14th century, but Scots who had hidden in a load of hay retook it in 1313. Most of the structure was built (it began as a more modest structure in the 14th century) by James I from 1425 to 1437. In 1513, Queen Margaret (a Tudor by birth) waited in vain at Linlithgow for husband James IV to return from the battle of Flodden. When their son, also born here, wed Mary of Guise, the palace fountain ran with wine. In 1746, fire gutted the building when government troops who routed Bonnie Prince Charlie at Culloden were barracked in the palace. Allow 2 hours.

See map p. 255. On A706, on the south shore Linlithgow Loch, Linlithgow. ☎ *01506-842-896.* www.historic-scotland.gov.uk. *Admission: £3 ($5.50) adults, £2.30 ($4.25) seniors, £1 ($1.85) children. Open: Apr–Sept daily 9:30 a.m.–6:30 p.m.; Oct–Mar daily 9:30 a.m.–4:30 p.m.*

St. Michael's Parish Church
Linlithgow

Next to Linlithgow palace stands the medieval kirk of St. Michael, site of worship for many a Scottish monarch since its consecration in 1242. The biggest pre-Reformation parish church in Scotland, most of what you currently see at St. Michael's was constructed in the 15th century. In the part of the church known as St. Catherine's Aisle, just before the battle of Flodden, King James IV apparently saw an apparition warning him against fighting the English (perhaps he should have listened). Despite being ravaged by the disciples of John Knox (who chided followers for their "excesses") and being transformed into a stable by Cromwell's forces, this remains one of Scotland's best examples of a parish church. Providing a dramatic focal point on the landscape, the aluminum spears projecting from the tower were added in the 1960s. Allow 1 hour.

See map p. 255. Adjacent to Linlithgow Palace, Linlithgow. ☎ *01506-842-188.* www. stmichaels-parish.org.uk. *Admission: free. Open: May–Sept daily 10 a.m.– 4 p.m.; Oct–Apr Mon–Fri 10:30 a.m.–3 p.m.*

Dining locally

The Boathouse
$$ South Queensferry FISH/SEAFOOD

What a vista! This restaurant is down a few steps from the main street of South Queensferry, which puts diners that much closer to the sea and views of the marvelous Forth rail and suspension road bridges. Typical dishes, including grilled herring or monkfish roasted with rosemary, garlic, and olive oil, are innovative but not overcomplicated.

See map p. 255. 19b High St., South Queensferry. ☎ *0131-331-5429. Fixed-price lunch: £12.50 ($23); main courses dinner: £12–£18 ($22–$33). MC, V. Open: Tues–Sat noon–2:30 p.m. and 5:30–10:30 p.m.; Sun 12:30–8 p.m. Closed Mon.*

Champany Inn
$$$ Champany Corner SCOTTISH

You find some of the best steaks in Britain in this converted mill. The restaurant also serves oysters, salmon, and lobsters, but beef is the main reason why people dine here. The meat served here is properly hung before butchering, which adds greatly to its flavor and texture. Next to the main dining room is the Chop House, offering somewhat less expensive cuts in a more casual atmosphere within the establishment. The wine list — some 2,000 bottles long — has won an award for excellence from *Wine Spectator* magazine.

See map p. 255. 3km (2 miles) northeast of Linlithgow, Champany Corner. ☎ *01506-834-532.* www.champany.com. *Reservations required. Fixed-price lunch: £16.75 ($31); main courses dinner: £17.50–£32.50 ($32–$60). AE, DC, MC, V. Open: Mon–Fri 12:30–2 p.m. and 7–10 p.m.; Sat 7–10 p.m. Main restaurant closed Sun.*

Livingston's
$$ **Linlithgow MODERN SCOTTISH/FRENCH**

This stone walled, slightly-hidden restaurant in converted stables includes a conservatory that overlooks a tidy little garden. On a seasonally changing menu, the saddle of venison is a favorite dish. Other options may include pigeon pie and brambles or a risotto of wild mushrooms and truffles made all the more delectable by a shaving of Parmesan. An elegant dessert selection is a chilled soup of strawberries and champagne accompanied by a chocolate mousse. Livingston's has an ample wine list as well, including bottles from California.

See map p. 255. 52 High St., Linlithgow. ☎ *01506-846-565. Reservations recommended. Fixed-price lunch: £13.50 ($25); fixed-price dinner: £30 ($55.50). MC, V. Open: Tues–Sat noon–2 p.m. and 6–9 p.m. Closed briefly in Jan, June, and Oct.*

The Clyde Valley

From its headwaters well south of Glasgow, the River Clyde meanders north. The Clyde Valley south of the city is best known locally for its garden nurseries and their sometimes-quaint tea shops. Near the town of **Lanark,** however, you can find a bona fide bit of history and an attraction that merits a daytrip.

Getting there

You can take the train to Lanark from Central Station in Glasgow or drive via the M74 motorway, following the signs from exit 9.

West of Glasgow, the Clyde widens as it empties into the sea. To get to places west, take the train that runs almost every half hour from Queen Street Station or head out on the M8 motorway, crossing the river at Erskine and following the northern shoreline. The area doesn't boast a host of attractions, but the drive can be very pretty, and in **Helensburgh,** the Mackintosh trail leads to the architect and designer's wonderful Hill House.

Seeing the sights

Glenarn Garden
Rhu near Helensburgh

Nestled in a protective hollow, Glenarn is a private garden established by the Gibson family in the early decades of the 20th century. The rhodendron collection is superb, and in early spring the flowering magnolias can be absolutely stunning. A large rock garden has also been built around a disused quarry. Allow 1 hour.

See map p. 256. Glenarn Road, off the A814, Rhu. ☎ *01436-820-493. Admission: £3 ($5.50). Open: mid-Mar–Sept dawn–dusk.*

Hill House
Helensburgh

Designed by Charles Rennie Mackintosh for publisher Walter Blackie, this timeless house on the hill above the town of Helensburgh (along the north banks of the Firth of Clyde) has been lovingly restored and opened to the public by the National Trust for Scotland. Inspired by the Scottish Baronial style, Hill House is still pure Mackintosh: from the asymmetrical juxtaposition of windows and clean lines that blend sharp geometry and gentle curves to the sumptuous but uncluttered interior with custom-made details (such as glass inlays, fireplace tiles and decorative panels) by both the architect and his artist wife Margaret Macdonald. Built at the beginning of the 20th century, practically the entire house is open to the public. The garden, overgrown when the National Trust took over the property in the early 1980s, has been restored to its original state thanks to photographs of the original garden taken in 1905 for a German design magazine. Allow 2 hours here.

See map p. 256. Upper Colquhoun Street, off the B832, Helensburgh. ☎ *01436-673-900.* www.nts.org.uk. *Admission: £8 ($15) adults, £6 ($11) seniors, £19 ($35) family. Open: Apr–Oct daily 1:30–5:30 p.m.*

New Lanark
Near Lanark

Founded first in 1784, by the early part of the 19th century, New Lanark was a progressive industrial mill and village under the guidance of Robert Owen, who decided that a contented work force was most likely to be a productive one. With that philosophy in mind, he set up free education for all employees and their children, a day-care center and social club, and a cooperative store along the banks of the River Clyde in the steep valley below the long-established market town of Lanark. Today, the New Lanark Conservation Trust runs the place (recognized by UNESCO as a World Heritage Site) as a tourist attraction. Admission includes an educational chair-lift ride that tells the story of what life here was once like as well as self-guided tours of the principle buildings, such as the factory where cotton was spun and the old schoolhouse. A walk upstream brings visitors to the three-tiered Falls of Clyde, worth the hike if you like waterfalls and walking. Allow 2 hours.

 From March through October, you can get a combination ticket from SPT/First ScotRail that combines transportation from Glasgow to New Lanark with admission to the attraction for about £11 ($20).

See map p. 256. Braxfield Road, outside Lanark. ☎ **01555-661-345.** www.new lanark.org. *Admission £5.95 ($11) adults, £3.95 ($7.25) children and seniors, £16.95 ($31) family of four. Open: daily 11 a.m.–5 p.m.*

Newark Castle
Port Glasgow

One of the few castles still standing in this part of Scotland, Newark dates to the 15th century. Its most prominent resident was Patrick Maxwell, who made notable additions to the castle but went down in history as a bully who murdered a couple of neighbors and regularly beat his wife. You can see a good deal of this well-preserved castle, from the tower house built in 1478 to a wood-paneled sleeping chamber and the high ceilings of the main hall, in addition to the old gate house. Allow 1 hour.

See map p. 256. On the A8, Port Glasgow. ☎ **01475-741-858.** www.historic-scotland.gov.uk. *Admission: £2.50 ($4.60) adults, £2 ($3.70) seniors and students, £1 ($1.85) children. Open: Apr–Sept daily 9:30 a.m.–6:30 p.m.*

Dining locally

If you've spent your day in the Clyde Valley, you'd do better to head back to Glasgow for dinner, but if you're running late in Lanark, I recommend the restaurant listed below.

Prego
$$ **Lanark ITALIAN**

This friendly, casual Italian eatery in the heart of Lanark is open for lunch and dinner. It specializes in fish dishes but also offers a good range of entrees and pasta meals. If you're lucky, the main courses may include a creamy risotto or a baked cod special served with mussels.

See map p. 256. 3 High St., Lanark. ☎ **01555-666-300.** *Main courses: £8–£15 ($15–$27.75). MC, V. Open: daily noon–2:30 p.m. and 5:30–9:30 p.m.*

Part IV
The Major Regions

The 5th Wave   By Rich Tennant

©RICHTENNANT

SCOTTISH
TOURS

"Looks like our trip into the town of Argyll
will be delayed while we let one of the
local farmers pass with his sheep."

In this part . . .

Some travelers just visit Edinburgh and Glasgow (discussed in Part III) and stop there. That's okay, but if you have more time, you really should get out and about and discover some of the rest of "real" Scotland — whether the medieval abbeys of southern Scotland, the picturesque ports of the Hebrides, or the sweeping vistas and rugged countryside of the Highlands.

Part IV focuses in on the major regions of Scotland. In the chapters that follow, you can find out about each region's best attributes — from harbor towns, whiskey distilleries, and world-class golf to ancient castles, loch cruises, and largely unspoiled islands. Each chapter has invaluable suggestions on how to get there and get around, which attractions to see, and, of course, where to stay and dine.

Chapter 14

Southern Scotland

In This Chapter

▶ Finding the best places to stay and eat
▶ Discovering the home of Sir Walter Scott
▶ Visiting the famous Borders abbeys
▶ Seeing one of the most picturesque ports in Scotland

*R*ichly historic southern Scotland is predominantly rural, with vast open spaces used for grazing livestock like the famous black-face lamb. The area consists of two administrative districts: the Borders, aptly named as it borders England, and the combined regions of Dumfries and Galloway in the southwest. Because most tourists enter Scotland by plane or train, arriving in either Glasgow or Edinburgh, many tend to travel *through* southern Scotland rather than journey *to* the region.

And truth be told, the area isn't as impressive as the Highlands (see Chapter 18) when it comes to natural beauty. Still, the southern part of the country offers attractions that make a visit here worthwhile: stately homes and the ruins of 12th-century abbeys, quaint towns, meandering rivers, and a ruggedly scenic peninsula that faces onto the Irish Sea.

Southern Scotland has no regional capital, per se, nor even a primary city. The main towns include Melrose, Jedburgh, and Galashiels in the Borders southeast of Edinburgh; Dumfries and Stranraer are the main hubs southeast and southwest of Glasgow, respectively.

 Because even the bigger towns in southern Scotland are quite small, the area has few stand-out restaurants. Your hotel may be your best option for dining and drinking.

Ideally, you could take two or three days to cover southern Scotland. But certain attractions may be within striking distance of daytrips from either Edinburgh or Glasgow, depending upon how long you allow your "day" to be.

Getting There

Buses and (to a lesser extent) trains run from Edinburgh and Glasgow to southern Scotland. Train service used to penetrate the Borders interior, but cutbacks in the 1960s eliminated lines. Some of these lines may be restored; for now, however, train service is limited to the east coast lines that run from the Scottish capital to Berwick on Tweed, just across the boundary in England.

Buses and trains from Glasgow service Dumfries and Galloway, with the western line terminating at the sea port Stranraer and the more central route continuing out of Scotland to Carlisle.

A car is probably the best mode of transportation to cover southern Scotland.

✔ **By car:** From Edinburgh, take the A68 toward Jedburgh, the A1 along the east coast, or, further west, the A701 to the M74. From Glasgow, the M74 runs south to Moffat, where the A701 continues to the town of Dumfries. You can also get to Dumfries by taking the A76, via Cumnock. If your destination is Galloway, take the A77 south via Ayr and Girvan. If you want to experience the area from England, the M1 to Newcastle links to the A1 or the A68 (via the A69). Coming from northwest England and the Lake District, take the M6 north to the M74 in Carlisle. Cross-country roads from Stranraer to Galashiels are predominantly two lane routes with a good bit of twists and turns.

✔ **By bus: Scottish Citylink** (☎ **0870-550-5050;** www.citylink.co.uk) routes cover the major towns in the region.

✔ **By train: First ScotRail** (☎ **0845-748-4950;** www.firstscotrail.com) travels to towns in the region, including Dumfries and Stranraer.

✔ **By ferry: Stena Line** (☎ **08705-707070;** www.stenaline.com) runs ferry services between Stranraer harbor and Belfast port in Northern Ireland.

Spending the Night

The selections I list below offer some of the best accommodations in the region. All are moderate to expensive, which is typical for southern Scotland, and many have good food for dinner and full bars for a friendly pint or nightcap. Some have earned star ratings from the tourist board (see Chapter 8 for a description of the rating system). Rates include full breakfast unless otherwise stated. And remember: You may well get a better deal than the advertised "rack" rates.

Most accommodations in the region are small bed-and-breakfasts. For more details and rates, contact the **Dumfries & Galloway Tourist Board,** ☎ **01387-253-862;** www.visit-dumfries-and-galloway.co.uk; or **The**

Southern Scotland

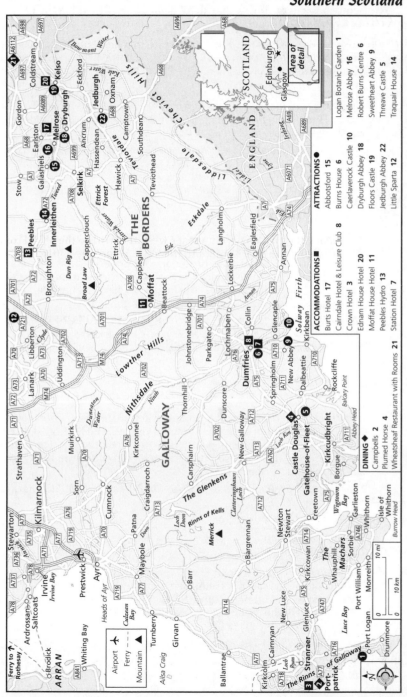

ATTRACTIONS ●
Abbotsford **15**
Burns House **6**
Caerlaverock Castle **10**
Dryburgh Abbey **18**
Floors Castle **19**
Jedburgh Abbey **22**
Little Sparta **12**
Logan Botanic Garden **1**
Melrose Abbey **16**
Robert Burns Centre **6**
Sweetheart Abbey **9**
Threave Castle **5**
Traquair House **14**

ACCOMMODATIONS ■
Burts Hotel **17**
Cairndale Hotel & Leisure Club **8**
Crown Hotel **3**
Edham House Hotel **20**
Moffat House Hotel **11**
Peebles Hydro **13**
Station Hotel **7**
Wheatsheaf Restaurant with Rooms **21**

DINING ◆
Campbells **2**
Plumed Horse **4**

Scottish Borders Tourist Board, ☎ 0845-22-55-121 (within the UK), ☎ 01506-832-121 (outside the UK); www.scot-borders.co.uk.

Burts Hotel
$$ Melrose

This small, whitewashed hotel is possibly best known for its award-winning food, and locals and guests from other hotels often pack the dining room. The building dates to 1722, but don't worry — the modest-sized rooms have all the modern amenities.

See map p. 271. Market Square, in the center of town. ☎ **01896-822-285**. *Fax: 01896-822-870.* www.burtshotel.co.uk. *Rack rates: £98 ($181) double. AE, DC, MC, V.*

Cairndale Hotel & Leisure Club
$$–$$$ Dumfries

This early 20th-century resort hotel with a stone facade is a wonderful place to go for a little R&R. The rooms are very comfortable, but the best features here are the spa and heated indoor pool. The hotel has some 91 units, with 22 suitable for family accommodations. Management has added a conference center to appeal to a business clientele, but the Cairndale still knows how to treat vacationing guests right.

See map p. 271. 132–136 English St., just off High Street. ☎ **01387-254-111**; *toll-free in U.S. 800-468-3750. Fax: 01387-250-555.* www.cairndalehotel.co.uk. *Rack rates: £69–£149 ($127–$281) double. AE, DC, MC, V.*

Crown Hotel
$$ Portpatrick

It may not offer the poshest accommodations in this quaint port town, but the popular and unpretentious Crown is right on the harbor, and several rooms, with big old-fashioned bath tubs, overlook the sea. The hotel has a popular local pub, too, so you may prefer a room in the back to avoid any noise from the bar below.

See map p. 271. 9 North Crescent. ☎ **01766-810-261**. *Fax: 01766-810-551. Rack rates: £72 ($133) double. AE, MC, V.*

Ednam House Hotel
$$$ Kelso

The Ednam occupies a great location overlooking the River Tweed. The Georgian mansion has a warming fire when it's cold and is awash in fishing mementos and other old furnishings and antiques. If you have the time, take high tea in the garden and have a meal in the restaurant.

See map p. 271. Bridge Street, just off the town square, one block north of the Kelso Bridge. ☎ **01573-224-168**. *Fax: 01573-226-319. Rack rates: £93–£130 ($172–$240) double. MC, V.*

Moffat House Hotel
$$ Moffat

This 18th-century mansion sits in the center of a garden in the heart of Moffat. The red-and-black-painted stone building is hard to miss, and lovely trees grace the back. Each individually decorated room is well stocked with amenities, and the restaurant serves excellent Scottish cuisine. A literary footnote: Poet James MacPherson (thought by some to be the poet Ossian) is believed to have written his disputed works here.

See map p. 271. High Street. ☎ *01683-220-039. Fax: 01683-221-288.* www.moffat house.co.uk. *Rack rates: £76–£94 ($140–$173) double. AE, MC, V.*

Peebles Hydro
$$$$ Peebles

Once a Victorian hydropathic hotel that claimed to cure whatever ailed you with a hot spring and mineral waters, the hotel's main features today, as the name suggests, are hydro-centric: a pool for the kids and a whirlpool and sauna for the adults. The hotel has lots of hallways and 30 acres of grounds for young ones to explore. Of the more than 125 units, 25 are geared toward families. Other activities at this chateau-style hotel include snooker, pitch and putt golf, and badminton.

See map p. 271. Innerleithen Road, on A72 just outside Peebles. ☎ *01721-720-602. Fax: 01721-722-999.* www.peebleshydro.com. *Rack rates: £182–£298 ($336–$551) double. AE, DC, MC, V.*

Station Hotel
$$–$$$ Dumfries

The Station's Victorian sandstone building lies near Dumfries's railroad station and the center of town. Part of the Best Western group, the comfortable 100-year-old rooms here have been renovated but still maintain a certain rustic charm. Don't worry about being close to the rail lines; there aren't any late-night trains.

See map p. 271. 49 Lovers Walk, just across from the train station. ☎ *01387-254-316. Fax: 01387-250-388.* www.stationhotel.co.uk. *Rack rates: £90–£120 ($166–$222) double. AE, DC, MC, V.*

Dining Locally

Campbells
$$ Portpatrick FISH/SEAFOOD

Facing the crescent-shaped harbor of Portpatrick, this family-run restaurant is welcoming and relaxed. Almost old-fashioned in its unpretentious ways, the décor here mixes rustic seaport with modernity. Fresh fish is the main reason to eat here, and the dishes tend to be unfussy and straightforward in presentation.

See map p. 271. 1 South Crescent. ☎ *01776-810-314. Reservations recommended. Main courses: £12–£20 ($22–$37). DC, MC, V. Open: Tues–Sun noon–2:30 p.m. and 6–10 p.m. Closed for 2 weeks in Feb.*

Plumed Horse
$$$ Crossmichael   SCOTTISH

With a Michelin star secured, Tony Borthwick's rather tiny restaurant in Crossmichael is considered by some to be the best in the region. Dishes, all certainly original recipes, may include the creamy signature fish soup or a fluffy quiche made with smoked haddock and spinach; you may also stumble upon main courses such as free-range chicken with truffle essence or a pot roast of pig cheeks.

See map p. 271. Main Street. ☎ *01556-670-333.* www.plumedhorse.co.uk. *Reservations required. Main courses: around £18 ($33). MC, V. Open: lunch reservations Tues–Fri and Sun 12:30 and 1 p.m.; dinner reservations Tues–Fri 7 and 8 p.m., Sat 7, 8, and 9 p.m. Closed Mondays. Closed for 2 weeks in Sept and Jan.*

Wheatsheaf Restaurant with Rooms
$$–$$$ Swinton   MODERN BRITISH

Located between Melrose and Eyemouth, from whose harbor the kitchen secures fresh seafood, the Wheatsheaf is a restaurant that pops up on many "best of" lists. You can eat in the pub as well as in the dining room. In addition to fresh fish, Wheatsheaf's menu often offers Borders lamb and organic pork from a local supplier.

See map p. 271. Main Street. ☎ *01890-860-257.* www.wheatsheaf-swinton.co.uk. *Reservations recommended. Main courses: £13–£18 ($24–$33). MC, V. Open: daily noon–2:30 p.m. and 6–9 p.m. Closed on Sun nights in Dec and Jan.*

Exploring Southern Scotland

The region's primary attractions are its stately, historic homes and ancient abbeys. The rolling hills and dense forests are attractive but don't offer the kind of natural splendor found in the Highlands of Scotland, although the coastal areas are reasonably dramatic and picturesque. The government's historic preservation society, Historic Scotland, runs quite a few of the attractions in the Borders and Dumfries and Galloway regions. I list several such attractions below, but for more details, visit www.historic-scotland.gov.uk. Don't feel as if you need to visit each and every abbey and castle in the area. Pick some representative ones, enjoy them, and move on.

The top attractions

Abbotsford
Roxburghshire

Abbotsford is the mansion that Sir Walter Scott built and lived in from 1817 until he died. Designed in the Scots baronial style, Abbotsford was constructed on land Scott acquired in 1811. Scott was one of Britain's earliest souvenir hunters, scouring the land for artifacts associated with the historical characters he rendered into fiction. Hence, Abbotsford contains many relics and mementos, including a gun apparently used by Rob Roy. One of Scott's other proud possessions is a sword given by Charles I to the Duke of Montrose. Especially interesting is Scott's study, home to his writing desk and chair. In 1935, two secret drawers were found in the desk; one contained 57 letters, part of the correspondence between Scott and his wife-to-be. You can also see Scott's library (with 9,000 rare volumes), drawing room, entrance hall, armories, and even the dining room where he died on September 21, 1832, in a bed facing the River Tweed. Abbotsford also has extensive gardens and grounds to visit and a private chapel added after Scott's death. Allow about 2 hours.

See map p. 271. Hwy. B6360, near Galashiels. ☎ *01896-752-043.* www.melrose. bordernet.co.uk/abbotsford. *Admission: £4.50 ($8.30) adult, £2.25 ($4) child. Open: Mar 15–Oct 31 Mon–Sat 9:30 a.m.–5 p.m.; June–Sept Sun 9:30 a.m.–5 p.m.; Mar–May and Oct Sun 2–5 p.m.*

Burns House
Dumfries

Most of the Robert Burns Heritage Trail is in Ayrshire (see Chapter 15), but the poet Burns was only 37 when he passed away in 1796 in this sandstone house, which is now a place of pilgrimage for his fans. Burns House has been preserved to look as it did when he lived there for the final few years of his short life, and it contains such articles as Burns's writing chair as well as some original manuscripts, letters, and printed editions. A highlight is the author's signature scratched into a windowpane. Allow about 1 hour.

See map p. 271. Burns Street, between Shakespeare and St. Michael's streets. ☎ *01387-255-297. Admission: free. Open: Apr–Sept Mon–Sat 10 a.m.–5 p.m., Sun 2–5 p.m.; Oct–Mar Tues–Sat 10 a.m.–1 p.m. and 2–5 p.m.*

Caerlaverock Castle
Near Dumfries

A historic target of English armies, Caerlaverock is one of Scotland's classic Medieval castles, complete with moat and twin-towered gatehouse, as well as some pretty serious battlements. It lies in ruins today, but you can still get the sense of what defending this castle may have been like. An exhibit on seige warfare, a nature trail, and an "adventure" park, which kids might enjoy, are all on the premises. A cafe is open during the summer and on weekends throughout the winter. Allow about 2 hours.

See map p. 271. B725, about 8 miles southeast of Dumfries. ☎ *01387-770-224.* www. historic-scotland.gov.uk. *Admission: £4 ($7.40) adults, £3 ($5.50) seniors and students, £1 ($1.85) children under 16. Open: Apr–Sept daily 9:30 a.m.–6:30 p.m.; Oct–Mar daily 9:30 a.m.–4:30 p.m.*

Dryburgh Abbey
Near St. Boswells

It's no wonder Sir Walter Scott chose this spot to be buried. The abbey ruins, now run under the auspices of Historic Scotland, lie amid giant cedar trees on the banks of the River Tweed. Of the four famed Borders abbeys, Dryburgh was the largest, arguably the most beautiful, and possibly the most attacked by English troops, although it's reasonably well intact today. Dryburgh's pleasant green surroundings make a lovely spot for a picnic lunch. Scott was interred in the side chapel in 1832. Allow about 1 hour.

See map p. 271. Off the A68, 8 miles southeast of Melrose on the B6404 near St. Boswells. ☎ *01835-822-381.* www.historic-scotland.gov.uk. *Admission: £3 ($5.50) adults, £2.30 ($4.25) seniors and students, £1 ($1.85) children under 16. Open: Apr–Sept daily 9:30 a.m.–6:30 p.m.; Oct–Mar daily 9:30 a.m.–4:30 p.m.*

Floors Castle
Near Kelso

Built by William Adam for the 1st Duke of Roxburghe in 1721 and today still home to the Duke (the 10th) and Duchess of Roxburghe, Floors Castle is one of the few fully intact and occupied castles in the Borders. It is said to be the largest inhabited castle in all of Scotland, although it's more of a mansion than a proper castle. After viewing the impressive art collection indoors (including paintings by Matisse and Odilion Redon), venture out and walk one of the nature trails through the woods or along the River Tweed. The walled garden also has an "Adventure Playground" for the kids. Allow about 3 hours.

See map p. 271. Hwy. A697, 2 miles northwest of Kelso. ☎ *01573-223-333.* www. floorscastle.com. *Admission: £5.75 ($10.60) adults, £4.75 ($8.80) seniors and students, £3.25 ($6) children under 16, £15 ($27.75) family. Open: Apr–Oct 10 a.m.–4:30 p.m. Closed Nov–Mar.*

Jedburgh Abbey
Jedburgh

This famous ruined abbey, founded by David I in 1138, is one of Scotland's finest. Under the Augustinian canons from Beauvais, France, it achieved abbey status in 1152 and went on to witness much royal pageantry, such as the marriage of Alexander III to his second wife, Yolande de Dreux. In 1544 and 1545, the English sacked the abbey during the frequent wars that ravaged the villages along the Scottish and English borders. The abbey's roof was burned, allowing rains to penetrate and further destroy much of

Sir Walter Scott: Inventor of historic novels

Today it may be hard to imagine the fame that Walter Scott, poet and novelist, enjoyed as the best-selling author of his day. His works are no longer so widely read, but Scott (1771–1832) was thought to be a master storyteller and today is considered the inventor of the historic novel. He created lively characters and realistic pictures of Scottish life in works such as *The Heart of Midlothian.* Scott's name is also linked to the Trossachs (a range of high hills and small mountains near the Highlands), which he used as a setting for his poem "The Lady of the Lake" and his tale of Rob Roy MacGregor, the 18th-century outlaw (an actual person who lived in the Trossachs region whose legend Scott popularized with his novel).

Born into a Borders family on August 14, 1771, and then settled in Edinburgh, Scott was permanently lame due to polio contracted as a child. He was troubled by ill health all his life, and later he suffered ailing finances as well. Scott spent his latter years writing in an effort to clear his enormous debts.

Scott made his country and its scenery fashionable with the English, and he played a key role in bringing George IV to visit Scotland. Although Scott became the most prominent literary figure in Edinburgh, his heart lay in the Borders, where he built his home. Starting with a modest farmhouse, he created Abbotsford, a mansion that became a key tourist destination in the mid-1900s (see the listing for Abbotsford in the section "The top attractions").

the interior detailing. After 1560, no efforts were made to repair the abbey. For about 300 years, a small section of it served as Jedburgh's parish church, but in 1875 other premises were found for day-to-day worship. Then, teams of architects set to work restoring the abbey to its original medieval design. The abbey is still roofless but otherwise fairly complete, with most of its exterior stonework still in place. Three pedimented gables remain at the doorway, and the solid buttresses and rounded arches in the Norman style are relatively intact.

See map p. 271. Hwy. A68. ☎ ***01835-863-925.*** www.historic-scotland.gov. uk. *Admission: £3.50 ($6.50) adults, £2.50 ($4.60) seniors and students, £1.20 ($2.20) children under 16. Open: Apr–Sept daily 9:30 a.m.–6:30 p.m.; Oct–Mar daily 9:30 a.m.–4:30 p.m.*

Little Sparta
Near Dunsyre

Not highlighted by many guide books, Little Sparta is a garden devised by one of Scotland's most intriguing artists in the 20th and 21st centuries, Ian Hamilton Finlay. It's a surprisingly lush plot of land given the harsh terrain of the Pentland Hills all around it. Dotted throughout the garden are stone sculptures (many with Finlay's pithy sayings and poems) created in collaboration with master stonemasons and other artists. Little Sparta has been called the "only original garden" created in Great Britain since World War II. Allow about 1 hour.

See map p. 271. Stonypath, Near Dunsyre, off the A702. ☎ *01899-810-252 Admission: free or voluntary donation. Open: mid-June–Sept Fri–Sun only 2–5 p.m.*

Logan Botanic Garden
Rhinns of Galloway

Run by the Royal Botanic Garden responsible for the beautiful spread in Edinburgh (see Chapter 11), the gardens on the old Logan estate have charms of their very own. Because of its southwest exposure (which guarantees mild Gulf Stream air flows) and some protective planting, the gardens have a micro-climate that allows the successful cultivation of palms, tree ferns, and other exotic plants such as towering, flowering columns of *echium pininana*s native to the Canary Islands. In addition to the more formal walled garden, Logan also has wilder plantings such as the *gunnera*, with its leaves larger than elephant's ears. Hand-held audio wands can be for used for self-guided tours, and there's an interpretative center with microscopes, too. This garden is definitely worth the trip if you fancy plants at all. Allow about 2 hours.

See map p. 271. B7065, 1 mile outside Port Logan, 14 miles south of Stranraer. ☎ *01776-860-231. Admission: £3.50 ($6.50) adults, £3 ($5.55) seniors and students, £1 ($1.85) children under 16, £8 ($14.80) family. Open: Mar–Oct daily 10 a.m.–6 p.m. (only until 5 p.m. in Mar and Oct).*

Melrose Abbey
Melrose

Legend has it that the heart of Scots King Robert the Bruce is buried somewhere on the grounds of this abbey, which sits in somewhat spectacular ruins. A 1996 archaeological dig uncovered a small conical lead casket along with a plaque saying that a heart had been found inside in 1921. The

---

Portpatrick

The site of a natural harbor that has been improved over the years, Portpatrick is where trade and people from Northern Ireland came ashore in Scotland from the 17th century to about midway through the 19th century. The more sheltered port at Stranraer was established some 7 miles inland, but Portpatrick remains one of the most picturesque towns in southwest Scotland. You won't find any tourist attractions, per se, but trails lead away from the village, both up and down the coast. Just south of the town, the path leads to the ruins of 15th-century Dunskey Castle, perched on the edge of a cliff above the sea. In the small inlet below is a small beach that seems to capture no end of golf balls hit astray from seaside courses somewhere along the coast. From Portpatrick, the 200-plus mile long Southern Upland Way, one of the greatest long-distance footpaths in Scotland, heads northeast across Scotland from coast to coast.

remains of one of the wealthiest abbeys in the country retain a regal beauty. The red sandstone Gothic alcoves and medieval statues and gargoyles (including one of a pig playing the bagpipes) make for an interesting walking tour. The abbey was built in the 1100s at the behest of Scotland's first king, David I (it's one of the famous Borders abbeys), and was later destroyed by the English and rebuilt by Robert the Bruce in the 14th century. None other than the famous novelist Sir Walter Scott led a 19th-century restoration project. Be sure to take the excellent free audio tour. Allow about 1½ hours.

See map p. 271. Abbey Street, in Melrose. ☎ *01896-822-562.* www.historic-scotland.gov.uk. *Admission: £3.50 ($6.50) adults, £2.50 ($4.60) seniors and students, £1.20 ($2.20) children under 16. Open: Apr–Sept daily 9:30 a.m.–6:30 p.m.; Oct–Mar daily 9:30 a.m.–4:30 p.m.*

Robert Burns Centre
Dumfries

This museum, commonly called the "RBC," in Dumfries's 18th-century watermill covers the poet's last years in the town. On display are many interesting items, such as a cast of Burns's skull, a scale model of 1790s Dumfries, and a sentimental audiovisual presentation of the poet's life. Also on display are original documents and relics belonging to Burns. The center has a cafe and bookshop as well. Allow about 1 hour.

See map p. 271. Mill Road, on the west bank of the River Nith. ☎ *01387-264-808. Admission (to slide show only): £1.50 ($2.75) adults. Open: Apr–Sept Mon–Sat 10 a.m.–8 p.m., Sun 2–5 p.m.; Oct–Mar Tues–Sat 10 a.m.–1 p.m., Sun 2–5 p.m.*

Sweetheart Abbey
New Abbey

The impressive remains of Sweetheart Abbey are worth the short jaunt from Dumfries. An unusual story lies behind the red sandstone structure: Lady Devorgilla of Galloway founded the abbey in 1273 in memory of her husband. She carried his embalmed heart around with her for 22 years, and when she was buried here, in front of the altar, the heart went with her, thus the name Sweetheart Abbey. Allow about 1 hour.

See map p. 271. Hwy. A710, New Abbey village, 7 miles south of Dumfries. ☎ *01387-850-397.* www.historic-scotland.gov.uk. *Admission: £2 ($3.70) adults, £1.50 ($2.75) seniors and students, £.75 ($1.40) children under 16. Open: Apr–Sept daily 9:30 a.m.–6:30 p.m.; Oct–Mar daily 9:30 a.m.–4:30 p.m. (except Oct–Dec closed Thurs–Fri and Jan–Mar closed Thurs afternoon, Fri and Sun morning).*

Threave Castle
The River Dee

One of the best things about this massive 14th-century tower house (a ruined proper castle) is how you get here. Ring a bell to call a boatman, who ferries you to the island in the River Dee on which the castle sits. Threave Castle was built by a former Lord of Galloway named Archibald the Grim (apparently for his battlefield disposition). The castle was last used in the 19th century as a prison for Napoleonic War soldiers. Birders enjoy an opportunity to get up close and personal with the swallows that nest in the ruins from April to September. *Note:* Leave your best shoes at home; the path from the parking area to the boat pickup can get muddy when it rains. Allow about 1 hour.

See map p. 271. Three miles west of Castle Douglas on A75 (follow signs from the roundabout). ☎ 07711-223-101. www.historic-scotland.gov.uk. *Admission: £2.50 ($4.60) adults, £1.90 ($3.50) seniors and students, £.75 ($1.40) children under 16. Open: Apr–Sept daily 9:30 a.m.–6:30 p.m. Closed Oct–Mar.*

Traquair House
Innerleithen

Dating from the tenth century, Traquair House is perhaps Scotland's most romantic house, rich in associations with Mary Queen of Scots and the Jacobite uprisings. The Stuarts of Traquair still live in the great mansion, making it the oldest continuously inhabited house in Scotland. One of the most poignant exhibits is in the King's Room: an ornately carved oak cradle in which Mary rocked her infant son, who was to become James VI of Scotland and James I of England. Other treasures include embroideries, silver, manuscripts, and paintings. Of particular interest is the brewery, which is still in operation. On the grounds are craft workshops — such as wrought ironwork and woodturning — as well as a maze and woodland walks. Allow about 2 hours.

See map p. 271. Innerleithen. ☎ 01896-830-323. www.traquair.co.uk. *Admission: £5.75 ($10.50) adults, £5.30 ($5.75) seniors, £3.20 ($6) children, £16.75 ($31) family of 5. Open: April–May and Sept daily noon–5 p.m.; June–Aug daily 10:30 a.m.–5:30 p.m.; Oct daily 11 a.m.–4 p.m.. Closed Nov–Mar.*

More cool things to see and do

- ✔ **Mary Queen of Scots' House,** Queen Street, Jedburgh (☎ **01835-863-331**). As the story goes, Mary was on a trip in 1566 to visit her betrothed, the Earl of Bothwell, when she became ill with fever. She allegedly stayed in this house to recover. Now the building is a visitor center that tells the tragic story of her life and features magnificent tapestries, oil paintings, antique furniture, coats of arms, armor, and some of the Queen's possessions.

- ✔ **The Old Bridge House Museum,** Mill Road, Dumfries (☎ **01387-256-904**). This museum is housed in the oldest building in Dumfries, a 1660 sandstone structure built into the Devorgilla Bridge. Today, the museum is devoted to Victorian life. A mid-19th century kitchen and antique dental tools are among the items on display.

- ✔ **The Trimontium Exhibition,** Market Square, Melrose (☎ **01896-822-651**). His is probably the last voice you'd expect to hear in the Borders, talking about a lost Roman legion that once explored this area, but Leonard Nimoy narrates the tour at this small, interesting museum devoted to Trimontium, the legendary three-peaked Roman fort and annexes of the ancient Tweed Valley. At one time the Roman army's headquarters in Scotland, Trimontium now looms over Melrose. Among the collection of first- and second-century artifacts are a Roman skull and facemask, tools, weapons, and pottery.

Shopping for Local Treasures

Southern Scotland isn't really a shopping destination. You'd do better to save your spending money for Edinburgh and Glasgow. None of the Borders towns has a major shopping district; the closest you get is the High Street in a place like Dumfries, which has a row of small craft shops and clothing stores. Almost all of the attractions listed in this chapter will have gift shops, however.

The town of Kelso is the home of **Pettigrews** (☎ **01573-224-234;** www. pettigrews.com), which produces a range of Scottish chutney and relish at its factory here. In the town of Moffat, you can visit the **Wollen Mill** (☎ **01683-220-134**), which has weaving demonstrations on Monday, Wednesday, and Friday and shops with tartan, whisky, and more for sale, seven days a week. And if you enjoy books, set aside some time to visit **Wigtown,** which is Scotland's book town where the main street has a host of secondhand and antiquarian bookshops.

Here are a couple of other picks worth visiting:

- ✔ **Broughton Gallery,** Broughton Place, Broughton (☎ **01899-830-234;** www.broughtongallery.co.uk). This fine little gallery (in a village near Biggar) has a good selection of Scottish items you won't find anywhere else. Most of the pieces are by Scottish and other British artists and include paintings, glassware, ceramics, jewelry, and even toys. The gallery will frame any paintings or prints you purchase. The shop is in an old tower house. The Broughton Gallery is open from late-March through mid-October and from mid-November through December 25, Thursday to Tuesday from 10:30 a.m. to 6 p.m.; closed Wednesdays.

- ✔ **Selkirk Glass,** on the A7, Selkirk (☎ **01750-20-954**). This factory shop and showroom is a popular stop for coach tours. But bargain hunters may appreciate the factory prices for most of the glassware. You can watch skilled craftsmen work in the factory, as well. Selkirk Glass is open Monday through Saturday from 9 a.m. to 5 p.m. and Sunday from 11 a.m. to 5 p.m.; closed holidays.

Hitting the Local Pubs

Most of the pubs in the Borders region are local and often nondescript, corner watering holes. Almost every town has one or two taverns, and whether unimpressive or not, they often can be a great place to meet the locals. Ask your hotel concierge or guesthouse host to recommend the nearest "local" to your accommodations, walking distance preferred.

Worth special note is the **Globe Inn,** 56 High St., Dumfries (☎ **01387-252-335;** www.globeinndumfries.co.uk). Established at the beginning of the 17th century, the Globe was one of poet Robert Burns's favorite haunts. You can even sit in Burns's favorite seat, just to the left of the fireplace. Other good places for a pint and meal are the **Crown** in Portpatrick and **Burts** in Melrose (see listing information for both in the "Spending the Night" section, earlier in this chapter).

Fast Facts: Southern Scotland

Area Codes

For a small country with less than 5 million people, Scotland has a bewildering number of local area telephone codes. Those for some of the major towns in southern Scotland: Dumfries is **01387;** Castle Douglas is **01556;** Kelso is **01573;** Melrose is **01896;** Moffat is **01683;** Peebles is **01721;** Selkirk is **01750;** and Stranraer is **01776.** You need to dial the area code only if you're calling from outside the town you want to reach.

ATM

All the major towns have ATMs at banks (smaller villages may have them in local shops), but these rural cash points may not be linked to international systems.

Emergencies

Dial ☎ **999** for police, fire, or ambulance.

Hospitals

The primary hospital for the region is Dumfries & Galloway Royal Infirmary, Bankend Road, Dumfries (☎ 01387-246-246). Just outside Melrose on the A6091, you'll find Borders General Hospital

(☎01896-826-000). Garrick Hospital (☎01776-703-276) is in Stranraer.

Information

For general information on the region, contact Borders Tourist Information, Shepherd's Mill, Selkirk (☎ 0870-608-0404; www.scot-borders.co.uk) or Dumfries & Galloway Tourist Board, Dumfries (☎ 01387-253-862; www.visit-dumfries-and-galloway.co.uk). VisitScotland's main number (☎ 0845-22-55-121) will connect you to local offices, or log onto www.visitscotland.com for more specific information. Or, if you're calling from a country outside the United Kingdom, dial ☎ 44-1506-832-121.

Internet Access

A convenient and affordable place to jump on the Net is Dumfries Internet Centre, 26/28 Brewery St., next to the Whitesands, Dumfries (☎ 01387-259-400).

Mail

The main post office in Dumfries is at 34 St. Michael St. (☎ 01387-253-415).

Chapter 15

Ayrshire and Argyll

. . . .

In This Chapter

▶ Getting to Ayrshire and Argyll
▶ Seeking out the best places to stay and eat
▶ Discovering the Burns Heritage Trail, Culzean Castle, the Isle of Arran, and more
▶ Hittin' the links in Troon and Turnberry
▶ Shopping for local goodies and finding the best pubs

. . . .

*T*he region of Ayshire stretches from the southern and western fringes of Glasgow south to southwest along the Firth of Clyde. Argyll covers the southwestern islands and western peninsulas of Scotland. While Ayrshire boundaries are well marked, Argyll is a bit more amorphous, encompassing a region that historically stretches into the Highlands.

One of Ayrshire's primary attractions is "Burns Country," because the area was the poet Robert Burns's birthplace as well as his predominant stomping grounds for most of his life. But Ayrshire also offers golfers some of the best links courses in the world. If you take the train from Glasgow to Ayr, the main town of Ayrshire, you can see one course after another in the sandy dunes along the shoreline.

Argyll, which means the "coast of the Gaels," encompasses islands such as Bute and Arran as well as the more remote Kintyre Peninsula. Kintyre is so sufficiently isolated that ex-Beatle Paul McCartney has long owned a ranch there where he and his family can retreat from prying eyes. It takes the better part of the day just to reach Kintyre, however, so I don't dwell on its charms for too long in this chapter. The port of Oban (pronounced oh-*bin*), gateway to the Hebrides and primary burgh of Argyll, and the town of Inveraray, on the shores of Loch Fyne, are more accessible, as is Loch Lomond, and all provide a pseudo-Highland experience.

You may not have time to see everything Ayrshire and Argyll have to offer, but visits to places such as the mansion and grounds of Culzean Castle or placid shores of Loch Lomond can still be accomplished as daytrips from Glasgow.

Getting There

Your options for getting in and out of the area include scheduled buses and trains that run from Glasgow to towns and terminals such as Wemyss Bay, Largs, and Ayr in Ayrshire and Oban in Argyll. If you're ambitious, however, and want to fully explore the Cowal or Kintyre peninsulas or the Clyde coastline, a car is your best choice.

✔ **By car:** From Glasgow, the main road to Ayrshire is the M77 (A77) from the city's south side. It's the fastest route to towns such as Troon, Ayr, and points further south, such as Culzean. You can also drive west on the M8, along the Clyde to Greenock or Gourock, connecting to the A78, which goes south along the Firth of Clyde to ports such as Wemyss Bay or Ardrossan. To get to Argyll, take the A82 from the West End of Glasgow north toward Tarbet (there are several Tarbets in Scotland, but this one is on the shores of Loch Lomond). From Tarbet, you can take the A83 to Inveraray and down the Kintyre Peninsula. The fastest route to Oban is the A82 from Tarbet: Go north along Loch Lomond to Crianlarich and Tyndrum, where the A85 goes west to Oban.

✔ **By train: First ScotRail** (☎ 0845-748-4950; www.firstscotrail. com) service overlaps with the the greater Glasgow rail service operated by **Strathclyde Passenger Transport (SPT)** (☎ 0141-333-3708; www.spt.co.uk). Between the two (and they're largely interchangable, unless you're a dedicated trainspotter), you have reasonably frequent service from Glasgow to Ayrshire and Argyll. Remember, however, that trains to Ayrshire depart from Central Station, while those heading toward Loch Lomond and Oban leave from Queen Street Station. A one-way journey to Ayr costs £5.50 ($10).

✔ **By bus:** From Glasgow, **Scottish Citylink** (☎ 0141-332-9644 or 0870-550-5050; www.citylink.co.uk) runs buses to Western Scotland, including towns such as Oban, Inverary, and Cambeltown. **Stagecoach Express** (☎ 01292-613-500) also runs buses to Ayr twice an hour during the week from Glasgow's Buchanan Street bus terminal. The round-trip fare to Ayr is £7.40 ($13.75).

✔ **By ferry: Caledonian MacBrayne** (☎ 01475-650-100; www. calmac.co.uk) — or "CalMac," as it's more colloquially known — serves 22 islands and 4 peninsulas over the West Coast of Scotland. From Gourock, you can reach Dunoon on the Cowel Peninsula or cross the Clyde north to Helensburgh (no cars). Ferries from Wemyss Bay go to Rothsay on the isle of Bute. The boat for Brodick on Arran departs from Ardrossan. Connections between train stations and ferry terminals are fairly well linked.

CalMac has some competition from another company, **Western Ferry** (☎ 01496-840-681), which, for example, runs a route to Dunoon from Greenock. And, **Seacat** (☎ 08705-523-523) hydrofoils arrive in the Ayrshire port of Troon from Belfast in Northern Ireland.

Ayrshire

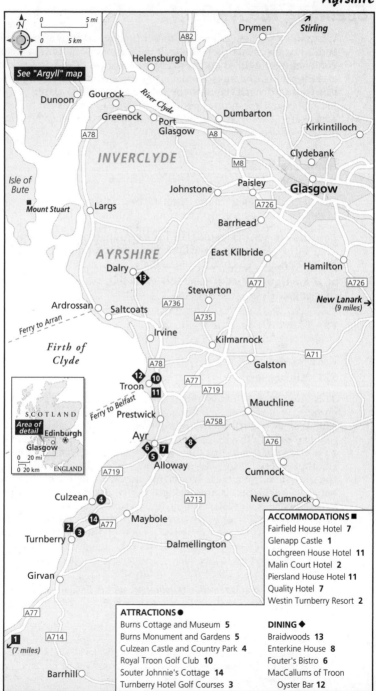

0 5 mi
0 5 km

See "Argyll" map

Drymen

↗ *Stirling*

A82

Helensburgh

Dunoon

Gourock

River Clyde

Dumbarton

Kirkintilloch

Greenock

Port Glasgow

A78

A8

Clydebank

M8

INVERCLYDE

Johnstone

Paisley

A726

Glasgow

Isle of Bute

■ *Mount Stuart*

Largs

Barrhead

AYRSHIRE

East Kilbride

Hamilton

Dalry ◆ **13**

Stewarton

A77

A726

New Lanark → (9 miles)

Ardrossan

Saltcoats

A736

A735

Ferry to Arran

Irvine

Kilmarnock

A71

Firth of Clyde

Galston

A78

◆ **12** ● **10**

Troon

■ **11**

A77

A719

Mauchline

SCOTLAND

Ferry to Belfast

Prestwick

A758

A76

Area of detail

Edinburgh

Glasgow ✱

0 20 mi
0 20 km ENGLAND

Ayr

● **6** ■ **7**

◆ **8**

● **5**

Alloway

Cumnock

A719

Culzean

◆ **4**

A713

New Cumnock

■ **14**

Maybole

■ **2** ■ **3** A77

Turnberry

Dalmellington

Girvan

■ **1** (7 miles)

A77

A714

Barrhill

ACCOMMODATIONS ■

Fairfield House Hotel **7**
Glenapp Castle **1**
Lochgreen House Hotel **11**
Malin Court Hotel **2**
Piersland House Hotel **11**
Quality Hotel **7**
Westin Turnberry Resort **2**

ATTRACTIONS ●

Burns Cottage and Museum **5**
Burns Monument and Gardens **5**
Culzean Castle and Country Park **4**
Royal Troon Golf Club **10**
Souter Johnnie's Cottage **14**
Turnberry Hotel Golf Courses **3**

DINING ◆

Braidwoods **13**
Enterkine House **8**
Fouter's Bistro **6**
MacCallums of Troon
  Oyster Bar **12**

Spending the Night

When it comes to accommodations, you may want to stay on the mainland in larger towns such as Ayr, Inveraray, or Oban for the sake of convenience. Some other choice accommodations, however, are available in more far-flung precincts. Some have even earned star ratings from the tourist board; see Chapter 8 for a description of the rating system. In the listings below, room rates generally include full breakfast, unless otherwise stated. And don't forget: You may well get a better deal than the advertised "rack" rates.

Alexandra Hotel
$–$$ Oban

On the northern end of the Oban seafront, this hotel affords views of the town and the waterfront. Once one of the largest buildings in town, this stately pile has been refurbished and modernized. You can play a little table tennis or snooker or simply paddle around in the large heated indoor pool. The friendly staff will make your stay very comfortable, and the hotel offers 24-hour room service. It also has accommodations especially created for travelers with disabilities. Rooms are modestly furnished but pleasing, with small bathrooms.

See map p. 289. North Pier, Oban. ☎ *01631-562-381. Fax: 01631-564-497. Rack rates: £40–£80 ($74–$148) double. AE, DC, MC, V.*

Ardanaiseig
$$$ Kilchrenan

This hotel is arguably the poshest and least accessible place listed in this chapter, so if you seek a bit of luxury in an out-of-the-way corner, read on. The Ardanaiseig (pronounced *ard*-na-sag) hotel is a stone Scottish baronial pile built in the 1830s on the shores of Loch Awe; it sits at the end of a curvy single-track road through the woods some 15 miles from Taynuilt (on the road to Oban). The gardens are especially colorful in spring when the rhododendrons are in bloom, but they have plenty of year-round interest as well. The public spaces include a large drawing room with views of the hotel's own wee island in the loch. Evening meals, supervised by head chef Gary Goldie, are especially memorable, and every day brings a different four-course menu. Guests can rent the gatehouse, called Rose Cottage, which sleeps up to five. Another small cottage was being built near the hotel's pier in late 2004. The hotel, which prefers not to take small children, closes for three weeks in January.

See map p. 287. 3 miles north of Kilchrenan, off the B845 from Taynuilt. ☎ *01866-833-333. Fax: 01866-833-222.* www.ardanaiseig-hotel.com. *Rack rates: £103–£138 ($190–$255) double. AE, MC, V. Closed Jan–mid-Feb.*

Argyll

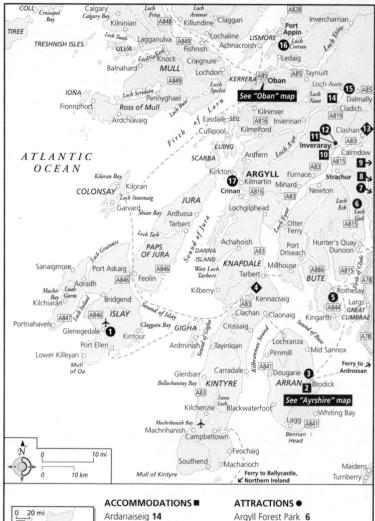

ACCOMMODATIONS ■

Ardanaiseig **14**
The Argyll Hotel **10**
De Vere Cameron House **8**
Drover's Inn **9**
Kilmichael Country House **2**
Loch Fyne Hotel **11**

DINING ◆

Anchorage Restaurant **4**
Loch Fyne Oyster Bar **13**

ATTRACTIONS ●

Argyll Forest Park **6**
Brodick Castle **3**
Inveraray Castle **12**
Kilchurn Castle **15**
Kilmartin House Museum **17**
Laphroaig Distillery **1**
Loch Lomond **7**
Mount Stuart **5**
Oban Seal & Marine Centre **16**

The Argyll Hotel
$$ **Inveraray**

This Best Western–managed waterfront hotel overlooking the picturesque Inveraray harbor is a pretty, white-stone building with green trim. Originally built in 1750 to accommodate guests of nearby Inveraray Castle, the Argyll is still putting up the castle's many visitors. You'll find a lovely atrium sitting room, a cozy formal dining area, and the beautiful wood-and-gilt Argyll Bar. Each room is nicely put together, with blond wood furniture. If you can, book a room with a view of Loch Fyne.

See map p. 287. Front Street. ☎ ***01499-302-466.*** *Fax: 01499-302-389.* www.the-argyll-hotel.co.uk. *Rack rates: £90 ($166) double. AE, DC, MC, V.*

De Vere Cameron House
$$$$ **Luss**

Posh and plush, the five-star Cameron House offers the premier lodgings along the banks of Loch Lomond. The midrange deluxe rooms face the loch, and the luxury suites are part of the original house and allow guests to have their meals in their own sitting room with dining table. Guests also can rent the hotel's 46-foot cruiser, the *Celtic Warrior,* moored in the hotel's private marina. The fine dining option is the Georgian Room, which is not suitable for children under 14; gentlemen are expected to don jackets and ties. Smollets is the name of the hotel's casual dining option.

See map p. 287. A82 north of Balloch, Dumbartonshire. ☎ ***01389-755-565.*** www.cameronhouse.co.uk. *Rack rates: £245–£285 ($453–$527) double. AE, MC, V.*

Drover's Inn
$ **Inverarnan**

The stuffed, snarling, and slightly worn animals near this inn's entrance give a pretty good hint as to the nature of this rustic tavern with restaurant and overnight rooms. The atmospheric pub usually has an open fire going, barmen in kilts, and plenty of travelers by foot and car nursing their drinks. The pub food is average, but the ambience of the place makes the Drovers a worthwhile stop. The inn has 10 overnight units in the original house built in 1705, and another 16 rooms in a new building in the rear. Rooms are run of the mill and worn but comfortable enough.

See map p. 287. A82 at by Ardlui. ☎ ***01301-704-234.*** www.droversinn.co.uk. *Rack rates: £46 ($85) double. MC, V.*

Fairfield House Hotel
$$$ **Ayr**

On the seafront near Low Green, this circa-1912 town house has been restored and converted into a 44-unit hotel. The staff is attentive and will help you arrange tee times at nearby golf courses. A noted designer of classic British interiors decorated the rooms in a country-house style. The units are large and luxurious, many done in chintz; most of the bathrooms

Oban

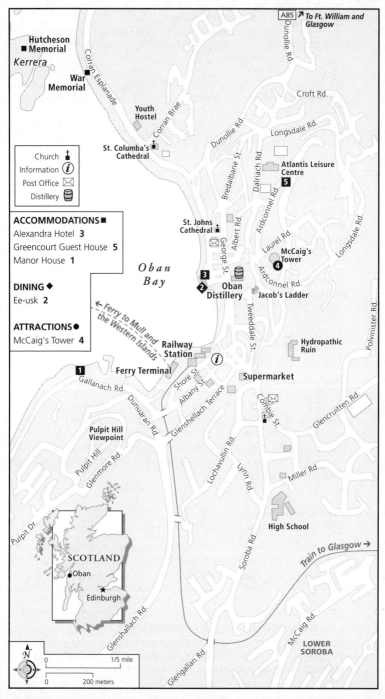

To Ft. William and Glasgow
A85

Hutcheson Memorial

Kerrera

War Memorial

Corran Esplanade

Corran Brae

Youth Hostel

St. Columba's Cathedral

Dunollie Rd.

Croft Rd.

Longsdale Rd.

Bredalbane St.

Dalriach Rd.

Atlantis Leisure Centre 5

Church
Information
Post Office
Distillery

ACCOMMODATIONS ■
Alexandra Hotel **3**
Greencourt Guest House **5**
Manor House **1**

DINING ◆
Ee-usk **2**

ATTRACTIONS ●
McCaig's Tower **4**

Oban Bay

St. Johns Cathedral

George St.

Albert Rd.

Ardconnel Rd.

Laurel Rd.

McCaig's Tower 4

Longsdale Rd.

3
2 Oban Distillery

Jacob's Ladder

Ardconnel Rd.

Polvinister Rd.

← Ferry to Mull and the Western Islands

Railway Station

Tweeddale St.

Hydropathic Ruin

1 Ferry Terminal

Gallanach Rd.

Dunuaran Rd.

Shore St.

Albany St.

Glenshellach Terrace

Supermarket

Combie St.

Glencruitten Rd.

Pulpit Hill Viewpoint

Pulpit Hill

Glenmore Rd.

Lochavullin Rd.

Lynn Rd.

Miller Rd.

Pulpit Dr.

High School

SCOTLAND

Oban

Edinburgh

Soroba Rd.

Train to Glasgow →

Glenshallach Rd.

Glengallan Rd.

McCaig Rd.

LOWER SOROBA

N

0   1/5 mile
0   200 meters

have bidets. The British AA guide rates the Fairfield House's restaurant highly for the "freshness and seasonality" of its cuisine.

See map p. 285. 12 Fairfield Rd. ☎ **01292-267-461.** *Fax: 01292-261-456.* www. fairfieldhotel.co.uk. *Rack rates: £110–£170 ($203–$314) double. AE, DC, MC, V.*

Glenapp Castle
$$$$ **Ballantrae**

This beautifully decorated pile close to the city of Stranraer offers Victorian baronial splendor with antiques, oil paintings, and elegant touches at every turn. Other accommodations in the region pale in comparison. The mansion was designed in the 1870s by David Bryce, a celebrated architect of his day, and it overlooks the Irish Sea. Lounges and dining rooms are elegant, and the spacious bedrooms and suites are individually furnished. Tall windows let in the afternoon and long summer evening light, making the rooms bright on many days. The hotel, open seasonally unless by special arrangement, stands on 12 hectares (30 acres) of lovely, secluded grounds that are home to many rare plants. Smoking is only permitted in the library.

See map p. 285. Ballantrae, Ayrshire, some 20 miles south of Ayr. ☎ **01465-831-212.** *Fax: 01465-831-000.* www.glenappcastle.com. *Rack rates: £365–£405 ($675–$750) double. Rates include dinner. Open only Apr–Oct. AE, V.*

Greencourt Guest House
$–$$ **Oban**

Of the many B&Bs and guesthouses in Oban, this one stands out for its warm reception and view over the town's bowling green. Greencourt only has six units, five with en suite bathrooms. Nonsmokers will appreciate the nonsmoking policy. Unlike many other homes along the winding streets of Oban, Greencourt has its own small parking area.

See map p. 289. Benvoullin Road. ☎ **01631-563-987.** *Fax: 01631-571-276.* www. greencourt-oban.co.uk. *Rack rates: £48–£64 ($88–$118) double. MC, V. Usually closed in Dec and Jan.*

Kilmichael Country House
$$$ **Isle of Arran**

This small, 300-year-old hotel is the best accommodation — and the oldest building — on the island. The lovely, spacious rooms hold antique wood furniture, fresh flowers, and pleasant pastel upholstery and drapes. The sitting room, formerly a chapel, has an impressive stained-glass window, and you'll enjoy sitting by one of the fireplaces on a blustery day. The hotel has an interesting collection of Japanese ornaments — but the tasty cuisine in the dining room is traditional Scottish.

See map p. 287. Glen Coy, near Brodick on a private road off the A841. ☎ **01770-302-219.** *Fax: 01770-302-068.* www.kilmichael.com. *Rack rates: £150–£190 ($277–$351) double. MC, V.*

Loch Fyne Hotel
$$ **Inveraray**

Just north of town, this old stone house perches on a lovely spot over the loch. It offers big rooms, a friendly desk staff, and a large pool and steam room. The last time I visited, the pool was full of kids. The attractive rooms aren't fancy, but little couches and beautiful views of the water make for a relaxing time between trips to the Jacuzzi or sauna. The food in the restaurant is quite satisfying and a good value.

See map p. 287. On the A83, just above the center of Inveraray. ☎ **01499-302-148.** *Fax: 01499-302-348. Rack rates: £65–£125 ($120–$231) double. MC, V.*

Lochgreen House Hotel
$$$ **Troon**

Adjacent to the fairways of the Royal Troon Golf Course, Lochgreen is a lovely country-house hotel set on 12 lush hectares (30 acres) of forest and landscaped gardens. The property opens onto views of the Firth of Clyde and Ailsa Craig. The interior evokes a more elegant, bygone time, with detailed cornices, antique furnishings, and oak and cherry paneling. Guests can meet and mingle in two luxurious sitting rooms with log fires or take long walks on the well-landscaped grounds. The spacious bedrooms have the finest mattresses.

See map p. 285. Monktonhill Road. ☎ **01292-313-343.** *Fax: 011292-318-661.* www. costley-hotels.co.uk. *Rack rates: £140–£235 ($260–$435) double. AE, MC, V. Free parking.*

Malin Court Hotel
$–$$ **Turnberry**

On one of the most scenic strips of the Ayrshire coast, this well-run hotel fronts the Firth of Clyde and the Turnberry golf courses. It's not a great country house, but rather a serviceable, welcoming retreat offering a blend of informality and comfort. Bedrooms are mostly medium in size. The staff can arrange hunting, fishing, riding, sailing, and golf activities.

See map p. 285. Turnberry. ☎ **01655-331-457.** *Fax: 01655-331-072.* www.malin court.co.uk. *Rack rates: £52–£75 ($96–$139) double. 20 percent discount for children under 16 staying separately from their parents. AE, DC, MC, V.*

Manor House
$$–$$$ **Oban**

At one time, the Duke of Argyll owned this Georgian residence on the coast road. Despite its formal exterior, the house is warm and inviting inside. The tasteful rooms have excellent views of the bay, fine antiques, and floral linens. The Manor House is known for its well-stocked bar and fine restaurant. Rates here include breakfast *and* dinner, but rates without dinner may be available — check the Web site or call for details.

See map p. 289. Gallanach Road. ☎ *01631-562-087. Fax: 01631-563-053.* www.manor houseoban.com. *Rack rates: £85–£102 ($157–$189) double. AE, MC, V.*

Piersland House Hotel
$$$ **Troon**

Designed by William Leiper in 1899, this hotel was originally occupied by Sir Alexander Walker of the Johnnie Walker whisky family and remained a private residence until 1956. The importation of some 17,000 tons of topsoil transformed the marshy surrounding property into a lush 1.6-hectare (4-acre) garden. The moderately sized guest rooms have traditional country-house styling.

See map p. 285. 15 Craigend Rd. ☎ *01292-314-747. Fax 01292-315-613.* www. piersland.co.uk. *Rack rates: £124 ($230) double, £180 ($333) suite with dinner. AE, MC, V.*

Quality Hotel
$$ **Ayr**

The Ayr railway station, a landmark since 1885, is still going strong. Connected to it is the Quality, with its red-sandstone Victorian exterior. It isn't the most modern hotel in town, but many visitors consider the Quality's high ceilings, elaborate detailing, and old-world charm reason to check in. Many of the guest rooms are quite spacious, if routinely furnished. All come with small shower-only bathrooms.

See map p. 285. Burns Statue Square. ☎ *01292-263-268. Fax: 01292-262-293.* www. choicehotelseurope.com. *Rack rates: £71 ($130) double. Children under 14 stay free in parent's room. AE, DC, MC, V.*

The Westin Turnberry Resort
$$$$ **Turnberry**

The 1908 pile is a remarkable and well-known landmark. You can see its white facade, red-tile roof, and dozens of gables from afar. The public rooms contain Waterford crystal chandeliers, Ionic columns, molded ceilings, and oak paneling. Each guest room is furnished in unique early-1900s style and has a marble-sheathed bathroom. The units, which vary in size, open onto views of the lawns, forests, and the golf course along the Scottish coastline. The spa and health facilities are exemplary.

See map p. 285. Maidens Road. ☎ *01655-331-000. Fax: 01655-331-706.* www. turnberry.co.uk. *Rack rates: £252–£475 ($466–$880) double. Off-season rates are lower. AE, DC, MC, V.*

Dining Locally

Ayrshire and Argyll are dominated by vast coastline, so some of the finest food you'll find in the region highlights locally-landed fish and seafood. While your hotel may satisfy your dining needs, below are some of the best dining options in the region.

Anchorage Restaurant
$$–$$$ **Kintyre Peninsula   FISH/SEAFOOD**

The Anchorage has won many awards (such as a Michelin "bib gourmand" for good food and moderate prices), and people come from all around Kintyre to sample the Mediterranean-influenced seafood here. House specialties include monkfish and scallops, but almost every dish incorporates local produce in novel recipes.

See map p. 287. Harbour Street, Tarbert. ☎ *01880-820-881. Reservations recommended. Main courses: £8–£16 ($15–$30). MC, V. Open: daily 7–10 p.m. during high season. Closed Jan to mid-Feb, 2 weeks in Nov, and Sun–Mon during off-season.*

Braidwoods
$$$ **Dalry   FRENCH/SCOTTISH**

One of the standout restaurants in Ayrshire, this simple cottage (known as a "butt and ben") has been converted into a small dining space in rural Ayrshire. Keith and Nicola Braidwood share the cooking chores. The place gets very busy on weekends. Holder of a Michelin star and other accolades, Braidwoods is expensive but worth the price.

See map p. 285. Saltcoats Road. ☎ *01294-833-544.* www.braidwoods.co.uk. *Reservations required. Fixed-price dinner: £32 ($60). AE, MC, V. Open: Tues 7–9 p.m., Wed–Sat noon–2 p.m. and 7–9 p.m., Sun noon–2 p.m.*

Ee-usk
$$ **Oban   FISH/SEAFOOD**

This modern restaurant's name, Gaelic for "fish cafe," sums up the place quite well, because it prepares a host of simple fish and shellfish dishes, from the creamy delights of smoked haddock Cullen skink to lightly breaded white fish to fresh shellfish platters. Located at the recently renovated North Pier in Oban, on nice days, you can sit in the sun on the bayside deck. Ee-usk has a good wine list and some rare Scottish ales.

See map p. 289. North Pier. ☎ *01631-565-666. Main courses: £10–£17 ($18.50–$31.50). MC, V. Open: daily noon–2:30 p.m. and 6–9 p.m.*

Enterkine House
$$$ **Annbank   MODERN SCOTTISH**

Dining at this highly rated, five-room country house hotel, done in Art Deco from the 1930s, can be a special treat. East of Ayr in the village of Annbank, Enterkine's menus emphasize local ingredients, whether seasonal game or fish landed at nearby Troon.

See map p. 285. Coylton Road, Annbank near Ayr. ☎ *01292-521-608. Reservations required. Fixed-price dinner: £37.50 ($69). AE, MC, V. Open: Sun–Fri noon–2:30 p.m. and 7–9 p.m., Sat 7–9 p.m.*

Fouter's Bistro
$$ Ayr MODERN SCOTTISH

In the heart of Ayr, Fouter's Bistro occupies the cellar of an old bank, retaining the original stone floor and a vaulted ceiling. The restaurant's name derives from the Scottish expression "foutering about," which is equivalent to fiddling about. But no one's goofing around here. Under new ownership in 2003, the restaurant has one of the best reputations in the region and emphasizes fresh local produce whenever possible.

See map p. 285. 2A Academy St. ☎ *01292-261-391.* www.fouters.co.uk. *Reservations recommended. Main courses: £9–£16 ($16.50–$30). AE, MC, V. Open: Tues–Sat noon–2 p.m. and 6:30–10:30 p.m.*

Loch Fyne Oyster Bar
$$–$$$ Cairndow SEAFOOD

On the road to Inveraray past Cairndow and the top of the loch is the famous Loch Fyne Oyster Bar. The company that owns it farms both oysters and mussels in the clear cool waters of Loch Fyne. With a glass of dry white wine at this casual (although almost often busy) restaurant, there are few things finer. Be sure to browse the nice gift shop next door.

See map p. 287. At the head of Loch Fyne on the A83. ☎ *01499-600-264. Reservations recommended and required for dinner Nov–Feb. Main courses: £8–£16 ($15–$30). AE, MC, V. Open: Mar–Oct daily 9 a.m.–10 p.m.; Nov–Feb daily 9 a.m.–7:30 p.m..*

MacCallums of Troon Oyster Bar
$$ Troon FISH/SEAFOOD

Near the ferry terminal at the harbor in Troon, this rustic seaside bistro is adjacent to the fresh fish market. Oysters, whole sardines, grilled langoustines, sole, and combination platters are usually on the menu here.

See map p. 285. The Harbour, Troon. ☎ *01292-319-339. Main courses: £10–£16 ($19–$30). AE, MC, V. Open: Tues–Sat noon–2:30 p.m. and 7–9:30 p.m.; Sun noon–3:30 p.m. (and 7–9:30 p.m. May–Sept).*

Exploring Ayrshire and Argyll

Just as Sir Walter Scott dominates Lothian and the Borders, the prominence of Robert Burns is felt southwest of Glasgow in Ayrshire. The heart of "Burns Country" is here, although it extends to Dumfries, as well (see Chapter 14). Down the Clyde Coast is another popular tourist attraction: Culzean Castle. Pronounced "cul-lane," it's more of a mansion than a castle and became a favorite of General Eisenhower, who has a wing named after him. This region of Scotland is home to some of the world's great links golf courses, including world-famous Royal Troon and Turnberry, with windswept coastal views and gorse-filled (bristly) dunes.

At one time, the royal burgh of Ayr was the most popular resort on Scotland's West Coast. On the reasonably picturesque Firth of Clyde, it's only some 56km (35 miles) southwest of Glasgow — about an hour by train or by car. For many years it was a busy market town with a more important and indeed larger port than Glasgow's until the 18th century. Today, Ayr offers visitors some 4km (2½ miles) of beach (more suitable for combing than swimming), cruises, fishing, and golf — as well as the top horse racing in Scotland.

Although the heyday of resort towns such as Largs on the Clyde Coast or Rothesay on the isle of Bute is long since past, they remain pleasant, relaxing places to visit. The isle of Arran is sometimes called Scotland in Miniature, because it combines mountains with more pastoral landscapes, offering visitors golf, a castle, and even a distillery. Oban and Inveraray have more in common with the Highlands and Western Islands and may provide substitutes for travelers who can't fully explore the open spaces further north. Argyll has also become the site of several archeological studies because this part of the country appears to be the spot in which the earliest humans to inhabit the land that became Scotland lived.

The top attractions

Argyll Forest Park
Near Arrochar

This 60,000-acre outdoor attraction offers lowland forest trails to the lofty peaks of the "Arrochar Alps." The terrain offers walking and hiking options for most skill levels and enough wildlife to please animal lovers as well. The park is home to acres of wildflowers, violets, bluebells, primroses, woodland birds, and even seals in the sea lochs. You can explore on your own or take a seasonal, ranger-led walk or safari. For park information and trail maps, visit the **Arrochar Tourist Information Center** (7 Alexandra Park in Dunoon; ☎ **01369-703-785**) or contact the park office in Arrochar. Allow 2 to 5 hours.

See map p. 287. ☎ *01369-840-666. Admission: free. Open: daily dawn to dusk.*

Brodick Castle
Isle of Arran

This impressive red-sandstone castle, which once belonged to the Dukes of Hamilton, sits by the bay and mountains surrounded by acres of park and gardens. The castle occupies the site of an old Viking fortress, and the oldest parts of the building allegedly date to the 13th century. The stately rooms hold an impressive collection of silver, porcelain, and paintings. Each room has both living expert guides and fun fact sheets ("junior guides") to make the castle interesting for even easily bored youths. Give yourself time to see the woodland gardens of exotic flowers. The castle also has a playground. Allow about 2 hours.

Burns: Humanitarian, poet, skirt chaser

Robert Burns (1759–1796) continues to hold a sentimental spot in the national consciousness of Scotland. In recent years, Ayrshire has begun to host an annual music and cultural festival "Burns an' a' that" (www.burnsfestival.com) in the spring to celebrate his life. Born in Alloway on a night so gusty that part of the cottage came down, Burns was the son of a simple and pious gardener who encouraged the boy to read and seek an education. Burns was, by trade, a hard-working though largely unsuccessful farmer who switched to being a tax collector later in his life.

But the world knows him as the author of poetry, often set to song, such as *Auld Lang Syne,* or narrative masterpieces, such as *Tam o'Shanter.* Other works, such as "A Man's a Man for a' That," show Burns's humanitarian leanings. Burns was also a prodigious pursuer of women ("Once heartily in love, never out of it") who fathered numerous children. In his short life, he wrote about 370 poems and songs. He died at 37, rather distinguished but resolutely destitute. His pregnant wife, Jean, is said to have had to beg a shilling from the poet's brother in order to feed her children on the day of his funeral.

See map p. 287. Brodick, Isle of Arran, 1 mile north of the pier. ☎ *01770-302-202. Admission: £7.50 ($14) adults, £6 ($11) seniors, students, and children under 16. Castle open: Apr–June and Sept–Oct daily 11 a.m.–4:30 p.m.; July–Aug daily 11 a.m.–5 p.m. Gardens open: Apr–Oct daily dawn to sunset. Closed Nov–Mar.*

Burns Cottage and Museum
Alloway

Although underfunded and basic, this tourist attraction is a must for even the casual Burns fan. Visitors can take a self-guided tour of the cottage, where the family lived for nine years. Decades after they left, it was expanded and used as a pub and inn before the local Burns Society had it restored to the original, more compact size. An audio track explains the various uses for the rooms — one of which held the family *and* their livestock before Burns's father built an addition. The cottage's original features include a box bed in the kitchen where the poet was born. The initial room has display cases with first editions of his books as well as many letters that Burns wrote and received. In the larger exhibition hall, a timeline helps place the bard in context with other historic and cultural events of his age. Cases contain various mementos and memorabilia such as the huge family bible. Allow about 1½ hours.

See map p. 285. Alloway (3km [2 miles] south of Ayr on B7024). ☎ *01292-443-700.* www.burnsheritagepark.com. *Admission: £3 ($5.50) adults, £1.50 ($2.75) children and seniors, £9 ($16.50) per family. Open: Apr–Oct daily 9:30 a.m.–5:30 p.m.; Nov–Mar Mon–Sat 10 a.m.–5 p.m.*

Burns Monument and Gardens
Alloway

About 1km (½ mile) from the Burns Cottage, just past the old kirk, this Grecian-classical monument, which was replicated in Edinburgh on Calton Hill, was erected in 1823 in a ceremony attended by the poet's widow, Jean Armour. The gardens overlook the River Doon and its famous arching bridge. Allow about 30 minutes.

See map p. 285. Drive 3km (2 miles) south of Ayr on B7024. ☎ *01292-443-700. Admission: £1 ($1.85) tokens from Tam o'Shanter Experience. Open: Apr–Sept daily 9:30 a.m.–5 p.m.; Oct–Mar daily 10 a.m.–4 p.m.*

Culzean Castle and Country Park
South Ayrshire

Situated on the cliffs above the sea about 20km (12 miles) south of Ayr, Culzean (pronounced *cul*-lane) Castle and Country Park provides one of the more scenic and soothing stops in Ayrshire. Culzean Castle is a fine example of architect William Adam's "castellated" style (that is, built with turrets and ramparts). Notwithstanding its architectural attributes — whether the celebrated round drawing room or the outstanding oval staircase — the pile is of special interest to many Americans because of General Eisenhower's connection. In 1946, the guest apartment was given to the general in thanks for his service as supreme commander of the allied forces. Undoubtedly, Culzean's location near so many outstanding golf courses, such as Turnberry and Troon (see listings in the section "Golfing heavens: Troon and Turnberry"), surely pleased the golf-mad ex-general and U.S. president. Fans of the Scottish cult horror film, *The Wicker Man,* will know that scenes at the home of the devilish character played by Christopher Lee were filmed here. Allow about 1 hour.

See map p. 285. Overlooking the Firth of Clyde. ☎ *01655-884-455.* www.culzean castle.net. *Admission (including entrance to the Country Park): £9 ($14) adults, £6.50 ($10) seniors and children, £23 ($37) families of 2 adults and 2 children. Open: Apr–Oct daily 10:30 a.m.–5 p.m. (last admission 30 minutes before closing). Closed Nov–Mar.*

Culzean Country Park became, in 1969, the first country park in Scotland. Thanks to the influences of the mild Gulf Stream, the grounds have some exotic plants that one would not expect to see in Scotland. The 228-hectare (565-acre) grounds contain a walled garden, aviary, swan pond, camellia house, orangery, adventure playground, and newly restored 19th-century pagoda, as well as a deer park, kilometers of woodland paths, and beaches. Culzean Country Park has gained an international reputation for its visitor center. The views towards the sea include the rounded rock of an island called Alisa Craig. An area some 16km (10 miles) offshore is a nesting ground and sanctuary for seabirds. Allow about 2 hours.

See map p. 285. On the land surrounding Culzean Castle. ☎ *01655-884-400. Admission: included in admission to Culzean Castle. Open: daily 9 a.m.–dusk.*

Arran: "Scotland in Miniature"

The Isle of Arran, in the Firth of Clyde off the coast of Ayrshire, is often called "Scotland in Miniature" because it combines pasture-filled lowlands with mountainous highland scenery. Indeed, the so-called Highland Boundary Fault Line bisects the island diagonally, just as it does the Scottish mainland. In addition to the geographic and topographic mimicry, Arran offers a castle, half a dozen golf courses (including one with 12 holes), and a whisky distillery. It's also a popular camping and cycling destination. Various attractions and activities on Arran range from hiking and rock climbing to pony trekking and sailing — plus good stretches of sandy, if wind-swept, beaches.

Inveraray Castle
Inveraray

This almost picture-perfect pile with fairy-tale spires and riveted roofs sits near Loch Fyne, just outside the town of Inveraray. From the impressive Armoury Hall to the fine collection of French tapestries and furniture, the building holds much over which to marvel. Belonging to the clan Campbell, the castle is home to the Duke and Duchess of Argyll. The grounds are particularly lovely in the fall when the leaves change color. Check out the small Combined Operations Museum in the stables, which covers the history of Inveraray's role in preparing troops for the D-Day invasion. Allow about 2 hours.

See map p. 287. On the A83 Trunk Road, 1km (¾ mile) northeast of Inveraray on Loch Fyne. ☎ *01499-302-203.* www.inveraray-castle.com. *Admission: £6 ($11) adults, £5 ($9.25) seniors and students, £4 ($7.50) children under 16, £15 ($27.75) family of 2 adults, 2 kids. Open: June–Sept Mon–Sat 10 a.m.–5:45 p.m., Sun 1–5:45 p.m.; April–May and Oct Mon–Thurs and Sat 10 a.m.–1 p.m. and 2–5:45 p.m., Sun 1–5:45 p.m., closed Fri closed Nov–Mar.*

Kilchurn Castle
Loch Awe

These stunning ruins, which date to the 16th century, are as much fun to get to as they are to explore — you can either walk up a steep path from the car park or hop on the steamboat ferry for the short ride from the Loch Awe pier. The castle, on the head of Loch Awe, has great views and is a popular place to take pictures, so don't leave your camera in the car. Built by Sir Colin Campbell, Kilchurn was one of the strongholds of this area that was controlled by Clan Campbell at one time. Allow about 2 hours.

See map p. 287. Car park: Hwy. A85 east of Loch Awe. Ferry: ☎ *01838-200-440. Admission: free. Ferry: £4 ($5.80) adults, £3 ($4.35) children under 16. Open: Apr–Nov daily dawn–dusk; call ahead at beginning and end of season. Closed Dec–Mar.*

Kilmartin House Museum
Kilmartin

Kilmartin House Museum preserves the history and culture of Scotland's early civilizations. An audiovisual presentation on the significance and sights of the Kilmartin Valley is interesting and artistically done, and the museum is full of fine artifacts from the early settlements of the area. You'll discover several items of interest in this scattered museum, from a replica of St. Columba's boat to a workshop where you can see old skills in action. This historically significant valley was where travelers coming from Ireland first settled on Scottish soil. The museum cafe offers fine regional food, traditional Scottish drinks, and coffee. Alas, as this book goes to press, the museum is threatened with closure because of funding shortfalls, so check if it's open before venturing out. Allow about 2 hours.

See map p. 287. Hwy. A816 between Lochgilphead and Oban, Kilmartin, Argyll. ☎ *01546-51-0278.* www.kilmartin.org. *Admission: £5 ($9.25) adults, £4 ($7.50) seniors and students, £2 ($3.70) children under 16, £10 ($18.50) family. Open: daily 10 a.m.–5:30 p.m.*

Laphroaig Distillery
Islay

Laphroaig (pronounced La *Froig*) is the home of a whisky that most people either love or loathe. It has a distinctive peaty flavor with a whiff of sea air (some say they can even taste a little seaweed). Even if you aren't a fan of the whisky, the distillery merits a visit. To visit the distillery and get a tour full of good anecdotes and information, you need to make an appointment. Allow about 1½ hours.

See map p. 287. Near Port Ellen, on the road to Ardbeg. ☎ *01496-302-418. Admission: free. Open: by appointment only.*

Loch Lomond
Argyll

Loch Lomond, the largest inland body of water in all of Great Britain, is about a 30-minute drive or train ride from the Glasgow city limits. At the loch's southern edge, in the otherwise unremarkable if pleasant town of Balloch, is **Loch Lomond Shores** (www.lochlomondshores.com). The activity complex includes an information center (open daily from 10 a.m.–5p.m.; ☎ 01389-722-199) on the adjacent national park — Scotland's first — that extends up the eastern shores of the loch. At the north end of Loch Lomond is the eccentric pub at the Drover's Inn, always worth a stop on the ride up (or down) the loch.

If you're a hiker, the trails up the eastern shore of the loch are preferable; this is the route that the West Highland Way (see the sidebar "Hiking the West Highland Way") follows. If you're a canoeing or kayaking enthusiast, the Loch Lomond Shores' visitor center has rentals (☎ **01389-602-576;** www.canyouexperience.com) for around £15 ($28) per hour. Up the western shores, before the notoriously winding road at Tarbet (where the train from Glasgow to Oban stops), visitors can take a cruise. Golfers usually are attracted to the Loch Lomond country club, near Luss, which has hosted the annual Barclays Scottish Open professional golf championships in past years (☎ **0141-887-2992**; barclaysscottishopen.co.uk).

McCaig's Tower
Oban

The distinguished landmark above Oban cityscape is this Classical structure, which seems out of place. Local banker John McCaig commissioned it around 1900 in order to employ three stonemasons who were out of work. Though never completed, the arches were intended to house statues of McCaig's family. You're free to walk through the monument and enjoy the city's best view of the town, bay, and surrounding area, especially at sunset. Floodlights illuminate the tower at night. Allow about 1 hour.

See map p. 289. Oban, between Duncraggan and Laurel roads. Admission: free. Open: daily 24 hours.

Mount Stuart
Bute

This mansion belongs to the Marquess of Bute's family, but it's open to the public for much of the year. Construction of the red-sandstone pile began around the early 1880s for the third Marquess. The interiors display certain eccentricities and interests of the man, such as a ceiling in an upstairs room that is covered in stars and constellations because of his interest in astrology. The garden dates back to the early 18th century, when the second earl of Bute moved the family here from the port town of Rothesay.

Hiking the West Highland Way

One of Scotland's best-known long-distance footpaths is the **West Highland Way,** established in the 1980s. The trail begins rather uneventfully northwest of Glasgow in the affluent suburb of Milngavie (pronounced mill-*guy*). But as the trail winds some 153km (95 miles) north along the eastern shore of Loch Lomond, through the desolate and almost pre-historic looking Rannoch Moor, along the breathtaking and historic Glen Coe, and ending finally in Fort William, it just gets better and better. At the northern terminus, you're at the foot of Ben Nevis, Scotland's highest mountain.

Trains run frequently throughout the day from the Queen's Street railway station in central Glasgow to Milngavie, the starting point of the walk. The 25-minute trip costs £2.15 ($4) one-way. In Fort William, you can catch the First ScotRail train back to Glasgow. Hikers can backpack and camp along the way or stay at inns conveniently dotted along the trail. Tour companies are available to haul your luggage from stop to stop along the way. For details on the West Highland Way, contact the National Park, Gateway Centre, Loch Lomond Shores, Ben Lomond Way, Balloch, G83 8QL; ☎ 01389-722-199 — or log onto www.west-highland-way.co.uk.

The grounds have a woodlands park, a huge walled area — the so-called "wee garden" — and a working vegetable plot, too. The garden is open from May to mid-October. Allow about 2 hours.

See map p. 287. A844 near Scoulag, south of Rothesay. Ferries (30-minute ride) to Rothesay from the mainland (Wemyss Bay) depart frequently. Trains to Wemyss Bay leave Glasgow Central. ☎ *01700-503-877.* www.mountstuart.com. *Admission: house and grounds £7 ($13) adults, £3 ($5.50) children; grounds only £3.50 ($6.50) adult, £2 ($3.75) children. Open: house May–Sept 30 Wed and Fri–Mon 11 a.m.–5 p.m.; gardens May–Sept 30 10 a.m.–6 p.m., also open Sat–Sun in April.*

Oban Seal & Marine Centre
Barcaldine

This seal sanctuary is a nursery and hospital for stray, sick, and injured seal pups. The center isn't elaborate, but it takes care of the cute creatures before releasing them back into the wild. Highlights of the animal rescue center include daily lectures and feedings. The marine center has exhibits on the natural habitats of sea creatures, including sharks. The setting, among tall, shady pine trees by the water's edge, is reminiscent of northern California. Allow about 2½ hours.

See map p. 287. A828, north of Oban, on the shores of Loch Creran. ☎ *01631-720-386. Admission: £6.50 ($12) adults, £5 ($9.25) seniors and students, £4 ($7.50) children under 16. Open: daily 10 a.m.–5 p.m.*

Souter Johnnie's Cottage
Kirkoswald

Some 13 miles south of Ayr, this cottage was the home of Burns's pal, the cobbler John Davidson. Davidson became the inspiration for the character "Souter Johnnie" in Burns's tale of Tam o'Shanter. The cottage contains Burnsiana and contemporary cobbler's tools, and in the churchyard are the graves of the real life Tam o'Shanter (Douglas Graham) and Souter Johnnie. Allow about 1 hour.

See map p. 285. Main Road, A77, Kirkoswald (6½km (4 miles) west of Maybole on A77). ☎ *01655-760-603.* www.nts.org.uk. *Admission: £3 ($5.50) adults, £2 ($3.75) children and seniors. Open: Apr 1–Sept 30 Fri–Tues 11:30 a.m.–5 p.m.*

Golfing heavens: Troon and Turnberry

For links-style golf, which emphasizes sandy dunes and rolling golf courses, you can hardly do better than the Ayrshire coastline. While there are a host of options for the avid golfer, the two best-known courses are Troon and Turnberry.

Troon

The resort town of **Troon,** 11km (7 miles) north of Ayr and 50km (31 miles) southwest of Glasgow, looks out across the Firth of Clyde toward the Isle of Arran. Troon takes its name from the curiously hook-shaped promontory jutting out into the sea: the "trone" or nose. From this port, a SeaCat ferry (☎ **08705-523-523;** www.steam-packet.com) sails daily to and from Belfast in Northern Ireland.

Troon and its environs offer several sandy links courses, most prominently the **Royal Troon Golf Club** (☎ **01292-311-555;** www.royal troon.co.uk). Royal Troon boasts two courses. The Old Course is a 7,150-yard (4-mile) seaside course that often hosts the prestigious Open Championship, which was played here as recently as summer 2004. Dignified Georgian and Victorian buildings and the Isle of Arran are visible from the fairways, which seem deliberately designed to steer your golf balls into danger. Hole 8, the famous "Postage Stamp," is only 123 yards in distance, but depending upon the wind, you may need a long iron to reach the green. The 6,289-yard (3.5-mile) Portland Course, is even more challenging, by some estimates, than the Old Course.

If you're in the mood to play both courses, a one-day fee — a whopping £200 ($370) — includes morning coffee, a buffet lunch, and two rounds: one on the Old Course and one on the Portland.

A much less expensive and still gratifying option is to play one of the municipal courses, such as Darnley or Lochgreen, run by the South Ayrshire Council; Darnley and Lochgreen run parallel to Royal Troon at spots. The clubhouse for the municipal courses is right across from the Troon Railway Station. Fees on the weekend range from £16 to £25 ($30–$46). Another option is a six-round, seven-day golf pass from the council for £72 ($133). For more information, log onto www.golfsouth ayrshire.com or call the South Ayrshire Golf information hotline at ☎ **01292-616-255.**

Non-golfing visitors will find plenty of room to relax on Troon's 3km (2 miles) of **sandy beaches** stretching along both sides of the harbor; the broad sands and shallow waters make it a safe haven for beach bums. From here you can take boat trips to Arran or the narrow strait north of Bute known as the Kyles of Bute.

Trains from Glasgow's Central Station arrive at the Troon station several times daily (trip time about 40 min.; £5 ($9.25) one-way ticket). Call ☎ **08457-484-950** for information. Trains and buses also connect Ayr with Troon, which is about a 10-minute ride.

Turnberry

The coastal settlement of Turnberry, 81km (50 miles) south of Glasgow on the A77, was once part of the Culzean Estate. It began to flourish early in the 20th century when rail service was developed, and a recognized golfing center with a first-class resort hotel was established. However, unlike Troon, which is a reasonably-sized port town/village, there isn't much to Turnberry except for the hotel and golf course.

From the original pair of 13-hole golf courses, the complex has developed into the two championship level courses, Ailsa and Kintyre, known world-wide as the **Turnberry Hotel Golf Courses.** Ailsa's 18 holes have been the scene of Open tournaments and other professional golfing events. Guests of the Westin Turnberry hotel get priority access, especially on the Ailsa course. The fees to play vary. Hotel residents pay between £45 and £105 ($83–$194) depending on the course and the season. If you're not staying at Westin Turnberry, rates range from £60 to £175 ($111–$324). Log onto www.turnberry.co.uk or call ☎ **01655-334-032** for details.

Other cool things to see and do

- ✔ **Inveraray Jail,** Church Square, Inveraray (☎ **01499-302-381**). This is a somewhat implausibly eerie but fun museum that takes on the history of Scottish crime and punishment. Wax figures and recorded voices attempt to re-create life in the old jail cells. A historic court-room is straight out of the 1820s; from there you get a glimpse of torture and death — from hot-iron branding and public whipping to (gulp) "ear nailing." The murderers and madmen aren't real, but little ones may find the prison section more frightening than fun.

- ✔ **Kilchurn Castle,** A85 east of Loch Awe (☎ **01838-200-440**). This castle offers well-maintained ruins that date to the 16th century. They're as much fun to get to as they are to explore — you can either walk up a steep path from the car park or hop on the steam-boat ferry for the short ride from the Loch Awe pier.

- ✔ **Museum of Islay Life,** Port Charlotte, Islay (☎ **01496-850-358**). This interesting little museum is housed in an old church. The museum focuses on the history of the island and island life, as well as the whisky-making process. It may seem a bit thrown-together, but it gives context to your visit to Islay.

- ✔ **Oban Distillery,** Stafford Street (☎ **01631-572-004**). Oban Distillery may not be the largest or most distinguished distillery in Scotland, but it's conveniently located in the heart of Oban and offers an informative tour of one of the oldest malt whisky makers in the country.

- ✔ **Tam o'Shanter Experience,** Murdoch's Lane, Alloway (☎ **01292-443-700**). This museum is adjacent to the gardens of the Burns Monument. Here you can watch a video on Burns's life and poetry — as well as one that depicts the Tam o'Shanter. The visitor center also has a well-stocked gift shop and a tearoom.

Shopping for Local Treasures

Although none of the towns in the region have extraordinary shopping opportunities, Ayr, Brodick, and Oban are nevertheless market towns. Many of the attractions listed in the section "The top attractions" have gift shops, and the Burns Museum in Alloway (see the detailed listing earlier in this chapter) is particularly good for souvenirs about the

Scottish bard. Along the shores of Loch Lomond, you can find a few galleries with local art. In addition, here are a few specialty shops.

- ✔ **Caithness Glass,** Railway Pier, Oban (☎ **01631-563-386**). This world-famous glass shop is a great place to find a unique memento. The colorful menagerie of items never disappoints and maintains the highest level of quality — no piece with even the slightest imperfection leaves the factory. Caithness Glass is open March through October, Monday through Saturday from 9 a.m. to 5 p.m., plus Sunday from 11 a.m. to 5 p.m. from April through October; November to February, Monday through Saturday from 10 a.m. to 5 p.m.

- ✔ **Crafty Kitchen,** Ardfern, midway between Oban and Lochgilphead (☎ **01852-500-303** or 01852-500-689). Part craft shop, part cafe, part art gallery, and part post office, Crafty Kitchen is one of the most memorable stores you'll find in the country. The crafts are unique and thoroughly Scottish, the cafe serves delicious vegetarian fare, and the gallery features Scottish artists and craftspeople. The shop is open April through October, Tuesday through Sunday from 10 a.m. to 5:30 p.m.; November and December, Saturday and Sunday from 10 a.m. to 5 p.m.

- ✔ **Inveraray Woolen Mill,** The Anvil, Front Street, Inveraray (☎ **01499-302-166**). A self-described "Pandora's box" of Scottish gifts, the mill has a great variety of items — more of a smorgasbord, I'd say. Among the quality gifts: Edinburgh crystal, cashmere, knitwear, woolly hats and gloves, and gourmet edibles. The architect who did much of Edinburgh's New Town designed the whitewashed building. Call for hours.

Doing the Pub Crawl

You'll find no shortage of pubs in Ayr and Oban, the largest towns in this area. In less-visited areas such as East Ayrshire, the Kintyre Peninsula, and the islands, most pubs are basic watering holes catering to the locals. In some small towns, in fact, the hotel pub is the only place to grab a dram of whisky or a pint. Many of the restaurants and hotels listed earlier in this chapter have public house licenses and welcome non-residents. In addition, consider the following:

- ✔ **Brodick Bar,** Brodick, Arran, just off Shore Road near the post office (☎ **01770-302-169**). This all-wood pub pours delicious ale and has a reputation for serving excellent pub grub — especially uniquely topped pizzas. During the day, you can get a light lunch; in the evening, the kitchen serves bistro food to accompany Scottish-brewed beer. Brodick Bar is open Monday through Saturday from 11 a.m. to midnight.

- ✔ **Oban Inn,** Stafford Street, Oban (☎ **01631-562-484**). This classic whitewashed pub, near the water just off the town's main street, has a warm, old-fashioned elegance. The upstairs bar is a little quieter than downstairs, but the downstairs room, with flags and exposed wooden beams, is a better place to meet people. The pub has an excellent selection of whisky and decent pub grub. Oban Inn is open daily from 11 a.m. to 1 a.m.

✔ **Rabbie's Bar,** Burns Statue Square, Ayr (☎ **01292-262-112**). The bar has walls covered with the pithy verses of Robert Burns and his portrait. However, don't come here expecting poetry readings in a quiet corner. The crowd, although not particularly literary, is talkative. Rabbie's Bar is open Monday through Saturday from 11 a.m. to 12:30 a.m.; on Sunday, it's open from noon to midnight.

Fast Facts: Ayrshire and Argyll

Area Codes

The area code for Arran is **01770**, Ayr is **01292**, Bute is **01700**, Campbelltown is **01586**, Inveraray is **01499**, Oban is **01631**, and Tarbert is **01880**. You need to dial the area code only if you're calling from outside the city you want to reach.

ATMs

Cash points at banks in bigger towns are common, but don't expect all or even any to be linked internationally.

Emergencies

Dial ☎ **999** for police, fire, or ambulance.

Hospitals

The most convenient hospital is Argyll & the Isles Hospital, off Soroba Road, at the south end of town in Oban (☎ 01631-567-500).

Information

Ayr tourist office is at 22 Sandgate, Ayr (☎ 01292-678-100). It's open from Easter to August, Monday through Saturday from 9 a.m. to 6 p.m. (in July and August, it's also open Sunday from 10 a.m. to 5 p.m.) and September to Easter, Monday through Saturday from 9:15 a.m. to 5 p.m. In Oban, the tourist office is in the Old Church, Argyll Square, (☎ 01631-563-122). April to mid-June and mid-September to October, it's open Monday through Friday 9:30 a.m. to 5 p.m. and Saturday and Sunday 10 to 4 p.m.; mid-June through mid-September, hours are Monday to Saturday 9 a.m. to 8 p.m. and Sunday 9 a.m. to 7 p.m.; and November through March, it's open Monday to Saturday 9:30 a.m. to 5 p.m. and Sunday noon to 4 p.m. If you prefer to gather tourist information online, visit www.visitscotland.com.

Internet Access

Cafe na Lusan, 9 Craigard Rd., Oban (☎ 01631-567-268), is open Tuesday through Thursday from 11 a.m. to 8 p.m., Friday through Saturday from 11 a.m. to 10 p.m., and Sunday from noon to 7 p.m. The charge is £1 ($1.45) for 15 minutes.

Post Office

The nearest main post offices are Corran Esplanade, Oban (☎ 01631-562-430), and Main Street South, Inveraray (☎ 01499-302-062).

Chapter 16

Fife and the Trossachs

- -

In This Chapter

▶ Easing your tired feet in cozy hotels

▶ Dining on local cuisine

▶ Discovering the stomping grounds of William Wallace and Robert the Bruce

▶ Enjoying a pint at the best local pubs

- -

Fife and the Trossachs are two regions teeming with attractions —
and many are within easy reach of Edinburgh and Glasgow. Each
has a flagship city: **St. Andrews** for Fife and the royal town of **Stirling**
for Central Scotland and the nearby Trossachs. Many of the hotels and
restaurants listed in this chapter are in or near these two cities.

If you're at all interested in golf, St. Andrews needs no introduction. Home
to one of the oldest courses in the world — as well as the association that
decides the rules for the sport — St. Andrews, also a college town with
cobblestone streets, is the golf mecca of the world.

Stirling is a royal burgh that was established by King David and was at
one time the de facto capital of Scotland. Its castle, a former home to
Scottish royalty including Mary Queen of Scots, remains intact. Many
people come to see the historic sites of the surrounding area, which
has seen its share of battles between freedom fighters and the English.
In fact, William Wallace, who has a towering monument here, and King
Robert the Bruce led decisive victories in and around Stirling. The
quaint town resembles an inland mini-Edinburgh.

Other things to see and do include visiting the Dunfermline birthplace
of Andrew Carnegie that is today a museum, the well-preserved ruins of
Doune castle (which Monty Python used in their film *The Holy Grail*), the
towering Wallace monument in Stirling, and the wooded glens of the
Queen Elizabeth Forest Park.

Getting to Fife and the Trossachs

You don't necessarily need a car if you're just going to St. Andrews or
Stirling, because both cities are navigable by foot. If your visit here is a
daytrip from Edinburgh or Glasgow, for example, consider taking a train

Fife

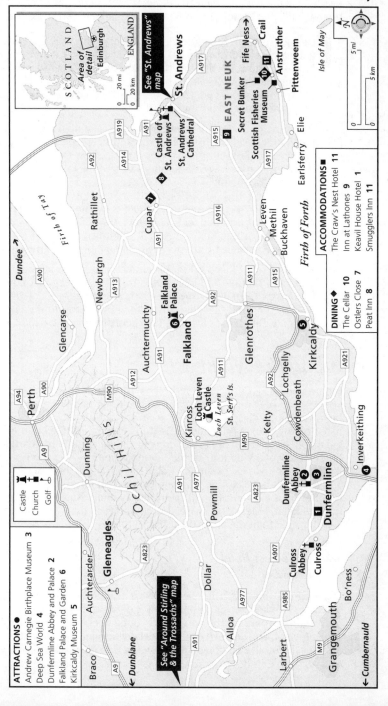

SCOTLAND
Area of detail
Edinburgh
ENGLAND

20 mi
20 km

Castle
Church
Golf

Dundee→

Firth of Tay

Perth

Ochil Hills

Gleneagles

Auchterarder

Dunblane→

Braco

Dunning

Powmill

Dollar

Alloa

Larbert

Grangemouth

Cumbernauld→

Bo'ness

Culross
Culross Abbey

Dunfermline
Dunfermline Abbey

Inverkeithing

Cowdenbeath
Kelty

Lochgelly
Lochgelly

Kinross
Loch Leven Castle
Loch Leven
St. Serf's Is.

Glenrothes

Kirkcaldy

Buckhaven
Methil
Leven

Falkland
Falkland Palace

Auchtermuchty

Newburgh

Glencarse

Rathillet

Cupar

Castle of St. Andrews
St. Andrews Cathedral
St. Andrews

See "St. Andrews" map

EAST NEUK

Secret Bunker
Scottish Fisheries Museum

Crail
Fife Ness→
Anstruther
Pittenweem

Elie
Earlsferry

Firth of Forth

Isle of May

5 mi
5 km

See "Around Stirling & the Trossachs" map

A94
A9
A90
A90
A92
A914
A913
A912
A91
A977
A823
A907
A977
A985
A91
M9
A823
M90
M90
A92
A911
A911
A915
A915
A921
A916
A91
A919
A917
A915
A917

or the bus. Even if you want to see an attraction that lies outside of the towns, additional trains and buses are available for short jaunts.

✔ **By car:** To get to St. Andrews from Edinburgh, cross the Forth Bridge and catch the A92 to the A91. From Glasgow to St. Andrews, take the M80 north towards Stirling, then take the A91. The A91 connects Stirling and St. Andrews. To get to Stirling from Edinburgh, take the M9; from Glasgow, take the M80. To get to Callander and Trossachs, catch the A84 from Stirling.

✔ **By train:** To get to Fife from Edinburgh, take the Fife loop, operated by First ScotRail, from Haymarket Station. To get to Stirling, trains depart from Edinburgh Waverley and Glasgow Queen Street stations. From Glasgow or Edinburgh to Stirling, take First ScotRail (☎ 0845-748-4950; www.firstscotrail.com). There is no direct train service to St. Andrews, but there's a stop some 13km (8 miles) away at the town of Leuchars, which is on the Edinburgh-Aberdeen route. For information, call ☎ 08457-484-950. After you arrive at Leuchars, you can take a bus to St. Andrews. You can't take a train into the Trossachs.

✔ **By bus:** From Glasgow, Edinburgh, Aberdeen, and Inverness, **Citylink** (☎ 0990-505-050) buses travel to Stirling. **Midland Bluebird** (☎ 01324-613-777) serves Aberfoyle and Callander from Stirling and Glasgow. To get to St. Andrews from Edinburgh, Glasgow, Dundee, or Stirling, take **Scottish Fife** (☎ 01334-474-238).

Spending the Night

Before you pick your accommodations, it's a good idea to decide what you want to see and in what order so you don't find yourself crisscrossing the area needlessly. For more accommodation choices than those listed below, such as smaller B&Bs (tons of comfortable but undistinguishable ones are in the area), consult the local tourism board for assistance. A few of my dining out recommendations — Creagan House and the Inn at Kippen, for example — also have rooms. Some of the hotels and inns I list have earned star ratings from the tourist board (see Chapter 8 for a description of the rating system). Rates below include full breakfast, unless otherwise stated. And remember: You may well get a better deal than the advertised "rack" rates.

The Craw's Nest Hotel
$$ Anstruther

Once an old minister's house, the Nest traded holiness for hospitality when the building became a fine hotel. It offers a little something for everyone: a games room for the young and young at heart, four-poster beds for romantic couples, and two rooms specially designed for travelers with disabilities. If you like to boogie, the hotel is also home to the largest dance floor in the region. If you enjoy a nice view, ask for a room in the wing overlooking the waters of the Forth and the Isle of May.

See map p. 307. Bankwell Road, off Pittenweem Road. ☎ *01333-310-691. Fax: 01333-312-216.* www.crawsnesthotel.co.uk. *Rack rates: £60–£94 ($111–$173) double. AE, DC, MC, V.*

Cromlix House
$$$–$$$$ Kinbuck

This accommodation is a sportsman's dream. Principally a hunting lodge, the Cromlix draws fishermen and hunters with its 3,000 acres of woodlands stretching to the River Allan. The owners even organize fishing and hunting trips. The three-story Victorian house is a restored pile that captures the elegance of affluence in the 19th century; the sitting rooms and guest rooms are decorated with fine art and period furniture, and common areas such as the library and conservatory have been restored.

See map p. 319. On the B8033 from the A9, 10 miles north of Stirling. ☎ *01786-822-125. Fax: 01786-825-450. Rack rates: £135–£260 ($250–$481) double. AE, DC, MC, V. Closed Jan.*

Golden Lion Hotel
$$ Stirling

Location, location, location. This 200-year-old building in the heart of Stirling houses one of the most popular accommodations in the area. Since its early days as a coaching inn (where horse-drawn coaches historically stopped), the Golden Lion has roared with hospitality. Now refurbished, the oldest and largest hotel in town is also quite modern. There's nothing fancy about the cookie-cutter rooms, but the hotel is clean, and for its proximity to attractions (only a couple of blocks from Stirling Castle), you can't beat the price. Another plus is a free parking garage.

See map p. 321. 8–10 King St., Stirling. ☎ *01786-475-351. Fax: 01786-472-755. Rack rates: £72–£86 ($133–$160) double. AE, DC, MC, V.*

The Inn at Lathones
$$$ Lathones

The Inn at Lathones is set in a picturesque spot just 5 miles from St. Andrews. It may be 400 years old, but the inn is thoroughly modern, and the rooms are equipped with stereos and huge baths. The bungalow-style inn has sidewalks that take you from one whitewashed building to the next. The main house, with a restaurant and front desk, is a comfortable area with fireplaces and sitting rooms. In an effort to cater to families, the inn offers a fun games room, an outdoor play area, and larger rooms that are ideal for a family of three or four.

See map p. 307. Five miles south of St. Andrews on the A915. ☎ *01334-840-494 or from the U.S. 800-544-9993. Fax: 01334-840-694.* www.theinn.co.uk. *Rack rates: £135–£180 ($250–$333) double. AE, DC, MC, V.*

Keavil House Hotel
$$$ **Crossford near Dunfermline**

This tranquil country hotel, part of the Best Western chain, is set on a dozen acres of forested land and gardens. The guest rooms are generous in size and well appointed, each with a bathroom. Master bedrooms contain four-poster beds. The hotel offers dining in its Cardoon Restaurant. Free parking is available for guests.

See map p. 307. Main Street, Crossford. Take A994, 3km (2 miles) west of Dunfermline. ☎ *01383-736-258. Fax: 01383-621-600. www.keavilhouse.co.uk. Rack rates: £100–£190 ($185–$351) double, £120–£225 ($222–$416) family suite. AE, DC, MC, V. Closed Dec 31–Jan 1.*

Montague House
$$–$$$ **St. Andrews**

Nearly every building on Murray Park is a guesthouse or B&B, but Montague is the standout — although the price doesn't reflect it. Each of the seven comfortable rooms is nicely appointed and creatively painted. If you book your stay far enough in advance, you may be able to get the Ceol-na-Mara ("Sound of the Sea") room, which has a bay window overlooking the water — be sure to ask if it's available. Montague House is well located between the old town area and the beaches.

See map p. 317. 21 Murray Park, just off North Street. ☎ *01334-479-287. Fax: 01334-475-827. www.montaguehouse.com. Rack rates: £60–£140 ($111–$259) double. MC, V.*

Old Course Hotel
$$$$ **St. Andrews**

Many dedicated golfers choose to stay at the Old Course Hotel, which overlooks the 17th fairway: St. Andrews's "Road Hole." Fortified by a real old-fashioned Scottish breakfast of finnan haddie (that's smoked haddock) and porridge, most guests then hit the links where Scots have been whacking away since the 15th century. Some £16 million ($30 million) was spent to transform the Old Course into a world-class hotel (with price tags to match), and the facade was altered to keep it in line with St. Andrews's more traditional buildings. The hotel's dining options are the contemporary **Sands** seafood bar and restaurant and the **Road Hole Grill.**

See map p. 317. Old Station Road, St. Andrews. ☎ *01334-474-371. Fax 01334-477-668. www.oldcoursehotel.co.uk. Rack rates: £225–£385 ($416–$712) double, £295–£955 ($546–$1,766) suite. AE, DC, MC, V.*

Portcullis
$$ **Stirling**

This fun little B&B sits in the shadow of Stirling Castle. The rooms are comfortable but unpretentious, and the staff is extremely friendly. The Portcullis has been around for hundreds of years and has the rustic feel of an old coach inn and tavern. The downstairs bar is a plus or a minus, depending on your point of view — it's perfect for a nightcap, not so perfect if you want to be in bed before 10 p.m. An added touch are the flowers that grow in the lovely walled-in beer garden.

See map p. 321. Next to Stirling Castle. ☎ *01786-472-290. Fax: 01786-44-6103.* www. theportcullishotel.com. *Rack rates: £80–£86 ($148–$159) double. AE, MC, V.*

Roman Camp
$$$ Callander

This cozy old hotel near Roman ruins is one of the more interesting places to stay in the area. Built in 1625 as a home for the Dukes of Perth, it hasn't changed much, retaining charming low ceilings, creaking corridors, and snug furniture. The drawing room and conservatory have lovely period furniture and antiques. The River Teith runs through 20 beautiful acres of grounds; you're welcome to fish in the river, but stay clear of the grazing sheep and cows.

See map p. 319. Off Main Street from the A84. ☎ *01877-330-003. Fax: 01877-331-533.* www.roman-camp-hotel.co.uk. *Rack rates: £120–£170 ($222–$314) double. AE, DC, MC, V.*

Smugglers Inn
$$ Anstruther

Back in the day (the building dates to the 13th century), this was a popular watering hole for smugglers. Although the rooms are small and the floorboards uneven, the classic whitewashed structure with black trim is quite comfortable and homey. The nautical theme is a bit kitschy, but don't worry, matey, it doesn't extend into the guest rooms. The Smugglers Inn has only nine rooms, so booking ahead is a wise idea.

See map p. 307. High Street. ☎ *01333-310-506. Fax: 01333-312-706. Rack rates: £60–£70 ($111–$130) double. AE, DC, MC, V.*

Stirling Highland Hotel
$$$ Stirling

Ever fall asleep in class? Then you're familiar with the ether-like effect of school. At the Stirling, an old converted high school, you can catch a good night's sleep or a much-needed nap in the classroom without facing detention. This well-managed accommodation is in easy hoofing distance of the castle (only 700 yards away) and all the decent restaurants in town. The architecture is Victorian and the furnishings heavy on tartan and floral patterns. The leisure room is quite nice, featuring a pool, steam room, gym equipment, table tennis, and more. The appropriately named Scholar's Restaurant and the Headmaster's Study bar are pleasant as well.

See map p. 321. Spittal Street. ☎ *01786-272-727. Fax: 01786-272-829.* www. paramount-hotels.co.uk. *Rack rates: £150 ($277) double. AE, DC, MC, V.*

Dining Locally

Your dining needs may be satisfied by your hotel, between a full breakfast in the morning and a meal in the dining room at night. But if you
decide to step outside of your hotel for a bite, this section guides you
toward some of the best options. As with accommodations, you may
gravitate toward St. Andrews or Stirling for places to eat out, but don't
forget the great restaurants outside those cities as well.

Andrew Fairlie at Gleneagles
$$$$ Auchterarder SCOTTISH/FRENCH

This may be the finest dining experience in the country. Fairlie is arguably
the most talented chef in Scotland: He not only has prowess in the kitchen,
but he also knows how to bring together a talented team. Dinners here are
seamless but not particularly stuffy affairs. If you have the money, go for
the tasting menu — it's six courses of pure delight. The signature dish is
smoked lobster, but other highlights include dishes such as foie gras terrine with apricot and grapefruit chutney or "twice-cooked" Gressingham
duck with oriental watercress salad.

See map p. 319. Gleneagles Hotel, Auchterarder. ☎ *01764-694-267. www.
gleneagles.com/restaurants-bars/restaurantsbars_html/andrew
fairlie.html. Reservations required. 3-course a la carte dinner: £55 ($101); tast-
ing menu: £75 ($139). AE, MC, V. Open: Mon–Sat 7–10 p.m. Closed Sun.*

Barnton Bar & Bistro
$–$$ Stirling PUB FOOD

The city of Stirling isn't exactly rich in dining options, but this casual place
is welcoming enough for a coffee, lunch, or an early evening meal. While
there's nothing particularly outstanding on the menu, Barnton is a friendly,
welcoming, and relatively inexpensive place in the middle of Stirling and
near the railway station. The premises are a converted pharmacy with a
games room to the rear, usually populated with university students.

See map p. 321. 3 Barnton St. ☎ *01786-461-698. Main courses: £5–£10 ($9.25–$18.50).
MC, V. Open: restaurant daily 10:30 a.m.–7:30 p.m.; bar Sun–Thurs noon–midnight,
Fri–Sat noon–1 a.m.*

The Cellar
$$$ Anstruther SEAFOOD/SCOTTISH

The Cellar is among the best restaurants in the region. Located in an
ancient fishing village and next door to a fisheries museum, the restaurant
is a hotspot for delicacies from the sea. In addition to staples such as crab,
scallops, and lobster, the mostly seafood menu includes dishes such as
crayfish and mussel bisque and monkfish with herb and garlic sauce. The
stone basement dining room is unassuming and comfortable, with can-
dlelight and fireplaces.

See map p. 307. 24 E. Green, off the courtyard behind the Fisheries Museum. ☎ *01333-310-378. Reservations recommended. Fixed-price lunch: £10.50 ($19), fixed-price dinner: from £28.50 ($51). AE, DC, MC, V. Open: year-round Tues–Sat 7–9 p.m., also summer Tues–Sat 12:30–2 p.m.*

Creagan House
$$–$$$ Stratheyre   SCOTTISH/FRENCH

Cherry and Gordon Gunn run this charming inn, well-situated for country walks, in a 17th-century farmhouse with a clutch of rooms. In the evenings, Gordon repairs to the kitchen where he cooks some sumptuous French-influenced meals using mostly local ingredients. Especially welcome are the vegetables, often grown just up the road, that he prepares to accompany the main courses, but these veggies are far from an afterthought. Don't be fooled by the baronial-style splendor of the dining room, however. It's a much, much more recent addition to the historic house, even though it looks historic itself.

See map p. 319. A84, north of Straheyre. ☎ *01877-384-638. www.creaganhouse. co.uk. Reservations required. Fixed-price dinner: £21.50 ($40). Open: one sitting 7:30–8:30 p.m. Closed Feb.*

Herman's
$$$ Stirling   AUSTRIAN/SCOTTISH

This simply decorated restaurant has a unique menu influenced by both Austria and Scotland. So, will it be jager schnitzel or roast Barbary duck breast? The aproned staff is excellent and helpful in decoding the menu. And don't even think about skipping the wonderful Austrian desserts. You can't beat the location here, just down the road from Stirling Castle.

See map p. 321. 58 Broad St. ☎ *01786-450-632. Reservations recommended. Main courses: £11.50–£16.50 ($21–$30.50). AE, DC, MC, V. Open: Mon–Fri noon–2:30 p.m. and 6–10 p.m., Sat–Sun noon–10 p.m.*

The Inn at Kippen
$$ Kippen   SCOTTISH

About a 10-minute drive west of Stirling on the A811, Kippen is a typical country village in the rolling hills north of Glasgow. Run by the same folk who once owned the well-regarded Olivia's in Stirling, the Inn at Kippen is a modernized version of the country tavern and hotel. The ground floor pub and restaurant specializes in Scottish fare with contemporary twists such as pink crab apple jelly accompanying a terrine of confit duck.

See map p. 319. Fore Road, Kippen. ☎ *01786-871-010. www.theinnatkippen. co.uk/dining.htm. Main courses: £8–£16 ($15–$30). AE, MC, V. Open: daily noon–2:30 p.m. and 6–9:30 p.m.*

Monachyle Mhor
$$$ Balquhidder SCOTTISH

Monachyle Mhor is another gem serving lunch and dinner in another 18th-century farmhouse, this one overlooking Loch Voil down a ramshackle one-lane road from the village of Balquhidder. The conservatory dining room (quite common in inns or older private homes, they have glass walls and often a glass ceiling) is modern and so is the cooking, with entrees such as roast chicken topped with foie gras, belly of pork served with sage and onion jus, and seared fish on a bed of shredded celeriac. Dinner is expensive (and worth it), but lunches are a bargain.

See map p. 319. Off the A84, Balquhidder; turn right at Kingshouse Hotel, and drive 9½km (6 miles). ☎ *01877-384-622.* www.monachylemhor.com. *Main courses lunch: £10 ($18.50); fixed-price dinner: £35 ($65). Open: daily noon–1:45 p.m. and 7–8:45 p.m. Closed Jan–mid-Feb. AE, MC, V.*

Ostlers Close
$$–$$$ Cupar MODERN SCOTTISH

Sophisticated and intensely concerned with the quality of its cuisine, this charming restaurant occupies a 17th-century building in the town of Cupar, west of St. Andrews. Dishes are based on seasonal Scottish produce and can include roasted saddle of venison; pan-fried scallops with fresh asparagus; a medley of seafood with champagne-butter sauce; or filet of Scottish lamb stuffed with skirlie, an old-fashioned but flavorful combination of onion, oatmeal, and meat juices.

See map p. 307. 25 Bonnygate, Cupar. ☎ *01334-655-574. Reservations recommended. Main courses: £10–£18 ($18.50–$33). AE, MC, V. Open: Tues–Fri 7–9:30 p.m., Sat 12:15–2 p.m. and 7–9:30 p.m. Closed 2 weeks mid-May.*

Peat Inn
$$$ Near Cupar MODERN SCOTTISH

The Peat was built in 1760 and is currently a restaurant, inn, and post office. The restaurant offers David Wilson's exceptional cuisine. Meals feature almost all local, seasonal ingredients. A dessert specialty is a trio of caramel-flavored sweets, including crème caramel, caramel-flavored ice cream, and a caramelized apple pastry, all drizzled with caramel sauce.

See map p. 307. Cupar, at the junction of the B940 and B941, 6 miles southwest of St. Andrews. ☎ *01334-840-206. Fax: 01334-840-530.* www.thepeatinn.co.uk. *Reservations required. Fixed-price lunch: £22 ($40); fixed-price dinner: £32 ($60). Open: Tues–Sat noon–1 p.m. and 7–9:30 p.m.*

The Seafood Restaurant
$$$ St. Andrews FISH/SEAFOOD

The Seafood Restaurant is a second branch for owner Tim Butler and his business partner, chef Craig Millar, who began further down the coast in St. Monans. Here, the location on the seafront is spectacular, and given the restaurant is essentially housed in a glass box, you can't miss the views. Dishes range from crab risotto to pan-seared scallops, with plenty of fancy accompaniments on the side.

See map p. 317. The Scores, St. Andrews. ☎ 01334-479-475. Fixed-price lunch: £16 ($30); fixed-price dinner: £30 ($55). AE, MC, V. Open: daily noon–2 p.m. and 6:30–10 p.m.

The Victoria
$ St. Andrews   INTERNATIONAL

This upstairs restaurant in Old St. Andrews looks like an ice cream shop, thanks to its big bar, high ceilings, and cool marble and iron tables. Alas, no ice cream is on the menu, but you can get large burgers, excellent home-made meat pies, and plenty of vegetarian items such as the Southwestern veggie burger, chili, wraps, or fajitas. And you'll have few complaints about the prices or the friendly service. On a warm day, soak in the fresh air out on the lovely beer terrace.

See map p. 317. 1 St. Mary's Place. ☎ 01334-476-964. Reservations not accepted. Main courses: £2.75–£6.25 ($5–$11). AE, DC, MC, V. Open: Mon–Sat 10 a.m.–7:45 p.m., Sun noon–5 p.m.

Exploring Fife and the Trossachs

North of the Firth of Forth, the region of Fife still likes to call itself a king-dom, a distinction that dates to Pictish pre-historic times when Abernethy was Fife's capital. Some 14 of Scotland's 66 royal burghs lay in this self-contained shire on a broad peninsula bound by the Forth to the south and the Tay River to the north. The highlight of Fife for golfers is **St. Andrews,** which many consider the most sacred spot of the sport. But the town, named after the country's patron saint, is also of ecclesiastical and schol-arly importance. Closer to Edinburgh, Dunfermline was once the capital of Scotland, and its abbey witnessed the births of royalty and contains the burial grounds of several royals, as well.

North of Glasgow is historic **Stirling,** with its castle set dramatically on the hill above the town. During the reign of the Stuarts in the 16th cen-tury, royalty preferred Stirling over Edinburgh, so it became the de facto capital of the country. The coronation of Mary Queen of Scots, only a child at the time, took place in Stirling. High on another hill north of the city center stands the prominent Wallace Monument, which is open daily. Nearby, Stirling Bridge is believed to be the crucial site of a 13th-century battle between English invaders and the rag-tag band of Scots led by William Wallace (forever immortalized — if fictionalized, as well — in the movie *Braveheart*). Just outside of the city is another, more famous battleground: Bannockburn. Somewhere around these fields outside of Stirling in 1314, a well-armed English army was never-theless routed by Scottish troops led by King Robert the Bruce.

More of a ruin than Stirling Castle, but perhaps more evocative, is **Doune Castle** near the town of Dunblane, which has its own attractive cathedral. Further northwest of Stirling are the Trossachs, a mountain range distinct from the Highlands but appealing for its wooded forests. The main attraction here is Loch Katrine, popularized by Sir Walter Scott's poem *The Lady of the Lake*. Two villages that provide gateways to the more mountainous regions north are Callander and Aberfoyle. They're often overrun by the bus tours in the high season because they offer places to rest, eat, and shop during the day.

Want to save a buck or two? Some attractions have two-for-one tickets. You can pay a single discounted price for admission to St. Andrews Castle and St. Andrews Cathedral, for example, or for Stirling Castle and Argyll's Lodging. In the case of Stirling Castle, this discount works only if you visit Argyll's Lodging first. If you visit the Castle first, you end up paying for both.

The top attractions

Andrew Carnegie Birthplace Museum
Dunfermline

In 1835, Andrew Carnegie (who later became an industrialist and philanthropist in America) was born about 200 yards (182m) down the hill from Dunfermline Abbey. The museum here comprises the 18th-century cottage in which he lived as a child and a memorial hall provided by his wife. Displays tell the story of the weaver's son who once worked as a bobbin boy in a cotton factory and eventually emigrated to the United States and became one of the richest men in the world. From the fortune he made, Carnegie gave away hundreds of millions of dollars before his death in 1919. Dunfermline received the first of the 2,811 free libraries he constructed throughout Britain and America and also received public baths and Pittencrieff Park and Glen, rich in history and natural charm. A statue in the park honors Carnegie. Allow about 2 hours.

See map p. 307. Moodie Street, Dunfermline. ☎ *01383-723-638.* www.carnegie birthplace.com. *Admission: £2 ($3.70) adults, £1 ($1.85) seniors, free for children under 15. Open: Apr–Oct Mon–Sat 11 a.m.–5 p.m., Sun 2–5 p.m. Closed Nov–Mar.*

Argyll's Lodging
Stirling

Sir William Alexander, the founder of Nova Scotia (or "New Scotland"), built this 17th-century town house, one of Scotland's finest Renaissance homes. The house has been preserved as it would have looked in 1680, when the 9th Earl of Argyll lived here following Sir William's death. Although you won't see many items belonging to Archibald Argyll and his family, the house has been furnished with accurate historic decorations and period furniture. You see tapestries, paintings, furniture and historic displays, such as clothing of the era, all giving you a very good idea of how the other half lived more than 300 years ago. Allow about 1 hour.

St. Andrews

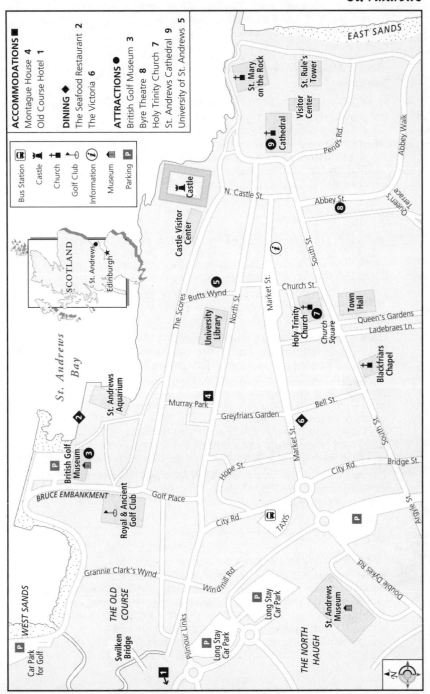

ACCOMMODATIONS ■
Montague House **4**
Old Course Hotel **1**

DINING ◆
The Seafood Restaurant **2**
The Victoria **6**

ATTRACTIONS ●
British Golf Museum **3**
Byre Theatre **8**
Holy Trinity Church **7**
St. Andrews Cathedral **9**
University of St. Andrews **5**

Bus Station | Castle | Church | Golf Club | Information | Museum | Parking

See map p. 321. Castle Wynd. ☎ *01786-461-146. Admission: £3 ($5.50) adults, £2.25 ($4) seniors and students, £1.20 ($1.75) children. Open: Apr–Oct daily 9:30 a.m.–6 p.m.; Nov–Mar daily 9:30 a.m.–5 p.m.*

Bannockburn Heritage Centre
Stirling

This famous battlefield site was the scene of King Robert the Bruce's victory over the English troops of Edward II. The decisive win secured Scottish independence from the British crown (at least for a little while). The museum contains life-size statues of William "Braveheart" Wallace and Robert the Bruce as well as a fascinating large-scale model of the Battle of Stirling Bridge. The audiovisual presentation does an excellent job of re-creating the battle and Bruce's story. Robert the Bruce picked the battle site — in his day it was a marsh, so he predicted that English horses would get stuck in the muck, helping to secure victory for the Scots. Allow about 2 hours.

See map p. 319. Glasgow Road, off M80. ☎ *01786-812-664. Admission: £2.30 ($4.20) adults, £1.50 ($2.75) seniors and children, £6.10 ($11) family. Open: Apr–Oct daily 10 a.m.–5:30 p.m.; Mar and Nov–Dec 23 daily 10:30 a.m.–4 p.m. Closed Dec 24–Feb.*

British Golf Museum
St. Andrews

Even non-golfers find this museum, devoted to the history and popularity of the game, interesting. Exhibits reveal the evolution of equipment and rules and remarkable facts and feats of the last 500 years of the game. Interactive touch-screen computers take you through the lives of famous players and even test your golf acumen. Be warned: There's a lot more to read than watch. The museum won the four-star "Excellent Standard" award from the Scottish Tourist Board in 1999. Although I wouldn't classify the museum as "kid-friendly," a section at the end lets them putt and dress up in turn-of-the-century golf outfits, which may occupy little ones while you read your way through the rest of the museum. Allow about 2 hours.

See map p. 317. Bruce Embankment. ☎ *01334-478-880. Admission: £4 ($7.40) adults, £2 ($3.70) children, £9.50 ($17.50) family. Open: Apr–mid-Oct daily 9:30 a.m.–5:30 p.m.; mid-Oct–Mar daily 11 a.m.–3 p.m.*

Deep Sea World
North Queensferry

In the early 1990s, a group of entrepreneurs sealed the edges of an abandoned rock quarry under the Forth Rail Bridge with a sheathing of concrete and positioned a 109m (364-ft.) cement-and-acrylic tunnel on the quarry's bottom. They then flooded the quarry with a million gallons of seawater, stocked it with a menagerie of creatures, and opened it as Scotland's most comprehensive aquarium. Compared to the aquariums you find in cities such as Baltimore or San Diego, this may seem amateurish. But from the

Around Stirling and the Trossachs

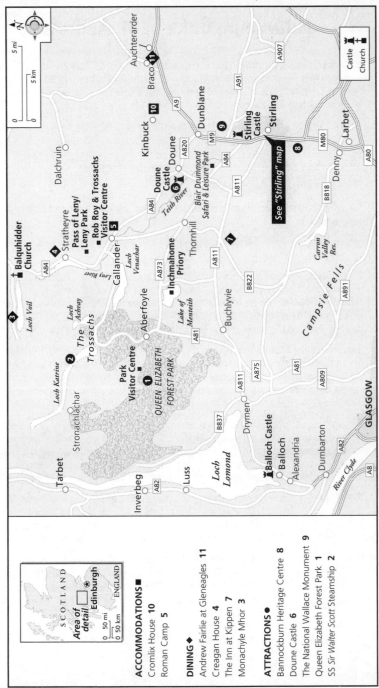

Castle
Church

Auchterarder
Braco **11**
Kinbuck **10**
Dunblane
9 Stirling Castle
Stirling
See "Stirling" map
8
Larbet
Denny
Dalchruin
Doune Castle
6 Doune
Teith River
Blair Drummond
Safari & Leisure Park
Carron
Valley
Res.
Strathyre
Pass of Leny/
Leny Park
Rob Roy & Trossachs
Visitor Centre **5**
† Balquhidder
Church
4
Thornhill
■ Inchmahome
Priory
Callander
Loch
Venachar
Leny River
3
Loch Voil
Loch
Achray
The
Trossachs
Aberfoyle
Lake of
Menteith
Buchlyvie
Campsie Fells
Loch Katrine
Park Visitor Centre
1
QUEEN ELIZABETH
FOREST PARK
Drymen
Stronachlachar
2
Balloch Castle
Balloch
Alexandria
Dumbarton
Tarbet
Inverbeg
Luss
Loch
Lomond
River Clyde
GLASGOW

N

5 mi
5 km

SCOTLAND
Area of
detail
Edinburgh
ENGLAND
50 mi
50 km

ACCOMMODATIONS ■
Cromlix House **10**
Roman Camp **5**

DINING ◆
Andrew Fairlie at Gleneagles **11**
Creagan House **4**
The Inn at Kippen **7**
Monachyle Mhor **3**

ATTRACTIONS ●
Bannockburn Heritage Centre **8**
Doune Castle **6**
The National Wallace Monument **9**
Queen Elizabeth Forest Park **1**
SS *Sir Walter Scott Steamship* **2**

Hitting the links in St. Andrews

Golf was played for the first time in the 1400s, probably on the site of St. Andrews's Old Course, and was enjoyed by Mary Queen of Scots in St. Andrews in 1567. Golfers consider this town to be hallowed ground. St. Andrews has five 18-hole courses (www.standrews.org.uk) and one course with only nine holes for beginners and children, all owned by a trust and open to the public. They are:

- ✔ **Old Course:** Where the Open is frequently played and dates to the 15th century

- ✔ **New Course:** Designed by Old Tom Morris in 1895

- ✔ **Jubilee Course:** Opened in 1897 in honor of Queen Victoria

- ✔ **Eden Course:** Opened in 1914

- ✔ **Strathtyrum Course:** The least difficult 18-holes, designed for those with high or no handicaps

- ✔ **Balgove:** The nine-hole course designed for beginners and hackers; turn up and play

For the 18-hole courses, except the Old Course, you should try to reserve your tee time at least one month in advance — except for Saturday play at Jubilee, Eden, or Strathtyrum, which can be reserved 24 hours in advance. The reservation office for all courses can be reached at ☎ **01334-466-666.** Online bookings for the New Course, Jubilee, Eden, and Strathtyrum can be made by logging on to www.linksnet.co.uk.

Reserving a tee time for the Old Course, which hosts the Open in 2005, is a whole different kettle of fish: You need to apply in writing one year in advance and even then there are no guarantees. By post, send applications to Reservations Office, Pilmour House, St. Andrews KY16 9SF, Scotland. You can also contact the reservations department at reservations@standards.org.uk.

Greens fees vary from course to course and depending on the time of year. Generally speaking, expect to pay between £22 and £115 ($40–$213) during the peak season (May through September) and from £16 to £80 ($30–$148) in the months of April and October. From November to March, you pay £56 ($104) to play the Old Course, using mats that protect the fairways, and between £11 and £27 ($20–$50) for the other 18-hole courses.

Virtually every hotel in town provides assistance to golfers. The **Royal and Ancient Golf Club,** founded in 1754, remains more or less rigidly closed as a private-membership men's club, however. It does traditionally open its doors to the public on St. Andrews Day (usually falls on November 30), though, for viewing of its trophy room.

If you're looking for more golf-related information, try the tourist office in St. Andrews at 70 Market St. (☎ **01334-472-021**). It's open year-round Monday through Saturday and on Sunday, too, during the high season. Call for hours.

Stirling

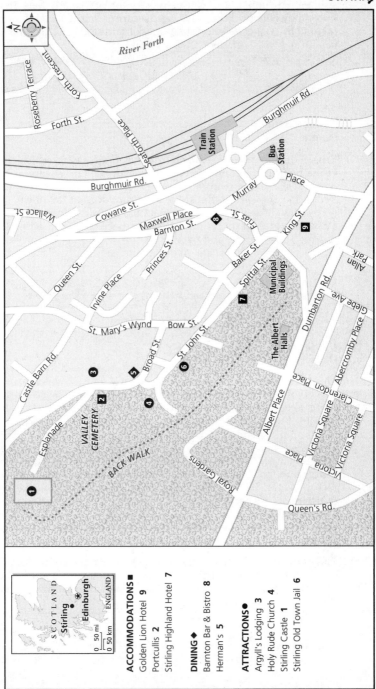

ACCOMMODATIONS ■
Golden Lion Hotel **9**
Portcullis **2**
Stirling Highland Hotel **7**

DINING ◆
Barnton Bar & Bistro **8**
Herman's **5**

ATTRACTIONS ●
Argyll's Lodging **3**
Holy Rude Church **4**
Stirling Castle **1**
Stirling Old Town Jail **6**

submerged tunnel, you can view kelp forests; sandy flats that shelter bottom-dwelling schools of stingray, turbot, and sole; and murky caves favored by conger eels and small sharks. For £100 to £125 ($185–$231) you can arrange a "shark dive." Allow about 2 hours.

See map p. 307. Battery Quarry, North Queensferry. ☎ *01383-411-880.* www.deep seaworld.com. *Admission: £8.25 ($15.25) adults, £6 ($11) children, £27 ($50) family of 4. Open: Apr–Oct daily 10 a.m.–6 p.m.; Nov–Mar Mon–Fri 10 a.m.–5 p.m.*

Doune Castle
Doune

Fans of the film *Monty Python and the Holy Grail* may recognize the exterior of Doune Castle, seeing as it served as a location for several scenes in the movie. The castle's restoration by Historic Scotland has been mostly limited to making certain the stone structure doesn't fall down, so visitors (especially those with good imaginations) actually get a better idea of what living here in the 14th century may have been like. The castle's low doors, narrow spiral stairs, and overall feeling of damp really drive home the experience of medieval life. Allow about 1½ hours.

See map p. 319. Northwest of Stirling, off the A84. ☎ *01786-841-742.* www. historic-scotland.gov.uk. *Admission: £3 ($5.50) adult, £2.30 ($4.25) seniors and children. Open: April–Sept daily 9:30 a.m.–6 p.m.; Oct daily 9:30 a.m.–4 p.m.; Nov–Mar Sat–Wed 9:30 a.m.–4 p.m.*

Dunfermline Abbey and Palace
Dunfermline

The ancient town of Dunfermline, about 22km (14 miles) northwest of Edinburgh, was the capital of Scotland at one time. The city is still known for its abbey and former royal palace (now largely gone). The abbey is on the site of two earlier structures: a Celtic church and an 11th-century house of worship dedicated to the Holy Trinity, under the auspices of Queen Margaret (later St. Margaret). Traces of both buildings are visible beneath gratings in the floor of the old nave. In 1150, the church was replaced with a large abbey, the nave of which remains as an example of Norman architecture. Later, St. Margaret's shrine, the northwest baptismal porch, and the spire on the northwest tower were added. While Dunfermline was the capital of Scotland, some 22 royal personages were buried in the abbey. However, the only memorial or burial places known are those of Queen Margaret and King Robert the Bruce, whose tomb lies beneath the pulpit.

The once-royal palace of Dunfermline stands adjacent to the abbey. The palace witnessed the birth of Charles I and James I, and the last king to reside here was Charles II in 1651. Today, only the southwest wall remains of this once-gargantuan edifice. Allow about 2 hours.

See map p. 307. St. Margaret's Street, off the M90. ☎ *01383-739-026.* www. historic-scotland.gov.uk. *Admission: £2.50 ($4.50) adults, £1.90 ($3.50) seniors, 75p ($1.40) children. Open: Apr–Sept daily 9:30 a.m.–6 p.m.; Oct–Mar Mon–Wed and Sat 9:30 a.m.–4:30 p.m., Thurs 9:30 a.m.–noon, Sun 2–4 p.m., closed Fri.*

Falkland Palace and Garden
Falkland

This hunting lodge and country home to eight (and counting) Stuart monarchs is an impressive specimen of Renaissance architecture. Among the rulers who resided on these stunning grounds were a young Mary Queen of Scots and her father, James V, who died here. The collection of artifacts inside is not as impressive as the architecture and painted ceilings. The jewels of the palace are the ornate Chapel Royal and the internationally lauded gardens. Also on the grounds is the world's oldest tennis court still in use. Queen Elizabeth II officially owns the palace, which the Scottish government maintains. Allow about 2 hours.

See map p. 307. High Street, just off the M90, at Junction 8. ☎ *01337-857-397. Admission: £4.50 ($8.30) adults; £3 ($5.50) seniors, students, and children. Open: Apr–Oct Mon–Sat 11 a.m.–5:30 p.m., Sun 1:30–5:30 p.m. Closed Nov–Mar.*

Holy Rude Church
Stirling

Among the many interesting aspects of this medieval church are bullet holes in the walls and on grave markers from the 1651 Stirling invasion by Cromwell's troops. Also, John Knox preached the Reformation here, and the inside features illuminating stained glass, 15th-century oak beams, and one of the oldest and grandest organs in the country. Rude (or *rood*) means "cross," and "holy rude" is the medieval term for Christ's cross. The grounds have one of the oldest bowling greens in Scotland and access to Lady's Rock and the Star Pyramid (see listing under "More cool things to see and do" later in this chapter). Allow about 1 hour.

See map p. 321. St. John Street. ☎ *01786-475-275. Admission: free. Open: May–Sept daily 10 a.m.–5 p.m. Closed Oct–Apr.*

Holy Trinity Church
St. Andrews

Called the "Town Kirk" in St. Andrews, this restored medieval church once stood on the grounds of the now-ruined St. Andrews Cathedral (see below). The church was moved to its present site in 1410, considerably altered after the Reformation of 1560, and restored in the early 20th century. John Knox preached his first sermon here in 1547. You'll find much fine stained glass and carvings inside. Allow about 1 hour.

See map p. 317. Opposite St. Mary's College, off South Street. ☎ *01334-474-494. Admission: free, but call in advance to make sure someone is in attendance. Open: daily 10 a.m.–noon and 2–4 p.m.*

Kirkcaldy Museum and Art Gallery
Kirkcaldy

The art collection in the second floor galleries here is perhaps the single best gathering of works by the so-called Scottish Colourists (indeed all

Scottish art) in the world. An entire room is devoted to the brightly hued still-life paintings and landscapes by S.J. Peploe as well as works by Hornel, Hunter, and Fegusson. Another highlight of the collection is a range of paintings by William Taggart. In addition, you can compare the abstract beauty of, say, Joan Eardley's "Breaking Wave" to a portrait by Scotland's currently best-selling, if critically panned, contemporary painter, Jack Vettriano. No comparison. This unassuming and humble attraction is arguably the best provincial art museum in Great Britain. What's more, all they request are donations from visitors. Allow about 1½ hours.

See map p. 307. War Memorial Gardens, next to the train station. ☎ *01592-412-860.* www.fifedirect.org.uk/museums. *Admission: free. Open: Mon–Sat 10:30 a.m.– 5 p.m., Sun 2–5 p.m.*

The National Wallace Monument
Stirling

Drive anywhere near Stirling and you're likely to see this tower, which commemorates William "Braveheart" Wallace, overlooking the surrounding plains. The view from the top of the 220-foot (and 246 steps!) tower is of Wallace's old fighting grounds, including the Stirling Bridge, where the "Guardian of Scotland" won a decisive battle against the English in 1297. Inside the monument are exhibits on the exploits of William Wallace, as told by an automatronic head of Scotland's favorite hero. It's nearly as silly as it sounds. You also can find an audiovisual display on battles that took place in the region and occasional talks on ancient weaponry. Built in the 1860s, the monument's popularity soared after the release of the 1995 movie *Braveheart.* A free shuttle runs from the visitor center to the base of the monument. If you don't want to drive to it, Stirling Castle offers excellent views of the monument. The top of the monument isn't wheelchair accessible. Allow about 1½ hours.

See map p. 319. Alloa Road, Abbey Craig; take Causewayhead Road from Stirling to where it meets Alloa Road (A907). ☎ *01786-472-140. Admission: £3.95 ($7.30) adults, £3 ($5.50) students, £2.75 ($5) seniors and children, £10.75 ($20) family. Open: Nov–Feb daily 10:30 a.m.–4 p.m.; Mar–May and Oct daily 10 a.m.–5 p.m.; June daily 10 a.m.–6 p.m.; July–Aug daily 9:30 a.m.–6:30 p.m.; Sept daily 9:30 a.m.–5 p.m.*

Queen Elizabeth Forest Park
Aberfoyle

East of Loch Lomond, the Queen Elizabeth Forest Park is 50,000 acres of hills, lochs, and woods. It's as fine a natural backdrop as you can get in the country. The forests teem with wildlife, and many trails wind through. If nature walks aren't your thing, the park has plenty of picnic spots, or you can drive through on the scenic Achray Forest Drive if you prefer. The park's visitor center has maps showing trails and picnic areas. Allow about 4 hours.

See map p. 319. David Marshall Lodge, off the A821. ☎ *01877-382-258. Admission: free. Open: park year-round daily dawn–dusk; visitor center Mar–mid-Oct daily 10 a.m.–6 p.m. Closed Nov–mid-Mar.*

Culross: Stepping back in time

Thanks largely to the National Trust for Scotland, this town near Dunfermline shows what a Scottish village was like from the 16th to 18th centuries. With its cobbled streets lined by stout cottages featuring crow-stepped gables, Culross is part city, part historic burgh; some restored buildings are only viewable from the outside because they serve as modern homes to Culross residents. One highlight of the village's history is that it may have been the birthplace of St. Mungo, who went on to establish the cathedral in Glasgow. The National Trust runs a visitor center in Culross (☎ **01383-880-359;** www. nts.org.uk), open daily noon to 5 p.m. from Good Friday through the end of September, which provides access to the town's palace and other sites. You can purchase admission tickets to the town's sites for £5 ($9.25).

St. Andrews Cathedral
St. Andrews

Near the Celtic settlement of St. Mary of the Rock, by the sea at the east end of town, you find the ruin of St. Andrews Cathedral and Priory. It was founded in 1160 and begun in the Romanesque style; however, the cathedral's construction suffered many setbacks. By the time of its consecration in 1318 in the presence of King Robert the Bruce, it had a Gothic overlay. At the time the largest church in Scotland, the cathedral established the city of St. Andrews as the ecclesiastical capital of the country, but today the ruins can only suggest its former beauty and importance. These days, visitors can see a collection of early Christian and medieval monuments as well as artifacts discovered on the cathedral site. Admission allows entry to nearby **St. Andrews Castle**, where the medieval clergy lived. Allow about 2 hours.

See map p. 317. A91, off Pends Road. ☎ *01334-472-563.* www.historic-scotland.gov.uk. *Admission: £4 ($7.50) adults, £3 ($5.50) seniors, £1.25 ($2.30) children. Open: Apr–Sept daily 9:30 a.m.–5 p.m.; Oct–Mar Mon–Sun 9:30 a.m.–4:30 p.m.*

SS Sir Walter Scott Steamship
Loch Katrine

For 100 years, this old-fashioned ship has taken passengers out on Loch Katrine to marvel at the beauty of the Trossachs. A bit of floating history, the ship is the last screw-driven steamship on the inland waters of Scotland. It runs between the Trossachs Pier and Stronachlachar and passes an eyeful of stunning views along the way. The ship is named after the renowned author who made Loch Katrine famous in his poem *The Lady of the Lake.* Be warned, however: This popular trip can get overcrowded in the summer, so if you can, go on a weekday. Allow about 4 hours.

See map p. 319. Loch Katrine, Trossachs. ☎ *01877-376-316. Admission: £6.50 ($12) adults, £3.75 ($7) children, £16 ($29) family. Departures: Apr–Oct daily 11 a.m., 1:45 p.m., 3:15 p.m. No sailings Nov–March.*

Stirling Castle
Stirling

Once the home of the kings of Scotland, this beautiful Renaissance castle was the residence of Mary Queen of Scots, her son James VI of Scotland (and later James I of England), and other Stuart monarchs. A natural fortress guarding the lowest point of the Forth Loch, the castle on a hill was the region's strategic military point throughout much of the 13th and 14th centuries. Even if you don't bother taking a tour of the impressive castle (though you should), now run by Historic Scotland, the ramparts and grounds surrounding the well-fortified landmark are worth a stroll — particularly the cemetery and the **Back Walk** along a wall that protected the Old Town from the desires of Henry VIII (to take the city for the English). In the castle proper, you can see both a palace built by James V and the **Chapel Royal,** which was remodeled by his grandson, James VI. Recently restored, the **Great Hall** is visible for miles thanks to the creamy, almost yellow exterior that apparently replicates its original color. Allow about 3 hours.

See map p. 321. Castle Wynd. ☎ *01786-450-000.* www.historic-scotland.gov.uk. *Admission: £8 ($15) adults, £2 ($3.75) children. Open: Apr–Oct daily 9:30 a.m.–5:15 p.m.; Nov–Mar daily 9:30 a.m.–4:15 p.m.*

Stirling Old Town Jail
Stirling

Tour guides in period dress take groups through the paces of penal life here, while a host of actors role-play as wardens and inmates to help enact the history of the jail. This building is a Victorian replacement for the rather less humane cells in the old Tolbooth across the street. Still, when you see the crank that inmates were made to turn as punishment, one wonders if prison existence had improved all that much. On the top of the building, an observation deck offers good views of the surrounding Old Town. Allow about 1½ hours.

See map p. 321. St. John Street. ☎ *01786-450-050.* www.instirling.com/sight/jail.htm. *Admission: £5 ($9.25) adults; £3.75 ($6.95) seniors, students, and children; £13.25 ($24.50) family. Open: Apr–Sept daily 9:30 a.m.–5:30 p.m.; Oct daily 9:30 a.m.–4:30 p.m.; Nov–Mar daily 9:30 a.m.–3:30 p.m.*

University of St. Andrews
St. Andrews

St. Andrews is the oldest university in Scotland and the third oldest in Britain after Oxford and Cambridge. Of its famous students, the most recent graduate is Prince William, grandson of Queen Elizabeth II and heir to the throne after Prince Charles. When classes are in session, you see packs of students walking around in their characteristic red gowns. The university grounds stretch west of the St. Andrews Castle between North Street and the Scores (a street). An ancient thorn tree, said to have been planted by Mary Queen of Scots, stands near the college's chapel. In 1645, the Scottish Parliament met in what was once the University Library and is now a students' reading room.

See map p. 317. www.st-andrews.ac.uk.

More cool things to see and do

- **Beheading Stone,** Stirling. It may seem ghastly, but you shouldn't skip this one, even if getting there is a bit of a walk around the back side of the castle (follow Stirling's Back Walk, which follows the Old Town walls, around the castle). But a walk is better than being dragged to meet your maker on a slab of rock, right? These days, the Beheading Stone (no admission fee) is under an iron cage, lest this old capital punishment become vogue again. In 1425, King James I had Murdoch, Duke of Albany, and his two sons executed here for misuse of power. What would today's politicians say to that?

- **Byre Theatre,** Abbey Street, St. Andrews (☎ 01334-475-000; www.byretheatre.com). This theater is the cultural center of St. Andrews; it features dramatic performances ranging from Shakespeare to musical comedies.

- **Lady's Rock and Star Pyramid,** Stirling. Located in the Stirling Castle cemetery (no admission fee), the rocky outcropping called Lady's Rock was once a popular vantage point from which to watch jousting tournaments and other events in the valley below. One of the more interesting items in the cemetery is the Star Pyramid, a large stone monument commemorating religious martyrs.

- **The Old Stirling Bridge**, off Union Street near Goosecroft Road, Stirling. At one of the narrowest points in the River Forth, the Old Stirling Bridge replaced a wooden bridge that was the central point of contention in a 1297 battle between William Wallace and his band of Scots and the English. Wallace secured victory over the English by destroying the wooden bridge. The current bridge dates from the late 15th century. It's accessible on foot from the town center, but driving to it is much easier.

- **Rob Roy Story,** Callander (☎ 01877-330-342). This museum in the Trossachs region, home of the Clan MacGregor, covers both versions of Rob Roy MacGregor. One is the legendary figure of Sir Walter Scott's novel and the movies, the tartan Robin Hood. And then there's the real Rob Roy, the cattle thief and blackmailer. Whatever the specifics, Rob Roy was certainly a hero to his people and an outlaw in defiance of the English. Life-size figures tell the tale of MacGregor's feud with the Duke of Montrose, and exhibits cover the man's life and legend.

- **Scottish Fisheries Museum,** Anstruther, 9 miles south of St. Andrews (☎ 01333-310-628). Honestly, this museum is more interesting than it sounds. On the quay outside are more than a dozen boats that are part of the museum's collection, and inside are informative exhibits on every aspect of the Scottish fishing trade, including whaling and a re-creation of a fisherman's cottage. Locals built the museum in tribute to their proud history and industry. Also here is a monument for Scottish fishermen who have been lost at sea.

✔ **Secret Bunker**, Troy Wood, 5 miles south of St. Andrews (☎ **01333-310-301**). This bunker is the former underground nuclear command center where Scotland's leaders supposedly would have lived in the event of a nuclear war. The farmhouse building doesn't look like much, but that's just a false front to the entrance of the fortified compound 100 feet underground. Kept from public knowledge for more than four decades, the nuclear bomb shelter has now been declassified, and you can see the nuclear command center and its facilities.

Shopping for Local Treasures

Shopping in Stirling and St. Andrews is typical of provincial towns and cities around Scotland, with the former offering the dubious bonus of a shopping mall called the Thistle Centre (just near the train station). This area also introduces tourists to another questionable shopping attraction in Scotland: Highland gateway towns. Both Aberfoyle and Callander fit this bill — one-street burghs cluttered with lots of tartan and woolens shops that attract coach tours, causing the sidewalks to occasionally overflow with tourists on summer days. Below are some suggestions for shops (with normal business hours) that are a cut above.

✔ **Jim Farmer,** 1 St. Mary's Place, Market Street, St. Andrews (☎ **01334-476-796**). Heads up, golfers. Did you lose a few too many balls in the water? Need a new pitching wedge or just a fancy set of club warmers? Jim will take care of you and maybe even help you take a stroke or two off your game. Shirts, hats, T-shirts, shoes, and more are on hand. Call for hours.

✔ **R.R. Henderson,** 6–8 Friar St., Stirling (☎ **01786-473-681**). Principally a kilt-making shop, this store also has a good range of other apparel, such as woolly mittens, tweed jackets, and cashmere sweaters. What sets Henderson's apart from other shops of its type is that it will custom-make tartans for you. You can also rent an entire kilt outfit (starting at £39.99 ($58) a day) if you're in the area for a special occasion or think it'd be fun to sport the local look. Call for hours.

✔ **St. Andrew's Fine Art,** 84A Market St., St. Andrews (☎ **01334-474-080**). One of the finest art galleries in the country, this shop seems much too small to hold all its excellent pieces — contemporary art crowds the walls. Whether you prefer prints or watercolors, oils or drawings, you're sure to find something to spark your interest here. The shop has specialized in Scottish art since 1800, but its stock goes well beyond the usual landscapes to include unique modern pieces. Call for hours.

✓ **The Scottish Wool Centre,** Aberfoyle, Stirling (☎ **01877-382-854**). More of an attraction than a shop, this is one store where the kids won't be bored. Besides exhibits that show everything you want to know about Scottish wool and more, the Spinner's Cottage gives you a chance to make your own wool. On weekends, dog lovers and shepherds (seriously) convene here to show off their Border collies and give sheepdog demonstrations. Call for hours.

Doing the Pub Crawl

If you're staying in Stirling or St. Andrews, check out some of these watering holes, which are a notch or two above the norm. Many of the following pubs keep late hours; call for the latest opening and closing times.

✓ **Central Bar,** corner of Market and College streets, St. Andrews (☎ **01334-478-296**). If you're looking for a quintessential old-fashioned pub, look no further. This fine bar, popular with students, has a good selection on tap, including "guest" ales, and an extensive international wine selection. Despite having one television, the Central Bar fills up when a game is on, all eyes squinting in one direction. Central Bar's open Monday through Saturday from 11 a.m. to 11:45 p.m., and Sunday from 12:30 p.m. to midnight.

✓ **The Jigger Inn,** Old Station Road, St. Andrews (☎ **01334-474-371**). Next to the Old Course Hotel lies a whitewashed brick building that was constructed in 1846 as a cottage for the railroad's stationmaster. Now it's the loveliest little pub in St. Andrews. Out back you'll find those who appreciate an open beer terrace that faces the famous Old Course. A note to golfers: No spikes are allowed in the pub. The Jigger Inn's open Monday through Saturday from 11 a.m. to 11 p.m., and Sunday from noon to 11 p.m.

✓ **Whistlebinkies,** 73–75 St. Mary's Wynd, Stirling (☎ **01786-451-256**). The name sounds like a place for kids, and young patrons are indeed welcome here and even get their own kid's menu. But adults will appreciate the comfortable booths and selection of good beers and whiskys as well. The fireplace and stained-glass windows are nice touches. The building, just down the hill from the Castle, dates to 1595 and originally housed the castle's blacksmith. Whistlebinkies is open noon to midnight.

Fast Facts: Fife and the Central Highlands

Area Code

The area code for Stirling is **01786,** St. Andrews is **01334,** and Aberfoyle and Callander (in the Trossachs) is **01877.** You need to dial the area code only if you're calling from outside the city you want to reach.

Emergencies

Dial ☎ **999** for police, fire, or ambulance.

ATMs

ATMs are readily available at banks in Stirling and St. Andrews.

Hospitals

The hospitals in the area are Stirling Royal Infirmary, Livilands Road, south of the town center (☎ 01786-434-000) and St. Andrews Memorial Hospital, Abbey Walk, south of Abbey Street (☎ 01334-472-327).

Information

You can find tourist offices at 41 Dumbarton Rd., Stirling (☎ 01786-475-019) and 70 Market St., St. Andrews (☎ 01334-472-021). Offices open only in the summer are located on Main Street, Aberfoyle (☎ 01877-382-352) and next to the castle, Stirling (☎ 01786-47-9901).

Internet Access

The best place to surf the Web in this area is at CommsPort, 83 Market St., St. Andrews. (☎ 01334-475-181; www.commsport.com). The shop's hours are Monday through Saturday from 8 a.m. until 5:30 p.m., and Sunday from 10:30 a.m. until 6 p.m. The cost is £6 ($9) per hour.

Mail

Post offices are at 127 South St., St. Andrews (☎ 01334-472-321), and 4 Broad St., Stirling (☎ 01786-474-537).

Chapter 17

Tayside and the Northeast

• •

In This Chapter

▶ Finding great places to stay and dine in this vast region
▶ Discovering Scone Palace in Perthshire
▶ Crawling the local pubs of Aberdeen

• •

*T*his chapter covers a significant area of Scotland: the oil-boom city, Aberdeen; North Sea ports such as Stonehaven, Peterhead, and Fraserburgh; several castles including Balmoral, the official royal family retreat; the Grampian Mountains; plus Dundee and Perth on the River Tay, which forms the southern boundary of the region. Compared to the Highlands (see Chapter 18), Tayside and the Northeast may prove to be a time-consuming distraction for many travelers, because driving distances between individual attractions can be lengthy. So, I've kept the chapter succinct and suggest that you either concentrate on the southern towns such as Perth or the Highland gateway of Pitlochry or trek through Royal Deeside and visit Aberdeen, the so-called Granite City.

The principal city in this region is Aberdeen. Also known as the oil capital of Europe, the port of Aberdeen receives oil pumped in the North Sea. It has plenty of bars and restaurants but is short on attractions of the traditional sort. Perth is a bustling town between two large open park areas, North and South Inch, which are about 1,000 yards apart. Both parks merit a stroll if you stop here. A royal burgh beside the River Tay, Perth has a couple of decent restaurants and lies near one of Scotland's most historic attractions: Scone Palace. Pitlochry is one of the most visited inland resort towns in Scotland, mainly because it's one of the few arteries to the Highlands beyond. The city's location — quite close to the geographic center of Scotland — makes it an excellent base for daytrips in most directions. Plus, the River Garry affords lovely views (including sightings of spawning salmon).

Getting There

Getting to and around this part of Scotland isn't quite as easy as it is in other parts of the country. Trains certainly run to Perth, Dundee, and Aberdeen, but the branch system isn't well developed. Bus service to the larger towns is reasonable, but in the end, you're likely to want a car to see the main attractions.

- ✔ **By car:** From Edinburgh, take the M90 north to Perth, where you have the option of using the A90 along the east coast to Aberdeen or the A9 inland to Pitlochry. From Glasgow, use the M80 (A80) to the M9 (A9), which takes you to Perth. In the Northeast, the most useful country road is A93, which goes past Braemar, Ballater, and Banchory on its way to Aberdeen.

- ✔ **By bus: Scottish Citylink** (☎ **0870-550-5050;** www.citylink.co.uk) routes cover the major towns.

- ✔ **By train: First ScotRail** (☎ **08457-48-49-50;** www.firstscotrail.com) travels to towns in the region, including Perth, Pitlochry, Dundee, Arbroath, and Aberdeen. You have to rely on buses or local taxis to venture further after you arrive in these towns. ScotRail service dovetails with long-distance trains from England, which are run by Great North Eastern Railway (☎ **08457-225-225**) and Virgin Trains (☎ **0870-789-1234**). You can also call National Railway Enquiries at the First ScotRail phone number above for details.

- ✔ **By ferry: NorthLink Orkney & Shetland Ferries Ltd.** (☎ **01855-851-144**) runs services between Aberdeen and Lerwick.

- ✔ **By plane:** The **Aberdeen Airport** (☎ **01224-722-331**) is 9½km (6 miles) north of town. Planes connect Aberdeen to Glasgow, Edinburgh, Dundee, and the Shetland and Orkney Islands. The **Dundee Airport** (☎ **01382-643-242**) is on Riverside Drive; it has service to Aberdeen and Edinburgh.

Spending the Night

Some of your best options for accommodations are in or near the major towns in Tayside and the Northeast. Because it's a fairly large area, you may want to choose your accommodations around the attractions on which you decide to concentrate. Some of the accommodations listed here have earned star ratings from the tourist board; see Chapter 8 for a description of the rating system. Rates include full breakfast unless otherwise stated. And remember: You may well get a better deal than the advertised "rack" rates.

Braemar Lodge
$$–$$$ **Braemar**

This homey, granite country house on the outskirts of town is an unpretentious, comfortable accommodation. The rooms are quite spacious, and most have views of the mountains. One of my favorite features is the oak-paneled bar, where guests can sip a whisky nightcap in front of a log fire. If the Victorian shooting lodge isn't down-home enough for you, log cabins with kitchens are also available for rent by the week.

Tayside and the Northeast

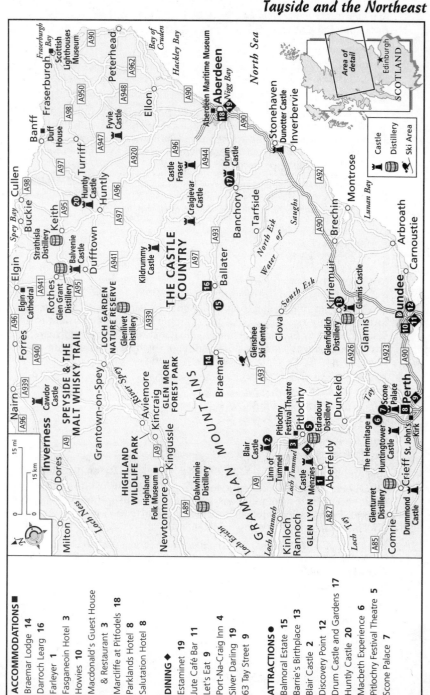

See map p. 333. 6 Glenshee Rd. ☎ *01339741-627.* www.braemarlodge.co.uk. *Rack rates: £80–£120 ($148–$222) double. DC, MC, V.*

Darroch Learg
$$$ Ballater

Set on a hill overlooking the road and River Dee beyond, this is one of the more highly regarded hotels in the entire region. Stately but friendly, with an excellent reputation for food, Darroch Learg is my choice if you're spending a night near the royal spread in Balmoral. A dozen overnight rooms in the main lodge are complemented with five more in a nearby annex. All are well appointed and comfortable.

See map p. 333. Braemar Road, on western side of town. ☎ *01339755-443. Fax: 01339755-252.* www.darrochlearg.co.uk. *Rack rates: £155–£230 ($286–$425) double. Prices include dinner. AE, DC, MC, V. Closed in Jan.*

Farleyer
$$–$$$ Aberfeldy

Not far off the beaten path is this luxurious 15th-century country house on a 30-acre estate in the beautiful Tay Valley. You're sure to like one of the lovely lounges or drawing rooms full of books, games, and a self-serve bar. Kids will enjoy running around the grounds and choosing from the good selection of movies available to watch in guest rooms. Salmon fishers, take note: The Farleyer's grounds offer some of the best salmon fishing on the River Tay.

See map p. 333. Weem, 2 miles from Aberfeldy, on the B846 over Tummel Bridge. ☎ *01887-820-332. Fax: 01887-829-879.* www.farleyer.com. *Rack rates: £85–£120 ($157–$222) double. AE, DC, MC, V.*

Fasganeoin Hotel
$$ Pitlochry

Just off the main drag, this house hotel is a few minutes' walk from the city. The rooms are comfy and cute, featuring a flower and antique motif, and some rooms have a cozy sunken floor. The peaceful grounds offer a lovely respite. For the price, you can't beat Fasganeoin (pronounced faze-gannon, it means "place for the birds" in Gaelic).

See map p. 333. Perth Rd., opposite the Blair Atholl Distillary. ☎ *01796-472-387. Fax: 01796-474-285.* www.fasganeoincountryhouse.co.uk. *Rack rates: £70–£80 ($129–$148) double. AE, DC, MC, V.*

Howies
$$ Dundee

Best known as a restaurant based in Edinburgh (see Chapter 11), the Howies in Dundee also offers four rooms upstairs. This boutique hotel is right in the heart of the action. Rooms are of standard size but are attractively decorated. Plus, the sturdy restaurant on the ground floor is a bonus.

See map p. 333. 25 South Tay St. ☎ *01382-200-399. Rack rates: £60 ($111) double. AE, MC, V.*

Macdonald's Guest House & Restaurant
$$ **Pitlochry**

This popular guesthouse and restaurant has a loyal following. The rooms are nicely decorated and the hospitality enormous (and you can't beat the price), but the best thing about the place is undoubtedly the food. Don't worry about getting to breakfast on time; it's served all day.

See map p. 333. 140 Atholl Rd. ☎ *01796-472-170. Fax: 01796-474-221.* www. smoothhound.co.uk/hotels/macdonal.html. *Rack rates: £64 ($118) double. AE, MC, V.*

Marcliffe at Pitfodels
$$$–$$$$ **Aberdeen**

Marcliffe is perhaps the best place to stay in Aberdeen; it's certainly the most often recommended, probably because it expertly combines high-class accommodation with intimate attention. The family-run, three-story hotel sits among trees and has a country feel despite its proximity to the city. All the individually decorated rooms are comfortable and spacious, the beds huge, and the antique furniture in good taste. Mikhail Gorbachev officially opened the place as a guest in 1993, and if it's good enough for the father of *glasnost,* it's good enough for you.

See map p. 333. North Deeside Road, off A92. ☎ *01224-861-000. Fax: 01224-868-860.* www.marcliffe.com. *Rack rates: £130–£295 ($240–$545) double. AE, DC, MC, V.*

Parklands Hotel
$$–$$$ **Perth**

This luxury accommodation occupies a stylish Georgian town house once owned by a lord provost (mayor). The hotel, which overlooks the woods of South Inch parkland and is near the railroad station, is a peaceful oasis in a bustling little town. The rooms are wonderfully decorated and very spacious, and the Victorian conservatory makes a lovely spot to enjoy high tea. The most remarkable thing about this fine hotel is how little it costs to stay here. *Tip:* Because Parklands caters to many business travelers, rooms are cheaper on the weekends.

See map p. 333. 2 St. Leonard's Bank. ☎ *01738-622-451. Fax: 01738-622-046.* www. theparklandshotel.com. *Rack rates: £99–£149 ($183–$275) double. AE, DC, MC, V.*

Salutation Hotel
$$ **Perth**

It's right on the main street of Perth, but the Salutation is a quiet haven of big beds and friendly service. After you've walked all over town and had your dinner, relax with a nightcap in the huge overstuffed couches by the fire in the lobby. The Salutation is also a historical footnote — the building was once a meeting place for Bonnie Prince Charlie and his troops. It's no wonder the staff has its act together — the spot has been welcoming guests since 1699.

See map p. 333. 34 South St., near the River Tay. ☎ *01738-630-066.* www. strathmorehotels.com. *Rack rates: £80–£100 ($148–$185) double. AE, DC, MC, V.*

Dining Locally

Your best option in the area may be in your hotel, but here are a few standouts to consider.

Estaminet
$ **Aberdeen   MEDITERRANEAN**

Estaminet (Flemish for "eating out") offers plenty to wet your whistle, but don't miss this college-crowd bar and restaurant's filling food. The "mussels with beer" special is self-explanatory and delicious. Meals range from made-to-order pizzas and burgers to nachos and a large selection of upscale pub grub. You have the option of sitting upstairs or relaxing in the more casual downstairs area, which is lighted by a large sunroof and dotted with stuffed couches and a warming fireplace.

See map p. 333. 8 Littlejohn St., between Broad and W. North streets. ☎ *01224-622-657. Reservations not accepted. Main courses: £4–£7 ($7.50–$13). AE, MC, V. Open: daily noon–midnight.*

Jute Café Bar
$–$$ **Dundee   INTERNATIONAL**

This nice café/bar is part of the Dundee Contemporary Arts complex in the so-called cultural quarter of the city, and it's one of the highlights of the city. After the restaurant closes for the night, it's a lively bar and one of the places to be seen in Dundee. The food here is as imaginative and as modern as the décor.

See map p. 333. 152 Nethergate. ☎ *01382-909-246.* www.dca.org.uk/cafe/welcome.asp. *Reservations not required. Main courses: £6–£12 ($11–$22). MC, V. Open: daily 11 a.m.–9 p.m.*

Let's Eat
$$–$$$ **Perth   SCOTTISH/SEAFOOD**

This popular, tasteful, tasty bistro used to be a theater dating back to the early 1800s. Decorated with lots of plants, it has an upscale feel, sans attitude. The international menu from chef proprietor Tony Heath includes dishes such as filet of sea bass with gazpacho broth, blackened Uist salmon, and other fresh fish and game dishes. The desserts are to die for, and the wine list is impressive as well.

See map p. 333. 77/79 Kinnoull St., at the corner of Atholl, near the North Inch. ☎ *01738-643-377. Reservations recommended. Main courses: £9.25–£18.95 ($17–$35). AE, DC, MC, V. Open: Tues–Sat noon–2 p.m. and 6:30–9:45 p.m.*

Port-Na-Craig Inn
$$–$$$ Pitlochry   SCOTTISH/SEAFOOD

A few years back, this place captured the attention of the Michelin inspectors, who bestowed upon the owners their award for good food at reasonable prices. Across the River Tummel from the main part of town, the Port-Na-Craig really prides itself on making everything possible from scratch, using mostly local ingredients. Dishes such as Gruyère risotto and roast venison with celeriac rémoulade and red onion relish are perennial crowd-pleasers.

See map p. 333. Off Foss Road. ☎ *01796-472-777. www.portnacraig.com. Reservations recommended. Main courses: £8–£18 ($15–$33). MC, V. Open: Tues–Sat 12:30–2 p.m. and 6–9 p.m., Sun 1–2:30 p.m.. Closed Dec 25 to mid-March.*

Silver Darling
$$$–$$$$ Aberdeen   SEAFOOD

Getting to this restaurant at the water's edge is a bit of an odyssey, but it's worth it. In the dining room overlooking the entrance to the harbor, you find succulent dishes such as grilled marinated tuna and swordfish, filet of trout poached in red wine and herbs, and turbot steamed on a bed of seaweed with scallop mousse. The menu may be pricey, but from the rooftop views overlooking the sea to some of the highest-quality food in the area, Silver Darling is worth the extra dough.

See map p. 333. Pocra Quay, North Pier. Follow the road from Aberdeen harbor along the water until you reach the beach, then turn right. ☎ *01224-576-229. Reservations required. Main courses: £17–£23 ($31–$42). AE, MC, V. Open: year-round Mon–Fri noon–2 p.m., Mon–Sat 7–9:30 p.m.; May–Sept Sun 7–9:30 p.m.*

63 Tay Street
$$–$$$ Perth   MODERN SCOTTISH

This restaurant rivals the better-known Let's Eat (see listing above) for good eating in Perth. The contemporary dining space overlooks the River Tay, and dishes include main courses such as rib-eye of Angus beef with new potatoes and mushroom jus. Fixed price lunches are a great deal at around £11 ($20).

See map p. 333. 63 Tay St. ☎ *01738-441-451. www.63taystreet.co.uk. Reservations recommended. Main courses: £8.50–£14.95 ($16–$27). MC, V. Open: Tues–Sat noon–2 p.m. and 6:30–9 p.m.*

Exploring Tayside and the Northeast

Tayside and the Northeast offer a vast array of sightseeing, even though they're relatively small areas of Scotland. Tayside, for example, is about 137km (85 miles) east to west and 97km (60 miles) north to south.

Carved out of the old counties of Perth and Angus, Tayside is named for its major river, the 192km-long (119-mile) Tay. The region is easy to explore, and the river's waters offer some of Europe's best salmon and trout fishing. Tayside abounds with heather-clad Highland hills, long blue lochs under forested bands, and miles of walking trails.

As you journey on the scenic roads of Scotland's Northeast, you pass moorland and peaty lochs, wood glens and rushing rivers, granite-stone villages and ancient castles, and fishing harbors as well as North Sea beach resorts.

The top attractions

Balmoral Estate
Ballater

Welcome to the vacation home of the Windsors. Because Balmoral is a working residence for the Queen and her family, visitor access is limited to the ballroom. On display are pictures of rooms as well as clothing and gifts belonging to the family. More interesting is the museum in the coach house. Pictures of the royal family from the last 150 years include shots from official visits, such as the visit of Czar Nicholas II and his family to Balmoral. You're free to walk the extensive grounds and gardens, and two-hour pony treks on the property are available. Because the castle is closed to tourists when the Queen is in town, it's a good idea to call in advance of your visit. Allow about 1½ hours.

See map p. 333. Balmoral, Ballater, off the A93, 8 miles from Banchory. ☎ *01339-742-334.* www.balmoralcastle.com. *Admission: £5 ($9.25) adults, £4 ($7.40) seniors and students, £1 ($1.85) children under 16. Open: mid-Apr–July daily 10 a.m.–5 p.m. Closed Aug–mid-Apr.*

Barrie's Birthplace
Kirriemuir

Due north of Dundee is where J. M. Barrie, the author of *Peter Pan,* was born in 1860, the ninth of ten children. The exhibit memorializing his birthplace is excellent and quite imaginative. Life-size figures, miniature stage sets, dioramas, and stage costumes illustrate the writer's life. A little fast-moving light around the room represents everyone's favorite sprite, Tinkerbell. The museum also contains manuscripts and artifacts from Barrie's life. Don't miss the washhouse; it was Barrie's first theater and the inspiration for the Wendy House. Allow about 1 hour.

Braemar Highland gathering

The average population of the village of Braemar is around 500 people. But when the village holds the Braemar Highland Games (☎ **01339-741-944**) every September, the population jumps by 20,000 or more, and that includes Queen Elizabeth, who usually attends. This purely Scottish experience of feats of strength and traditional dance is a lot of fun for outsiders, as well. Plenty of crafts and delicious food abound. The history of the gatherings predates Scotland as a country, when kings had their best warriors compete to see who were the toughest. Of all the Highland games, Braemar's is possibly the biggest and best.

See map p. 333. 9 Brechin Rd. ☎ *01575-572-646. Admission: £2.20 ($4) adults; £2 ($3.70) seniors, students, and children under 16; £6 ($11) family. Open: Apr–Oct Sat–Wed noon–5 p.m. Closed Nov–Mar.*

Blair Castle
Blair Atholl

This fine, fairy-tale-white castle up the road from Pitlochry has much to see. It's chockfull o' stuff: art, armor, flags, stag horns, and more items not typically found on the standard furniture-and-portrait castle tour. Between the 30 rooms and the grounds (including a walled garden), the castle has something for just about everyone. The most common theme in the Duke of Atholl's decorating is hunting. Deer antlers decorate the long hallway and ballroom, and the weaponry collection spans hundreds of years. You'd be hard pressed to find so many guns and swords in one place anywhere else. Blair Castle's long history includes a couple of Jacobite sieges and a sleepover by Queen Victoria. Although the castle is the ancient seat of the Dukes and Earls of Atholl, and although Duncan Atholl was the king murdered in Shakespeare's *Macbeth,* the real Duncan didn't live in this castle. Allow about 2 hours.

See map p. 333. Blair Atholl, off the A9, 6 miles west of Pitlochry. ☎ *01796-481-207.* www.blair-castle.co.uk. *Admission: £6.50 ($12) adults, £5.50 ($10) seniors, £4 ($7.50) children under 16, £18 ($33) family. Open: daily 9:30 a.m.–6 p.m.*

Discovery Point
Dundee

This port is home to the famous RRS *Discovery,* the scientific ship Captain Robert Scott took into Antarctica. One of the last of the wooden three-masted ships, she set sail in 1901 and lived a long life of polar adventure. Here you can tour the ship and get all the details of her construction and of Scott's historic trip. The coolest part (literally) is the Polarama, a hands-on exhibit of life in the Arctic that includes a whiff of polar air. By the way, RRS stands for "Royal Research Ship." Allow about 2 hours.

See map p. 333. Discovery Quay. ☎ *01382-201-245. Admission: free. Open: Apr–Oct Mon–Sat 10 a.m.–5 p.m., Sun 11 a.m.–5 p.m.; Nov–Mar Mon–Sat 10 a.m.–4 p.m., Sun 11 a.m.–4 p.m.*

Drum Castle and Gardens
Banchory

This lovely little castle is the oldest intact building in the care of the National Trust. It's full of beautiful antique furniture and lovely rooms staffed by knowledgeable guides. Nothing in particular in the Irvine family collection is remarkable, but you're likely to enjoy the walk through the house, which includes a nice collection of early 20th-century toys and an impressive vaulted library. Don't miss the castle grounds, which hold a restored 16th-century chapel, a holly grove, rose bushes, and a walled garden. Allow about 2 hours.

See map p. 333. Drumoak, Banchory. Follow signs on the A93, 10 miles from Aberdeen. ☎ *01330-811-204.* www.drum-castle.org.uk. *Admission: £7 ($10) adults; £5.25 ($7.60) seniors, students, and children under 16; £19 ($28) family. Open: July–Aug daily 10 a.m.–6 p.m.; Apr–June and Sept–Oct daily noon–5 p.m. Closed Nov–Mar.*

Edradour Distillery
Pitlochry

You get a good primer on the whisky-making process at this mini-distillery. Edradour holds the distinction of being the smallest distillery in Scotland. It's a cute site, too, with little whitewashed buildings with red doors and a stream bubbling through the property. The friendly staff of six or seven puts out a whopping 12 casks a week using the smallest size spirit stills that the law allows. Of course, it's quality, not quantity, that counts. The tours and dram of whisky are free. Allow about 1½ hours.

See map p. 333. Off the A924, just outside Pitlochry. ☎ *01796-472-095.* www.edradour.co.uk. *Admission: free. Open: Mar–Oct Mon–Sat 9:30 a.m.–5 p.m.; Nov–Feb Mon–Sat 10 a.m.–4 p.m.*

Huntly Castle
Huntly

This simple castle has been housing royals on and off for about five centuries. Robert the Bruce laid his head here, but Mary Queen of Scots refused her invitation (a wise choice, seeing as a kidnapping was in the works). The nicest features are the heraldic friezes on the building constructed by past Earls of Huntly and now protected from the elements. You'll also see Catholic images; the castle held fast to its religion during the Reformation, which saw the banishment of Catholicism in Britain. Don't leave without visiting the pretty River Deveron. Allow about 1 hour.

See map p. 333. On the A96. ☎ *01466-793-191. Admission: £3 ($5.50) adults, £2.50 ($4.60) seniors and students, £1 ($1.85) children under 16, £4 ($7.50) family. Open: Apr–Sept daily 9:30 a.m.–6:30 p.m.; Oct–Mar Mon–Sat 9:30 a.m.–4:30 p.m, Sun 2–4:30 p.m.*

Macbeth Experience
Bankfoot

You may be weary of roadside attractions inside visitor centers, as you well should be, but the Macbeth Experience is an interesting one-room attraction. In an attempt to distinguish the real Macbeth from the Shakespearean version, this audiovisual production makes the argument that the famous Thane of Cawdor was really a good and just king, not the bloodthirsty usurper of old English propaganda. Here's a warning if you have small kids: The dark theater and pyrotechnics can be a little frightening. Allow about 1 hour.

See map p. 333. Perthshire Visitor Centre, Bankfoot, just off the A9 between Perth and Pitlochry. ☎ *01738-787-696.* www.macbeth.co.uk. *Admission: £2 ($2.90) adults, £1.50 ($2.20) seniors and students, £1 ($1.45) children under 16, £5 ($7.25) family. Open: Apr–Sept daily 9 a.m.–8 p.m.; Oct–Mar daily 9 a.m.–7 p.m.*

Pitlochry Festival Theatre
Pitlochry

This big theater on the south side of the River Tummel is the jewel of Pitlochry. The theater recently went through a major overhaul, although it certainly didn't need a renovation to improve on its popularity with visitors and locals. Scots come here from all over to see new and classic professional performances, usually six shows a season and running simultaneously. Besides plays, the Pitlochry also schedules concerts, films, and literary and culinary events. Be sure to book tickets in advance.

See map p. 333. Across the river from Main Street. ☎ *01796-484-626.* www.pitlochry.org.uk. *Tickets: £14–£16 ($20–$23).*

Scone Palace
Near Perth

Scone (pronounced scoon) is hallowed ground because it's where most of the early Scottish kings were crowned. Until about 700 years ago, the palace was the home of the Stone of Destiny, an actual stone also known as the Stone of Scone, and important rulers such as David I, Macbeth, and Robert the Bruce were crowned on it. Edward I stole the stone in 1296 and took it to Westminster Abbey, however, in hopes of breaking the line of Scottish royalty; the plan didn't work, and even without the stone Scottish kings continued to be crowned at Scone. The stone (stolen from Westminster Abbey by Scottish nationalists in 1950 but recovered and returned to the abbey shortly after) was returned officially to Scotland in the 1990s and is now on display in Edinburgh Castle.

The castellated Scone Palace you find today only dates to 1803, incorporating parts of earlier buildings. It's full of fine furniture, ivories, clocks, and needlework, and of particular note is the renowned porcelain collection. Scone Palace also has a hall dedicated to the coronation of kings. Reading material is available, but if you have any questions, ask one of the expert guides posted throughout the palace. The grounds are also quite nice, but you must contend with the shrieking peacocks that live there. A replica commemorates the location of the Stone of Destiny outside the palace on Moot Hill, just in front of the little chapel. To the left of the chapel is a playground area with huge tire swings, slides, and even a zipwire, which is the thing most kids love best about this place. Allow 2 to 3 hours.

See map p. 333. Braemar Road, on the A93. ☎ 01738-552-300. www.scone-palace.co.uk. *Admission: palace and grounds £6.95 ($13) adults, £5.95 ($11) seniors and students, £4 ($7.40) children under 16, £22 ($41) family. Open: Apr–Oct daily 9:30 a.m.–5:30 p.m. Closed Nov–Mar.*

Other cool things to see and do

- ✔ **Aberdeen Maritime Museum,** Shiprow, Aberdeen (☎ 01224-337-700). Ever wanted a whale's-eye view of a scale model of an off-shore oil rig? This ⅓-scale, £1 ($1.85) million detailed model is the highlight of this three-story museum devoted to the seafaring history of Aberdeen — a city sustained by North Sea oil drilling.

- ✔ **Auchingarrich Wildlife Centre,** near Comrie (☎ 01764-679-469). This center offers up-close-and-personal encounters with furry animals. The headliner of the place is the Highland cow, a shaggy, horned variation of the common dairy cow. Visitors can hold baby sheep and marvel at beasts such as the meerkat and emu.

- ✔ **Balvenie Castle,** A941 just outside of town toward Craigellachie (☎ 0131-668-8600). Here you see the ruins of an old castle belonging to the fourth Earl of Atholl. The castle is intact enough for you to walk a couple stories up into the bedroom where Mary Queen of Scots once stayed.

- ✔ **Duff House,** Banff (☎ 01261-818-181; www.duffhouse.org.uk). The tour of this fine country house rivals many castle tours; it features a fine collection of Chippendale furniture and portraits by top artists such as El Greco. Among the grounds' attractions are a Victorian glasshouse vinery, playground, mausoleum, distillery, and the Duff House Royal Golf Course.

- ✔ **Dunotter Castle,** near Stonehaven (☎ 01569-762-173). This castle is best known for its breathtaking views. Much of the structure still stands, but no inside tour of the castle is available, and informative signs are scant. The tragic history of the place includes a siege by William "Braveheart" Wallace, who set the castle on fire, roasting the soldiers inside.

- ✔ **Glamis Castle,** 12 miles north of Dundee and 5 miles west of Forfar (☎ 01307-840-393; www.glamis-castle.co.uk). This castle is notable for being the childhood home of the late Queen Mother and of Queen Elizabeth, as well as the birthplace of the late Princess Margaret. A royal residence since 1372, it's actually more famous for being the (historically inaccurate) setting for Shakespeare's *Macbeth.*

- ✔ **Scottish Lighthouses Museum,** Kinnaird Head, on the A98 (☎ 01346-511-022). This museum is a must-see for lighthouse enthusiasts and is recommended if you have any interest in the towers of all shapes and sizes that have kept sailors safe at sea for more than 200 years.

Shopping for Local Treasures

With its cluster of tartan and woolens shops, Pitlochry offers the classic Highland gateway shopping experience, where you may just find the perfect wooly jumper to keep you warm. Both Dundee and Aberdeen offer a full range of shops these days, with many of the stores you would expect to find in provincial centers. Also consider visiting the shops I list below.

✔ **Baxter's Highland Village,** Fochabers, 9 miles east of Elgin (☎ **01343-820-666;** www.baxters.com). This shop is the home and retail outlet for Baxter's food products, primarily jams and soups. Besides the food shop, you can also stop in the store for modern kitchen and housewares. Highland Village is open Sundays from 11 a.m. to 6 p.m., Monday through Wednesday from 10 a.m. to 6 p.m., Thursday and Friday from 10 a.m. to 8 p.m., and Saturday from 10 a.m. to 7 p.m.

✔ **Le Chocolatier,** 29 Scott St., Perth (☎ **01738-620-039**). This heavenly shop offers lots of tasty handmade sweets, from butter fudges to chocolates for diabetics. Le Chocolatier is open Monday through Saturday from 9 a.m. to 5 p.m.

✔ **Macnaughtons of Pitlochry,** Station Road, Pitlochry (☎ **01796-472-722**). Macnaughtons is actually a big complex made up of several storefronts that sell high-quality clothes. The range of apparel includes kilts, cashmere, tartans, and tweed, as well as other Scotland-related gifts. Macnaughton's of Pitlochry is open Monday through Saturday from 9 a.m. to 5 p.m.

✔ **McEwan Gallery,** on A939, 1 mile west of Ballater, Tomintoul, Ballater, Deeside (☎ **01339-755-429**). A great shop if you're looking for art, many of the items sold here are Scotland- or golf-related and make nice high-end souvenirs. McEwan Gallery is open Tuesday through Sunday from 11 a.m. to 5 p.m. in summer and by appointment in winter.

Doing the Pub Crawl

Aberdeen has a range of traditional pubs, stylish bars, and nightlife options. I list some of my favorites below.

✔ **The Lemon Tree,** 5 W. North St., at Queen Street (☎ **01224-642-230;** www.lemontree.org). This is an eclectic place that's a whole-foods shop and popular lunchroom by day and a theater and music venue by night. Call or visit The Lemon Tree's Web site for schedules and show times.

✔ **Old Blackfriars,** 52 Castlegate, at the top end of Union Street (☎ **01224-581-922**). This excellent pub features local ales. The friendly place is cozy yet big enough for milling. Old Blackfriars is open Monday through Saturday from 11 a.m. to midnight, and Sunday from 12:30 p.m. to 11:30 p.m.

✔ **The Prince of Wales,** 7 St. Nicholas Lane, down an alley off Union Street at George Street (☎ **01224-640-597**). Possibly the best place to grab a pint in Aberdeen, The Prince of Wales is an old-fashioned pub with private booths, wood furniture, stone floors, and an excellent spectrum of ales (such as Orkney Dark Island). If you're a little hungry, try the Guinness pie. The only problem with this place is that it can get crowded, but that's the price of popularity. The Prince of Wales is open Monday through Saturday from 11 a.m. to midnight, and Sunday from noon to midnight.

Fast Facts: Tayside and the Northeast

Area Code

The area codes for this region are: Perth **01738**, Aberfeldy **01887**, Pitlochry **01796**, Dundee **01382**, Aberdeen **01224**, Braemar **01339**, and Elgin **01343**. You need to dial the area code only if you're calling from outside the city you want to reach.

ATMs

Your best bets for banks with ATM machines are in Aberdeen, Dundee, and Perth.

Emergencies

Dial ☎ **999** for police, fire, or ambulance.

Hospitals

Hospitals in the area are Aberdeen Royal Infirmary, Foresterhill, on the west end of Union Street (☎ 01224-681-818), and Perth Royal Infirmary (☎ 01738-623-311), Taymount Terrace, on the west side of town. Aberfeldy's cottage hospital (☎ 01887-820-3140) is on Old Crieff Road. Dundee Royal Infirmary (☎ 01382-434-664) is on Barrack Road.

Information

Tourist offices are located at: The Square, Aberfeldy (☎ 01887-820-276); 22 Atholl Rd.,

Pitlochry (☎ 01796-472-215); 4 City Sq., Dundee (☎ 01382-434-664; www.angus anddundee.co.uk); The Mews, Mars Road, Braemar (☎ 01339-741-600); Lower City Mills, West Mill Street, Perth (☎ 01738-627-958; www.perthshire. co.uk); Elgin (☎ 01343-542-666); and St. Nicholas House, Aberdeen (☎ 01224-288-828).

Internet Access

The best place for Internet access in the region is CommsPort, 31–33 Loch St., Aberdeen (☎ 01224-626-468; www. commsport.com). The shop is open Monday through Wednesday and Friday through Saturday from 8 a.m.–6 p.m., Thursday from 8 a.m.–7 p.m., and Sunday from 10 a.m.–5 p.m. Access to the Web costs £3 ($4.35) per hour.

Mail

Post offices are located at 371 George St., Aberdeen (☎ 01224-632-904); 3 Main St., Perth (☎ 01738-624-637); and 92 Atholl Rd., Pitlochry (☎ 01796-472-965).

Chapter 18

The Highlands

*A*fter Edinburgh and Glasgow, the Highlands is the next most visited region in Scotland — and for good reason. The tourist trail through the Highlands includes breathtaking Glen Coe and beautifully desolate Rannoch Moor; the scenic "Road to the Isles," west of Fort William in Lochaber; remote western peninsulas such as Morvern and Ardnamurchan; the city of Inverness; the Great Glen and, of course, Loch Ness. And that's only the beginning!

The Highland boundary line runs diagonally across Scotland, from the isle of Arran (which it bisects) to the Moray Firth. The many lochs and mountains in the area force all forms of transportation to navigate around them.

It's easy to be overwhelmed when you're trying to visit an area of this size. Using maps to plot your course, take a pencil and mark off the attractions you want to see. Then figure out the best order in which to see them, whether coming or going.

Inverness is the capital of the Highlands and the region's largest city; despite its size, Inverness is an easy place to get around on foot. The River Ness runs through the town, which has shops, restaurants, bars, and accommodations as well as a nice castle and museum but few other attractions. I suggest that you use Inverness as a comfortable base from which to explore other parts of the Highlands.

Fort William lies at the foot of Ben Nevis (the highest mountain in Great Britain), at the far end of Loch Linnhe. This location, on the roads leading north through the Great Glen to Loch Ness and going west towards Glenfinnan, means that tourists regularly pass through Fort William, which has shops and restaurants to accommodate visitors.

West Coast villages and towns worth seeing include Arisaig, Mallaig, Plockton, and Ullapool. In the east lie Tain and Dornoch, and Durness is in the far north. Durness features a small memorial in memory of the late Beatle John Lennon, who often went there on vacations. If you're looking for really wild and sparsely populated territory, you need to travel north of the fishing port Ullapool, which is a veritable metropolis compared to the settlements you find further north.

Getting There

Inverness is well served by buses and trains. If you're making the big leap north from Glasgow or Edinburgh, you may want to consider taking public transportation to reach the capital of the Highlands. Then, after you arrive, you can rent a car. You can also take the train from Glasgow to Fort William and transfer there for another train up to Mallaig — possibly the most scenic train ride in the entire UK. Local bus services crisscross the Highlands, but, for optimal mobility, a car is quite useful.

✔ **By car:** The A82 runs nearly the entire length of the Highlands from Loch Lomond and Crianlarich north to Fort William and then into Inverness. From the east, the A9 from Perth leads north to Inverness and then on to Tain, as well. Other key roads in the region include the A830 (the so-called Road to the Isles) from Fort William to Mallaig; the A87 from Invergarry to the Kyle of Lochalsh; the A835 from Inverness to Ullapool; and the A836 from Tain to Tongue and the far north coast.

✔ **By bus: Scottish Citylink** (☎ **0870-550-5050**; www.citylink.co. uk) routes hit all the major Highland towns.

✔ **By train: First ScotRail** (☎ **0845-748-4950**; www.firstscotrail. com) travels to major towns in the region, including Fort William and Mallaig on the West Highland Lines and Inverness, Tain, Kyle of Lochalsh, and even Thurso. You have to rely on buses or local taxis after you arrive by train, however. ScotRail service to Inverness dovetails with long-distance trains from England run by Great North Eastern Railway. You can also call National Railway Enquiries at the First ScotRail phone number above for details.

✔ **By plane: Inverness/Dalcross Airport** (☎ **01463-23-2471**) is at Dalcross, 8 miles east of Inverness. The airport handles flights to and from Glasgow and Edinburgh.

✔ **By ferry: Caledonian MacBrayne** (☎ **01475-650-100**; www.calmac. co.uk) — or CalMac, as it's more colloquially known — serves 22 islands and 4 peninsulas over the West Coast of Scotland. In the Highlands, this includes service from Mallaig to Skye and Ullapool to the Outer Hebrides.

The Highlands

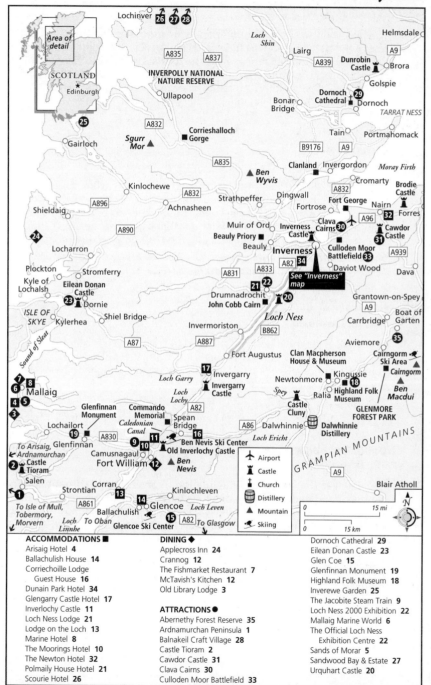

ACCOMMODATIONS ■

Arisaig Hotel **4**
Ballachulish House **14**
Corriechoille Lodge
  Guest House **16**
Dunain Park Hotel **34**
Glengarry Castle Hotel **17**
Inverlochy Castle **11**
Loch Ness Lodge **21**
Lodge on the Loch **13**
Marine Hotel **8**
The Moorings Hotel **10**
The Newton Hotel **32**
Polmaily House Hotel **21**
Scourie Hotel **26**

DINING ◆

Applecross Inn **24**
Crannog **12**
The Fishmarket Restaurant **7**
McTavish's Kitchen **12**
Old Library Lodge **3**

ATTRACTIONS ●

Abernethy Forest Reserve **35**
Ardnamurchan Peninsula **1**
Balnakeil Craft Village **28**
Castle Tioram **2**
Cawdor Castle **31**
Clava Cairns **30**
Culloden Moor Battlefield **33**

Dornoch Cathedral **29**
Eilean Donan Castle **23**
Glen Coe **15**
Glenfinnan Monument **19**
Highland Folk Museum **18**
Inverewe Garden **25**
The Jacobite Steam Train **9**
Loch Ness 2000 Exhibition **22**
Mallaig Marine World **6**
The Official Loch Ness
  Exhibition Centre **22**
Sands of Morar **5**
Sandwood Bay & Estate **27**
Urquhart Castle **20**

Spending the Night

You may want to stay in tourist-friendly Inverness or Fort William, but the rest of the Highlands towns hide some real treats, too. Some accomodations have earned star ratings from the tourist board; see Chapter 8 for a description of the rating system and information on self-catering accommodations, of which there are quite a few in the Highlands. Rates listed here include full breakfast, unless otherwise stated. You may well get a better deal than the advertised "rack" rates.

Arisaig Hotel
$$ Arisaig

With views of the lovely bay at Arisaig, its small harbor, and the isles beyond, this hotel captures the essence of the Western Highlands and island experience without even trying. Rooms are tidy and well appointed, if not exceptionally large. The best ones face onto the sea. A restaurant and popular local pub as well as a playroom for children are on premises.

See map p. 347. A830 at Arisaig harbor. ☎ **01687-450-210.** *Fax: 01687-450-310.* www.arisaighotel.co.uk. *Rack rates: £70–£90 ($129–$166) double. AE, MC, V.*

Ballachulish House
$$$ Ballachulish

The small eight-room hotel on the road to Fort William is renowned for its meals, which have earned recognition from the persnickety Michelin guide. Dinner is a five-course gourmet excursion using mostly local produce. Rooms are generally spacious.

See map p. 347. Off A82 on A825. ☎ **01855-811-266.** *Fax: 01855-811-498.* www.ballachulishhouse.com. *Rack rates: £125–£188 ($230–$347) double. AE, MC, V.*

Ballifeary House Hotel
$$ Inverness

You won't find a closer accommodation to Inverness — without hearing car horns and pedestrians — than this hotel. Ballifeary House is in a quiet residential area within easy walking distance of Inverness center and along the River Ness. The Edwardian villa has lovely sitting rooms and immaculate guest rooms that exude comfort. The hotel is entirely nonsmoking, and the large free parking area is convenient. Take note: The minimum age for guests here is 15.

See map p. 357. 10 Ballifeary Rd. ☎ **01463-235-572.** *Fax: 01463-717-583.* www.ballifearyhousehotel.co.uk. *Rack rates: £60–£70 ($111–$130) double. MC, V.*

Corriechoille Lodge Guest House
$$ **Near Spean Bridge**

This oasis of a guesthouse has a sitting room with a view of the Nevis Range Mountains. An old stone fishing lodge has been converted into this four-star (bordering on five, no doubt) accommodation with all the trimmings.

See map p. 347. Just off the A82, 2 miles east of Spean Bridge. ☎ *01397-712-002.* www.corriechoille.com. *Rack rates: £56–£62 ($103–$115) double. MC, V. Closed early Nov–late Mar.*

Dunain Park Hotel
$$$ **Dunain near Inverness**

In a tourist-strategic position between Loch Ness and Inverness, the Dunain is a wonderful old Georgian country house surrounded by woods and gardens. Some of the well-dressed rooms have four-poster beds, and some are in separate quaint cottages. The indoor heated swimming pool and sauna are nice. With only 13 rooms, booking ahead is wise.

See map p. 347. Fort William Road, on the A82, 2 miles south of Inverness. ☎ *01463-230-512. Fax: 01463-224-532.* www.dunainparkhotel.co.uk. *Rack rates: £140–£218 ($260–$403) double. AE, DC, MC, V.*

Glengarry Castle Hotel
$$–$$$ **Invergarry**

You'd be hard pressed to find a prettier spot for a country house hotel. This 26-room Victorian mansion is on extensive wooded grounds with its own castle ruins (the real Glengarry Castle) and nice views of Loch Oich. It also has tennis courts and rowboats for guest use. Some of the hotel's warmly decorated rooms have four-poster beds, and all are beam-roofed and spacious. The hotel may seem highbrow, but the staff is friendly and personable — and the price is a bargain for all that.

See map p. 347. Invergarry, where the A87 and A82 meet. ☎ *01809-501-254. Fax: 01809-501-207.* www.glengarry.net/hotel.php. *Rack rates: £84–£156 ($155–$288) double. AE, MC, V. Closed early Nov–late Mar.*

Glen Mhor Hotel
$$–$$$ **Inverness**

This cozy Victorian hotel sits on the River Ness just below the city's castle. The lobbies and the restaurant, Nico's Bistro (see listing in the section "Dining Locally"), are lovely spots with overstuffed chairs, tartan upholstery, and oak paneling. The rooms are large and the beds perfectly firm. Be sure to ask for a river view (it carries no extra charge).

See map p. 357. 9–12 Ness Bank. ☎ *01463-234-308. Fax: 01463-713-170.* www.glenmhor.com. *Rack rates: £120 ($222) double. AE, MC, V.*

Inverlochy Castle
$$$$ **Fort William**

Undoubtedly Fort William's most highly rated accommodation, this hotel is beautifully situated between Ben Nevis and the water. The castle indeed offers an experience fit for royalty: Queen Victoria stayed here for a week in 1873 and wrote in her diary, "I never saw a lovelier or more romantic spot." That sentiment still rings true today. The sitting rooms and dining area are breathtaking — flawlessly decorated and illuminated by chandeliers. The attention to fine detail and maximum comfort extends to the guest rooms, as well, which all have lovely views. The food is gourmet, and after you've had your fill of rich food and posh surroundings, you can tour the 500-acre grounds.

See map p. 347. Torlundy, 3 miles north of Fort William, on the A82. ☎ *01397-702-177. Fax: 01397-702-953.* www.inverlochycastlehotel.com. *Rack rates: £290–£550 ($536–$1,000) double. AE, MC, V. Closed Jan–Feb.*

Loch Ness Lodge
$$ **Drumnadrochit**

This hotel is full of tourists year-round. Look out your window and you're likely to see a plastic reproduction of the "monster" and the Loch Ness Exhibition Centre. That said, the rooms are quite comfortable and rather large, the staff is used to accommodating out-of-towners, and this is a prime location for exploring all the Loch Ness sights. The lodge, which dates to 1740, also hosts traditional music and *ceilidhs* (traditional Scottish group dances).

See map p. 347. Drumnadrochit, Loch Ness. On the A82, midway between Inverness (13 miles north) and Fort Augustus. ☎ *01456-450-342. Fax: 01456-450-429.* www.lochness-hotel.com. *Rack rates: £90–£120 ($166–$222) double. AE, DC, MC, V.*

Lodge on the Loch
$$$–$$$$ **Onich**

A stay at the Lodge on the Loch should leave an indelible memory of your visit to the Highlands, not because the building or rooms are spectacular but because the location is prime. With some of the finest vistas in the country, this serene family-run retreat overlooks Loch Linnhe five miles or so west of Glencoe. The house was built in 1870 as a country home, and today the cozy rooms are decorated in Art Nouveau and Shaker styles. Take time to explore the grounds to the shore or through the gardens.

See map p. 347. On A82, 10 miles south of Fort William. ☎ *0871-222-3462. Fax: 0871-222-3416.* www.freedomglen.co.uk. *Rack rates: £160–£300 ($296–$555) double. MC, V.*

Marine Hotel
$$ Mallaig

This hotel is centrally located in the increasingly bustling fishing and ferry port of Mallaig, where you can catch the ferry across the Sound of Sleat to the Isle of Skye. The staff is memorably accommodating, and the house is lovely. Some rooms have views of the sea and port; all are comfortable and modestly decorated. With the wind and rain in this part of the country, you'll probably appreciate the central heating more than any other amenity.

See map p. 347. On the right from A830, adjacent to the railway station. ☎ *01687-462-217. Fax: 01687-462-821.* www.marinehotel-mallaig.co.uk. *Rack rates: £60–£80 ($111–$148) double. MC, V.*

The Moorings Hotel
$$–$$$ Fort William

On a quiet residential stretch outside Fort William's center, this labyrinthine hotel is bigger than it looks. The large, comfortable rooms stretch back to the Caledonian Canal; some units have views of the locks and the boats going through. The staff is helpful, the beds are comfortable, and all rooms have satellite television. Superior rooms have Internet access.

See map p. 347. On the B8004, just off the A830 toward Mallaig, next to Neptune's Staircase. ☎ *01397-772-797. Fax: 01397-772-441.* www.moorings-fortwilliam.co.uk. *Rack rates: £82–£110 ($150–$204) double. AE, DC, MC, V.*

Moyness House
$$ Inverness

The Moyness is arguably the finest B&B in town (the other contender is Ballifeary House, whose review appears earlier in this section), and it's in a quiet residential location within easy strolling distance of Inverness center. The gracious hosts have perfectly restored and improved the hotel (which is entirely nonsmoking). Each room in this whitewashed, circa-1880 Victorian villa is individually and comfortably done up. The guesthouse has a free parking lot.

See map p. 357. 6 Bruce Gardens, just off A82, south side of the River Ness. ☎ *01463-233-836. Fax: 01463-233-836.* www.moyness.co.uk. *Rack rates: £70–£76 ($129–$140) double. AE, MC, V.*

The Newton Hotel
$$$ Nairn

Just before you enter the little coastal town of Nairn from the west, you should spot this castle-like hotel. It could be just the thing you need after a busy day of sightseeing. The overnight rooms are quite large, and the comfortable public rooms are decorated with antique furniture. In addition to the usual room facilities, other nice touches include a complimentary morning paper and heated bathroom floors. In the morning, you have the win-win choice of breakfast in your room or in the lovely glass-enclosed atrium dining area. As a guest at this four-star hotel, you have free use of the gym, pool, sauna, and steam room of its nearby sister hotel.

See map p. 347. Inverness Road, on A96. ☎ *01667-453-144. Fax: 01667-454-026.* www.morton-hotels.com/newton/index.html. *Rack rates: £114–£196 ($210–$362) double. AE, DC, MC, V.*

Polmaily House Hotel
$$ Drumnadrochit

For an Edwardian country house, Polmaily sure knows how to provide modern family friendly accommodations. The high-ceilinged bedrooms are large and elegant, and the hotel also features a heated indoor pool, movies for the TV, an Internet room, horse stables (you can even get lessons), tennis courts, sailing, and fishing. Parents will appreciate the baby-sitting service, organized children's activities, indoor and outdoor play areas, and family-size suites.

See map p. 347. On the A831 toward Cannish. ☎ *01456-450-343. Fax: 01456-450-813.* www.polmaily.co.uk. *Rack rates: £80–£144 ($148–$266) double. MC, V.*

Scourie Hotel
$$ Scourie

Scourie is one those places that believes guests have better things to do than sit in their rooms and watch TV. (There are no TVs here, by the way, although they'll provide you with a radio if asked.) Rooms are quite homey and spacious. Part of an original coaching inn, the hotel overlooks Scourie Bay. It's a top spot for fishing enthusiasts, too.

See map p. 347. ☎ *01971-502-396. Fax: 01971-502-423.* www.scourie-hotel. freeserve.co.uk. *Rack rates: £60–£80 ($111–$148) double. MC, V.*

Dining Locally

Applecross Inn
$$ Applecross FISH/SEAFOOD

This may not be the easiest place in Scotland to reach, but many visitors feel the twists and turns of the road to Applecross are well worth it if a meal at the inn (which also has overnight rooms) is on the itinerary. This one-time fisherman's cottage sits right on the shores of the Inner Sound of Raasay, looking out toward the mountains of Skye. Naturally, seafood dishes make up the majority of the menu, but expect local venison or sausages, too. The Applecross, with an excellent selection of real ale, was also rated one the country's best pubs.

See map p. 347. Shore Street. ☎ *01520-744-262. Fax: 01520-744-440.* www. applecross.uk.com/inn/index.htm. *Reservations required. Main courses: £8–£16 ($15–$30). MC, V. Open: daily noon–9 p.m.*

Café 1
$$–$$$ Inverness INTERNATIONAL

The small, well-chosen menu here is often a delight, especially when it includes such finely prepared items as wild mushroom risotto, prime Angus beef, and succulent smoked haddock. The menu always has something for vegetarians as well. The décor behind the stone exterior is simple and modern, and you'll find the service polite and professional.

See map p. 357. 75 Castle St. ☎ *01463-226-200. Reservations recommended. Main courses: £8–£13 ($15–$24). AE, DC, MC, V. Open: Mon–Sat noon–2:30 p.m. and 6–10 p.m.*

Crannog
$$$ Fort William FISH/SEAFOOD

This restaurant sits on stilts out over the waters of Loch Linnhe and offers fine views. The fish and seafood is so fresh that you'll swear the staff went out and caught it right after you ordered. And you're not far off — the restaurant deploys its own fleet and runs a smokehouse, too. Enjoy a fine meal in the nautically themed dining room to the sound of water gently lapping against the wooden structure, which was once a bait store. The plate of langoustine with hot garlic butter is highly touted. By the way, *crannog* is the Gaelic word for an artificial island on the banks of a loch — how appropriate.

See map p. 347. The Pier. ☎ *01397-705-589. Reservations recommended for dinner. Main courses: £12–£16 ($22–$30). MC, V. Open: daily noon–2:30 p.m. and 6–9:30 p.m.*

The Fishmarket Restaurant
$$ Mallaig FISH/SEAFOOD

Situated right on the harbor and serving dishes that incorporate freshly caught fish, this restaurant is a casual place for a meal. Typical main courses include poached haddock with whisky mussels and chervil, roasted whole seabass with fennel and ginger, or traditional fish and chips. Prawns (shrimp) come in by the ton here at Mallaig and thus serve as one of the restaurant's specialties.

See map p. 347. Station Road. ☎ *01687-462-299. Fax: 01687-462-623. Reservations recommended. Main courses: £10–£15 ($18.50–$28). MC, V. Open: Mon–Sat noon–3 p.m. and 6–8:30 p.m., Sun 12:30–7 p.m.*

McTavish's Kitchen
$ Fort William SCOTTISH

Abundant local publicity makes this restaurant a popular place for tourists. On the ground floor, a self-service restaurant with sturdy if not supreme food is convenient for visitors making forays into Fort William for supplies. The upstairs dining room serves delectable Scottish fare alongside traditional options like spaghetti Bolognese and features Scottish entertainment nightly during the high season.

See map p. 347. West End High Street. ☎ *01397-702-406.* www.mctavishs.com.
Main courses: £5–£10 ($9–$18.50). MC, V. Open: daily noon–2 p.m. and 6–10 p.m.
Upstairs closed Oct–May.

Nico's Bistro
$$–$$$ Inverness SCOTTISH

This upscale restaurant is very laid-back considering the quality of food and service it dishes out. Happy patrons have included Prince Charles and Princess Anne. You can't go wrong with one of the catches of the day, such as sea scallops sautéed in olive oil or fried whole langoustines. The chef is proud of his "prize-winning" haggis, and the excellent veggie options include a compote of woodland mushrooms. The lounge is perfect for a pre-dinner beer or an after-dinner cocktail, and outdoor seating is available.

See map p. 357. 9–12 Ness Bank. ☎ *01463-234-308. Main courses: £8–£16 ($15–$29). AE, DC, MC, V. Open: daily 11:30 a.m.–10 p.m.*

Old Library Lodge
$$$ Arisaig MODERN SCOTTISH

Located in a 200-year-old stone building (formerly a library, hence the name) just down the street from the Arisaig Hotel, this restaurant (which also has overnight rooms) garnered three stars from the Scottish tourist board. Dishes from the evening menu include grilled Mallaig scallops on a celeriac puree, fillets of lamb with a port wine sauce, and collops of monkfish with a warm vinaigrette sauce.

See map p. 347. ☎ *01687-450-651. Fax: 01687-450-219.* www.oldlibrary.co.uk. *Fixed-price 3-course dinner: £24 ($44). MC, V. Open: daily 6–9 p.m. Closed Nov–Mar.*

Riva
$$ Inverness ITALIAN

Fine wine, Italian cuisine, and service on the River Ness — could you ask for more? Perhaps a singing waiter? Ask for Ronaldo. The intimate bistro-style seating here is nice and lively. The subtly flavored meals turn staples such as baked filet of sole or tagliatelle with red peppers into something memorable. You'll also find an ideal complement to the dinner in the smartly planned wine selection. Lunch prices are a particular bargain, but nothing here is terribly expensive, which probably explains Riva's local popularity.

See map p. 357. 4–6 Ness Walk, by the Ness Bridge. ☎ *01463-226-686. Reservations recommended. Main courses: £8–£12 ($15–$22). AE, MC, V. Open: daily 10:30 a.m.–10 p.m.*

The River Café and Restaurant
$–$$ Inverness SCOTTISH

This small, simple venture by the water is a favorite among locals because of its good eats at even better prices. During the day, it acts very much like a cafe with croissant sandwiches or stuffed baked potatoes. In the evening, the candles come out and the cuisine is more formal with specialties such as filet of Scottish salmon or chili con carne, all at take-away prices. Not bad for a sit-down place by the river.

See map p. 357. 10 Bank St. ☎ *01463-714-884. Reservations recommended. Main courses: £5–£8 ($9–$15). MC, V. Open: Sun–Tues 10 a.m.–8:30 p.m., Wed–Sat 10 a.m.– 9:30 p.m.*

rocpool
$$$ Inverness   MODERN SCOTTISH

This is the most ambitious, modern, and stylish restaurant in the city of Inverness. The menu at rocpool may range from lamb loin with black pudding to halibut with tzatziki (Greek-style roe) and Oriental salad. Desserts are impressive and so are the unisex restrooms.

See map p. 357. 1 Young St. ☎ *01463-717-274. Main courses: £12–£20 ($22–$37). MC, V. Open: Oct–May Mon–Sat noon–10:30 p.m.; June–Sept Mon–Sat noon–10:30 p.m., Sun 6–10 p.m.*

Exploring the Highlands

You can find plenty of tourist attractions between Inverness and Fort William, but please don't confine yourself to the well-known Loch Ness hot spots. In addition to those heavily touristed sites, you have a wide choice of things to see throughout the Highlands: ancient monuments, lovely lochs, picturesque towns, natural areas for hiking, sandy and unspoiled beaches, and a good number of excellent castles.

Guided tours

The Highlands lends itself to smartly operated theme tours, whether relating to the area's rich historic heritage or unique natural history. Here are a couple of the best:

✔ **Dolphin Ecosse** (☎ **01381-600-323;** www.dolphinecosse.co.uk): The Cromarty bottlenose dolphins are the only known group living in the North Sea. This tour takes you out to see the dolphins in action. As many as 130 dolphins live in the area, and they're generally friendly and unafraid to approach the boat. The tour also covers other local coastal attractions, such as seals, natural rocks, and caves. Guests are provided with coffee and biscuits, as well. Tours depart from Cromarty Harbor, on the A832 at the junction of Bank Street and High Street in Cromarty. Tickets cost £20 ($37) per person, free for children under 3. The tour lasts 2 hours and 45 minutes.

✔ **Jacobite Cruises** (☎ **01463-233-999;** www.jacobite.co.uk): Jacobite Cruises, which take visitors out on Loch Ness, are perhaps the most efficient and best organized tours of the loch. The boats are large, which means less rocking and rolling. You can choose from a number of different excursions, lasting one to four hours depending on the cruise. The company offers combination tickets in case you want to get off at Urquhart and tour the castle or visit the monster exhibits in Drumnadrochit. Boats leave from Tomnahurich Bridge, Glenurquhart Road, Inverness. To reach the launching point, stay on the same road as the Ness Bridge in Inverness, which eventually becomes Tomnahurich Bridge. Trips run from April through October, and fares start at £8 ($15).

The top attractions

Abernethy Forest Reserve
Loch Garten

Some seven miles from Aviemore in the Cairngorms, this aviary reserve operated by the Royal Society for the Protection of Birds (RSPB) offers an observation center to spy on osprey, which were once thought to be extinct in Scotland and still, horribly, remain targets of assorted idiots. But since the mid-1950s, the osprey have returned from Africa to nest here in the spring. The observation center deploys telescopes and video cameras to help visitors see the young birds of prey at play.

See map p. 347. Near Boat of Garten. ☎ **01479-821-409** *or 01479-810-363.* www.rspb.org.uk/reserves/guide/a/abernethyforest/index.asp. *Admission: £2.50 ($4.60). Open: Apr–Aug daily 10 a.m.–6 p.m.*

Ardnamurchan Peninsula

One of the more easily reached but seemingly remote areas of the Highlands, the Ardnamurchan Peninsula is the most westerly point in the entire British mainland. One highlight is the ruins of Castle Tioram (see the listing later in this section), but the peninsula also has pretty beaches and tide pools, a natural history and visitor center near Glenmore, lots of hiking trails, and a lighthouse at the craggy point, which can feel like the end of the earth on a windy day. From Kilchoan on the peninsula, you can take a ferry to Tobermory on the Isle of Mull.

See map p. 347. Take the A861 from Lochailort or the small ferry service to Corran a few miles north of Ballachulish.

Balnakeil Craft Village
Near Durness

This artist community, just on the outskirts of Durness near Cape Wrath, has plenty of galleries selling local artwork. The craft village is housed in a former military communications installation with lots of flat-roofed institutional looking buildings. Still the place is friendly, communal, and, yes, vaguely hippy-esque. The cafe serves tasty natural foods, and the bookshop is well-stocked with local titles. If you've come this far, you may as well carry on to the end of the road to see the old ruins of a church and a nice sandy beach.

See map p. 347. Off the A838, west of Durness.

Inverness

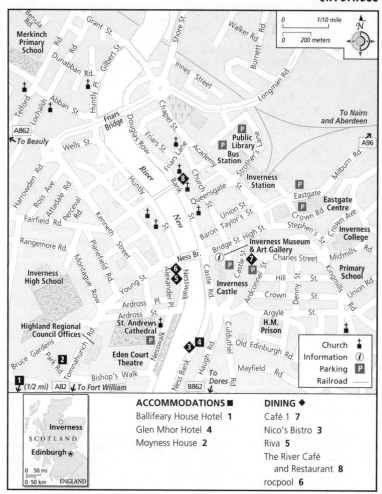

ACCOMMODATIONS ■
Ballifeary House Hotel 1
Glen Mhor Hotel 4
Moyness House 2

DINING ◆
Café 1 7
Nico's Bistro 3
Riva 5
The River Café
    and Restaurant 8
rocpool 6

Ben Nevis
Near Fort William

At 1,344m (4,418 ft.), Ben Nevis is the tallest mountain in the United Kingdom, although it's difficult to see just how tall it is from the usual vantage points around Fort William. Ben Nevis may not make for the best picture, but it's a popular climb among locals and hearty visitors. The round-trip hike is ten miles and takes up to eight hours. If you're setting out for the hike, you need to wear good boots and have both warm- and cold-weather gear, because the temperature and weather can fluctuate unpredictably at certain heights: Don't be fooled by fools in shorts and t-shirts. Also, don't attempt the hike too late in the day — you don't want to be stuck out there all night and you may get lost hiking around in the dark. The tourist office in Fort William has trail maps if you're planning to make the big climb. Allow about 8 hours.

See map p. 347. Path leaves from Glen Nevis Road, just outside Fort William. ☎ *01397-703-781 (Highlands of Scotland Tourist Board).* www.visit-fort william.co.uk/mf_bennevis.html.

Castle Tioram
Near Blain on Loch Moidart

This classic medieval fortress, now in ruins (although there are hopes that it will be restored someday), sits along the picturesque shores of Loch Moidart. A key outpost for clan Macdonald for hundreds of years, a rich Scotsman has bought the pile of stone and wants to fix it up and live here. Some historic authorities have other plans. Until a final decision is made, Castle Tioram (pronounced *cheer*-um) remains a unique place to visit, seeing as it sits on an island that can only be accessed by crossing a spit of land at low tide. Like so many castles in Scotland, Tioram was sacked and burned during Jacobite uprisings — in this instance apparently to keep it from falling into the hands of forces loyal to the Hanovers in London. There are good hiking trails nearby the castle, too.

See map p. 347. Off the A861 from Blain.

Cawdor Castle
Cawdor

Cawdor is one of my favorite castles, largely because the room-by-room self-guided tour cards are well written, humorous, and full of candor and personal details. The house, with both its drawbridge and medieval tower intact, is also full of treasures from around the world. The gardens are wonderful, with wildflowers, lots of fountains, and a maze of holly bushes. Legend has it that a king determined the location of the castle by giving instructions to build it wherever his donkey decided to rest. The animal stopped in the shade of a tree, and deep within the castle, the tree still stands today. Although Macbeth was the Thane of Cawdor, the Scottish king never resided here. The gift shop is among the best of any castle, and the separate wool shop has some unique items. Allow about 3 hours.

See map p. 347. On the B9090, off the A96 between Inverness and Nairn. ☎ *01667-404-615.* www.cawdorcastle.com. *Admission: £6.50 ($12) adults, £5.50 ($10) seniors and students, £3.70 ($4.80) children under 16. Open: May–mid-Oct daily 10 a.m.–5:30 p.m. Closed Oct 11–Apr.*

Clava Cairns
Culloden

If you're visiting the nearby Culloden Moor Battlefield (see the next listing), Clava Cairns is a good place to stop for a short break. Basically a 4,000-year-old graveyard, the Clava Cairns are significant because they're the most intact Bronze Age tombs in Scotland. You'll find little more to see than large circular pits and a few standing stones in a grove of trees, but you can walk into the ring and passage cairns. The place is slightly eerie, with a sort of extraterrestrial feel. Allow about 1 hour.

See map p. 347. Take the B9006 from Inverness, beyond the Culloden Battlefield, go right on B851, and stay straight through the crossroads. ☎ *01667-460-232. Admission: free. Open: year-round 24 hours.*

Culloden Moor Battlefield
Culloden Moor

This marshy field is where the hopes of Bonnie Prince Charlie's Jacobite uprising of 1745 (begun at Glenfinnan, see "Glenfinnan Monument," later in this section) ended in complete defeat in 1746. The bloody battle (the last fought in Great Britain) was over in about an hour, and Charlie was among the few men who got away unharmed. After the Jacobite defeat, Highland life was censored and restricted by a London administration tired of rebellion. The visitor center at the battlefield is long on interesting details; in it you'll find a museum and an excellent film about the battle. Take the time to walk through the battlefield, which has clan stones and cairns in memory of those who lost their lives in the fight. The road to the visitor center goes right over part of the battlefield. The terrain is just as it was during the battle, when the boggy conditions played a role in the Jacobites' defeat. Tours are available for an extra £3 ($4.35) for adults and £2 ($2.90) for children. Allow about 2½ hours.

See map p. 347. Culloden Moor, 5 miles east of Inverness on the B9006, which runs parallel to the A96. (Bus: No. 12 on the Highland County Bus, ☎ *01463-71-0555, from Inverness. Tour bus by Guide Friday,* ☎ *01463-22-4000.)* ☎ *01463-79-0607.* www. nts.org.uk. *Admission: £5 ($9.25) adults; £3.75 ($7) seniors, students, and children under 16; £13.50 ($25) family. Open: site year-round, daily; visitor center, restaurant, and shop Apr–Jun and Sept–Oct daily 9 a.m.–6 p.m.; Jul–Aug daily 9 a.m.–7 p.m.; Feb–Mar and Nov–Dec daily 11 a.m.–4 p.m. Closed Jan.*

Dornoch Cathedral
Dornoch

Before 2000, the most interesting thing to happen in Dornoch, about eight miles south of Tain, was the last witch burning in Scotland in 1722. Now the village and its cathedral founded in 1224 is on the map as the spot where Madonna married film director Guy Ritchie. Never mind the fine stonework and stained-glass windows dedicated to Andrew Carnegie — Gwyneth Paltrow and Sting actually stood here. Allow about 1 hour.

See map p. 347. On the main square. ☎ *01862-810-296.* www.visitdornoch.com/ pages/cathedral.html. *Admission: free. Open: daily 9 a.m.–dusk.*

Eilean Donan Castle
Dornie

Grab your camera: Eilean Donan is probably the most photographed stone pile in Scotland (after Edinburgh Castle, that is). On an islet in Loch Duich,

Plockton: The prettiest Highland village?

Not far from Eilean Donan lies Plockton, arguably the prettiest village in the Highlands, on the shores of Loch Carron. The crescent-shaped, harborside main drag here is lined with cute cottages, and the sidewalks are punctuated with palm trees that defy the northern latitudes. Plockton gained fame in the UK as the location for a BBC TV series, *Hamish Macbeth,* starring a then little-known Robert Carlyle as a laid-back, pot-smoking policeman. Today, Plockton features some good grub at the pubs in the Plockton Hotel and nearby Plockton Inn.

this quintessential castle (which lay in ruins from about 1719–1912) is accessible by an arched bridge. Originally built in the early 1200s by Alexander II to deter Viking invaders, the castle underwent substantial restoration following serious destruction at the hands of Hanoverian troops during the Jacobite uprising of 1719. Inside are a piper gallery, Jacobite relics, and military objects as well as a war memorial to Clan MacRae, which held the castle on behalf of another clan, MacKenzie. B-movie fans will be excited by the fact that *Highlander* was filmed here. Allow about 2 hours.

See map p. 347. Dornie, Kyle of Lochalsh, on the A87. ☎ *01599-555-202.* www.eilean donancastle.com. *Admission: £4 ($7.50) adults; £3.20 ($6) seniors, students, and children under 16; £9.50 ($17.50) family. Open: Apr–Oct 10 a.m.–5:30 p.m. Closed Nov–Mar.*

Glen Coe
Glencoe

It's hard to believe that such a beautiful valley has such a bloody historical event associated with it. Glen Coe is where the massacre of February 1692 took place, when Campbell of Glenlyon and his soldiers brutally killed at least 40 members of the MacDonald clan — including women and children. What makes their murders truly repulsive is the fact that Campbell's troops had been staying as guests of MacDonald. Thus in the lore of the land, Glen Coe is right up there with Culloden when it comes to tragic bloodshed. In spite of the area's grim history, a lovely glen runs about ten miles from the King's House in the east to the shores of Loch Leven and the village of Glencoe in the west. The National Trust for Scotland Visitor Centre has trail maps of the area and audiovisual presentations that explain local geography and the clan slayings. You can also see a monument to the massacre in Carnoch. Ranger-led walks take place throughout the summer. Allow about 2 hours.

See map p. 347. Glen Coe Visitor Centre, Glencoe, Ballachulish. ☎ *01855-811-307.* www.nts.org.uk. *Admission: £4.50 ($8.30) adults; £2.95 ($5.50) seniors, students, and children under 16; £9.95 ($18.40) family. Open: daily 10 a.m.–5 p.m.*

Glenfinnan Monument
Glenfinnan

This monument marks the hopeful start of the 1745 Jacobite rebellion led by Bonnie Prince Charlie, who was trying to reclaim the English and Scottish crowns for his Stuart family lineage. Be sure to take your camera; this monument and now-sacred historical ground amid Highland scenery is a great spot for pictures, especially if you're lucky enough to see the steam train cross the arched viaduct behind the visitor center. (Fans of the Harry Potter films will recognize the setting.) The Jacobites allegedly left from this spot to successfully push all the way to Derby in England before turning back and ultimately finding defeat at Culloden (see "Culloden Moor Battlefield" earlier in this section). The Jacobite cause has captured the Scots' collective imagination, and the visitor center provides a good primer on the Jacobites and Prince Charlie. The monument can be vaguely magical, especially on one of my visits when a lone piper broke the silence of twilight with mournful playing from a heather-filled hillside. Allow about 2 hours.

See map p. 347. On A830, next to Loch Shiel, 18 miles west of Fort William. ☎ *01397-722-250. Admission: £2.50 ($4.60) adults; £1 ($1.85) seniors, students, and children under 16. Open: Site year-round daily. Visitor center Apr–Jun and Sept–Oct daily 10 a.m.–5 p.m.; Jul–Aug daily 9:30 a.m.–5:30 p.m. Closed Nov–Mar.*

Highland Folk Museum
Kingussie

About a dozen miles southwest of the resort Aviemore, in Kingusse (pronounced king-*yous*-ee), this interesting museum describes the last 400 years of Highland life in a re-created old crofters' (small farmers') home, painstakingly built by craftspeople using only period tools and technology. The collection of everyday objects, furniture, machines, and more is enormous. Particular items of interest include a fiddle from 1772, bagpipes played at the Battle of Waterloo, a 19th-century harp, and an excellent video presentation, "A Way of Life No More." In the summer, craftsmen in period costume demonstrate Highland skills, and tours run regularly throughout the day, according to demand. Allow about 2 hours.

See map p. 347. Duke Street, on the A86, off the A9. ☎ *01540-661-307.* www.highlandfolk.com/kingussie/default.htm. *Admission: £3.50 ($5.10) adults, £2.50 ($3.65) seniors and children under 16, £7 ($10) family. Open: Apr–Aug Mon–Sat 9:30 a.m.–5:30 p.m.; Sept–Oct Mon–Fri 9:30 a.m.–4:30 p.m.; Nov–Mar Sat–Sun tours by appt. only.*

Inverewe Garden
Near Poolewe

The most impressive garden in the Highlands is here on the south-facing shores of Loch Ewe. Because of the North Atlantic drift that carries warmer waters up from the Caribbean, the climate here is amazingly temperate. The plants are a testament to the ideal growing conditions. In late summer, you can see cabbages the size of basketballs in the large vegetable patch within the walled garden. The sprawling 50-acre garden, however, encompasses much more than just vegetables, including rhodondendron and pine walks, a "bambooselem," two ponds, and a rock garden. Diverse planting means something is in bloom all year round, from azaleas in spring to Kaffir lillies in the autumn.

See map p. 347. On A832. ☎ *01455-781-200. Fax: 01455-781-497.* www.nts.org.uk. *Admission: £7 ($13) adult, £5.60 ($10.35) children, £19 ($35) family. Open: Apr–Oct daily 9:30 a.m.–9 p.m.; Nov–Mar daily 9:30 a.m.– 4 p.m.*

Inverness Museum and Art Gallery
Inverness

This museum's permanent collection includes period dress, old bagpipes, a cast of the death mask of Bonnie Prince Charlie, prehistoric stones, the history of the city, and lots and lots of taxidermied animals. The collection of Highland silver is the largest of its kind. The two-story building also holds an innovative art gallery with rotating exhibits. This place is definitely worth a look-see, and you can't argue with the price. Allow about 1½ hours.

See map p. 357. Castle Wynd, off Bridge Street. ☎ *01463-237-114.* www.inverness museum.com. *Admission: free. Open: Mon–Sat 9 a.m.–5 p.m.*

The Jacobite Steam Train
Fort William and Mallaig railway stations

The 42-mile train ride between Fort William and the port town of Mallaig is one of the most picturesque journeys you'll find anywhere. The trip lasts only a couple of hours each way; you can take it round-trip or one-way to Mallaig, where the ferry goes to the Isle of Skye. Not every train going this route is the historic steam train, so inquire about schedules if you want to ride the real thing. As you chug along past mountains, skirting lochs, and by the sea, you'll pass the Glenfinnan Monument and miles and miles of dramatic, unspoiled scenery. It's hard to believe that the rail line wasn't

Ullapool

Ullapool is the busiest fishing port on the northwest coast of Scotland. Established reasonably recently in 1788 by the British Fisheries Society, the town's become a popular resort — the last outpost before the sparsely populated north. So if you need to stock up at a supermarket, stop in Ullapool. It also has some good casual restaurants that feature freshly landed fish and seafood, like crabs, and the **Ceilidh Place** (☎ 01854-612-103) is a hub of cultural activity with frequent music and dance events through the high season. The Ullapool Museum and Visitor Centre, 7–8 West Argyle St. (☎ 01854-612-987; www.ullapool.co.uk/museum.html), is open year-round; call for open times. Admission is £3 ($5.50) adults, 50p (90¢) children.

built for the delight of visitors; rather, it was created to bring catches of fish inland. At the Glenfinnan station, a small train museum is worth a look, and you can take a break in a cafe located in an old train car. Allow about 5 hours round-trip.

See map p. 347. Fort William and Mallaig railway stations. ☎ *01463-239-026.* www. steamtrain.info. *Tickets: £25 ($46) round-trip or £20 ($37) one-way adults; £15 ($27.75) round-trip or £10 ($18.50) one-way children under 16. Open: mid-June–Sept one round-trip daily Mon–Fri, from Fort William at 10:20 a.m., from Mallaig at 2:10 p.m.; July 30–Sept one round-trip Sun from Fort William at 12:45 p.m., from Mallaig at 5:05 p.m. Closed Oct–mid-June.*

Loch Ness

Okay, this is it: The dark, deep (274m or 900 ft. to be exact), mysterious, and legendary Loch Ness. In addition to looking for the elusive monster, you should seek out other local attractions, such as Urquhart Castle (see the listing later in this section for more information). As you drive along the loch, strategically placed plaques offer information and some history of the area. But the best way to experience the loch is probably by boat (see the listing under "Guided tours," earlier in this chapter). As for the monster, little is known for certain. Although no one can say if it exists, it's apparently against the law to kill it. Is it out there? Although the dark waters of the loch may not be terribly conducive to photosynthesis, thereby stunting the food chain, it offers plenty of room for a large beast to hide. No one can say definitively. Keep an eye out, just in case.

See map p. 347.

Loch Ness 2000 Exhibition
Drumnadrochit

Visiting this attraction is rather like reading *Loch Ness For Dummies* (if there were such a book). In other words, it covers all the bases without burying you in details. Focusing mainly on monster myths and the technology of scientific monster hunting, Loch Ness 2000 offers a reasonably entertaining walking tour through a series of light and video displays. The exhibition is a little cavernous and kitschy, but who doesn't like a good laser show? And while the kids may marvel at the smoke and mirrors, you'll actually learn a couple things about the long history of sightings, research, and theories on the monster. Allow about 1 hour.

See map p. 347. Drumnadrochit, Loch Ness, on the A82. ☎ *01456-450-573.* www. loch-ness-scotland.com. *Admission: £5.95 ($11) adults, £4.50 ($8.30) seniors and students, £3.50 ($6.50) children under 16, £14.95 ($27.50) family. Open: daily 9 a.m.–8 p.m.*

Mallaig Marine World
Mallaig

This small aquarium is a good place to pass some time with children while you're waiting for the ferry to Skye or just during your amble through

Mallaig. Located on the harbor, the attraction provides some perspective on the interesting and diverse sea life of the area. In addition to the maze of tanks, it has models, photographs, and a video about the town's fishing tradition, all of which are usually appreciated by the 12-and-under crowd. Guided tours and talks are available. Allow about 1½ hours.

See map p. 347. The Harbour. ☎ *01687-462-292.* www.road-to-the-isles.org. uk/marine-world.html. *Admission: £3.50 ($6.50) adults, £2.50 ($4.60) seniors and students, £2 ($3.70) children under 16, £8 ($15) family. Open: Apr–Oct Mon–Sat 9 a.m.–7 p.m., Sun 10 a.m.–6 p.m.; Nov–Mar Mon–Sat 9 a.m.–7 p.m.*

The Official Loch Ness Exhibition Centre
Drumnadrochit

This is the "other" Loch Ness exhibit, the older and less expensive one, which requires from visitors a little more by way of literacy skills than its flashier competition (see the listing "Loch Ness 2000 Exhibition"). The focus of this exhibit is less on the Loch Ness monster than the loch itself, which actually has a very interesting history. A film covers the history of Nessie sightings and explains how many are actually sightings of something else, such as sea otters. The exhibition is full of pictures, including other freak beast lore and a series on John Cobb's fatal attempt to beat the world's water speed record (see the John Cobb Cairn below in "Other cool things to see and do"). Allow about 1½ hours.

See map p. 347. On the A82. ☎ *01456-450-342.* www.lochness-centre.com. *Admission: £5 ($9.25) adults, £3.50 ($6.50) seniors, £3.75 ($7) students, £3 ($5.50) children under 16. Open: Mar–June and Sept–Oct daily 9:30 a.m.–5:30 p.m.; July–Aug daily 9 a.m.–7:30 p.m.; Nov–Feb daily 10 a.m.–3 p.m.*

Sands of Morar
Near Mallaig

Bonnie Prince Charlie apparently roamed these beautiful bleached beaches 250 years ago while fleeing his oppressors. Set against postcard-pretty seas, looking across at the islands Rhum and Eigg, Morar has become a popular locale for filmmakers intent on capturing the quintessential Scottish backdrop. *Highlander* and, to much better effect, *Local Hero* were filmed here. Unfortunately, the sands can get rather crowded — at least by local standards — with sun-seeking locals and tourists in the summer.

See map p. 347. Just off the A830, about a mile south of Morar.

Sandwood Estate
Near Blairmore

Purchased in the early 1990s by the John Muir Trust, the Sandwood Estate has *the* beach that, by most accounts, is the most beautiful and unsullied on the entire mainland of Great Britain. Yes, getting there and back from the nearest road requires a 14-km (9-mile) hike on a peat-and-stone trail, but then why do you think it's so pristine? The entire estate covers many

Skiing the Highlands

Outside of Nevis Range Gondola and Skiing (see "Other cool things to see and do," later in this chapter), the Highlands offer other legitimate ski resorts. **Glencoe** has some moderately challenging slopes, great views, and a cute ski and mountaineering museum at the base (open off-season). Glencoe Mountain Resort is at Kingshouse, Glencoe, on the A82 (☎ **01855-851-226;** www.glencoemountain.com). The **Cairngorms** offer unpredictable weather, but when the snow base is good, the whole family can enjoy skiing as well as other non-ski activities. CairnGorm Mountain (☎ **01479-861-261;** www.cairngormmountain.com), located 9 miles from the town of Aviemore, offers great skiing within Britain's largest nature reserve. Alas, it seems climate change has made snow rather rare in the Highlands, and some resorts have tottered on closure.

thousands of acres and encompasses crofts and peat bogs as well as dunes and craggy coastline.

See map p. 347. Take the B801 from the A838 to Blairmore. www.jmt.org/cons/sand.

Urquhart Castle
Drumnadrochit

Despite the impressive ruins, this large and significant castle (pronounced *ur*-ket) has no strong clan association. Because its location on Loch Ness was important for trade routes through the Highlands, the castle has changed hands many times since the 13th century. One of the last groups to occupy it (before the tourists invaded) was Cromwell's army in the 1650s; later it was blown up to prevent Jacobite occupation. A recent addition to the visitor center is an A/V display of views and history that plays before you see the real thing. Allow about 2 hours.

See map p. 347. Near Drumnadrochit., on the A82. ☎ *01456-450-551.* www.historic-scotland.gov.uk. *Admission: £5 ($9.25) adults, £3.75 ($7) seniors and students, £1.50 ($2.75) children under 16. Open: July–Aug daily 9:30 a.m.–8:30 p.m.; Apr–June and Sept daily 9:30 a.m.–6:30 p.m.; Oct–Mar daily 9:30 a.m.–4:30 p.m.*

Other cool things to see and do

- ✔ **Brodie Castle,** 7 miles east of Nairn (☎ **01309-641-371;** www.nts.org.uk). It may be a bit austere — one may even say gloomy — but the castle has a good deal to explore. This is a particularly good stop for art fans; the collection of paintings is large, as is the volume of books.

- ✔ **Clanland/Storehouse of Foulis,** Evanton, 20 minutes north of Inverness (☎ **01349-830-000;** www.clanland.com). Clanland isn't as bad as it sounds. The interactive displays here focus on local music, food, topography, and clan history. You can watch a video that's a tribute to the powerful Highland Clan Munro. A small display focuses on seals that frequent the nearby beaches.

✔ **Dunrobin Castle,** Golspie, 50 miles north of Inverness (☎ **01408-633-177**). This fine castle once belonged to the earls and dukes of Sutherland and holds an excellent collection of tapestries and Louis XV–period furniture. The pieces are all amazingly intricate, and the family heirlooms on display are in good shape.

✔ **Fort George,** just off the A96 on the B9006 in Ardersier (☎ **01667-462-777**). Fort George still functions as a working army barracks, but it's also open to visitors, who may walk through the entire complex. Highlights include the magazine room stocked with old muskets and uniforms from the Napoleonic War, a museum filled with trophies and medals, and a drawbridge.

✔ **Glenmore Forest Park,** at Kincraig on the B9152 (☎ **01540-651-270;** www.forestry.gov.uk). This park isn't simply a place of stunning scenery full of Scottish flora and fauna. The attractions within the attraction include Wolf Territory and the Brightwater Burn otters (a burn is a stream or creek). You can drive through the main reserve and walk to the other attractions.

✔ **John Cobb Cairn,** between Drumnadrochit and Invermoriston. This memorial cairn (a pile of stones) is a place of pilgrimage for many who want to honor Cobb, who lost his life on Loch Ness in 1952 while making a second attempt at the world water speed record.

✔ **Nevis Range Gondola and Skiing,** 6 miles north of Fort William (☎ **01397-705-825;** www.nevisrange.co.uk/winter). This resort on Ben Nevis offers the only gondola in Scotland. The trip takes you halfway up Aonach Mor mountain, a panoramic 2,000-foot landmark that houses a restaurant, bar, and shops. You can hike paths around the area before returning down in the gondola in the warmer weather, or you can ski or snowboard to the bottom if the conditions are good. You'll find plenty of mountain bike trails around the base as well, and bike rentals are available. *Warning:* The winter resort has been on the brink of closure due to lack of snow.

✔ **Tain Through Time,** Tower Street in Tain (☎ **01862-894-089;** www.tainmuseum.demon.co.uk). This attraction is a combination museum, medieval church, audiovisual show, and self-guided tour. It offers a look at local archaeology and the religious history of this ancient burgh, with plenty of activities and displays geared toward kids.

Shopping in the Highlands

The only major shopping center in the area worth noting is the **Eastgate Shopping Centre,** 11 Eastgate, off High Street, in Inverness (www.inverness-eastgate.com). It has more than 50 shops in one spot, and that's a big deal for the Highlands. This American-style mall doesn't necessarily cater to tourists, but discerning shoppers can find plenty of bargains. Eastgate is open from 9 a.m. until 5:30 p.m. most days, closing at 8 p.m. on Thursdays and at 5 p.m. on Sundays. While you're on your shopping spree, make sure to take a gander at the fascinating ornamental clock that kicks into high gear at the top of every hour.

Also, Balnakeil Craft Village (see the listing in "The top attractions") is a good place to find unique gifts, while Ullapool (see the sidebar "Ullapool") has some interesting small shops. You may also consider:

- ✔ **Edinburgh Woollen Mills,** 13 High St., Fort William (☎ 01397-703-064) and 60 High St., at Monzie Square, Fort William (☎ 01397-704-737). Typical of woolen mill shops, these sister shops offer plenty of variety in finely crafted woolen and tweed apparel. The best part is their excellent bargains. Call for hours.

- ✔ **Highland Stoneware Pottery,** Mill Street, Ullapool (☎ 01854-612-980; www.highlandstoneware.com) and Lochinver, north of Ullapool on the coast road (☎ 01571-844-376). In just under three decades, Highland Stoneware has gained an international following. Visitors and orders for its unique freehand-decorated pottery come to the two shops from all over the world. The stores are open Monday through Friday from 9 a.m. to 6 p.m. and Saturdays in season only (Easter through October) from 9 a.m. to 5 p.m. They're closed two weeks around Christmas and New Year's.

- ✔ **Moniack Castle Wines,** Beauly Road, on the A862, 7 miles from Inverness (☎ 01463-831-283). This popular winery and gourmet food shop makes six wines and three liqueurs from natural ingredients such as birch bark. You can also purchase top-quality marmalades, sauces, jams, and chutneys, all made here, like the wine, from local ingredients. Moniack is open Monday through Saturday from 10 a.m. to 5 p.m.

- ✔ **Riverside Gallery,** 11 Bank St., Inverness (☎ 01463-224-781). This funky two-floor gallery on the east side of the River Ness has a wide range of traditional and contemporary pieces by Scottish artists. The gallery is open Monday through Friday from 9 a.m. to 5:30 p.m. and Saturday from 9 a.m. to 4:30 p.m.

- ✔ **The Whisky Shop,** Drumnadrochit, next to Loch Ness 2000 Exhibition (☎ 01456-450-321). This small chain of gourmet shops skips the key chains and postcards and goes for high-quality Scottish items. Excellent whisky products are obviously the main trade; you'll also find an impressive collection of china, silver, glassware, and gourmet jams and sweets, all 100 percent Scottish made. Call for hours.

Doing the Pub Crawl

The West Highlands have a good number of atmospheric, quintessentially Scottish pubs where you can relax and enjoy a bit of pub grub. Many of the rural inns have public bars and welcome anyone, whether guests of the hotel or not. Listed below are a few additional favorites.

- **Ben Nevis Pub,** 103–109 High St., Fort William (☎ **01397-702-295**). GOOD FOOD, GOOD BEER, GOOD COMPANY reads the motto along the roof beams of this old pub, and it's true on all accounts. The fireplace and pool table are nice, and you can often find live music on Thursday and Friday nights. Ben Nevis Pub is open daily from 11 a.m. to 1 a.m.

- **Claichaig Inn,** Glencoe, follow the sign from the A82 or walk across a footbridge from the visitor center (☎ **01855-811-252**). This rustic pub's wood-burning stove and staff's sunny disposition both warm the woody lounge and bar. The views are excellent, too. Climbers, tourists, and locals come here for a wee rest stop and excellent ales on tap. The pub's open Sunday through Thursday from 11 a.m. to 11 p.m., Friday from 11 a.m. to midnight, and Saturday from 11 a.m. to 11:30 p.m.

- **Mr. G's,** 9–21 Castle St., Inverness (☎ **01463-233-322**; www.mr-gs.co.uk). Mr. G's is the best place for dancing in Inverness. Flanked by two bars and some big booths, the center stage dance floor is augmented by a huge video screen on the wall above and a high-tech light show. The club's hours vary depending on the act, but its late license allows it to stay open until 3 a.m.

Fast Facts: The Highlands

Area Code

The area code for Aviemore is **01479**; Dornoch **01862**; Drumnadrochit **01456**; Fort William **01397**; Glencoe **01855**; Inverness **01463**; Nairn **01667**; and Ullapool **01854**. You need to dial the area code only if you're calling from outside the city you want to reach.

ATMs

ATMs are definitely few and far between in the Highlands, with the exception of Inverness and Fort William, where the most convenient ATMs may be at the Safeway (Morrisons) Supermarkets.

Emergencies

Dial ☎ **999** for police, fire, or ambulance.

Hospitals

The main hospital in the area is Raigmore Hospital, Inshes Road, Inverness (☎ 01463-704-000).

Information

For general information on the region, contact the Highlands Information Centre, Grampian Road, Aviemore (☎ 01479-810-363; www.highlandfreedom.com). Other tourist offices include: Castle Wynd, just off Bridge Street, Inverness (☎ 01463-23-4353); and Cameron Square, about halfway down the High Street, Fort William (☎ 01397-703-781). Summer offices are located at 62 King St., Nairn (☎ 01667-452-763) and 6 Argyle St., Ullapool (☎ 01854-612-135).

Internet Access

The best place to jump on the Web is the Electric Post Office, 93 High St., Nairn (☎ 01667-451-617). It's open daily from 10 a.m. to 10 p.m., and the cost is £4 ($6) per hour.

Mail

A central post office is located at 2 Greig St., Inverness (☎ 01463-233-610).

Chapter 19

Hebridean Islands

*T*he allure of the Hebridean (Heb-ri-*dee*-an) Islands isn't difficult to understand: The history, culture, and beauty of the landscape are all unique and captivating.

Getting to the Hebrides is half the fun, and when you arrive, you can be sure of a peaceful retreat from the mainland. But you should know a few things before you set out for these islands: Because the islands get fewer visitors than other places in Scotland, many businesses, including attractions and hotels, close in the off-season; due to some rather devout Protestantism, Sundays turn many smaller villages into virtual ghost towns; the Western Islands, home of the majority of Gaelic-speaking people in Scotland, have many signs posted only in Gaelic; and the Hebridean Islands get some of the most dramatic weather in Scotland — in summer, sunshine can be followed by rain falling horizontally.

Although the Hebrides chain is made up of several islands, this chapter covers only the more notable ones. Island hopping through the Hebrides can be fun, but it's also time-consuming. Alternatively, you can take excursions from the mainland to different isles for a taste of island life.

Getting to the Islands

One of the best things about any visit to the islands is the ferry ride. A network of boats links the Outer and Inner Hebrides to the mainland and, in some cases, to one another. You'll probably want a car to explore the islands, but you can get around easily enough without one.

Hebridean Islands

Ferry - - -
Mountain ▲

DINING ◆
Gannets **6**
Gruline Home Farm **4**
Rodel Hotel **11**

ATTRACTIONS ●
The Black House **19**
Butt of Lewis **20**
Calanais Standing Stones **17**
Doune Broch **18**
Duart Castle **5**
Eigg **8**
Iona Abbey and Nunnery **2**
North and South Uist **9**
St. Clement's Church **10**
Staffa and Fingal's Cave **3**
Torosay Castle and Gardens **5**
Western Isles Museum **16**

ACCOMMODATIONS/DINING ■
Ardhasaig House **13**
Ardvourlie Castle Guest House **14**
Argyll Hotel **1**
Cabarfeidh Hotel **15**
Harris Hotel **12**
St. Columba Hotel **1**
Seaforth Hotel **15**
Tobermory Hotel **7**
Western Isles Hotel **7**

✔ **By ferry:** The main provider of ferry services is **Caledonian MacBrayne** or CalMac (www.calmac.co.uk), as it's more colloquially known. The company serves 22 islands and 4 peninsulas over the western coast of Scotland. For general enquiries, call ☎ **01475-635-235** or **08705-650-100** or fax 01475-637-607. For reservations, call ☎ **08705-650-000** or fax 01475-635-235.

Main offices of CalMac in the region include Armadale, Skye (☎ **01471-844-248**); Craignure, Mull (☎ **01680-812-343**); and a host of others. You can find contact information for each office at www.calmac.co.uk/contact-us.html.

✔ **By train: First ScotRail** (☎ **0845-748-4950;** www.firstscotrail.com) runs trains to Kyle of Lochalsh, Mallaig, and Oban, terminuses on the mainland from which you can get connecting ferries to the islands. Regular passenger trains don't run on the islands. On Mull, however, a narrow gauge train runs the short trip from Craignure to Torosay Castle (☎ **01680-812-494;** www.mullrail.co.uk).

✔ **By bus:** From Glasgow, **Scottish Citylink** (☎ **0141-332-9644** or **0870-550-5050;** www.citylink.co.uk) runs buses to ferry ports such as Oban or Ullapool. After you reach the islands, bus services are run by local authorities and coverage is limited; each island basically has its own bus company, and my experience is that you have to be a patient and probably very ecologically minded visitor to use them. Renting a car on the islands is certainly more convenient.

✔ **By car:** You can drive onto Skye over the bridge at Kyle of Lochalsh, on the A87, which is the main road on the Isle of Skye. On Mull, the main road is the A849, which links Tobermory to Fionnophort via Craignure. You can also drive your car onto ferries to get to the main islands.

✔ **By plane:** The airport on Lewis (☎ **0345-222-111**) is 6.4km (4 miles) east of Stornoway, and you can arrange to fly there from Inverness or Glasgow, though flights are limited and very expensive. Inter-island flight services are offered from Barra, but it's not necessary to fly to these islands. Plus, taking the ferry is part of the fun of travel to the Hebrides.

Spending the Night

Because the islands have limited dining and drinking options, the accommodations listed in this section tend to include those where food and drink are part of the package. The larger islands offer more accommodations options; you should contact local tourist offices if you want to spend the night on a smaller island. Breakfast is included except where otherwise noted. See Chapter 8 for an explanation of the star ratings given by VisitScotland.com — also known as the Scottish Tourist Board — and for suggestions on self-catering cottages, which are a possible option on any island tour.

The Isle of Skye

0 | 10 mi
0 | 10 km

N

Ferry to Tarbert — Rubha Hunish
Kilmaluag
Skye Museum of
Island Life — A855
3
Balgown
Staffin Bay
Ferry to
← Lochmaddy
Vaternish Point
Staffin
Kilt
Rock
Redpoint
Lower
Diabaig
Ben
Geary
Idrigil — Uig
Culnaknock
Fearnmore
Loch Torridon
Dunvegan
Head
Loch
Snizort
A856
A855
RONA
Lusta
B886
The Storr
Sound of Raasay
Shieldaig
Dunvegan
Castle
Kensaleyre
Boreraig
Milovaig
2
Bernisdale
Borve
Beinn Bhan
1
Dunvegan
Carbost
Brochel
Applecross
B884
Healabhal
Bheag
Roskhill
Portree
B885
4
RAASAY
Toscaig
Castle ♜
Ferry - -
Mountain ▲
SKYE
5
6
Oskaig
Clachan
CROWLIN
ISLANDS
Inner Sound
Loch Kishorn
B883
A850
Portnalong
7
Peinchorran
Longay
Duirinish
Balmacara
Taliske O Carbost
Sligachan
Sconser
SCALPAY
Pabay
Kyle of
Lochalsh
A87
Loch Alsh
Beinn
Bhreac
8
CUILLIN
HILLS
Bla Bheinn
(Blaven)
Luib
A850
9
Broadford
Breakish
A850
Kyleakin
Kylerhea Ferry
Glenbrittle
Sgurr
Alasdair
Loch
Scavaig
B8083
Torrin
10
Beinn na
Seamvaig ▲
Glenelg
Loch Brittle
Sea of
the Hebrides
SOAY
Elgol
Loch Eishort
Isle Ornsay
11
Dunsgiath
Castle ♜
SLEAT
Teangue
12
Loch Hourn
CANNA
Clan Donald
Visitor Centre
Knock
Castle ♜
A851
Sound of Sleat
KNOYDART
Sound of Canna
Killmory
13
14
Ardvasar
Aird of Sleat
RHUM
(RUM)
Kinloch
Point of Sleat
Ferry to
Mallaig

**Area of
detail**
SCOTLAND
⊛
Edinburgh
0   20 mi
0   20 km   ENGLAND

DINING ◆
Chandlery **5**
Creelers **10**
Kinloch Lodge **11**
Three Chimneys Restaurant **1**

ATTRACTIONS ●
Armadale Castle Gardens & Museum of the Isles **14**
Aros Heritage Centre and Aros Experience **6**
Dunvegan Castle **2**
Skye Museum of Island Life and Flora MacDonald's Grave **3**
Talisker Distillery Visitor Centre **7**

ACCOMMODATIONS ■
Ardvasar Hotel **13**
Cuillin Hills Hotel **4**
Dunollie Hotel **9**
Hotel Eilean Iarmain **12**
The Rosedale **4**
The Royal Hotel **4**
Sligachan Hotel **8**

Ardhasaig House
$$–$$$ Ardhasaig, Harris

This small, six-unit hotel is fairly remote, but the reward for making it here is the view of the nearby bay and mountains. The bar is surprisingly modern, and the food is always interesting; the menu changes pretty much on a daily basis, emphasizing what is fresh and locally available. Rooms are comfortably (if basically) furnished and some include antique furniture while all have views either of the hills or of the sea. In 2004, the old stone barn was converted into a self-contained suite with a king size sleigh bed and sheepskin rugs.

See map p. 371. A859, 3 miles north of Tarbert, Ardhasaig. ☎ *01859-502-066. Fax: 01859-502-077. www.ardhasaig.co.uk. Rack rates: £110 ($203) double. MC, V. Closed Nov.*

Ardvasar Hotel
$$ **Ardvasar, Skye**

This lovely hotel, pub, and restaurant is a good bet for a stay in the southern part of Skye. Near Armadale Castle and the ferry terminal (from Mallaig), the Ardvasar Hotel sits on the edge of the Sound of Sleat. Rooms are sizable and comfortable, with lovely views of the water and the rugged landscape of the island's interior. The food is about as good as it gets in the area, and the pub bustles with grinning locals: It has been accurately described as the hub of the local community.

See map p. 373. Just off the A851 before the ferry terminal, Ardvasar. ☎ *01471-844-223. Fax: 01471-844-495. www.ardvasarhotel.com. Rack rates: £85 ($157) double; £130 ($240) double with dinner. MC, V.*

Ardvourlie Castle Guest House
$$$–$$$$ **Aird Amhulaidh, Harris**

This castle sits on a remote spot near the Lewis-Harris border, along the main road connecting the two. Nearby hills rise up behind the castle, which overlooks Loch Seaforth. Ardvourlie was built in 1863 for the Earl of Dunmore and has been restored with period furnishings and fabrics. The dining room has real gas lighting, and the Victorian motif extends to the well-designed guest rooms and the wood paneling and brass faucets in the huge bathrooms. The sculptured lawns, home to 7,000 trees, are worth a stroll. With only four rooms available, booking in advance is a must. I could go on and on about the gourmet meals, but seeing as the room rate includes dinner (and breakfast), you'll see for yourself. Payment is in cash or traveler's checks only.

See map p. 371. Just south of the Harris-Lewis border on the A859, Aird Amhulaidh. ☎ *01859-502-307. Fax: 01859-502-348. Rack rates: £200 ($370) double. Children under 12 half price. Rate includes dinner. No credit cards.*

Argyll Hotel
$$–$$$ **Argyll, Iona**

This environmentally conscientious hotel, originally built in 1868 as the village inn, complements the spiritual nature of Iona, where St. Columba made his historic pilgrimage over 1,000 years ago. The outstanding and obliging hospitality makes up for what may be lacking in smallish units. But why hang out in your room when you can spend time in the sitting rooms or the garden room, all of which face the water? The package that includes dinner comes recommended — not least because some of the ingredients in your meal are actually grown in the hotel's own organic garden.

See map p. 371. 200 yards from the harbor, Argyll. ☎ *01681-700-334. Fax: 01681-700-510.* www.argyllhoteliona.co.uk. *Rack rates: £64–£174 ($118–$321) double (includes dinner). MC, V.*

Cabarfeidh Hotel
$$ Stornoway, Lewis

The finest modern accommodation on Lewis sits in the middle of an eight-acre garden just outside of Stornoway. The rooms are large and well upholstered, and the staff is top-notch. The restaurant specializes in local seafood and has various areas, from a conservatory to a garden room.

See map p. 371. Manor Park, between Laxdale and Newmarket, Stornoway. ☎ *01851-702-604. Fax: 01851-705-572.* www.calahotelscom/hotels/caber.shtm. *Rack rates: £108 ($199) double. AE, DC, MC, V.*

Cuillin Hills Hotel
$$–$$$ Portree, Skye

About a ten-minute walk from the center of Portree, this 19th-century hunting lodge features excellent views of Portree Bay and nearby Cuillin crags. The hotel has 27 rooms and is popular with hikers, birders, and sportsmen — the comfort and friendliness appeal to everyone. The conservatory is a great place to relax, and the rooms are full of quality furniture and also have large bathrooms. The surrounding grounds encompass some 15 acres. On a historical note, the lodge was built for the Macdonald clan that once ruled the island. The restaurant here regularly earns praise for its seafood and traditional Scottish dishes.

See map p. 373. Off the main road, just north of town, Portree. ☎ *01478-612-003. Fax: 01478-613-092.* www.cuillinhills-hotel-skye.co.uk. *Rack rates: £120–£220 ($222–$407) double. AE, MC, V.*

Dunollie Hotel
$$ Broadford, Skye

The Dunollie Hotel sits on the old harbor wall in Broadford, with views across to Loch Kishorn and the Applecross hills. You may even catch a glimpse of a whale or dolphins in the sea. Refurbished a few years ago, the 84-unit hotel is a welcoming holiday base from which to explore the Isle of Skye. The Dunollie offers a combination of Skye charm and modern-day comforts; its friendly, well-trained staff ensures that your stay on the "Misty Isle" is an enjoyable one.

See map p. 373. On the A87, Broadford. ☎ *01471-822-253. Fax: 01471-822-060.* www.british-trust-hotels.com. *Rack rates: £95 ($175) double; £131 ($242) double with dinner. MC, V.*

Harris Hotel
$$ Tarbert, Harris

You can't find a much more convenient location in Harris than this hotel near the ferry terminal. The pretty, whitewashed building, built in 1865, has 1970s-era décor, a comfortable selection of rooms (including family units), a large garden, and a wonderful sun lounge. One guest, *Peter Pan* author J.M. Barrie, mischievously etched his initials in a window.

See map p. 371. Near the Tarbert ferry terminal, 23 miles from Leverburgh, Tarbert. ☎ *01859-502-154. Fax: 01859-502-281.* www.harrishotel.com. *Rack rates: £79–£109 ($146–$201) double; £123–£153 ($227–$283) double with dinner. MC, V.*

Hotel Eilean Iarmain
$$$ Isleornsay, Skye

The Eilean Iarmain combines quintessential Highland hospitality with tranquility and beautiful surroundings. Many of the century-old building's original antiques are intact, and each of the 12 rooms contains period furniture. The finest room is perhaps *Te Bheag,* or "Whisky One," which contains a canopy bed that apparently was once used in Armadale Castle. The views of the Isleornsay harbor from the country house hotel are picture-postcard perfect, especially at sunset. In addition to the units in the main building, suites have been added to the converted 19th-century stable blocks. Another plus: The hotel is open year-round.

See map p. 373. A8561, Isleornsay. ☎ *01471-833-332. Fax: 01471-833-275.* www.eileaniarmain.co.uk. *Rack rates: £125–£190 ($231–$351) double. AE, MC, V.*

The Rosedale
$$–$$$ Portree, Skye

This nice white set of former fishermen's houses near the water's edge is warmly decorated, giving the place a snug B&B feel. An eccentric layout of stairs and corridors connects lounges, bar, and restaurant. The main building has cozy rooms simply decorated while those in another wing are more individually decorated. Most of the units in either wing, however, overlook the harbor. Dinners normally reflect seasonal produce.

See map p. 373. On the harbor, Beaumont Crescent, Quay Brae, Portree. ☎ *01478-613-131. Fax: 01478-612-531.* www.rosedalehotelskye.co.uk. *Rack rates: £60–£116 ($111–$214) double. MC, V. Closed mid-Nov–mid-Mar.*

The Royal Hotel
$$ Portree, Skye

In a great spot between the pier and town, just opposite the tourist information office, the Royal is a fine, recently refurbished hotel. The rooms aren't fancy but are quite comfortable, and for a little extra cash you can get a "superior" room with nicer views. Some of the units can comfortably accommodate families. Another treat for this part of the world is the hotel's gym and steam room. Entertainment, particularly Scottish folk music, is brought in most nights in the summer. In addition to a restaurant, the Royal is also home to the casual eatery, Well Plaid.

See map p. 373. Bank Street, Portree. ☎ **01478-612-525**. *Fax: 01478-613-198.* www . royal-hotel-skye.com. *Rack rates: £88–£93 ($162–$172) double; £118–£124 ($218–$229) double with dinner. AE, DC, MC, V.*

St. Columba Hotel
$$$ Argyll, Iona

Between the sun lounges and the lovely dining area at this hotel, you won't be at a loss for pretty views of the water even if your room faces the other direction. This more upscale hotel (a converted and expanded church manse dating from 1846) edges out the Argyll Hotel (see listing earlier in this chapter) only in its larger and better-furnished rooms. A hotel car collects you and your bags at the boat jetty when you arrive. The service is fine and the food generally quite good, although if you love seafood, this is the best dining option on the island. St. Columba, as you may expect, is very close to the island's main attraction, the Abbey.

See map p. 371. One quarter mile from Iona jetty, Argyll. ☎ **01681-700-304**. *Fax: 01681-700-688.* www.stcolumba-hotel.co.uk. *Rack rates: £120–£138 ($222–$255) double with dinner. MC, V.*

Seaforth Hotel
$$ Stornoway, Lewis

The Seaforth is the most modern hotel is these parts. The contemporary-style furnishings and décor don't attempt to conform to tradition, and the hotel looks vaguely like it could be located just about anywhere in the world. Nevertheless, rooms are comfortable, and most come with all modern conveniences — although not every room has a private bath.

See map p. 371. 11 James St., Stornoway. ☎ **01851-702-740**. *Fax: 01851-703-900.* www . calahotels.com/hotels/sea.shtm. *Rack rates: From £85 ($157) double. AE, MC, V.*

Sligachan Hotel
$$ Sligachan, Skye

This fun little 22-room hotel books live music and has plenty to occupy the wee ones, such as video games, a playroom, outdoor rec equipment, and a playground. It was built in the 1830s and retains much of its original stonework, a classic look that complements the stunning location at the head of a sea loch and the foot of the Cuillin Hills. Most of the rooms (rather basic and a touch old-fashioned) have a view (choose between the loch and the hills), and cots are available for young kids. Located in the middle of Skye, the Sligachan is ideal for visiting both sides of the island. The popular Seumas' Bar serves meals for young kids, too.

See map p. 373. 9 miles south of Portree on the A87, Sligachan. ☎ **01478-650-204.** *Fax: 01478-650-207.* www.sligachan.co.uk. *Rack rates: £80–£100 ($148–$185) double. MC, V.*

Tobermory Hotel
$$ Tobermory, Mull

All the buildings at the harbor in Tobermory are brightly painted in pastel colors, and the Tobermory Hotel is no exception — it was pink on my last visit. A stay here is like a visit with a favorite grandmother, if that grandmother lives in a pretty fisherman's cottage on the waterfront of a lovely harbor town on the northern end of a Hebridean Island. With comfy beds, home cooking, and a smile to greet you at the door, it's like coming home. The hotel has three family rooms and offers extra cots as well as a toy box, games, and books for the kids.

See map p. 371. 53 Main St., Tobermory. ☎ **01688-302-091.** *Fax: 01688-302-254.* www. thetobermoryhotel.com. *Rack rates: £82–£102 ($151–$188) double. AE, MC, V.*

Western Isles Hotel
$$ Tobermory, Mull

Fans of the great black-and-white movie *I Know Where I'm Going!* (see Chapter 2) should recognize this hotel on the hill above Tobermory. A Victorian stone-front building overlooking the bay below, it exudes charm and hospitality. The staff is cheery and helpful, and the rooms are nicely furnished, some with a tartan or floral theme and canopy beds. The hotel occupies a desirable spot, and several rooms have views of the harbor. Still, the best vista in the house is from the refurbished conservatory.

See map p. 371. Main Street, Tobermory. ☎ **01688-302-012.** *Fax: 01688-302-297.* www. mullhotel.com. *Rack rates: £99–£124 ($183–$229) double. AE, MC, V.*

Dining Locally

Few restaurants on the Hebridean Islands can thrive independently of a hotel (not enough locals to keep them in business), so most of your dining options are likely to come from the previous section. However, a few other restaurants stand out. Also, it isn't listed below, but you should seek out the fish and chip van at Tobermory harbor — it produces possibly the best "fish suppers" in all of Scotland.

Chandlery
$$$ Portree, Skye   FRENCH

The Chandlery (in the Bosville Hotel) occupies a lovely setting on the cliff overlooking Portree harbor. With minimalist décor in the dining area, the place has an airy feel. The staff is efficient and professional, serving up such gourmet treats as a starter of carved Gaelic rose of melon. Seafood specialties include monkfish and a steamed lobster that would make a

Maine native blush with pleasure. If you're staying at the hotel, you can enjoy the Chandlery's excellent breakfasts, as well.

See map p. 373. In the Bosville Hotel, Bosville Terrace, Portree. ☎ *01478-612-846. Reservations recommended. Main courses: £13–£16 ($24–$30). AE, MC, V. Open: Jan–Mar daily 8 a.m.–9:30 p.m.; Apr–Dec daily 8 a.m.–10 p.m.*

Creelers
$$–$$$ Broadford, Skye   SEAFOOD/MEDITERRANEAN

Don't be put off by the size of this tiny, simply decorated restaurant: The food is usually outstanding. Among some Cajun- and Mediterranean-influenced dishes, diners also find traditional dishes such as haggis with neeps and tatties (turnips and potatoes), scrumptious mushroom and broccoli pie, and plenty of local seafood. The pride of the menu is the "authentic" seafood gumbo made with local fish and shellfish.

See map p. 373. Broadford. ☎ *01471-822-281. Reservations not accepted. Main courses: £8–£15 ($15–$28). AE, MC, V. Open: daily noon–2 p.m. and 5–10 p.m.*

Gannets
$–$$ Tobermory, Mull   SCOTTISH

Don't let the plastic tablecloths and somewhat cheesy décor put you off; Gannets has friendly service and excellent Scottish cuisine, such as Tobermory smoked trout or homemade pork in cider and cream. The restaurant is right on the main street overlooking the harbor, and its prices are attractive as well.

See map p. 371. 25 Main St., Tobermory. ☎ *01688-302-203. Reservations not accepted. Main courses: £5–£10 ($9.25–$18.50). MC, V. Open: Apr–Oct daily 10 a.m.–10 p.m.; Nov–Mar daily 10 a.m.–3:30 p.m.*

Gruline Home Farm
$$$ Gruline, Mull   SCOTTISH

Meals here have an excellent reputation, but they're served only by prior arrangement, so don't consider dropping in for a bite as I foolishly did. Dishes are made from mostly local produce.

See map p. 371. Off the BB8035, southwest of Salen. ☎ *01680-300-581. Reservations required. Fixed-price dinner: £30 ($55). Open: call for availability.*

Kinloch Lodge
$$$ Isleornsay, Skye   SCOTTISH

Kinloch is the home of the Macdonalds, and the lady of the house, Lady Clarie Macdonald, has become well-known in the Scottish culinary world. The lodge regularly hosts special cooking weekends when guests see demonstrations, do some cooking, and, of course, eat themselves silly. In addition to the restaurant, Kinloch has 14 overnight rooms in the 17th-century hunting lodge.

See map p. 373. By the A851, 3 miles north of Isleornsay. ☎ *01471-833-214.* www . kinloch-lodge.co.uk. *Reservations required. Fixed-price dinner: £38 ($70). AE, MC, V. Open: dinner only; call for availability.*

Rodel Hotel
$$ Rodel, Harris MODERN BRITISH

A godsend on a Sunday in the Hebrides (it's open!), the Rodel Hotel combines some excellent local produce with contemporary touches, which extend to the art on the walls. Near St. Clement's Church (see "The top attractions," later in this chapter), the restaurant features dishes such as "trawlerman" fish soup with crusty bread, homemade pâté with oatcakes, roast rib of beef with Yorkshire pudding, and pan-roasted monkfish tails with garlic, rosemary, and white wine.

See map p. 371. ☎ *01859-520-210. Fax: 01859-520-219.* www.rodelhotel.co.uk. *Fixed-price dinner: £19.50 ($36) for three courses. MC, V. Open: daily noon–5 p.m. and 5:30–9:30 p.m.*

Three Chimneys Restaurant
$$$–$$$$ Colbost, Skye SCOTTISH

It's easy to understand why this whitewashed shore-side restaurant is probably the most popular on Skye. Serving superb Scottish cuisine with produce from the island, chef proprietor Shirley Spear offers the highest-quality seafood and Highland game dishes, such as venison and wild hare, along with homemade soups, breads, and puddings. Cozy twin fireplaces warm the dining area. The menu changes seasonally; in the summer, try one of the organically grown salads with herbs and veggies.

See map p. 373. 4 miles from Dunvegan on the B884 road to Glendale, Colbost. ☎ *01470-511-258.* www.threechimneys.co.uk. *Reservations required. Fixed-price 4-course dinner: £48 ($89). MC, V. Open: Mon–Sat noon–2 p.m. and 7–9 p.m. Closed Sun and Nov–Mar.*

Exploring the Hebrides

From the spiritual mecca of Iona to the tourist kitsch of the Aros Experience to the many ancient and royal attractions in between, the Hebridean Islands offer a lot, with no shortage of natural beauty. Indeed, the islands are attractions in themselves, but you'll find plenty to see besides the scenery.

The biggest island in the Hebrides is the **Isle of Skye.** Thanks to a controversial bridge (well, the toll is controversial), visitors can drive onto it at Kyle of Lochalsh or take a ferry from the mainland harbor of Mallaig further south. Skye offers stunning landscapes, historic attractions, and a good deal of accommodation and dining options. Fifty miles long and 23 miles wide, Skye is a treat to drive across, with a beautiful landscape between the sea and the Cuillin Hills. **Portree,** the capital of the island, is a small, quaint town on the water and a comfortable base from which to explore all the Skye attractions.

Next in accessibility is **Mull,** home to the picturesque port of **Tobermory,** some castles, and the added value of little sister island **Iona.** Mull is known as the rainiest of the Hebridean Islands. After you arrive in **Craignure** (which has little to offer other than the nearby castles of Duart and Torosay), you can either head north to **Tobermory** or west toward **Fionnphort** to catch the ferry to the island of Iona. Give yourself an hour no matter which way you decide to go — the roads turn into single lanes in both directions. Tobermory, the largest town on Mull, is worth a visit. Brightly painted houses and storefronts in shades of blue, red, and yellow give Tobermory the look of a little Copenhagen and the feel of an Italian fishing village. To see Mull and Iona in a day, Bowman's Tours (ferry and coach) run from Oban from April through October. Fares are around £30 ($55). Call ☎ **01631-566-809** for more information.

Beyond Skye are the connected islands of **Lewis** and **Harris** (the latter being famous for its tweed), the primary isles of the Outer Hebrides. On Lewis and Harris, you arrive at the ferry terminal in Tarbert. The southern coastal drive is an attraction in itself — the rocky moonscape soon transforms into a Gulf Stream miracle of beaches and blue waters. Lewis is larger and has more attractions than its southern cousin, and its town of **Stornoway** is the largest on the dual islands.

Some of the other islands — **Barra, Coll, Eigg, Rhum,** and **North** and **South Uist** — are smaller, sparsely populated, and not entirely geared to tourism, although a few can provide daytrip opportunities.

The top attractions

Armadale Castle Gardens & Museum of the Isles
Armadale, Skye

The Armadale estate covers more than 20,000 acres traditionally belonging to the clan Donald or Macdonald, known as the Lords of Isles, but now held in trust. The old castle is in ruins but occupies a magnificent spot with 19th-century woodland gardens, nature trails, and sea views. It isn't difficult to understand the allure of this place. On the grounds you can find a museum full of information about and artifacts of the Macdonalds. The museum is usually of interest to non-Macdonalds, but those who share the common surname may want to visit the library and study center, which assists with genealogical research. The castle grounds are home to a large variety of different trees and plants, all flourishing thanks to the Gulf Stream breezes, and the gardener gives occasional tours of his award-winning grounds. Allow about 2 hours.

See map p. 373. Armadale Road, just north of the pier on the A851, Sleat. ☎ *01471-844-305.* www.clandonald.com. *Admission: £4 ($7.40) adults; £3 ($5.50) seniors, students, and children under 16; £12 ($22) family. Open: Mar–Oct daily 9 a.m.–5:30 p.m. Closed Nov–Feb.*

Aros Heritage Centre and Aros Experience
Portree, Skye

A more touristy roadside attraction had not been built on Scottish soil when the Aros Experience, with its life-size historical mannequins, first opened. However, the more recent addition of the Heritage Centre has shifted this attraction's focus to a theatre that hosts drama, music, and movies. Allow about 1 hour.

See map p. 373. Viewfield Road, just south of town on the A87. ☎ *01478-613-649.* www.aros.co.uk. *Admission: £3 ($4.35) adults; £2 ($2.90) seniors, students, and children under 16; £7 ($10) family. Open: summer daily 9 a.m.–11 p.m.; off-season daily 9 a.m.–6 p.m.*

The Black House
Arnol, Lewis

Another Historic Scotland property, this attraction steps back a couple of hundred years in island living. Visitors explore a restored traditional Hebridean thatched house, a "black house," which was a structure that served as both home and barn. This one on Lewis is about as quaint as can be. Visitors are free to poke around and visit the information center for more background on this way of life; the center doesn't paint a pretty picture of the rather rough living. This house, built in 1885 and occupied until 1964, is the only authentically maintained traditional black house. Allow about 1½ hours.

The burning peat fire has been known to sometimes fill the house with smoke, but that's the cost of authenticity.

See map p. 371. 11 miles north of Stornoway, off the A858. ☎ *01851-710-395.* www.historic-scotland.gov.uk. *Admission: £3 ($5.50) adults, £2.30 ($4.25) seniors and students, £1 ($1.85) children. Open: Apr–Sept Mon–Sat 9:30 a.m.–6:30 p.m.; Oct–Mar Mon–Thurs and Sat 9:30 a.m.–4:30 p.m.*

Butt of Lewis
Lewis

These beautiful high cliffs overlooking the ocean are worth the drive to the tip of Lewis. You see seabirds, seals, and spectacular windblown waves crashing against the rocks. The only building on the Butt is a magnificent lighthouse, which adds even more grandeur to the scene. Look for the large hole in the ground near the parking area; legend has it that the Vikings cut the hole in an attempt to drag the island back to Norway with them. Allow about 1 hour here.

See map p. 371.

Calanais Standing Stones
Lewis

Known as the "Scottish Stonehenge," this ancient cross-shaped formation of large stones is the most significant archaeological find of its kind in the country. There's no charge to see the stones, which were erected sometime around 3,000 BC, but visitors should not miss the visitor center, which helps put the site in context. The exhibit explores theories on the stones' function and shows what life would have been like at the time they were erected. If you're here during the summer solstice, you'll find tents pitched near the monoliths — Calanais is a popular spot for New Agers to come and celebrate the longest day of the year. Allow 2 hours.

See map p. 371. Off the A859, 12 miles west of Stornoway. ☎ *01851-621-422.* www.historic-scotland.gov.uk. *Admission: stones: free; visitor center: £2 ($3.70) adults, £1.50 ($2.75) seniors and students, £1 ($1.85) children under 16. Open: stones: year-round, 24 hours; visitor center: Apr–Sept Mon–Sat 10 a.m.–7 p.m.; Oct–Mar Wed–Sat 10 a.m.–4 p.m.*

Cuillin Hills
Skye

These dark and massive hills are a point of pride for the residents of Skye. Considered some of the best climbing and walking real estate in Scotland, the 3,000-foot peaks lie along the southern part of the island. You should consider spending an afternoon hiking the hills, but if you're not an experienced walker, you may want to enquire about professional guides at the tourist office.

See map p. 373.

Doune Broch
Carloway, Lewis

This interesting home (a "broch" is a stone tower used for defensive purposes and as a home) from the Iron Age is in remarkably good condition — good enough for you to walk through and on. The ruins — properly called Dun Carloway — provide insight into life long ago, a life that seems oddly comfortable. Regardless of the time of year and weather outside, stepping into the broch provides instant protection from any chill. Allow 1½ hours.

See map p. 371. On the A858, west side of Lewis. ☎ *01851-643-338. Admission: free. Open: broch: year-round, 24 hours; visitor center: Apr–Oct Mon–Sat 10 a.m.–6 p.m.*

Duart Castle
Near Craignure, Mull

Fans of the 1945 film *I Know Where I'm Going!* should recognize the drawing room in this fine castle. Overlooking the Sound of Mull and best seen from the ferry from Oban, Duart was abandoned in 1751 but, thanks to the efforts of Fitzroy Maclean, was restored from ruins in 1911. When you're inside, make your way up the narrow, twisting stairs and you can walk outside on the parapet at the top of the castle. As the ancestral home of the clan Maclean, one floor is devoted to clan history, with various references to the 17th-century battle cry: "Another for Hector!" Today, Duart Castle remains the home for the 28th chief of clan Maclean. There are no special gardens to tour, but visiting the grounds is free of charge. Allow 1½ hours.

See map p. 371. Off the A849, 3 miles southeast of Craignure. ☎ *01680-812-309.* www. duartcastle.com. *Admission: £4.50 ($8.30) adults, £4 ($7.40) seniors and students, £2.25 ($4.20) children under 16, £11.25 ($21) family. Open: Apr daily 11 a.m.–4 p.m.; May–mid-Oct daily 10:30 a.m.–5:30 p.m. Closed mid-Oct–Mar.*

Dunvegan Castle
Dunvegan, Skye

The seat of the Macleod chiefs, Dunvegan is Scotland's oldest castle with continual ownership by the same family, going on 800 years now. In addition to antiques, oil paintings, rare books, and clan heirlooms — some dating well into the Middle Ages — the castle is home to the legendary Fairy Flag, thought to bring "miraculous powers" to the clan Macleod. Also on display at Dunvegan are personal items belonging to Bonnie Prince Charlie and a reasonably creepy dungeon as well as mementos from visits by Queen Elizabeth, Sir Walter Scott, and Dr. Samuel Johnson. Don't miss the stunning grounds, mainly planted with azaleas and rhododendrons. Particularly impressive is the Walled Garden, a perfectly manicured display of unique flora, statues, and tranquil fountains and pools. After you take in the castle, and especially if you have kids with you or you like wildlife, why not take a short seal boat ride? You get up close and personal with the seals who live on the tiny islands in the bay below the castle — and if you don't, you get a refund on the price of the ride. Allow 2 hours.

See map p. 373. Duirinish Peninsula, on the 850, on the west side of Skye. ☎ *01470-521-206.* www.dunvegancastle.com. *Admission: castle: £6.50 ($12) adults, £6 ($11) seniors and students, £4 ($7.50) children under 16; seal tour: £5 ($9.25) adults, £2.50 ($4.60) children 5–15, free for children under 5. Open: mid-Mar–Oct daily 10 a.m.–5 p.m.; Nov–mid-Mar daily 11 a.m.–4 p.m.*

Eigg

The isle of Eigg lies just off the west coast of Scotland and can be reached from either Mallaig or Arisaig. The latter offers summer cruises (on the *Sheerwater*), which often have the bonus of whale-sightings on the hour-long trip. Eigg is the most populated of the so-called Small Isles, but it's hardly crowded. A few years ago the inhabitants set up a trust to buy the island from the laird. Visitors can take a variety of walks on the island, including the slightly strenuous hike up the major geographical feature, Sgurr Ridge. Easier is the trek to see chapel ruins on Kildonan Bay. A small tea room and place to rent bicycles are located at the small pier. Eigg is close enough to Arisaig that you can easily make a daytrip of it and get a small dose of island life. For information on sailings from Arisaig on the *Sheerwater,* log onto www.arisaig.co.uk or call ☎ **016878-450-224.**

See map p. 371. www.isleofeigg.org.

Iona Abbey and Nunnery
Iona

This spiritual landmark is a significant shrine to the early, early days of Christianity in Scotland. The abbey (of both historic and sacred value) was established by St. Columba, the Irish pilgrim who almost single-handedly brought religion to a pagan land in the sixth century. The abbey is a large building in very good shape, having undergone several restorations since the 13th century. Crosses laid into the abbey floor mark the graves of several monks buried under the monastery, and three impressive crosses stand on the grounds, which you should give yourself extra time to explore. The St. Columba interpretive center is free but open only in the summer from 11 a.m. to 5 p.m. Allow about 1½ hours.

See map p. 371. Iona. ☎ *01681-700-512.* www.historic-scotland.gov.uk. *Admission: £3.30 ($6) adult, £2.50 ($4.60) seniors and students, £1.20 ($2.20) children; tour: £2 ($2.90) contribution requested. Open: Apr–Sept daily 9:30 a.m.–6:30 p.m.; Oct–Mar daily 9:30 a.m.–4:30 p.m. (depending on ferry from Mull).*

North and South Uist

Although no single attraction on North and South Uist (pronounced yewst) stands out, the islands can be worth a visit if you're already on Lewis and Harris or northern Skye — and have a full day to cross the mostly rural landscape and take in the sights, scenery, and landmarks. At the Balranald Nature Reserve, you can spot waders and seabirds. The ruins of Flora MacDonald's birthplace are near Milton. And the Kildonan Museum and Heritage Centre covers local culture, history, and archaeological finds. You can drive through the Uists, but buses also run the length of the islands.

See map p. 371.

St. Clement's Church
Rodel, Harris

You may wonder if it's worth the drive to the southern tip of Harris to see this far-flung attraction. It is. At the end of the wonderful drive on the amazing coastal route full of white beaches and aqua-blue waters, you arrive at this small but well-preserved 16th-century church, named after a saint who is popular in Norway. The most impressive feature inside the cruciform church is the carved tomb of Alexander MacLeod of Dunvegan, who built the church. Panels include apostle effigies and other religious symbols. Allow 1 hour.

See map p. 371. On the A859, Rodel. Admission: free. Open: daily dawn to dusk.

Skye Museum of Island Life and Flora MacDonald's Grave
Kilmuir, Skye

This "museum" consists of seven black houses (structures acting as both home and barn), each showing how people lived on Skye a century ago. The re-created crofter (farm) homes contain antique domestic items, agricultural tools, and photographs of island life. If you follow the path from the museum up to Kilmuir Cemetery, you can see the grave of the legendary Flora MacDonald, the woman credited with saving Prince Charlie's hide. Bonnie Prince Charlie lived in hiding on Skye after the battle of Culloden and escaped disguised as MacDonald's maid. She was later arrested for her assistance and held in the Tower of London for eight months; she was moved to North Carolina in the United States during the Revolutionary War and then back to Skye before she died. This lovely little museum, full of old pictures and documents, tells her story and the island's. Allow 1 hour.

See map p. 373. On the A855, north from Portree. ☎ *01470-552-206.* www.skye museum.co.uk. *Admission: £1.75 ($3.25) adults; £1 ($1.85) seniors, students, and children under 16. Open: Apr–Oct Mon–Sat 9 a.m.–5:30 p.m. Closed Nov–Mar.*

Staffa and Fingal's Cave

Just a short boat trip from Mull, the uninhabited isle of Staffa is an attraction worth seeing if you're spending time in the Mull-Iona area. Visitors enjoy watching the sea crash against the dramatic, vertical rock formations here, especially the cathedral-like columns of Fingal's Cave. The cave is one of the natural wonders of the world and is famous for being the inspiration for Mendelssohn's *Hebridean Overture.* Birders, take note: Staffa is home to a large puffin colony. Unfortunately, in the mid-season, some of the boats won't sail if they don't get enough reservations. Various ferry services offer trips to Staffa: Iolaire (☎ **01681-700-358**) departs from Fionnphort and Iona, while Turus Mara (☎ **0800-858-786** or 01688-302-808; www.turusmara.com) departs from Ulva Ferry, on the west side of Mull. Excursions are generally available from Easter through September.

See map p. 371.

Talisker Distillery Visitor Centre
Carbost, Skye

As whisky distillery tours go, Talisker's may be among the best. Enthusiastic and expert guides take visitors through the distillery, expounding on the virtues of their single malt whisky and its unique production process. Although the single malt they produce is one of the most distinctive whiskies in all of Scotland, about 90 percent of the nearly 2 million liters of whisky made at Talisker annually goes into blends such as Dewar's and Johnnie Walker. At the end of the tour, do a tasting and note the smoky peat taste that's so characteristic of whiskies made on the islands. Allow 1 hour.

See map p. 373. On the B8009, just off the A863, which joins the A87 at Sligachan. ☎ *01478-614-308. Admission: £3.50 ($6.50). Open: July–Sept Mon–Sat 9:30 a.m.–5 p.m.; Apr–June and Oct Mon–Fri 9:30 a.m.–5 p.m.; Nov–Mar Mon–Fri 2–5 p.m.*

Torosay Castle and Gardens
Craignure, Mull

Unlike nearby Duart Castle, Torosay is a relatively modern house, built in the Victorian era. Access here is more limited, too, because most of Torosay is still a private home. For many visitors, the surrounding gardens are the real attraction. The 12 acres of well-manicured grounds abound with fine and unique flora, Romanesque statues, and ivy-covered walls. You're welcome to explore the greenhouse and are encouraged to stop and smell the roses; this stop is a treat for anyone with a green thumb. Photography buffs appreciate the views of the Sound of Mull and background mountains, and children usually enjoy the small-scale train that runs to Torosay from Craignure. Allow 1½ hours.

See map p. 371. Off the A849. ☎ *01680-812-421.* www.torosay.com. *Admission: castle and gardens: £5 ($9.25) adults, £4 ($7.40) seniors and students, £1.75 ($3.25) children under 16, £12 ($22) family; gardens only: £4 ($7.40) adults, £3 ($5.50) seniors and students, £1.25 ($2.30) children, £10 ($18.50) family. Open: Apr–mid-Oct 10:30 a.m.– 5:30 p.m.*

Western Isles Museum (Museum nan Eilean)
Stornoway, Lewis

This museum is home to excellent exhibits on various aspects of island life. Although the museum has no permanent collection, the displays, usually borrowed from other museums and collections around the islands and the Scottish mainland, are of excellent quality and significant historical importance. This museum is definitely worth a visit — and you can't beat the price. Allow 1½ hours.

See map p. 371. Francis Street, Stornoway. ☎ *01851-709-266. Admission: free. Open: Apr–Sept Mon–Sat 10 a.m.–5:30 p.m.; Oct–Mar Tues–Fri 10 a.m.–5 p.m., Sat 10 a.m.– 1 p.m.*

Other cool things to see and do

✔ **Aros Castle,** near Salen, Mull. Today, the castle's just a monumental pile of rocks in the shape of a ruined castle keep, on a hill overlooking Salen Bay. But it was at one time a stronghold of the MacDougalls and the Lords of the Isles. Aros, at least during my visit, was not fenced off.

✔ **Mull Theatre,** Tobermory, Mull (☎ **01688-302-828;** www.mull theatre.com). This surprisingly accomplished dramatic company tours Scotland and performs at its own wee theatre in Dervaig.

✔ **Skye Scene Highland Ceilidh,** Portree, Skye (☎ **01470-542-228**). Guarantee that your trip to the Highlands is complete with a *ceilidh* (a social get-together with music, dancing, and sometimes singing). They can be great fun.

✔ **Skye Serpentarium,** Harrapool on the A850, Skye (☎ 01471-822-209). The staff is crazy about their collection of reptiles, many of which were seized (while being smuggled into the country) by customs officials and sent to this serpentarium.

✔ **Tobermory Distillery,** Tobermory, Mull (☎ 01688-302-645). The only distillery on Mull, Tobermory produces five different single malts with unpeated malted barley (not typical of island whisky). A visitor center is located on the premises.

✔ **Ulva** is the small isle located just across a narrow straight from the settlement of Ulva Ferry on Western Mull. To hail the actual ferry, go to the side of the building that faces the water from the slip. During the Clearances from 1840 to 1881, when thousands of people were evicted from their lands in northern Scotland, so many inhabitants of Ulva were shipped out that the population went from about 850 to less than 60 — and the remaining residents were forced to live in one small corner near the ferry called Desolation Point. A cafe serving fresh oysters occupies this corner now.

Shopping the Hebridean Islands

Despite their remoteness, the Hebridean Islands are home to a fair number of excellent craft and specialty shops.

✔ **Edinbane Pottery,** on the A850, between Portree and Dunvegan, Edinbane, Skye (☎ 01470-582-234; www.edinbane-pottery.co.uk). This workshop produces an excellent selection of glassware and ceramics in a style you won't find anywhere else. The pottery is open daily from 9 a.m. to 7 p.m.

✔ **Isle of Mull Cheese,** Sgriob-Ruadh Farm, near Tobermory (☎ 01688-302-235; www.btinternet.com/~mull.cheese). This farm produces award-winning cheeses using only milk produced on the premises. From spring through the end of September, the shop is open daily from 10 a.m. to 4 p.m.

✔ **Isle of Mull Silver & Goldsmiths,** Main Street, Tobermory, Mull (☎ 01688-302-345; www.mullsilver.co.uk). Part manufacturer, part retail shop, this little jewelry store makes pieces in-house and has an impressive selection from other suppliers throughout Scotland. The shop is open Monday through Saturday from 9:30 a.m. to 1 p.m. and 2 p.m. to 5 p.m. Hours may be extended in the summer.

✔ **Isle of Mull Weavers,** near Craignure, Mull (☎ 01680-812-381). This wee shop has none of the jackets and kilts you normally find in Scottish weavers' stores. Instead, here you get the genuine article — bundled Shetland wool yarn and tweed by the yard. Isle of Mull Weavers is open April to October daily from 9 a.m. to 5 p.m. and November to March Monday through Saturday from 9 a.m. to 5 p.m.

- **Lewis Loom Centre,** Stornoway, Lewis (☎ 01851-704-500; www. lewisloomcentre.co.uk). Most people stop here for the best traditional tweed and knitwear anywhere around. The center offers some deals, as well, because you're eliminating the middleman of a typical shop. Lewis Loom Centre is open Monday through Saturday from 9 a.m. to 6 p.m.

- **Luskentyre Harris Tweed Company,** Plockropool, Harris (☎ 01859-511-217). This little shop and loom is housed in a shed located on a rocky road. It sells warm hats, scarves, socks, and other clothes, and weavers give demonstrations of warping, bobbin winding, and wool plying (you can even find out what those things are!). Take a left at the Golden Road, south of Harris from the A859, and follow it to Plockropool. Call for hours.

- **Over the Rainbow,** Portree, Skye (☎ 01478-612-555; www.skye-knitwear.com). The colorful knitwear in this shop is of the finest quality. The clothes, blankets, and rugs are all made using local materials and techniques. The shop also sells excellent designer jewelry and watches. Over the Rainbow is open daily from 9 a.m. to 9 p.m. in the summer and daily from 9 a.m. to 6 p.m. during the off-season.

- **Tobermory Handmade Chocolate,** Tobermory, Mull (☎ 01688-302-526). More than a specialty shop, this local chocolatier is famous on the island for its unique handmade confections. It's located just off the main road, a block before the ferry terminal and tourist office. The shop is open March through October Monday through Saturday from 9:30 a.m. to 5 p.m., plus Sunday from 11 a.m. to 4 p.m. in July and August.

Doing the Pub Crawl

Many of the inns and restaurants listed at the beginning of this chapter offer pub life, too. Below are two more to consider. Call for the latest opening and closing times.

- **Isles Inn,** Somerled Square, Portree, Skye (☎ 01478-612-129). This cozy, friendly pub in the center of Portree is a popular joint featuring traditional music most nights, especially in the summer. The fireplace and the thatched-roofed bar add a bit of warmth and kitsch to a clean and amiable drinking experience.

- **Mishnish,** Main Street, Tobermory, Mull (☎ 01688-302-009). This quayside bar is rather big for such a diminutive town. The nautically themed pub, full of barnacle-encrusted sea glass, has two main areas, comfortable red velvet booths, and a warming fireplace. Small back rooms allow a little privacy or a game of snooker.

Fast Facts: The Hebridean Islands

Area Code

The area codes for the main towns and islands in the Hebrides are: Portree, Skye **01478**; Tobermory, Mull **01688**; Iona **01681**; Stornoway, Lewis **01851**; Tarbert, Harris **01859**. You need to dial the area code only if you're calling from outside the city you want to reach.

Emergencies

Dial ☎ **999** for police, fire, or ambulance.

Hospitals

The main hospitals in the Hebrides are Gesto Hospital, Lower Edinbane, Portree, Skye (☎ 01470-582-262); and one in Salen, Mull (☎ 01680-300-392).

Information

The main tourist office is Western Isles Tourist Board, 26 Cromwell St., Stornoway, Lewis (☎ 01851-703-088; fax: 01851-705-244; www.visithebrides.com). Other tourist offices include: Bayfield House, just off Somerled Square, Portree, Skye (☎ 01478-612-137); Pier Road, Tarbert, Harris (☎ 01859-502-011); Pier Road, Lochmaddy, North Uist (☎ 01876-50-0321); Pier Road, Lochboisdale, South Uist (☎ 01878-700-286); Main Street, Castlebay, Harris (☎ 01871-810-336); in the Caledonian MacBrayne ticket office at the far northern end of the harbor, Tobermory, Mull (☎ 01648-302-182); and opposite the quay, Craignure, Mull (☎ 01680-812-377).

Mail

You can find post offices at Gladstone Buildings, Quay Brae, Portree, Skye (☎ 01478-612-533), and 36 Main St., Tobermory, Mull (☎ 01688-302-058).

Chapter 20

Orkney and Shetland Islands

In This Chapter

▶ Uncovering accomodations and restaurants on the islands
▶ Discovering ancient sites and settlements

Making the trip to the northern island groups of Orkney and Shetland may seem like time and money poorly spent. That's not necessarily true, but if you do plan to visit the area, you should know that getting there does take extra effort.

But when you reach the islands, you discover that they abound with grand views, old ruins, and a heritage unlike the rest of Scotland. The location is so far north that midsummer nights get no darker than twilight. As far as the weather's concerned, these islands can be quite chilly with a steady breeze, and winters offer scant sunlight and often bring snow.

Visitors also find that accommodation, dining, shopping, and drinking options are limited. In the off-season, the quiet gets even quieter. So, keep in mind that although the Orkney and Shetland Islands offer an escape from the crowds, in many ways you're escaping conveniences, too.

 Given the limited tourist offerings on the islands, I keep this chapter short and succinct, combining the accommodation and dining options into one section.

Getting There

For many travelers, the simplest way to see the islands is to join a tour that covers the major sights in the area. If you're not on a tour, you can get to both Orkney and Shetland by ferry or by airplane. The major islands of the groups have ferry services that connect them to one another.

✔ **By ferry: NorthLink Ferries** (☎ **0845-600-0449;** www.northlink
ferries.co.uk) operates the most frequent services from the
mainland to the Orkneys, whether from Aberdeen to Kirkwall or
from Scrabster to Stromness. Smaller companies also run boats
from John O'Groats to Burwick (passengers only) and Gills Bay
to St. Margaret's Hope.

✔ **By car:** If you've rented a car for your time in Scotland, you can
take it with you when you visit Orkney by booking passage on one
of the **NorthLink Ferries.** You can make arrangements with many
car-rental agencies for free vehicle pick-up and delivery at ferry
landings and airports in Scotland.

✔ **By plane: Kirkwall Airport** (☎ **01856-872-421**) is 3 miles from the
center of Kirkwall, Orkney. **Sumburgh Airport** (☎ **01950-460-654**) is
25 miles south of Lerwick, Shetland. British Airways serves both airports from several cities in the UK, including Edinburgh, Glasgow,
and London; flights may connect in Aberdeen. Flights link the two
islands in the summer only.

Spending the Night and Dining Locally

Your choices of accommodations and restaurants are limited on Orkney
and Shetland. I've listed the best options in this section. Rates include
full breakfast unless otherwise stated. And remember: You may well get
a better deal than the advertised "rack" rates.

Ayre Hotel
$$ Kirkwall, Orkney

This renovated 18th-century town house has plenty of room and hospi-
tality for everyone. Besides the cozy, simply-decorated rooms and the
friendly service you'd expect from a hotel that has been in the same family
for two decades, the Ayre has a pair of popular bars and offers live enter-
tainment a couple nights a week. The whitewashed building is conve-
niently located near the town center as well as by the water. Ask for a room
with a view of the sea.

See map p. 395. Ayre Road, Kirkwall, Orkney. ☎ *01856-873-001. Fax: 01856-876-289.*
www.ayrehotel.co.uk. *Rack rates: £90–£100 ($166–$185) double. AE, MC, V.*

Burrastow House
$$–$$$$ Near Walls, Shetland   SCOTTISH

If there's better food on the Shetlands, I haven't found it. If you're planning
to spend the evening on Shetland, definitely book a dinner reservation
at Burrastow House. The menu's heavy on fish and game (sorry, vegetarians), and dishes are prepared and garnished with local produce. While
sheep graze on the grass outside, you'll be grazing on mussel stew, lamb,

The Shetland Islands

Muckle Flugga Lighthouse · Lamba Ness
Herma Ness
UNST
Haroldswick
Baltasound
A968
Point of Fethaland
Cullivoe
Belmont
Gutcher
YELL HASCOSAY
FETLAR
A968
Mid Yell
Yell Sound
Colgrave Sound
Burravoe
OUT SKERRIES
Stenness
Hillswick
Esha Ness
Saint Magnus Bay
A970
Brae
A968
Vidlin
WHALSAY
MUCKLE ROE
Voe Laxo
Symbister
PAPA STOUR
PAPA LITTLE
A970
Kergord
Melby Ho
A971
North Sea
Wats Ness
MAINLAND
Bridge of Walls A971
Walls
Whiteness
VAILA
Lerwick ISLE OF NOSS
The Deeps
Scalloway
BRESSAY
FOULA
Hamnavoe
Bard Head
Ham
WEST BURRA
Kettle Ness
MOUSA
Sandwick
ST. NINIAN'S ISLAND
A970
Fitful Head
To Orkney & Aberdeen
Airport
Ferry
Sumburgh

Area of detail

SCOTLAND

Edinburgh

ENGLAND

ACCOMMODATIONS & DINING
Burrastow House **4**
Grand Hotel **3**

ATTRACTIONS
Jarlshof **1**
Scalloway Castle **2**

monkfish, homemade soups and breads, and more. It's delicious, traditional food served in a traditional-looking, oak-paneled dining area.

If you're looking to spend the night, Burrastow offers the northernmost accommodations in Scotland.

See map p. 393. 3 miles from Walls, Shetland. ☎ *01595-809-307.* www.users. zetnet.co.uk/burrastow-house-hotel. *Reservations required for dinner. Main courses: £10–£20 ($18.50–$37). Open: Sun–Mon 12:30–2 p.m., Tues–Sat 12:30– 2 p.m. and 7:30–9 p.m. Rack rates: £140 ($259) double including dinner. MC, V. Closed Nov–Mar.*

Foveran Hotel & Restaurant
$$ Near Kirkwall, Orkney   SCOTTISH

On 34 acres of beautiful grounds overlooking the waters of Scapa Flow, this lovely little hotel with a fireplace and IKEA-like furniture is a popular spot for visitors. The architecture and décor are Scandinavian, and the attitude of the staff is friendly and informal. Most rooms have sea views.

If you decide to eat in-house, you get excellent Scottish grub, renowned in its own right for the locally grown produce, Orkney beef and lamb, fresh seafood, and excellent desserts.

See map p. 395. On the A964/Orphir Road, St. Ola, just outside Kirkwall, Orkney. ☎ *01856-872-389. Fax: 01856-876-430. www.foveranhotel.co.uk. Rack rates: £83–£90 ($153–$166) double. Main courses: £10.50–£18 ($17–$29). Open: Daily 7-9 p.m. MC, V. Closed Jan.*

Grand Hotel
$$ Lerwick, Shetland

If you want to spend the night in the Shetlands, the Grand Hotel is your place. Located in the middle of the capital, Lerwick, this old-fashioned structure is quite grand. The building has an impressive castellated design with gables and turrets, and it's only a block from the water. The service is top-notch, and the rooms are as fancy as the building. The digs may look old, but the facilities are quite modern. In addition to the bar and coffee shop, the hotel has its own beauty salon and even a nightclub, the only one in the Shetlands.

See map p. 393. 149 Commercial St. ☎ *01595-692-826. Fax: 01595-694-048. Rack rates: £75–£110 ($138–$203) double. MC, V.*

Stromness Hotel
$$ Stromness, Orkney

Established in 1901, the 42-unit Stromness Hotel underwent a major refurbishment not long ago. Many of the rooms in this traditional stone building with bay windows overlook the harbor and Scapa Flow. To give guests a sampling of Orkney culture, the hotel hosts live traditional music shows.

See map p. 395. The Pierhead, Victoria Terrace, Stromness, Orkney. ☎ *01856-850-298. Fax: 01856-850-610. www.stromnesshotel.com. Rack rates: £60–£92 ($111–$170) double. MC, V.*

Exploring Orkney and Shetland

Attraction for attraction, Orkney, with its host of ancient landmarks bearing World Heritage Site status, has more going for it than the Shetlands. The Orkney Islands' top sights are on what the Orcadian's (the islands' residents) call the Mainland. Orkney also offers spectacular seascapes

The Orkney Islands

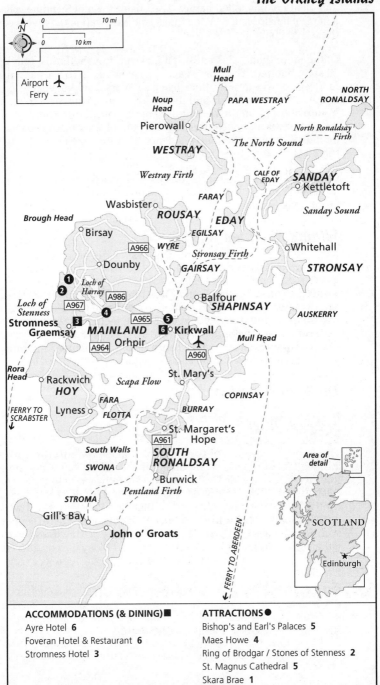

| Airport ✈ |
| Ferry - - - - |

ACCOMMODATIONS (& DINING) ■
Ayre Hotel **6**
Foveran Hotel & Restaurant **6**
Stromness Hotel **3**

ATTRACTIONS ●
Bishop's and Earl's Palaces **5**
Maes Howe **4**
Ring of Brodgar / Stones of Stenness **2**
St. Magnus Cathedral **5**
Skara Brae **1**

and plenty of unspoiled nature. The quaint town of **Stromness** has been a natural harbor since Viking times, and **Kirkwall** is the lovely capital of the island chain.

Of the more than 100 islands that make up the **Shetlands,** only about 20 are inhabited. The Norse gave the island chain to Scotland through a marriage dowry in 1469, but the legacy of its Scandinavian origins shows in the faces of the locals and the architecture of the main town, **Lerwick.** Nature abounds in the beautiful scenery, from Shetland ponies that roam freely to seals and porpoises that live and play along the coasts. Like the people of Orkney, Shetland residents' identities are more strongly tied to their islands than to Scotland.

 Be sure to stop at the tourist offices in Kirkwell (Orkney) and Lerwick (Shetland) and pick up the handy maps showing both large and small attractions.

Joining a guided tour

A guided tour is a smart, convenient way to get around and see the sights on the islands.

- ✔ **Wildabout Orkney Tours** (☎ 01856-851-011; www.orknet.co.uk/wildabout) offers excursions covering all the island's highlights, history, and nature you'd ever want, including Skara Brae, Maes Howe, and the Stones of Stenness. Guides provide commentary on Orkney's archaeological, historic, and scenic points of interest. A special tour of wildlife and the night sky takes place in the winter.

The top attractions

Bishop's and Earl's Palaces
Kirkwall, Orkney

The impressive ruins of the Bishop's Palace date to the 12th century, although most of what's standing today is about 400 years more recent. Rumor has it that King Haakon of Norway returned here to die after losing the battle of Largs (southwest of Glasgow) in 1263. Earl Patrick Stuart built the Earl's Palace next door to the Bishop's Palace in the 1600s. Stuart, an illegitimate nephew of Mary Queen of Scots, was later executed for treason. In its day, the Earl's Palace was one of the finest examples of Renaissance architecture in Scotland — and today it's considered the best surviving piece of such work remaining in the country. Allow about 2 hours.

See map p. 395. Broad Street, across Palace Road from Magnus Cathedral. ☎ *01856-871-918.* www.historic-scotland.gov.uk. *Admission for both palaces: £2.50 ($4.60) adults, £1.90 ($3.50) seniors and students, £1 ($1.85) children under 16. Open: Apr–Sept daily 9:30 a.m.–6:30 p.m. Closed Oct–Mar.*

Jarlshof
Shetland

This settlement was first uncovered by a storm in 1897. Subsequent archaeological digs have further revealed settlements and remarkable artifacts from different civilizations. More than three acres of remains that span some 3,000 years, from the Bronze Age onward, are now accessible to visitors. Sites include an oval Bronze Age house, an Iron Age *broch* (stone house and fortification) and wheelhouses, a medieval farmstead, and the relatively modern 16th-century laird's house. Allow about 2 hours.

See map p. 393. A970, Sumburgh Head, 22 miles south of Lerwick on the southern end of Shetland Island, near the airport. ☎ *01950-460-112.* www.historic-scotland.gov.uk. *Admission: £3.30 ($6) adults, £2.50 ($4.60) seniors and students, £1 ($1.85) children under 16. Open: Apr–Sept daily 9:30 a.m.–6:30 p.m. Closed Oct–Mar.*

Maes Howe
Orkney

Dating to 2750 BC, this burial cairn is the finest megalithic tomb in the UK. The large mound covers a stone-built passage, a burial chamber, and smaller cells. Look for the inscriptions along the walls written by Vikings who pillaged the tomb's treasures in the 12th century. Allow about 1½ hours.

See map p. 395. On the A965, 9 miles west of Kirkwall. ☎ *01856-761-606.* www.historic-scotland.gov.uk. *Admission: £3 ($5.50) adults, £2.30 ($4.25) seniors and students, £1 ($1.85) children under 16. Open: Apr–Sept daily 9:30 a.m.–6:30 p.m.; Oct–Mar Mon–Sat 9:30 a.m.–4:30 p.m., Sun 2–4:30 p.m.*

Ring of Brodgar/Stones of Stenness
Orkney

These two standing-stone circles, mini-Stonehenges of the north, date to the third millennium BC. These impressive ceremonial sites are amazing and imposing to walk through. The tallest stone of the Stenness group is a whopping 4.8m (16 ft.) high. The two circles are within walking distance of each other. Twenty-seven of the 60 stones in the Ring of Brodgar remain standing; only 4 of 12 at Stenness are still upright. When the fog rolls in, the rings are quite a sight. The origin of the stones is not certain, but they're believed to have been used for some kind of ancient ceremony. Allow about 2 hours.

See map p. 395. Five miles north of Stromness, on the A965. ☎ *01856-841-815. Admission: free. Open: Year-round, 24 hours.*

St. Magnus Cathedral
Kirkwall, Orkney

Dominating the town of Kirkwall, this red and yellow sandstone cathedral honors the patron saint — and martyr — of the islands. Back near the beginning of the 12th century, after being killed by his cousin, Magnus was buried in the town of Birsay and, according to legend, a heavenly light shone upon his grave. This event conferred upon him a cult following. Magnus's nephew, Earl Rognvald, initiated construction of the cathedral in 1137. Today, it retains all its grand features, from narrow naves to huge sandstone columns to beautiful stained glass. Relics of Magnus and Rognvald lie in the cathedral, surrounded by a mix of Norman, Romanesque, and Gothic architecture. The cathedral also holds a memorial to the HMS *Royal Oak,* which a German sub torpedoed and sank off the Orkney coast during World War II, killing 833 crewmembers. On a calm day, on the road south from Kirkwall over Scapa Flow, you can see the underwater outline of the *Royal Oak,* now a National War Grave. Allow about 1 hour.

See map p. 395. Broad Street. ☎ *01856-841-815.* www.orkneyjar.com/history/stmagnus/magcath.htm. *Admission: free. Open: Apr–Sept Mon–Sat 9 a.m.–6 p.m., Sun 2–6 p.m.; Oct–Mar Mon–Sat 9 a.m.–1 p.m. and 2–5 p.m.*

Scalloway Castle
Scalloway, Shetland

These amazing ruins dominate the town of Scalloway and date back to the time when the town served as the capital of Shetland. Earl Patrick Stuart — not a popular figure in these parts thanks to his corruption and brutality — built Scalloway Castle in 1600. In fact, he used forced labor to do it. After he was executed, the medieval building fell into disrepair, but the ruins make for good photographs. If the front door is locked, you can usually get the key at the Shetland Woolen Company next door or at the Royal Hotel nearby. Allow about 1 hour.

See map p. 393. Scalloway center, on the A970. ☎ *01856-841-815.* www.historic-scotland.gov.uk. *Admission: free. Open: Apr–Sept Mon–Sat 9 a.m.–5 p.m.; Oct–Mar Mon–Fri 9 a.m.–5 p.m.*

Skara Brae
Orkney

This prehistoric beachside village — the best-preserved village of its type in northern Europe — was once home to a few Stone Age families. It was first uncovered by a storm in 1850. Covered passage tunnels allow you to walk through the Pompeii-like site of a half-dozen rooms and see preserved beds and fireplaces. The visitor center contains a replica house (Skaill House) that lets you experience what life may have been like when Skara Brae was someone's home. The walk along the shoreline is a windy adventure. Allow about 2 hours.

See map p. 395. B9056 off the A967, 19 miles northwest of Kirkwall. ☎ *01856-841-815.* www.orkneyjar.com/history/skarabrae. *Admission: £5 ($9.25) adults, £3.75 ($7) seniors and students, £1.30 ($2.40) children under 16. In summer, admission includes Skaill House. Open: Apr–Sept daily 9:30 a.m.–6:30 p.m.; Oct–Mar Mon–Sat 9:30 a.m.–4:30 p.m., Sun 2–4 p.m.*

Other Cool Things to See and Do

✔ **Orkak,** 10 Albert St., Kirkwall, Orkney (☎ **01856-873-536**). Orkak has become one of Scotland's leading designers of gold and silver jewelry. The locally made items at the Orkak Visitor Centre and Shop are excellent, much of it styled with a Celtic theme.

✔ **Stromness Museum,** 52 Alfred St., Stromness, Orkney (☎ **01856-850-025**). This museum covers a good range of interesting topics, including the German fleet that roamed the Scapa Flow at one time and the local presence of the Hudson Bay Company (one of the biggest employers in town). Visitors see displays on the area's whaling and fishing industries, as well.

✔ **Tankerness House,** Broad Street, next to St. Magnus Cathedral, Kirkwall, Orkney (☎ **01856-873-191**). Tankerness House is an interesting little museum that covers aspects of Orcadian life during the last 5,000 years. The building dates to 1574, when it was a residence for church officials.

✔ **Up Helly Aa Exhibition,** St. Sunniva Street, Lerwick, Shetland. January finds Lerwick hosting **Up Helly Aa,** its famous **Fire Festival,** on the last Tuesday of the month (www.shetland tourism.com/pages/up_helly_aa.htm). A thousand locals, torches held high, are cheered on as they storm an effigy of a Viking longboat and set it aflame. These heroes and their witnesses follow up the fire with a long night of eating, drinking, music playing, and dancing. The celebrations spread out from here, and more remote communities hold their local versions of the event over the three months that follow.

Fast Facts: Orkney and Shetland

Area Code

The area code for Kirkwall and Stromness is **01856**; Lerwick is **01595**. You need to dial the area code only if you're calling from outside the city you want to reach.

Emergencies

Dial ☎ **999** for police, fire, or ambulance.

Hospitals

The main hospitals on the islands are Balfour Hospital (☎ 01856-873-166), New Scapa Road, Kirkwall, Orkney, and Gilbert Bain Hospital (☎ 01595-743-300), Scalloway Road, Lerwick, Shetland.

Information

You can get information on visiting the islands from Orkney Islands Tourist Board, 6 Broad St., Kirkwall, Orkney (☎ 01856-872-856; www.visitorkney.com), or Shetland Islands Tourist Board, Market Cross, Lerwick, Shetland (☎ 01595-693-434; www.shetlandtourism.co.uk).

Mail

Post offices are at 15 Junction Rd., Kirkwall, Orkney (☎ 01856-872-974), and 46 Commercial St., Lerwick, Shetland (☎ 01595-693-201).

Part V
The Part of Tens

The 5th Wave
By Rich Tennant

"Okay, we got one cherry lager with bitters and a pineapple slice, and one honey malt ale with cinnamon and an orange twist. You want these in pints, or parfait glasses?"

In this part . . .

*1*f you want quick listings of some of the most outstanding spots in Scotland, you've come to the right place. Part V gives you the scoop on great Scottish golf courses, from the world-famous St. Andrews to some notable ones with which you may be less familiar. There are also lists of the most evocative castles, engaging historic sites, and natural attractions that'll likely knock your socks off. If Scotland's ample and first-rate whiskies interest you, check out the rundown of distinctive distilleries that you can tour. You may find that after you've visited these locales, they become your favorites.

Chapter 21

Ten Outstanding Golf Courses

In This Chapter

▶ Rubbing shoulders with the golf elite at St. Andrews

▶ Doing the duffer's dance on the heathered countryside

*I*t would be unfair to say *definitively* that the golf courses listed in this chapter are the ten best in Scotland. Scotland has so many great courses to choose from that selecting the top ten without facing argument from some faction or other is impossible. The fact of the matter is that you can find many more top-notch courses in Scotland than you'll have time to play unless you're planning to move there permanently. Even then, it would probably take a lifetime to hit all the best courses. Each course in this chapter has its own special attraction. Some are more famous than others; some are more difficult than others.

For every course, call ahead for information about tee times and requirements to play (if any exist).

Carnoustie

Although golfers have been playing here since 1560, somehow Carnoustie has remained one of Scotland's lesser-known championship courses. It's increasingly popular, in part because it has been the site of recent British Open tournaments. The course has one of the toughest and longest finishes in the country.

Carnoustie, east of Dundee. Par 72. ☎ 01241-853-789.

Gairloch Golf Club

It may be only nine holes, but this course is still very much a challenging and tricky one. Combine this challenge with a location along a golden beach and overlooking Skye and the Hebrides and you have a great course.

Gairloch. Par 35. ☎ **01445-712-407.**

Muirfield

Muirfield is the best championship course near Edinburgh (only 20 to 30 minutes away), and it's regularly a location for qualifying play before the British Open (which people here just call the "Open"). If you're not an expert, you'll be more comfortable playing on one of the other two courses at Muirfield.

Muirfield. Par 71. ☎ **01620-842-255.**

Prestwick

The original home of the Open, this course remains a monument to the early days of golf (1860s). It has bumpy fairways, deep bunkers, and many blind shots, but this old-school course is well worth the time and the challenge.

Prestwick. Par 71. ☎ **01292-477-404.**

Royal Dornoch Course

This course doesn't have a single bad hole, and its only downside is its location in the far north. You have plenty of room off the tee, but placing your drive depends greatly upon the wind and the pin positions. The course is challenging but accessible to nearly everyone.

Dornoch. Par 70. ☎ **01862-810-219.**

Royal Troon

Despite popular belief, nonmembers aren't prohibited from playing this famous and fabulous course in Ayrshire on the Clyde Coast. The course frequently plays host to the Open, and each hole provides a challenge. The 8th hole, or Postage Stamp, is the shortest in Open history. If you don't have the chops for Royal Troon, go to one of the excellent municipal courses nearby.

Troon. Par 71. ☎ **01292-311-555.**

St. Andrews

The Old Course at St. Andrews is arguably the most famous golf course in the world. All the "greats" have played here, apparently even Mary Queen of Scots. This often windy and always challenging seaside links golf course is the one in Scotland that most frequently hosts the British Open. It's definitely the mecca of golf, if ever there was one.

St. Andrews. Par 72. ☎ **01334-475-757.**

Traigh

This is probably the most picturesque nine-hole course in Scotland, and possibly in the world. Just two miles up the road from Arisaig and set right along the country's most attractive shoreline, Traigh offers not only challenging golf (for a short course) but brilliant views, too.

Arisaig. Par 34. ☎ **01687-450-337.**

Turnberry

The Ailsa Course at Turnberry is home to a fair amount of British Open drama; golf heroes such as Jack Nicklaus, Tom Watson, and Greg Norman have all competed for the top prize here. The links-style course that runs along the South Ayrshire seashore, against the backdrop of the grand Turnberry hotel, is one of the most picturesque in Scotland. Book a room at the hotel to be guaranteed a tee time.

Turnberry. Par 72. ☎ **01655-331-000.**

Western Gailes

With its unique layout of greens tucked away in hollows, the course here requires finesse, accuracy, and precision. This natural links-style course hugs the coastline less than an hour's drive from Glasgow and can be played practically all year round, because its sandy fairways and greens drain quickly and the weather is generally moderate (if typically windy).

Irvine. Par 72. ☎ **01294-311-649.**

Chapter 22

Ten Can't-Miss Castles and Historic Sites

In This Chapter

▶ Walking the grounds of great Scottish battles

▶ Hunting down the crown jewels

▶ Discovering the most fascinating castles

*I*n a country with hundreds of ancient castles and ruins, choosing just ten of the best is certainly difficult. If you're a history buff or get a special charge out of walking in the footsteps of some of history's giants, put the attractions and locations in this chapter on your must-see list. But for each of these, you may prefer two others; remember, these are simply my favorites.

Bannockburn

King Robert the Bruce beat Edward II's English troops here in a decisive battle that secured Scottish sovereignty after the freedom struggles associated with William "Braveheart" Wallace. See Chapter 16 for more on this historic area.

Heritage Centre: Glasgow Road, near Stirling. ☎ **01786-812-664.**

Calanais Standing Stones

The "Scottish Stonehenge" is one of the most significant archaeological find of its kind in the country (see Chapter 19). Much mystery surrounds the purpose and origin of these stones (whose arrangement dates back some 5,000 years), which remain an attraction to pilgrims who camp out here during the summer solstice.

Isle of Lewis. ☎ **01851-621-422.**

Castle Tioram

The ruins of this ancient castle on Loch Moidart (see Chapter 18) have one of the most romantic (and remote) settings in the Western Highlands. Although access is limited, you can scale the hill upon which the castle sits and let your imagination do the rest.

Near Blain, Ardnamurchan, off the A861.

Culloden Moor Battlefield

British forces loyal to the Hanoverian king in London defeated Bonnie Prince Charlie's Jacobite rebellion here in 1746, ending a valiant but ultimately unsuccessful movement for restoration of the Stuart crown. No other military movement followed Charlie after his loss here. A visitor center with museum provides the complete history of the battlefield. (Flip to Chapter 18 for more on this historical site.) As you stare out over the moody moorlands, you may be able to imagine the desolation felt by the defeated Highland troops.

Culloden Moor, 5 miles east of Inverness. ☎ **01463-790-607.**

Culzean Castle

A mansion more than a castle, Culzean remains a classic example of the work of Robert Adam, Scotland and England's preeminent architect in the Georgian style. In addition to the castle, Culzean offers lots of parkland and gardens to explore. Culzean makes this list of must-see attractions because it appeals to a range of visitors, from buffs of historic buildings and those keen on formal gardens to beachcombers, hikers, and families with children. You can find details on Culzean and its surroundings in Chapter 15.

Overlooking the Firth of Clyde, South Ayrshire. ☎ **01655-884-455.**

Doune Castle

Made famous thanks to the film *Monty Python and the Holy Grail,* Doune Castle is one of the best because it has been modestly restored, giving visitors a feel for what life in a medieval castle truly was like during Doune's heyday. See Chapter 16 for more details.

Northwest of Stirling, off the A84. ☎ **01786-841-742.**

Edinburgh Castle

This castle is the country's most popular attraction, and it holds the historic Stone of Destiny as well as Scotland's crown jewels. For my money, too much of the attraction is devoted to military history. But that's to be expected, considering the castle remains an active military barracks. For the complete scoop on Edinburgh Castle, jump to Chapter 11.

Castlehill, Edinburgh. ☎ **0131-225-9846.**

Eilean Donan Castle

After Edinburgh Castle, Eilean Donan is probably the most photographed castle in Scotland. It has been restored and offers some interesting exhibits as well as a good bit of history, including defending the area from Vikings and serving as a Jacobite stronghold. See Chapter 18 for more information on this castle.

Dornie, Kyle of Lochalsh, on the A87. ☎ **01599-555-202.**

Glasgow Cathedral

Glasgow Cathedral is the oldest pre-Reformation cathedral still standing soundly on the Scottish mainland. It marks the place where this industrial powerhouse of the 19th and 20th centuries began over 1,000 years earlier. Flip to Chapter 12 for details.

Cathedral Square, Castle Street, Glasgow. ☎ **0141-552-6891.**

Melrose Abbey

Of all the historic abbeys in the Borders region (see Chapter 14), the one in Melrose may be the most interesting. Built in the 12th century, it's said to be the place where the heart of King Robert the Bruce was buried.

Melrose, on Abbey Street. ☎ **01896-822-562.**

Chapter 23

Ten Distinctive Distilleries

In This Chapter
▶ "Nosing" about for the good stuff
▶ Taking tours of distilleries large and small

Scotland has many, many distilleries, but not all are created equal. Whisky is undoubtedly Scotland's best known export and a good deal of the distilleries across the country are open to the public, many with tours of their facilities that explain exactly how whisky is made (and how it's different from American or Canadian whiskeys). This chapter lists some of the best to visit.

Dalwhinnie

Originally called Strathspey distillery, Dalwhinnie has the distinction of being the country's "highest distillery," in elevation, I mean, at about 326m (1,073 ft.) above sea level. The tour of this distillery is good, too, but perhaps not on a par with either the dramatic setting, where you may see snow on surrounding hills in early summer, or the sparkling white buildings with their pagoda-type roofs.

Dalwhinnie. ☎ **01528-522-208.**

Edradour

Edradour is the smallest distillery in Scotland, putting out only 12 casks a week, and one of the last remaining so-called farm distilleries that used to be commonplace in Perthshire. Edradour is produced by three people, using traditional methods and seemingly antique equipment. They pride themselves on using skills passed down through generations. The picturesque buildings and grounds are memorable.

Between Edradour and Pitlochry. ☎ **01796-472-095.**

Glenfiddich

Readers who haven't heard of Glenfiddich probably have little interest in this chapter. Glenfiddich is one of the three biggest selling whiskies in the world, which explains why some 125,000 visitors come here annually. It was the first distillery to recognize the potential of tourism and open a visitor center, and it's a good choice for those who want a well-organized tour of a large, modern distillery.

Dufftown, at the A941 and B975. ☎ **01340-820-373.**

Glen Grant

Grant is one of the big names in Scottish spirits. Beautiful gardens are a highlight of any visit to this fine, family-run distillery. After the decent tour, take your dram of whisky (apparently the favorite of Italians) outside and taste it cut with a drop or two of water from the Glen Grant burn (that's what the Scots call a brook).

Rothes. ☎ **01542-783-318.**

Glenlivet

The Glenlivet is among the most popular single malts sold. The tours here have a reputation for being the most entertaining and informative of any in Scotland. Thus, if you're in the area and can only visit one distillery, you may want to make it this one.

Ten miles north of Tomintoul. ☎ **01542-783-220.**

The Glenturret

It may be one of the smallest distilleries in the country, but the tours and audiovisual presentation here make Glenturret one of the most unforgettable. Illegal distilling at this site began as early as 1717. Because visitors can quite easily get here and back in an afternoon drive from either Glasgow or Edinburgh, Glenturret is very popular, but staff manages to handle the crowds adeptly. The tour covers practically all of the facility and includes a film presentation.

Northwest of Crieff, off the A85. ☎ **01764-656-565.**

Laphroaig

For fans of peaty flavors, Laphroaig from the isle of Islay (pronounced *eye*-la) is often a preference and is perhaps best known of all island single malts. The taste of this whisky carries hints not only of the local peat but of the sea air as well.

Port Ellen. ☎ **01496-302-418.**

Strathisla

This fine Highland single malt is better known for being the main ingredient in Chivas Regal, one of the most popular blends in the world. The distillery tour here usually ends with an informative and unique "nosing" of different whiskies from the various regions of Scotland.

Keith, on Seafield Avenue. ☎ **01542-783-044.**

Talisker

The tour at this distillery is among one of the best in the country. Talisker produces whisky with the peaty flavor of the island. In addition to producing its own distinctive brand, Talisker produces whisky used in popular blends such as Johnnie Walker. See Chapter 19 for additional information about the Isle of Skye and this distillery.

Carbost, Skye. ☎ **01478-640-314.**

Tobermory

The tour here is short, but the tasting is tall. Tobermory is on the waters of its picturesque namesake town (see Chapter 17), and it's one of the tastiest things going on there. Unlike visits to other distilleries, which involve long treks to get there, Tobermory is right in the harbor town — arguably the prettiest in the Hebridean islands. It's easy enough to include on even a half-day visit to the isle of Mull.

On the harbor in Tobermory, Mull. ☎ **01688-302-645.**

Chapter 24

Ten Stunning Natural Attractions

Scotland is more than vibrant cities, historic monuments, castles, golf courses, pubs, wool, and distilleries. The country is also home to some of the prettiest countryside you could ever imagine. Whether you like to hike, watch birds, or just hunt for perfect photographic backdrops, take in as many of these top nature spots as you can.

Arthur's Seat and Holyrood Park

It's rare to find a hike of such natural beauty in any city. But Edinburgh is no ordinary metropolis. You can walk to the top of Arthur's Seat or cheat and drive to the park — either way, you find plenty to soak in, especially the views. Chapter 11 contains more information on this Edinburgh landmark.

At the foot of the Royal Mile, Edinburgh.

Ben Nevis

The tallest mountain in Great Britain is also a popular climb. You certainly don't have to hike all the way to the peak, but if that's your plan, just make sure you have the stamina and plenty of warm clothes. The climb is a rite of passage among Scots, but it's also a fun bit of exercise for anyone. Nevis also has a gondola and ski area if you enjoy coming down more than going up. Check out Chapter 18 for details.

Fort William, Western Highlands.

Butt of Lewis

The views from these beautiful high cliffs over the ocean are worth the drive to the tip of Lewis. Grab your camera: You encounter seabirds, seals, and heavy winds blowing spectacular waves against the rocks. Check out Chapter 19 for more info.

Isle of Lewis, Outer Hebrides.

Cuillin Hills

These dark, brooding hills make a stunning backdrop for your drive through Skye. You can also get out and hike the area. Some of the trails are easy, but don't attempt to climb the peaks unless you're an experienced hiker. You can find details on this area in Chapter 19.

Isle of Skye, the Hebrides.

Glen Coe

This lovely valley runs some ten miles and is fairly breathtaking every bit of the way — even though it's best known as the site of a bloody massacre. You can climb Ossian's Ladder, a trail up the hillside, to an infamous cave or take a more moderate ranger-led hike. See Chapter 18 for more information on the valley.

Glencoe, Ballachulish, Western Highlands.

Inverewe Garden

I'm cheating a bit with this recommendation, because Scotland's many marvelous gardens aren't exactly natural attractions so much as man-made wonders. But no matter how it came to be, Inverewe Garden is one of the loveliest gardens in the country. It shows off some glories of nature: towering trees, flowering shrubs, and almost tropical species that survive thanks to the warming North Atlantic flow from the Gulf of Mexico. (The so-called North Atlantic drift brings warm seas and its effects to all southwest-facing coastlines of Scotland. And indeed the Gulf Stream keeps all of Great Britain, and even parts of Europe, from having a more Siberian climate.) For a more complete description of this garden and for visitor information, check out Chapter 18.

Near Poolewe, Wester Ross, Highlands.

Loch Lomond

A 45-minute drive north from Glasgow puts you at this excellent loch. The pretty scenery is best explored on a boat tour, but plenty of spots along Lomond make good picnic stops as well. Plus, coming here allows you to get a taste of the Highlands without straying too far from the big city. Flip to Chapter 15 for details.

Northwest of Glasgow, Argyll.

Loch Ness

Monster hunting aside, this huge loch in the middle of Scotland is a lovely natural wonder. As you drive along it, consider stopping to read the numerous plaques containing fascinating information related to the loch. The best way to see the loch is by boat; sign up for one of the excellent tours. Find out more about Loch Ness in Chapter 18.

Between Fort George and Inverness, Highlands.

Rannoch Moor

There's something spectacularly desolate and almost prehistoric about the Rannoch Moor, which you pass through on the way to Glen Coe and Fort William. You can almost imagine dinosaurs roaming this strangely spectacular scenery, almost entirely treeless and full of bracken and ground-hugging foliage amid bogs and ponds. For more on the Highlands, flip to Chapter 18.

Highlands.

Sands of Morar

Between Arisaig and Mallaig on Scotland's beautiful West Coast, the beaches of Morar are so spectacular that they've been used in several movies, most notably Bill Forsyth's *Local Hero*. The light is magical in the evenings, especially during summer when the sun slowly sets in the north-western skies. Find out more about the Sands of Morar in Chapter 18.

Road to the Isles, Western Highlands.

Quick Concierge

- -

Fast Facts

American Express

The Amex offices in Edinburgh and Glasgow exchange money and traveler's checks as well as perform other services for cardholders. The Edinburgh office is at 69 George St. at Frederick Street (☎ 0131-718-2501; Bus: 13, 19, or 41). It's open Monday through Friday from 9 a.m. to 5:30 p.m. and Saturday from 9 a.m. to 5 p.m.; on Wednesday, the office opens at 9:30 a.m. The Glasgow office is located at 115 Hope St. (☎ 0141-222-1401; Underground: St. Enoch) and is open Monday through Friday from 8:30 a.m. to 5:30 p.m. (except Wednesday when it opens at 9:30 a.m.), and Saturday from 9 a.m. to noon.

ATMs

In Scotland, ATMs (automated teller machines) are called *cash machines*. In the cities as well as in many of the larger towns, ATMs now often connect to international systems such as Cirrus or Plus. Most give cash advances on major credit cards as well.

Business Hours

Most businesses are open Monday through Saturday from 9 or 9:30 a.m. to 5 or 5:30 p.m., with some exceptions. Many businesses and shops are closed Sunday, although many shops in the cities open on Sunday afternoons. Most cities also have extended shopping hours on Thursday until 8 p.m. Outside of Edinburgh and Glasgow, businesses may close for lunch, generally from 12:30 to 1:30 p.m.

Banks are normally open from 9 a.m. or 10 a.m. until about 5 p.m. on weekdays. Banks are good places to exchange currency and get credit card cash advances.

Restaurants and pubs have different restrictions on hours of operation depending upon their licensing, which is controlled by local councils. Although some bars may not open until late afternoon, most serve drinks from noon to midnight and maybe later on weekends. Some pubs in residential and rural areas, however, close at 11 p.m. Many restaurants stop serving food at 2:30 p.m. and resume at 5:30 or 6 p.m. Nightclubs in cities and larger towns have late-night hours, staying open until between 1 and 3 a.m. — but doors may not open until 10 p.m.

Cameras and Film

Most pharmacies sell photo supplies and many have photo-developing services, as well. One-hour film processing is available in larger cities. These services and products are more expensive abroad than in the U.S. If you have to buy photo supplies or film while you're in Scotland, go to a camera shop or department store. Never buy film from a souvenir stand near a tourist attraction, where the markup is high.

Credit Cards

The toll-free emergency numbers for major credit cards are: Visa ☎ 0800-891-725; MasterCard ☎ 0800-964-767; American Express ☎ 0800-700-700; and Diner's Club ☎ 702-797-5532 (members can call collect).

Currency Exchange

You can change money at any place with the sign BUREAU DU CHANGE. You find these signs at banks, which give you the best rates; major post office branches; and many hotels and travel agencies. (See Chapter 5 for more information on dealing with money in Scotland.)

Customs

UK customs restricts the value of goods you can bring into Scotland to about £150 ($277). U.S. citizens returning to Scotland after an absence of at least 48 hours are allowed to bring back, once every 30 days, $800 worth of merchandise duty-free.

Driving

In Scotland, cars travel on the left side of the road. (See Chapter 7 for more details on driving in Scotland.)

Drugstores

Drugstores are called *pharmacies* or *chemists* in Scotland. The regulations for over-the-counter and prescription drugs differ from those in the U.S., so you may not find commercial pharmaceuticals or your preferred medicine. Consider bringing your own products from the U.S.

Electricity

The electric current in Scotland is 240 volts AC, which is different than the U.S. current, so most small appliances brought from the U.S., such as hair dryers and shavers, don't work (and the current could damage the appliance). If you're considering bringing your laptop or iron from home, check the voltage first to see if it has a range between 110v and 240v. If the voltage doesn't have a range, the only option is to purchase an expensive converter. If the voltage does have a higher range, then you still need to buy an outlet adapter because your prongs won't fit in the Scottish sockets. You can buy an adapter for about $10 at an appliance store or even at the airport.

Embassies and Consulates

Embassies are located in the capital of Great Britain, London. Edinburgh has consulates for Australia (69 George St.; ☎ 0131-624-3700), Canada (30 Lothian Rd.; ☎ 0131-245-6013), and the United States (3 Regents Terrace; ☎ 0131-556-8315).

Emergencies

For any emergency, contact the police or an ambulance by calling ☎ 999 from any phone. You can also call the National Health Service Helpline, ☎ 0800-22-4488, which offers health-related advice and assistance from 8 a.m. to 10 p.m. daily. (See Chapter 9 for details on accessing health care in Scotland.) Every city and regional chapter lists local hospitals. For emergencies, treatment is free, although you will be billed for long stays.

Internet Access

Many hotels offer Internet access (though it's usually rather expensive), and Internet cafes are popular, especially near central railway stations. See the major city and regional chapters for more information.

Language

English is the principal language spoken in Scotland, although heavy accents and local vernacular (especially words used by lowland Scots) can make it difficult to comprehend. Ask the natives to speak more slowly if you can't understand them. Gaelic is spoken in the Highlands and islands, where signs are frequently in both Gaelic and English.

Liquor Laws

The minimum drinking age in Scotland is 18. Liquor stores, called *off-licenses* (or *off-sales*) sell spirits, beer, and wine and generally operate from 11 a.m. to 10 p.m.

Maps

Decent street maps and city plans are sold at most tourist information centers and major newsstands. For detailed *ordinance survey* maps, try the major booksellers such as Waterstone's or Borders.

Police

For emergencies dial ☎ **999**.

Post Office

Most branches of the post office are open Monday through Friday from 9 a.m. to 5 p.m. and Saturday from 9 a.m. to noon. Smaller, rural branches may be open weekdays from 9 a.m. to 1 p.m. and 2:15 to 5:30 p.m. as well as Saturday from 9 a.m. to 1 p.m. Many post offices close early on one day of the week, but how early and what day depends on the office.

Sending a postcard from Scotland to North America or Australia and New Zealand costs 43p (80¢). Letters (under 20 grams) cost 63p ($1.16). Mail usually takes one week (sometimes less) to get to the United States. For information on mail services in Scotland and the UK, call ☎ 08457-641-641 or visit www.royal mail.com. See the major city and regional chapters for more post office information.

Safety

Violent crime rates are low in Scotland. There are few guns in the country, and most police officers don't carry them, either. As a tourist, the most important thing you can do is guard yourself against theft. Pickpockets look for people who seem to have the most money on them and who appear to know the least about where they are. Be extra careful on crowded trains in the big cities and when taking money from ATMs.

Smoking

In November 2004, the Scottish government announced its intention to ban smoking in all public spaces, including business offices, restaurants, and pubs. The prohibition is expected to take effect in April 2006. In the meantime, smoke-filled pubs and bars are common, although most restaurants have non-smoking sections and increasingly try to keep the dining room completely non-smoking. Smoking is already prohibited on all trains and buses.

Taxes

The tax is 17.5 percent and applies to pretty much everything. It's called VAT (value-added tax), and it works like local sales taxes do in the United States. But tourists are entitled to a refund of most of it (see Chapter 5 for more information). VAT is non-refundable for services such as hotels, meals, and car rentals.

Telephones

The country code for Scotland is **44**. To make international calls from Scotland, dial 00 and then the country code, local code, and telephone number. The U.S. and Canadian country code is **1**, Australia is **61**, and New Zealand is **63**. If you can't find a number, a directory is available by dialing a variety of numbers (thanks to privatization of the service), including ☎ 118-811 or ☎ 118-800 for domestic numbers and ☎ 118-505 for international numbers.

Scotland has pay phones that accept coins and credit cards, although the use of cellphones (called *mobiles*) means you see fewer pay phones. If you're interested in renting a cellphone to use during your visit, check out Chapter 10 for more information.

Time Zone

Scotland follows Greenwich mean time, which is five time zones ahead of eastern standard time in the United States (eight hours ahead of the Pacific Coast). So,

when it's noon in New York, it's 5 p.m. in Glasgow. The clocks are set forward by one hour for British *summer time* in late March, which expires at the end of October. The high latitude blesses the country with long days in the summer, with sunset as late as 10 or even 11 p.m. But the opposite is true in winter, when the sun sets as early as 3:30 or 4 p.m.

Weather Updates

For weather forecasts of the day and 24 hours in advance, and for severe road-condition warnings, call the Met Office at ☎ 0870-900-0100. An advisor offers forecasts for the entire region and beyond at your request.

Toll-Free Numbers and Web Sites

Major airlines serving Great Britain

Aer Lingus
☎ 800-474-7424 from U.S.
☎ 0845-084-4444 from UK
www.aerlingus.com

Air France
☎ 800-237-2747 from U.S.
☎ 0845-0845-111 from UK
www.airfrance.com

American Airlines
☎ 800-433-7300
www.aa.com

BMI
☎ 44-01332-854-854 from U.S.
☎ 0870-6070-555 (short haul) or 0870-6070-222 (long haul) from UK
www.flybmi.com

British Airways
☎ 800-247-9297 from U.S.
☎ 0870-850-9-850 from UK
www.britishairways.com

Continental Airlines
☎ 800-231-0856
www.continental.com

Delta Air Lines
☎ 800-241-4141 from U.S.
☎ 0800-414-767 from UK
www.delta.com

Easyjet
☎ 44-870-6000-000 from U.S.
☎ 0871-244-2366 from UK
www.easyjet.com

Icelandair
☎ 800-223-5500 from U.S.
☎ 354-50-50-100 from Iceland
www.icelandair.is

KLM
☎ 800-374-7747 from U.S.
☎ 08705-074074 from UK
www.klm.com

Lufthansa
☎ 800-399-5838 from U.S.
☎ 44-0-870-8377-747 from UK
www.lufthansa.com

Northwest Airlines
☎ 800-225-2525
www.nwa.com

Ryanair
☎ 353-1-249-7700 from U.S.
☎ 0871-246-0000 from UK
www.ryanair.com

Scandinavian Airlines
☎ 800-221-2350 from U.S.
☎ 0870-60 727 727 from UK
www.scandinavian.net

United Airlines
☎ 800-538-2929 from U.S.
☎ 0845-8444-777 from UK
www.united.com

Virgin Atlantic Airways
☎ 800-862-8621 from U.S.
☎ 0870-380-2007 from UK
www.virgin-atlantic.com

Car-rental agencies serving Scotland

Auto Europe
☎ 888-223-5555 from U.S.
☎ 00-800-223-5555-5 from UK
www.autoeurope.com

Avis
☎ 800-230-4898 from U.S.
☎ 44-870-60-60-100 from UK
www.avis.com

Budget
☎ 800-527-0700 from U.S.
☎ 0-11-44-8701-565656 from UK
www.budget.com

Enterprise
☎ 800-261-7331 from U.S.
☎ 0870-350-3000 from UK
www.enterprise.com

Hertz
☎ 800-654-3131 from U.S.
☎ 08708-44-88-44 from UK
www.hertz.com

Thrifty
☎ 800-847-4389 from U.S.
☎ 1-918-669-2168 from UK
www.thrifty.com

Major hotel and motel chains in Scotland

Best Western International
☎ 800-780-7234 from U.S.
☎ 0800-39-31-30 from UK
www.bestwestern.com

Comfort Inns
☎ 800-654-6200 from U.S.
☎ 0800-44-44-44 from UK
www.hotelchoice.com

Days Inn
☎ 800-329-7466
www.daysinn.com

Hilton Hotels
☎ 800-445-8667 from U.S.
☎ 00-800-888-44-888 from UK
www.hilton.com

Holiday Inn
☎ 800-465-4329 from U.S.
☎ 0800-40-50-60 from UK
www.holiday-inn.com

Hyatt Hotels & Resorts
☎ 888-591-1234 from U.S.
☎ 0845-888-1234 from UK
www.hyatt.com

Inter-Continental Hotels & Resorts
☎ 800-327-0200 from U.S.
☎ 0800-028-9387 from UK
www.intercontinental.com

ITT Sheraton
☎ 888-625-5144
www.starwood.com

Marriott Hotels
☎ 888-236-2427 from U.S.
☎ 0800-221-222 from UK
www.marriott.com

Omni
☎ 800-843-6664
www.omnihotels.com

Quality Inns
☎ 877-424-6423 from U.S.
☎ 0800-44-44-44 from UK
www.qualityinns.com

Radisson Hotels International
☎ 888-201-1718 from U.S.
☎ 0800-374-411 from UK
www.radisson.com

Ritz Carlton
☎ 800-241-3333 from U.S.
☎ 0800-234-000 from UK
www.ritzcarlton.com

Sheraton Hotels & Resorts
☎ 800-325-3535 from U.S.
☎ 353-21-4279-200 from UK
www.sheraton.com

Westin Hotels & Resorts
☎ 800-228-3000 from U.S.
☎ 353-21-4279-200 from UK
www.westin.com

Where to Get More Information

If you're looking for more information on Scotland, start with the **Scottish Tourist Board** or, as it prefers to be called these days, **VisitScotland.com** (☎ **0845-225-5121;** www.visitscotland.com). The Web site has information on accommodations, attractions, and general topics, and you can get details on special offers and promotions. You can also find recommended attractions as well as listings for hotels, guesthouses, B&Bs, self-catering lodging, caravan and camping sites, serviced apartments, and hostels. Keep in mind that hotels, restaurants, and attractions generally pay to be included in these listings, however, so they haven't necessarily been evaluated on any level.

Plenty of Web sites offer helpful and interesting information on Scotland; listed below are a few of the better ones. (Remember, though, that things can change quickly in cyberspace, so a site may have been transformed by the time you read this.)

✔ www.geo.ed.ac.uk/scotgaz/scotland.html: A one-stop shop for info on Scotland's shopping, recreation, attractions, weather, tours, and more. This site also has good interactive maps.

✔ www.travelscotland.co.uk: A great site for news, sports, history, attraction information, and Scotland travel chats. This site even has a clan finder tool to help you locate the regions of your Scottish ancestors.

✔ www.geo.ed.ac.uk/home/scotland/scotland.html: A great place to get Scottish history, maps, and demographics. You can also search the encyclopedic reference guide on this Web site. *Warning:* Turn the sound off (or at least turn the volume down) on your computer before opening this site — a headache-inducing soundtrack of Scottish muzak plays nonstop while the site is open.

✔ www.frommers.com/destinations/scotland: Offers complete and up-to-date information on Scotland as well as message boards and more.

Index

Ratho

• *T* •